Contents

Foreword XIII

Introduction 1

Welcome to Using Visual InterDev 6 1

How to Use This Book 2

What You Need To Use This Book

What's Not Covered in This Book 3

About Sample Code and Updates 4

Some Final Thoughts 4

I Visual InterDev Fundamentals

1 Creating Web Projects with the Site Designer 5

Creating Web Projects with the Site Designer 7

Defining a New Visual InterDev 6 Web Project 8

Identifying the Source Code Location 8

Selecting the Web Server to Host Your Web Project 11
    Setting the Published Web Name 11
    Creating Your First Visual InterDev 6 Web Project 12
    Adjusting the Web Project Properties 15

Using a Site Diagram to Structure Your Web Project 17
    Creating a New Site Diagram 17
    Adding New Documents to Your Site Diagram 19
    Adding Existing Web Documents to Your Site Diagram 21
    Moving Web Documents in the Site Diagram 22

    Removing Documents from the Site Diagram 22

Applying Themes and Layouts to Your Web Project 24
    Using Themes 25
    Using Page Layouts 27

Customizing Your Page Layouts 30

2 Using the Visual InterDev 6 Editor 33

A Quick Tour of the Integrated Development Environment (IDE) 34
    The Main Editor Window 35
    Using the Editor Modes 37
    Using the Visual InterDev 6 Dockable Windows 39
    Stacking Your Dockable Windows 42
    Navigating the Visual InterDev 6 Menus 44

Using the Visual InterDev 6 Toolbars 45
    Creating Your Own Custom Toolbar 47

All About the IDE Views 48
    Using the Existing Views 49
    Creating Your Own Custom Views 51

Modifying the IDE Settings 52
    Environment Options 53
    Text Editor Options 54
    Data Tools Options 54
    Projects Options 55
    Other Options Pages 56

3 Building Web Pages with the Page Designer Tools 57

Creating a Template Document 58
    Controlling the Page Layout with the HTML TABLE Element 58
    Adding an Image to the Template 63
    Adding Sample Text to the Template 66

Using the PageNavBar Design-Time Control 67
    Adding a Sample Site Diagram 68
    Adding a Banner to the Template Document 69
    Adding a Link Menu to the Template Document 71
    Adding Global Links to the Template 74

Building a Sample Web Site with the Template Document 75
    Creating the Pages with the Template Document 76
    Creating the Site Diagram 77

Using the PageTransitions Design-Time Control 81
    Adding the PageTransition Controls to Your Documents 82

4 Using Visual InterDev 6 to Manage Your Web Projects 85

Supporting Development Teams with Visual InterDev 6 86
    Creating a Shared Visual InterDev 6 Project 86

Utilizing the Visual InterDev Project Model 88
    Master Mode 89
    Local Mode 90
    Offline Mode 90
    Establishing the Working Mode for the Project 91
    Using the Working Modes for Effective Team Development 92
    Comparing to Master Mode 94
    Working in Isolation 95

Verifying Links with the Visual InterDev 6 Link View 96
    Using the Link View Features to Manage Your Web Site 97
    Filtering Your Link View 98
    Working with Objects 100

Opening an Object from Within Link View 101
Checking External Links 103

Repairing the Links 103

Deploying Completed Web Applications 105
    Copying a Web Site 106

II Web Page Design Techniques 109

5 Designing Quality Input Forms for the Web 111

Dealing with the HTML Display Space 112
    HTML Is Autoformatting 112
    HTML Forms Are Stateless 113
    Most HTML Forms Are Single-Mode Documents 114

Creating Single-Mode POST Forms 115
    The Details of Posting Data 116
    Building the POSTFORM.HTM Document 116
    Adding the POSTVALUES.ASP Document 121

Creating Single-Mode GET Forms 123
    Why Use GET to Send Data? 123
    Building the GETFORM.HTM Document 124
    Adding the GETVALUES.ASP Document 127

Controlling Layout with the TABLE Element 128
    Building the TABLEFORM.HTM Document 129

6 Building Basic Web Forms with Intrinsic HTML Controls 133

What Are the Intrinsic HTML Controls? 134
    The Advantages and Disadvantages of HTML Intrinsic Controls 134

Contents

Coding with the <INPUT> Tag 135
Building the INPUTS1 Web Project 135

Using the Textbox Input Control 136

Using the Password Input Control 141

Using the Checkbox Input Control 143

Using the Radio Input Control 147

7 Building Advanced Web Forms with Intrinsic HTML Controls 153

The Other Input Controls 154
Creating the INPUTS2 Web Project 154

Using HTML SELECT to Create Dropdown and Listbox Elements 155
Creating Drop-down Boxes with HTML SELECT 156
Creating Listbox Controls with HTML SELECT 159

Accepting Multiple Text Lines with the HTML TEXTAREA Control 164

Collecting Filenames from the Client with the HTML FILE Type INPUT Control 167

Adding Graphical Buttons Using the HTML IMAGE Type INPUT Control 170

8 Using Style Sheets with Your Web Pages 175

What Is a Style Sheet? 176
The Style Sheet File Format 178
How to Link Style Sheets to Your Document 179
How to Apply Styles in Documents 179

Using the Visual InterDev 6 Style Sheet Editor 180
Starting the Style Sheet Editor 182
Adding the FIRST.CSS File to Your FIRST.HTM Document 184
Defining Font Styles 185
Defining Background Styles 187

Defining Borders, Margins, and Padding Styles 191
Defining Layout Styles 193
Defining List Styles 195
Defining Style Classes 198
Defining Unique ID Styles 200

9 Adding Multimedia to Your Web Applications 205

The Pros and Cons of Multimedia for Your Web Applications 206

Adding Sound and Video 207
Adding Sound to Your Web Documents 207
Using the ActiveMovie Control to Add Video 212

Using the DirectX Animation Controls to Add Advanced Graphics 216
Locating the DirectAnimation Controls in Visual InterDev 6 217
Using the Sprite Control 218
Moving Graphics with the Path Control 220
Drawing Complex Shapes with the Structured Graphics Control 224

10 Creating and Using Image Maps 233

What Are Client-Side Image Maps? 234
Advantages of Client-Side Image Maps 234
Client-Side Image Map Drawbacks 235

Creating a Client-Side Image Map 235
Importing an Image File into Your Web Project 236
Placing the Image on Your Web Document 237

Adding Map Coordinates to Your Image Files 239
Understanding the <MAP> and <AREA> HTML Tags 239
Defining Your Own Image Map 241

Using Visual InterDev 6

Adding the Target HTML
Documents 244
Testing the Image Map Document 244

III Using Visual Basic Script 245

11 Programming with Visual Basic Scripting Language 247

Visual Basic Script Quick Start 248
   Creating a Simple VBScript Application 249

Using Script Variables 253
   Declaring Variables 253
   Variable Types in VBScript 254
   Setting the Scope of VBScript Variables 255

Using Program Control Structures 259
   Using the For...Next Loop Structure 259
   Using the Do...Loop Structure 261
   Using the If...Then...Else Structure 264
   Using the Select...Case...End Select Structure 267

12 Expanding Your Scripts with Built-In Methods 271

Using the Built-In Methods 272

Using the VBScript Math Methods 273

Using the VBScript String Methods 277

Using the VBScript Date/Time Methods 284

Using the VBScript Data Conversion Methods 290

Other VBScript Methods 293
   Using the Output Formatting Methods 294
   Using the User Input/Output Methods 296

13 Adding Event Handling to Your Visual Basic Scripts 301

Linking Your VBScript to Event Messages 303
   Using Instrinsic Event Declaration 303
   Using Attribute Event Declaration 304
   Using Explicit Event Declaration 305

About Event Bubbling 306

Setting Up the VBScript Event Web Project 307

Using Window Events 308

Using Document Events 313

Using Form Events 318

Using Element Events 325

Adding Event Coding to Link Elements 331

14 Client-Side Scripting with the MSIE Object Model 335

What Is Client-Side Scripting? 336
   Why Use Client-Side Scripts? 337

Adding Client-Side Script Blocks 338
   Using the <SCRIPT> Tag 338
   Adding Event-Handling Script Blocks 340
   Adding Scripts via HTML Attributes 341
   Using FOR...EVENT to Add Scripts 343
   About Multiple Script Blocks and Shared Script Blocks 344

Using the Microsoft Internet Explorer Object Model 346
   The Microsoft Internet Explorer Object Hierarchy 347
   Preparing the DOCOBJ Project 349
   Using the Window and Frame Objects 349
   Using the History, Navigator, and Location Objects 359

Exploring the Document Object 364
    Using the Link Object 373
    Using the Form and Element Objects 375

15 Using Server-Side Scripting with the Built-In ASP Objects 379

What Is Server-Side Scripting? 380
    Understanding How Server-Side Scripts Work 382
    Creating a Simple Server-Side Script with VBScript 385

Accessing the Host Server with the Server Object 389

Sharing Data with All Users with the Application Object 392
    Coding the Application Object Example 394

Tracking User Values with the Session Object 397
    Adding the Session Sample Page 399

Sending Output to Clients with the Response Object 403
    Adding the Response Object Sample Page 405

Accepting Data from the Client with the Request Object 409
    Laying Out the REQUEST.ASP Page 410
    Displaying the Cookies Collection 411
    Displaying the QueryString Collection 412
    Displaying the Form Collection 413

IV Databases and the Web 415

16 Accessing Web Databases 417

General Tasks for Accessing Web Databases 418
    OLE DB and ADO 419
    Using SQL Server and Oracle Databases 420
    Using Microsoft Access Databases 420

Using the Data Environment Designer 421
    Creating the WEBDB Project 421
    Internet Data Connections and ODBC 422
    Creating Data Connections 426
    Creating Data Commands 429

Editing Database Data with the Query Designer Tool 433
    Using the QDT Data Grid to Edit Tables 433
    Editing Existing Records with Update Queries 435
    Adding New Records with Insert Values Queries 436
    Deleting Existing Record with Delete Queries 438

17 Creating Data-Bound Web Forms 439

Designing Good Data-Bound Web Forms 440
    Using Data-Bound Design-Time Controls 441
    Client-Side Versus Server-Side DTC Scripting 443
    Using the Scripting Object Model 444

Creating the DBFORM Project and Adding the Data Connection and Data Command Objects 445
    Creating the DBFORM Project 446
    Adding the Data Connection 447
    Adding the Data Command 448

Building Data-Bound Entry Forms with DTCs 451

18 Creating Databases for the Web 477

Using Visual InterDev 6.0 to Create Database Items 478
    What Is and Isn't Possible with Visual InterDev 6.0 Data Tools 479

Using Visual InterDev 6

Using ISQL to Create a New Device and Database 480
Creating a New Database Project with Visual InterDev 6.0 481

Adding New Tables to an Existing Database 483
   Using the Database Diagram to Add the Customers Table 484
   Adding a Trigger to the Customers Table 486
   Using the Query Designer to Add the Sales Table 488
   Using the Table Script to Add the Product Table 489
   Defining Table Relationships with the Database Diagram 491

Using the Visual InterDev 6.0 Data Tools to Add Records to the Database 493
   Entering Records Using the Query Designer Grid 494
   Creating an Insert SQL Script with the Script Template 495
   Creating an Insert Query with the Query Designer 497

Adding New Views to an Existing Database 498
   Using the Query Designer to Add the TotalSales View 499
   Using the View Script to Add the ProductSales View 500

Adding a Stored Procedure to an SQL Server Database 502
   Executing a Stored Procedure with Visual InterDev 6.0 Data Tools 503

19 Using ActiveX Database Objects (ADO) 505

The Basics of ActiveX Data Objects (ADO) 506
   The ActiveX Data Object Model 506

Special ADO Properties 508
   ConnectionString 508
   CommandText 509
   CommandType 509
   CursorLocation 510
   CursorType 511
   LockType 512
   Mode 513

Setting Up the ADODB Web Project 514
   Building the ADODB Project 514
   Using the ADOVBS.INC Include File 514
   Creating the ADO Programming Objects in the ADOSTUFF.INC File 517
   Adding Support Methods to the ADOSTUFF.INC File 518

Connecting to a Database with the Connection Object 520
   Using Server-Side ADO to Open a Data Connection 522

Retrieving Records with the Recordset Object 524
   Using Text Recordsets 524
   Using a Table Command Type 526

Setting Execution Rules with the Command Object 528
   Creating UPDATE Queries with the Command Object 528
   Creating INSERT and DELETE Queries with the Command Object 530

Running Parameter Queries with the Parameter Object 532
   Executing a Text Parameter Query Statement 533
   Executing a Microsoft Access Parameter QueryDef 535
   Executing a Microsoft SQL Server Parameter Stored Procedure 538

V Using ActiveX Technologies 541

20 Using Advanced Design Time Controls 543

Introducing Design-Time Controls (DTCs) 544
 Design-Time Controls Versus Other Components 544
 The Advantage of Design-Time Controls 545
 Controls Available in Visual InterDev 6 546

Incorporating DTCs into Your Pages 546
 Understanding the Scripting Object Model 547
 Manipulating Control Properties 548
 Viewing Runtime Text 550

Using Data-Bound DTCs in Forms 552
 Adding the Recordset 552
 Binding Form Controls to the Data Source 554
 Introducing Recordset Navigation 556
 Adding Buttons 558
 Using the Grid Control 560

Adding Multimedia DTCs 562
 The Page Transitions Control 563
 The Timeline Control 564

21 Adding Reports and Graphs to Your Web Applications 569

The Advantages of Reporting Formats 570
 Using Columnar Reports 570
 Using Tabular Reports 572
 Using Graphical Chart Reports 573

Preparing for the Reporting Examples 574

Using HTML Tables to Produce Formatted Columnar Reports 575
 Adding a Data Connection 575
 Using VBScript and ASP to Access SQL Server Data 577
 Creating the Report Heading and Print Loop 580
 Displaying Data Detail with HTML Tables 581

Building Tabular Reports with the REPORT.ASP Document 583
 A Quick Tour of REPORT.ASP 584
 Building Your Report Information File 586

Using ASPChart to Display Database Recordsets 590
 Installing ASPChart 591
 Creating the CHARTING.ASP Document 592

22 Adding Active Content to Your Web Application 597

Harnessing the Power of Active Content 598
 Designing to Take Advantage of Active Content 598
 Using the Active Content Solution Framework 599

Preparing the Active Content Project 600

Building an Online Magazine with the Content Linker Objects 601
 Laying Out the VID News Central Contents Page 602
 Activating the Contents Page with ASP Code 604
 Adding the Text File to Control Online Content 606

Creating Rotating Banner Ads with Ad Rotator Component 609
 The Text File that Runs the Ad Rotator 610
 Creating the Ad Banner Display Page 611
 Adding a Hit Check Page to Monitor Ad Usage 612
 Building the Ad Rotator Control File 613

23 Adding Active Documents to Your Web Projects 617

What Are Active Documents and Why Should You Use Them? 618
   Microsoft Office Active Documents 618
   Visual Basic ActiveX Documents 620

Adding Microsoft Office Documents to Your Web Project 621
   Adding an Excel Spreadsheet 622
   Adding a Word 97 Document 625

Adding Visual Basic ActiveX Documents to Your Web Project 627
   ActiveX Documents and Browser Security 627
   The VB ActiveX Document Installation Package 628
   About the Setup Information File 629
   Including ActiveX Documents in Your Web Project 630
   Inspecting the ActiveX Document Startup HTML Page 632
   Testing the Visual Basic ActiveX Document Automatic Installation 634

VI More Active Server Programming 637

24 Looking at ASP Behind the Scenes 639

Setting Up the BehindTheScenes Web Application 640

Using GLOBAL.ASA in Your Web Applications 641
   The Life of GLOBAL.ASA 642
   Sharing Data and COM Objects with the GLOBAL.ASA 643
   The Difference Between Storing Pointers in the Contents Collections 644
   Using the GLOBAL.ASA Events 645
   Adding <OBJECT> Tags 647
   Referencing Type Libraries 649

Taking Advantage of Server-Side Include Files 652
   How Server-Side Include Files Work 653
   Creating SSIs for Your Web Applications 653
   Using SSIs in Your Web Applications 656

Learning About Server Variables 657

25 Managing Files with ASP 663

Preparing the FileSystemObject Web Application 664

Inspecting Disk Storage with the System File Object 666
   Creating Folders and Files with the FileSystemObject 667
   Reading Server Drives 671
   Viewing Folders on the Server 674
   Viewing Files in the Folder on the Server 678

Reading and Writing Text Files with the TextStream Object 681
   Building the Web Tip Sample Document 683

26 Adding Security to Your Web Applications 691

Defining Security Requirements 692
   Understanding Authority Access 692
   Understanding Membership Access Security 693

Using Operating System Security 695
   Advantages of Operating System Security 696
   The Downside of Operating System Security 697
   Securing an Application Folder 698

Contents

27 Using Program-Based Security 707

Advantages of Program-Based Security 708

The Downside of Program-Based Security 709

Building a Program-Based Security System 711
  Checking for Valid Users 714
  Collecting User Login Data 715
  Validating the Logged-In User 717

A Blueprint for Creating Your Own Program-Based Security 721

28 Adding Error Handling to Your Web Application 723

Understanding Error Handling with Visual InterDev 724
  Cleaning Up Syntax Errors 724
  Dealing with Web-Related Errors 727
  Handling Code-Related Runtime Errors 729
  The Best Defense Is a Good Design 730

How Visual InterDev Reports Errors 732
  Accessing the Built-In Err or Object 734
  Turn On Error Handling with Resume Next 735
  Adding Error Handling to Active Server Pages 736

Creating an Error Trap Include File 738
  Building the SSI File to Handle ASP Errors 739
  Using the ERRORTRAP.INC File in Your ASP Documents 745

29 Using DHTML to Dynamically Alter HTML Content and Positioning 749

What Is Dynamic HTML? 750
  Listening for Events 751

The Power of the STYLE Attribute 755
Using the DIV and SPAN HTML Elements 756
Creating the DHTML Web Project 758

Altering HTML Content at Runtime 758
  Using the ONMOUSEOVER Event and the innerHTML Property 759

Creating Visual Drag-and-Drop Interfaces 762
  Laying Out the REPOSITION.HTM Document 763
  Using the event Object to Enable Drag-and-Drop for Web Documents 767

VII Appendixes 771

A Using Microsoft FrontPage and FrontPage Server Extensions 773

Advantages of Mixing Microsoft FrontPage and Visual InterDev 6 774

Recommended Installation Steps 775
  Remove FrontPage from the Client 776
  Remove FrontPage Server Extensions—Twice 776
  Install the Option Pack Without FrontPage Server Extensions 777
  Install the FrontPage Server Extensions Separately 777
  Install Microsoft FrontPage Without the Personal Web Server 777

Sharing Projects Between Microsoft FrontPage and Visual InterDev 6 778
  Connecting to Existing FrontPage Webs with Visual InterDev 6 779
  Connecting to Existing Visual InterDev 6 Webs with FrontPage 783

Troubleshooting FrontPage and Visual
InterDev 6 Problems 787
    Cannot Locate Web Server 787
    Visual InterDev 6 VINAVBAR
    Component Broken   788

B Online Resources   791

Using Visual InterDev 6 Web Site   791

Related Web Sites 792

Related Newsgroups 793

Related Mailing Lists 794

About Other Online Resources 794

C Glossary 795

    Index 821

Foreword

Where Is the Web Taking You?

If you are a corporate developer, it may not be the "worldwide" part of the Web that motivated you to pick up this book, but rather the Web in your own back yard—your intranet or extranet. The last couple of years have uncovered a compelling economy in corporate applications created the "Webway," where thin clients really *are* better than the standard client/server fatties—especially if you care about cost.

If, on the other hand, you develop Web sites for the public, it may be the siren call (or fire alarm?) of e-commerce that has brought you to this book. And I'm not just talking shopping baskets here, but the entire range of dynamic, personalized interactions your site must provide to bring visitors back again and again. You want to get intimate with your visitors, and serve up the content you know they want.

In either case, the fundamental technical challenge is the same: to hitch data to the Web in a way that makes sense for you and your users. You've come to the right place. Visual InterDev 6.0 is the most powerful tool available today for building Web sites that are driven by data. With Visual InterDev, it matters little where the data lives—it works with almost every commercially available database. In other words, *your* data.

This book is an excellent, detailed introduction to Visual InterDev 6.0 for both the corporate and public Web site developer. You'll learn the basics of creating a Web site with Visual InterDev and, more importantly, how to harness data to make your Web site really work for you.

Susan Warren
Visual InterDev Product Manager
Microsoft Corporation
October 1998

About the Author

Mike Amundsen works as an IS Consulting and Training Specialist for Design-Synergy Corporation, a consulting and project management firm specializing in information technology services. He travels the U.S. and Europe teaching and consulting on Windows development topics.

Mike's other book projects include authoring the two previous editions of *Sams Teach Yourself Database Programming with Visual Basic*; the *MAPI, SAPI, and TAPI Developer's Guide* published by Sams Publishing, and contributing to a number of books on Visual Basic, Visual InterDev, and other topics. Mike has contributed to several periodicals, including several *Cobb Journals*, *Visual Basic Programmers Journal*, and *VB Tech* magazine.

When he's not busy writing or traveling to client sites, Mike spends time with his family at his home in Kentucky. You can reach Mike at tysdbvb@amundsen.com or visit his Web site at www.amundsen.com.

Contributing Authors

Steve Banick is a network administrator and graphic designer who is currently the client software developer for TELUS PLAnet Internet Services in Alberta, Canada. His published works as a contributing and lead author include: *Special Edition Using Microsoft Commercial Internet System*, *Special Edition Using Visual InterDev*, *Web Management with Microsoft Visual SourceSafe 5.0*, *Special Edition Using Microsoft Internet Information Server 4.0*, *Platinum Edition Using Windows NT Server 4.0*, *Platinum Edition Using HTML 4, Java 1.1 and JavaScript 1.2*, *Using FrontPage 98*, *FrontPage Unleashed 98*, and *Special Edition Using Photoshop 5.0*.

L. Michael Van Hoozer is a director for BSI Consulting and has ten years of system development experience. Mike has strong ties to Microsoft in that he has been very involved with the alpha and beta testing of products including Visual Basic, Visual InterDev, and the rest of the Visual Studio suite of tools. Mike is the author of *Sams Teach Yourself Microsoft Visual InterDev in 21 Days* (Sams.net Publishing, April, 1997), and he contributed several chapters to *Visual InterDev Unleashed* (Sams.net Publishing, August, 1997).

Dedication

This one's dedicated to Claire. You were at my side all the way. Thanks.

Acknowledgments

Although many folks have helped shape the contents of this book, several people deserve special recognition in helping complete this book.

First, my thanks go to Steve Banick (*Special Edition Using Visual InterDev 6.0* from Que Corporation) and Michael Van Hoozer (*Sams Teach Yourself Microsoft Visual InterDev 6 in 21 Days* from Sams Publishing). Without their contributions to this book, it never would have seen the light of day.

Next, I must thank the folks at Microsoft for their help in putting this book together. The Visual InterDev 6.0 team has been very supportive throughout the process, including David Lazar and Susan Warren (product managers for Visual InterDev 6.0). I must also mention three members of the Internet Developer Support group of the Microsoft Technical Support Division. Tony Pacheco, Andrea Fox, and Rob Reno all helped me learn a great deal about Visual InterDev 6.0 and provided top-notch support and encouragement throughout the beta cycle of Visual InterDev 6.0.

I also must say thank you to all those who helped me review and revise the text as it was developing. Several volunteers provided helpful comments. However, I would like to especially thank Kelly Householder for his suggestions and support.

Finally, I must tip my hat to the folks at Macmillan Publishing who got saddled with me and did such a good job pulling this book together and getting it out the door. Brad Jones, Kelly Marshall, and Matt Purcell bore the heaviest burden. Nancy Albright and Tonya Simpson were very patient (and persistent) in helping me revise the text and provide the proper elements to the book. I must also thank Andrew Fritzinger for his untiring technical editing. "Tech Edit," as it's known in the business, is a difficult and often thankless task. Andrew provided me with excellent feedback and suggestions on how to improve the coding for this book.

It's one thing to develop the content for a technically accurate book. It's quite another to put it all together in a way that is consistent, useful, and enjoyable to read. If this book succeeds in all this, it is because of the excellent work of the folks at Macmillan.

As can be expected with a book of this scope, many more people provided sample code, review comments, and even moral support throughout the entire process. To all those I've not yet mentioned (you know who you are!), thanks for your help. It's been quite an experience!

Mike Amundsen
Erlanger, Kentucky
September, 1998

Tell Us What You Think!

As the reader of this book, *you* are our most important critic and commentator. We value your opinion and want to know what we're doing right, what we could do better, what areas you'd like to see us publish in, and any other words of wisdom you're willing to pass our way.

As the Executive Editor for the Advanced Programming team at Macmillan Computer Publishing, I welcome your comments. You can fax, email, or write me directly to let me know what you did or didn't like about this book—as well as what we can do to make our books stronger.

Please note that I cannot help you with technical problems related to the topic of this book, and that due to the high volume of mail I receive, I might not be able to reply to every message.

When you write, please be sure to include this book's title and author as well as your name and phone or fax number. I will carefully review your comments and share them with the author and editors who worked on the book.

Fax: 317-817-7070

Email: `adv_prog@mcp.com`

Mail: Brad Jones
Executive Editor
Advanced Programming Team
Macmillan Computer Publishing
201 West 103rd Street
Indianapolis, IN 46290 USA

INTRODUCTION

Welcome to *Using Visual InterDev 6*

Welcome to *Using Visual InterDev 6*. This book was designed to help you learn how to use Visual InterDev 6 to build powerful Web applications. To that end, the book has been divided into several sections of related chapters.

Part I, "Visual InterDev Fundamentals," will help you get a good feel for the Visual InterDev 6 environment and the basic skills of creating Web applications, adding and editing documents in the Web, and managing the documents after they've been created.

Part II, "Web Page Design Techniques," focuses on techniques for building effective Web documents and input forms and using style sheets, images, and other media to establish a complete look and feel for your Web apps.

Part III, "Using Visual Basic Script," reviews the Microsoft Visual Basic Scripting language. This section will give folks new to Visual Basic Scripting a good grounding in the language and will give those with Visual Basic Scripting experience a handy reference for future use. Both client- and server-side scripting is covered.

Part IV, "Databases and the Web," introduces the new database features of Visual InterDev 6. You'll learn how to use the data environment, the new design-time controls (DTCs), and the Visual Data Tools to build database tables, stored procedures, and queries. You'll also learn to use the ActiveX Data Object library to create custom Active Server Page solutions.

Part V, "Using ActiveX Technologies," provides examples of how to add reports and graphs, active contents, and other component-based material to your Web applications.

Part VI, "More Active Server Programming," shows you how to manage server-based text files, add security and error handling to your Web apps, and how to take advantage of DHTML features like scriptlets, visual filters, and other cool Microsoft Internet Explorer technologies.

Bonus Chapters

Bonus Web chapters have been set up on the *Using Visual InterDev 6* companion Web site at `http://www.amundsen.com/uvi6`. "Creating Scriptlets for Microsoft Internet Explorer 4.0" covers everything you need to know about incorporating scriptlets into your Web applications. "Applying Visual Filters and Transitions with DHTML" covers how to create your own entries in the Toolbox window, how to use visual filters to alter text and graphics, how to work with the `blendTrans` method, and how to create sophisticated display transitions between images.

How to Use This Book

There are really three different ways you can use this book, depending on your current skill level and needs. The material is grouped together both in related subject areas and in order of complexity. The easier material appears in the first chapters, and the more advanced examples appear toward the end of the book.

If you're new to Visual InterDev 6 and to Web application building in general, you can start reading from Chapter 1 and move sequentially through the book. This will help you become familiar with the Visual InterDev 6 environment first and move progressively through simple HTML examples, client and server scripting, database coding, component-based examples, and, finally, to examples of advanced client and server coding.

If you are already comfortable with Visual InterDev 6 and have experience building Web apps, you might want to focus on the sections that interest you most. Because the material is divided into related subject areas, you can easily jump to the database section, then move back to the scripting section, then jump ahead to the ActiveX section. You might find that some chapters assume you have completed earlier examples; however, none of the chapters require you to have already created other material. Also, you will find that every chapter has extensive reference to other sections in the book. This will help you when you are jumping around and need to get a quick look at previously presented items.

Finally, after you've completed your tour through the text, you can use this book as a companion reference. Much work has been done to provide a quality index that you can use to find what you're looking for quickly. And the new "See Also" items in each chapter give you additional suggestions on related material that appears elsewhere in the text.

What You Need To Use This Book

You'll need a copy of Visual InterDev 6 (of course) running on either Windows 95/98 or Windows NT (Workstation or Server). The specs suggest 32MB of RAM, but I strongly suggest 64MB or more, especially if you will be running this on NT machines with SQL Server. As a rule, the more RAM, the better!

Almost all the examples in this book will work using the Visual InterDev 6 Professional Edition. However, a few database chapters use features found only in the Enterprise Edition. However, you can still get a great deal out of those chapters if you are using the Professional Edition.

For the record, this book was composed on a P200 laptop with 64MB of RAM and 4GB of hard drive storage. The machine was running Windows NT4 Workstation with Service Pack 3. The rest of the software came directly from the Visual Studio 6.0 CDs including the Personal Web Server, Visual InterDev 6.0, and all the other support programs.

What's Not Covered in This Book

To keep things relatively simple, only Visual Basic Scripting language is covered in this book. You won't find any JScript examples here. This is not because Visual Basic Scripting is better—building a book without covering too much territory is just easier. If you prefer JScript, you can still get a lot out of the book. Converting the client-side examples to JScript will not be too difficult.

Although there are several chapters on databases, this book does not offer a complete tutorial on database technology. The focus here is on how to use databases within your Web applications. If you want to dive deeper into database techniques, including how to design effective tables and queries, you will need to tap the vast market of other books targeting databases. All the examples here use either SQL Server or Microsoft Access database formats. However, there is nothing here that would work with other formats including dBase, FoxPro, Oracle, and others.

This book does not provide extensive advice on installing IIS4 and all the other parts of a Web server. If you are responsible for installing and supporting a Web server, you'll need to find some other texts that cover this area.

About Sample Code and Updates

You'll notice that there is no accompanying CD-ROM with this book. However, you can still get electronic copies of the coding examples by visiting the supporting Web site at `http://www.amundsen.com/uvi6`. You'll also find any fixes or updates to the text at this Web site.

The Web site will also have links to other Visual InterDev 6-related sites and to some special offers for readers. Even if you don't need to download the code samples, you might want to visit the site just to keep up to date on any changes in either the book or in Visual InterDev 6 itself.

Some Final Thoughts

The release of Visual InterDev 6.0 marks a major upgrade in Microsoft's premier Web application development tool. If you have used VI 1.0, you'll find lots of changes. I have enjoyed using Visual InterDev 6.0 and have enjoyed putting this book together. I hope you will also enjoy reading it.

I am always interested in comments and suggestions from readers. Please feel free to contact me by sending e-mail to `uvi6@amundsen.com` or by visiting the Web site at `http://www.amundsen.com/uvi6`.

PART I

Visual InterDev Fundamentals

1 **Creating Web Projects with the Site Designer** 7

2 **Using the Visual InterDev 6 Editor** 33

3 **Building Web Pages with the Page Designer Tools** 57

4 **Using Visual InterDev 6 to Manage Your Web Projects** 85

CHAPTER 1

Creating Web Projects with the Site Designer

Learn how to create a new Visual InterDev 6 Web project

Use site diagrams to structure your Web projects

Apply themes and layouts to Web projects

PART I   Visual InterDev Fundamentals
CHAPTER 1   **Creating Web Projects with the Site Designer**

Defining a New Visual InterDev 6 Web Project

The first thing you must do when using Visual InterDev 6 to build your Web solutions is to define and create your Visual InterDev 6 Web projects. Web projects contain all the HTML documents, graphics files, server-side components, and control files needed by Visual InterDev 6 to complete a Web application.

Most of the items in your Visual InterDev 6 Web project will be deployed as public parts of the Web solution on the Web server. However, some of these project pieces exist only to help Visual InterDev 6 keep track of details for supporting the development interface and for communicating to the Web server. At this point, understanding the meanings and uses of every item in a Web project is not important. However, it is important to know that you have several items to track and manage when you create a new Web project.

Creating new Web projects involves making a handful of important decisions:

- Where on the network will you locate the project control files and source code?
- Which Web server will you select to host the project?
- What name will you use to publish the completed project on the Web server?

In the next several sections, you'll learn some of the details behind these three key bits of information. After a review of the three major points, you'll use Visual InterDev 6 to actually create your first Web project.

Identifying the Source Code Location

The first task to complete in creating a new Visual InterDev 6 Web project is to decide where the project source code and control files will be located. This location is not the actual Web that will be published for users to visit with their browsers. This location is the place where you will hold all the items required by Visual InterDev 6 to manage and control your Web project.

Projects and Visual InterDev

You can think of a project as a self-contained group of files and folders that make up a Web site. Microsoft refers to all Web sites, or Web applications within Visual InterDev, as projects.

Microsoft FrontPage extensions required for the host Web

Visual InterDev 6 uses the Microsoft FrontPage Server Extensions to talk directly to the Web server that hosts the Visual InterDev 6 project. Even if you are using a non-Microsoft server for your Web projects, that machine will need to have Microsoft FrontPage Extensions installed so that Visual InterDev 6 can "talk" to the Web host when creating new projects.

Defining a New Visual InterDev 6 Web Project

When you decide on a Web project's source code location, you can use any available disk space where you have rights to create new files and folders. Typically, this will be a location on your own workstation or on a mapped disk drive somewhere on the network.

After you determine the drive and path for your Visual InterDev 6 project, you must come up a with a new folder name for the project. Typically this is a descriptive name such as MyWeb or Accounting. However, you can also use more structured names such as Project01 or AcctWebProj. The only restrictions that exist for creating the top-level project folder are the same restrictions that exist for creating new Windows operating system folder names. Usually, this top-level folder name is also used as the published Web name on the Web server that hosts the project. However, this is not a requirement.

A Visual InterDev 6 project folder has several default subfolders and disk files. These folders and disk files will be added to the source code location by Visual InterDev 6 when you create your project. The default folders and files for a project folder named MyWeb are summarized and described in Table 1.1.

TABLE 1.1 Default subfolders and files for a Visual InterDev 6 Web project

Folder	File	Description
MyWeb	MyWeb.sln	The solution text file. This file contains the details for locating all the associated projects for a complete solution.
	MyWeb.sou	The solution binary file. This file contains additional machine-readable details for all the associated projects for a complete solution.
	MyWeb.vip	The project text file. This contains the details for defining the Web project.
MyWeb.vic	The project cache file	This binary file contains additional information on the definition of the project.

continues…

Use only mapped network drives for Visual InterDev 6 Web projects

It is important to use only mapped disk drives when locating your Visual InterDev 6 Web projects. Although the Visual InterDev 6 editor will allow you to use a UNC named share (for example \\myserver\myshare\mywebcode) as a location for a new project, some items in a Visual InterDev 6 Web project cannot use named shares. To avoid problems with your Web projects, use only mapped drive letters (L:\mywebcode) as locations for your Web projects.

Avoid spaces when naming folders

Although folder names with spaces (for example, \My Web Project\) are legal names, they are not recommended. They are sometimes difficult to type and, in some cases, third-party tools, such as source control packages or other software, might not be capable of properly handling folder names with spaces.

Visual Studio solutions

Visual Studio (including Visual InterDev) uses the term *solution* to represent the projects that comprise your active workspace. In older versions of Visual Studio, solutions were known as *workspaces*.

Do not edit contents of the _ScriptLibrary folder

The _ScriptLibrary folder contains several HTML and Active Server Page (ASP) documents used by Visual InterDev 6 at runtime. It is important that you do not edit these documents in any way. Doing so can permanently break your Web project and render it unusable.

The _ScriptLibrary and ASP

To use the _ScriptLibrary and fully realize the power of Visual InterDev, you must be using Microsoft Internet Information Server (IIS) 4.0 or higher. IIS 4.0 introduced a considerably more powerful version of Microsoft's Active Server Pages processor as well as server-side debugging features with Visual InterDev.

TABLE 1.1 Continued

Folder	File	Description
MyWeb\MyWeb_Local		This contains a "local" copy of all the items in the project.
MyWeb\MyWeb_Local	Global.asa	This is used at runtime to manage application and session information for the Web project.
MyWeb\MyWeb_Local_private		This contains control files used by Visual InterDev 6 to manage the project code.
MyWeb\MyWeb_Local_Layouts		This contains a set of files and subfolders that define the optional page navigation definitions used in the project.
MyWeb\MyWeb_Local_Themes		This contains a set of files and subfolders that define the optional style sheets and background graphics used in the project.
MyWeb\MyWeb_Local_ScriptLibrary		This contains a set of read-only Web documents used as runtime support for the project.
MyWeb\MyWeb_Local_vti_cnf MyWeb\MyWeb_Local_vti_log MyWeb\MyWeb_Local_vti_pvt		Read-only folders. This contains information used to manage the project at runtime.
MyWeb\MyWeb_Local\images		This contains any custom images used in your Web project.

Most of the files and folders you see in Table 1.1 will never be edited or even viewed within Visual InterDev 6 during the life of the Web project. However, they are still very important files. They are listed here so that you will know that they exist and have an understanding about how they are used in the project.

SEE ALSO

▶ *For more on the details of Visual InterDev 6 project files, see page 640*

Selecting the Web Server to Host Your Web Project

After establishing a location for the Web project source code and control files, you must select a Web server that will host your completed project. This is the machine that has Microsoft Personal Web Server (PWS) or Internet Information Server (IIS) installed and running. This machine must also have FrontPage Server Extensions installed.

The host Web server does not have to be the same machine that holds the project source code. In fact, in production settings the host Web server is usually a different machine. However, it is quite common to store the source code in another folder on the hosting Web server, especially for test projects and prototypes.

The key thing to keep in mind is that, as far as the Web server is concerned, the machine that will host your Visual InterDev 6 project is independent of the machine that holds your source code. In other words, after you have completed the source code of your Web project and deployed it to the hosting Web server, deleting one of the two items does not affect the other at all. Removing the Web from the host Web server will not delete the source code, and erasing the source code files will not erase the files from the hosting Web server.

Each project has only one host Web server

You can deploy the completed Web application to any number of Web servers, but every project has only one master project Web host. After you select a Web server to host your project, moving it to another server is difficult. For this reason, it is important to choose your hosting Web server carefully.

Setting the Published Web Name

After establishing a source code location and selecting a host Web server for the project, you must decide on a name to use for the Web that appears on the host Web server. This name is usually the same as the folder name you selected for the source code location. However, this is not required.

For example, if you used the folder name MyWeb for the source code location and selected MyServer as the hosting Web server for the project, the default Web name on the Web server would be MyWeb. This means you could use the following Universal Resource Locator (URL) to connect to the completed Web on the server:

```
http://myserver/myweb/
```

Use the default Web name whenever possible

Although you have the option to use different names for the source code folder and Web names, it is not a recommended practice. Using two different names can become confusing for both Web developers and server administrators and might lead to mistakes when it is time to update or delete selected Web projects.

As mentioned earlier, you do not have to use the source code folder name as the published Web name. You could use any other legal folder name as the published Web name. For example, you might want to publish the documents at the MyWeb source code location as TestFormsWeb on the Web server called MyServer. You might do this to make the published Web name more meaningful for users or to conform to a preestablished naming convention for the Web sever. You can also use this option when you already have a published Web on the host Web server with the same name as your project source code folder name.

SEE ALSO
▶ *For more about hosting a Web with Microsoft FrontPage Extensions, see page 773*

Creating Your First Visual InterDev 6 Web Project

Now that you have a good understanding of the three key parts of a Visual InterDev 6 Web project definition, you're ready to create your first Visual InterDev 6 Web project.

Creating a Visual InterDev 6 Web project

1. If you have not already done so, start Visual InterDev 6.
2. When Visual InterDev 6 starts, a New Project dialog box should appear. If it does not, select **File**, **New Project** from the main menu.
3. With the New Project dialog in view, enter a disk drive and path name in the **Location** field—for example, c:\UVI\Source\.
4. Next, enter a new folder name in the **Name** field—for example, MyFirstWeb.
5. Click the **New Web Project** icon in the right section of the dialog box.
6. Finally, press **Open** to create the source code location (see Figure 1.1).

Defining a New Visual InterDev 6 Web Project

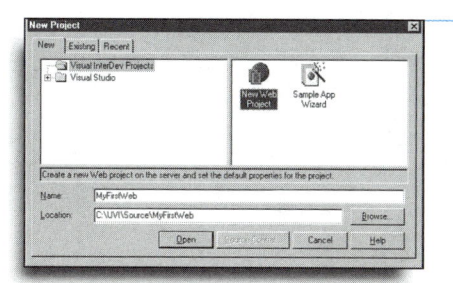

FIGURE 1.1
Filling out the New Project dialog.

After establishing the source code location, you must use the Web Project Wizard to select an available Web server to host the Visual InterDev 6 project. This wizard automatically appears when you open a new Web project.

Selecting an available Web server to host the Visual InterDev 6 project

1. At the first screen of the Web Project Wizard, enter the name of a valid PWS or IIS Web server in the **What server name do you want to use?** field—for example, `MyServer`. Do not enter `\\MyServer` or `http://MyServer`.

2. If the server you are using requires an SSL connection, check the **Connect using Secure Sockets Layer** check box.

3. Select the **Master mode** as the mode you want to work in (see Figure 1.2).

4. Press the **Next** button to continue creating the new Web project.

After selecting a Web server to host your Visual InterDev 6 project, you must decide on a public Web name for the project. This will be the name that will be used to connect browsers to the published documents.

Web authoring and SSL

If you're working on a site that requires confidentiality and security, you should always use SSL. Your Web server must be configured for SSL for this type of connection to function.

PART **I** Visual InterDev Fundamentals

CHAPTER **1** **Creating Web Projects with the Site Designer**

FIGURE 1.2

Selecting the hosting Web server.

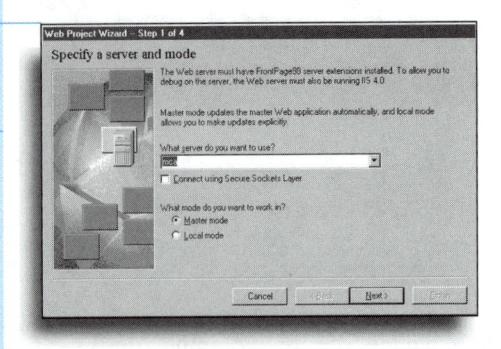

Setting the project's Web name

1. In Step 2 of 4 of the Web Project Wizard, select either **Create a new web project** or **Connect to an existing web project**. For this example, click the radio button for **Create a new web project**.

2. If you selected **Create a new web project**, enter a value in the **Name** field. For this example, accept the default source code folder name (MyFirstWeb).

3. If you selected **Connect to an existing web project**, use the pull-down list to select an existing Visual InterDev 6 Web project.

4. Press the **Next** button to continue the Web Project Wizard (see Figure 1.3).

5. In Step 3 of 4 of the Web Project Wizard, press **Finish** to complete the creation of the new project.

FIGURE 1.3

Setting the published Web name.

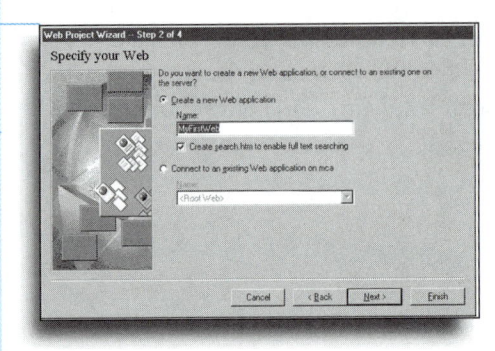

Defining a New Visual InterDev 6 Web Project

PART I
CHAPTER 1

15

In this example, you skipped the Apply a layout and Apply a theme steps in the Web Project Wizard. You'll learn more about how to apply themes and layouts in the last section of this chapter.

SEE ALSO
➤ *To learn more about using the Visual InterDev 6 Editor, see page 48*

Adjusting the Web Project Properties

Now that you have established a new Web project, you can inspect and adjust the project properties. These are values that can affect how the project is deployed to the server, the default starting page for the project, and other important values.

You can view the project properties in two ways. First, you can use the Properties window to view a list of the project properties (see Figure 1.4).

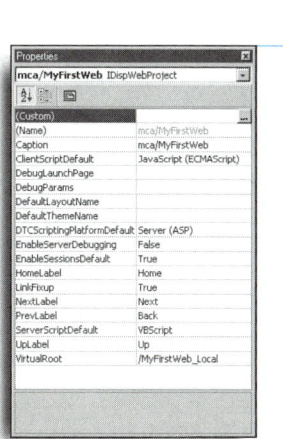

Attaching to an existing Web

It is not required that you create a new Web on the server for each Visual InterDev 6 project you create. In some cases, you will want to create a new local Visual InterDev 6 project and connect it to an existing Web on your Web server so that you can perform updates or modifications to an existing Visual InterDev 6 Web application.

FIGURE 1.4
Viewing the project properties with the Properties window.

You can also view the project properties by calling up the Project Properties dialog box. You can do this by right-clicking the project name in the Project Explorer window and selecting **Properties** from the context menu, by pressing the **(Custom)** browse button in the Properties window, or by pressing the Property Pages icon at the top of the Properties window (the right-most icon in the list). Figure 1.5 shows an example of the Project Properties dialog.

Project properties

As you work more with Web projects, you will discover that manipulating the project properties to suit your needs is a requirement, not just a useful feature.

PART **I** Visual InterDev Fundamentals

CHAPTER **1** **Creating Web Projects with the Site Designer**

FIGURE 1.5

Viewing the Project Properties dialog.

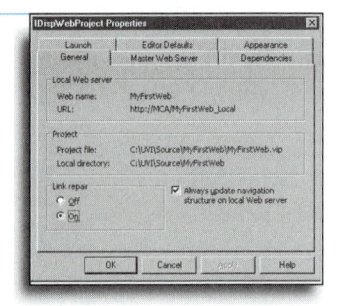

There are six tabs on the project properties dialog:

- **General**—Contains general information about the project, including the local Web server name and the source code project location.
- **Master Web Server**—Contains information about the hosting Web server for the project.
- **Dependencies**—Contains a list of all the associated custom components and dependent subprojects.
- **Launch**—Contains information about the default page used when launching the project in debug mode and the debug settings.
- **Editor Defaults**—Contains information about the default scripting platforms for both server- and client-side scripting.
- **Appearance**—Contains details about the applied theme and layout documents, along with the default navigation bar labels.

You usually do not need to adjust the properties of the Web project at this level. Most of the property settings can be left to their defaults. As you progress through the book, you'll occasionally return to these dialogs to adjust the property settings. For now, you can leave them at their default values.

Using a Site Diagram to Structure Your Web Project

Now that you have created a valid Web project and have established a Web on the host server, you're ready to begin laying out your Web site. To do this, you use the Visual InterDev 6 site diagram.

The site diagram is a document that enables you to design a Web site by literally dragging and dropping pages on an open space that looks much like a whiteboard. This drawing space can be populated by HTML documents, Active Server Pages, style sheets, text files, links to other Webs, and so on. The site diagram enables you to build your basic site design visually and then quickly test this design in your browser.

When you are satisfied with the appearance of the site, you can begin to edit the contents of the various pages in your diagram. Later in this chapter, you'll see how you can even apply predefined navigation bars and set default font and color styles to the entire site or just selected pages in the site.

SEE ALSO
> To learn more about managing your Web projects, see page 85

Creating a New Site Diagram

The first step in the process is to create a new site diagram for your Web. This diagram will act as the "blueprint" for your Web site. For this example, use the same Visual InterDev 6 project that you created earlier in this chapter.

Adding a new Visual InterDev 6 site diagram

1. With a valid Visual InterDev 6 project loaded, select **Project, Add Web Item, Site Diagram**.
2. When the **Add Item** dialog appears, enter `MySiteDiagram` in the **Name** field.
3. Be sure the **Site Diagram** icon is highlighted and press **Open** to add the new document to your project (see Figure 1.6).

> **Site diagrams are not sent to the Web host**
>
> Visual InterDev 6 uses the site diagram file to manage the navigation information within a single Visual InterDev 6 Web project. This information is used to modify HTML and ASP documents in the project. The actual site diagram file is not needed by the Web host server, and it is not copied to the Web server.

FIGURE 1.6

Adding a new site diagram to the project.

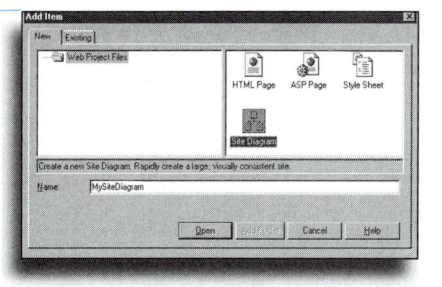

Editing the Startup Document's Name and Title

When the document is loaded into the Visual InterDev 6 editor, a small square appears with a house icon in the bottom-left corner. This represents the default start page of the Web project. This new document will be saved as DEFAULT.HTM to your Web. The word **Home** appears inside the box. This represents the title of the document.

You can edit these values at any time by right-clicking over the box and selecting **Property Pages** from the drop-down menu. This brings up the Property Pages dialog box (see Figure 1.7).

FIGURE 1.7

Viewing the site diagram Property Pages.

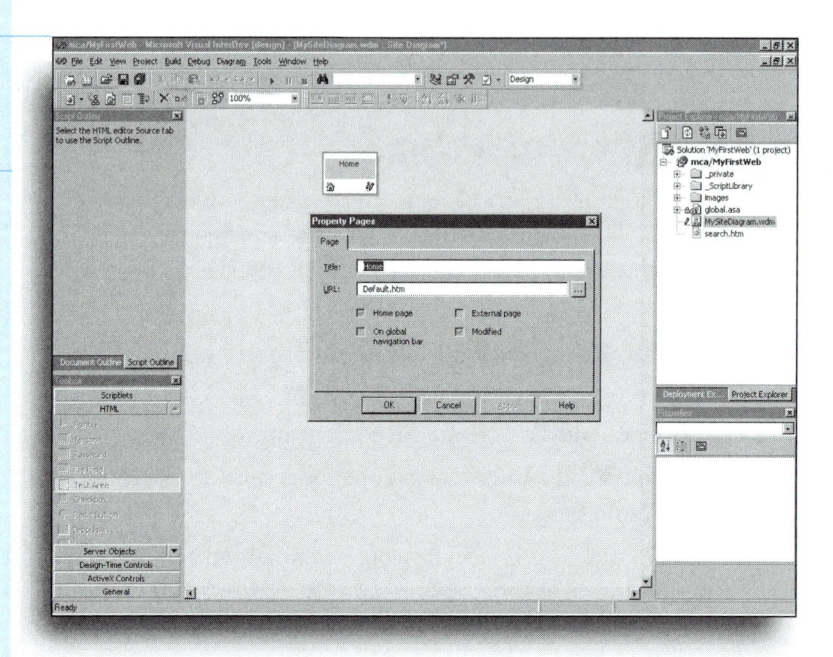

Using a Site Diagram to Structure Your Web Project

For this example, change the **Title** property to **My First Web** and press **OK** to save the change and dismiss the dialog box.

So far, you have set the properties of the new document, but you haven't actually saved those changes to the site diagram file. To do this, press Ctrl+S to save the open diagram.

Now that you know how to update the diagram, you're ready to add new documents to your Web project.

SEE ALSO
➤ *For more on setting document properties, see page 58*

Adding New Documents to Your Site Diagram

You can use the site diagram to create brand new documents for your Web. When you do this, you are actually adding boxes to a diagram that represent Web documents for your project. As you add these boxes to your diagram, you will also be establishing the name and title of each document that will eventually be added to the actual Web project.

Adding new documents to the site diagram

1. With the site diagram loaded into the Visual InterDev 6 editor, right-click over any blank space in the diagram.
2. Select **New HTML Page** from the context menu.
3. When the new document box appears on the diagram, use your mouse to drag the document box close to an existing box in the diagram (in our example, the **Home** page box).
4. When the dotted connecting line appears, release the mouse button to drop the document. A solid line should appear showing that the two documents are linked together (see Figure 1.8).

For practice, continue to add documents in this way until your site diagram looks like the one in Figure 1.9.

Be sure to save the site diagram before you move on to the next section in this chapter.

Always save your site diagram changes

Each time you modify the site diagram you must be sure to save it back to the project. When you do, Visual InterDev 6 will also update the actual HTML and ASP documents affected by the change. If you fail to save the diagram file, none of the changes will be made to the associated HTML and ASP document.

Use the site diagram as a design tool

You can use the site diagram as a way to quickly illustrate the planned design of an entire Web site. You can even print the diagram and include it in documentation packages.

PART I Visual InterDev Fundamentals

CHAPTER 1 **Creating Web Projects with the Site Designer**

FIGURE 1.8

Adding a new document to a site diagram.

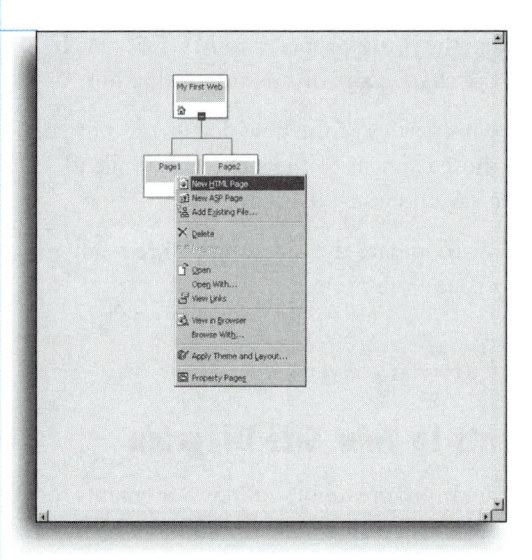

FIGURE 1.9

Building the MyFirstWeb site diagram.

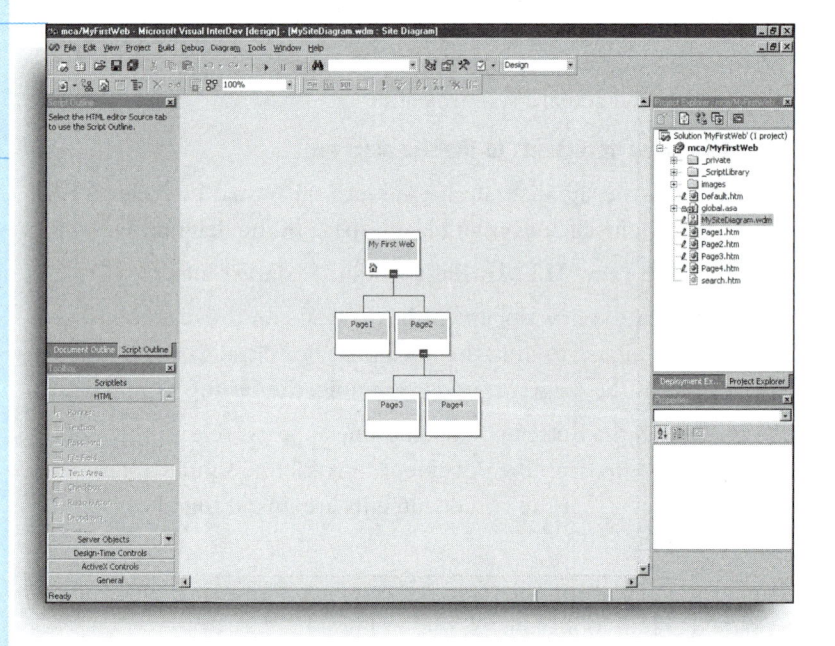

Using a Site Diagram to Structure Your Web Project

PART I
CHAPTER 1

21

Adding Existing Web Documents to Your Site Diagram

Along with creating new Web documents for the site diagram, you also can add existing Web documents to the diagram. Drag the document from the Project Explorer to the diagram that is loaded in the editor, and drop it in the location you want.

Adding an existing Web document to the site diagram

1. First, be sure the site diagram is loaded into the Visual InterDev 6 editor.
2. Next, locate a document in the Project Explorer window that you want to add to the site diagram. For this example, locate the SEARCH.HTM document.
3. Now drag the desired document from the Project Explorer over to the site diagram.
4. When you have moved the mouse to the correct location, drop the document by releasing the mouse button. The existing document now appears in the site diagram (see Figure 1.10).

> **Using site diagrams to spot potential problems**
>
> As you evolve your Web site by adding existing documents and creating new pages, you can use site diagrams to spot potential problems with your site structure and layout. Don't build yourself into a corner—leave your site room to grow without causing headaches during maintenance.

> **FIGURE 1.10**
> Adding an existing document to the site diagram.

> **Add existing documents any time**
>
> You can use Visual InterDev to build your Web documents as usual and later add them to the site diagram by dragging them from the Project Explorer. You do not have to make your site diagram complete before you start editing your documents.

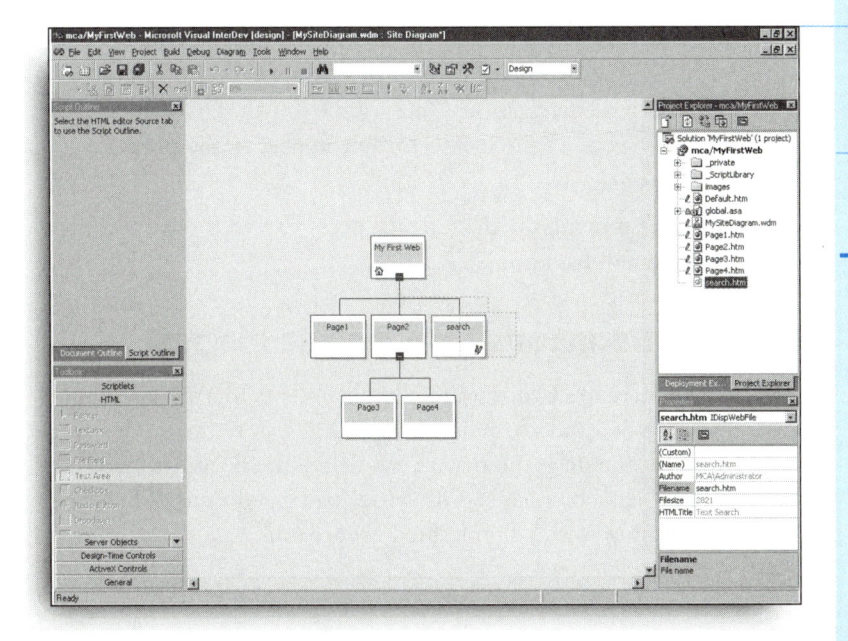

Moving Web Documents in the Site Diagram

You can also move documents around within the site diagram. This enables you to change the navigational structure of the Web project quickly and easily. Not only can you move a single page from one location in the diagram to another, you can also move whole groups of pages.

Moving a group of documents in a site diagram

1. First, be sure the site diagram is loaded into the Visual InterDev 6 editor space.
2. Next, use the mouse to draw a rectangle around the group of documents you want to relocate within the diagram. For this example, draw a rectangle around pages 3 and 4.
3. When you release the mouse, you'll see that the selected documents are now highlighted in the diagram.
4. Now move the entire group of documents by dragging one of the boxes to the desired location. You'll see that all the highlighted boxes move along with the one you selected. For this example, move pages 3 and 4 until they are under page 1.
5. When you drag the group close to another document in the diagram, the dotted connector line appears showing you where the navigational line will be drawn. Drop the group when you see the connector line appear in the proper location.
6. After moving the documents, press Ctrl+S to save the updated diagram.

Removing Documents from the Site Diagram

Just as there are two ways to add documents to a site diagram, there are two ways to remove them. You can remove a document from just the diagram, or you can delete the document from the Web project completely. Of course, you can do this with a single document or with a highlighted group, too.

Connecting pages

Remember that when you connect pages in the site diagram, you are working on the links behind the global site navigation. This does not implicitly add a hyperlink to a page, however.

Always refresh your browser pages when altering site diagrams

If you have been using your browser to test these pages, you might find that an old version of the page has been stored in your browser's memory. Be sure to press the refresh button to make sure the most recent version of the page has been loaded.

Using a Site Diagram to Structure Your Web Project

Removing a document from the diagram does not delete the physical file from your project. It only takes the document out of the diagram and removes any references to it in HREF links or navigation bars.

Deleting the document from the Web project actually deletes the physical file from the project and also removes any references to it in your Web site.

For this example, you must first add two new documents to the current diagram. It does not really matter what the names and locations of the pages are, as long as they are both added off the same branch. Use Figure 1.11 as a guide in adding two new pages to your diagram. Be sure to save the diagram before continuing to the next step.

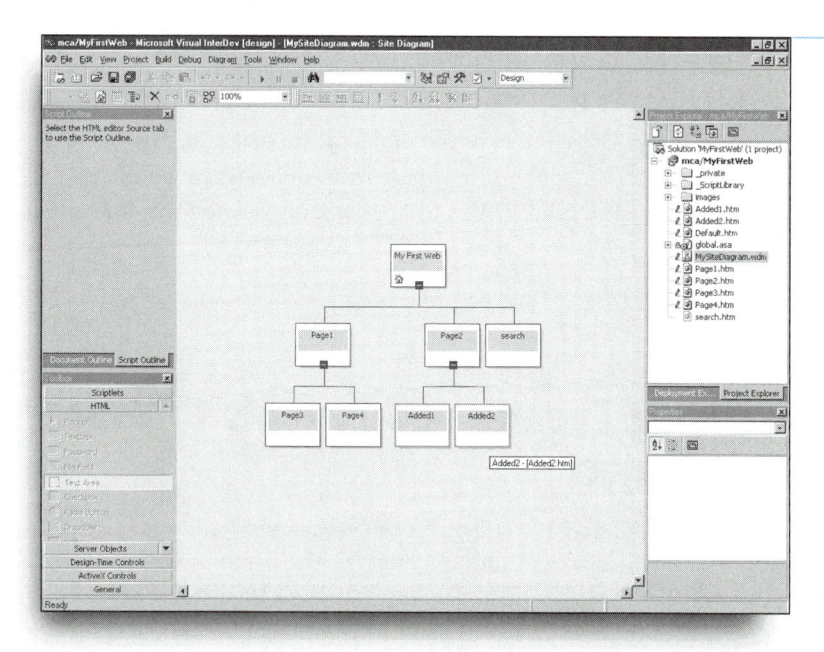

Deletes are permanent

If you decide to physically delete a file from your Web project, you will not be able to recall it very easily. If you think you might use the document in the future, remove it from navigation bars and move the file to a subfolder for later retrieval.

FIGURE 1.11
Results of adding two new documents to the diagram.

Now that you have two new pages in the diagram, you're ready to experiment with the delete options for site diagrams.

Deleting documents from a site diagram

1. With the site diagram loaded, right-click over the document you want to delete (for this example, select **Added1.htm**).
2. Choose **Delete** from the context menu.
3. When the Delete Pages dialog appears, select **Remove these pages from all navigation bars**.
4. Press **OK** to complete the action.
5. You'll see the document disappear from the diagram, but remain in the listing of the Project Explorer.
6. Now select another document to delete (for example, **Added2.htm**).
7. Right-click over the document and select **Delete** from the context menu.
8. This time, select **Delete these pages from the web project** and press **OK**.
9. Press Ctrl+S to save the updated site diagram. Now, you'll see the document disappear from the diagram and from the Project Explorer. You have physically deleted this document.

SEE ALSO
➤ *For more on using the Visual InterDev 6 Editor to manage project documents, see page 48*

Applying Themes and Layouts to Your Web Project

Now that you have created your project and built your site diagram, you can start adding details to the pages using the Visual InterDev 6 themes and layouts. You use Visual InterDev 6 themes to provide a consistent look and feel to your pages. Visual InterDev 6 layouts provide a consistent set of navigation controls and headings or footers to all the pages. By combining a theme and layout and applying them to your project, you can easily build a good-looking framework for your Web site in just minutes.

Applying Themes and Layouts to Your Web Project

The Visual InterDev 6 theme contains several parts, including a background gif, default navigation buttons, headers and footers, and a set of font types, sizes, and colors. Visual InterDev 6 ships with close to 60 different themes you can use in your Web projects.

Although the Visual InterDev 6 themes provide a consistent look to your documents, the layouts provide common navigation bars and a consistent page layout. Almost 20 different layouts are installed with Visual InterDev 6. Each one has its own set of buttons, headers, and footers.

In the most typical cases, you'll apply a single theme and layout to your entire Web project. However, Visual InterDev 6 enables you to select a subset of pages and to apply a different theme or layout to this subset. In this way, you can create unique-looking subsections of large projects. You can even customize page layouts by adding certain navigation controls to an individual page.

In the next three sections, you'll learn how to apply themes and layouts to your Visual InterDev 6 projects and how to customize page layouts to meet your specific needs.

SEE ALSO
> *To learn more about themes, see page 58*

Using Themes

You can apply a theme to a project in several different ways. Which method you use is entirely up to you:

- Project Properties dialog—You can access the Project Properties dialog and set the theme property for the project.
- Project Explorer context menu—You can right-click over the project name in the Project Explorer and select the **Apply Theme and Layout** item from the menu.
- Highlight pages in the site diagram—You can use the mouse to select one or more pages in a site diagram and then use the right-click context menu to select the **Apply Theme and Layout** option.

Create your own themes

Microsoft provides a special developer's kit for creating your own Visual InterDev 6–compatible themes. You can get more information about creating your own themes by visiting `http://www.microsoft.com/frontpage`.

The one-two punch of themes and layouts

Although it is possible to use only a theme or only a layout, usually you'll want to combine the two features to create a rich, consistent look and feel for your Web site.

For this example, you use a second option to apply a theme to the project.

Applying a theme to your Web project

1. Locate the project name in the Project Explorer window and right-click over it.
2. Select **Apply Theme and Layout** from the context menu.
3. Press the **Apply theme** radio button to activate the list of available themes.
4. Click on a theme to see a sample in the preview window (for example, click once on the **Redside** theme).
5. When you have decided which theme to apply, press **OK** to add it to your project. This will copy the theme components to a subfolder in your project and modify all the existing HTML and ASP documents in your project to match the selected theme.

You can test the look of the new theme by loading any HTML or ASP document into the editor. From the site diagram, all you must do is double-click on any document in the diagram to view the page in the editor. Figure 1.12 shows the SEARCH.HTM page as it looks in the editor with the Redside theme applied to the project.

Applying a theme to a set of Web pages makes sure they all have a consistent look. However, applying a theme does not add navigation buttons or default headers and footers to your pages. To do this, you must apply a layout to the project.

Check out the theme preview pane

As you search for an appropriate theme for your site, you can use the preview pane on the right side of the dialog box to see how the color scheme and fonts will look in a typical browser. Although this is only a small sampling of the theme, it can help you narrow your selections.

PART I
CHAPTER 1

Applying Themes and Layouts to Your Web Project

27

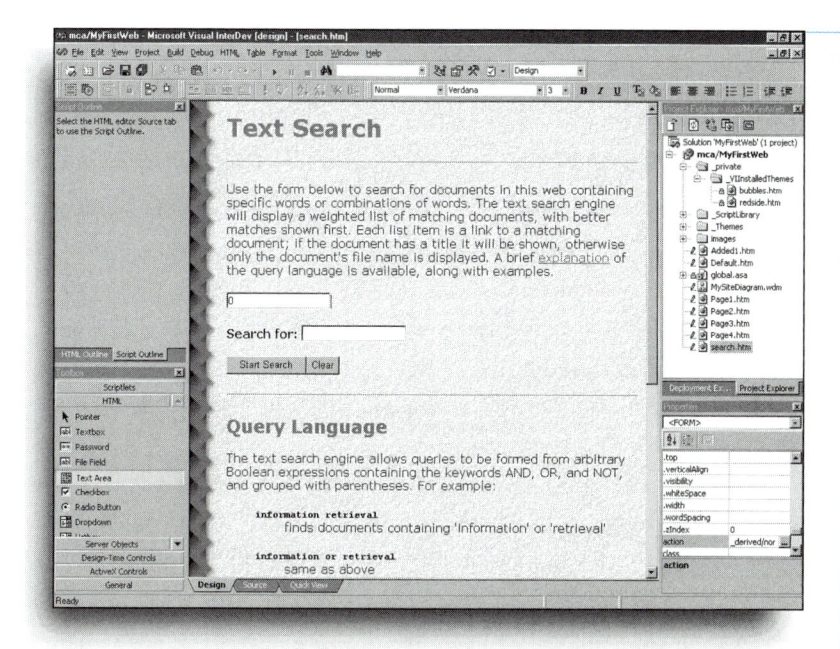

FIGURE 1.12
Viewing the Redside theme applied to the SEARCH.HTM page.

Using Page Layouts

You can use page layouts to add a constant set of navigation bars, headers, and footers to a project. As with applying themes, adding layouts can be done in several different ways:

- Project Properties dialog—You can access the Project Properties dialog and set the theme property for the project.

- Project Explorer context menu—You can right-click over the project name in the Project Explorer and select the **Apply Theme and Layout** item from the menu.

- Highlight pages in the site diagram—You can use the mouse to select one or more pages in a site diagram and then use the right-click context menu to select the **Apply Theme and Layout** option.

For this example, you use a second option to apply a layout to the project.

Applying a page layout to your Web project

1. Right-click over the project name in the Project Explorer window.
2. Select **Apply Theme and Layout** from the context menu.
3. Press the **Layout** tab to expose the list of available layouts.
4. Select the **Apply layout and theme** radio button to activate that list of layouts.
5. Select the desired layout from the list. Use the Preview window on the right to see how the layout will appear in the documents. For this example, select the **Top and Left 7** layout.
6. Press **OK** to apply the layout to the project. This will copy the layout components to a subfolder in your project and update all the HTML and ASP documents in your project to contain the layout elements.

When you apply a layout to one or more pages, you are actually adding several Design-Time Controls (DTCs) to the pages. These DTCs read control information in your project folders and display graphical buttons and headings on each page automatically.

To see how these DTCs look in design mode, you can double-click any document in the project to bring it into the editor. Figure 1.13 shows the **My First Web** home page loaded in design mode.

Notice that several design-time controls appear on the page. You will not see these design-time controls when the document is actually loaded into your browser. Instead, you see a large title banner and several clickable buttons that enable you to navigate through the Web site.

To test this, right-click over the HTML page in Design mode and select **View in Browser** from the context menu. This loads the current page into your default Web browser and shows you how it will look to visitors on the Web (see Figure 1.14).

Some DTCs are just for looks

Some of the design-time controls (DTCs) added by the Visual InterDev 6 layouts are there only to give Web designers visual cues. For example, **LayoutDTC** just displays the message **Add Your Content Above Here** or **Add Your Content Below Here**. It has no properties or methods and does not provide any functionality at runtime.

PART I

CHAPTER 1

Applying Themes and Layouts to Your Web Project

29

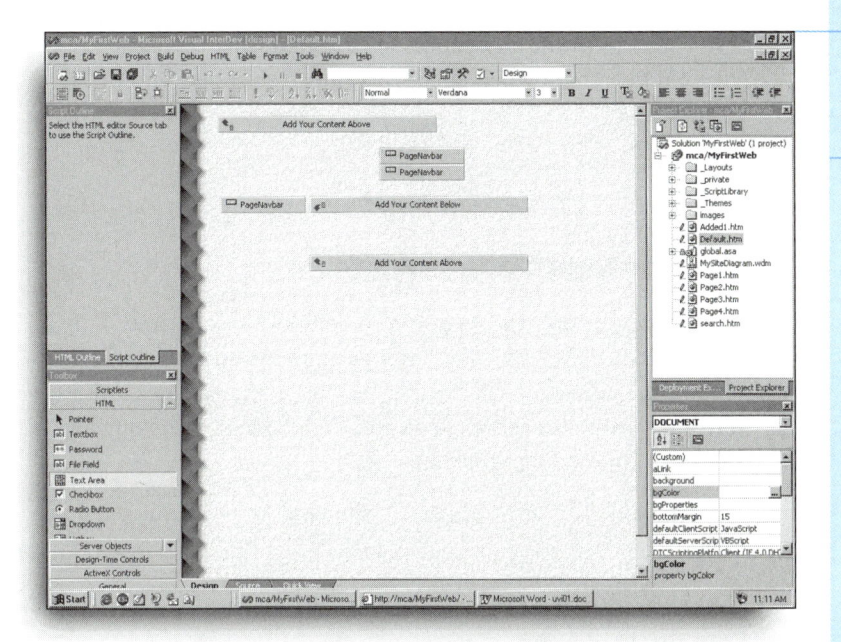

FIGURE 1.13

Viewing a page layout in Design mode.

FIGURE 1.14

Viewing the new page layout in a browser window.

When you work with pages that contain layout DTCs, you must be careful to place content only above or below the DTCs, as indicated. This ensures that your content does not overwrite critical parts of the navigation scheme, and that it will not be deleted or hidden when clients download the page into their browsers.

SEE ALSO
➤ *To learn more about using layouts, see page 58*

Customizing Your Page Layouts

You can customize the page layout controls if you want. This enables you to set up unique navigation buttons on certain pages or to remove buttons. For example, you might decide to add the **Home** button to every page in the Web to help users quickly return to the welcome screen.

You can also add or remove the following layout items from the page:

- Global navigation buttons
- Top-level pages
- Parent pages
- Sibling pages
- Child pages
- Back and Next pages
- Banner
- Home page

It is very unlikely that you will add all these items to a single page layout control. A typical page that uses the layout controls will have several controls on the page: one to handle the banner, one to handle the child pages, and so on. When you select a layout from the dialog list, you actually tell Visual InterDev 6 to add a specific set of page layout controls to your documents.

For our example, alter the page layout controls on the Home page and the three top-level pages (Page1, Page2, and Search).

Create a global navigation bar

You can create a global navigation bar that appears on one page by marking a set of pages with the **Add to Global Navigation Bar** option. These pages will always appear in a navigation set at the top of your pages.

Applying Themes and Layouts to Your Web Project

Customizing a page layout by editing PageNavbar properties

1. With the site diagram loaded in the editor, double-click the Home page to load it into the Visual InterDev 6 Editor.
2. Right-click over the desired PageNavbar control and select **Properties** from the context menu. For this example, select the second navbar control on the page.
3. Make the needed adjustments to the General properties. For this example, change the **First level pages** radio button to **Global navigation bar**.
4. If you want, click the **Home** or **Parent** check boxes to turn them on or off. For this example, make sure both items are checked on.
5. Press **OK** to save the changes and dismiss the dialog box (see Figure 1.15).
6. Do the same steps for Page1, Page2, and the Search pages.

The PageNavBar control

The PageNavBar control is your tool for controlling your site's navigational bar (navbar... get it?). The PageNavBar control is replaced with the global navigation information that you specify in a site diagram. Convenient, isn't it?

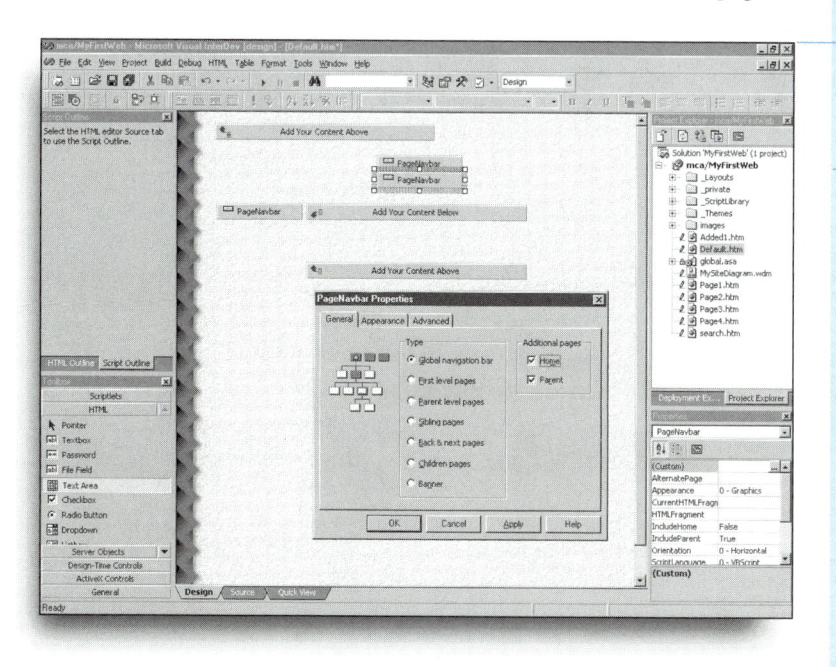

FIGURE 1.15
Modifying the page layout control properties.

PART I   Visual InterDev Fundamentals

CHAPTER 1   **Creating Web Projects with the Site Designer**

The PageNavbar control can be displayed as buttons, plain text, or customized HTML code. You can use the **Appearance** tab of the PageNavbar control dialog box to do this. Figure 1.16 shows the home page of the chapter's sample Web with the left-side navigation control set to display HTML text using an inline JScript command that offers mouse-activated DHTML coloring for Microsoft Internet Explorer browsers.

FIGURE 1.16

Viewing a modified navigation bar.

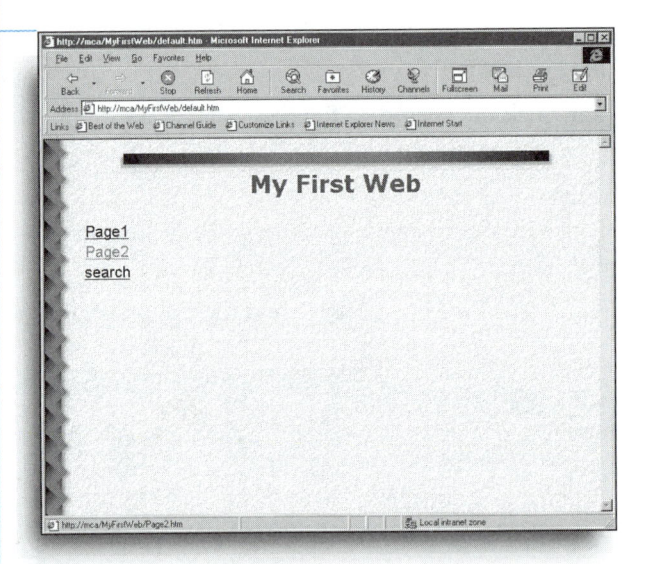

You can also place additional PageNavbar controls on the document if you want and use them to display any of the various navigation options you need. In fact, you can build your own custom navigation scheme using the DTC PageNavbar controls. However, because every new page in the project should sport the same navigation theme, doing all this by hand could get tedious.

CHAPTER 2

Using the Visual InterDev 6 Editor

Learn how to take advantage of the Visual InterDev 6 environment

Add your own custom toolbars

Create and store your own environment views

Modify your editor settings, including font sizes and colors

A Quick Tour of the Integrated Development Environment (IDE)

The Visual InterDev 6 Integrated Development Environment (IDE) is a powerful set of tools. It has been designed to give you access to everything you need when designing, coding, testing, and deploying a Web application. The good news is that there are lots of features and options in the Visual InterDev 6 IDE. The bad news is that there are lots of features and options!

There are three main modes of navigating the Visual InterDev 6 IDE:

- The dockable windows
- The menus
- The toolbars

Visual InterDev 6 has several windows that provide access to most of the major operations, including document editing, project files, database handling, debugging, and many others. These windows can be *docked* along the borders of the main frame. By simply dragging the window close to the edge of the work frame (or close to other docked windows), they will suddenly "stick" in a certain location. You'll learn more about docking windows in the next section.

Visual InterDev 6 also has extensive menu options. The key to getting comfortable with Visual InterDev 6 menus is to remember that you can get a quick set of applicable menu options by just right-clicking the mouse over your target item (file, control element, and so on). This calls up a context menu that highlights the possible actions for this item.

Finally, there are 16 prebuilt toolbars that you can use with Visual InterDev 6. These toolbars will usually automatically appear whenever you need them. However, in some cases you must manually pull these toolbars out onto the page. You can also create your own custom toolbars to handle tasks that do not regularly appear on the prebuilt toolbars.

A familiar interface

The Visual Studio interface has evolved since Visual InterDev 1.0 and other previous versions of other Visual Studio products. However, for as much as it has evolved, it still is very familiar to users who have spent much time in previous versions. Consider this an "evolutionary upgrade."

PART I
CHAPTER 2

A Quick Tour of the Integrated Development Environment (IDE)

35

The Main Editor Window

The center of the Visual InterDev 6 IDE is dominated by the main editor window. This is where all the documents and input grids appear. Usually, the main editor window contains HTML or ASP documents. At this time, the window has three tabs at the lower left:

- **Design** mode—This offers a WYSIWYG (what-you-see-is-what-you-get) view of the document. You can actively edit the page as if it were a formatted document (see Figure 2.1).

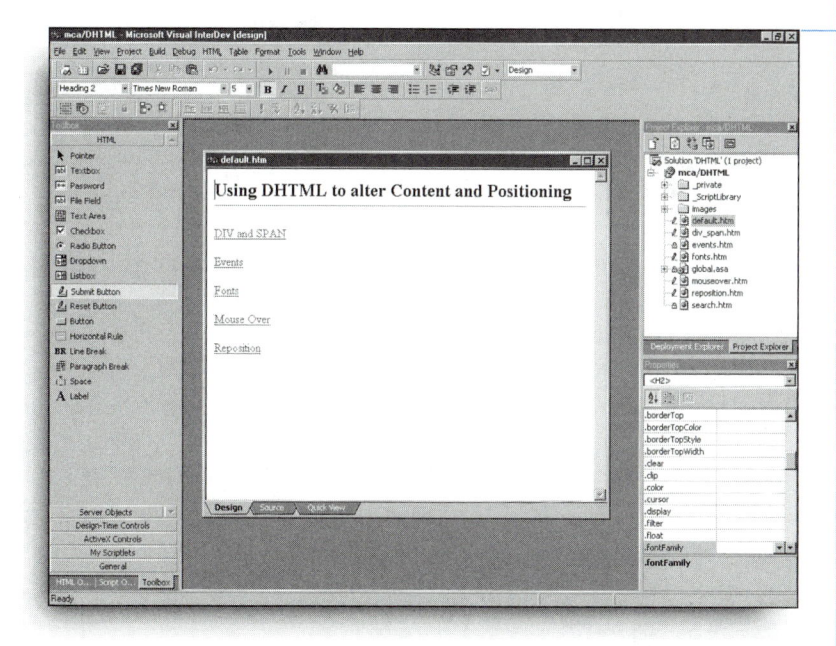

FIGURE 2.1
Viewing the main editor window with a loaded HTML document in Design mode.

- **Source** mode—This displays the document in plain source code format. You can see the highlighting of the various control elements, along with comments and other text not normally seen in Design mode (see Figure 2.2).

PART I Visual InterDev Fundamentals

CHAPTER 2 Using the Visual InterDev 6 Editor

FIGURE 2.2

Viewing the main editor window with a loaded HTML document in Source mode.

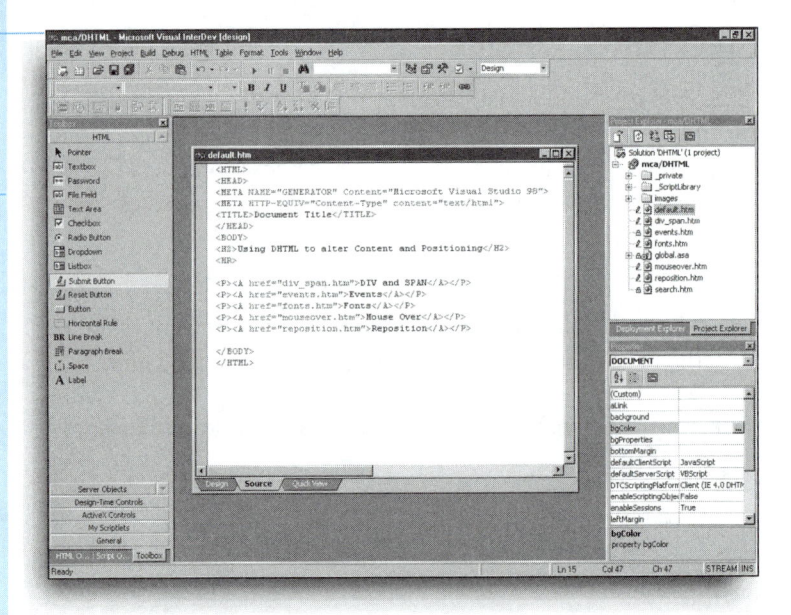

- **Quick View** mode—This displays the document as it would appear in an HTML client browser. All client-side script elements are active, including navigational links. However, server-side script is not interpreted, and any server-side elements will be missing from this view (see Figure 2.3).

FIGURE 2.3

Viewing the main editor window with a loaded HTML document in Quick View mode.

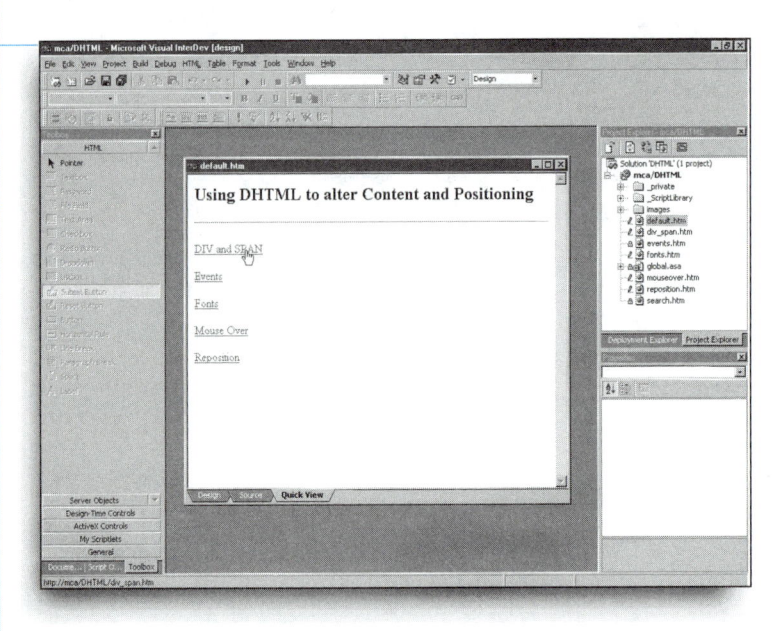

A Quick Tour of the Integrated Development Environment (IDE)

PART I
CHAPTER 2

37

Notice that, as long as you are working with pure HTML documents, the only difference between the Design and Quick View modes is that the Quick View mode is an actual running instance of a browser and Design mode is just an editor that looks like a browser.

Using the Editor Modes

As an example of how these three modes of the editor work together, you can create a new project and add an HTML document to the project.

Creating a new Visual InterDev 6 project

1. Start Visual InterDev 6.
2. You should see the New Project dialog box. If not, select **File**, **New Project** from the main menu.
3. Enter the project name in the **Name** input box. For this example, type `Editor`.
4. Click **Open** to open the new project.
5. At the next dialog, enter a valid Web server in the input box and click **Next** to continue.
6. At the next dialog, accept the default Web name (**editor**) and click the **Finish** button to create the new project.
7. Visual InterDev 6 will create several folders on your local machine and on the Web server.

When Visual InterDev 6 is finished building your empty project, you'll see the three main windows (Project Explorer, Properties, and Toolbox) along with a blank space where your document editing will take place. You're now ready to add a new HTML document to the new project.

Adding a new HTML document to the project

1. Right-click the mouse over the project name in the Project Explorer window.
2. Select **Add Item** from the context menu.
3. Select **HTML Page** from the submenu.
4. Enter the name of the new document in the **Name:** input box (for this example, enter `default.htm`).

> **Modes and editors**
>
> Although each tab reflects a different mode within the same editor, you can safely consider each of these modes as its own editor. For example, the Source mode is the Source Editor, and so on. This approach is used throughout this book.

> **Your screen might be different**
>
> If you have already begun to customize your Developer Studio, your screen might look a bit different.

PART **I** Visual InterDev Fundamentals

CHAPTER **2** **Using the Visual InterDev 6 Editor**

5. Click **Open** to add the new document to your project. Visual InterDev 6 will load the new blank document into the editor.

Now that you have a new document in your Visual InterDev 6 editor, you can test out the three different editing modes. First, switch to Design mode and type the following at the top of the document:

```
Testing the Design Mode
```

Now locate the style pull-down on the HTML toolbar and select **Heading 1** from the list. This will set the text to HTML's H1 style (see Figure 2.4).

FIGURE 2.4

Setting the text to **Heading 1** style.

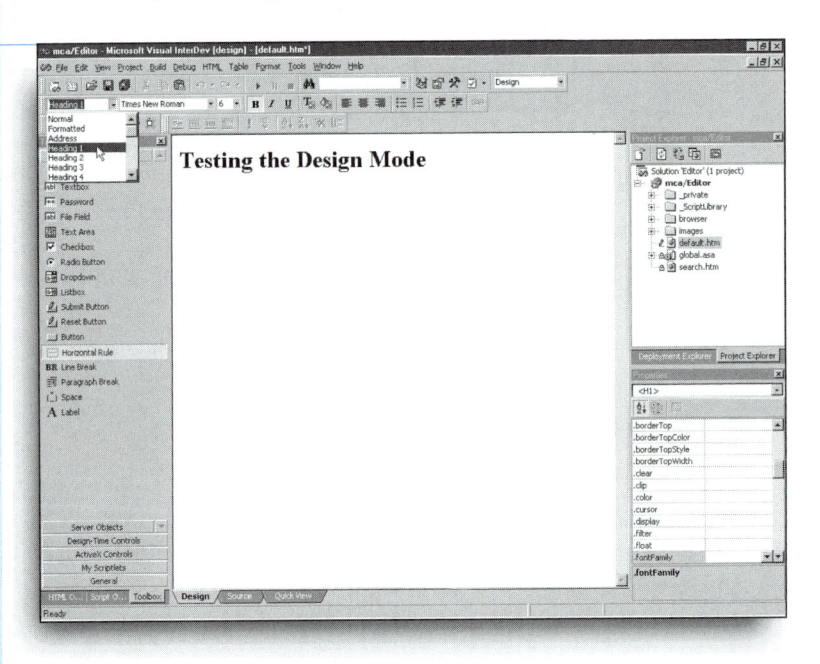

Next, switch to Source mode by pressing the **Source** tab at the bottom of the editor window. Now you will see the plain HTML coding used to create the DEFAULT.HTM document. You can edit the document in Source mode any time you want. You can even drag items from the Toolbox window and drop them on the page in Source mode.

A Quick Tour of the Integrated Development Environment (IDE)

Using drag-and-drop in Source mode

1. With the HTML document loaded in the editor, make sure the Source mode is active by clicking the **Source** tab at the bottom of the editor page.
2. Locate the Toolbox window and click the **HTML** bar to display the built-in HTML controls.
3. Drag the selected control from the toolbox and drop it on the HTML document in the desired location. For this example, drag the **Horizontal Rule** from the toolbox and drop it right underneath the **Testing the Design Mode** text. This will add the <HR> tag to the document (see Figure 2.5).

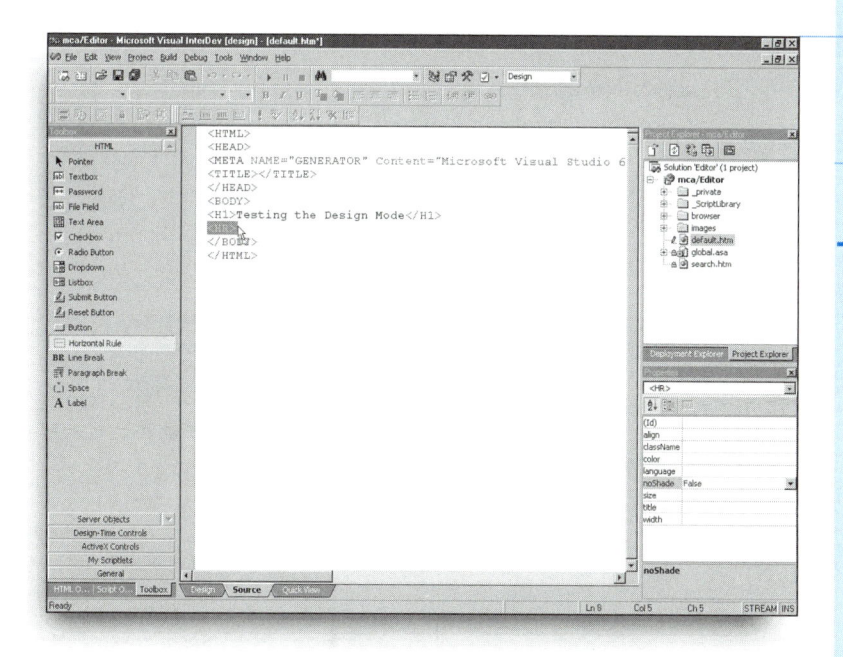

FIGURE 2.5
Adding the horizontal rule in Source mode.

The editors

Although the Design Editor in Visual InterDev 6 is a big step forward for Microsoft's WYSIWYG Web editing, it still lacks a lot of features to truly consider it WYSIWYG. The key behind this mode is to make your work easier, however it likely will not replace working in raw source code mode. One other note is that the Design mode produces pretty obscure and haphazard HTML code when you switch back to Source mode.

As mentioned earlier, the Quick View mode simply renders the current document in an active browser window.

Using the Visual InterDev 6 Dockable Windows

Visual InterDev 6 offers 18 windows that each hold specific data. Not all these windows are active or applicable at the same time.

PART I Visual InterDev Fundamentals

CHAPTER 2 Using the Visual InterDev 6 Editor

The Task List

The Task List can prove to be an invaluable tool during your development. Not only can you use it to track your own progress and that of your team, but Visual InterDev also uses it to track debugging information and problems with your application.

Customization temptation

When you first start to customize Visual InterDev, your temptation might be to open every toolbox you think you'll ever need and start to get to work. What you'll likely learn as you work more with the tool is that more isn't always better. You'll learn to customize the tool to your own work habits, as opposed to the "out of the box" provisions.

The three main windows that can always be accessed are shown in Table 2.1 along with their shortcut keys and a brief description.

TABLE 2.1 Three Main Visual InterDev 6 Windows

Window Name	Shortcut Key	Description
Project Explorer	Ctrl+Alt+J	Contains information about all the projects loaded into Visual InterDev 6
Properties Window	F4	Enables you to edit the various property settings for the current object (project, document, control, and so on)
Toolbox	Ctrl+Alt+X	Holds the various control elements that can be used within a Visual InterDev 6 project

Because these windows are used so often, they usually appear automatically in every predefined Visual InterDev 6 view. However, you can close them any time to gain more space on the screen. To call them back, you can use the shortcut keys shown in Table 2.1 or use the **View** menu instead (see Figure 2.6).

FIGURE 2.6

Accessing the **View** menu to see the entries for the three main windows.

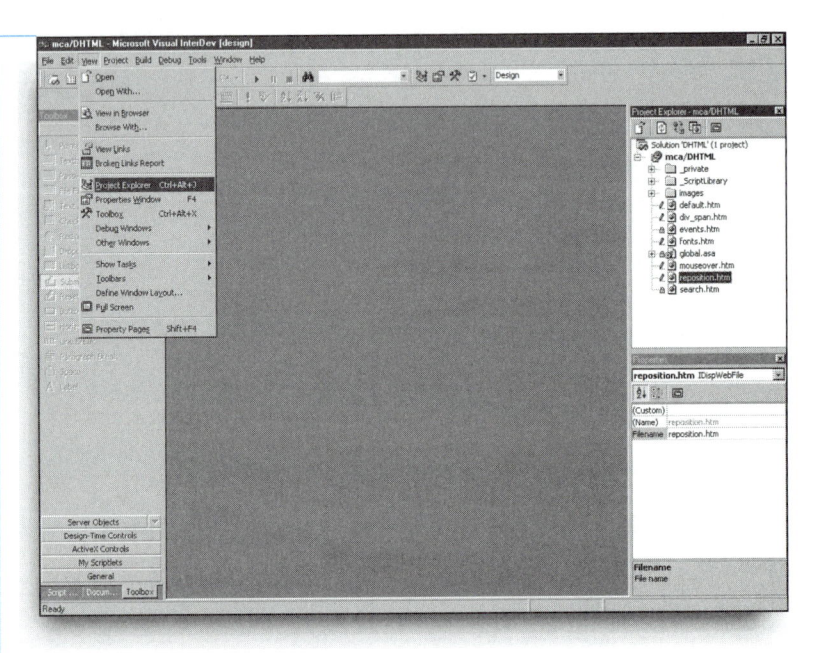

A Quick Tour of the Integrated Development Environment (IDE)

Besides the three main windows, there are several other commonly used windows. These are listed in Table 2.2 along with the shortcut key and a brief description for each entry.

TABLE 2.2 Other Visual InterDev 6 Windows

Window Name	Shortcut Key	Description
Task List	Ctrl+Alt+K	Enables users to build a TO DO list to share with other members of the project
Visual Component Manager	None	Enables access to a database of completed components that can be added to a Visual InterDev 6 project
Deployment Manager	None	Holds details for copying one or more projects to distant Web servers
Object Browser	Ctrl+Alt+B	Provides access to all the project's objects and their properties and methods
HTML Outline	Ctrl+Alt+T	Shows an outline view of all the important HTML elements in the current document
Output	Ctrl+Alt+O	Displays status messages sent by various operations, such as deployment, data access, and so on
Data View	None	Shows a list of all the databases in the project, along with their diagrams, tables, views, and stored procedures
Script Outline	Ctrl+Alt+S	Shows an outline of all the client- and server-side scriptable elements in the current document

The most commonly used windows shown in Table 2.2 are the Script Outline and the HTML Outline (see Figure 2.7).

The HTML Outline window is active when you have a loaded document in the editor and the editor is in either Design or Source mode. The Script Outline window is active only when the editor has a loaded document and the editor is in Source mode.

There are also six different windows for handling debugging operations. These and other windows are available at various times throughout the life of a project. You'll learn more about these other windows later in this book.

PART **I**   Visual InterDev Fundamentals

CHAPTER **2**   **Using the Visual InterDev 6 Editor**

FIGURE 2.7

Viewing the HTML Outline and Script Outline windows.

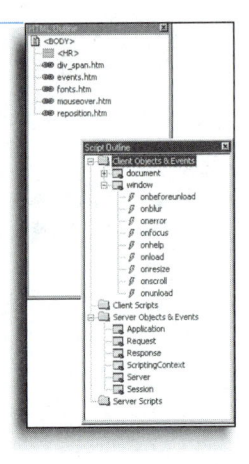

SEE ALSO

➤ *Scripting and the Script Outline is covered beginning on pages 248 and 303*

➤ *You'll learn about integrating components and controls into your pages beginning on page 546*

➤ *The Visual InterDev data environment is explored on page 421*

Stacking Your Dockable Windows

Another handy feature of the Visual InterDev 6 IDE is that you can stack the dockable windows in any way you want. This gives you the ability to have several windows available in your IDE without taking up too much screen space. Figure 2.8 shows the Script Outline, HTML Outline, and Toolbox windows all arranged in a single stack.

Notice the three tabs at the bottom of the stack. You can click each tab to bring that window to the top of the stack.

The act of stacking windows is a bit tricky. You first must select a window to act as the stack *host*. Then you must find another window that will be placed on the stack. After this has been selected, you must carefully move the window over the stack host until you see the new tab appear at the bottom of the host (see Figure 2.9).

Maximizing screen space

Creative docking can be helpful in maximizing your screen real estate. I typically dock and combine the Project Explorer, Properties, and Data View windows into one vertical window on the right side of Visual InterDev. On the left side I keep the standard dock of the HTML Outline, the Toolbox, and the Script Outline.

A Quick Tour of the Integrated Development Environment (IDE)

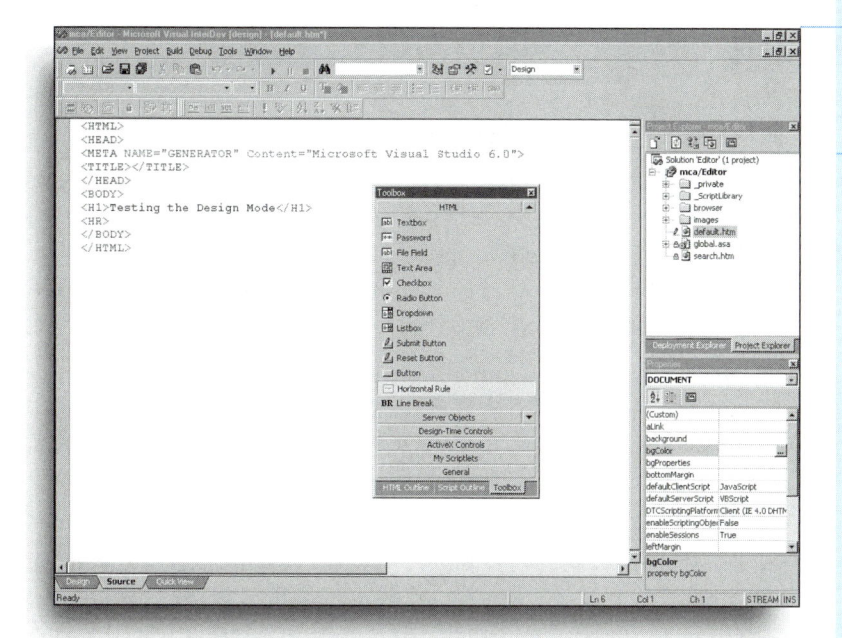

FIGURE 2.8
Viewing stacked dockable windows.

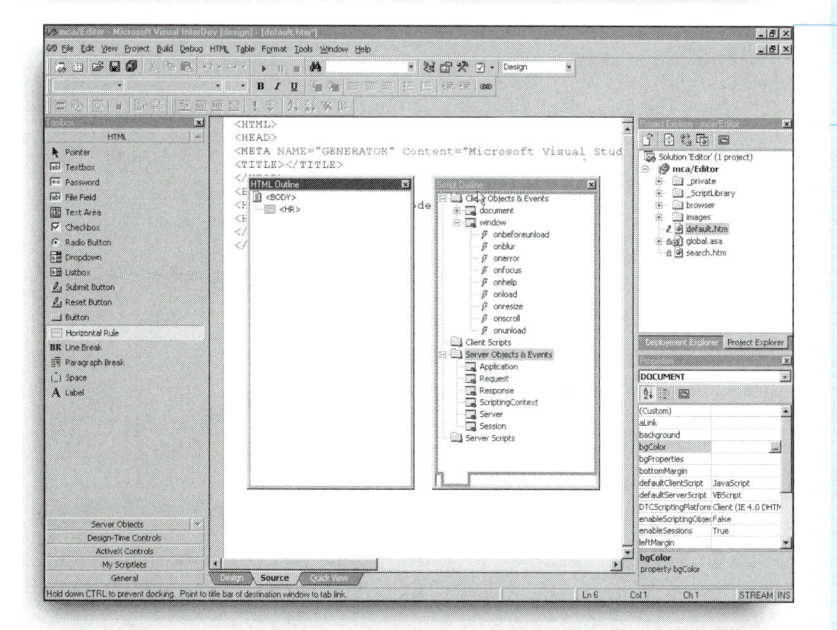

FIGURE 2.9
Adding a window to the stack.

Navigating the Visual InterDev 6 Menus

The Visual InterDev 6 menus are easy to work with and contain all the commands you need to manage your projects. Although most of the menus make sense, a few items deserve mention here.

First, the **Build** menu is not valuable for Visual InterDev 6 projects. This menu option is used for Visual J++ projects and is not used for Visual InterDev 6.

Next, the **New File** option from the **File** menu should be used only to add to the **Miscellaneous Files** section of the Project Explorer. These are files used to document the project. Any files added to the **Miscellaneous Files** section cannot be accessed from within your Web.

Next, there is a set of handy editing options in the **Advanced** submenu of the **Edit** menu. This menu offers several helpful editor features. For example, you can turn on whitespace viewing to see where you have placed spaces in your HTML document. You can also convert spaces to tabs and back again.

Using the Advanced submenu to modify viewing whitespace

1. Load an HTML document into the editor (for this example, double-click the DEFAULT.HTM document).
2. Select the **Source** tab to view the HTML code.
3. Place your cursor on an empty line within the body of the document.
4. Select **Table**, **Insert Table**.
5. When the Table dialog appears, click **OK** to add a new table to the page.
6. Now select **Edit**, **Advanced** from the Visual InterDev 6 main menu.
7. Finally, select **View White Space** to make sure it is checked on. You should now see blue dots, and in some cases arrows, to show the whitespace within your HTML document (see Figure 2.10).

Using miscellaneous files

Why add files to **Miscellaneous Files**? You can use this section to keep important documents and files that are not directly part of your Web application. You might want these files close in your Visual InterDev solution, but not in the Web itself. This could be development files, such as a software development plan.

Viewing whitespace

You can use this option to spot potential problems in your code.

Blue dots and arrows

Blue dots represent spaces, whereas blue arrows represent tabs.

Using the Visual InterDev 6 Toolbars CHAPTER 2   45

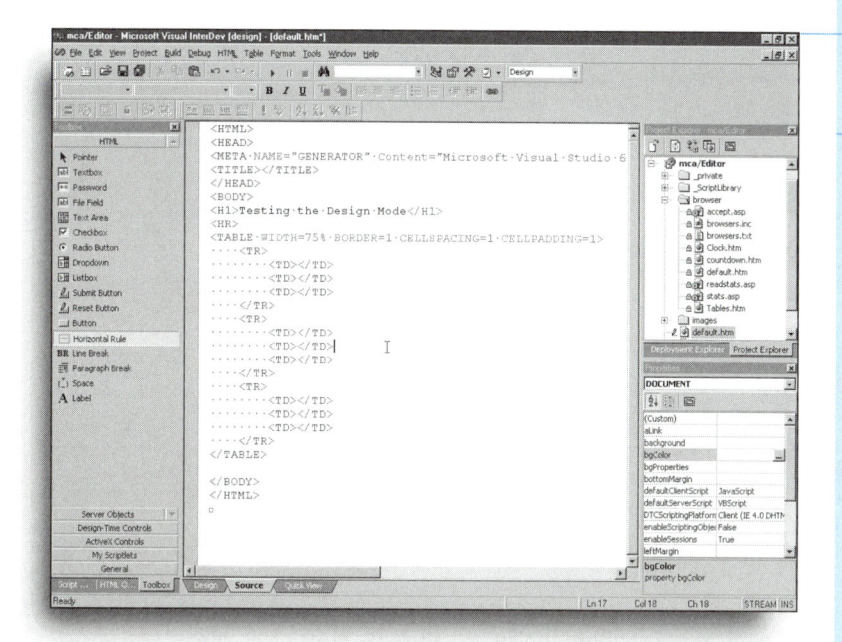

FIGURE 2.10
Viewing whitespace in the editor.

You can now use the **Tabify selection** and **Untabify selection** menu options of the **Advanced** menu to toggle whitespace between tabs and simple spaces. You'll see that tabs appear as arrows, and simple spaces appear as dots. You can use these features to confirm the type of whitespace you have in your HTML documents. This same submenu also offers the **Make Uppercase** and **Make Lowercase** options.

> **You can only tabify source code**
>
> The **Advanced** menu options (**Tabify selection**, **Untabify selection**, and so on) are available only when you are in the Source mode of the editor. You cannot apply tabs to the code while you are in Design or Quick View modes.

Using the Visual InterDev 6 Toolbars

Along with the extensive menu collection, Visual InterDev 6 has 14 predefined toolbars. Like menu options and dockable windows, these toolbars usually appear and disappear depending on the type of document that is loaded and the type of operation you are performing. However, you can always manually add toolbars by selecting the **Toolbars** option of the **View** menu (see Figure 2.11).

PART **I** Visual InterDev Fundamentals

CHAPTER **2** **Using the Visual InterDev 6 Editor**

FIGURE 2.11

Accessing the **View**, **Toolbars** menu options.

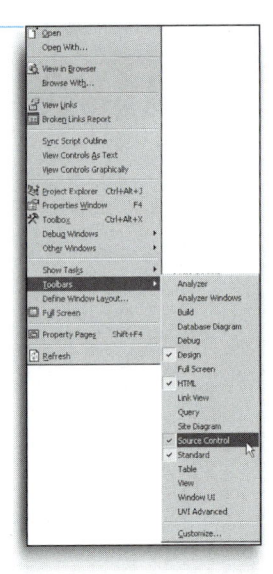

Toolbars can be docked or floating above the page. It's easy to add one of the prebuilt toolbars and then dock that new toolbar into the existing set at the top of the page.

Adding an existing toolbar to the Visual InterDev 6 IDE

1. With the Visual InterDev 6 editor open and a document visual on the page, select the **View** menu.
2. Select the **Toolbars** option in the drop-down menu.
3. In the list of available menus, select the one that you want to add to the IDE. For this example, select the **Debug** toolbar.
4. When you select the item, it will appear in the IDE either as a floating toolbar or already docked at the top.
5. If the toolbar is already docked, pull it out over the editor window by holding the mouse down over the double bars on the left margin of the toolbar and pulling the toolbar off the top of the window (see Figure 2.12). You now have a new floating toolbar.

Perfection in views

The unfortunate thing about each of the built-in views is that none of them are perfect. You'll likely want to use them as a starting point to making your own workspace.

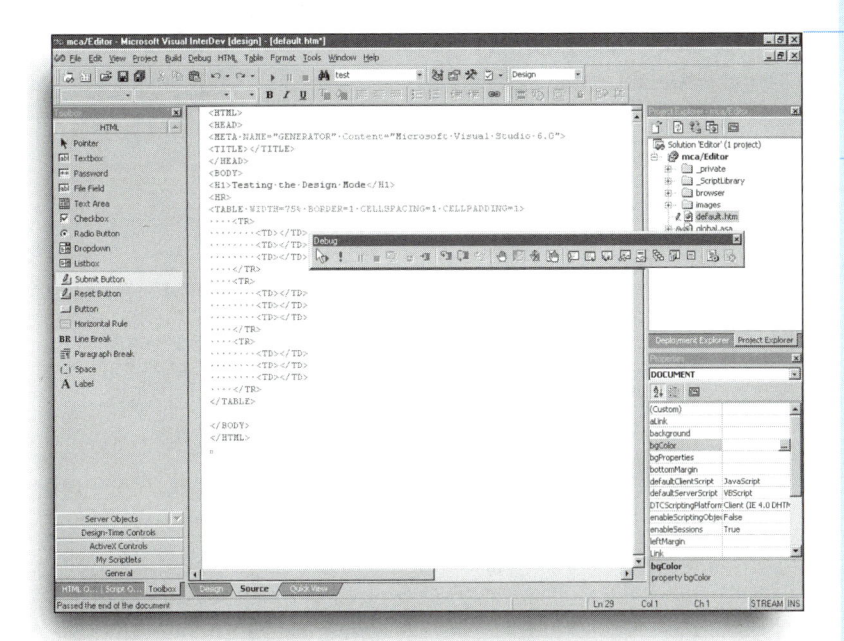

FIGURE 2.12

Pulling a toolbar off the top of the Visual InterDev 6 IDE.

Creating Your Own Custom Toolbar

You can also create your own custom toolbar to hold all your favorite features of Visual InterDev 6. All you must do is add a new blank toolbar and then populate it with menu options using drag-and-drop operations from the Customize dialog box. After you create the new toolbar, Visual InterDev 6 will remember it and display it in future sessions.

As an example, you can build a toolbar that contains the advanced source code options described in the "Navigating the Visual InterDev 6 Menus" section earlier in this chapter. This means you'll build a toolbar with the **View White Space**, **Tabify Selection**, and **Untabify Selection** menu options.

Custom toolbars

If you find yourself working often from a few individual toolbars, you're likely better off to create one custom toolbar that combines the features you use most.

Creating a custom toolbar in Visual InterDev 6

1. If you haven't done so already, open an existing Web project in Visual InterDev 6. For this example, you can use the Editor project that was created earlier in this chapter.

2. Select the **View** option on the main menu.

3. Select the **Toolbars** option to expose the submenu list of available toolbars.
4. Select the **Customize** option at the bottom of the list to display the Customize dialog.
5. Click the **Toolbars** tab.
6. Click **New** to add a new toolbar and enter the toolbar name in the **Toolbar name:** input box. For this example, enter UVI Chap2 Example (see Figure 2.13).
7. Click **OK** to create the empty toolbar. You'll see it appear next to the dialog box.
8. Click the **Commands** tab and click once on a main menu item in the left-hand **Categories** list box. For this example, click the **Edit** entry.
9. Scroll down through the **Commands:** list box on the right until you find the desired command to add to the toolbar. For this example, locate the **SelectionTabify** item in the list.
10. Drag the desired command from the list and drop it on the empty toolbar. This will add the entry to the toolbar.
11. You can continue to add items from any command list to the new toolbar. For this example, add the **SelectionUntabify** and the **Show White Space** entries to the new toolbar.

FIGURE 2.13

Adding a new toolbar to Visual InterDev 6.

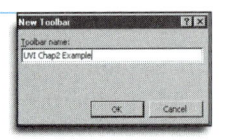

You can now dock this toolbar at the top of Visual InterDev 6 and use it any time you want.

All About the IDE Views

One of the ways in which Visual InterDev 6 helps you manage the integrated development environment is to provide a set of prebuilt views. These views consist of a specific set of toolbars and dockable windows arranged in a familiar pattern.

Visual InterDev 6 automatically switches to one of the prebuilt views, depending on the operations you are performing. You can modify the prebuilt views to fit your preferences. You can also create your own unique views if you want.

You can access the views by selecting **View** from the menu bar.

Using the Existing Views

Six prebuilt views ship with Visual InterDev 6. They are shown in Table 2.3 along with a short comment on their use.

TABLE 2.3 **Prebuilt IDE Views in Visual InterDev 6**

View Name	Comments
Design	The default view when starting a new project and editing documents with Visual InterDev 6.
Edit HTML	The view presented when you are editing an HTML document. The prebuilt version of this view is identical to the Design view.
DevStudio	An editing view that looks like the Developer Studio 97 interface used with Visual InterDev 1. Those familiar with Developer Studio 97 or Visual InterDev 1 can use this view.
Visual Basic	This view mimics the window layout of Microsoft Visual Basic. Those familiar with Visual Basic can use this view.
Full Screen	This view removes all toolbars and presents only the contents of the editor. This is a good view if you want to see the maximum amount of the document you are editing.
Debug	The view that is presented when you switch to Debug mode while in Visual InterDev 6.

Figures 2.14 and 2.15 show the Design and DevStudio views. These are probably the two most commonly used prebuilt views in Visual InterDev 6.

PART I Visual InterDev Fundamentals

CHAPTER 2 **Using the Visual InterDev 6 Editor**

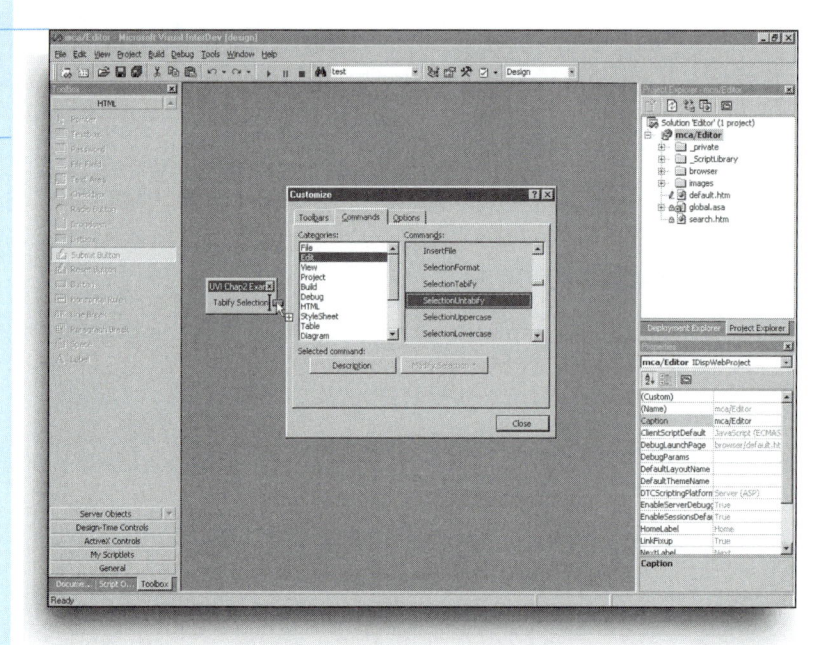

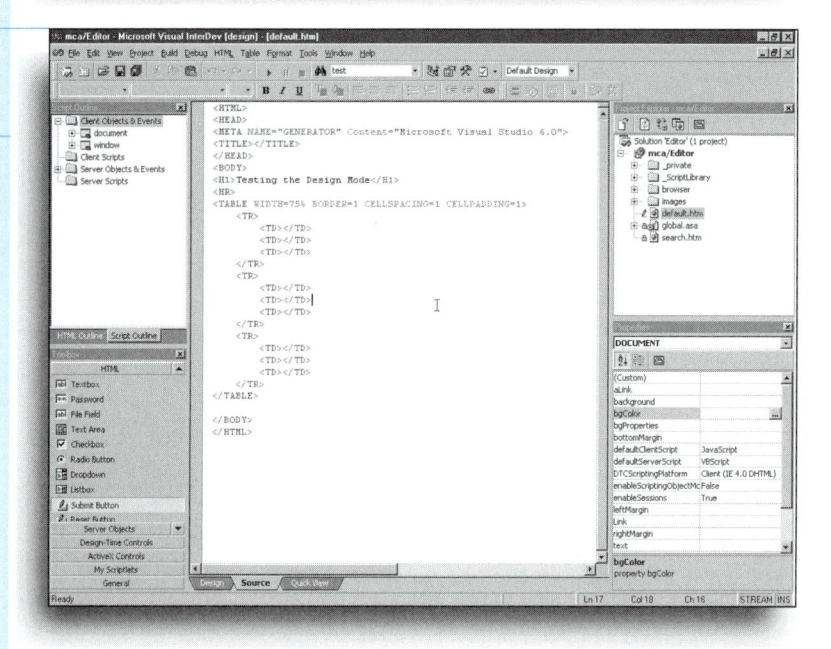

FIGURE 2.14

The Design view.

FIGURE 2.15

The DevStudio view.

All About the IDE Views | CHAPTER 2

You can easily change views by selecting the **Load/Save Window UI** drop-down list from the Window UI toolbar or the Standard toolbar (see Figure 2.16).

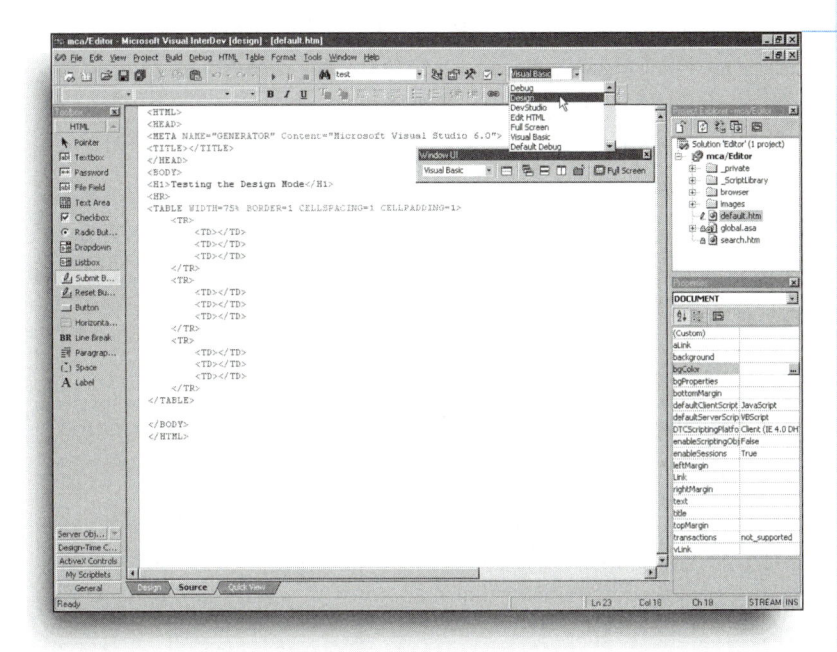

FIGURE 2.16
Selecting a new IDE view.

Creating Your Own Custom Views

You can also add your own custom views to Visual InterDev 6. These views will be stored and can then be recalled as needed. This way, you can spend time arranging the windows just the way you like and then save the configuration for later sessions.

Creating a custom view

1. Load an existing project in Visual InterDev 6. For this example, you can use the Editor project created in "Using the Editor Modes," earlier in this chapter.
2. Load a document into the editor. For this example, load the DEFAULT.HTM document into the editor.
3. Select **View** from the main menu.
4. Select **Define Window Layout**.

5. When the Define Window Layout dialog box appears, type `UVI CH02 View` in the **View Name:** input box.

6. Click the **Add** button to add a new view to the collection.

7. Select the **UVI CH02** view from the **Views:** list.

8. Click the **Apply** button to store the current window layout for this view.

9. Click **Close** to dismiss the Define Window Layout dialog box.

Now that you have created a new view in the Visual InterDev 6 collection, you can rearrange the windows, resize them, and even add and delete toolbars. After you have the view looking the way you like, you can update Visual InterDev 6 to make sure it remembers your view for the next session.

Updating an existing view

1. Select **View** from the main menu.

2. Select **Define Window Layout** from the **View** menu.

3. Locate, in the list, the name of the view you want to update and click once on that name. For this example, select **UVI CH02 View.**

4. Click the **Update** button to save the current window layout under the selected name.

5. Click **Close** to dismiss the dialog box.

Now you can switch between any of the prebuilt views and your new custom view any time you want.

Modifying the IDE Settings

Several predefined settings determine how the Visual InterDev 6 IDE behaves. This includes font sizes and colors, indent sizes, default startup behavior, and several others. All these settings are controlled from a single dialog box called the Options dialog box. You can reach the Options dialog box by selecting **Tools, Options.**

Customizing customized views

Remember that you can go back and modify your customized view any time. You're never stuck with how you choose things.

Modifying the IDE Settings CHAPTER 2

The Options dialog box is actually a series of dialogs all accessed through a tree list to the left of the input dialog. There are nine main sections in the Options dialog list. Many of these main sections have more than one screen for handling the various optional settings in Visual InterDev 6. The next several sections offer quick summaries of each of these main sections.

Environment Options

The **Environment** section has seven pages (see Figure 2.17):

- **General**—Sets global values, such as startup behavior.
- **Help System**—Enables you to select the help content and default language for the help files.
- **International Settings**—Use this to set the default language and fonts for Visual InterDev 6 menus and dialog boxes.
- **Keyboard**—Use this to create and modify your own keyboard macros for use within Visual InterDev 6.
- **Saving**—Use this to establish when files will be saved.
- **Source Control**—Use this to set defaults for Visual InterDev 6 and Visual SourceSafe interaction, including the VSS username to use when logging into VSS from within Visual InterDev 6.
- **Task List**—Use this to modify the various task keywords used throughout your documents.

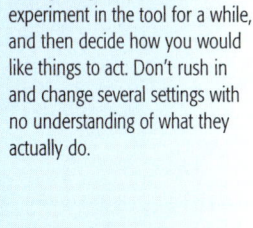

Experiment with caution

Make sure you know what you're changing when you modify IDE settings. A good practice is to experiment in the tool for a while, and then decide how you would like things to act. Don't rush in and change several settings with no understanding of what they actually do.

Source control

Actually, Visual InterDev supports any revision control system that supports the Microsoft SCC-Source Code Control specification. However, Visual InterDev is ideally suited for Visual InterDev. If you want more information on Visual SourceSafe, you should look into another book, such as *Web Site Management Using Visual SourceSafe 5.0* by Steven Banick.

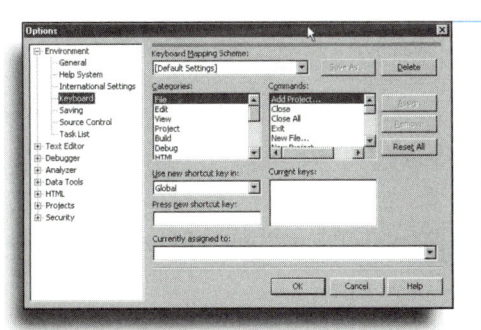

FIGURE 2.17
Viewing the **Keyboard** page of the **Environment** options dialog.

Text Editor Options

The **Text Editor** section has the following pages, which enable you to establish the various fonts and colors used throughout Visual InterDev 6 as well as language-specific settings for tabs and other behaviors (see Figure 2.18):

- **General**—Use this to adjust cut-and-paste behavior and active margins.
- **Font And Colors**—Use this to set the colors, fonts, and sizes of all the editing panes in Visual InterDev 6.
- **Per Language**—This is a set of pages that enables you to control editor behavior by language for **HTML**, **PL/SQL**, **Plain Text**, **SQL**, **T-SQL**, and **T-SQL7**.
- **Tabs**—This is another set of pages that enables you to control how the editor manages tabs by the same languages referred to under the explanation of **Per Language**.

> **Brass tacks**
>
> This is where you get down to the details: deciding how you want your editors to look and behave. You can copy the behaviors from other editors you might have worked with in the past to make your ideal editor.

FIGURE 2.18

Viewing the **Font And Colors** page of the **Text Editor** options dialog.

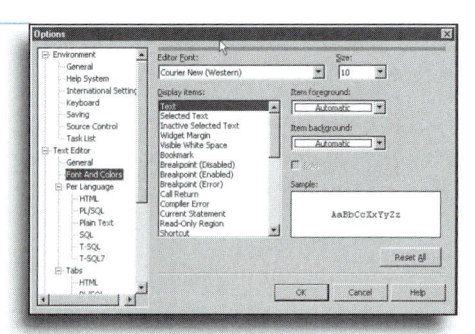

Data Tools Options

The **Data Tools** options section presents three pages of settings (see Figure 2.19):

- **Data Environment**—Use this dialog to control how data connections and data commands are treated within the Visual InterDev 6 editor.

Modifying the IDE Settings   PART I   CHAPTER 2   55

- **Data View**—This enables users to control query timeout options and how to render system objects in the data view window.
- **Database Projects**—Use this page to control how Visual InterDev 6 database projects behave, including which scripts are automatically created and how they are saved.

SEE ALSO
➤ *For a better understanding of the Visual InterDev Data Environment, see page 421*

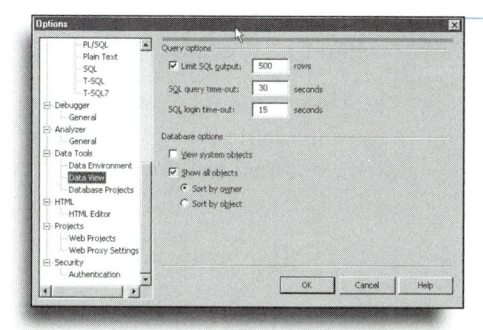

FIGURE 2.19
The Data Tools Options is used to customize the Data Environment behavior.

Projects Options

The **Projects** options section has two pages, which control how projects get created for the Web server and how Visual InterDev 6 contacts the Web server through a proxy server (see Figure 2.20):

- **Web Projects**—Use this page to control whether projects are created with a GLOBAL.ASA file, how files are opened, and which document types are not included when deploying the project to a remote server.
- **Web Proxy Settings**—Use this page to establish a custom proxy server for use in contacting target Web servers, as well as creating a list of hosts that do not use proxies.

Proxies

Remember that you communicate with your Web server via HTTP. Make sure that your proxies have been configured to allow you to do so if you are behind a firewall.

FIGURE 2.20

Viewing the Project Settings page of the **Web Projects** options dialog.

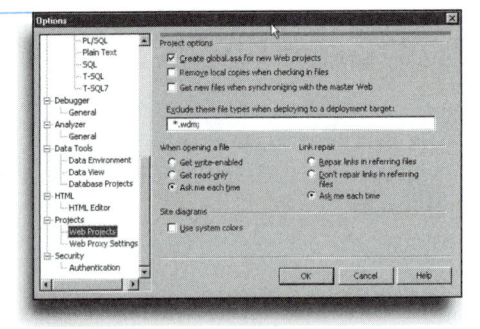

Other Options Pages

The **Debugger** and **Analyzer** options items each have only one page: the **General** page. This page contains options for controlling how Visual InterDev 6 debugging and Web server analysis is handled. Usually, you do not need to modify these values.

The **HTML** options page also has only one **General** page. You can use this page to control how the Visual InterDev 6 editor will render DTCs and how it will load and display ASP and HTML documents.

The **Security** options page can be used to manage your certificate settings for the Visual InterDev 6 editor. You can also use a default test certificate if you do not already have the certificate installed.

SEE ALSO

➤ *For more detail on security and your Web application, see page 691*

CHAPTER

3

Building Web Pages with the Page Designer Tools

Design and use your own page template

Learn how to use the PageNavBar control

Add the Page Transition control to your pages

Now that you know how to use the Visual InterDev 6 Site Designer to design Web sites and how to use the Visual InterDev 6 editor to create Web pages, you're ready to get deeper into the details of building Web pages. In this chapter, you learn some techniques that will help you quickly design and create Web documents that have a consistent look and feel.

You'll learn how to create a template document that can act as the boilerplate for your Web pages. You'll also learn how to use the PageNavBar and the PageTransition design-time controls to help you easily add page banners, navigation menus, and page-to-page transition graphics. Most importantly, you'll learn how these controls can be used to automatically update the navigation menus of your entire Web site without having to rewrite any documents in the design.

> **As with anything, exercise discretion**
>
> The PageNavBar and PageTransition DTCs provide a lot of temptation to designers. Make sure that you are using them to enhance and improve your site, as opposed to cluttering it for users.

Creating a Template Document

One of the most important aspects of creating Web pages is to be able to generate documents that have a common "look and feel" throughout the Web site. This usually means that you have a similar layout for the pages and that you use the same background colors and font styles from page to page. Although there will be times when a particular page will require a custom layout, starting from a template or model page will make it easier to add new pages to your site and enable you to focus more on the content of the page instead of the layout itself.

There are several techniques for generating Web pages that have a common look and feel. In this chapter, you learn how to use the HTML TABLE element to design a standard page layout. The TABLE element is commonly used to control placement of text on a Web document.

> **What about using FRAMESET?**
>
> If you want, you can use the HTML **FRAMESET** element to generate a common layout for your Web site. However, some low-level browsers do not support the use of **FRAMESET** and might not be able to render your documents. Additionally, **FRAMESET**s can slow down your site's loading and rendering time. You should use **FRAMESET** pages selectively.

Controlling the Page Layout with the HTML *TABLE* Element

A typical Web page layout is shown in Figure 3.1.

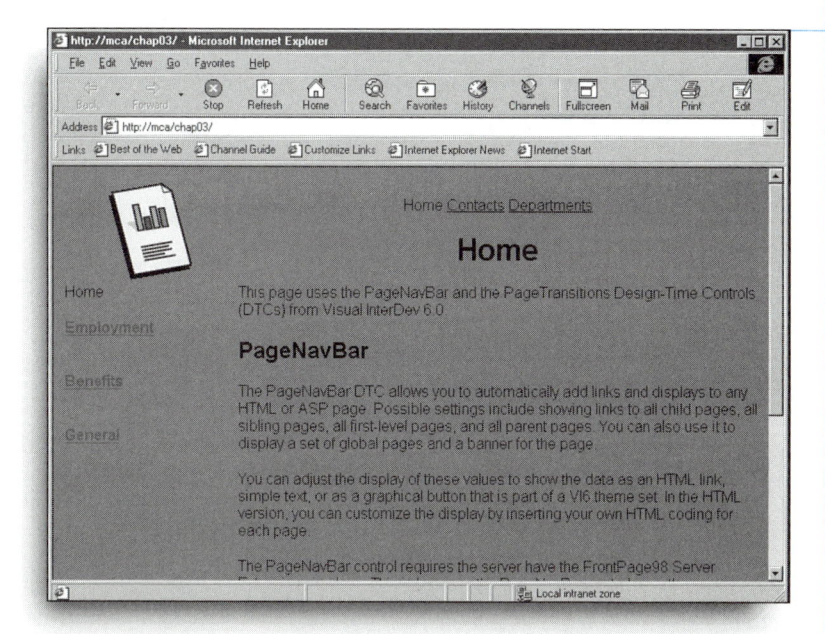

FIGURE 3.1
A typical page layout.

Notice that there are five basic elements to the page layout:

- A graphical image in the top-left corner
- An immediate navigation menu in the left margin
- A global navigation menu in the top right
- A title banner in the top right
- The actual page content in the bottom right

This layout was created using the HTML TABLE element. A blank page was created with a single table containing two rows and two columns. In this example, the first column width is set to 25 percent. Then the actual contents of each table cell (image, menu, banner, content) were added. When you have the basic template, you can customize each page as needed.

There are three tasks to creating a template document for your project. First, you must create the new HTML document and add it to your project. Next, you must add an empty table to the document to hold the page contents. Finally, you must adjust the table's column settings, such as width and alignment, to reflect your desired layout.

Site navigation

Most Web sites offer a variation on this theme, if not a duplication of it. Surprisingly, the past few years have seen very little evolution in site design and navigation.

Test in other browsers

If you are designing for the Internet or an intranet that does not have one standard Web browser, make sure to test your layout in several different browsers. This lets you see firsthand how your layout will appear in the various browsers out there and determine whether it needs adjustment.

Creating a layout template HTML document

1. Create a new Visual InterDev 6 Web project or open an existing one.
2. Right-click the mouse over the project name and select **Add** from the context menu.
3. Select **HTML Page** from the submenu.
4. In the Add Item dialog, enter a new name in the **Name:** input box (for this example, enter `template`) and press the **Open** button to open the new document in the Visual InterDev 6 editor.

Now that you have the new document added to your project and loaded in the Visual InterDev 6 editor, you're ready to add the empty HTML table that will control the layout of the page.

Adding an empty HTML table to the document

1. With the document loaded in the Visual InterDev 6 editor, select **Table** from the main menu.
2. Select **Insert Table** from the menu list to bring up the Insert Table dialog.
3. When the Insert Table dialog appears, set the **Rows:** and **Columns:** values as desired. In this example, set both values to **2**.
4. Set the **Width:** value as needed. For this example, set the width to **100** and set the measurement type to **percent**.
5. Set the **Border size** property as needed. In this example, set it to **0**.
6. Press **OK** to create the new HTML table in your document (see Figure 3.2).

Because you created this sample table with borders turned off (**Border size: 0**), you won't be able to see the table while you are viewing the document in Design mode. However, you can force Design mode to display the table borders by pressing Ctrl+Q or selecting **Visible Borders** from the **View** menu. You can also press the Visible Borders button on the **Design** toolbar (see Figure 3.3).

Creating a Template Document

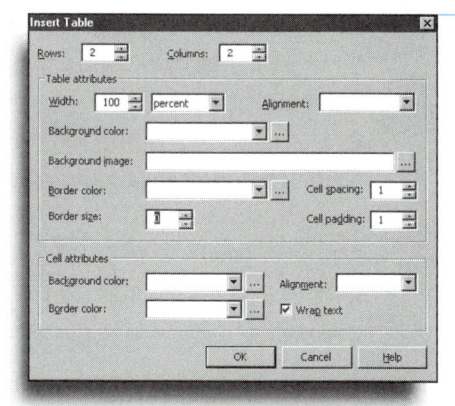

FIGURE 3.2
Using the Insert Table dialog to add a new table to the document.

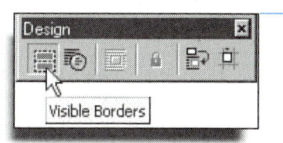

FIGURE 3.3
Forcing Visual InterDev 6 to display the table borders.

Now that you have the empty table on your template document, you must adjust the table cell settings, including column width and alignment, to reflect your desired layout. For this example, you'll set the left column to cover only 25 percent of the page. This will provide the thin left margin that will hold the graphical image and the immediate navigation menu.

You'll also set the alignment of the table as follows:

- Top-left cell—Align content in the exact middle of the cell.
- Bottom-left cell—Align content to the top of the cell.
- Top-right cell—Align content in the center of the cell.
- Bottom-right cell—Align content to the top-left of the cell.

Setting the column properties of an HTML table

1. Be sure the document that holds the HTML table is loaded in the Visual InterDev 6 editor.
2. Place your cursor inside the table cell you want to adjust. For this example, place your cursor in the top-left cell of the table.

Remember to turn off the borders!

Make sure to turn off your table's borders when you are finished designing unless you specifically want them to be visible.

Remember browser differences

Keep in mind that different browsers (such as Internet Explorer and Netscape Communicator) render tables and alignment a bit differently. Make sure to test your layout thoroughly with different browsers to make sure it works.

PART I Visual InterDev Fundamentals

CHAPTER 3 **Building Web Pages with the Page Designer Tools**

  3. Right-click the mouse to bring up the context menu and select **Properties** from the menu to bring up the Properties dialog.
  4. Set the table cell properties as desired. For this example, set the **Horizontal:** alignment to **center** and the **Vertical:** alignment to **middle**. Also set the **Width:** to **25** and the measurement to **percent**.
  5. After you have set all the properties you want, press the **Apply** button to save the values to the document (see Figure 3.4).
  6. With the dialog still in view, click another cell in the table. For this example, click the bottom-left cell.
  7. Set the desired properties for the selected cell. For this example, set the **Horizontal:** alignment to **left** and the **Vertical:** alignment to **top**. Press **Apply** to save the settings to the document.
  8. Click the top-right cell in the table and set the **Horizontal:** alignment to **center** and the **Vertical:** alignment to **middle**. Press **Apply** to save the settings.
  9. Click the bottom-right cell in the table and set the **Horizontal:** alignment to **left** and the **Vertical:** alignment to **top**. Press **Apply** to save the settings.
  10. Press **OK** to dismiss the dialog and return to the Visual InterDev 6 editor.

If you have a better layout

If you have a better idea for a layout, feel free to replace the instructions provided here with your own ideas.

FIGURE 3.4

Setting the table detail cell properties.

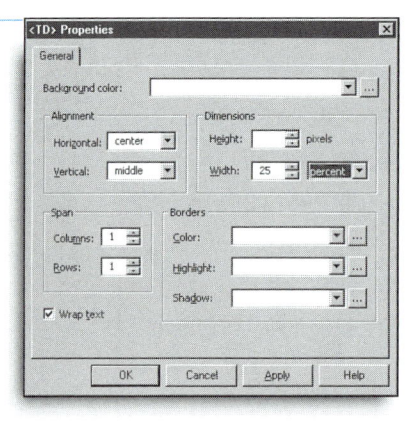

You have now completed your template page layout for this project. Be sure to save the document by pressing Ctrl+S or selecting **S**ave template.htm from the **F**ile menu.

You're now ready to add the default graphical image and sample text to the template.

SEE ALSO
➤ *You can read more about using the Design and Source Editors on page 34*

Adding an Image to the Template

Now that you have completed the HTML table definition, you're ready to add a default graphical image to the top-left cell. By adding the image to the template, it will act as the default image for all pages you add to your project. Later, you can remove the image or replace it with one more appropriate for the specific page you are building.

For this example, you add the REPORT.GIF image to the template. In the sample project in this book, this image was already added to the images folder of the project. If you are working with a new Visual InterDev 6 project, you might not have an image in your images folder. So, before you add the image to the page, you'll learn how to add an image file to your project.

For this example, you add a single GIF (graphical information file) format file to the project. It does not matter which image you add, as long as it is in a compatible format for display on Web pages. You can safely use GIF- or JPG-formatted image files in your Web documents. The following steps show you how you can navigate to any folder on the local machine or available local network shares to locate and add an image file. If you do not have any GIF or JPG images available, you can download the sample project files from the *Using Visual InterDev 6* Web site.

Where are the image files?

All the image files used in this book can be found at the *Using Visual InterDev 6* Web site. Check Appendix B, "Online Resources," in the back of the book for the exact location of this site.

Adding a graphical image file to your project

1. Be sure you have a valid Visual InterDev 6 project loaded.
2. Select the Images folder from the Project Explorer window.

PART **I** Visual InterDev Fundamentals

CHAPTER **3** **Building Web Pages with the Page Designer Tools**

Image formats

Keep in mind that you can use any image format that your Web browser supports, such as GIF, JPG, PNG, even Macromedia Flash (.SWF) if your browser is configured properly.

3. Right-click over the images folder and select **Add** from the context menu.
4. Select **Add Item** from the submenu.
5. When the Add Item dialog appears, select the **Existing** tab.
6. Set the **Files of type:** drop-down at the bottom of the dialog box to **Image Files**. You'll see a long list of file types that are valid image formats.
7. Use the **Look in:** drop-down box at the top of the dialog box to locate a folder that contains valid images (see Figure 3.5).

FIGURE 3.5

Selecting an image file to add to the project.

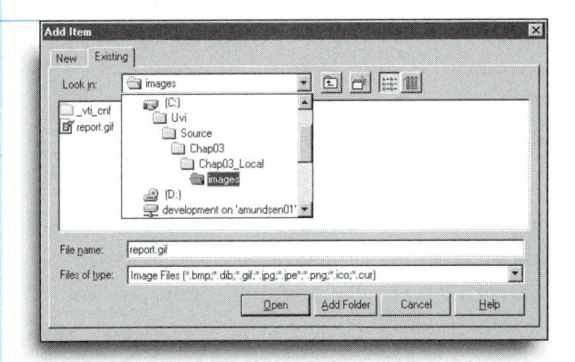

8. When you locate a folder with the desired image (in this example, REPORT.GIF), click once on the image file to select it.
9. Press the **Open** button to add the image file to your project.

Now that you have an image file in your project, you're ready to add it to the TEMPLATE.HTM document.

Adding a graphical image to an HTML document

1. First, be sure the desired document is loaded in the Visual InterDev 6 editor. For this example, load the TEMPLATE.HTM document.

Creating a Template Document

2. With the editor in Design mode, place your cursor in the exact location where you want the image to appear. For this example, place your cursor in the top-left cell of the table.
3. Select **HTML** from the main menu.
4. Select **Image** from the **HTML** menu to display the Insert Image dialog.
5. Press the **Browse** button to bring up the Create URL dialog.
6. Click the Images folder in the **Projects:** tree view on the left to reveal the list of image files loaded in the project folder.
7. Select the desired image from the **Contents of 'images'** list on the right. In the example in the book, the REPORT.GIF file is selected (see Figure 3.6).

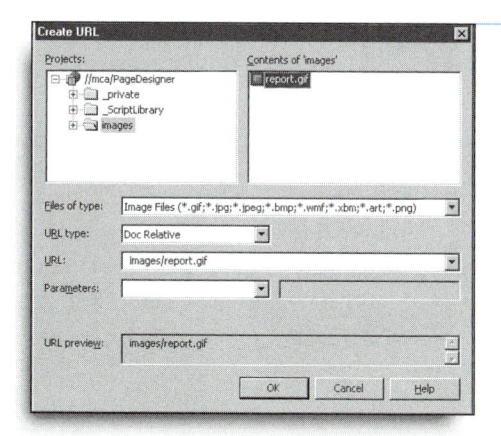

FIGURE 3.6
Using the Create URL dialog to select an image file.

8. Press **OK** to return to the Insert Image dialog box.
9. Enter some descriptive text in the **Alternate text:** input. For this example, enter Report Image.
10. Press **OK** to add the image to the document. Your final page should look like the one in Figure 3.7.

Navigational graphics

Typically, when you add images to your site's navigational structure, you'll want to use graphics of a fairly small size. This ensures a quick load time and enough "breathing room" for any other graphics your page might reference.

A shortcut for adding an image

You can also add an image to your page by dragging it from the Project Explorer and dropping it onto your page. Who doesn't appreciate time savers?

Provide alternative text

One thing many designers are forgetting with today's Web site is that not everyone visiting a Web site is using a graphical browser. Text browsers such as Lynx, or users who have images disabled in their standard Web browsers, will lose out on your site's navigational structure if you do not provide alternative text. Additionally, alternative text typically appears onscreen before the image loads. This enables your site's visitors to quickly recognize buttons before the image even appears. This, in turn, makes their experience less tedious.

FIGURE 3.7

Viewing the added image in the HTML document.

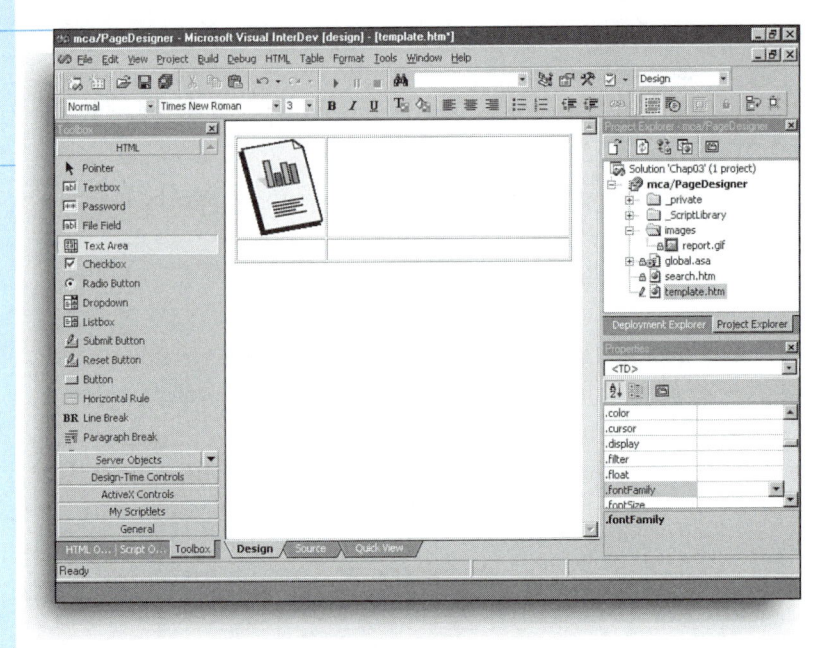

Adding Sample Text to the Template

After you have the template document layout complete and you've added the default graphical image, you must add some sample text to the page to help remind you of the content that should appear in each cell of the layout. For this example, you'll use the following sample text in the document:

- Top-right cell—`global navigation` on one line and `banner title` below it
- Bottom-left cell—`immediate navigation menu`
- Bottom-right cell—`page content`

You can add this text in Design mode simply by placing your cursor in the table cell and typing the text. When you are finished, your document should look like the one in Figure 3.8.

Now that you have completed the basic template document, you're ready to enhance it with some of the new Visual InterDev 6 Page Designer design-time controls.

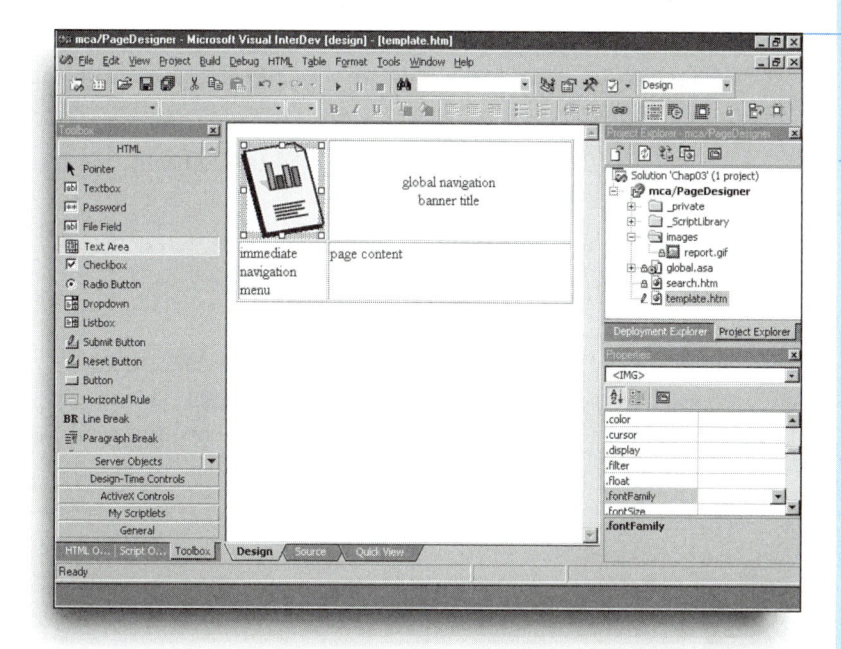

FIGURE 3.8
Adding sample text to the template document.

SEE ALSO
➤ Visual InterDev themes and layouts let you create a standardized navigational structure much like these instructions. For information on using themes and layouts, see page 24

Using the PageNavBar Design-Time Control

Visual InterDev 6 ships with several design-time controls (DTCs) that provide a special set of features for Visual InterDev 6 projects. DTCs provide a familiar set of dialogs that enable you to set properties at design-time. However, when the project is actually running, these controls produce standard HTML and scripting language that can be read by most browsers. This all happens without your having to write your own script or HTML. In this way, the DTCs enable you to add high-level functionality to your pages without going through all the pain of actually coding them yourself.

Two of the DTCs are specifically targeted for helping design Web pages. For this reason they are sometimes referred to as the Page Designer controls. The two controls are

- The PageNavBar DTC, which is used to add navigation features to a Web page
- The PageTransitions DTC, which is used to add entry and exist transitions or "wipes" to a Web page

In this section of the chapter, you learn how to use the PageNavBar DTC to automatically add banner titles, link menus, and global navigation links to your template document. After you've added these DTCs to your documents, they will automatically provide links and banners to all your pages.

SEE ALSO
▶ *Design-time controls are covered in more detail on page 544*

Adding a Sample Site Diagram

> **FrontPage navigation bars**
>
> The Visual InterDev PageNavBar DTC is much like the PageNavBar control in Microsoft FrontPage 98. If you've used those navigational bars, you might want to flip past this section.

The PageNavBar DTC works in conjunction with the project's site diagram. You will not be able to see the effects of adding PageNavBar DTCs to your document until you add a site diagram, too. For this example, you build a simple site diagram that you can use to see how the PageNavBar and the site diagram work together.

Adding a site diagram to an existing Web project

1. Right-click the mouse over the project name in the Project Explorer window.
2. Select **Add** from the context menu.
3. Select **Site Diagram** from the submenu.
4. Enter a name for the new diagram in the **Name:** input box. For this example, use `template` as the name.
5. Press **Open** to add the site diagram to the project and open it in the Visual InterDev 6 editor.
6. When the site diagram appears, the first page, called Home, appears in the document. This is the DEFAULT.HTM page for the site diagram.

Using the PageNavBar Design-Time Control | PART **I** CHAPTER **3** | **69**

7. Drag the TEMPLATE.HTM page from the Project Explorer and drop it on the site diagram close to the Home document where it will be attached as a child page of the Home document (see Figure 3.9).

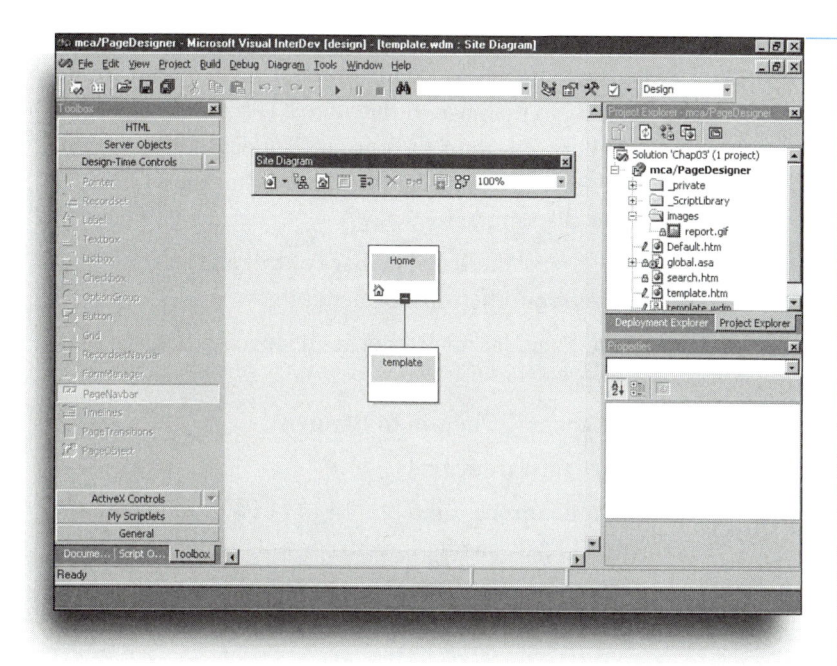

FIGURE 3.9
Creating the sample site diagram.

8. Press Ctrl+S to save the diagram. This will add the DEFAULT.HTM document to your project.

SEE ALSO
➤ *You learn about using the Site Designer on page 17*

Adding a Banner to the Template Document

The PageNavBar DTC provides a long list of possible displays for the Web page. The simplest of these options is the Banner option. This enables you to use the PageNavBar DTC to display the established name for the document as a banner. You can also adjust the way the banner is displayed by changing the default settings of the PageNavBar control.

Adding the Banner PageNavBar control to your document

1. First, be sure the desired document is loaded in the Visual InterDev 6 editor and the editor is in Design mode.
2. Select the **Design-Time Controls** tab of the Toolbox window to see a list of the available DTCs.
3. Locate the PageNavBar DTC in the list and drag it from the Toolbox to the page in the editor. Drop the control exactly where you want the output to appear. In this example, drop the control in the top-right cell of the HTML table after the sample text.
4. Right-click over the PageNavBar control and select **P**r**operties** from the context menu.
5. When the PageNavbar Properties dialog appears, select the **General** tab.
6. Set the **Type** radio button to **Ba**n**ner**.
7. Select the **Appearance** tab.
8. Set the **Appearance** radio button to **H**TML to expose the template HTML coding for the control.
9. In the **Current page template:** input, edit the entry from **#LABEL#** to **<H1>#LABEL#</H1>**. This will force the control to display the page banner in Heading1 style (see Figure 3.10).
10. Press **OK** to save the settings to the document.

Now save the current document (press Ctrl+S) and then view it in your default browser. To do this, right-click over the document and select **View in B**r**owser** from the context menu. Your document should now look like the one in Figure 3.11.

When you add the PageNavBar DTC to a document and set it to Banner display, it will automatically show the name set in the site diagram. This is an important point. The PageNavBar does not use the document's HTML Title value or the actual disk filename of the document. You must use the Visual InterDev 6 site diagram to alter the string displayed in the Banner PageNavBar.

DTC choices

The **Design-Time Controls** tab lists several DTCs that you can use. For now, stick to the PageNavBar. As you proceed through the chapters in this book, you will begin using other controls.

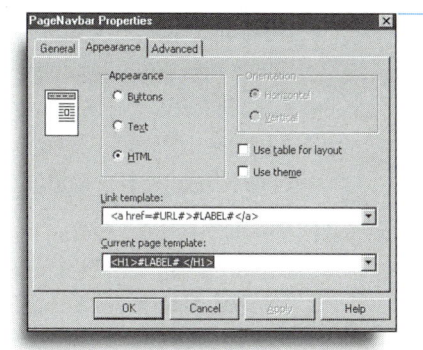

Using the PageNavBar Design-Time Control | CHAPTER 3

FIGURE 3.10
Adding the Banner PageNavBar control to the document.

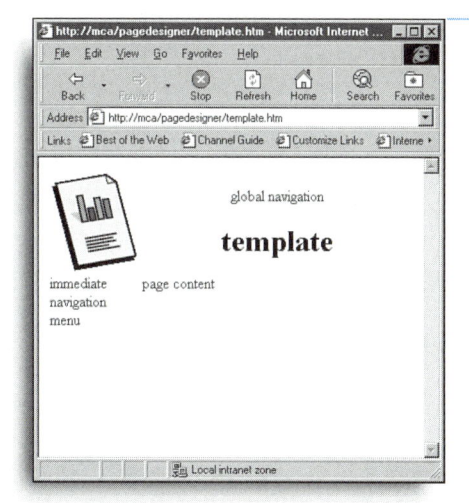

FIGURE 3.11
Viewing the TEMPLATE.HTM document with the Banner PagNavbar DTC.

Adding a Link Menu to the Template Document

You can also use the PageNavBar DTC to display the links to the current document that were established with the Visual InterDev 6 Site Designer. There are six different link types that you can display with the PageNavBar DTC:

- **First Level Pages**—Use this setting to display links to the top-level set of pages in a site diagram.
- **Parent Level Pages**—Use this setting to display links to the pages directly above the current page in the site diagram.

- **Sibling Pages**—Use this setting to display links to all the pages that are at the same level of the current page in the site diagram.
- **Children Pages**—Use this setting to display links to all the pages directly below the current page in the site diagram.
- **Back & Next Pages**—Use this setting to display links to the next and previous pages in the site diagram.
- **Global Navigation Pages**—Use this setting to display links to a special set of pages marked as global navigation pages.

You can also use the PageNavBar DTC to show the direct parent and the home page of the site diagram, no matter which setting you select. For this example, you add a PageNavBar DTC that will show the children pages as well as the parent and home page in the site diagram.

Adding a child link PageNavBar DTC to your document

1. First, make sure the desired document is loaded in the Visual InterDev 6 editor and that the editor is in Design mode. For this example, load the TEMPLATE.HTM document in the Visual InterDev 6 editor.
2. Select the **Design-Time Controls** tab of the Toolbox window and locate the PageNavBar DTC in the list.
3. Drag the PageNavBar DTC from the Toolbox window and drop it exactly where you want the set of child links to appear in your document. For this example, drop the DTC in the bottom-left cell of the HTML table where the words **immediate navigation menu** appear.
4. Right-click the PageNavBar DTC and select **Properties** from the context menu.
5. Select the **General** tab of the PageNavbar Properties dialog box and set the **Type** radio button to **Children pages**.
6. Set the **Additional pages** check boxes as desired. For this example, check both the **Home** and **Parent** check boxes on.
7. Press the **Appearance** tab and set the **Appearance** radio button to **HTML**.

Page relationships

The best way to think of your Web site is as a family of pages. The relationship between your pages (siblings, parents, third-removed cousins from your mother's side) is represented in the site diagram. You can use the diagram to rearrange the relationship as needed. Now is your chance to see your little-known cousins get married and get promoted up in the navigational bar!

Using the PageNavBar Design-Time Control

8. Modify the **L**ink template: from **<a href=#URL#>#LABEL#</a>** to **<H3><a href=#URL#>#LABEL#</a></H3>** (see Figure 3.12).

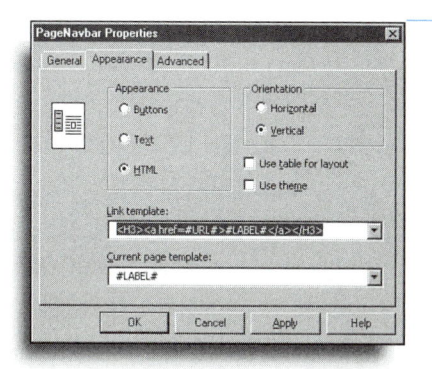

FIGURE 3.12
Setting the **Link template** value of the PageNavBar DTC.

9. Set the **Orientation** radio button to **V**ertical.

10. Press **OK** to save the settings to the document.

Now save the updated document and view it in your default browser. You should now see that the link **Home** appears at the left side of the page (see Figure 3.13).

FIGURE 3.13
Viewing the completed document with the child link DTC.

DTCs and IIS 4.0

Remember that your Web server must be running Internet Information Server 4.0 (or higher) for this design-time control (and others) to function.

What if there are no global pages?

If there are no pages in the Web marked as global navigation pages, you will not see any text appear in the final documents. The global navigation PageNavBar DTC is smart enough to simply stay hidden if you have not added any global pages to the Web.

Because the TEMPLATE.HTM document has no defined child pages, you will not see any other children appear in the link list. Because the only parent to the TEMPLATE.HTM document is the Home page, you also will not see both the **Home** and **Parent** links appear. The PageNavBar DTC is smart enough to display only the **Home** link instead.

Adding Global Links to the Template

You must add one more PageNavBar control to your TEMPLATE.HTM document. This DTC will be used to display a set of links at the top of the document that point to the same set of pages every time. This will be the global navigation bar. Typically, this set of links points to the most commonly used pages in the Web project. For this example, you add the control now and create the global pages later in the chapter.

Adding a global navigation PageNavBar DTC to your document

1. First, make sure the desired document is loaded in the Visual InterDev 6 editor and that the editor is in Design mode. For this example, load the TEMPLATE.HTM document in the Visual InterDev 6 editor.

2. Select the **Design-Time Controls** tab of the Toolbox window and locate the PageNavBar DTC in the list.

3. Drag the PageNavBar DTC from the Toolbox window and drop it exactly where you want the set of child links to appear in your document. For this example, drop the DTC in the upper-right cell of the HTML table where the words **global navigation** appear.

4. Right-click the PageNavBar DTC and select **P**roperties from the context menu.

5. Select the **General** tab of the PageNavbar Properties dialog box and set the **Type** radio button to **G**lobal navigation bar.

6. Set the **Additional pages** check boxes as desired. For this example, set the **Home** check box on.

7. Press the **Appearance** tab and set the **Appearance** radio button to **H**TML.

Building a Sample Web Site with the Template Document

8. Next, select the last item in the **Link template:** list (see Figure 3.14). **<a href=#URL#>#LABEL#</a>**.

9. Finally, press **OK** to save the settings to the document.

Now save the TEMPLATE.HTM document. You now have a completed template page that you can use to quickly generate new documents for your Web site. In the next section of this chapter, you learn how to create new pages with the template document and how to use the Site Designer to arrange those pages into a complete Web site.

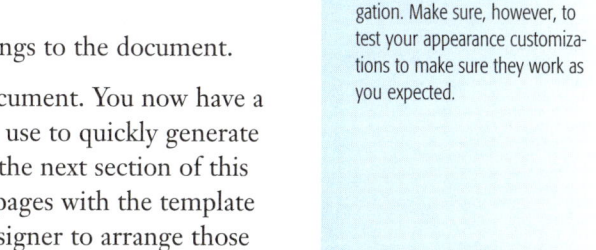

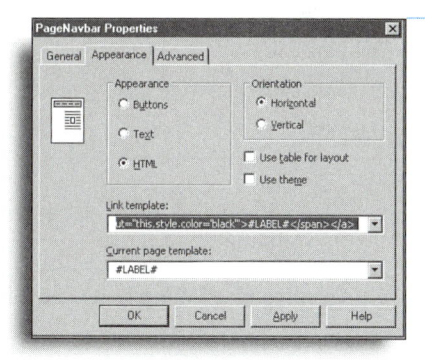

> **Test appearance customizations**
>
> By letting you customize the appearance of items, Visual InterDev is giving you a great deal of power over your site navigation. Make sure, however, to test your appearance customizations to make sure they work as you expected.

FIGURE 3.14
Adding the global navigation PageNavBar DTC to your document.

> **Building a template pool**
>
> Using Visual InterDev to create a selection of templates for your application will likely save you a lot of time in the future. You can create, debug, and test an idea to perfection and then use it throughout your site as you need it.

Building a Sample Web Site with the Template Document

Now that you have a completed template document, you're ready to use it to add pages to the Web project. To do this, you must first load the template document into the editor, and then save it using the new (final) document name. In this way, you are actually copying the template to new documents in your project.

After you've added all the new pages you need for the site, you can use the Visual InterDev 6 Site Designer to link the pages together so that the PageNavBar DTCs will be able to properly display the links, banners, and global navigation bar.

Creating the Pages with the Template Document

The first step is to save copies of the template document with new names. This creates a set of pages that will comprise the documents in the Web. For this example, you must add several documents to your Web project. Table 3.1 shows the document names, filenames, and the group in which they belong (global navigation or child page).

TABLE 3.1 Documents to Add to the Web Project

Group	Name	Filename
Home Page	Home	DEFAULT.HTM
Child Page	Customers	CUSTOMERS.HTM
Child Page	Vendors	VENDORS.HTM
Global Page	Contacts	CONTACTS.HTM
Global Page	Departments	DEPARTMENTS.HTM

You can use the list of documents in Table 3.1 as you go through the following steps.

Creating new Web pages from a template document

1. First, load the desired template document in the Visual InterDev 6 editor and be sure the editor is in Design mode. For this example, load the TEMPLATE.HTM document in the editor.
2. Select the **File** menu option from the main menu.
3. Select **Save template.htm As** from the **File** menu.
4. When the Save File As dialog appears, enter the name of the new document in the **File name:** input field. For this example, enter `default.htm` for the new document name.
5. Press **Save** to save the document under a new name.

Using your own pages

Of course, if you have your own site you'd prefer to work with, feel free. You can replace references to the pages in this table with your own pages to suit your site's needs.

Be sure to Save As

You don't want to save over your template, so make sure to use the Save File As option. Just to be safe, however, make two copies of your template to avoid potential disasters.

Building a Sample Web Site with the Template Document

6. If the document already exists, you will see a dialog box asking you whether you want to replace it. For this example, press the **Yes** button (see Figure 3.15).

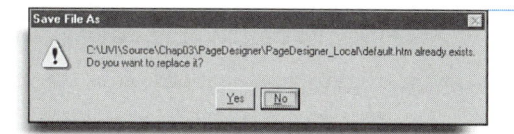

FIGURE 3.15
Visual InterDev warns you when you are about to replace a file by the same name.

7. If the document already exists, you will see a second dialog asking you to confirm the replacement. Select **Yes** to continue the replacement.

8. With the new document in your editor, make any needed changes to the content of the page. For this example, change the **page content** text to the name of the document: **default.htm**. This will help you identify the documents as you are testing the Web diagram.

9. After you are finished editing the document, close it by selecting **Close** from the **File** menu.

Repeat these steps for each of the pages listed in Table 3.1. When you are finished, you should be able to see all five documents in your Project Explorer window. You should be able to load each document in the Visual InterDev 6 editor and see that they all have the same layout and same set of DTC controls. The only difference will be the content text in the bottom-right table cell.

Be sure to save all these documents before you continue.

Creating the Site Diagram

Now that you have created all the sample pages using the template document, you are ready to use the Visual InterDev 6 Site Designer to create the actual document Web. To do this, you must create a new site diagram file and drag the various pages from the Project Explorer window onto the site diagram.

Reusing the existing diagram

If you want, you can reuse the site diagram you built earlier in this chapter. Although it's okay to have more than one site diagram in a project, it might get a bit confusing if you have more than one diagram for the same project.

The most effective way to organize content

Most developers and designers would argue that organizing your content by subject matter is the most effective way. Consider the type of material you are organizing for your site's navigation and how people perceive it. Would a person go to a News section to read about a company's history? Not likely. Make sure your navigation follows a common sense thread that user's will be able to understand.

Every page is an island

Keep in mind that you don't need to have every page in your site linked to the navigation bar. There may be pages that are of a "diminished" importance and only need to be linked from a single page. Don't try to jam pack your navigation bar with every possible page.

Before you add the new site diagram, be sure to erase the existing TEMPLATE.WDM from the project. This was a sample diagram you added early in the project for testing only. It is no longer needed.

Adding a site diagram to an existing Web project

1. Right-click the mouse over the project name in the Project Explorer window.
2. Select **Add** from the context menu.
3. Select **Site Diagram** from the submenu.
4. Enter a name for the new diagram in the **Name:** input box. For this example, use master as the name.
5. Press **Open** to add the site diagram to the project and open it in the Visual InterDev 6 editor.
6. When the site diagram appears, you might see the first page, called **Home**, appear in the document. This is the DEFAULT.HTM page for the site diagram. If you do not see it, you can drag the existing DEFAULT.HTM document from the Project Explorer window and drop it in the site diagram.
7. Drag the CUSTOMERS.HTM and the VENDORS.HTM pages from the Project Explorer and drop them on the site diagram close to the **Home** document where they will be attached as a child page of the **Home** document (see Figure 3.16).
8. Finally, press Ctrl+S to save the diagram. This will add the DEFAULT.HTM document to your project.

Next, you must add the two global navigation pages to the diagram. When you add these pages, you must add them independent of other pages and then mark them as part of the global navigation collection.

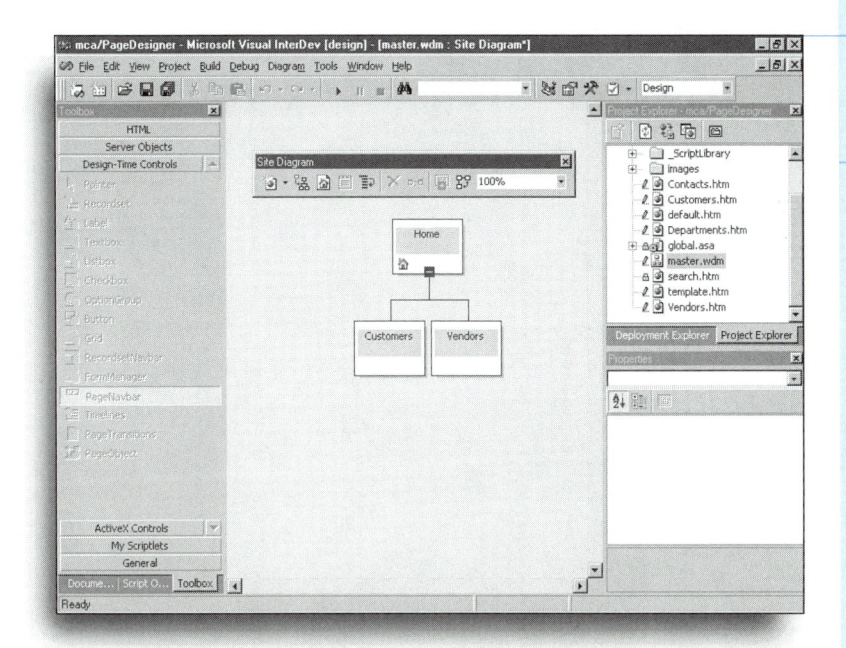

Building a Sample Web Site with the Template Document | PART **I**
CHAPTER **3**

79

FIGURE 3.16
Creating the site diagram for the sample Web site.

Adding global navigation pages to the site diagram

1. First, be sure to load the proper site diagram in the Visual InterDev 6 editor. In this example, you should load the MASTER.WDM document in the editor.

2. Drag a page from the Project Explorer window onto the site diagram. Be careful not to allow this page to connect to any other page in the diagram. It should stand alone on the diagram. For this example, drag the CONTACTS.HTM document onto the site diagram and place it at the bottom of the page.

3. Click once on the added page (CONTACTS.HTM) to select it.

4. Use the **Site Diagram** toolbar to mark the selected page as part of the global navigation collection by pressing the **Add to Global Navigation Bar** button on the Site Diagram toolbar (see Figure 3.17).

FIGURE 3.17

Marking the global navigation pages.

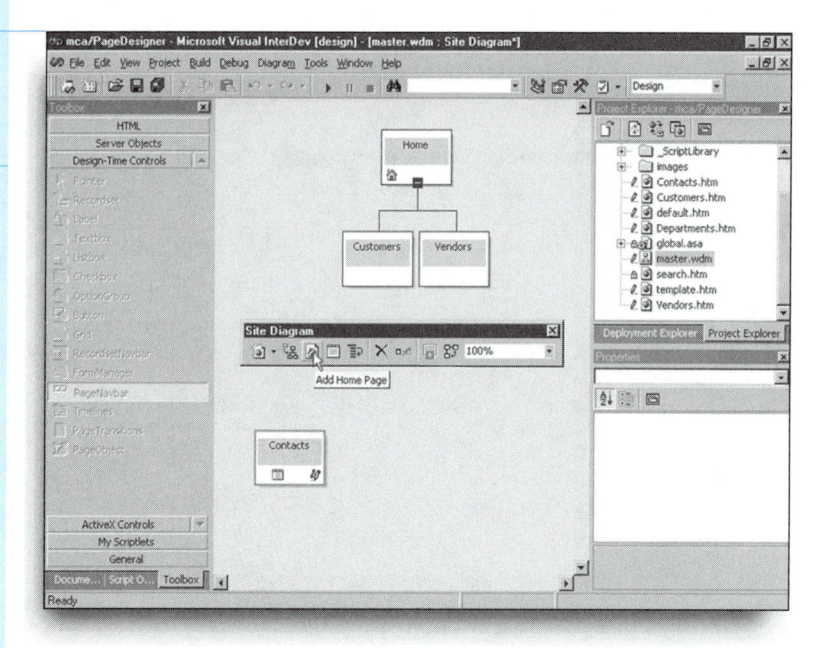

5. Repeat step 2 for each document you want to add to the global navigation. For this example, add the DEPARTMENTS.HTM page to the site diagram and mark it as a member of the global navigation collection.

6. After adding all the pages you want, save the diagram by pressing Ctrl+S.

You have now added all the pages to your site diagram. You can now test the pages by right-clicking over the DEFAULT.HTM document and selecting **View in Browser** from the context menu. You should now see a page that looks like the one shown in Figure 3.18.

You should notice that the links in the top global navigation collection use some client-side JScript to provide color changes when you hover the mouse over the text. Notice also that as you click on the various pages, the link list on the left changes, but the global links do not. The banner title for each page also changes. All this occurs even though you have not written a single bit of HTML or script! This is the work of the PageNavBar DTCs.

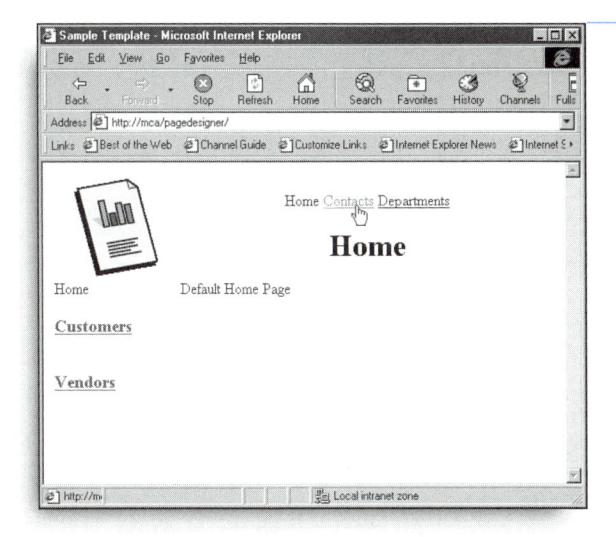

Using the PageTransitions Design-Time Control

FIGURE 3.18
Results of using the site diagram and PageNavBar DTCs.

SEE ALSO
➤ *Another method of page navigation is to use the content linker server-side ASP component. To learn about it, see page 601*

Using the PageTransitions Design-Time Control

The other design-time control created to help design Web documents is the PageTransitions DTC. This DTC provides entry and exit transitions between pages. The control provides 23 different transition options, including box in/out, fade in/out, and many others. By adding the PageTransitions DTC to your page, users will see a smooth transition when they change from one page to the next within your Web application.

The PageTransitions DTC uses the `revealTrans` method, which is specific to Microsoft Internet Explorer browsers. This means that you will be able to see the transitions only when viewing the documents with Microsoft Internet Explorer–compatible browser clients. However, because the actual code that performs the transition is surrounded in HTML comments, adding the

The PowerPoint connection

If you've used Microsoft PowerPoint or seen a presentation created using PowerPoint, you've probably experienced Page Transitions. The Visual InterDev Page Transitions are identical to those offered in PowerPoint.

PageTransition DTC will not cause errors in non–Microsoft Internet Explorer browsers such as Netscape Navigator.

SEE ALSO

➤ *Page Transitions and the PageTransition DTC are also covered on page 562*

Adding the PageTransition Controls to Your Documents

It's easy to add the PageTransitions DTC to a document. In this section, you see how you can add it to any document in your Web and adjust its properties to control the type of transitions users will see.

Adding a PageTransitions DTC to your document

1. First, be sure to load the target document (HTML or ASP) in your Visual InterDev 6 editor and make sure the editor is in Design mode. For this example, load the DEFAULT.HTM document in the editor.
2. Click the **Design-Time Controls** tab of the Toolbox window to display the list of available controls.
3. Locate and drag the **PageTransitions** DTC from the Toolbox and drop it at the very top of the document (see Figure 3.19).
4. Right-click over the **PageTransitions** DTC and select the **P**r**operties** option from the context menu.
5. When the PageTransitions Properties dialog appears, select the **Page Transition** tab.
6. Set the **Page Enter T**r**ansition** property to **Random**, and set the **Page Exit T**r**ansition** property to **Random** (see Figure 3.19).
7. Press **OK** to save the settings to the document.

Using the PageTransitions Design-Time Control

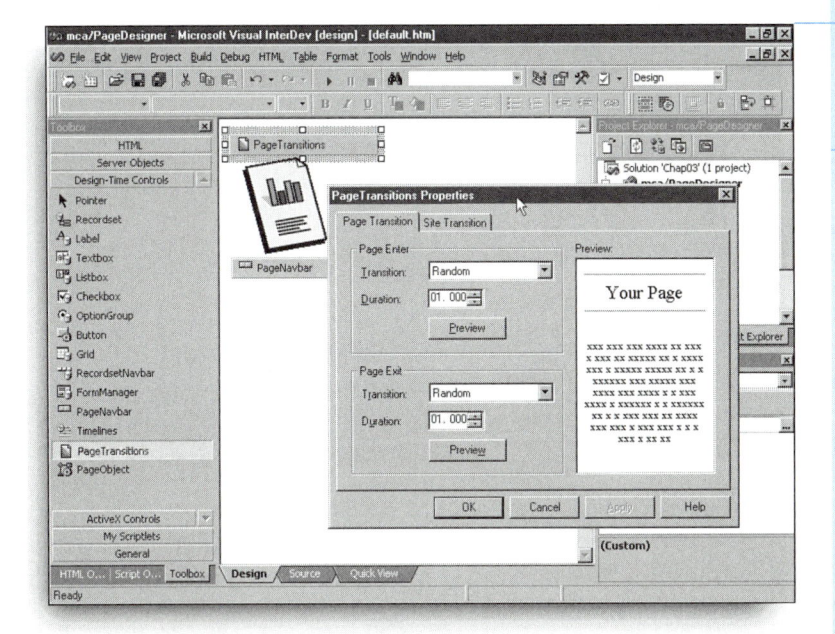

FIGURE 3.19
Using the PageTransitions DTC on a document.

After adding the PageTransitions DTC to the DEFAULT.HTM document, save it (press Ctrl+S) and view the document in a Microsoft Internet Explorer browser. As you move from the DEFAULT.HTM document to another and back again, you'll see various page transitions used when entering and exiting the DEFAULT.HTM document. If you want, you can add the PageTransition DTC to all the documents in your Web project.

Use Page Transitions with care

If you use the PageTransitions DTC on every page in your site, you'll likely drive your users batty. Some might argue that Page Transitions are as bad as the infamous Netscape `<BLINK>` tag that flashed text to users. Use Page Transitions wisely and with discretion to enhance your site, not to compromise it.

CHAPTER 4

Using Visual InterDev 6 to Manage Your Web Projects

Learn how to support team development with Visual InterDev 6

Understand the differences in Master and Local editing mode

See how you can check internal and external links in a project

Use the Copy Web and Deploy Web options to install completed Web applications

Supporting Development Teams with Visual InterDev 6

One of the powerful new features of Visual InterDev 6 is the capability to support teams of Web developers, all working on the same project. Visual InterDev 6 now enables users to easily connect to an existing Web on the master server and link a new project to that Web.

After the new project is linked to an existing Web, developers can then work in a new Local mode where any changes to the site can be saved and tested on the developer's machine. In this way, the developer can isolate his or her work from the rest of the team. After the pages are completed and tested, the developer can upload the changes to the master Web host for other team members to see.

Another new feature for Visual InterDev 6 is the Merge Differences dialog window. This feature first appeared in Microsoft's Visual SourceSafe version control tool. Now, when two developers both make changes to the same document, Visual InterDev 6 is able to automatically merge the two documents into a single page. If the changes conflict with each other, the developer saving the document will be presented with a dialog noting the conflicting areas and prompted for input as to how to proceed. After all conflicts are merged, the document is placed on the server for others to see.

Creating a Shared Visual InterDev 6 Project

The first step in supporting team development with Visual InterDev 6 is to create a shared project for the team. This is actually quite easy. It just takes a little planning and timing.

First, a standard Web project should be created. The Web project will act as the "starter" project for all the team members. After the project is built, other team members can create their own personal Visual InterDev projects and link their personal project to the starter project. In this way, all team members are able to work with their own copies of the starter project.

Visual InterDev 6 enables team members to synchronize their personal copies of the project and to easily upload their own changes and download the changes made by others in the team.

So there are really only two tasks to creating shared projects for Visual InterDev 6. The first is to create the starter project. The second is to create a personal project and link it to the starter project.

Creating a shared starter project for team use

1. Load Visual InterDev 6. If the New Project dialog does not appear, select **New Project** from the **File** menu.
2. When the New Project dialog appears, use the **Browse** button to locate and select the location for the new project.
3. Enter a project name in the **Name:** input box. For this example, enter Manage as the project name.
4. Click **Open** to create the shared starter project.
5. When the Web Project Wizard dialog appears, select a Web host server that can be seen by all the members of the project team. Accept the default working mode of Master mode. Then, click the **Next** button to continue the wizard.
6. At the second page of the Web Project Wizard, accept the default choice to create a new Web application. Also, accept the default Web name for the project. For this example, it should be set to Manage.
7. Click the **Finish** button to allow the Web Project Wizard to add all the needed folders and files in your project.

You have now completed the first task in creating a shared project for Visual InterDev 6 developer teams. At this stage, you have accomplished two tasks. First, you have created a Web application on your Web server that provides the URL structure for your Web site. Second, you have created a Visual InterDev project that enables you to design and develop the site.

At this point, other developers can create their own projects against the Web application in order to personally develop their portions of the application. This personal project should be linked to the starter project that already exists on the Web server.

Creating a personal Visual InterDev 6 project and linking it to an existing Web project

1. Go to another machine in the LAN or start a new instance of Visual InterDev 6 on your workstation. You can also perform this task on your own machine, but the features are better demonstrated in a networked, team environment.

2. When the New Project dialog appears, use the **Browse** button to locate and select the location for the new project.

3. Next, enter a project name in the **Name:** input box. For this example, enter Dev1 as the project name.

4. Click **Open** to create the shared starter project.

5. When the Web Project Wizard dialog appears, select a Web host server that can be seen by all members of the project team. Again, accept the default of Master mode. Then, click the **Next** button to continue the wizard.

6. At the second page of the Web Project Wizard, instead of creating a new Web on the Web host, click the **Connect to an existing web application on** *web_server_name*.

7. Select the existing Web name to which you want to connect this project from the list of Webs displayed in the drop-down list. For this example, locate and select the **Manage Web** project.

8. Click the **Finish** button to allow the Web Project Wizard to add all the needed folders and files in your project.

Notice that Visual InterDev 6 will download any pages from the existing Web site onto the machine that has the personal project. Some pages can be viewed in gray. This means that they are available on the server, but that you do not have a read/writable copy of the document project.

Utilizing the Visual InterDev Project Model

So far, you have learned how to create an initial Web application and project. You have also learned how to connect to an existing

Utilizing the Visual InterDev Project Model

Web application and create a project against that Web. In this section, you learn how to isolate an individual developer's work from the rest of the team. Visual InterDev 6 supports developer isolation through its powerful project model and working modes. There are three basic working modes of Visual InterDev 6:

- Master mode
- Local mode
- Offline mode

Master Mode

Master mode is the default working mode for Visual InterDev. You accepted this default mode in the previous examples. Master mode dictates that all your changes will be saved automatically to the master Web server. Figure 4.1 demonstrates the Master mode development process.

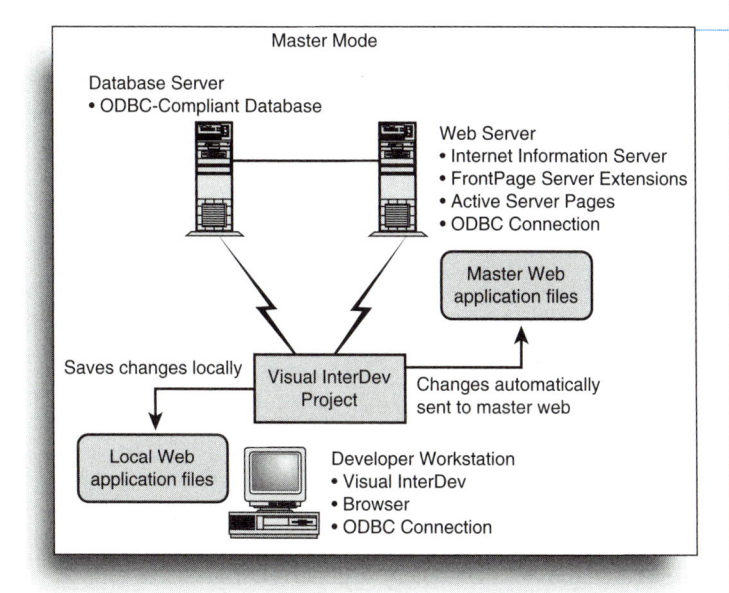

FIGURE 4.1
Working in Master mode.

Any time you create a project, Visual InterDev creates two sets of files: the master set that resides on your Web server and a local set of files that resides on your developer machine.

Local file duplication

If you are developing on a standalone machine, both sets of files will physically reside on the same machine in different directories.

In the example in Figure 4.1, you see a development machine, a Web server, and a database server. When you create a Web application, Visual InterDev 6 constructs a local set of application files on the development machine as well as a master set of files on the Web server machine. Because the project is working under Master mode, all changes are simultaneously saved to the local version as well as the master version.

Local Mode

Local mode enables a developer to isolate his or her work from the rest of the team. Any changes are automatically saved in the local version, which resides in a directory structure named *name_of_project_*Local. The developer can develop and test his or her part of the application and then update the master Web server when finished. Figure 4.2 demonstrates this process.

FIGURE 4.2

Working in Local mode.

Two sets of files will be maintained

Again, if you are developing on a standalone machine, two sets of files will be maintained on the same machine in different directory structures.

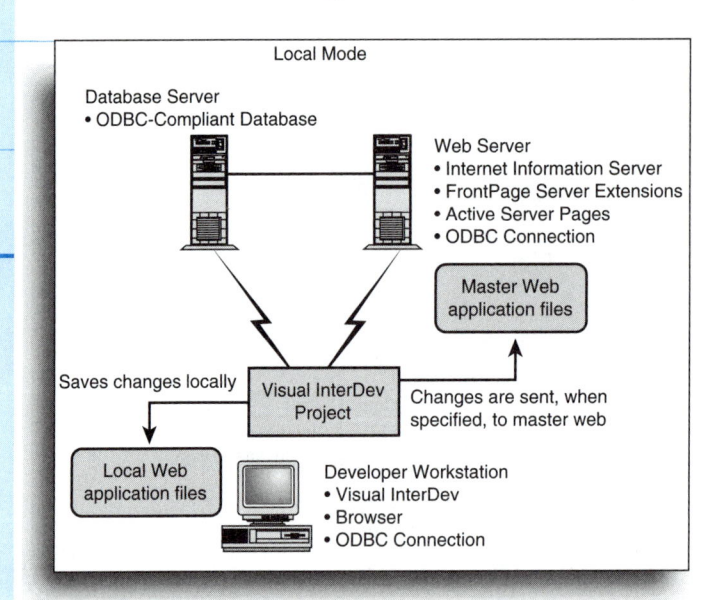

Local Mode

Database Server
• ODBC-Compliant Database

Web Server
• Internet Information Server
• FrontPage Server Extensions
• Active Server Pages
• ODBC Connection

Master Web application files

Saves changes locally → Visual InterDev Project → Changes are sent, when specified, to master web

Local Web application files

Developer Workstation
• Visual InterDev
• Browser
• ODBC Connection

Offline Mode

The third working mode that Visual InterDev supports is Offline mode. Offline mode enables you to continue working on the files within the project without a connection to a Web server. You are somewhat limited because you can only execute functions that do not rely on Web server interaction. The following list provides functions that you can execute while in Offline mode:

- Open a project.
- Edit local working copies of files.
- Preview changes to HTML files using Quick View.
- Save your changes to the local working copies of the files.

Because you do not have a connection to a Web server while in Offline mode, there are some functions that you cannot carry out:

- Update the master version of files on the Web server.
- Retrieve the latest versions of files from the master Web server.
- Release the working copies of files back to the master Web server.
- Move files in the project.

Establishing the Working Mode for the Project

You basically have two methods of setting the working mode for the project. First, you can establish a working mode at the time you create the project. As mentioned earlier, the Web Project Wizard enables you to select either Master or Local mode during step 1 of the process. You can also change the working mode for the project from within the Visual InterDev IDE after you have opened or created the project. To accomplish this task, select the project root and click the right mouse button to reveal the shortcut menu. From the list of menu items, choose **Working Mode**. This action will reveal the three working modes, enabling you to select one from the list. The icon for the currently selected mode for the project will appear slightly depressed and highlighted, as shown in Figure 4.3.

FIGURE 4.3

Viewing the working mode for the project.

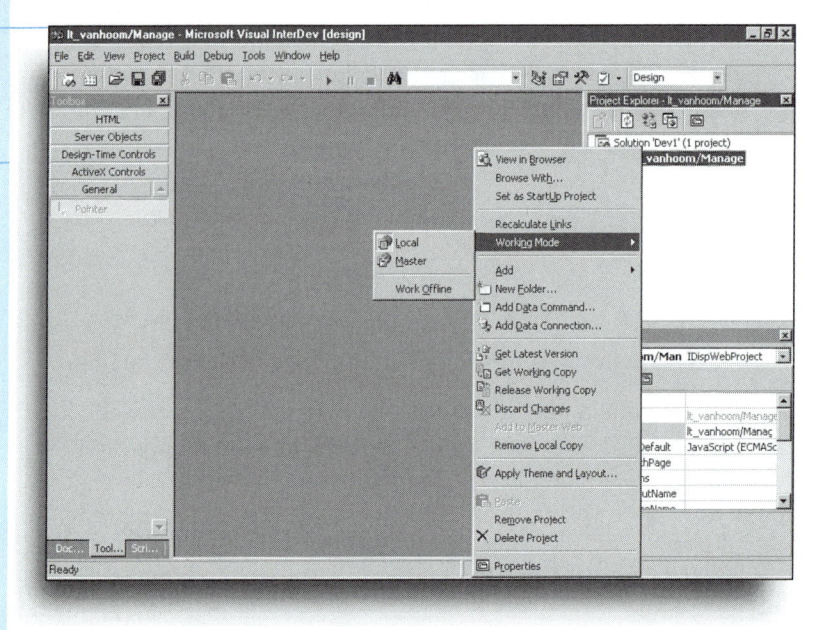

You can also change the working mode for the project by selecting the **Project** menu. Then choose **Web Project**, **Working Mode**, which reveals the same list of menu items as shown in Figure 4.3.

SEE ALSO

➤ *You can set the working mode when you first create a project. You learned how to create projects on page 8*

Using the Working Modes for Effective Team Development

Now that you are familiar with the basic working modes that Visual InterDev supports, you will get a chance to realize the benefits of these distinct working modes and how Visual InterDev 6 can improve the effectiveness of your team.

Working in Local mode

1. If necessary, open the Dev1 project that you created earlier.
2. In the Project Explorer, right-click the **Manage** project root.

Utilizing the Visual InterDev Project Model

PART I
CHAPTER 4

93

3. Select **Working Mode**, **Local** to set the project working mode to local.

4. Create a new HTML Web page by right-clicking the project root and selecting **Add**, **HTML Page**. Enter `Page1.htm` for the name and click **Open** from the **Add Item** dialog window.

5. Using the Design editor, add the text `My Local Page` on the first line of the Web page. Use the icons on the toolbar to center the text and make it bold. Figure 4.4 displays the results of these changes as seen through the Design view.

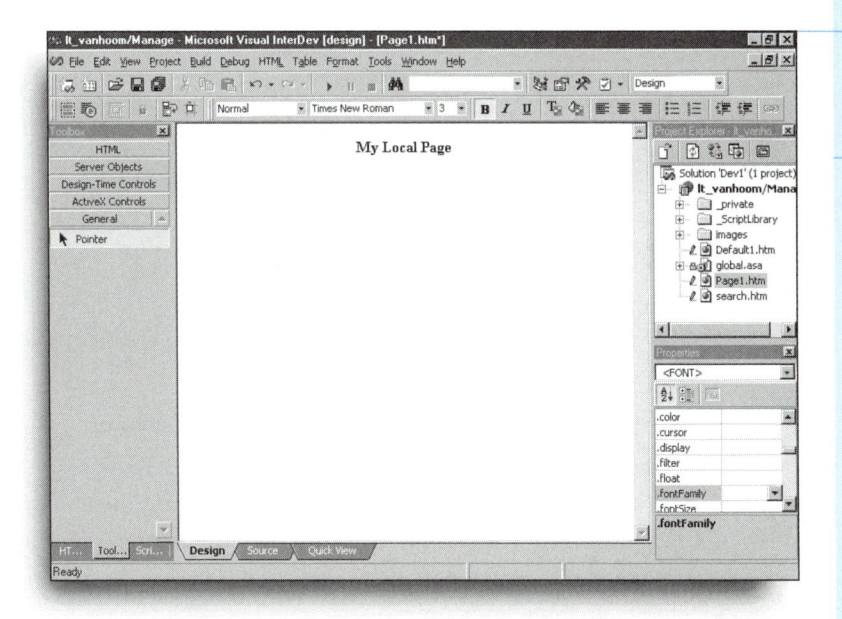

FIGURE 4.4
Making changes to the local version.

6. Save your changes to this file.

7. Select the file and choose **View in Browser** from the shortcut menu. The page will be loaded from the local version and displayed in the browser, as depicted in Figure 4.5.

Local development woes

If you do not have a Web server on your local development machine, the file will be loaded with a file URL, and server script will not work.

FIGURE 4.5

Viewing the local version through the browser.

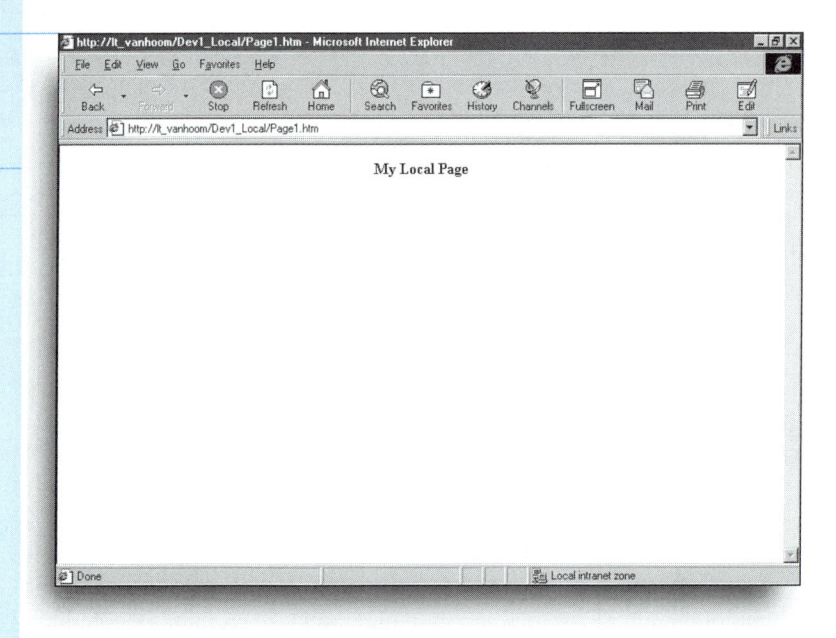

Comparing to Master Mode

Now that you have created a new HTML Web page within your local version of the application, you can add this file to the master Web server for the rest of the team to see.

Updating the master Web server and comparing the differences

1. Right-click the PAGE1.HTM file in the Project Explorer and select **Add to Master Web** from the shortcut menu. This action adds the newly created file to the master Web server.

2. Using the Design editor, open a working copy of PAGE1.HTM and change the font size of the title to **6**. Also, change the text from **My Local Page** to My Local Home Page. Remember, you are still working in Local mode against the local version of this file.

3. Save your changes.

4. From within Visual InterDev, right-click the PAGE1.HTM file in the Project Explorer and select **Compare to Master Web** from the shortcut menu. This action displays the Differences dialog window enabling you to compare the differences between the local version and the master Web version. Note the different font sizes and title text.

5. Close the Differences dialog window.

6. To update the master Web server with your changes, select the file and choose **Release Work**i**ng Copy** from the shortcut menu. This action will update the master version of the Web application with any changes that you have made to your files.

7. Right-click the page again and choose **Compare to** **M**aster **Web**. You will receive a dialog window stating that the local and master files are identical.

Working in Isolation

For most projects in which you have a team of developers, Local mode should be the working mode of choice. As you have learned, Local mode enables you to isolate your part of the application from the work of other developers. You can develop, debug, and test your pages while being insulated from the changes that other developers are making to their parts of the application. They are also insulated from your changes. The benefit is that Local mode enables each individual to develop in peace and promotes the idea of fully testing your work before you check it back in to the master Web server version. In this way, you can reduce the chance of code being overwritten as well as the chance that the master version contains faulty code.

To update the master Web server, you can select one or more files in the Visual InterDev project explorer and choose the **Release Work**i**ng Copy** command to update files on the master Web server. You can also update multiple files by selecting the files in the Visual InterDev Project Explorer and choosing **Project**, **W**eb Files, **Release Work**i**ng Copy**. To update the master Web server with your entire set of local files, change your working mode from Local mode to Master mode. This action will synchronize your local version with the master version of the application.

You can also obtain new files that other team members have created and saved on the master Web without updating the master Web with your changes. This one-way synchronization from the master Web server enables you to retrieve pages that you might need to test locally with your part of the application even without having to place your untested pages on the master Web.

Retrieving other team members' work while working in isolation

1. Go back to the first networked machine from which you completed the first exercise. In the Project Explorer, right-click the **Manage** project root.
2. Select **Working Mode**, **Master** to set the project working mode to master.
3. Create a new HTML Web page by right-clicking the project root and selecting **Add**, **HTML Page**. Enter Default.htm for the name and click **Open** from the Add Item dialog window.
4. Using the Design editor, add the text Master Home Page on the first line of the Web page. Use the icons on the toolbar to center the text and make it bold. Change the font size to 6. Save your changes.
5. Return to the Dev1 project machine and choose **Project**, **Web Project**, **Synchronize Files**. This action will retrieve all the latest updates from the master Web server, including the newly created DEFAULT.HTM.

Verifying Links with the Visual InterDev 6 Link View

Managing the files contained within your Web application is a vital and sometimes laborious task. Visual InterDev 6 provides a graphical tool called the Link view that enables you to visually examine the files within your Web site and their relationships. You can expand or contract the view to explore different aspects of your site. For example, you might want to focus solely on a certain section or group of Web pages or objects. The Link view provides a rich graphical tool to help you conceptualize the design and structure of your Web site.

SEE ALSO
➤ *Although the two may seem similar and are often confused for one another, the Link View is a different feature than the Site Designer. You learned how to use the Site Designer on page 17*

Verifying Links with the Visual InterDev 6 Link View | PART **I** CHAPTER **4** | **97**

Using the Link View Features to Manage Your Web Site

You can use Link view to see a multitude of files, including HTML Web pages, images and sound files, ActiveX controls, and Java applets. You can basically examine any file that is a part of your Web site using the Link view. The Link view diagram also reveals characteristics about the page. For example, the Link view diagram will show cascading style sheet files if they were applied to the page. Link view enables you to filter what is displayed in the diagram as well as to open-end edit objects using the object's default editor.

Using Link view to view the structure of your Web application

1. Open the Island Hopper A application in Visual InterDev. This application is included on the MSDN CDs included with Visual Studio. If you have not installed this sample application, perform a search for it within MSDN help and follow the instructions for installing the sample application. After it is installed, you must create a project against the application.

2. Right-click the HEADLINES.ASP file in the Project Explorer and choose **View Links** from the shortcut menu. Figure 4.6 displays the Link view diagram for the site.

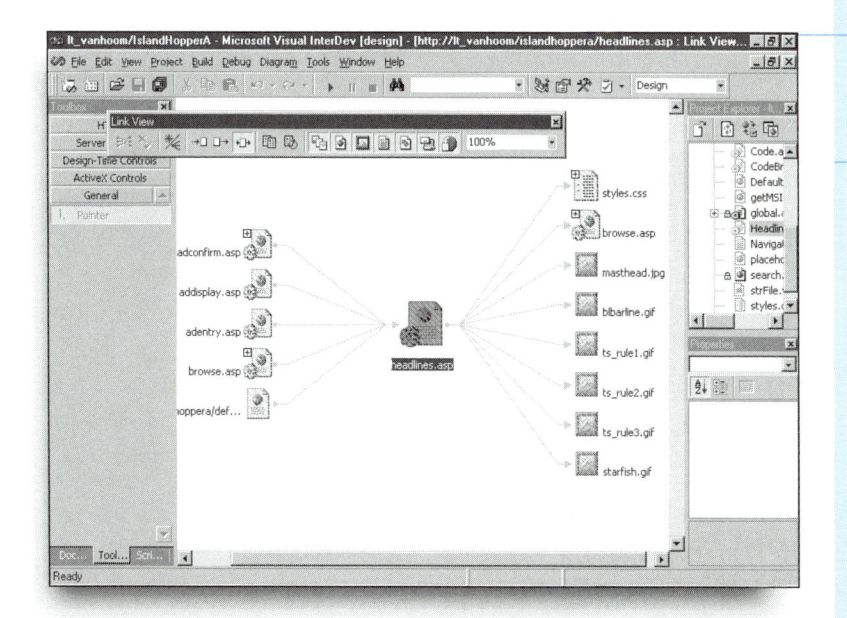

FIGURE 4.6
Viewing the links for the headlines page.

This illustration depicts a robust Web site diagram with graphical icons representing the file type for each item in the view, and lines and arrows indicating the relationship between the files. The arrows and circles located at the ends of the lines serve as visual indicators that describe the nature of the relationship. A circle next to an object indicates that it is the parent, and the arrow next to an object signifies that it is the child.

From Figure 4.6, you can determine that the Active Server Page in the middle of the diagram is the parent of all the surrounding files. You can describe the relationship another way by stating that the ADCONFIRM.ASP file is the child of the HEADLINES.ASP Web page.

The object contained in the middle of Figure 4.6 appears with a large icon, and all the surrounding items display with smaller icons. The large icon signifies that the developer opened a Link view for this object. A plus sign (+) in the top-left corner of an item icon indicates that the item contains links to the other items. You can expand the links for one of these items by clicking the +.

The next few sections walk you through the process of interacting with a diagram to obtain a more granular view of the site.

Filtering Your Link View

The Link view enables you to filter the amount and type of information displayed in your diagram, so you can more easily decipher and understand your Web site structure. You can choose the **Diagram** menu to display a menu list of available filter choices as depicted in Figure 4.7.

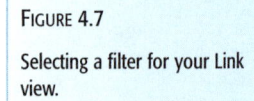

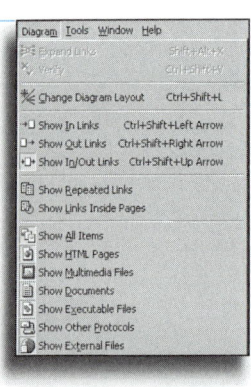

FIGURE 4.7

Selecting a filter for your Link view.

Verifying Links with the Visual InterDev 6 Link View

As you can see, Visual InterDev 6 provides many choices to filter the objects that are displayed within your Link view diagram. Table 4.1 provides an explanation for each available filter option.

Accessing the Link view commands

All the options displayed in Figure 4.7 are also available from the Link View toolbar.

TABLE 4.1 Filter Categories

Category	Description
Show In Links	Displays the inbound links—in other words, the pages that refer to this page
Show Out Links	Displays the outbound links—in other words, the items and pages that the page refers to
Show In/Out Links	Displays both the inbound and outbound links for the page
Show Repeated Links	Displays any repeated links for the page
Show Links Inside Pages	Displays the links inside the individual pages in the diagram
Show All Items	Displays all objects
Show HTML Pages	Displays HTML Web pages
Show Multimedia Files	Displays images and multimedia files
Show Documents	Displays document files (MS Word, PowerPoint, and so on)
Show Executable Files	Displays program files, such as EXEs and DLLs
Show Other Protocols	Displays links to non-HTTP objects, such as news servers, Mail, and Telnet
Show External Files	Displays objects external to the project

You can use any of these filters to limit the types of files that are displayed in your Link view diagram. Initially, all the available items will be enabled. Selecting a filter option from the list toggles the choice on and off. In order to show only images and multimedia files in your diagram, you must turn off all the other filter choices by selecting them.

For example, the default behavior of the Link view diagram chooses to display all items.

Filtering the site diagram to show only multimedia files

1. Using the Link view diagram for the headlines page, click the Show All Items icon on the Link View toolbar. This action should deselect the option and hide all the related items for the page.

2. Click the Show Multimedia Files icon on the toolbar. This action displays only the images and multimedia files related to the page, as shown in Figure 4.8.

FIGURE 4.8

Viewing the images for the headlines page.

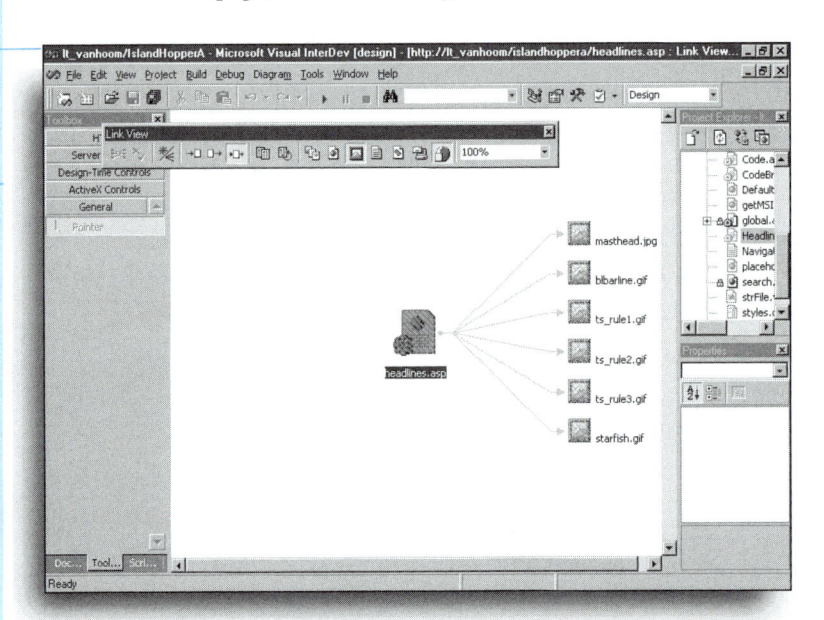

Working with Objects

The purpose of opening a Link view for your objects is to examine and understand the structure and relationships that exist within the Web site. Upon further review of your site, you might want to interact with the objects contained in the diagram. The Link view enables you to directly access the object and activate the default editor for one or more objects. When the object is selected, you can click the right mouse button to display the shortcut menu. For example, Figure 4.9 depicts the shortcut menu for an Active Server Page.

PART I
CHAPTER 4

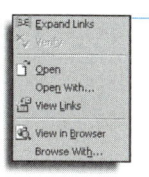

Verifying Links with the Visual InterDev 6 Link View

101

FIGURE 4.9
Opening the object from within the Link view.

Figure 4.9 displays the menu options that are available for all Link view objects. Table 4.2 lists and describes each of these options.

TABLE 4.2 **Object Shortcut Menu Options**

Menu Item	Description
Expand Links	Expands the diagram to include the links of the selected object
Verif**y**	Verifies a broken link
Open	Opens the object using its default editor
Ope**n** With	Enables you to choose an editor to open the selected file
View **L**inks	Creates a new Link view diagram for the object
View in **B**rowser	Enables you to preview the Web page using the default browser
Browse Wit**h**	Enables you to choose a browser to browse the selected page

Opening an Object from Within Link View

As stated previously, you can open objects depicted on the Link view diagram. For example, to open the ADCONFIRM.ASP file, right-click the file and choose **Open** from the shortcut menu. Figure 4.10 demonstrates the results of choosing to open the Ad Confirm ASP file from the shortcut menu in the Link view.

As you can see from the illustration, the selected .asp file is opened using the Source view, enabling you to make changes to the page.

PART I   Visual InterDev Fundamentals

CHAPTER 4   **Using Visual InterDev 6 to Manage Your Web Projects**

FIGURE 4.10

Editing an ASP page.

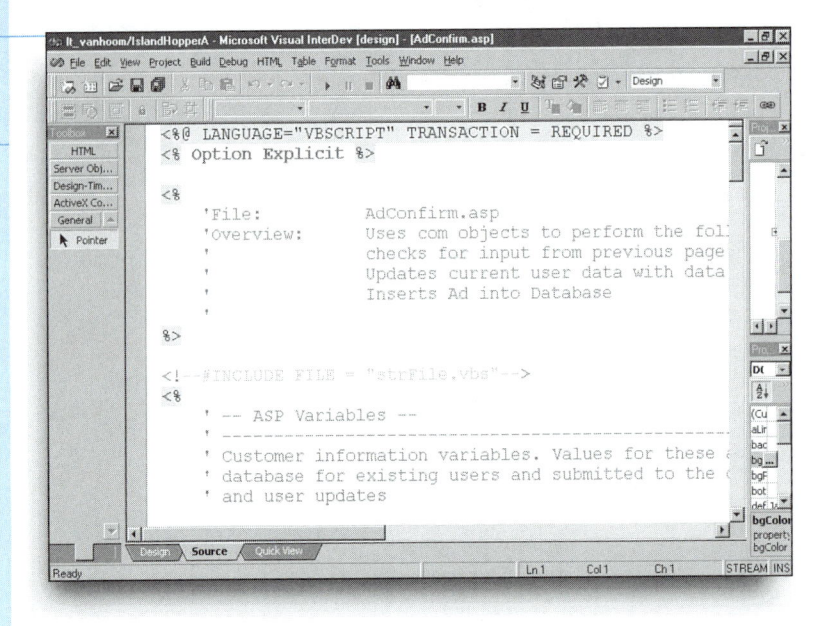

Selecting multiple files in the diagram

You also can select multiple files by dragging the mouse cursor over the objects that you want to select in the diagram. To accomplish this task, click the mouse in the diagram and drag it across the objects that you want to select. A rectangle will display as you drag the mouse to guide you through the selection. When the rectangle encloses all the objects, release the mouse button. All the objects contained in the rectangle will then be selected.

You can also select multiple objects in the Link view diagram by holding down the Ctrl key and clicking the left mouse button on each object that you want to select. After you have made your selections, you can click the right mouse button to choose an action. For example, you might want to open and work with an image and a Web page at the same time. You can select both the image and the HTML Web page file from within the Link view and choose **Open**. Both objects are opened with their respective default editors, enabling you to make any necessary changes.

Another example involves expanding the links for your objects. You might want to expand the links for a portion or all of your Web site to gain a comprehensive look at its structure. In this case, you could individually select the objects using the previously described method, or you can choose **Select All** from the **Edit** menu to select all the items in the diagram. Then, you can select **Expand Links** from the shortcut menu to expand the links for all the selected objects.

The ability to interact instantly with your objects from within the Link view provides a significant time saver to your development effort. Whether you want to preview the design of a Web page or directly modify an image file, Visual InterDev truly promotes the idea of an integrated development environment through the implementation of this feature.

Checking External Links

So far, you have learned how to use Link view to see the links on an internal Web application. You also can view the links for any URL address by choosing the **Tools** menu and selecting **View Links on WWW**. You are then prompted to enter a URL address for the Web page that you want to see in Link view. You can use this feature for your own internal intranet addresses as well as for external Internet URL addresses. Figure 4.11 depicts a Link view diagram for the Macmillan Publishing Web site.

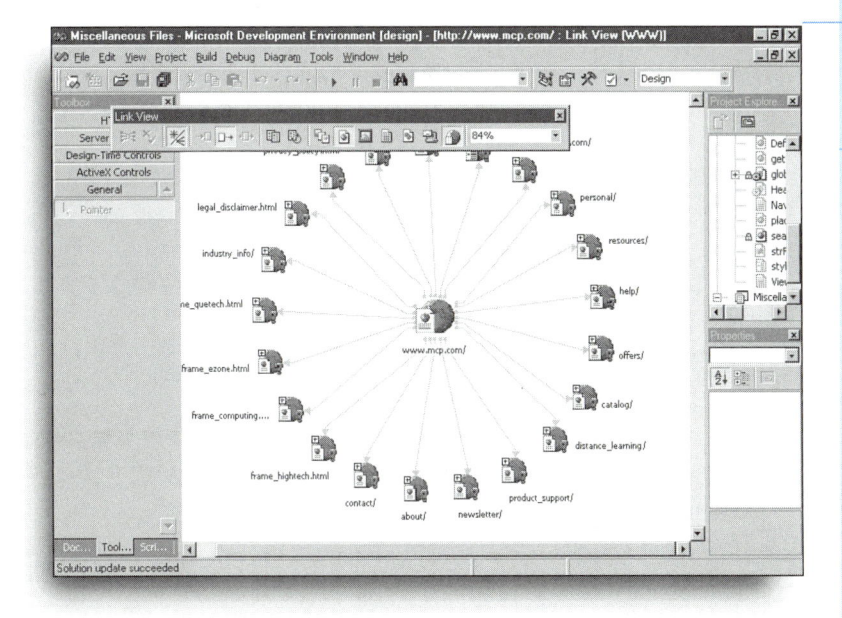

FIGURE 4.11
Viewing the links for a URL on the Web.

Repairing the Links

Visual InterDev 6 provides an automated feature to ensure that your files remain consistently linked. The automatic **Link repair** option is enabled by default. To set this property, right-click the project root from within the Project Explorer and choose **Properties**. The **General** tab will display as shown in Figure 4.12.

FIGURE 4.12

Enabling automatic link repair.

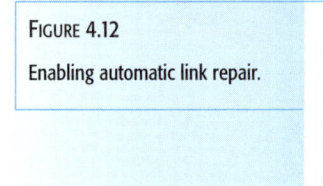

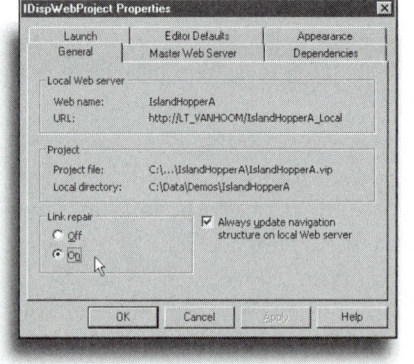

This option is enabled by default. When you have set this option, Visual InterDev will track the files and make you aware of the impact when you change, delete, or move a file. For example, when you rename a file in your project, you receive a warning message similar to the one displayed in Figure 4.13.

FIGURE 4.13

Resolving a conflict: the proactive approach.

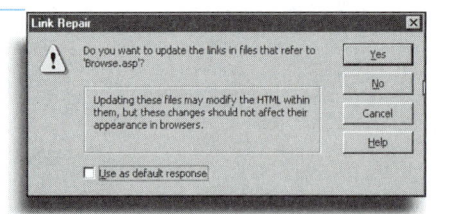

This dialog box enables you to update the links in files that refer to this object so that a conflict won't arise when you try to run your application.

For those occasions on which you have a broken link, you can place your mouse cursor over the object and use the ToolTips help to identify the conflict. For example, Figure 4.14 displays a ToolTips message for an application that contains a broken link.

In this example, the file location information is displayed along with an error message for this object, which describes the conflict in the link relationship. The image file has been moved and cannot be found. Based on this information, you can repair the damage by copying the image file back to the images folder.

Deploying Completed Web Applications | CHAPTER 4 | 105

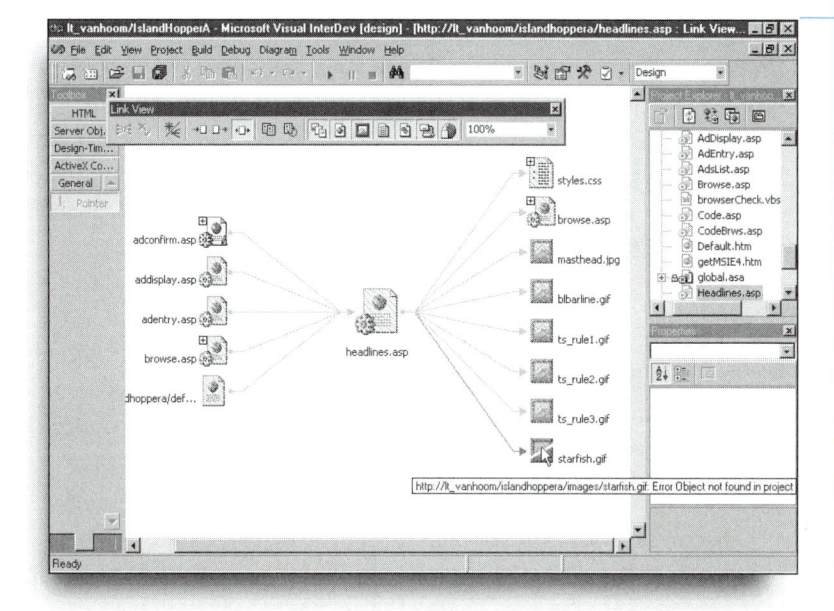

FIGURE 4.14
Using ToolTips to identify the problem.

You can also create a broken links report by choosing **View**, **Broken Links Report**. This action will create a list of tasks in the task list enabling you to view any broken links contained with the structure of your site.

Deploying Completed Web Applications

Visual InterDev 6 contains a powerful feature that enables you to copy an entire Web site to another location. With any project, you will usually have a development, testing, and production environment. These three environments can be used to contain the different stages of your application. These concepts apply whether your development team consists of the three-person team of me, myself, and I, or a team of 50 people.

First, you must create a development environment that supports the initial design and development of your Web-based application. Next, you must create a testing area that reflects individually tested modules. This testing environment supports the integration testing of all the components within your application.

The testing, or staging, area is the final checkpoint before the application is released to the end users. By having a separate testing environment, you can separate modules that are still being worked on versus those that have been adequately tested. In this way, you can ensure that individual developers don't hinder the work of their cohorts. The production environment represents the third stage. This environment supports the use of your Web site by its constituents. This environment contains your fully tested Web-based application and separates the work of the developers from the users. Modules that are still being developed won't cause the user's version of the application to crash, because they operate in separate worlds.

Visual InterDev 6 supports the use of these environments by enabling you to copy your entire Web site across the different environments. Because you have established a unique directory structure for each site, you can use Visual InterDev 6 to promote your site between each stage of development. These environments are logical in nature and could reside either in a different directory on the same machine or on different physical machines. In this way, you can ensure that all the components in your Web site are migrated properly without you having to identify and copy the individual files contained in your site.

Copying a Web Site

The Copy Web feature enables you to copy an entire Web site to another server or to the same server with a new name. One of the new capabilities of Visual InterDev 6 involves the copying of components as well. In Visual InterDev 1, the Copy Web function pertained only to Web site content such as HTML and ASP pages, as well as images and so on. Visual InterDev 6 now supports copying components as well. This feature includes not only the physical copying of business objects and components to another machine or area on a Web server, but also the proper registration of these components on the machine.

To copy a Web site, select **Project**, **Web Project**, **Copy Web Application** to display the Copy Project dialog box. Figure 4.15 illustrates the options that are available on this window.

Having the proper security to copy your Web

You must have administrator privileges on the destination server to execute the Copy Web command. This security restriction is a function of the server operating system, not Visual InterDev. Visual InterDev attempts to execute the command on the destination server using your user ID and password. If you have the correct administrator privileges, the Web site will be copied.

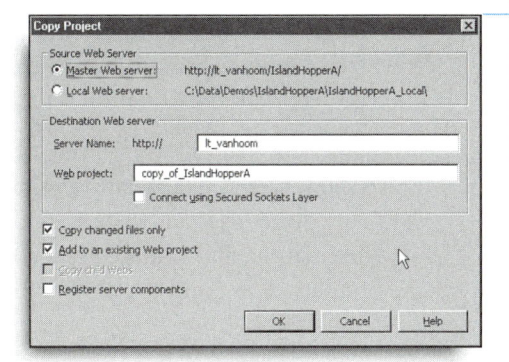

FIGURE 4.15
Copying a Web site.

The first two options on this dialog box enable you to choose the project that you are copying. You can either copy from your **Local Web server** or **Master Web server** project. The next section of the dialog box enables you to specify the **Destination Web server**. You can enter or change the name of the destination server machine. You can also enter a new name for the destination Web project. You can enable a Secure Sockets Layer (SSL) connection by clicking the check box next to this option.

The options at the bottom of this dialog box enable you to customize what is being copied. First, you can choose to **Copy changed files only**. This option is useful when you have initially copied a Web site to the destination and you are copying an updated version to the destination. This option can be applied to the three stages of application development, when you are constantly migrating updated versions of your application from development to testing and from testing to production. You can save a lot of time during the application promotion process by selecting this option because only the files that have changed are copied to the destination location.

The **Add to an existing Web project** option is similar to the one that you have used to create new projects. You can choose to add this Web to an existing site or create a new Web for this site.

The **Copy child Webs** option is enabled only if you are copying the root Web. In this case, you can check this option to copy all the child Webs that exist within the root Web.

The **Register server components** option is new in Visual InterDev 6 and enables you to register any components within your project on the destination server.

To make a copy of this Web, accept the defaults for the destination Web server and destination Web project name. After you confirm your entries and click **OK**, the Web is copied to the new destination, and you receive a confirmation notice, such as the one shown in Figure 4.16.

FIGURE 4.16

A successful copy.

Security settings for the Web on the destination Web server

The newly copied Web site assumes the security settings of the root Web on the destination server machine.

After the site has been copied, you must create a Visual InterDev 6 project to access and interact with the copied Web site.

PART II

Web Page Design Techniques

- 5 **Designing Quality Input Forms for the Web** 111
- 6 **Building Basic Web Forms with Intrinsic HTML Controls** 133
- 7 **Building Advanced Web Forms with Intrinsic HTML Controls** 153
- 8 **Using Style Sheets with Your Web Pages** 175
- 9 **Adding Multimedia to Your Web Applications** 205
- 10 **Creating and Using Image Maps** 233

CHAPTER 5

Designing Quality Input Forms for the Web

Learn how the HTML display space behaves

Create forms that use POST to send data

Create forms that use GET to send data

Use tables to control form layout

Dealing with the HTML Display Space

One of the most common tasks of a Web programmer is the development of quality input forms. The creation of static display pages is a real art, but building input forms that work well on the Web can be a challenge, too.

One of the reasons form design for Web apps can be difficult is that the HTML display space (the space where you place the controls and text) is quite different from the well-known Windows display space. It automatically reformats text to fit the client, enables event messages to pass between document elements, and even gives programmers greater access to all aspects of the document—including the capability to easily manipulate document content during runtime.

Even more important, the HTML display space does most of its magic without any request from users or programmers. In some cases, this auto-adjusting aspect of HTML displays can be a source of frustration or confusion. However, when you understand some of the basics of the HTML workspace, you'll be able to take advantage of its power.

SEE ALSO
➤ *For details on building input forms for the Web, see page 133*

HTML Is Autoformatting

The biggest difference between HTML form space and Windows form space is that HTML form space is capable of *autoformatting* the display. For example, if the user resizes the browser window, the HTML display space will automatically reformat the text to make sure word wrapping matches the current display. This can include the placement of complex elements, such as images, table collections, and even multiframe borders, within the display. Although it is possible for standard Windows forms to achieve the same level of flexibility, it can be done only with a good deal of coding and debugging. The HTML display space does all this automatically.

Dealing with the HTML Display Space

The HTML display space is also smart enough to enable users to adjust the size of the text displayed within the client window. By just selecting an option in the client browser, the HTML display space will adjust *all* the text it receives. Not only that, but the HTML display space will adjust all text fonts relative to each other! This means that if the programmer sets the text sizes to 24 point for titles and 12 point for standard text, when users adjust their browsers to enlarge all the text, the titles might be bumped up to 48 point and the standard text enlarged to 24 point. Again, none of this has to be handled ahead of time by the programmer. The HTML display space has this capability built in.

Of course, there can be a downside to this kind of power. Clients now have the capability of adjusting much of the display behavior of your Web applications. If you are a programmer that has enjoyed having a great deal of control over the layout of your forms, you'll find HTML display space can be quite frustrating. There are times when no matter what you do, you cannot guarantee that a particular icon or line of text will appear at a specific spot in the HTML window every time for every user. The variations of client browsers, video display sizes, and user preferences make it quite difficult to control the minute aspects of HTML display.

> **Learn to love the auto formatting of HTML**
>
> If you've been building Windows dialog boxes, you might find yourself desperately trying to control the exact layout of an HTML document—don't! HTML browsers (and their users) will make their own decisions about font and window size and there's not much you can do about it anyway.

SEE ALSO
► *For more information on how to interact with the Microsoft Internet Explorer client browser space, see page 335*

HTML Forms Are Stateless

Another important aspect of HTML is that the environment is *stateless*. This means that information is not kept in memory as you move from one HTML document to the next. Each page in the Web application exists in its own "world." It is also important to keep in mind that each time you request a document from the Web server, your browser starts a conversation with the server, gets the document, and then closes the conversation. Each document request has the same pattern (start, request, and close). This means that the server remembers nothing of any previous requests by the client and does not keep track of data on previous forms or documents the client had requested earlier.

This stateless nature of the World Wide Web doesn't mean you can't pass data from one form to another, it just means that it must be done carefully and consistently. If you are used to creating programs for the Windows operating system, you know that most languages enable you to define memory space (variables) that is global in scope. The variables can be seen by every form or code section in your application. Web applications have difficulty accomplishing this task. You must send data from your forms back to the server in a special collection, and have documents on the server that are prepared to accept that data and store it for later use. You'll learn two different methods for passing data from your forms to the server later in this chapter.

The key thing to keep in mind is that data collected from input forms can't simply be placed in storage variables for use by other documents in your Web application. You must send them back to the server for handling.

Stateless is good

One of the biggest advantage of a stateless programming model is that it can process client requests much faster. Because your Web server does not need to keep track of large blocks of memory for every connected user, it can answer requests from many users without showing much stress.

SEE ALSO
- To learn how to use the POST method to pass data, see page 115
- To learn how to use the GET method to pass data, see page 123

Most HTML Forms Are Single-Mode Documents

The last aspect of HTML form design that will be covered here is the aspect of *operating mode*. You might not think of it much, but each data entry form you use (no matter what operating system or language) has one or more modes of operation. Some forms are built for *display mode* only. These forms enable users to view data, but they can't add, edit, or delete information. Other forms enable users to both view and edit the data. Other forms enable users only to add new records to the database, but not delete records or edit existing records. These types of forms are sometimes called *single-mode forms*. They enable users to do only one type of operation.

Other forms enable users to both display and edit data on the same page. Forms that enable users to perform multiple operations are sometimes called *multimode forms*. This is typical of many forms built for Windows or other graphical user interface (GUI) operating systems. In fact, most users have become used to the behavior of multimode forms. The capability to view existing records, edit them, delete them, or add new ones all on the same page has become quite common for Windows applications.

Although multimode forms are common for standalone and network applications, they are not very common for Web applications. The fact that Web forms must operate in a stateless environment and constantly send and request data from distant Web servers makes the creation of multimode forms a complex process. For this reason, most Web forms are designed as single-mode forms. They enable users to enter data that is sent to the server; a new form is returned to the user showing the results of the previous data entry.

In fact, this single-mode form concept is so common for Web applications that the HTML display space has a built-in element for handling this input and send behavior: the `<FORM>` element. You'll learn more about the `<FORM>` element in the rest of this chapter. The key thing to remember is that the most common way to collect data in Web documents is to define a set of input elements as part of the HTML `<FORM>` and send the contents of those input elements back to the server for processing. This is the essence of single-mode forms.

SEE ALSO
➤ For information on how to create advanced multimode input forms for the Web, see page 543

> **Don't confuse single-mode forms and modal dialog boxes**
>
> You might have heard the phrase *modal dialog* to describe dialog boxes in Windows applications. This is not the same thing as a single-mode form. Modal dialogs are used to halt program execution until the dialog box is dismissed. Single-mode dialog boxes are used to allow users to perform a single task.

> **Multimode Web forms**
>
> It is possible to create multimode Web forms with Visual InterDev using the FormManager Design-Time Control (DTC). This is a special control that enables programmers to define each mode for the form and establish behaviors for each element on the form during each defined mode. You'll learn more about the FormManager DTC in Chapter 20, "Using Advanced Design-Time Controls."

Creating Single-Mode *POST* Forms

The most common design for Web input forms is the single-mode POST form. This form contains `<INPUT>` HTML elements to collect data from the user and the `<FORM>` element to define the start and end of the input items. The form also includes **Submit** and **Reset** buttons to enable users to send the data to the server or clear the form and try again.

In this section, you learn the basic theory of posting data from a Web client to the Web server, and how to create the HTML client document for user input and an ASP server document to accept the data.

The Details of Posting Data

There actually are two ways to send data from the browser client to the Web server: POST and GET. The POST method packages the NAME and VALUE attributes of the INPUT elements of a Web form and sends them to the Web server in a separate portion of the conversation between the client and server. The GET method sends the NAME and VALUE attributes as an additional part of the URL (uniform resource locator). When you use the GET method, the client can see the various values in the browser's URL display.

The POST method is also capable of passing more data than the GET method. The POST method hides the NAME and VALUE attributes in the transmission between client and server. Because the GET method displays the NAME and VALUE attributes for all users to see, it is also not very cosmetically appealing.

The key thing to understand is that the receiving document must know ahead of time the method used to send data from client to server. Although POSTing data is the preferred method, some destination URLs (for example, ISAPI DLLs or some CGI scripts) might require the use of the GET method.

POST it if you can

Because the **POST** method enables a larger amount of data to be passed and because the data is passed in the hidden conversation body, not on the URL line where users can see it, you should use the **POST** method to send data to the server unless you are specifically prevented from doing so by the server-side component or some other programming restriction.

SEE ALSO

➤ *For more on how* NAME, ID, *and* VALUE *apply to HTML Input controls, see page 133*

Building the POSTFORM.HTM Document

Now that you know the theory behind creating POST forms, it's time to build one. For this example, you build a simple form with two input fields (**Name** and **Telephone**) along with the **Submit** and **Reset** buttons. In the next section, you add an ASP document to accept the data from the POST Web form.

Creating Single-Mode *POST* Forms

Creating a POST form with Visual InterDev is easy. If you haven't done it already, start Visual InterDev and create a new Web project called Forms (see Chapter 1, "Creating Web Projects with the Site Designer," for more information on starting a new Web project). Now it's time to add a new HTM document to the project and format it as a Web form.

Adding a new HTM document to your project

1. Right-click on the project name in the project window.
2. Select **Add** from the menu.
3. Select **Add HTML Page** from the next menu.
4. Enter the name of the new document (POSTFORM) and press **Open**.
5. The document will appear in your project window.

After adding the document, you're ready to create the input form. For this example you want to add a <FORM> element, two lines of text, two input controls, and the **Submit** and **Reset** buttons. You also add a heading line and a horizontal bar to the form. Figure 5.1 shows how the form will look when you are finished creating it.

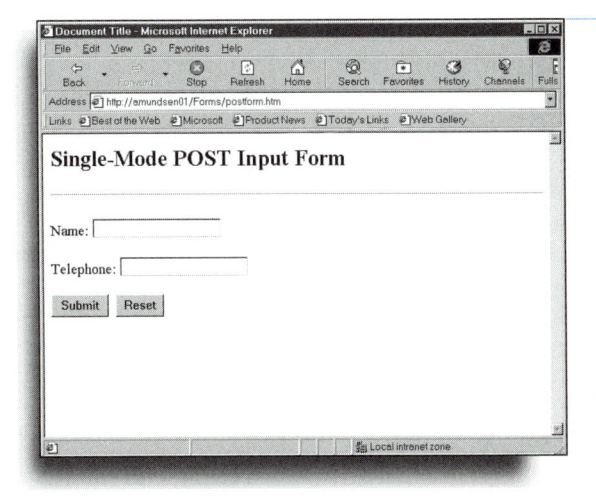

FIGURE 5.1
Laying out the POSTFORM.HTM document.

The first task is to load the document into the editor and add a heading and horizontal bar to the top of the form.

Adding a heading and horizontal bar to an HTML document

1. Open the HTM document for editing by double-clicking it in the project window (select **POSTFORM.HTM**).

2. Select the **Design** tab in the Visual InterDev editor and type a form header (for this example, type Single-Mode POST Input Form).

3. With the cursor still on the same line as the heading, set the text style to **Heading 1** by selecting it from the list of styles on the toolbar.

4. Click the **HTML** tab of the toolbox window and locate the Horizontal bar (**HR**) element.

5. While the editor is still in Design mode, drag the **HR** element from the toolbox up onto the page and drop it at the end of the heading line. This will place the horizontal bar directly underneath the last line of text.

6. Press Return once to mark the end of the paragraph. This will enable you to set a new text style for the remaining portion of the form.

The next task is to add the two input controls and their prompt text to the document.

Adding input controls and prompts

1. In the **Design** tab of the Visual InterDev editor, move your cursor to a new line on the document and type the label of the first input control into the document (for this example, type Name:). Be sure to add two spaces after the text to place some room between the label and the input control.

2. Now add the textbox INPUT element by dragging a Textbox control from the **HTML** tab of the toolbox window onto the page. Drop it at the end of the label text on the same line.

3. With the INPUT element in focus (shaded outline around it), locate the ID attribute in the property window and set it to a meaningful name (in this case, use txtName). Also set the NAME attribute to the same value (txtName).

4. Press Return to mark the end of the paragraph.

Creating Single-Mode *POST* Forms

5. Repeat steps 1–4 for each input element in your form. In this example, add a second line of text, `Telephone:`, and add another textbox INPUT element with its NAME and ID attributes set to **txtPhone**.

After adding all the input elements and their prompts, you're ready to add the **Submit** and **Reset** buttons for the form.

Adding the Submit and Reset buttons to an HTML document

1. With the Visual InterDev editor in Design mode, locate the **Submit** button in the **HTML** tab of the toolbox window and drag it onto the document; drop it on a new line underneath the last input element.
2. Set the NAME and ID attributes of the **Submit** button to `btnSubmit`.
3. Now locate the **Reset** button in the **HTML** tab of the toolbox window and drag the button onto the document; drop it on the same line as the **Submit** button.
4. Set the NAME and ID attributes of the **Reset** button to `btnReset`.

The final step in completing the POST form is to add the FORM element to the document. This can be a bit tricky because the Visual InterDev FORM element is not as smart as you might hope. The FORM element has the following format:

```
<form method=POST action="postvalues.asp">
<!-- place input elements and buttons here -->
</form>
```

As you can see, there are two tags for the FORM element. The <FORM> tag marks the start of the form area. The <FORM> tag has two attributes. The METHOD attribute defines the data transfer method. In the preceding example, the POST method is used. The ACTION attribute defines the URL that is the destination of the data transfer. This usually contains an ASP document or a COM object DLL. It can also contain the name of a CGI script or ISAPI.DLL file located on the server.

The end of the form area is marked by the </FORM> tag. Any <INPUT> element that is placed between the <FORM> and </FORM>

NAME versus ID

The ID attribute is used by scripting languages to identify unique items in the HTML document. The NAME attribute is used to offer a friendly description of the element. Although not required, it is a good idea to make both values the same. It is possible to have several HTML elements with the same name. However, every element ID should be unique in a document.

tags will be included in the data transmission back to the server. In order for this to work properly, the **Submit** and **Reset** buttons must also be placed between the `<FORM>` and `</FORM>` tags.

Now that you know what the `<FORM>` tags are used for, you're ready to add them to your POSTFORM.HTM document.

Marking an HTML document with the *<FORM>* and *</FORM>* tags

1. With the HTM document already in the editor, select the **Source** tab to view the source code.
2. Locate the line in the HTML code that defines the first `INPUT` element for the form (in this case, locate the `txtName` input element).
3. Be sure there is a blank line just above the first `INPUT` element. If there is none, press the Return key to add a blank line to the document.
4. Type `<FORM METHOD=POST ACTION="postvalues.asp">` to mark the start of the HTML form and indicate the data transfer method as `POST` and the URL of the document to receive the data.
5. Locate the first blank line after the end of the form inputs and buttons. If there is no blank line, press Return to make the new line.
6. Place the cursor on the blank line after the end of the form inputs and buttons and type `</FORM>` into the document. This marks the end of the HTML input form.

When you have completed all these steps, you have a finished HTML input form that uses the `POST` method to send data back to the server. Your completed HTML code for the POSTFORM.HTM document should look like the code in Listing 5.1.

LISTING 5.1

❶ This line marks the beginning of the Web form.

LISTING 5.1 The HTML Code for the POSTFORM.HTM Document

```
1  <H1>Single-Mode POST Input Form </H1>
2  <HR>
3  <form method=POST action="postvalues.asp">         ──────── ❶
4  <P>Name: <INPUT id=txtName name=txtName></P>
5  <P>Telephone: <INPUT id=txtPhone name=txtPhone></P>
```

Creating Single-Mode *POST* Forms

```
6 <P><INPUT id=btnSubmit type=submit value=Submit
  ➥name=btnSubmit> 
7 <INPUT id=btnReset type=reset value=Reset name=btnReset></P>
8 </form>
```

> **LISTING 5.1 CONTINUED**
>
> ❷ This line marks the end of the Web form.

The code shown in Listing 5.1 is all the code that will appear in the <BODY> of the HTML document. Notice that you were able to complete almost all this form using the WYSIWYG editor and drag-and-drop techniques. Save this document and view it in the **Quick View** tab of the Visual InterDev editor. It should look like the one shown in Figure 5.1.

Now that the form is complete, you must build an ASP document that will accept the data and, for this example, display it to the client.

SEE ALSO
➤ *For more on using Visual InterDev 6 to build Web forms, see page 57*

Adding the POSTVALUES.ASP Document

It is quite easy to create ASP documents that can accept data from client-side entry forms. In this example, you build a document called POSTVALUES.ASP that will accept the data from the POSTFORM.HTM document and then display it to the user.

The first step is to add a new ASP document to the project.

Adding a new ASP document to your project

1. Right-click over the project name in the project window.
2. Select **Add** from the menu.
3. Select **Active Server Page** from the submenu.
4. Enter the name of the new ASP document (postvalues) and click **Open**.
5. The document will appear in your project window.

Now all you must do is add a few lines of Visual Basic Script to the ASP document. First, double-click the POSTVALUES.ASP document in the project window to load it into the Visual InterDev editor. Then add the text shown in Listing 5.2 to the <BODY> portion of the document.

LISTING 5.2 Adding Visual Basic Script to the POSTVALUES.ASP Document

```
1  <%
2  '
3  ' retrieve values from a POST form
4  '
5  Dim strName
6  Dim strPhone
7
8  strName = Request.Form("txtName")
9  strPhone = Request.Form("txtPhone")
10
11 Response.Write "You entered the following responses:<HR>"
12 Response.Write "Name: " & strName & "<BR>"
13 Response.Write "Phone: " & strPhone & "<BR>"
14 %>
```

LISTING 5.2

❶ Notice that the member name `txtName` matches the NAME and ID attribute used in the client-side form.

❷ The `<BR>` element sends out a line break.

Be sure to enter `<%` at the beginning of the code section and `%>` at the end. This marks the start and end of the server-side script block.

Note the use of the `Request.Form` method in lines 8 and 9 of Listing 5.2. These are the two lines that accept the data from POSTFORM.HTM and store it in memory variables on the server. Lines 11–13 use the `Response.Write` method to send HTML coding back to the client to display the values.

Be sure to save the ASP document in your Web project. Then mark the POSTFORM.HTM document as the start page (right-click on POSTFORM.HTM and select **Set as Start Page**). Then press F5 to run the project in your default browser. You should be able to enter data in your form, then press the **Submit** button and see the resulting server-side script page send data to you (see Figure 5.2).

Using `Request("MyValue")` instead of `Request.Form("MyValue")`

You can simplify your parameter-passing code by dropping the `.Form` object word from the `Request.Form("MyValue")` ASP code. If data was passed using the POST method, the line `Request("MyValue")` will still return the same information to the ASP document.

SEE ALSO
▶ *For more on how to use the ASP Request object, see page 411*

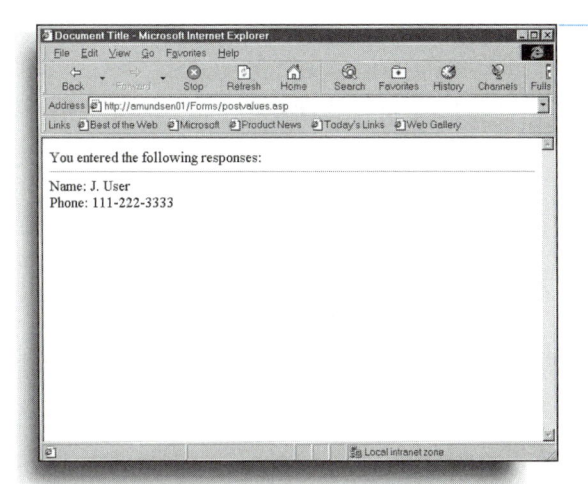

FIGURE 5.2
Viewing the results of POSTVALUES.ASP.

Creating Single-Mode *GET* Forms

As mentioned earlier in this chapter, there are two methods of sending data from the client to the server. In the first section, you built a form that uses the POST method of sending data. In this section, you build a form that looks the same but uses the GET method to send data. You also create a new ASP document that is able to accept data sent using the GET method.

Why Use *GET* to Send Data?

Although the POST method of data transfer is the preferred way to move data from the client back to the server, there are times when you might need to use the GET method. Although it has its limits, the GET method is still used quite frequently, especially at Web servers that use old-style DLLs and CGI scripts that do not follow the COM (Component Object Model) interface rules.

The first thing you should remember is that sending data via the GET method is actually sending data alongside the URL that is mentioned in the <FORM> tag. This means that you are limited in the total amount of data you can send. In general, only small amounts of data should be sent via the GET method. The GET method works well for passing startup parameters for forms,

Using GET to debug your forms

You can also use the GET method to debug forms that seem to be passing the wrong parameter values. Because the GET method places all parameter values on the URL line, it is easy to use your browser to inspect the values to make sure your form is working properly.

FIGURE 5.3

Viewing the passed data in the browser URL line.

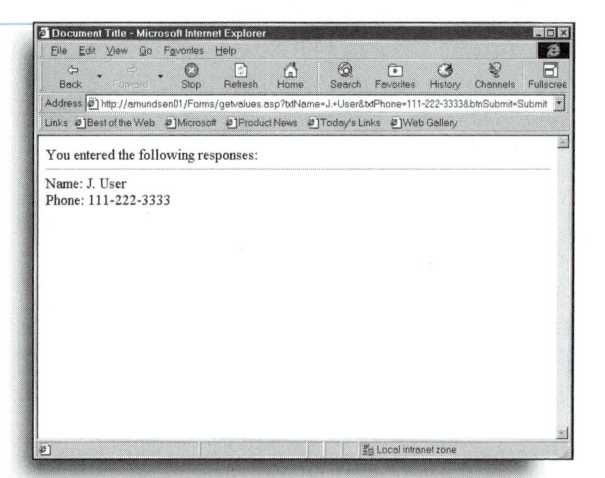

sending simple request parameters for the server to use when building data queries for the user, or in cases where the data you want to send is quite small. In any other case, the POST method is better.

Finally, when you use the GET method you must keep in mind that the entire data stream (including the names of the INPUT controls and the actual data) will be displayed to the user in the location input box of the browser (see Figure 5.3).

As you can see from Figure 5.3, the user can see all the values entered in the form (along with the **Submit** button name) in the URL field of the browser. Normally, the ability to see passed data is not a very important matter. However, if you are passing passwords or other vital information back to the server, you might not want to let the user see this data.

SEE ALSO
➤ *To learn how to build forms that use* POST *instead of* GET, *see page 115*

Building the GETFORM.HTM Document

The first step is to add a new form to your Web project called GETFORM.HTM. Then you can lay out an input form just like the one you built for the POSTFORM.HTM document. In fact, the only difference between the GETFORM.HTM and the POSTFORM.HTM documents is the details of the `<FORM>` tag. Instead of using the `POST` method, you use the `GET` method, and you use a different URL in the `ACTION` attribute, too.

First, you must add a new document to the project. To do this, just right-click on the project name in the project window, select **Add**, **HTML Page** from the menus, enter `GETFORM` as the name, and press **Open**. This adds the new form to your project.

Now, in order to save time and typing errors, you can simply copy the HTML code from the POSTFORM.HTM document and place it inside the `<BODY>` of the GETFORM.HTM document.

Copying HTML code from one file to another

1. Load the document into the editor that has the code you want to copy by double-clicking on it in the project window (in our example, double-click on **postform.htm**).

2. Select the **Source** tab in the Visual InterDev editor and, using your mouse, select all the text you want to copy. In this example, place the cursor on the line that is immediately after the line with the `<BODY>` tag and press the left mouse button. Now, holding the mouse button down, drag the mouse to the line that is immediately before the line that has the `</BODY>` tag and release the mouse button. All this text should now be selected.

3. After releasing the mouse button, move your mouse over the selected text and press the right mouse button. Select **Copy** from the context menu. This places a copy of the selected text onto the Windows Clipboard.

4. Now load the document into the editor that you want to hold the copy of the HTML code you just selected. To do this, double-click the desired document in the project window (for this example, double-click **GETFORM.HTM**).

5. Select the **Source** tab for the loaded document and place the cursor on the location where you want to paste the copied HTML code. In this example, place your cursor on the line immediately after the `<BODY>` tag.

6. When the cursor is positioned exactly where you want, right-click the mouse and select **P**aste from the context menu. This will paste all the code from the Clipboard into the current document.

7. If the HTML code is not placed where you want it, you can press Ctrl+Z to undo the paste operation and then reposition the cursor to try again.

After you have pasted all the code from the POSTFORM.HTM document into the GETFORM.HTM document, you need only change the two attributes of the <FORM> tag. Locate the <FORM> tag in the code window and change the METHOD attribute from POST to GET and the ACTION attribute from **POSTVALUES.ASP** to **GETVALUES.ASP** When you're finished, your HTML code should look like the code in Listing 5.3.

LISTING 5.3

① Notice the use of the GET method instead of POST.

LISTING 5.3   The Completed HTML Code for GETFORM.HTM

```
1 <H1>Single-Mode GET Input Form </H1>
2 <HR>
3 <form method=GET action="getvalues.asp">
4 <P>Name: <INPUT id=txtName name=txtName></P>
5 <P>Telephone: <INPUT id=txtPhone name=txtPhone></P>
6 <P><INPUT id=btnSubmit type=submit value=Submit name=
 ➥btnSubmit> 
7 <INPUT id=btnReset type=reset value=Reset name=btnReset></P>
8 </form>
```

Again, the only difference in this code from the code in Listing 5.1 are the values of the METHOD and ACTION attributes of the <FORM> tag.

Save this document to your Web project before you add the GETVALUES.ASP document mentioned in the next section.

SEE ALSO
➤ *For more on how to use* `Request.QueryString`, *see page 381*

Creating Single-Mode *GET* Forms PART II
CHAPTER 5

127

Adding the GETVALUES.ASP Document

Now that the GETFORM.HTM entry form is complete, you must build an ASP document to accept the data values passed from the client. This document will look a lot like the POSTVALUES.ASP document. The only difference is that you will edit the lines that accept the data from the client.

Because only a few lines will change, you can create the new ASP document and then copy the code from POSTVALUES.ASP into GETVALUES.ASP and make the minor changes needed.

First, add the new ASP document by right-clicking the project name in the project window, selecting **Add**, **Acti̱ve Server Page** from the menu tree, entering GETVALUES.ASP as the document name, and clicking **Open**. The new document will appear in your project window.

Now, using the steps outlined in the previous section, copy the ASP code body from POSTVALUES.ASP into GETVALUES.ASP. When you're finished, the code in GETVALUES.ASP should look exactly like the code in Listing 5.2. The only change that is needed is to replace the Request.Form statements with Request.QueryString statements. Whenever you use the GET method to send data to ASP documents, you must use the Request.QueryString statement to collect the data at the server. Listing 5.4 shows how the GETVALUES.ASP document looks after you make the changes to lines 8 and 9 of the code listing.

LISTING 5.4 **The Completed ASP Code for the GETVALUES.ASP Document**

```
1  <%
2  '
3  ' retrieve values from a GET form
4  '
5  Dim strName
6  Dim strPhone
7
8  strName = Request.QueryString("txtName")
```

continues...

LISTING 5.4

① When you use GET to send data to the server, you should use QueryString to retrieve the object, not Form.

LISTING 5.4   **Continued**

```
9  strPhone = Request.QueryString("txtPhone")
10
11 Response.Write "You entered the following responses:<HR>"
12 Response.Write "Name: " & strName & "<BR>"
13 Response.Write "Phone: " & strPhone & "<BR>"
14 %>
```

Again, note that lines 8 and 9 are now using the `Request.QueryString` method to retrieve data from the client GET form. This is the only change you must make to the document.

After the changes have been completed, save the document. You can then test your project by marking the GETFORM.HTM document as the start page (right-click over the document and select **Set as Start Page** from the menu) and pressing F5 to run the document in your default browser. After filling out the form and pressing the **Submit** button, you should see the same results shown in Figure 5.3.

You can test the **Reset** button, too. This button automatically clears out any input controls on the form and lets you start again. To test this, enter data into the two input boxes on the form and then click the **Reset** button to clear the fields.

Make your ASP scripts accept both POST or GET values

You can build your ASP documents to accept either POST or GET values by simply using the line `request(<input name>)` instead of `request.Form()` or `request.QueryString()`.

Controlling Layout with the *TABLE* Element

You might have noticed that it is difficult to align a set of prompts and input elements in a straight line in the HTML display space. This is because many browsers do not support what is called *absolute positioning* of control elements. Although the Visual InterDev editor does support the use of absolute positioning, you will find that many people who are viewing your Web application will not be able to take advantage of the feature. They will still see the controls unaligned.

There is, however, another way to easily produce forms that show aligned elements. This is through the use of the HTML <TABLE> element. You can define a set of columns and rows to

Controlling Layout with the *TABLE* Element

hold prompts and input elements. Then, when the client browser displays the elements, they appear in a fixed table instead of in a jagged line (see Figure 5.4).

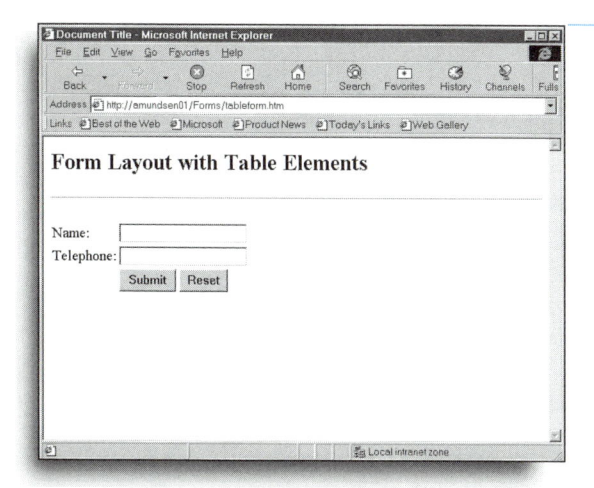

FIGURE 5.4
The results of using TABLE elements to align controls.

The process of using TABLE elements to produce aligned forms can be a bit confusing. The added layer of TABLE tags clutters the HTML code up a bit. Also, you must do some planning ahead of time to build the tables properly before you add the prompts and inputs. However, the results are worth the effort.

In the next section, you build a new form that works just like the POSTFORM.HTM document you built earlier. However, this one will use the TABLE elements to create a fully aligned form.

Building the TABLEFORM.HTM Document

The first thing to do is add a new HTML document to your Web project. To do this, right-click on the project name in the project window, select **Add**, **HTML Document** from the menus, enter TABLEFORM as the name, and press **Open** to add the new form to your project. Optionally, you can add a heading to the form (Form Layout with Table Elements) and a horizontal bar.

Using absolute positioning instead of tables

If you are using only Microsoft Internet Explorer 4.x and higher, you might be able to use absolute positioning to manage the size and location of HTML controls on your form. The drawback to using absolute positioning is that some clients might not honor the settings, and the resulting page can be difficult to read.

Now you're ready to load the form into the Visual InterDev editor and create the HTML codes needed to display an aligned input form. This process involves first adding the table and then placing the controls inside the table cells. The final step is to wrap the entire table in a `<FORM>...</FORM>` tag set.

Here's how you add a table to your HTML document to hold the input form controls.

Adding a table to your HTML document

1. With the document loaded into the Visual InterDev editor, select the **Design** tab to set the editor in WYSIWYG mode.
2. Place the cursor on a blank line where you want the table to appear.
3. Now select **T**able, **I**nsert Table from the main menu to bring up the Insert Table dialog box (see Figure 5.5).
4. Enter the number of **R**ows for your table (in this example, enter 3).
5. Enter the number of **C**olumns for your table (in this example, enter 2).
6. Set the **W**idth attribute to 1 and select **pixels** as the unit value. This will force the table to appear only as large as needed to host the prompts and input controls.
7. Set the **Border si**z**e** to 0 to make the table invisible on the form.
8. Click **OK** to add the defined table to your document.

Now add the prompts to the form. Place your cursor in the first cell on the first line of the table and type `Name:`. Now place your cursor in the first cell of the second line of the table and type `Telephone:`. Note that the table cells resize to fit your text.

Next, add the INPUT text box elements. Just drag a Textbox control from the **HTML** tab of the toolbox window and drop it in the second cell on the first line of the table. You must be sure to drop it exactly inside the cell. If you accidentally drop the control somewhere else, just press Ctrl+Z to undo the action and try again. Also, after dropping the text box in the table for the name, be sure to set its NAME and ID attributes to txtName. Next, you can

Controlling Layout with the *TABLE* Element

drop a text box in the table for the telephone input. Set its NAME and ID attributes to `txtPhone`.

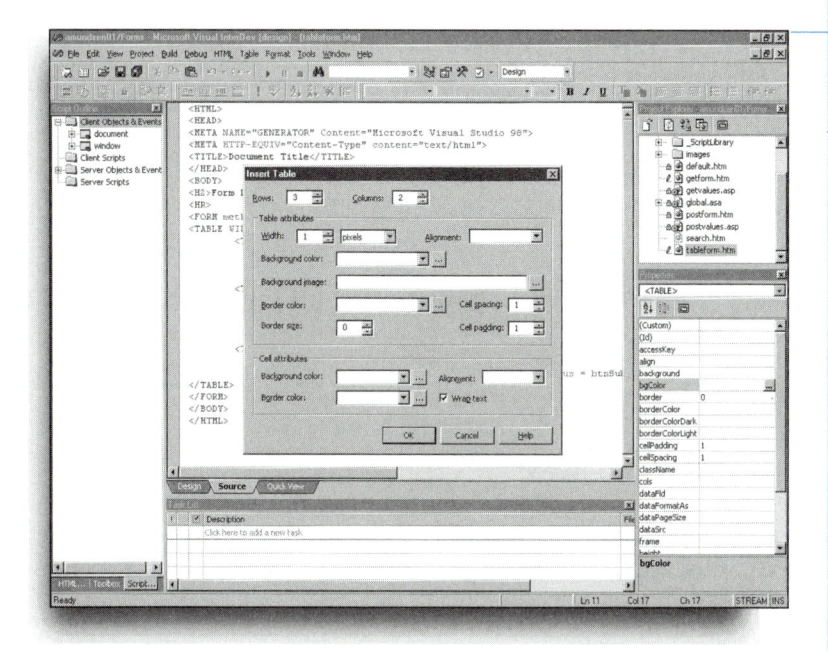

FIGURE 5.5
The Insert Table dialog box.

Now, drag and drop a **Submit** button and a **Reset** button from the **HTML** section of the toolbox into the second cell on the third line of the table. Place them next to each other in the same cell. Be sure to set their NAME and ID attributes to `btnSubmit` and `btnReset`, respectively.

The next step is to place the FORM tags in the document. To do this, switch to **Source** view in the Visual InterDev editor and drag the FORM element from the toolbox onto a blank line above the <TABLE> element. You can then cut and paste the </FORM> tag to the first blank line after the </TABLE> element.

Finally, you must set the ACTION attribute of the <FORM> tag to `postvalues.asp`. This sends the results of the data entry to the POSTVALUES.ASP document you built earlier in this chapter.

When you are finished building the form, the HTML code will look like the code in Listing 5.5.

PART II Web Page Design Techniques

CHAPTER 5 **Designing Quality Input Forms for the Web**

LISTING 5.5

① This line marks the start of the HTML table.

② This line marks the end of the HTML table.

LISTING 5.5 **The Completed HTML Code for the *TABLE* Form**

```
 1 <BODY>
 2 <H2>Form Layout with Table Elements</H2>
 3 <HR>
 4 <FORM method=post action=postvalues.asp>
 5     <TABLE WIDTH=1 BORDER=0 CELLSPACING=1 CELLPADDING=1>────①
 6        <TR>
 7           <TD>Name:
 8           <TD><INPUT id=txtName name=txtName>
 9        <TR>
10           <TD>Telephone:
11           <TD><INPUT id=txtPhone name=txtPhone>
12        <TR>
13           <TD>
14           <TD><INPUT id=btnSubmit type=submit value=
               ÂSubmit status = btnSubmit>
15              <INPUT id=btnReset type=reset value=Reset name=
                ÂbtnReset>
16           </TD>
17        </TR>
18     </TABLE>───────────────────────────────────②
19 </FORM>
20 </BODY>
```

After you complete the TABLEFORM.HTM document, be sure to save it to the project. You can test the form by marking it as the start page (right-click on the document in the project window and select **Set as Start Page** from the context menu) and pressing F5 to launch the document in your default browser. You should see an input form that has its controls properly aligned as in Figure 5.4.

SEE ALSO
➤ *For more on using HTML Intrinsic controls to build Web forms, see page 153*

CHAPTER 6

Building Basic Web Forms with Intrinsic HTML Controls

Learn about the intrinsic HTML controls

Work with the <INPUT> tag

Understand and use the various types of <INPUT> element controls

What Are the Intrinsic HTML Controls?

This chapter and the one that follows it is devoted to showing you how to use the most basic HTML INPUT control elements. These HTML controls can be used to build forms that enable users to enter text data, make logical choices in check boxes, and select from a fixed set of items in a radio button collection.

The control elements covered in this chapter are part of the HTML intrinsic set. They are called the intrinsic controls because they are built into every client browser. These input controls are not downloaded from the Web server to the client station, and they need no additional client code to create them. They are intrinsic to the very browsers themselves.

SEE ALSO
➤ To learn about the Advanced data-bound design-time controls (DTCs), see page 441

The Advantages and Disadvantages of HTML Intrinsic Controls

Intrinsic controls have several advantages over any custom-built or third-party input controls. First, because they are already built into the browser, you can be sure that Web forms that use these controls will work with almost any client HTML browser. Second, the creation and operation of the intrinsic controls is almost always faster than any customer-built input control. Finally, the behavior and the "look and feel" of the intrinsic controls are quite familiar to users. If you add custom-built controls to your Web forms, you might find that they confuse users or that users do not use the new controls properly.

There are a few disadvantages to intrinsic controls, too. First, because the controls are designed to run on all browsers, regardless of the operating platform, they are—by design—rather simple. It is difficult to create feature-rich input controls that must run on Windows, Apple, UNIX, and other operating systems. Second, because the controls *do* run on other operating systems, occasionally they behave slightly differently from one system to the next. Although the controls do not fail, they might not

---

Use intrinsic HTML controls for generic browsers

If your Web application needs to support generic browsers (not just Microsoft Internet Explorer 4 and above), you should stick to using the intrinsic HTML controls.

exhibit all the features or behaviors that you expect. For this reason, it is important to test your controls on all browsers that might be running your Web applications.

Finally, because the intrinsic controls were designed for HTML coding, they do not always easily cooperate with scripts that attempt to set or get their values or other attributes. The exact method for manipulating HTML intrinsics can vary between controls, browsers, and operating systems. Again, carefully test your Web forms against as many browser and operating platforms as possible.

Coding with the <INPUT> Tag

The rest of this chapter covers the four most commonly used HTML intrinsic controls. These controls all use the <INPUT> tag as part of their definition. Along with the <INPUT> tag, they have a TYPE attribute, which defines how the control will appear in the client browser. In this chapter, you learn to use four of the most common input control types:

- Textbox—Used to get a single line of text from the user.
- Password—Similar to the textbox, but only echoes * back to the user.
- Checkbox—Presents a small box where the user can add or remove a check mark to indicate on or off, yes or no.
- Radio—Presents a set of round on/off inputs in a group. Only one of the items in the group can be on at any time.

SEE ALSO
➤ For information on general design of Web forms, see page 111
➤ To learn about the advanced HTML input controls, see page 153

Building the INPUTS1 Web Project

All the HTML documents in this chapter can be collected in a single Web project. If you have not already done so, now is the time to create a new Web project to hold the HTML documents for this chapter. To do this, you must start Visual InterDev and create a new project.

Creating a new Web project

1. Select **F**ile, and then **New Project** from the Visual InterDev main menu.
2. When the New Project dialog appears, click on the New Web Project icon on the right.
3. Press the **B**rowse button to navigate to the disk folder where the new project should reside.
4. Click **OK** when you have selected the home folder for the project.
5. Now enter a **N**ame for the Web project (in this case, enter INPUTS1) and click the **O**pen button.
6. If the input box **What server do you want to use?** is blank, enter the name of the Web server that will host your project.
7. Be sure to select **M**aster mode as the operating mode for the project, and press **N**ext.
8. Accept the default project name (in this case **inputs1**) and click **N**ext.
9. Click **F**inish to skip the Theme and Layout dialog boxes.
10. Visual InterDev will create your project folder, populate it with subfolders and documents, and return you to the Visual InterDev IDE ready for work.

Now that you have created the Web project, you're ready to start experimenting with the HTML intrinsic input controls.

SEE ALSO

➤ *For more on creating a new project with Visual InterDev 6, see page 7*

Using the Textbox Input Control

The most commonly used input control is the textbox type. This control accepts a single line of text as input. The HTML format for the textbox type input control and its attributes is shown in Listing 6.1.

Using the Textbox Input Control

LISTING 6.1 The Basic HTML Coding for the Textbox Input Control

```
1  <INPUT
2     ID=txtField1
3     NAME=txtField1
4     SIZE=30
5     MAXLENGTH=20
6     VALUE="Starting Value"
7     ACCESSKEY="c"
8     READONLY=0
9     TABINDEX=1
10    DISABLED
11  >
```

The ID and NAME attributes (lines 2 and 3) are quite similar. HTML and script languages use one or both of these fields. It is a good idea to use both of them when defining your input controls.

The SIZE attribute (line 4) sets the display size (in characters) of the control on the page. The MAXLENGTH attribute (line 5) sets the maximum number of characters you will allow to be entered into the control.

The VALUE attribute (line 6) contains the data entered by the user. You can "seed" the input control with default data by setting the VALUE attribute when you build the form.

The attributes on lines 7–10 are supported by the Visual InterDev editor, but are not commonly used. If you use these attributes, you must test your Web applications to make sure your client browser honors them.

Using the textbox input control on your Web documents is easy. First, add a new document to your Web project called TEXTBOX.HTM.

Adding a new HTML document to your Web project

1. Right-click over the project name in the Project Explorer.
2. Select **A**dd from the context menu.
3. Select **H**TML **P**age from the submenu that appears.

Where's the TYPE=TEXT attribute?

You might notice that Visual InterDev 6 does not use the TYPE=TEXT attribute for the text INPUT element. That is because the default type for an INPUT element is TEXT.

Microsoft Internet Explorer supports Windows-like attributes

If you are building your Web solution for Microsoft Internet Explorer-compatible browsers, you can give your users a more Windows-like user experience by taking advantage of the optional attributes of the INPUT control supported by Microsoft Internet Explorer browsers.

4. Enter the document **Name** (for this example use TEXTBOX).

5. Press **Open** to load the document into the Visual InterDev 6 editor.

Now you must drop a textbox control from the toolbox onto your Web document.

Adding a textbox control to your HTML document

1. Set the Visual InterDev 6 Editor in Source mode by selecting the **Source** tab at the bottom of the edit window.

2. Next, click the **HTML** tab of the toolbox window and locate the **Textbox** control in the list.

3. Drag the control from the toolbox on the loaded document in the editor and drop it within the <BODY> section of the document by releasing the mouse button.

Notice that the Visual InterDev Editor creates a very simple textbox definition. It contains only the <INPUT> tag and the ID and NAME attributes. You must add any other attributes manually or in script code when the document is loaded.

For this example, set the NAME and ID attributes to txtInput. Also, add a SIZE attribute of 30 and a MAXLENGTH attribute of 20. When you're finished, the HTML coding should look like the code in Listing 6.2.

LISTING 6.2 **Defining the *txtInput* Text Box**

```
1  <INPUT
2      ID=txtInput
3      NAME=txtInput
4      SIZE=30
5      MAXLENGTH=20
6  >
```

Use SIZE and MAXLENGTH attributes for input controls

It is a good idea to use the SIZE and MAXLENGTH attributes for your input controls. These help add a bit of client-side input validation to your forms and give users a better idea of how the input elements are to be used.

Now you can test the textbox input control by selecting the **Quick View** tab in the editor. This will display the HTML document as it would appear to the client browser. Enter text in this control and notice that event; although it shows you a space 30 characters wide (based on the SIZE attribute), you can enter only 20 characters (based on the MAXLENGTH attribute).

Now switch back to the **Source** tab and add a small bit of client-side script to the page. First, make sure the document has the `DefaultClientScript` property set to `VBScript`. To do this, select **DOCUMENT** from the property window pull-down list. Then set the `DefaultClientScript` property to `VBScript` (see Figure 6.1).

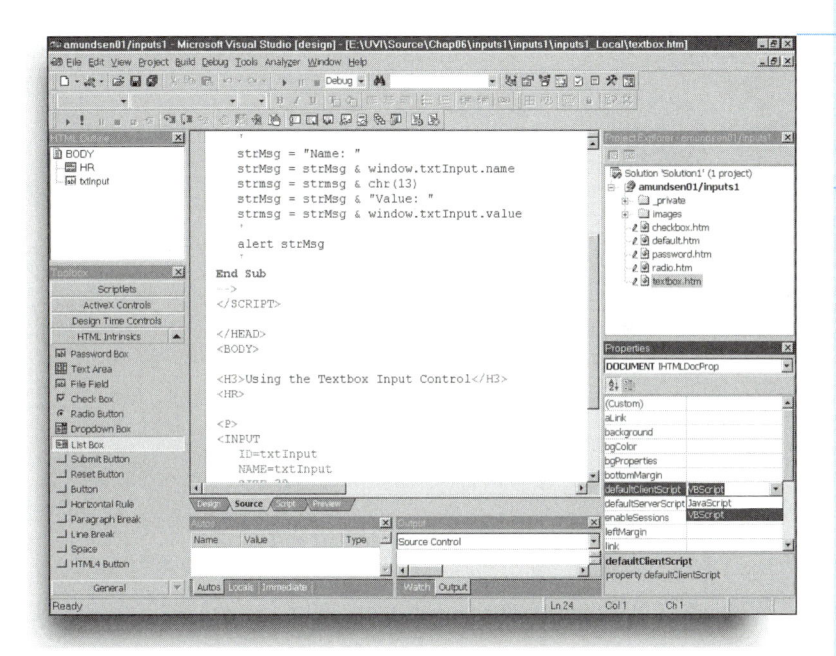

FIGURE 6.1
Setting the `DefaultClientScript` property.

Now you must add a client script event code block to your document using the Visual InterDev Script Outline window (see Figure 6.2).

Adding some client-side Visual Basic Script to the HTML document

1. With the editor still in Source mode, select the **Client Objects and Events** item from the script outline tree.

2. Click the document node to expose the list of events for the document object.

3. Double-click the `onclick` event to add the client-script code block to your document.

Now you're ready to add some code to the script block. In this example, you write some Visual Basic script that will display the

---

Microsoft Internet Explorer is required to run client-side Visual Basic Script

The examples in this book use Visual Basic Script as the client-side scripting language. You'll need to use Microsoft Internet Explorer as the client browser in order to execute client-side Visual Basic Script.

PART II Web Page Design Techniques
CHAPTER 6 **Building Basic Web Forms with Intrinsic HTML Controls**

name of the input control and the value entered by the user. Listing 6.3 contains the Visual Basic Script you must enter in the `document_onclick` event.

FIGURE 6.2

Adding a code block using the Script Outline window.

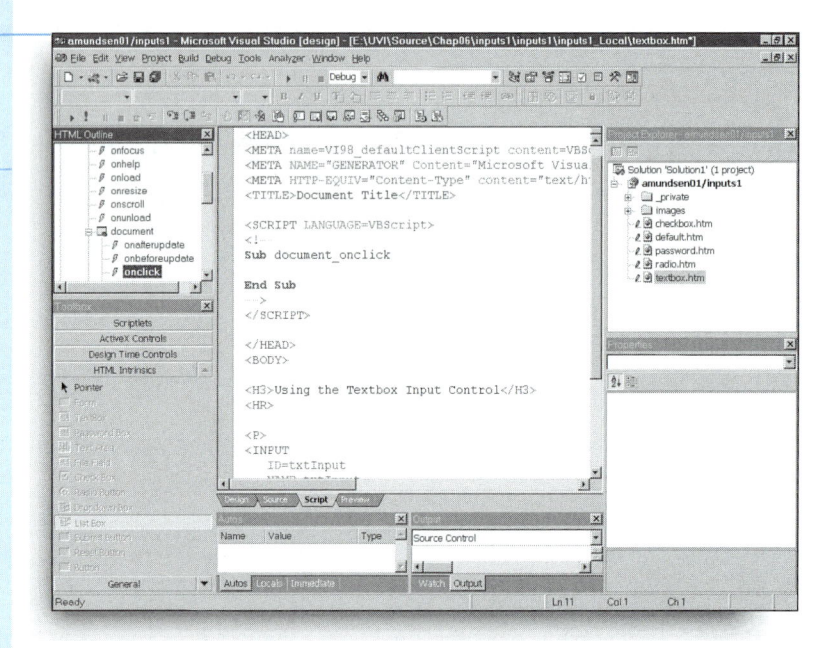

LISTING 6.3

① This line displays the NAME attribute of the HTML INPUT control you set when you built the Web document.

② This line displays the VALUE attribute of the HTML INPUT control that was set when the user typed in the text.

LISTING 6.3 **Coding the *document_onclick* Event for the Text Box**

```
1  <SCRIPT LANGUAGE=VBScript>
2  <!--
3  Sub document_onclick
4      Dim strMsg
5      '
6      strMsg = "Name: "
7      strMsg = strMsg & window.txtInput.name
8      strmsg = strmsg & chr(13)
9      strMsg = strMsg & "Value: "
10     strmsg = strMsg & window.txtInput.value
11     '
12     alert strMsg
13     '
14 End Sub
15 -->
16 </SCRIPT>
```

Using the Password Input Control

In Listing 6.3, the local variable `strMsg` is filled with the `NAME` attribute in line 7 and the current value of the text box in line 10. This string is then displayed in an alert box (line 12).

You can test this code by switching to the **Quick View** tab of the editor, typing some text, and clicking your mouse anywhere on the document space.

You can access many other attributes of the textbox `INPUT` control using this same technique. For now, it is important to remember that the `VALUE` and `NAME` properties are the ones most commonly used.

SEE ALSO
➤ *For more on Visual Basic Scripting, see page 247*
➤ *For information on the Microsoft Internet Explorer Scripting model, see page 337*

Using the Password Input Control

Another often-used input control is the password type. This control works just like the textbox control. The only difference is that when users type data into the control, only asterisks (*) are echoed back on the screen. This way people who are looking over the user's shoulder can't see the actual letters typed in a password input box.

The HTML format for the password type input control is almost identical to the format for the textbox type input control. Listing 6.4 shows how the password type input control HTML coding looks.

> **The VALUE attribute of the password control is not encrypted**
>
> Even though the password HTML control hides user input in the browser window, the actual contents typed into the control are not encrypted in any way. Sending the `VALUE` attribute of a password control to another page results in sending a plain text version of the password.

LISTING 6.4 HTML Coding Format for the Password Input Control

```
1  <INPUT
2     TYPE=password
3     ID=txtPassword
4     NAME=txtPassword
5     SIZE=10
6     MAXLENGTH=10
7  >
```

LISTING 6.4

❶ Adding this line to the default input control turns it into a password control.

The important difference appears in line 2. The TYPE attribute identifies this not as the standard textbox input control, but as a password type input control.

For this example, create a new document for your Web project called PASSWORD.HTM. Load this document into the Visual InterDev Editor and drag a password control from the HTML section of the toolbox window on the HTML document. Set its attributes to match those in Listing 6.4.

Set the `DefaultClientScript` property of the document to `VBScript` using the property window. Now use the script outline window to create the `document_onclick` Visual Basic script block and enter the Visual Basic script to display the value of the `txtPassword:` control. Listing 6.5 shows how this should look in your document.

LISTING 6.5 Displaying the *VALUE* Attribute of the *txtPassword* Control

```
1 <SCRIPT LANGUAGE=VBScript>
2 <!--
3 Sub document_onclick
4    alert "Your password is: " & window.txtPassword.value
5 End Sub
6 -->
7 </SCRIPT>
```

Save the document and then switch to the **Quick View** tab in the editor to display the results. When you view the document in the **Quick View** tab, you can enter data into the input field but can see only a line of ****** echoed to the browser. When you click on the document, an alert box appears announcing (to everyone looking over your shoulder) the password you just entered (see Figure 6.3).

SEE ALSO
➤ *For more on passwords and user security, see page* 707

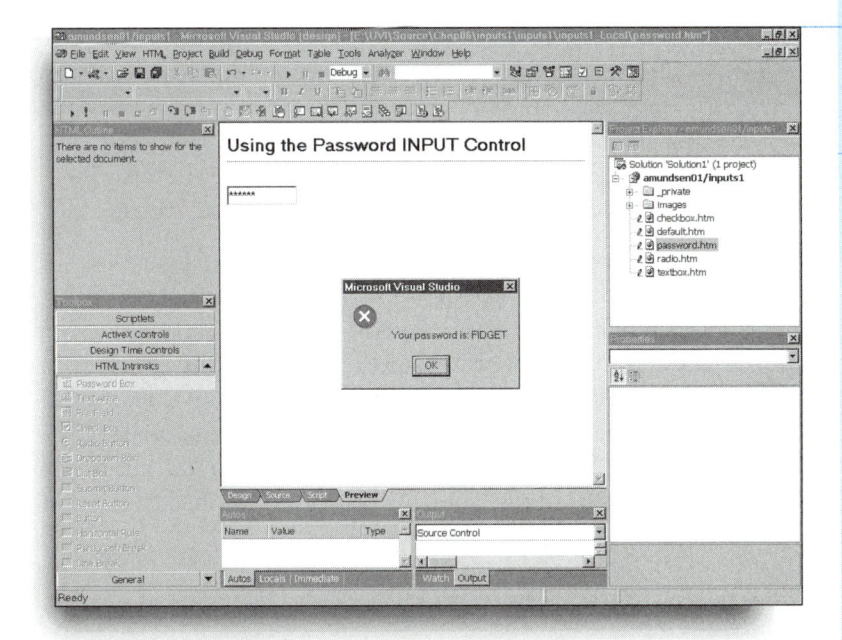

FIGURE 6.3
Displaying the VALUE attribute of the password control.

Using the Checkbox Input Control

The checkbox type input control is a bit different than the input controls you've used so far in this chapter. The checkbox control does not enable users to enter any character data. However, they can click on a small box to make the check mark appear or disappear. The checkbox is the best input control for collecting yes/no or true/false answers from users.

The HTML coding format of the checkbox type input control is shown in Listing 6.6.

LISTING 6.6   The HTML Coding Format for the Checkbox Input Control

```
1  <INPUT
2      TYPE=checkbox
3      ID=chkPlanes
4      NAME=chkPlanes
5      CHECKED
6  >
```

LISTING 6.6

❶ Adding the CHECKED attribute means that the moment the document is loaded in the browser, this option will be selected.

It looks much like the password and textbox type input controls. Note the use of the TYPE keyword to identify this as a check box. Also notice that a new optional attribute appears in line 5. If the CHECKED attribute is present in the definition, the check box will be already checked when the document is loaded. In this way, you can set default values for check boxes on your Web forms.

For this example, add a new HTML document to your Web project called CHECKBOX.HTM and load it into the Visual InterDev Editor. Next, set its DefaultClientScripting property to VBScript. Now enter three lines of text on the document: Planes, Trains, and Automobiles. Be sure each word is on a different line in the document. Now drag three checkbox controls from the HTML tab of the toolbox window onto the document, each next to one of the words. When you're finished, your document should look like the one in Figure 6.4.

FIGURE 6.4

Laying out the CHECKBOX.HTM document.

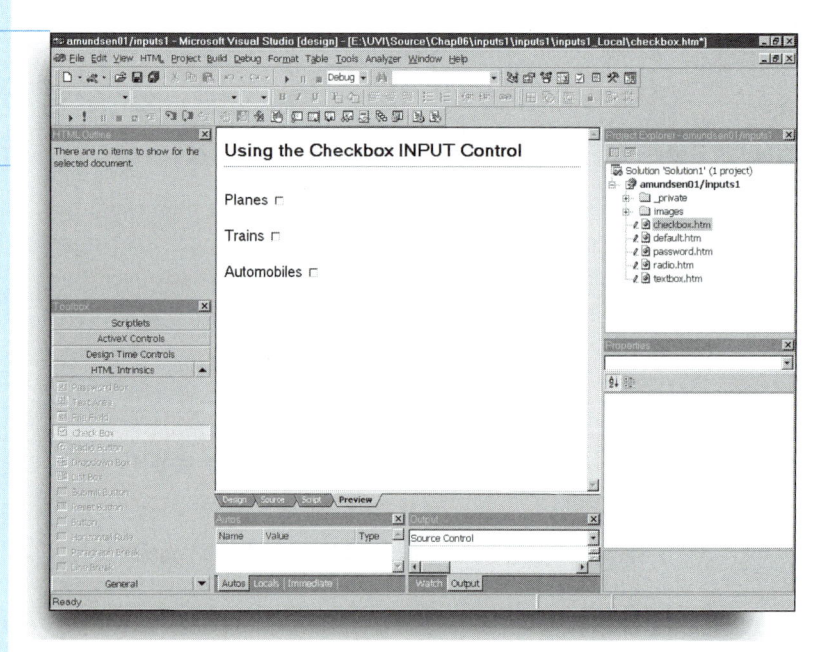

Set the NAME and ID attributes of each of the controls to chkPlanes, chkTrains, and chkAutos, respectively. Also, add the CHECKED attribute to the first checkbox control in the document. Your completed HTML code should look like the code in Listing 6.7.

Using the Checkbox Input Control

LISTING 6.7 Viewing the Completed HTML Code for the CHECKBOX.HTM Document

```
1  <P>
2  Planes
3  <INPUT
4      TYPE=checkbox
5      ID=chkPlanes
6      NAME=chkPlanes
7      CHECKED
8  >
9  </P>
10
11 <P>
12 Trains
13 <INPUT
14     TYPE=checkbox
15     ID=chkTrains
16     NAME=chkTrains
17 >
18 </P>
19
20 <P>
21 Automobiles
22 <INPUT
23     TYPE=checkbox
24     ID=chkAutos
25     NAME=chkAutos
26 >
27 </P>
```

Now you're ready to add some Visual Basic script that will display the list of items the user checked. This code will review the CHECKED property of each of the three controls and present this in an alert message box.

First, create the document_onclick event code block using the Script Outline window. Next, enter the code in Listing 6.8 for the document_onclick event.

The order of attributes in an element doesn't matter

The exact order of the attributes in the <INPUT> elements does not matter. Attributes can all be placed on a single line or spread over several lines in the document. Most of the examples in this book have been reformatted to make them easier to read.

LISTING 6.8

You determine whether the check box was selected by inspecting the checked property with Visual Basic Script.

LISTING 6.8 Coding the *document_onclick* Event for the CHECKBOX.HTM Document

```
1  <SCRIPT LANGUAGE=VBScript>
2  <!--
3  Sub document_onclick
4     dim strMsg
5     '
6     If chkPlanes.checked=True then
7        strMsg = "Planes" & chr(13)
8     End If
9     '
10    If chkTrains.checked=True then
11       strMsg = strMsg & "Trains" & chr(13)
12    End If
13    '
14    If chkAutos.checked=True then
15       strMsg = strMsg & "Autos" & chr(13)
16    End If
17    '
18    alert strMsg
19    '
20 End Sub
21 -->
22 </SCRIPT>
```

Notice that the code in Listing 6.8 inspects the checked property of each of the three controls (lines 6, 10, and 14). If the CHECKED property returns True, the strMsg variable is updated with some text. Finally, this string is displayed using the alert method in line 18.

Save this document and run it in Preview mode. You should see that the first check box appears already checked when the document is loaded (see Figure 6.5).

Also notice that you could check as many of the boxes as you like. More than one check box can be checked on. This is important to remember when you create your document with the radio type input control in the next section.

SEE ALSO

▶ *To learn more about using HTML controls, see page 153*

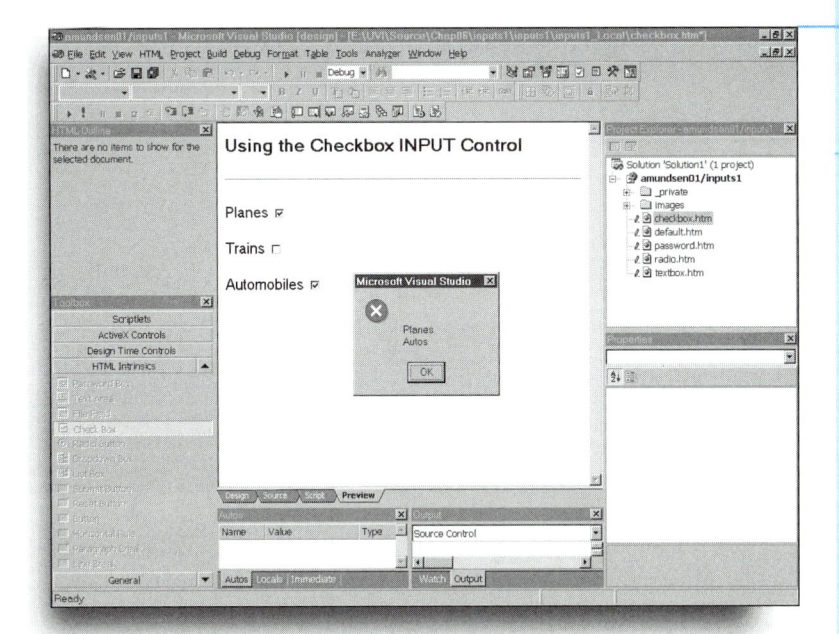

FIGURE 6.5
Previewing the CHECKBOX.HTM document.

Using the Radio Input Control

The final input control covered in this chapter is the radio type input control, which looks similar to the checkbox type input control. However, its attributes and runtime behavior are very different.

The difference between check box and radio controls is that radio controls are defined in groups instead of individually. By defining them in a group, you describe a set of mutually exclusive options for the user. Although users can select as many of the check box options at one time as they want, they can select only one of the radio options at any one time.

This mutually exclusive nature of the radio type input controls means you must also treat the controls differently when you are writing script against them. You must address the radio controls as a group in order to discover which of them has been selected by the user. You'll see how to do this later in this section.

The basic HTML coding format of the radio input control is shown in Listing 6.9.

PART II Web Page Design Techniques
CHAPTER 6 Building Basic Web Forms with Intrinsic HTML Controls

LISTING 6.9

① Radio type input controls have a VALUE attribute. Check box type input controls do not.

② Notice that the NAME and ID attributes of these two radio buttons are the same. This makes them part of a group.

LISTING 6.9 HTML Coding Format for the Radio Type Input Control

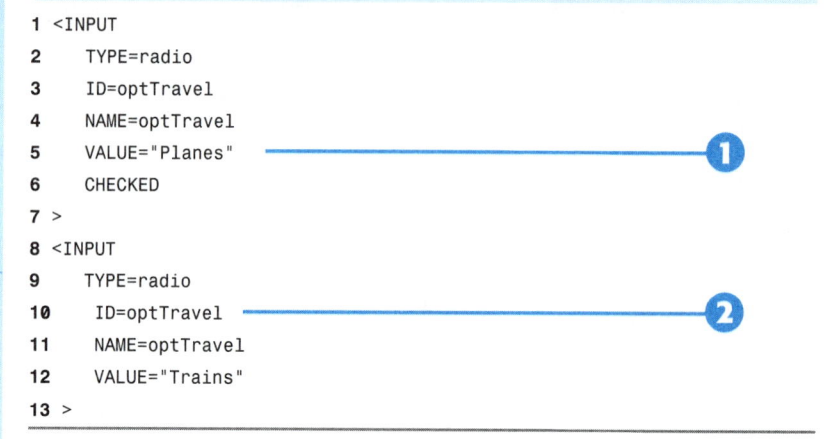

```
 1 <INPUT
 2     TYPE=radio
 3     ID=optTravel
 4     NAME=optTravel
 5     VALUE="Planes"
 6     CHECKED
 7 >
 8 <INPUT
 9     TYPE=radio
10     ID=optTravel
11     NAME=optTravel
12     VALUE="Trains"
13 >
```

Because radio type input controls are worthless unless there are at least two from which the user can choose, Listing 6.9 shows two radio type input control definitions. The first thing you should notice is that the ID and NAME attributes of both controls are the same. This is a requirement.

Radio buttons return On if their VALUE attribute is not set

If you forget to establish unique VALUE attributes for each radio button in a group, the only return value you'll get is On. No matter which button is selected, the return value will always be On.

Always set one of the radio controls to CHECKED

You should always set one of the radio controls as the default by adding the CHECKED property. This will reduce errors when users click the Submit button before they select a radio button.

Listing 6.9 shows that radio type input controls require a VALUE attribute. The VALUE attribute is returned when you use the **Submit** button on a form. If you fail to include this attribute, your forms will not work correctly.

Note also that you can add the CHECKED attribute to one (and only one) of the radio input controls in a group. This makes the selected radio button show its on state when the form is loaded.

For this example, create one more HTML document called RADIO.HTM and add it to your Web project. After loading the new document into the Visual InterDev Editor, set its DefaultClientScripting property to VBScript.

Next, enter three lines of text into the document: Planes, Trains, and Automobiles, each on a separate line. Then drag three radio type input controls from the **HTML** tab of the toolbox window onto each line of the HTML document. When you're finished, it should look like Figure 6.6.

Using the Radio Input Control CHAPTER 6

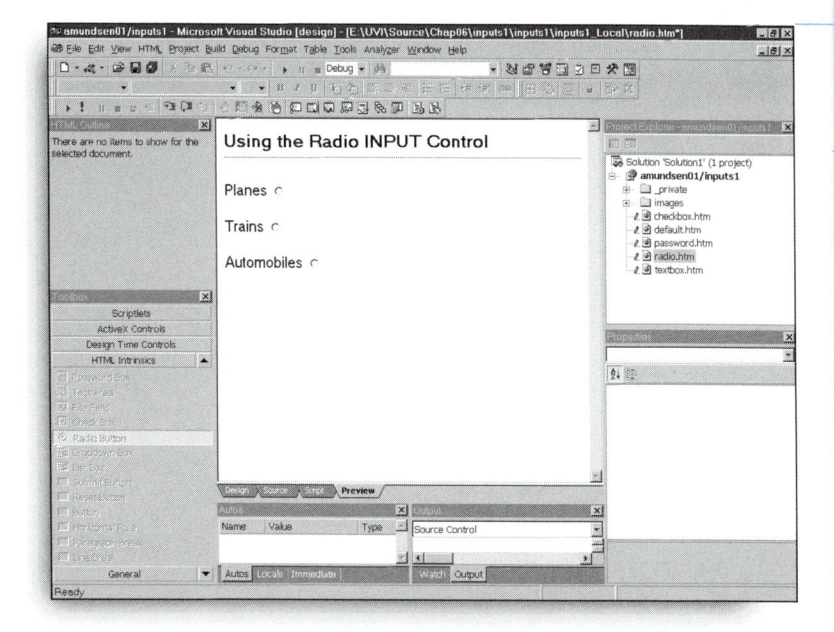

FIGURE 6.6
Building the RADIO.HTM document.

After adding all three radio type input controls to the form, switch to the **Source** tab, and set the ID and NAME attributes of all three radio controls to optTravel. By setting the NAME and ID attributes the same, you create a radio "group" that allows only one of the buttons to be selected at one time.

However, you must set the VALUE attributes of each control differently. The VALUE attribute is sent when a Web form is submitted to the server. You can also check the VALUE attribute using scripting code. For this example, set the VALUE attributes of the three controls to Planes, Trains, and Automobiles, respectively.

Finally, add the CHECKED attribute to the first of the three radio buttons. When you are finished, your HTML code should look like the code in Listing 6.10.

LISTING 6.10

① This is the defualt choice in this example.

LISTING 6.10 Completed HTML Coding for the RADIO.HTM Document

```
1  <P>
2  Planes
3  <INPUT
4      TYPE=radio
5      ID=optTravel
6      NAME=optTravel
7      VALUE="Planes"
8      CHECKED                                                    ──①
9  >
10 </P>
11
12 <P>
13 Trains
14 <INPUT
15     TYPE=radio
16     ID=optTravel
17     NAME=optTravel
18     VALUE="Trains"
19 >
20 </P>
21
22 <P>
23 Automobiles
24 <INPUT
25     TYPE=radio
26     ID=optTravel
27     NAME=optTravel
28     VALUE="Autos"
29 >
30 </P>
```

Now you're ready to add some client-side script to the document that will report the radio type input control that was selected by the user. To do this, use the Script Outline window to expose the document object's `onclick` event. Double-click on this event to add the client-side script block to your project.

Writing the Visual Basic script to discover the selected radio type input control is done quite differently from previous examples in this chapter. Because there are three controls in the document that all have the same NAME and ID attributes, you can't use

Using the Radio Input Control

the following code to display the value of the selected radio type input control:

```
alert window.optTravel.value
```

Instead, you must tell the browser which button in the collection you want to display, as in the following:

```
alert window.optTravel(0).value
```

This line displays the value of the first radio type input control in the collection. Note that the collection numbering starts with 0 instead of 1.

Of course, the trouble with all this is that you do not know ahead of time which radio type input control in the list has been checked. You can do this with the following code:

```
if window.optTravel(0).checked = true then
    alert window.optTravel(0).value
end if
```

This code will work for the first item in the collection, but what if that is not the item that was selected? In fact, in order to discover which input control in a collection was checked, you must inspect the CHECKED property of all the radio type input controls in the collection. This can be done in a For...Next loop.

Listing 6.11 shows the complete Visual Basic Script code that you can add to the document_onclick event to inspect all the radio type input controls and display the VALUE attribute of the one control that was selected by the user.

LISTING 6.11 **Visual Basic Script Code to Display the *VALUE* of the Selected Radio Type Input Control**

```
1  <SCRIPT LANGUAGE=VBScript>
2  <!--
3  Sub document_onclick
4  '
5      for i = 0 to window.optTravel.length-1
6          if window.optTravel(i).checked = true then
7              alert window.optTravel(i).value
8          end if
9      next
```

LISTING 6.11

❶ Use the length property to determine the total number of radio controls in the group.

❷ Even if you have used the VALUE attribute of the radio input control, you can still use the checked property in Visual Basic Scripting.

continues...

PART II   Web Page Design Techniques

CHAPTER 6   **Building Basic Web Forms with Intrinsic HTML Controls**

LISTING 6.11   **Continued**

```
10      '
11 End Sub
12 -->
13 </SCRIPT>
```

Although you've seen most of the code in Listing 6.11 already, an interesting bit of Visual Basic script has not been covered. Line 5 of Listing 6.11 uses the length property of the optTravel collection to return the total number of radio type input controls in the collection. Also, because the collection numbering starts at 0, the length property must be adjusted by -1.

Save this document to your Web project and display it in the **Quick View** tab of the Visual InterDev Editor. You'll be able to select one (and only one) of the three option buttons. Clicking anywhere on the document will cause the alert dialog to appear showing the VALUE attribute of the one radio type input control selected by the user (see Figure 6.7).

FIGURE 6.7

Previewing the RADIO.HTM document.

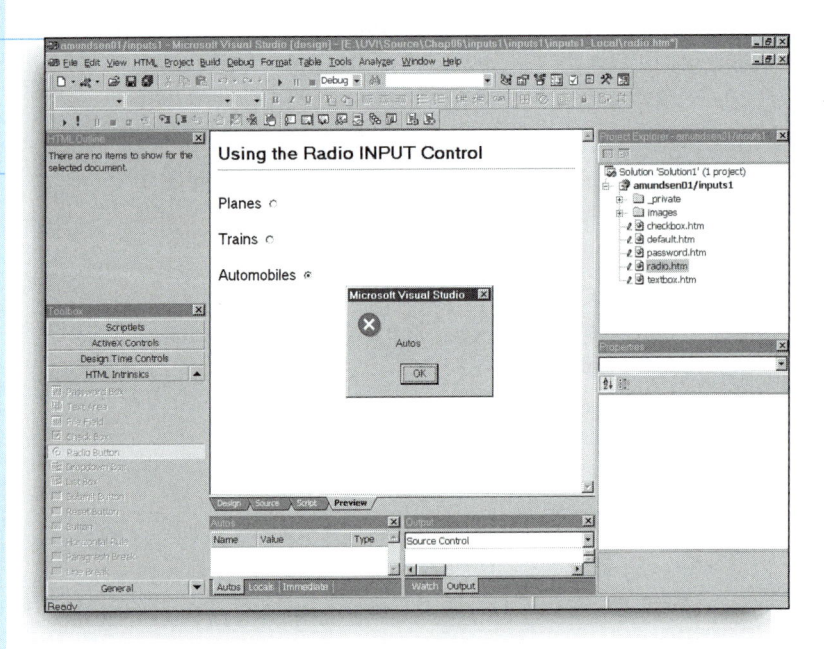

SEE ALSO

▶ *For more on accessing controls and control groups with Visual Basic Scripting, see page 335*

CHAPTER 7

Building Advanced Web Forms with Intrinsic HTML Controls

Learn how to use HTML SELECT to build Dropdown and Listbox input controls

Collect filenames from local machines with the HTML FILE type input control

Use the TEXTAREA control to get multiple-line input from clients

Use the HTML IMAGE type input control to submit form data to servers

The Other Input Controls

The HTML input controls covered in this chapter go beyond the basic input controls covered in the previous chapter. These controls either use the standard INPUT tag in a different way or use a totally different HTML tag to collect user input. Five HTML input controls are covered here:

- Drop-down controls
- List box controls
- Multiple-line text boxes
- Filename input box
- Graphical submit buttons

Drop-downs and list boxes are two variations on the use of the SELECT and OPTION HTML tags. You'll learn how to construct these input controls, fill them with data, and retrieve the selected items from the client browser for packaging and delivery to the Web server.

The multiple-line text box enables users to enter extended comments into client browser forms, and the filename input box enables them to browse their own workstation's file structure and select a filename for delivery to the Web server.

Technically, a graphical submit button is not an input control, but it uses the HTML INPUT tag, so it is included here. You can use this format of the INPUT tag to provide a more interesting submit button for your HTML forms.

SEE ALSO
➤ *For more on basic HTML input controls, see page 133*

Creating the INPUTS2 Web Project

Throughout this chapter, you'll build Web pages that host each of the controls. You'll also add some Visual Basic Script to inspect control properties and display them to the client. Each of the pages can be part of a Visual InterDev Web project. Before you begin reviewing the examples here, you can create the host Web project to hold all the documents.

Using HTML *SELECT* to Create Dropdown and Listbox Elements

PART II
CHAPTER 7
155

To do this, you must first start Visual InterDev and then create a new Web project. Select **File**, then **New Project** from the main menu and, after navigating to the proper folder that will house the source code for the Web project, enter `inputs2` as the name and click **Open**. Accept the default Web server name or, if none appears, enter a valid name and click **Next**. Now you can click **Finish** to skip the Theme and Layout dialog boxes. Visual InterDev will now churn away building your Web project and finally display the Visual InterDev IDE ready for work.

SEE ALSO
➤ *For details on how to create new Visual InterDev 6 Web projects, see page 7*

> **Combining host Web projects for examples**
>
> Throughout this book you will be building host Web projects to test various documents and techniques. If you want to, you can create a single Visual InterDev 6 project to hold all the examples. This will reduce the number of Webs you generate on the Web server.

Using HTML *SELECT* to Create Dropdown and Listbox Elements

Two of the more common advanced HTML controls are the Dropdown and Listbox input controls. These controls enable users to select one or more items from a list of items in the browser form. If you are used to programming for Windows applications, the HTML Dropdown control works like the combo box, and the HTML Listbox control works like the Listbox control you see on Windows forms.

Actually, the Dropdown and Listbox controls are just variations of the HTML SELECT control. The SELECT control is designed to give users a list of options and return the selected item (or items). The only difference between the two is that the Listbox version shows more than one row of data in the client browser. When one row is presented, a button appears letting users know that they can press the button to get the complete list. When multiple rows are presented, no button appears, but a scrollbar will appear if the list goes beyond the allotted space on the browser page.

> **Is it a control or an element?**
>
> HTML programmers refer to each item on a document as an element (as in the RADIO element). Windows programmers typically refer to items on a form as controls (as in the BUTTON control). You'll see both terms used interchangeably in this book.

With both the Listbox and Dropdown versions, the set of selectable options are created using the HTML OPTION tag. This tag is actually nested inside the `<SELECT>...</SELECT>` tag pair.

In the next two sections, you'll learn how to define and use the two versions of the HTML SELECT control.

Creating Drop-Down Boxes with HTML *SELECT*

Creating drop-down boxes with HTML SELECT is very simple. The basic format for the Dropdown version of the HTML SELECT control is shown in Listing 7.1.

LISTING 7.1 Basic HTML Coding of the Drop-Down HTML *SELECT* Control

```
1  <SELECT
2      NAME=ddlTest
3      ID=ddlTest>
4      <OPTION value=ItemA>Item A
5      <OPTION value=ItemB SELECTED>Item B
6      <OPTION value=ItemC>Item C
7      <OPTION value=ItemD>Item D
8  </SELECT>
```

Notice that the only meaningful attributes of the drop-down version of the SELECT control itself are the ID and NAME attributes. However, the OPTION tags nested inside the SELECT control are the ones that determine the list of values available to the client browser.

The VALUE attribute defines the value that will be returned to the Web server or displayed in a client scripting routine. The text outside the OPTION tag is the text that will be displayed in the list box. Note that you can use the SELECTED attribute of the OPTION tag to create a default selection item for the Dropdown control.

Using the drop-down version of the SELECT control is very easy. First, add a new page to your Web project called DROPDOWN.HTM. To do this, just right-click over the project name, select **Add**, then **HTML Page** from the menus, enter dropdown as the name, and press **Open** to create the new page and load it into your browser.

Now select the **HTML** tab in the toolbox window and locate the **Listbox** item in the toolbox. With the editor in Design mode, drag this HTML control onto the new page and drop it at the top of the page. You'll notice that it appears on the page as a small, empty control. Now you're ready to add items to the Dropdown control.

Always supply a default select value

You can avoid some data entry errors on your Web forms if you always mark one of the OPTION items in the SELECT list as SELECTED. This will mark it as the default value even if the users do not actually select an item from the list.

Using HTML *SELECT* to Create Dropdown and Listbox Elements

Adding items to an HTML *SELECT* Dropdown control

1. Highlight the Dropdown control (a gray border will appear).
2. While your mouse is over the gray border, right-click the mouse and select **Properties** from the context menu.
3. When the Property Page appears, enter a name for the control (for this example, enter ddlTest, as in Figure 7.1).

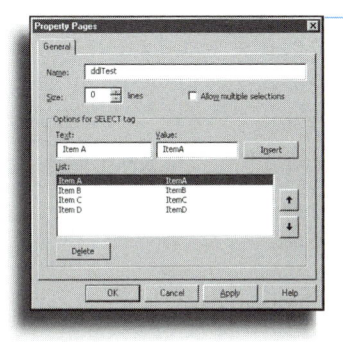

FIGURE 7.1
Using the Dropdown control properties dialog box.

4. Enter the options you want to display in the dialog box by pressing the **Insert** button and entering data in the **Text** and **Value** fields of the dialog. Remember that the **Value** field will be returned in script and form submit routines. For this example, enter Item A for the TEXT and ItemA for the VALUE attributes.
5. Continue to add items to the option list until you have added all the entries you need. For this example add four items (Item A through Item D).
6. If you want, you can remove an item from the list by pressing the **Delete** button at the lower-left of the dialog.
7. You can rearrange the order of items in the list by pressing the up and down arrows next to the options list.
8. After you are satisfied with the contents and order of the option list, press **OK** to save the definition and exit the dialog.

Now you're ready to add an HTML BUTTON control to the page. You'll use this button to accept a click event from the user and run some Visual Basic Script to display some of the runtime properties of the Dropdown control.

Is it a property or an attribute?

If you have experience with Windows programming, you are probably familiar with the word *property* to describe unique settings for user controls. If you do a lot of HTML programming you use the word *attribute* to describe the settings of HTML controls. These are both different names for the same thing. You can see both words used interchangeably in this book.

Just drag a BUTTON control from the **HTML** tab of the toolbox window onto the HTML document and drop it underneath the Dropdown control. With the BUTTON control still in focus (surrounded by a thick gray border), use the properties window to set the **NAME** and **ID** properties to btnShow and set the **Value** property to Show.

When you complete the process of adding the HTML Dropdown and BUTTON controls, you can press the **Source** tab on the Visual InterDev Editor to view the results. Your HTML code should look something like the code in Listing 7.2.

A note about HTML formatting

You might find that the actual formatting of the HTML code in your documents is not the same as the examples shown in this book. The examples here have been altered to make it easier to see the various HTML elements and attributes and their settings. The exact format of the HTML does not affect the way it will run. However, reformatting the HTML code makes it much easier to read.

LISTING 7.2   **The HTML Source Code for the Dropdown Control**

```
1   <P>
2   <SELECT
3      NAME=ddlTest
4      ID=ddlTest>
5      <OPTION value=ItemA>Item A
6      <OPTION VALUE=ItemB SELECTED>Item B
7      <OPTION value=ItemC>Item C
8      <OPTION value=ItemD>Item D
9   </SELECT>
10  </P>
11
12  <P>
13  <INPUT
14     TYPE=button
15     ID=btnShow
16     NAME=btnShow
17     VALUE=Show
18  >
19  </P>
```

Now, with the **Source** tab active, let's add some Visual Basic Script to react when users press the **Show** button. First, select **DOCUMENT** from the property window and make sure the DefaultClientScript property is set to VBScript. Next, use the Script Outline window to locate the btnShow object and double-click the onclick event to add it to your HTML document.

Using HTML *SELECT* to Create Dropdown and Listbox Elements

Now you're ready to add Visual Basic Script that will display the NAME attribute of the control and the VALUE attribute. When a user selects an item from the list, the VALUE attribute will be set to match the VALUE attribute of the OPTION tag selected by the user. Listing 7.3 shows the Visual Basic Script that will do what you need.

LISTING 7.3 Adding Client-Side Script to Show the Selected Value of the Dropdown Control

```
1  <SCRIPT LANGUAGE=VBScript>
2  <!--
3  Sub btnShow_onclick
4     Dim strMsg
5     '
6     strMsg = strMsg & "NAME: " & chr(9)
7     strMsg = strMsg & window.ddlTest.name & chr(13)
8     strMsg = strMsg & "VALUE: " & chr(9)
9     strMsg = strMsg & window.ddlTest.value  & chr(13)
10    '
11    alert strMsg
12    '
13 End Sub
14 -->
15 </SCRIPT>
```

After you add the Visual Basic Script, save the document and test it by running it in the **Quick View** mode of the editor by selecting the **Quickview** pane of the editor. You can now pull down the list box, select an item, and press the **Show** button. When you do, you'll see a message dialog box appear telling you the control's name and value settings (see Figure 7.2).

SEE ALSO
▶ *For more on using Visual Basic Scripting, see page 247*

Creating Listbox Controls with HTML *SELECT*

Creating the HTML Listbox control is almost identical to creating the Dropdown control. The only difference between the two is the addition of the SIZE attribute to the HTML SELECT tag.

PART II   Web Page Design Techniques

CHAPTER 7   **Building Advanced Web Forms with Intrinsic HTML Controls**

This controls how many rows of the list are shown. However, with the list box you also have the option of allowing users to select more than one item from the list. You can do this by adding the MULTIPLE attribute to the SELECT definition.

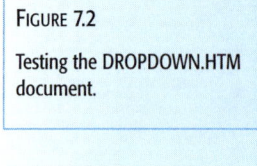

FIGURE 7.2

Testing the DROPDOWN.HTM document.

Using the Dropdown control in an HTML form

If you use the Dropdown control in an HTML <FORM>...</FORM> tag set, the browser will send the ID property of the Dropdown control along with the value selected by the user. You can use server-side script to recall this value by asking for the Dropdown control's ID.

Using the MULTIPLE attribute with HTML SELECT

Actually, you can use the MULTIPLE attribute with both the Dropdown and Listbox versions of the HTML SELECT control. However, multiple-selection behavior in a Listbox is rather confusing to view and use. For this reason, it is recommended that you use the MULTIPLE attribute only with the Listbox version of the HTML SELECT control.

For this example, add a new HTML document to the Web project called LIST.HTM and set its DefaultClientScript property to VBScript. After loading it into the Visual InterDev editor, drag a Listbox control from the HTML tab of the toolbox window and drop it on the page.

With the control still in focus (a thick gray border surrounds the control), right-click over the control and select **Properties** to bring up the Listbox property page. Set the control's NAME property to lstTest and add four items to the option list (Item A through Item D). Finally, set the **Size** value to **5** and check the **Allow Multiple Selections** option on the dialog. When you're finished, click **OK** on the dialog to save the definition (see Figure 7.3).

Next, drag a button control from the **HTML** tab of the toolbox window onto the page and drop it underneath the Listbox control. Use the properties window to set the NAME and ID attributes to btnShow and the VALUE attribute to Show.

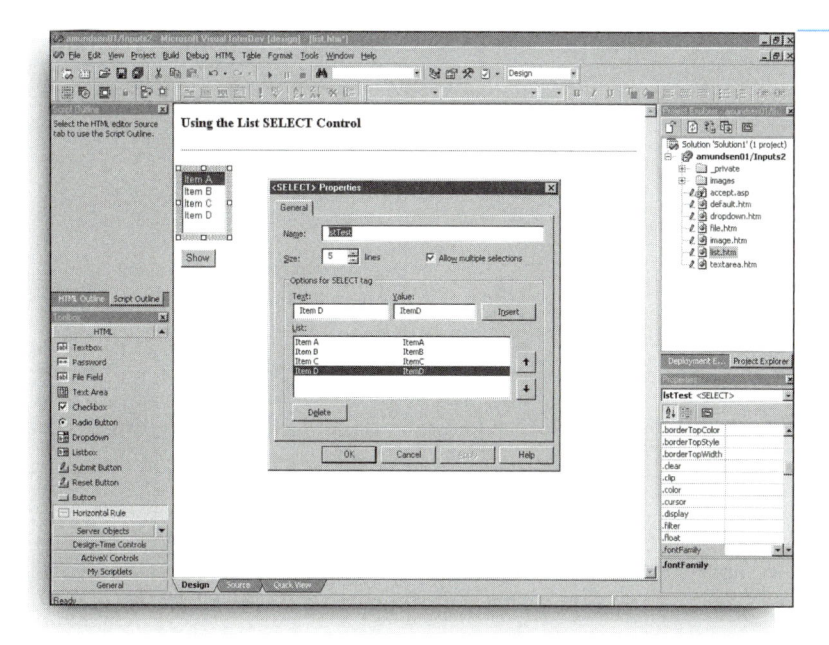

Using HTML *SELECT* to Create Dropdown and Listbox Elements

FIGURE 7.3
The completed Listbox property page.

Next, switch to the **Source** tab and locate the HTML **SELECT** definition for the Listbox control. Be sure to add the SELECTED attribute to ItemB on the option list.

When you're finished, your HTML code should look like the code in Listing 7.4.

LISTING 7.4 **Completed HTML Code for the List Box**

```
1  <P>
2  <SELECT
3     NAME=lstTest
4     ID=lstTest
5     SIZE=5
6     MULTIPLE>
7     <OPTION value=ItemA >Item A
8     <OPTION VALUE=ItemB SELECTED>Item B
9     <OPTION value=ItemC>Item C
10     <OPTION value=ItemD>Item D
11  </SELECT>
12  </P>
```

continues...

LISTING 7.4 Continued

```
13
14  <P>
15  <INPUT
16     TYPE=button
17     ID=btnShow
18     NAME=btnShow
19     VALUE=Show
20  >
21  </P>
```

Now you're ready to add Visual Basic Script code to display the NAME and VALUE attributes of the Listbox control. To do this, be sure the **Source** tab is active and use the script outline window to locate the btnShow object. Double-click the onclick event to add it to your HTML document. Now you can add Visual Basic Script to the event that will run when the user clicks the button.

Using the Listbox control with HTML forms

When you post an HTML form that contains a Listbox control, your server will receive the control's ID along with a comma-delimited list of the selected values (as in Listbox="Mike,Mary, "John"). If only one value is selected, you will see only the ID and the single selection.

Because you have allowed the user to select multiple items in the list, you must write your Visual Basic Script so that it is ready to accept more than one item. To do this, use a FOR...NEXT loop to walk through all the items in the list to see whether they were selected. If the item was selected, it will be added to the final output for the message.

Listing 7.5 shows the Visual Basic Script code that will inspect the list items, determine which ones were selected, and add them to the output for display.

LISTING 7.5 Adding Visual Basic Script to View Selected List Box Items

```
1  <SCRIPT LANGUAGE=VBScript>
2  <!--
3  Sub btnShow_onclick
4      '
5      Dim i
6      Dim strMsg
7      '
```

Using HTML *SELECT* to Create Dropdown and Listbox Elements

```
8     strMsg = strMsg & "NAME: " & chr(9)
9     strMsg = strMsg & window.lstTest.name & chr(13)
10    strMsg = strMsg & "VALUE: "
11    '
12    for i=0 to window.lstTest.length-1
13      if window.lstTest(i).selected=true then
14        strMsg=strMsg & chr(9)
15        strMsg=strMsg & window.lstTest(i).value
16        strMsg=strMsg & chr(13)
17      end if
18    next
19    '
20    alert strMsg
21    '
22 End Sub
23 -->
24 </SCRIPT>
```

Notice that the code in Listing 7.5 uses the `length` property of the Listbox control (line 12) to determine how many items are in the list. Because item numbering begins at `0`, the `length` property is adjusted to make sure the loop does not attempt to read past the end of the list. In line 13, the `selected` property of the list item is inspected. If the user had selected the item, the `selected` property will be set to `TRUE`. Lines 14–16 simply format a part of the text output to contain the `VALUE` attribute of the selected item. Finally, after the list has been fully inspected, the results are displayed to the client browser in a message box (line 20).

Save this page and test it by pressing the **Quick View** tab. You'll see a list box and should be able to select multiple items in the list. When you press the **Show** button, a dialog will appear showing the control's name and the list of selected items (see Figure 7.4).

SEE ALSO
➤ *For more on client-side scripting, see page 335*

How to select multiple items in a list

To select more than one item in the list, hold down the Ctrl key and click each item you want to select. You can also click the first item in the list and, while holding the Shift key, select the last item in the list. This will select all the items in the list.

FIGURE 7.4

Viewing the results of the Listbox control.

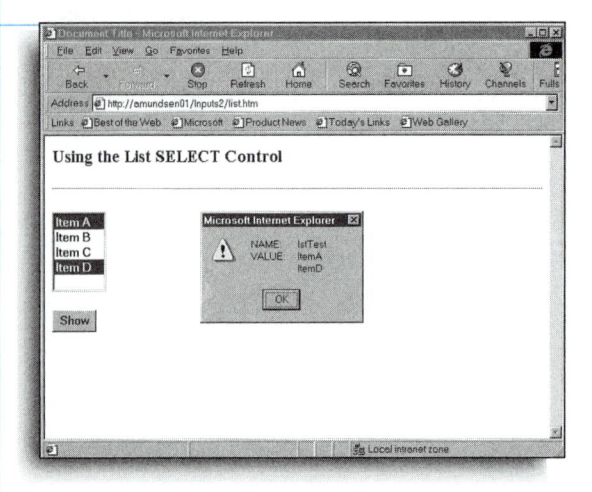

Accepting Multiple Text Lines with the HTML *TEXTAREA* Control

Another input control that is common on Web application forms is the TEXTAREA control. This is the HTML version of a "memo" field. Users can add multiple lines of text, even line breaks and paragraph markers. The basic HTML syntax for the TEXTAREA control is shown in Listing 7.6

LISTING 7.6 HTML Syntax for the *TEXTAREA* Control

```
1  <TEXTAREA
2      ID=txaTest
3      NAME=txaTest
4      WRAP=Virtual
5      ROWS=5
6      COLS=40>
7  This is default text for the TEXTAREA Control.
8  </TEXTAREA>
```

The ID and NAME attributes function as you would expect. The ROWS and COLS attributes can be used to set the height and width of the TEXTAREA control on the document.

Accepting Multiple Text Lines with the HTML *TEXTAREA* Control

The WRAP attribute enables you to control how word wrapping will be handled within the Web page. There are three possible settings for the WRAP attribute:

- OFF—Do not wrap text within the TEXTAREA control on the page.
- SOFT—Perform word wrapping within the document, but return only a single long string of text.
- HARD—Perform word wrapping within the document and return a string that is formatted exactly as it is in the document.

If you do not include the WRAP attribute, SOFT is used as the default behavior.

You can also see from Listing 7.6 that you can supply default text for the control. This is text that will appear inside the TEXTAREA control when the page is first loaded into the browser. The key thing to notice here is that you do not use the VALUE= syntax to set the default text of the TEXTAREA control. You should also note that the default text is outside the closing > of the <TEXTAREA> HTML tag, but before the </TEXTAREA> tag.

For this example, add a new HTML document to your Web project called TEXTAREA.HTM and set its `DefaultClientScript` property to VBScript. Then drag the TEXTAREA control from the **HTML** tab of the toolbox window and drop it on the page. Use the property window to set the NAME and ID properties to txaTest, set the ROWS property to 5, and the COLS property to 40, and set the WRAP property to SOFT.

Next you can add an HTML BUTTON control below the TEXTAREA control and set its NAME and ID properties to btnShow and its VALUE property to Show. After you have added the HTML code, add a single line of text within the <TEXTAREA>...</TEXTAREA> tags. Any text will do. Now, your document should look like Listing 7.7.

SOFT and HARD versus VIRTUAL and PHYSICAL

Some browsers do not recognize the settings **SOFT** and **HARD** for the **WRAP** attribute. Instead, they use the keywords **VIRTUAL** and **PHYSICAL**, respectively. Be sure to test your code with various browsers to make sure it is working as you expect.

LISTING 7.7 Completed HTML Code for the TEXTAREA.HTM Document

```
1  <P>
2  <TEXTAREA
3      ID=txaTest
4      NAME=txaTest
5      WRAP=Soft
6      ROWS=5
7      COLS=40>
8  This is some text for the TEXTAREA Control.
9  </TEXTAREA>
10 </P>
11
12 <P>
13 <INPUT
14     TYPE=button
15     ID=btnShow
16     NAME=btnShow
17     VALUE=Show
18 >
19 </P>
```

Using TEXTAREA with HTML forms

When you use **TEXTAREA** controls with HTML **FORM** tags, the browser will send the contents of the **TEXTAREA** along with the ID attribute. If you use **WRAP=HARD**, the carriage returns and line feeds inserted by the user will also be sent.

Now you're ready to add a tiny bit of Visual Basic Script to display the contents of the TEXTAREA control. Use the script outline window to locate the btnshow object and double-click the onclick event. This will create a client-side script block. Now add the single line of Visual Basic Script in Listing 7.8.

LISTING 7.8 Adding Visual Basic Script to Display the Value of the *TEXTAREA* Control

```
1 <SCRIPT LANGUAGE=VBScript>
2 <!--
3 Sub btnShow_onclick
4     alert window.txaTest.value
5 End Sub
6 -->
7 </SCRIPT>
```

When you've added this line of Visual Basic Script, save the document and click the **Quick View** tab to see the page in action.

Collecting Filenames from the Client

Add some text to the TEXTAREA control. Be sure to include at least one carriage return. When you're finished adding text, press the **Show** button to see the dialog box that displays the VALUE attribute of the control (see Figure 7.5).

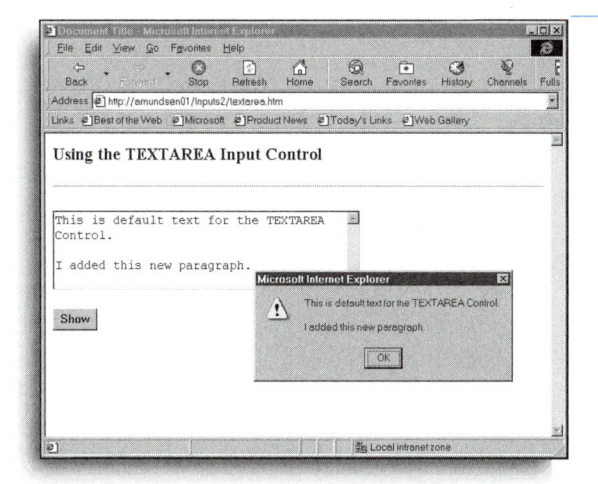

FIGURE 7.5
Viewing the VALUE attribute of the TEXTAREA control.

SEE ALSO
➤ *For more on using the simple text input control, see page 133*

Collecting Filenames from the Client with the HTML *FILE* Type *INPUT* Control

One of the new HTML controls included in Visual InterDev 6 is the FILE type INPUT control. This control presents a single text box and an associated button. Users can press the button and see a file selection dialog that enables them to locate any file or folder available to the local workstation. Upon selection of the file, the VALUE property of the control contains the exact drive, path, and filename of the selected file. This is the HTML equivalent of the Windows Common Dialog control.

The basic HTML syntax for the FILE type INPUT control is shown in Listing 7.9.

LISTING 7.9 Typical HTML Coding for the *FILE* Type *INPUT* Control

```
1  <INPUT
2     TYPE=File
3     ID=filTest
4     NAME=filTest
5     SIZE=20
6  >
```

As you can see, there's not much to the coding of the control. Its primary duty is to display a file selection dialog that enables users to indicate a complete filename and pass it back to the Web server.

File uploading requires a server-side component

Although the `FILE` type `INPUT` control enables users to select a client-side file, you need a special server-side component to actually accept the file and place it on the server. You can find a demonstration copy of a server-side component for uploading files at the *Using Visual InterDev 6* Web site (see Appendix B, "Online Resources").

For this example, add a new HTML document to your Web project called FILE.HTM and set its `DefaultClientScripting` property to `VBScript`. Next, drag the **File Field** control from the **HTML** tab of the toolbox window and drop it on the page. Use the property window to set the `ID` and `NAME` properties to `filTest` and set the `SIZE` property to `20`.

Next, add an HTML button to the page (under the **File Field** control) and set its `NAME` and `ID` properties to `btnShow` and its `VALUE` property to `Show`. Your completed HTML code should look like the code in Listing 7.10.

LISTING 7.10 Completed HTML Code for the FILE.HTM Document

```
1  <P>
2  <INPUT
3     TYPE=File
4     ID=filTest
5     NAME=filTest
6     SIZE=20
7  >
8  </P>
9
10 <P>
11 <INPUT
12    TYPE=button
13    NAME=btnShow
14    ID=btnShow
```

```
15      VALUE=Show
16  >
17  </P>
```

Now you're ready to add the client-side Visual Basic Script code that will display the control name and the file selected by the user. To do this, you must use the Script Outline window to locate the btnShow object and double-click the onclick event. This will add the event code block to your document.

Now you must add Visual Basic Script that will display the NAME and VALUE properties of the FILE type INPUT control. Listing 7.11 shows the Visual Basic Script code that will do just that.

LISTING 7.11 Adding Visual Basic Script to Display the *NAME* and *VALUE* Properties of the *FILE* Type *INPUT* Control

```
1  <SCRIPT LANGUAGE=VBScript>
2  <!--
3  Sub btnShow_onclick
4      Dim strMsg
5      '
6      strMsg = strMsg & "NAME: " & chr(9)
7      strMsg = strMsg & window.filTest.name & chr(13)
8      strMsg = strMsg & "VALUE: " & chr(9)
9      strMsg = strMsg & window.filTest.value & chr(13)
10     '
11     alert strMsg
12     '
13 End Sub
14 -->
15 </SCRIPT>
```

Now save the document and switch to the **Quick View** tab to test the page. Press the **Browse** button to bring up the file locator dialog (see Figure 7.6).

When you select a file and return to the Web page, you can press the **Show** button to see a dialog that displays the control NAME and VALUE properties.

PART II Web Page Design Techniques

CHAPTER 7 Building Advanced Web Forms with Intrinsic HTML Controls

FIGURE 7.6

Testing the `FILE` type `INPUT` control.

Opening files on the client workstation

The `FILE` type `INPUT` control merely passes you back the complete name of a file on the client workstation. If you want to read, display, or copy the contents of the selected file, you must use scripting commands. Visual Basic Script offers a whole series of objects, methods, and properties for dealing with disk files. These are covered in Chapter 25, "Managing Files with ASP."

SEE ALSO

➤ *For more information on accessing disk files, see page 663*

Adding Graphical Buttons Using the HTML *IMAGE* Type *INPUT* Control

The last `INPUT` control covered in this chapter is the `IMAGE` type `INPUT` control. This is not really an `INPUT` control at all, but a replacement for the **Submit** button on a form. If you want to add a bit of creativity to your Web forms, you can replace the standard `<INPUT TYPE=Submit...>` with an `<INPUT TYPE=Image...>` control.

The basic HTML coding of the `IMAGE` type input control is shown in Listing 7.12.

LISTING 7.12 Basic HTML Code of the *IMAGE* Type *INPUT* Control

```
1  <input
2     TYPE=image
3     ID=imgTest
4     NAME=imgTest
```

Adding Graphical Buttons Using the HTML *IMAGE* Type *INPUT* Control

```
5    SRC=images\easel.gif
6    WIDTH=200
7    HEIGHT=172
8    >
```

You can see in Listing 7.12 that the SRC attribute in line 5 contains a reference to a GIF file in the Web project. This will be the actual image displayed on the form.

The last two attributes (WIDTH and HEIGHT) are optional. However, you can use these values to alter the size of the button on the form. In the case shown in Listing 7.12, the image will actually be shown twice its original size. The client browser handles all the details of scaling the graphic image.

Now add one more document to your Web called IMAGE.HTM and set its DefaultClientScript property to VBScript. Now you're ready to add the IMAGE type INPUT control to the page. There's only one problem: There is no IMAGE type INPUT control in the **HTML** tab of the toolbox window. Visual InterDev does not ship with the IMAGE type INPUT control defined in the toolbox. This means you must build your own in code.

To do this, open the **Source** view of the Visual InterDev editor and enter the exact HTML code shown in Listing 7.12 into the <BODY> section of the document. You must get your own image reference. The one used in Listing 7.12 was included with FrontPage 98.

After adding the HTML code, you must add some Visual Basic code that will show the control NAME and SRC property when the user clicks the IMAGE type INPUT control. Locate the imgTest object in the Script Outline window and double-click the onclick event to add the client-side script block to your document.

Now add the code from Listing 7.13 to the script block.

> **Don't confuse the IMG control and the INPUT TYPE=IMAGE control**
>
> It is easy to confuse the HTML image control (**IMG**) with the image input control (**INPUT TYPE=IMAGE**). Although it is possible to add **IMG** controls to a Web form, the **INPUT TYPE=IMAGE** control works more efficiently in an HTML form, and it can be easier to work with when you write your client-side scripts.

LISTING 7.13 Adding Visual Basic Script to the IMAGE.HTM Document

```
1 <script LANGUAGE="VBScript">
2 <!--
3 Sub imgTest_onclick
```

continues...

Building Advanced Web Forms with Intrinsic HTML Controls

LISTING 7.13 Continued

```
4    Dim strMsg
5    '
6    strMsg = "NAME: " & chr(9)
7    strMsg = strMsg & window.imgTest.name
8    strMsg = strMsg & chr(13)
9    strMsg = strMsg & "SRC: " & chr(9)
10   strMsg = strMsg & window.imgTest.src
11   '
12   alert strMsg
13   '
14 End Sub
15 -->
16 </script>
```

Using multiple INPUT TYPE=IMAGE controls on a form

If you want to have multiple images within an HTML form, you should set the ID and NAME attributes of each button to a unique value. This value will be passed to the server in the form *<name>*.x and *<name>*.y. This is an old convention that was used to send information for server-side image maps from client to server.

In the code in Listing 7.13, all you are doing is accessing the NAME and SRC properties and displaying them for the user. If you added this control to a real input form, pressing it would commit the POST or GET action that would transmit the contents of all the INPUT controls back to the server.

Now save your page and press the **Quick View** tab in the Visual InterDev editor to test the page. When you click on the image, you see the dialog pop up telling you the NAME and SRC properties of the image (see Figure 7.7).

FIGURE 7.7

Testing the IMAGE type INPUT control.

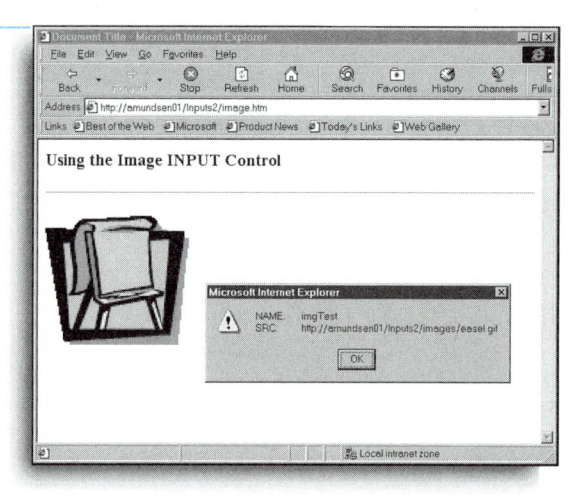

SEE ALSO
➤ *For more information on sending client data to Web servers, see page 111*

CHAPTER
8

Using Style Sheets with Your Web Pages

Use the Visual InterDev 6 Style Sheet Editor

Add inline, embedded, external, and imported style sheets

Create effective Web pages with style sheets

What Is a Style Sheet?

The HTML format was originally designed as a "markup language" for navigating the Internet. In fact, HTML stands for Hypertext Markup Language. However, the early versions of HTML allowed only minimal markup features. As late as HTML 3.2, there were very few standard methods for creating visually pleasing pages. And as more people began to use the Web, more people saw the need for a truly flexible—and extensible—way to add visual styles to HTML documents.

To solve this need for an extensible markup language, the Cascading Style Sheet (CSS) specification was developed. CSS is a way to define all the major parts of display styles, including

- Fonts
- Background
- Margins and borders
- Spacing, positioning, and alignment

With CSS markup coding in your document you can turn a rather plain-looking page (see Figure 8.1) into one that is much more appealing to the eye (see Figure 8.2).

Style sheets and typography

If you have ever worked with traditional typography and page layout, you should find Cascading Style Sheets very familiar. Style sheets attempt to duplicate the flexibility of print and have adopted many similarities to its print background.

FIGURE 8.1

A typical HTML document before CSS coding.

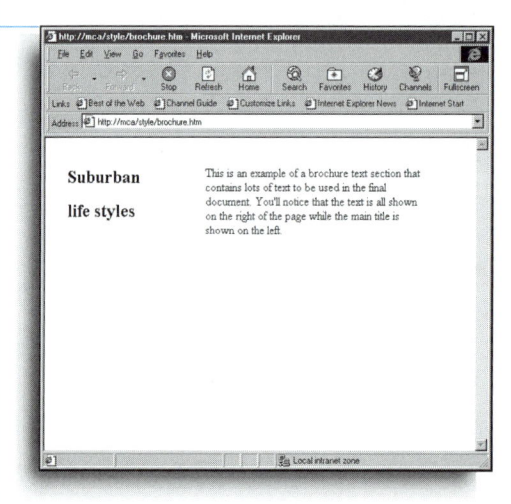

FIGURE 8.2
The same HTML document after applying CSS coding.

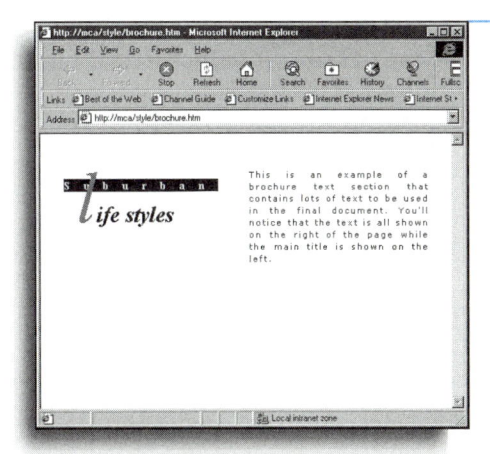

The CSS specification is also designed to "degrade gracefully." If the document requests a particular font or background that is not available for the current browser, secondary fonts or styles can be substituted. The CSS method for defining styles also is done in a way that will not cause problems for client browsers that do not support CSS. In other words, non-CSS browsers can simply ignore the CSS markups and continue to display the documents as if no CSS coding were included.

There are just a few basic steps to adding style sheets to your Web documents. You first must define the styles. The most common way to do this is with the Visual InterDev 6 Style Sheet Editor. This places all the styles in a single document called the *style sheet file*.

After the style sheet file is built, you must link your HTML documents to the existing style sheet. This is done with a `<LINK>` element in the `<HEAD>` section of the HMTL document.

Finally, when the style sheet is linked to your HTML document, you can add additional attributes to existing text-level and block-level elements in order to apply the styles in the style sheet file to your text.

The next three sections of this chapter explain these tasks in greater detail.

Graceful degradation with style sheets

Keep in mind that when a user visits your page without a browser that supports CSS, he or she will see the raw formatted text. When you use CSS instead of traditionally using an image file to accomplish an effect, consider the impact on the end user. You might want to continue using the old techniques until you know all your visitors support CSS.

Be prepared for a surprise when applying styles in various browsers

Because the CSS specification is designed to allow browsers to ignore the parts they don't understand, you should be prepared to see unexpected results appear when some browsers load your document using CSS tags. If you plan to implement your HTML documents on the Internet, carefully test your CSS tags in various browsers to make sure users will see what you want them to see.

The Style Sheet File Format

As mentioned previously, after defining a series of styles you can place them all in a single document called a style sheet file. This file has a special format understood by HTML browsers. Listing 8.1 shows a typical example of a style sheet document.

LISTING 8.1 **A Typical Style Sheet Document**

```
 1  BODY
 2  {
 3      BACKGROUND-COLOR: aqua;
 4      COLOR: maroon;
 5      FONT-FAMILY: Arial, sans-serif
 6  }
 7  #MyCSSID
 8  {
 9      COLOR: blue;
10      FONT-SIZE: large
11  }
12  ADDRESS.MyCSSCLASS
13  {
14      FONT-STYLE: italic;
15      FONT-VARIANT: normal
16  }
17  .MyNewClass
18  {
19      BACKGROUND-COLOR: blue;
20      FONT-FAMILY: 'Arial Rounded MT Bold', sans-serif
21  }
```

> **SEE ALSO**
> ➤ For more on creating HTML documents with Visual InterDev 6, see page 57

Style sheet files

As you can see by Listing 8.1, there isn't much to a style sheet file. If you are comfortable doing so, you can safely edit these files in a text editor or in the Visual InterDev Source Editor if you prefer not to use the Style Sheet Editor.

It's all just plain text

The Cascading Style Sheet information is all stored as plain text in a document. This means that you can also use a simple text editor to edit these documents. Although this is not recommended, it is good to know that it is possible if you are at a client site and need to apply a quick fix to a CSS document.

Notice that there are several different style types in this document. The first type redefines the default style for the <BODY> section of the document (lines 1–6). Lines 7–11 define a unique ID that can be applied anywhere in the document. Lines 12–16 define a special class of the ADDRESS element called MyCSSClass. This is a style that can be applied only to the ADDRESS element on a page. Finally, a "free" class style is defined in lines 17–21.

What Is a Style Sheet?

Because the class is not preceded by an element name, this class can be applied to any existing element in the document (that is, <H1>, <SPAN>, <DIV>, <P>, and so on).

SEE ALSO
➤ *For more information on using* <DIV> *and* <SPAN> *in your HTML documents, see page 749*

How to Link Style Sheets to Your Document

The syntax for linking an HMTL document to an existing CSS file is to add the following line to the <HEAD> section of an HTML document:

```
<LINK rel="stylesheet" href="css/brochure.css">
```

In this example, the file BROCHURE.CSS is stored in the subfolder called css. The LINK statement indicates that there is a style sheet relationship (rel) between the current document and the BROCHURE.CSS file.

The real advantage of using a CSS file is that you can easily manage styles across an entire Web project by modifying just one document. This can be done because the actual style information is not stored in the HTML document itself. Only a link to the style sheet exists in each HTML document. Thus, by changing a style value in the style sheet file, all linked documents will reflect the change the next time they are loaded.

SEE ALSO
➤ *For information on creating subfolders in your Visual InterDev 6 projects, see page 33*

How to Apply Styles in Documents

Basically, the CSS specification enables you to add various font and style attributes to all the existing section and text-level markup elements. For example, you can define a style that alters the <H1> element so that all <H1> text appears in reverse colors. Or you can create a CSS definition that uses Arial 12-point font for all text within the <BODY> of the document.

The CSS specification enables you to create your own custom markup codes, too. For example, you can create "classes" that

---

CSS file locations

Always remember to refer to your CSS file by its directory location, just like any other URL. For example, if the CSS file is located one directory up from your document, prefix it with a directory up ..\.

The <LINK> element belongs in the <HEAD> element

If you want to use the <LINK> element to link CSS documents to your HTML document, you must place that element between the <HEAD> and </HEAD> elements.

are applied to one or more existing elements. These classes can be applied to existing elements using the `class=` attribute:

```
<H2 Class="MyClass">
```

You can also create your own unique ID codes for handling styles. You can then apply the styles simply by referencing the ID code:

```
<P ID="MyCSSID">
```

This is text with the `MyCSSID` style applied:

```
</P>
```

You'll learn more about creating classes and unique IDs in the next section of this chapter.

> **Stlye classes versus IDs**
>
> The difference between classes and IDs is subtle. Although they can often be used interchangeably, the general rule is to use classes to apply only to a specific existing element (like **H1**) and IDs to apply to any element (like **H1** or **P**).

Using the Visual InterDev 6 Style Sheet Editor

Now that you understand the basics of style sheets and how they work, you're ready to start creating your own style sheet documents. Visual InterDev 6 has a very handy Style Sheet Editor that you can use to create your style sheets. This editor enables you to visually create the various styles and see how they will look in a test document. When you are satisfied that the style looks the way you like, you can save the entire group of styles as a .CSS file. When you have a .CSS file available, you can simply apply it to any existing Web documents.

For all the examples in this section of the chapter, you apply styles to a single document. The entire document text is shown in Listing 8.2.

> **Build the plain document first**
>
> Because it is possible that some users might view your Web document with a browser that does not support style sheets, it is a good idea to build your document without CSS markings and view that first. Later you can apply CSS tags to improve the visual appearance of the document.

LISTING 8.2 The FIRST.HTM for Testing Styles

```
1  <H1>This is H1 Text</H1>
2
3  <P>
4  This is normal text.
5  </P>
6
```

```
 7  <P>
 8  This is also normal text in a second paragraph.
 9  you will be able to see the difference between these two
10  paragraphs when you create a special "style class" and
11  apply that style class to this paragraph.
12   </P>
13
14  <P>
15  This paragraph shows more clearly how top and
16  bottom margins are applied to HTML tags including
17  the P element.</P>
18
19  <UL>
20  <STRONG>List Items</STRONG>
21  <LI>Item One
22  <LI>Item Two
23  <UL>
24  <LI>Sub Item Two A
25  <LI>Sub ITem Two B
26  </UL>
27  <LI>Item Three
28  </UL>
29
30  <ADDRESS>
31  www.amundsen.com
32  </ADDRESS>
```

Listing 8.2 shows all the text in the body of the HTML document. Add a new document to your STYLES project called FIRST.HTM and enter the text from Listing 8.2 into the document while in Source mode. You'll use this document to test the various styles you create in the rest of the chapter.

The completed document should like the one shown in Figure 8.3.

SEE ALSO
▶ *For more on adding documents to an existing Web project, see page 33*

FIGURE 8.3

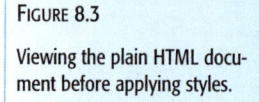

Viewing the plain HTML document before applying styles.

Helpful tip: Hold on to your style sheets

Nothing says you can't use a style sheet you create in one project, such as the one in this chapter, in another project. Keep an archive of style sheets that you like to use for incorporation into other sites.

Starting the Style Sheet Editor

It's easy to create a new style sheet with the Style Sheet Editor. First, start up Visual InterDev 6 and create a new project called Style on your current Web server. Don't worry about applying a theme or layout to the new Web project. After you select the host Web server and project name, just press the **Finish** button to build a simple Web project.

When Visual InterDev 6 is finished creating your default project, you're ready to add your first style sheet.

Adding a new style sheet to an existing Web project

1. Right-click over the project name in the Project Explorer window.
2. Select **Add Item** from the context menu.
3. Select **Style Sheet** from the submenu.
4. When the Add Item dialog appears, enter a name for the style sheet (in this example use `first`) and press the **Open** button. You'll then see the Visual InterDev 6 Style Sheet Editor appear, ready for your work (see Figure 8.4).

PART **II**

CHAPTER **8**

183

Using the Visual InterDev 6.0 Style Sheet Editor

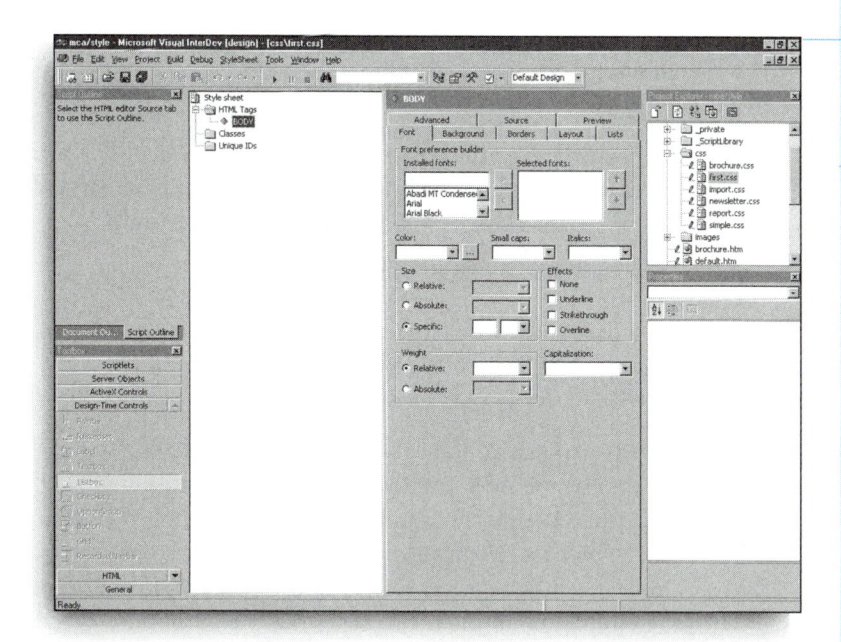

FIGURE 8.4
The Visual InterDev 6 Style Sheet Editor ready for use.

When the editor is in view, you see a tree view on the left and a multitabbed dialog box on the right. The tree view shows you the current style definitions in the file. There are only three main style types you must deal with:

- *HTML Tags*. This enables you to set styles for any existing HTML tag.
- *Classes*. This enables you to create a special type of style definition called a *class*. You can then apply these classes to existing HTML tags to add a customized style to your document.
- *Unique IDs*. This enables you to create another special type of style definition called an *ID*. You can then apply these IDs to any portion of your HTML document.

The difference between a class and an ID is subtle, but important. Classes are used to organize styles around existing HTML tags. For example, you can create a set of classes that expand on the H1 HTML tag. These could be H1.Big, H1.reverse, and H1.warning. The following is an example:

The Visual InterDev 6 Style Sheet Editor is the default CSS editor

If you double-click a CSS document in your project, Visual InterDev 6 will automatically launch the Style Sheet Editor for you with the document loaded. If you do not want to use the CSS editor that ships with Visual InterDev 6, you can right-click over the CSS document and select **Open With** to associate a new CSS editor for Visual InterDev 6.

```
<H1 class="big">Big Heading</H1>
<H1 class="reverse">Resverse Colors</H1>
<H1 class="warning">Don't Press Delete!</H1>
```

Style IDs, however, are designed to act independently of HTML tags. For example, you might define a `#Warning` ID that could be applied to more than one HTML tags. Here's an example:

```
<H1 ID=#Warning>About the Delete Button</H1>
<P ID=#Warning>
It's not a good idea to press the Delete button unless
you are quite sure you do not need to save the data at all.
</P>
```

You'll see how you can define and apply classes and IDs later in this chapter. For the most part, you'll concentrate on building style sheets that modify the way HTML tags display text in your document. The next several sections show you how to use the Visual InterDev 6 Style Sheet Editor to create a style sheet file that has examples of all the major types of style definitions you'll use in your Web documents.

Adding the FIRST.CSS File to Your FIRST.HTM Document

For now, even though you have not added any special style definitions to your style sheet file, close the file so you can link the style sheet file to your HTML document. To do this, select **File**, **Close** from the main menu. You'll see a dialog asking if you want to save the style sheet file. Click **Yes**.

Now that you have a stored style sheet file, you can link it to your HTML document.

Linking a style sheet file to an HTML document in Visual InterDev 6

1. Double-click the **FIRST.HTM** document in the Project Explorer window for the STYLES project. The document will appear in the Visual InterDev Editor.

2. With the HTML document loaded in your editor, switch to Source mode by clicking the **Source** tab at the bottom of the editor window.

Using classes and IDs to your benefit

You can create as many unique IDs and classes as you need. If you must create a subtle distinction between one block of `<P>` text and another, create a custom class. If you prefer to create your own unique IDs for formatting, go ahead. Keep in mind that the classes and IDs you create and don't use are ignored by the Web browser. There is minimal overhead in creating new styles, so you might want to plan ahead.

Inline styles

Although style sheets support inline styles, where you can define style attributes within the HTML document itself, I recommend you use external files as in this chapter. This makes updating easier, and it also makes your styles available to other pages.

Using the Visual InterDev 6.0 Style Sheet Editor | PART **II**
CHAPTER **8**

3. To make room for the style sheet, you link the `<HEAD>` section of the document. Move your cursor to the line that has the `</HEAD>` tag on it and press Enter to add a new blank line to the page. The style sheet link will go on this blank line.

4. Move your cursor to the Project Explorer window and locate the FIRST.CSS document in the list. Drag this from the Project Explorer over to the HTML document in the editor and drop the item on the blank line in the `<HEAD>` section. You'll then see the complete `<LINK...>` coding appear in your HTML document. That's it!

After you drop the style sheet file inside your HTML document, the `<HEAD>` section should look similar to the one shown in Listing 8.3.

LISTING 8.3 **Results of Dropping a Style Sheet File in an HTML Document**

```
1 <HEAD>
2 <META NAME="GENERATOR" Content="Microsoft Visual Studio 6.0">
3 <LINK rel="stylesheet" href="css/first.css">
4 </HEAD>
```

Now you're ready to start adding style definitions to the style sheet file and viewing the results in the FIRST.HTM document.

SEE ALSO
➤ *For more on using the Visual InterDev 6 editor, including drag-and-drop operations, see page 33*

Defining Font Styles

With the Visual InterDev 6 Style Editor up and running, you can select the **Font** tab to enter information to define a font style. For example, you can highlight the BODY HTML tag and set a font style for the entire BODY section of the document to 12-point Tahoma.

Setting the *BODY* font style

1. With the Visual InterDev 6 Style Sheet Editor up and running, click the **Font** tab in the dialog on the left.

Use multiple CSS files for a single document

It is possible to apply more than one CSS file to the same HTML document. For example, you could have a CSS document that defines paragraph styles and another that defines margins and layouts. Just add both the new documents to the `<HEAD>` section of the HTML page and you're all set.

PART II Web Page Design Techniques

CHAPTER 8 Using Style Sheets with Your Web Pages

Installed fonts: The facts

Remember that installed fonts are exactly that: the installed fonts on your computer. There is no guarantee that your site's users will have the same fonts that you do. This example assumes everyone has Tahoma. However, what are the odds that someone using a Macintosh will? It's something to consider.

---

2. In the tree view on the left, be sure to highlight the word **BODY** in the **HTML Tags** section.

3. In the **Font** tab dialog, use the scrollbars in the font list (below the **Installed fonts** input box) to scroll through the font selections. Locate and double-click the **Tahoma** font to add it to the list of **Selected fonts**.

4. Finally, enter sans serif in the **Installed fonts** input box and click once on the right arrow button to add this to the **Selected fonts** list. You've just defined your first font style! (See Figure 8.5.)

FIGURE 8.5

Defining a font style for the BODY.

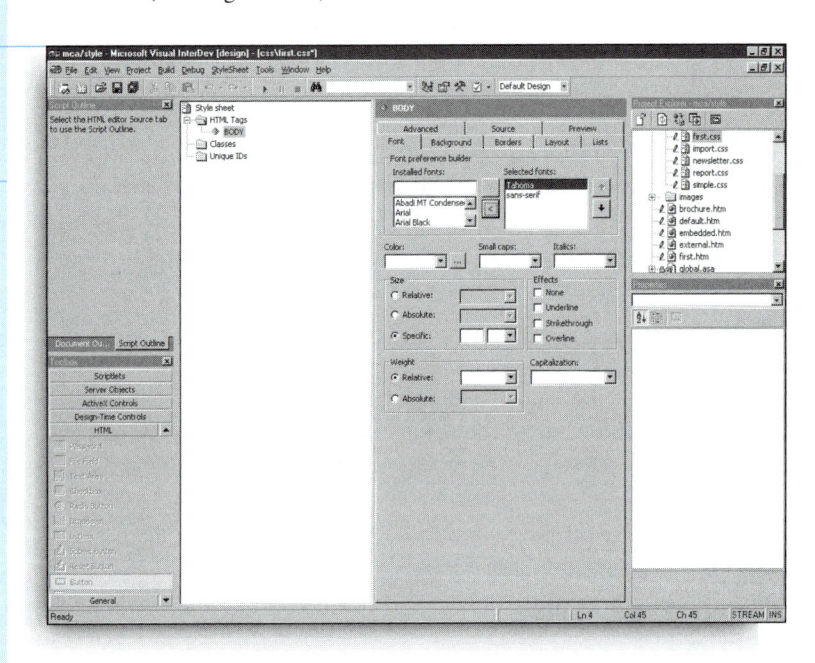

Failures in font requests

Until everyone is using a browser that can download fonts at the drop of a hat, fonts will continue to be a heartache among Web developers. Carefully consider the impact of the wrong font on your site's visual consistency and layout. Plan your site around the lowest common denominator in your visitors.

When building your selected font list, you can add as many fonts to the list as you like. The client browser will attempt to use the first item in the list. If the browser cannot locate a font with the name you requested, the browser will read the next font in the preference list and attempt to locate and use that font. This will continue until the browser finds a font request it can fulfill or the browser runs out of fonts.

In the preceding example, you added sans serif to the list of fonts. This is not an actual font—it is the name of a font family. Almost all client browsers will have at least one font in their collection that belongs to the sans-serif font family. Therefore, it is always a good idea to end every font selection list with a font family name.

The valid font family names are

- Serif (for example, Times)
- Sans serif (for example, Arial or Helvetica)
- Cursive (for example, Zapf-Chancery)
- Fantasy (for example, Western)
- Monospace (for example, Courier)

You can also use the Visual InterDev 6 Style Sheet Editor to view the actual style sheet that will be saved to your Web project. To do this, select the **Source** tab in the dialog box. You should see a display that looks like the one in Listing 8.4.

LISTING 8.4 Viewing the Resulting Style Sheet Source

```
1 BODY
2 {
3 FONT-FAMILY: Tahoma, sans-serif
4 }
```

Now, when you view the FIRST.HTM document, you'll see the results of setting the new font for the body of the document. This style update appears even though you have not edited the HTML document itself. This is the power of linked style sheets (see Figure 8.6).

Defining Background Styles

You can also use the **Background** tab of the Style Sheet Editor to create style definitions for backgrounds. You can create background styles for the entire document body or for any existing HTML tag.

Always add font families to font styles

Sometimes the client browser cannot fulfill your font request. In this case, the browser will revert to the original font for the HTML tag (usually Times Roman, serif). To avoid undesirable displays, you should always add a font family to the end of every font selection list in a style.

PART II   Web Page Design Techniques

CHAPTER 8   **Using Style Sheets with Your Web Pages**

FIGURE 8.6

Viewing FIRST.HTM with new BODY font style.

Setting the background style for the HTML *BODY* tag

1. With the Visual InterDev 6 Style Sheet Editor loaded, select the **Background** tab in the dialog box.

2. Locate the **Background colors** section and press the browse button (...) to call up the Color Picker dialog box.

3. Select a color from the various blocks in the dialog; in this example, select **Plum**.

4. Check the **Use color names** box at the bottom left of the dialog box. This will save the color as a readable name instead of a hex numerical value.

5. Press **OK** on the Color Picker dialog box to save the color selection (see Figure 8.7).

Now when you select the **Source** tab to view the style sheet file, you see something like the text in Listing 8.5.

It's best to use color names

When you save color values with Visual InterDev 6, it is a good idea to use color names instead of the hex numeric values. This will make the resulting documents easier to understand. However, this does not guarantee color matching between computer systems and platforms.

LISTING 8.5   **Viewing the Style Sheet Source After Setting the Background Color**

```
1  BODY
2  {
3      BACKGROUND-COLOR: plum;
4      FONT-FAMILY: Tahoma, sans-serif
5  }
```

PART **II**

Using the Visual InterDev 6.0 Style Sheet Editor

CHAPTER **8**

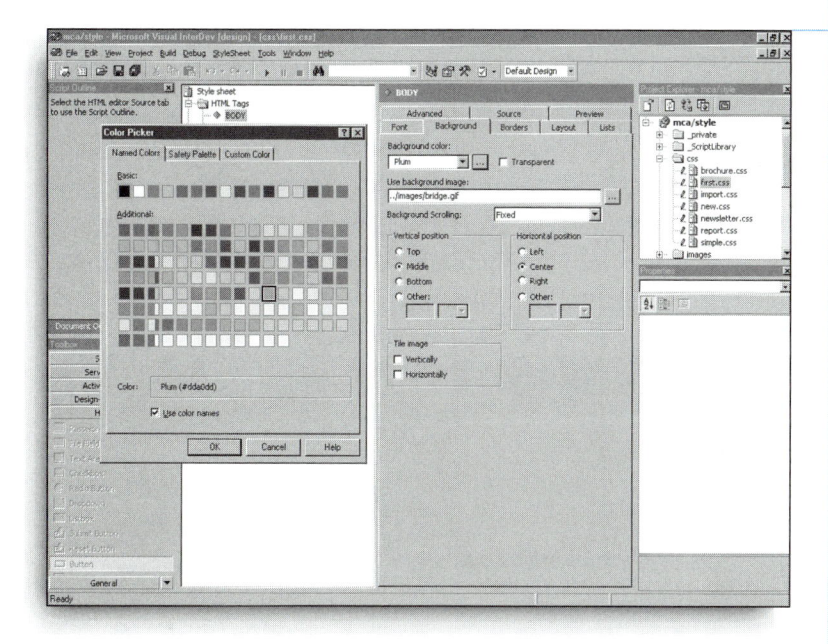

189

FIGURE 8.7
Setting the background color style for the BODY.

You should notice from the dialog box that you can also select a graphic image file to act as the background and then control this image's placement on the page. You must have an image already imported into your Web document before you can apply it as the background for your page. When you have an image available, you can add it to your style sheet file.

Adding a background image to your style sheet

1. With the Visual InterDev 6 Style Sheet Editor up and running, select the **Background** tab.
2. Click the browse button (...) next to the **Use background image** input box.
3. Use the Select Background Image dialog box to locate an image in your Web project and click on that image in the dialog box (see Figure 8.8).
4. Notice that the URL for locating the image is placed in the **URL** field in the dialog box.
5. If needed, you can adjust the **URL type** box to use Doc Relative, Root Relative, or Absolute URL addressing. For this example, use Doc Relative addressing.

Backgrounds: Styles versus <BODY>

Basically, every Web browser out there supports the <BODY BACKGROUND=" "> attribute to set a document's background graphic. Remember that only browsers that support CSS will see the backgrounds created using the CSS background attribute.

6. When you have selected the graphic you need, press **OK** to add the URL to your style sheet.

7. When you return to the style sheet Background dialog box, set the **Vertical** and **Horizontal** position values. For this example, use `Middle` and `Center`, respectively.

8. Finally, you can adjust the tiling property of the background image, too. For this example, check off the **Vertical** and **Horizontal** tiling boxes.

FIGURE 8.8

Adding a background image to the style sheet.

URL types

If you're not quite sure what type of URL type to use, remember this: An absolute URL will always map to your resource by its complete address (that is, `http://www.banick.com/images/banick.gif`). This complicates matters, however, when you go back to do site maintenance. If you change your directory structure, you must go back and fix those absolute references. Doc Relative references, however, are moved with the directory. As long as the location of the image in relation to your document doesn't change, Doc Relative is usually the best.

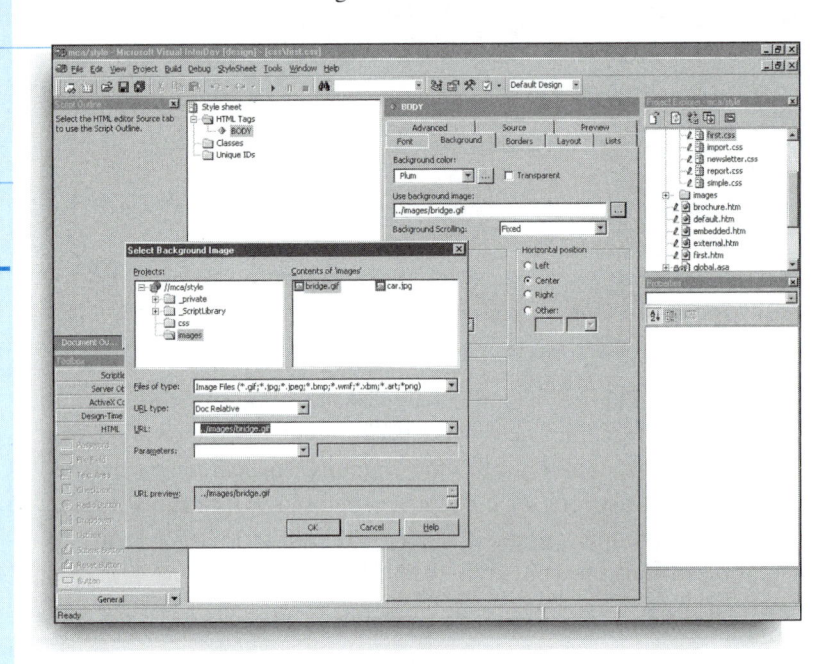

Your style source should now look like the text in Listing 8.6.

LISTING 8.6 Style Sheet Source After Adding a Background Image

```
1  BODY
2  {
3      BACKGROUND-COLOR: plum;
4      BACKGROUND-IMAGE: url(../images/bridge.gif);
5      BACKGROUND-REPEAT: no-repeat;
6      FONT-FAMILY: Tahoma, sans-serif
7  }
```

Using the Visual InterDev 6.0 Style Sheet Editor | PART II CHAPTER 8 | 191

Now, when you view the FIRST.HTM document in your browser you see both the new background color and the fixed background graphic (see Figure 8.9).

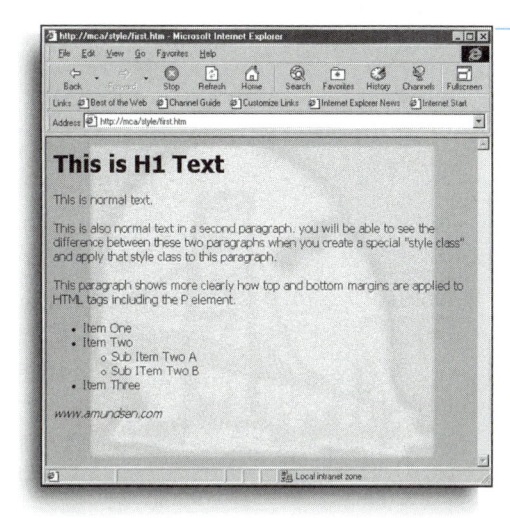

FIGURE 8.9
Results of setting the background styles.

SEE ALSO
➤ *For more on adding images to your Web documents, see page 207*

Defining Borders, Margins, and Padding Styles

You can also define border, margin, and padding styles in your style sheet file. This will help you control how blocks of text appear in the document. For example, you could add margin styles to the `<P>` element to make sure each paragraph has the margins you want. The following is a step-by-step example of setting the margins for the `<P>` element.

Setting the margin style for an HTML tag element

1. Select the **Borders** tab in the Visual InterDev 6.0 Style Sheet Editor dialog box.
2. Locate the **Margins** inputs and for the **Top** value, enter .25 and select in from the drop-down next to the input. Then enter 0.5 and in for the **Bottom**, 1.0 and in for the **Left**, and 0.5 and in for the **Right** margin (see Figure 8.10).

Margins in CSS

Margins and padding in style sheets can be referenced with several different units: inches, pixels, points, and relative units. Keep in mind that point sizes and inches are subject to the size of the screen for positioning. Pixels are often the best for precise layout.

PART II Web Page Design Techniques

CHAPTER 8 Using Style Sheets with Your Web Pages

3. When you save the style sheet, the new margins will be active in your document.

FIGURE 8.10

Adding margin style definitions.

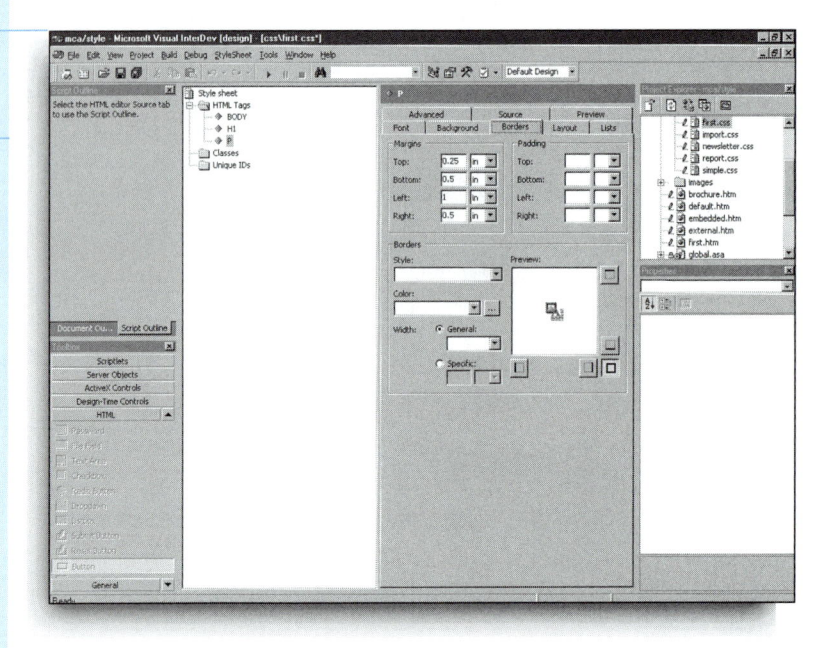

Your style sheet source should now look like the code in Listing 8.7.

LISTING 8.7 Style Sheet Source After Adding Margins for the <P> Element

```
1  BODY
2  {
3      BACKGROUND-COLOR: plum;
4      BACKGROUND-IMAGE: url(../images/bridge.gif);
5      BACKGROUND-REPEAT: no-repeat;
6      FONT-FAMILY: Tahoma, sans-serif
7  }
8  P
9  {
10     MARGIN: 0.25in 0.5in 0.5in 1in
11 }
```

Notice that you can also add borders to any HTML tag and control the padding of space between elements, too.

Now check out the progress of your HTML document by viewing the FIRST.HTM page in your browser (see Figure 8.11).

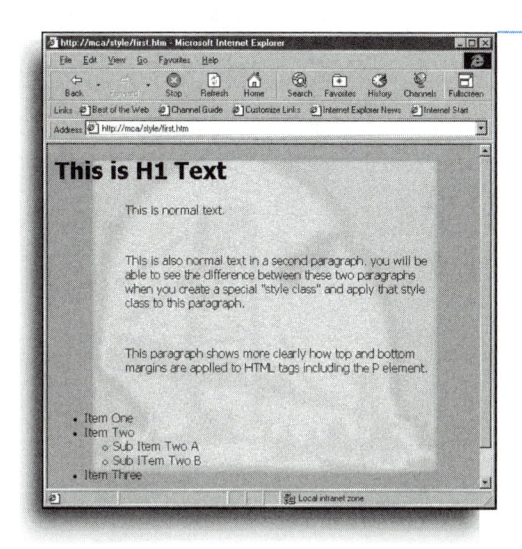

FIGURE 8.11
Results of setting border styles.

Defining Layout Styles

You can also define more general layout styles for your documents. This includes line and letter spacing, text justification, and even which cursor appears when you move the mouse over the designated text.

In this example, you add some style definitions for the <H1> tag.

Adding layout styles to an HTML tag element

1. Highlight the **HTML Tags** folder in the left tree view of the Visual InterDev 6 Style Sheet Editor.
2. Right-click over the **HTML Tags** item and select **Insert HTML Tag** from the context menu.
3. Enter H1 in the dialog box and press **OK** to add the H1 tag to your list.
4. Highlight the **H1** tag in the tree, and then select the **Layout** tab in the dialog box at the right.

PART II Web Page Design Techniques
CHAPTER 8 **Using Style Sheets with Your Web Pages**

Cursor styles

Changing the cursor styles in relation to an element on your page is a great step toward better interfaces. Using this attribute, you can make your pages behave more like conventional Windows applications (or MacOS applications, for that matter).

5. In the **Text layout** section, select **Right** for **Alignment**.
6. In the **Spacing between** section, select **Specific** for **Letters** and enter 2 and pt in the inputs next to the **Letters** box.
7. In the **Cursor style** pull-down, select **Help** from the list (see Figure 8.12).
8. Close the dialog box by selecting **File**, **Close** from the main menu.

FIGURE 8.12
Adding layout styles.

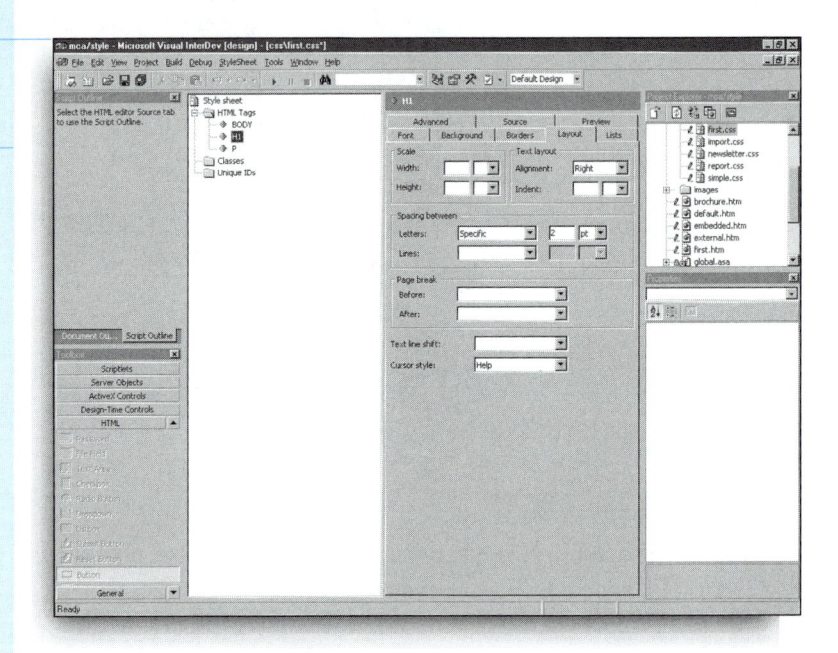

Your style sheet source should now look like the code in Listing 8.8.

LISTING 8.8 Style Sheet Source After Adding Layout Styles

```
1  BODY
2  {
3      BACKGROUND-COLOR: plum;
4      BACKGROUND-IMAGE: url(../images/bridge.gif);
5      BACKGROUND-REPEAT: no-repeat;
```

Using the Visual InterDev 6.0 Style Sheet Editor | CHAPTER 8

```
6     FONT-FAMILY: Tahoma, sans-serif
7   }
8   P
9   {
10    MARGIN: 0.25in 0.5in 0.5in 1in
11  }
12  H1
13  {
14    CURSOR: help;
15    LETTER-SPACING: 2pt;
16    TEXT-ALIGN: right
17  }
```

LISTING 8.8

❶ CURSOR: help will change the cursor when it is over the <H1> tag.

❷ Text will always align to the right of the document.

The resulting HTML document is shown in Figure 8.13.

FIGURE 8.13
The results of adding layout styles.

Defining List Styles

Style sheets can also be used to define custom bullets for the unordered list (<UL>) HTML tag. This allows you to apply a fixed standard bullet or use a custom graphic image for your bullets. In this example, you add a new graphic bullet to the <BODY> HTML tag.

Adding a custom graphic bullet to the *BODY* style

1. Highlight the **BODY** entry in the **HTML Tags** list of the Visual InterDev 6 Style Sheet Editor.

Images for bullets

Using an image for a list bullet is a great way to improve the appearance of your page. Keep in mind, however, the impact of another graphic on your page for download speeds. The built-in bullets are very fast to render; weigh the pros and cons of adding another graphic to enhance your page.

PART II   Web Page Design Techniques

CHAPTER 8   **Using Style Sheets with Your Web Pages**

2. Select the **Lists** tab in the dialog on the right.
3. Click the **Bulleted list** radio button.
4. Press the browse button (...) to bring up the Select Bullet Image dialog box.
5. In the Select Bullet Image dialog box, locate a graphic in your current Web project. The example shown in Figure 8.14 selects BUTTON.GIF from the Images folder.
6. After selecting the graphic, select the desired URL type. `Doc Relative` is used in this example.
7. Press **OK** to add the selected image to your style definition.

FIGURE 8.14

Adding a custom graphic bullet to the style sheet.

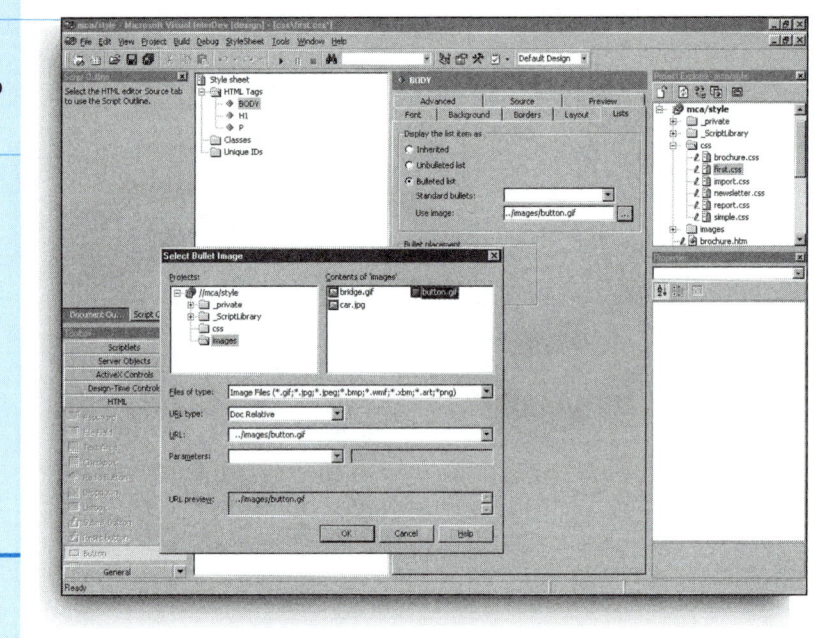

Image buttons need extra attention

If you decide to use custom images for your buttons, be sure you always include the images in your Web project. If you fail to copy the images into the project, users will see only the default nongraphic buttons.

Your style sheet source will now reflect the added List definition (see line 5 in Listing 8.9).

LISTING 8.9   **Style Sheet Source After Adding the List Definition**

```
1  BODY
2  {
3      BACKGROUND-COLOR: plum;
4      BACKGROUND-IMAGE: url(../images/bridge.gif);
```

Using the Visual InterDev 6.0 Style Sheet Editor PART II CHAPTER 8 **197**

```
5     BACKGROUND-REPEAT: no-repeat;
6     FONT-FAMILY: Tahoma, sans-serif
7      LIST-STYLE: url(../images/button.gif);
8  }
9  P
10 {
11    LIST-STYLE: inside;
12    MARGIN: 0.25in 0.5in 0.5in 1in
13 }
14 H1
15 {
16    CURSOR: help;
17    LETTER-SPACING: 2pt;
18    TEXT-ALIGN: right
19 }
```

LISTING 8.9

① This is the location of the button image.

After adding the new list styles to the sytle sheet, your HTML document should look close to the one in Figure 8.15.

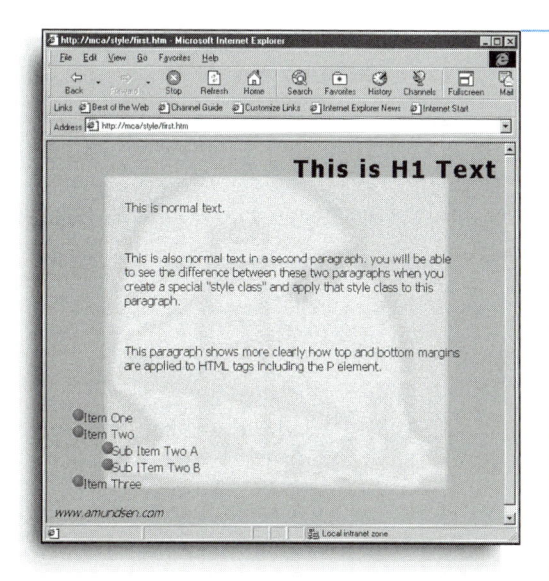

FIGURE 8.15
The results of adding list styles.

SEE ALSO
➤ *For information on adding drop-down lists to your Web documents, see page 155*

Defining Style Classes

One of the nice features of the CSS specification is that you can create your own specialized style classes. These classes can then be applied to one or more existing HTML tags to provide added flexibility to your presentation. For example, you could define two classes of paragraph style: `Emphatic` and `Justified`. Each of these styles could then be applied to existing paragraphs.

Creating a paragraph class style class

1. Right-click over the **Classes** section in the tree view.
2. Select **Insert Class** from the context menu.
3. Enter `Emphatic` as the **Name**.
4. Check the **Apply only to the following tag** box and enter `P` as the tag name. Press **OK** to add the class name to the style sheet.
5. With **P.Emphatic** highlighted in the tree view, select the **Font** tab in the dialog on the right.
6. Set **Italics** to `Yes`.
7. Set **Size** to `Relative` and select **Smaller** from the list.
8. Set **Weight** to `Relative` and select **Bolder** from the list.

Now you can add a class style for the `Justified` paragraph type.

Creating a justified paragraph class style

1. Right-click over the **Classes** section and select **Insert Class**.
2. Enter `Justified` as the name, check the **Apply only** box, and enter `P` as the tag element. Press **OK** to save the tag name.
3. With **P.Justified** selected in the tree view, select the **Layout** tab in the dialog.
4. In the **Text Layout** section, select `Justify` for the **Alignment** value.

With the two new classes added to your style sheet definition, the style sheet source should now look like the text in Listing 8.10.

Examples of style classes

Consider the example of a newspaper online. The newspaper could use several different style classes for the <P> tag to represent the type of story. Human Interest stories might get a different background color than hard-hitting news. Entertainment could have a strong border to separate it from the weather. You can use these style classes to create visual distinction in your pages.

Justification and alignment

Remember that justification and alignment effects slow down the rendering speed for your pages. Particularly noticeable is Justify for alignment: This requires the Web browser to compute all the text, flow it into position, and then make the alignment changes before the user can see it.

Using the Visual InterDev 6.0 Style Sheet Editor | PART II CHAPTER 8 | **199**

LISTING 8.10 Style Sheet Source After Adding the New Paragraph Classes

```
1  BODY
2  {
3      BACKGROUND-COLOR: plum;
4      BACKGROUND-IMAGE: url(../images/bridge.gif);
5      BACKGROUND-REPEAT: no-repeat;
6      FONT-FAMILY: Tahoma, sans-serif
7       LIST-STYLE: url(../images/button.gif);
8  }
9  P
10 {
11     LIST-STYLE: inside;
12     MARGIN: 0.25in 0.5in 0.5in 1in
13 }
14 H1
15 {
16     CURSOR: help;
17     LETTER-SPACING: 2pt;
18     TEXT-ALIGN: right
19 }
20 P.Justified ───────────────── ❶
21 {
22     TEXT-ALIGN: justify
23 }
24 P.Emphatic ─────────────────── ❷
25 {
26     FONT-SIZE: smaller;
27     FONT-STYLE: italic;
28     FONT-WEIGHT: bolder
29 }
```

LISTING 8.10

❶ Here's the new paragraph class called `Justified`.

❷ Here's the new paragraph class called `Emphatic`.

It should also be noted that you can define a style class that is not applied to only one HTML tag. This "free class" can then be applied to any existing HTML tag.

After adding the two new style classes, you can apply them to paragraphs in the FIRST.HTM document. To do this, you must open the FIRST.HTM document in the **Source** tab of the Visual InterDev 6 editor and alter two lines in the document.

First, locate the <P> marker at the start of the second paragraph of text. Replace that <P> with the following line:

```
<P class="Justified">
```

Once a P.Justified, always a P.Justified

When you define a style class as belonging to a particular element (as in <P>), you can only apply that class to the <P> element. For example, the `P.Justified` class could not be applied to a heading element like `H1.Justified`.

Next, replace the `<P>` element that starts the third paragraph with the following:

`<P class="Emphatic">`

As you can see, all you need to do is add the `class=<classname>` attribute to the existing `<P>` element to get the desired effect. Figure 8.16 shows the results of applying the custom class styles.

FIGURE 8.16

The results of applying the custom class styles.

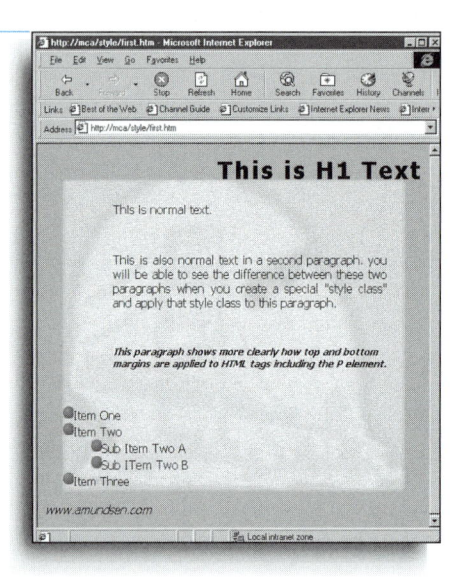

Defining Unique ID Styles

Another way to define a class is to give it a unique ID within the style sheet file. This unique ID can then be applied to any HTML tag element you want. The advantage of unique IDs is that you can apply them freely to a wide range of both text-level and block-level elements. In this example, you create a new unique ID style to apply to the `<ADDRESS>` HTML tag.

Creating a unique ID style

1. Right-click over the **Unique ID** section of the **Style** tree view and select **Insert Unique ID** from the menu.
2. Type `SmallCaps` as the **ID Name** and press **OK** to save the ID to the style sheet.

Using the Visual InterDev 6.0 Style Sheet Editor

3. After you have added the unique ID you can create any type of style definition you want.
4. For this example, select the **Font** tab and set the **Color** to Navy, the **Small Caps** to Yes, and the **Weight** to Absolute and Bold(700).

Now your style sheet source should look like the one in Listing 8.11.

LISTING 8.11 Style Sheet Source After Adding a Unique ID

```
1  BODY
2  {
3      BACKGROUND-COLOR: plum;
4      BACKGROUND-IMAGE: url(../images/bridge.gif);
5      BACKGROUND-REPEAT: no-repeat;
6      FONT-FAMILY: Tahoma, sans-serif
7       LIST-STYLE: url(../images/button.gif)
8  }
9  P
10 {
11     LIST-STYLE: inside;
12     MARGIN: 0.25in 0.5in 0.5in 1in
13 }
14 H1
15 {
16     CURSOR: help;
17     LETTER-SPACING: 2pt;
18     TEXT-ALIGN: right
19 }
20 P.Justified
21 {
22     TEXT-ALIGN: justify
23 }
24 P.Emphatic
25 {
26     FONT-SIZE: smaller;
27     FONT-STYLE: italic;
28     FONT-WEIGHT: bolder
29 }
30 #SmallCaps ──────── ❶
31 {
```

LISTING 8.11

❶ This is a unique style ID for this style sheet.

continues...

Web Page Design Techniques
Using Style Sheets with Your Web Pages

LISTING 8.11 Continued

```
32      COLOR: navy;
33      FONT-VARIANT: small-caps;
34      FONT-WEIGHT: bold
35  }
```

Notice that the `SmallCaps` definition (beginning on line 28) starts with a # symbol. This is inserted by the Visual InterDev 6 Style Sheet Editor. The # marks this item as a unique ID.

Now you can apply the `#SmallCaps` ID to an HTML element in the FIRST.HTM document. To do this, replace the `<ADDRESS>` tag with `<ADDRESS ID="SmallCaps">`. Figure 8.17 shows the result of applying the `#SmallCaps` ID to the `<ADDRESS>` tag in your FIRST.HTM document.

Unique IDs Can Be Applied to Any Element

Unlike style classes that are tied to a specific element (as in `P.Justified`), unique style IDs are "free" to be applied to any HTML element. For example, both `<H1 ID=#SmallCaps>` and `<P ID=#SmallCaps>` are valid uses of a unique style ID.

FIGURE 8.17

The results of applying the unique ID to your document.

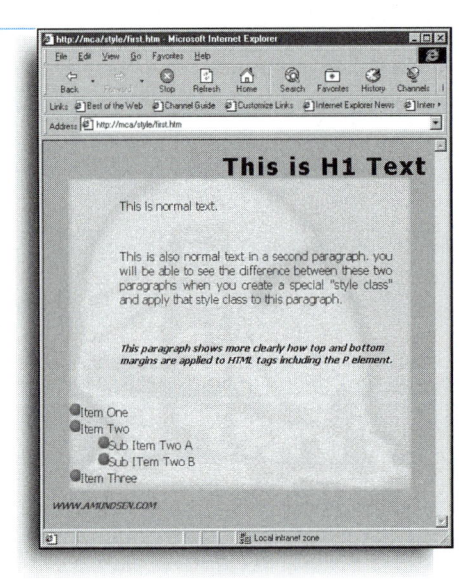

That's the basics of using the Visual InterDev 6 Style Sheet Editor to add styles to your HTML documents. There are lots of additional things you can do to create great-looking HTML documents.

Using the Visual InterDev 6.0 Style Sheet Editor

For example, you can create standard CSS files that you can apply regularly to your documents. You might create a REPORT.CSS that contains typical styles for creating report covers for online presentations. You could also create a CODE.CSS that has numerous style settings for making source code easy to read, such as coloring different code sections and special monospaced fonts for source code.

Finally, you can use CSS files to build creative layouts for online materials, such as brochures and newsletters. This can include ways to create drop-caps for the first letters in paragraphs, special margins, and even reverse printed titles.

The possibilities are endless!

SEE ALSO
➤ *For information on animating your HTML documents with Dynamic HTML, see page 750*

Organize Your Style Sheets Into Groups

Because you can apply more than one style sheet to any document, you can build style sheet groups to handle different values. For example, MARGINS.CSS, HEADINGS.CSS, LISTS.CSS, FONTS.CSS, etc. This allows you to easily modify elements within a style sheet without affecting other styles.

CHAPTER 9

Adding Multimedia to Your Web Applications

Learn how to add sound and video to your Web applications

Learn how to use the DirectAnimation controls to draw complex graphical images

The Pros and Cons of Multimedia for Your Web Applications

Visual InterDev 6 has some great tools for supporting sound, video, and complex graphics for your Web applications. In this chapter, you learn how you can add these features to your Web apps with very little trouble.

Adding a bit of sound, a video clip, or some custom line drawing and animation can greatly increase the value of your Web application for your users. Often, a little bit of multimedia can make the difference between a ho-hum Web page and one that really grabs the user's attention.

Another advantage of using multimedia for your Web apps is that it can widen the reach of your application. There are many times when you can get your point across much better with an audio or video clip rather than with lots of text on a page.

Employing detailed graphics and line drawings can also greatly improve your application's functionality. This is especially true for applications that are targeted for visually oriented users (graphic artists, designers, engineers, and so on). Often the most important documents in your Web application will be multimedia files (video clips, artists renderings of new products, and so on).

However, adding multimedia has its drawbacks. First, most of the features you'll learn about here require ActiveX support. This means that you need Microsoft Internet Explorer in order to take advantage of these enhancements to your Web applications.

Second, overuse of multimedia can quickly degrade performance for your Web application—even for the Web server itself. You must be sure not to go overboard when adding multimedia features to your Web documents. A few well-chosen animations or one or two video clips is all that is usually needed in order to get your user's attention and deliver important information.

Targeting a specific browser

It is often a tough call to decide whether you should target a specific browser. When you cater to Microsoft Internet Explorer users on your site while neglecting Netscape Communicator/Navigator users, you might be building yourself into a corner. Carefully consider how this could impact your site and its visitors. If you have to, consider an approach that will gracefully degrade for users who do not have Microsoft Internet Explorer.

Finally, some users find extensive multimedia a bit annoying. If your application does not need the multimedia in order to deliver the main message, consider leaving it out or providing alternative pages for users who do not want to download large audio and video files to their workstations.

With the preliminaries now out of the way, it's time to learn how you can add sound, video, and complex graphics to your Web pages!

SEE ALSO

> If you want to experiment with other types of multimedia, look at pages 749

Adding Sound and Video

The easiest multimedia features to add to your Web applications are sound and video clips. Sound clips can be as simple as the familiar Windows login or logout tones or as involved as a famous speech or musical performance. Video files can be anything from short news clips to long taped presentations for wide distribution.

In the next two sections, you'll see how easy it is to add sound and video to your Web pages.

Adding Sound to Your Web Documents

The Microsoft Internet Explorer supports an HTML element you can use to add background sound to a Web document. This enables you to identify a sound that will be played immediately after the page is downloaded to the client browser. You can also control the number of times the item repeats—from 0 repeats to infinite.

Here's the basic syntax for the BGSOUND HTML element:

```
<BGSOUND SRC="sounds/telephone.wav" LOOP=INFINITE>
```

Slow pages

Everyone who has surfed the Web has experienced that torturous page that takes two minutes to download and brings your computer to a crawl after it appears. Keep in mind that the more multimedia files you add to your page, the more agonizing the experience for your users—this is especially true considering most users don't have the latest whiz-bang processors and graphics cards.

The legalities of multimedia

Always keep in mind the legality of multimedia files you use on your site. Most material out there is under copyright restrictions, and cannot be freely reproduced on your site. If you, or your company, did not create the content you will be using, always make sure to obtain the proper permission. The last thing you want to do is make yourself out to be a legal target and have your Web site display a banner that reads "Closed due to copyright infringement."

INFINITE LOOPs might use infinite disk space

In some cases, using a `LOOP` value of `INFINITE` might consume all the available workstation disk space. This happens when the browser attempts to download a copy of the sound file for each repetition. You should use the `INFINITE` setting with great caution.

File associations and default actions

If a user chooses that, by default, he wants an audio file to be opened by a particular program, the Web browser will automatically open the file. Only when a user does not have a default action or program specified is he prompted.

Note that there are only two attributes for the BGSOUND element:

- SRC is a required attribute that contains the URL of the sound file to play.
- LOOP is an optional attribute that determines the number of times the sound file will be played. If missing (or set to 1), the sound file will play only once. Setting the LOOP attribute to INFINITE will cause the sound file to continue to play as long as the page is loaded in the browser.

With the BGSOUND HTML element, you can also play sound files from the Microsoft Internet Explorer browser by adding a simple URL link to the sound file. For example:

```
<a href="http://mca/Multimedia/sounds/GLASS.WAV">
<img src="images/wav.gif" WIDTH="32" HEIGHT="32"></a>
```

In this example, the user will see a small icon appear on the HTML document. By clicking on the icon, the GLASS.WAV file will be downloaded to the client station. This will force a File Download dialog to appear on the client station (see Figure 9.1).

FIGURE 9.1
Viewing the File Download dialog.

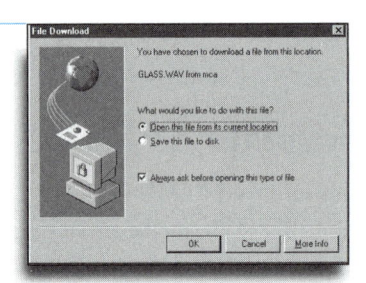

Selecting the **Open** option will cause the associated program to automatically load and play the sound file (see Figure 9.2).

FIGURE 9.2
Playing the sound file with the associated program.

Adding Sound and Video

If the client station has no associated program that can handle the sound file, or if the workstation does not have sound services installed, users will see a message similar to the one in Figure 9.3.

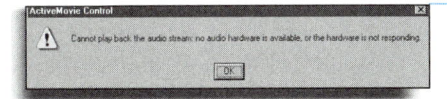

FIGURE 9.3
Error message while attempting to play a sound file.

You can also execute a sound file from client-side script. Listing 9.1 shows how you can accomplish this with Visual Basic Scripting. In this case, a section of text is defined in the document using the <DIV>...</DIV> tags. When a user clicks on the section, the Visual Basic Scripting from Listing 9.1 will execute.

The horror of error messages

Most novice users will be confused by such error messages as the one shown in Figure 9.3. Most experienced users will be disgusted. Plan accordingly around your anticipated audience's capabilities.

LISTING 9.1 Sample Visual Basic Scripting to Play a Sound File

```
1 Sub SoundByte_onclick
2    ' cue up MIDI file
3    window.open "sounds/canyon.mid","Sounds"
4    '
5 End Sub
```

You might also have noticed that this last example does not use a WAV format file. Instead, a MID (or MIDI) format file is used. Several sound formats are available. The difficulty is in knowing just what format is understood by your user's workstations. The Microsoft WAV format is the most common among Windows users. Every machine that has the Windows operating system installed has a WAV format player available. You might also be able to use MID and RMI formats on Windows machines.

The RA, AU, RAM, and AIFF formats are also quite common among Internet users. However, running these sound formats requires an audio player that might not be available on the workstation.

Consider audio format

The ideal format for an audio file depends entirely on what type of audio you are playing. WAV files are typically samples recorded from another source. MIDI files are instrumental music. Real Audio RA and RAM files are intended for compressed, streaming audio. Plan your multimedia file format around the type of content you are sending downstream.

Where are the sound files?

The sound files used in this example can be downloaded from the *Using Visual InterDev 6* home page (see Appendix B, "Online Resources" for the address). You can also use any sound file you have readily available.

Now that you know how to add sound to your Web pages, start up Visual InterDev 6 and add a new HTML page called SOUND.HTM to the current project. In this document, you'll add a background sound, some direct HTML links, and an example that uses Visual Basic Scripting to play a sound file.

The first thing you must do is add one or more sound files to your Web project. You can do this using the Visual InterDev 6 Project Explorer.

Add sound files to your Web project

1. Right-click the project name in the Project Explorer window and select **New Folder** from the context menu.
2. Enter the name of the new folder (sounds) and press **OK** to create the new folder.
3. Right-click over the newly added folder (**sounds**) and select **Add** from the context menu.
4. Select **Add Item** from the submenu.
5. Press the **Existing** tab of the Add Items dialog box and navigate to the folder that holds the sound files you want to add.
6. From the **Files of Type** drop-down menu, choose **Audio Files (*.wav; *.ra; *.ram; *.au; *.aiff)** to display the sound files.
7. Note that you can select multiple files in the same folder. Just highlight the items with your mouse or hold the Ctrl key down as you click on each file to add to your Web project.
8. After you have selected all the files in the folder, press the **Open** button to add them to the Web project.
9. Repeat steps 3 through 8 until you have added all the files you need.

Now you're ready to add sounds to your HTML document. With the target HTML document loaded in the Visual InterDev 6 editor (SOUNDS.HTM), move to the Project Explorer window and highlight one of the sound files. Now drag the file over the HTML document and drop it on a blank line. This will create a new HREF link in the document. Do this for each sound file you want to play in the document. Listing 9.2 shows how the BODY section of the document looks after adding links to four sound files. The text portion of the links has been edited for clarity.

LISTING 9.2   Results of Dropping Sound Links on an HTML Page

```
1  <a href="http://mca/Multimedia/sounds/GLASS.WAV">
   ➥Breaking Glass</a>
2  <a href="http://mca/Multimedia/sounds/tada.wav">
   ➥ Windows LogOff Sound</a>
3  <a href="http://mca/Multimedia/sounds/CANYON.MID">
   ➥Sample MIDI File</a>
4  <a href="http://mca/Multimedia/sounds/Beethoven's
   ➥%20Fur%20Elise.rmi">Fur Elise</a>
```

Now add a background sound to the document by adding the following HTML line in the <HEAD>...</HEAD> section of the page:

```
<bgsound SRC="sounds/tada.wav">
```

Be sure to use a valid sound filename for all the examples shown here.

Finally, add a simple HTML button to the page and set its **NAME** and **ID** values to btnSound and add the Visual Basic Script from Listing 9.3.

> **Sound strategies**
>
> Many Web sites offer remote controls for audio files. These remote controls allow visitors to turn on and off the sound files, rather than be forced to experience audio that they have an intense personal distaste for.

LISTING 9.3   Adding Visual Basic Script to Launch a Sound File

```
1   <script ID="clientEventHandlersVBS" LANGUAGE="vbscript">
2   <!--
3   Sub btnSound_onclick
4       ' cue up MIDI file
5       window.name = "Sounds" ' name this window
6       window.open "sounds/canyon.mid","Sounds"
        ➥'open in same window
7       '
8   End Sub
9   -->
10  </script>
```

When you're finished, your document should look close to the one shown in Figure 9.4.

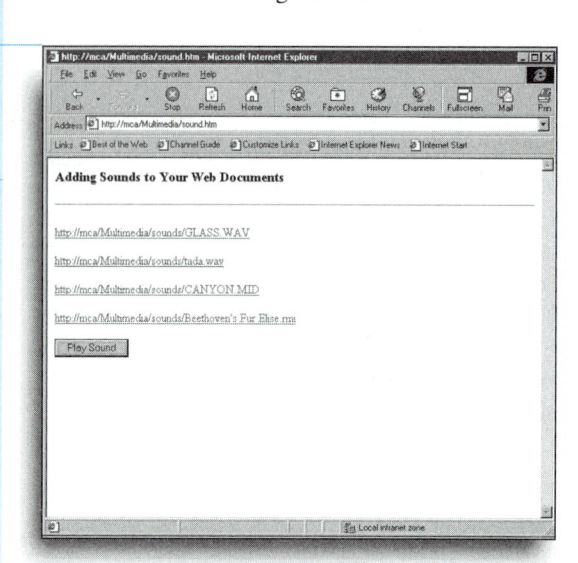

FIGURE 9.4

Viewing the completed SOUND.HTM document.

Label your sound files

Sound files, like all multimedia files, should be clearly labeled for visitors. If a visitor doesn't know she's about to download a large sound file that she doesn't want, she might take out her frustrations by not visiting your site again. Some sort of visual indication (be it text or images) that lets visitors know that a multimedia file will be opened by their actions will let them brace themselves for the consequences.

Save the document, mark it as the startup page, and press F5 to launch the document in your browser. If you have sound services installed on your workstation, you should now be able to hear a sound clip when you first load the page and play each of the sound clips behind the links and the command button.

Using the ActiveMovie Control to Add Video

You can also add video files to your Web pages using the ActiveMovie control. This ActiveX control ships with current versions of the Windows operating system and is also available with the Microsoft Internet Explorer installation.

ActiveMovie and the Windows Media Player

ActiveMovie has given way to Microsoft's Windows Media Player on Windows 95, 98, and NT. The concept and controls are the same but Media Player supports more formats.

The ActiveMovie control can be placed on any standard HTML document. You can then edit the object's settings in order to present the video file in a window embedded in the Web document. Figure 9.5 shows the ActiveMovie control as it appears in a Web document.

Notice the control buttons and displays that appear at the bottom of the video image. You can control just what appears (and what is enabled) using properties of the ActiveMovie control.

PART II
CHAPTER 9

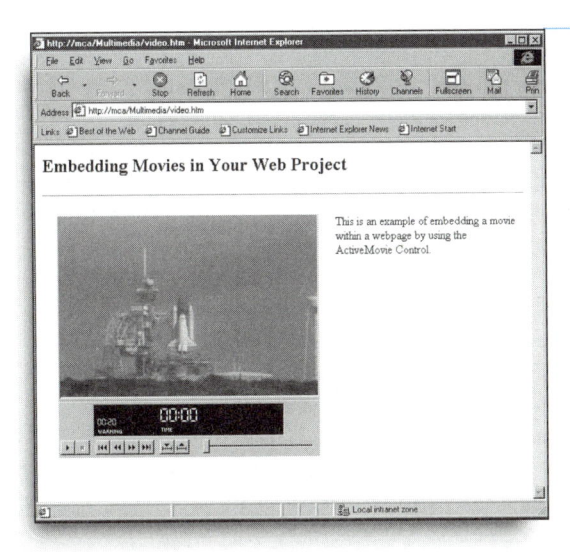

Adding Sound and Video

FIGURE 9.5
Using the ActiveMovie control to view a video file.

The OBJECT tag of the ActiveMovie control can be a bit intimidating. First, you do not need to type this information into your browser. It appears automatically when you drop the ActiveMovie control on the page. However, you do need to edit the PARAM values. Luckily, you need to know only a few of the essential PARAM settings. Listing 9.4 shows the OBJECT tag for the ActiveMovie control.

The presence of controls

Although removing playback controls is typically more visually aesthetic, it might be irritating or confusing for your visitors. ActiveMovie does support controls of media files by right-clicking the video image, but most users (especially novices) don't realize this. Consider the impact of removing the controls on users who might want to use them.

LISTING 9.4 Typical *OBJECT* Tag for the ActiveMovie Control

```
1   <OBJECT align=left
2       classid=CLSID:05589FA1-C356-11CE-BF01-00AA0055595A
        ➥height=322
3       hspace=20
4       id=ActiveMovie1
5       width=357 VIEWASTEXT>
6       <PARAM NAME="_ExtentX" VALUE="9446">
7       <PARAM NAME="_ExtentY" VALUE="8520">
8       <PARAM NAME="EnableContextMenu" VALUE="-1">
9       <PARAM NAME="ShowDisplay" VALUE="-1">
10       <PARAM NAME="ShowControls" VALUE="-1">
11       <PARAM NAME="ShowPositionControls" VALUE="-1">
12       <PARAM NAME="ShowSelectionControls" VALUE="-1">
13       <PARAM NAME="EnablePositionControls" VALUE="-1">
14       <PARAM NAME="EnableSelectionControls" VALUE="-1">
```

continues…

LISTING 9.4 Continued

```
15      <PARAM NAME="ShowTracker" VALUE="-1">
16      <PARAM NAME="EnableTracker" VALUE="-1">
17      <PARAM NAME="AllowHideDisplay" VALUE="-1">
18      <PARAM NAME="AllowHideControls" VALUE="-1">
19      <PARAM NAME="MovieWindowSize" VALUE="0">
20      <PARAM NAME="FullScreenMode" VALUE="0">
21      <PARAM NAME="MovieWindowWidth" VALUE="-1">
22      <PARAM NAME="MovieWindowHeight" VALUE="-1">
23      <PARAM NAME="AutoStart" VALUE="-1">
24      <PARAM NAME="AutoRewind" VALUE="-1">
25      <PARAM NAME="PlayCount" VALUE="1">
26      <PARAM NAME="SelectionStart" VALUE="0">
27      <PARAM NAME="SelectionEnd" VALUE="-1">
28      <PARAM NAME="Appearance" VALUE="1">
29      <PARAM NAME="BorderStyle" VALUE="1">
30      <PARAM NAME="FileName" VALUE="http://mca/Multimedia/
        ➥video/movie.avi">
31      <PARAM NAME="DisplayMode" VALUE="0">
32      <PARAM NAME="AllowChangeDisplayMode" VALUE="-1">
33      <PARAM NAME="DisplayForeColor" VALUE="16777215">
34      <PARAM NAME="DisplayBackColor" VALUE="0">
35      <PARAM NAME="Enabled" VALUE="-1">
36      <PARAM NAME="Rate" VALUE="1">
37  </OBJECT>
```

Long listings

Adding ActiveX controls, particularly ActiveMovie, creates incredibly long code listings. When you are trying to keep your code clean and neat, temptation is to remove the line feeds and keep the control code as a block. Don't do it! Keep each line clearly visible so that you can modify the attributes easily. The white-space (blank lines, spaces, tabs) in a Web document add negligible delay to the downloading of the page.

The most important PARAM value is the FileName PARAM on line 30. This is the video file to display within the window. You can also adjust the PARAMs that control the appearance and functionality of the buttons and progress displays (lines 10–18). By setting the FullScreenMode PARAM to –1 (true) you can force the ActiveMovie control to expand to fill the entire workstation. It is also a good idea to set the AutoStart and AutoRewind PARAMs (lines 23 and 24) to –1 (true).

Now that you have the basic idea of how the ActiveMovie control can be used, it's time to create a Web page that displays a video in your Microsoft Internet Explorer browser.

Adding Sound and Video

The ActiveMovie control might not have been installed when you installed your copy of Visual InterDev 6. If not, the first thing you must do is add the ActiveMovie control to your toolbox. To do this, edit the Toolbox window to include the new control.

Add the ActiveMovie control to your toolbox

1. Click the **ActiveX Controls** tab of the Toolbox window to open the list of loaded ActiveX controls.
2. Right-click over any item in the list and select **Customize Toolbox** from the context menu.
3. When the Customize Toolbox dialog appears, select the **ActiveX Controls** tab.
4. Locate and select the desired control (**ActiveMovieControl Object**) in the list. Be sure to set the check box **On**.
5. Press **OK** to add the selected control to the toolbox.

Next, make sure you have a valid AVI video file in the Web project. The example in this chapter uses the file MOVIE.AVI. You can download this file from the *Using Visual InterDev 6* Web site. Alternatively, you can use any valid AVI file you have available. Just be sure to add it to the Web project using the step-by-step procedure earlier in the chapter for adding sound files to your project.

Now that you have a copy of the ActiveMovie control added to your Visual InterDev 6 toolbox and a valid AVI file in your Web project, you're ready to create a new HTML document to play your video file.

First, add a new HTML document to the project called VIDEO.HTM. Next, switch the Visual InterDev 6 editor to **Source** mode and drag and drop the ActiveMovie control onto a blank line in the document between the `<BODY>` and `</BODY>` tags. You'll see the control object appear as a visual rectangle. You must switch it to text view instead. To do this, right-click on the borders of the ActiveMovie control and select **Always View as Text**. Now you should see the HTML `<OBJECT>` tag for the ActiveMovie control.

> **Where's the MOVIE.AVI file?**
>
> The video file used in this example can be downloaded from the *Using Visual InterDev 6* home page (see Appendix B for the address). You can also use any AVI file you have available for this example.

> **AVIs are big**
>
> The Microsoft Video for Windows AVI (or Audio Visual Interleave) format is no space saver. AVI files tend to be big and bloated. To their credit, however, they do tend to be of much better quality than, say, a Real Video file. Consider the size of video that is being sent to the browser. Even though ActiveMovie can play the video as it is being streamed to the computer, it still can be slow due to the size. AVIs are often best for intranets and high-bandwidth Web sites. A final note: Always warn visitors about the size of the video, just in case!

The last step is to add the PARAM values to the control so that it will play the video file when the page is first loaded. Listing 9.5 shows the PARAM elements to add to the ActiveMovie object. Be sure to use the proper value for the FileName PARAM based on your Web server and the location of your video file.

LISTING 9.5 PARAM Elements to Add to the ActiveMovie Object

```
1  <OBJECT
2      align=left
3      classid=CLSID:05589FA1-C356-11CE-BF01-00AA0055595A
4      height=322
5      width=357
6      hspace=20
7      id=ActiveMovie1
8      VIEWASTEXT>
9      <PARAM NAME="AutoStart" VALUE="-1">
10     <PARAM NAME="AutoRewind" VALUE="-1">
11     <PARAM NAME="FileName" VALUE="http://mca/Multimedia/
       ➥video/movie.avi">
12 </OBJECT>
```

AutoStart and AutoRewind

You can use the AutoStart and AutoRewind parameters to control the experience for your site's visitors. However, keep in mind the preferences of your visitors. If it maintains consistency with your site's design, consider user selectable options for AutoStart and AutoRewind.

Why not use the property page?

The ActiveMovie control's property page is missing key PARAM settings. For this reason, it is better to convert the control to text and edit the PARAMs yourself.

If you compare Listing 9.5 with Listing 9.4 you'll get an idea of the number of optional parameters you can use with the ActiveMovie control. In fact, the only required PARAM for the control is FileName. The rest are optional.

After completing the PARAM tags, save the document, mark it as the startup page, and press F5 to launch it in your browser. The results should look like those of Figure 9.5.

Using the DirectX Animation Controls to Add Advanced Graphics

The rest of this chapter is devoted to three ActiveX controls that implement the Microsoft DirectX Animation services. These controls enable you to add predefined sprites, control the movement of graphical objects along a preset path, and draw and animate polygons.

Using the DirectX Animation Controls to Add Advanced Graphics

- The Sprite control accepts a set of images and displays them in sequence to show animation.
- The Path control accepts an image and moves it along a predetermined path.
- The Structured Graphics control gives you low-level access to drawing, coloring, and moving various polygons within a predefined area.

Although each control offers several options, you can also combine these three controls in various ways to get complex graphics displays. For example, you can use the Structured Graphics control to draw a shape and then use the Path control to move that shape about the document. You can also apply the Path control to a sprite.

One of the key benefits of these controls is that they all operate on the client side. In other words, you can use them to provide advanced graphics services without having to make calls to the Web server for additional data or images. This means that the graphics are rendered very quickly and that they are very responsive to user input.

As with the other controls covered in this chapter, these are ActiveX controls that were designed for use with Microsoft Internet Explorer. You should keep this limitation in mind when adding the controls to your Web application.

Locating the DirectAnimation Controls in Visual InterDev 6

The DirectAnimation controls covered in this chapter should have been installed when you installed your copy of Visual InterDev 6. To confirm this, click on the **ActiveX Controls** tab of the Toolbox window. You should see a list that is similar to the one in Figure 9.6.

If you do not see these three controls in your toolbox, you can add them by following the steps for adding the ActiveMovie control outline earlier in this chapter (see Figure 9.7).

DirectAnimation's DirectX relations

DirectAnimation can be considered part of the DirectX suite for Windows 95, 98, and NT. DirectX empowers developers to create multimedia experiences (games, audio, video) without having to write low-level support for the myriad of hardware devices on the market. The hardware manufacturer creates a DirectX driver (DirectAudio for sound cards, DirectVideo for video cards, Direct3D for 3D cards, and so on) and developers use Microsoft's DirectX platform to create applications. Consider the alternative, which is to write a program and develop hardware drivers for every piece of equipment out there. Yuck.

It's a Microsoft world

A common thread throughout this book has been "This only works in Microsoft Internet Explorer." DirectAnimation is no different. Plan around visitors who might not be using Microsoft Internet Explorer as their Web browser so that they do not miss out on the experience. After all, who really wants to switch browsers just to visit a Web site?

FIGURE 9.6

Viewing the DirectAnimation controls in the Toolbox window.

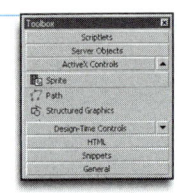

FIGURE 9.7

Adding the missing DirectAnimation controls to the toolbox.

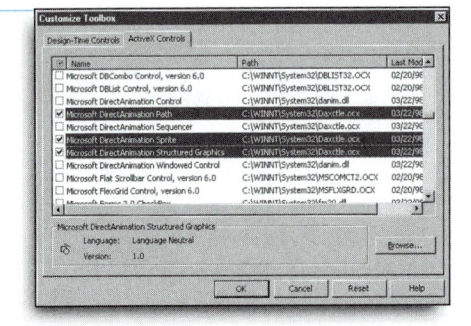

Other DirectAnimation controls

There are actually more than three controls that comprise DirectAnimation. Other controls include Microsoft DirectAnimation Sequence and Microsoft DirectAnimation Windowed Control.

Add the following three control files to your toolbox:

- Microsoft DirectAnimation Path
- Microsoft DirectAnimation Sprite
- Microsoft DirectAnimation Structured Graphics

All three of these items are stored in the DAXCTLE.OCX file.

After you have them loaded in your toolbox, you're ready to start using them in your Visual InterDev 6 projects.

Using the Sprite Control

The GIF advantage

Of course, the real advantage behind animated GIFs isn't their size, it's their support. You can safely assume almost everyone can see an animated GIF. Can you say the same for a DirectAnimation sprite?

The Sprite control enables you to create a single graphical element that is actually a combination of several graphics. By combining them in a sequence you can give the appearance of animation. This enables you to create items that look as if they are a type of animated GIF. However, sprite-animated graphics are usually faster and can be smaller than some animated GIFs.

Using the DirectX Animation Controls to Add Advanced Graphics

For this example, you use a special GIF file that contains 18 different frames. Each frame holds a slightly different view of the earth as it spins on its axis. You can use the Sprite control to present each frame in sequence and give the appearance of a spinning globe (see Figure 9.8).

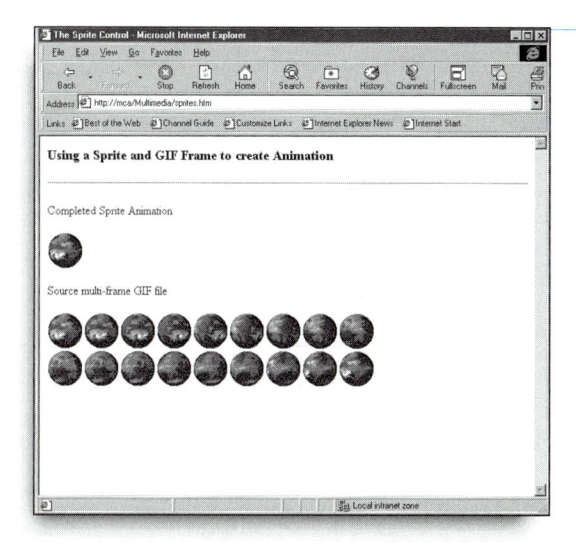

FIGURE 9.8
Viewing the GIF frames as a sprite.

It's relatively easy to create an HTML document that displays a multiframe GIF as a sprite. First, add a new HTML document to the current project called SPRITES.HTM. Next, with the Visual InterDev 6 editor in Source mode, drag and drop a DirectAnimation Sprite control onto a blank line in the body of the page. Finally, right-click over the border of the sprite control and select **Always View As Text** from the context menu. You should now see the complete `<OBJECT>...</OBJECT>` tag for the Sprite control.

Now use the information in Table 9.1 to update the various `PARAM` values of the object. You must change only the ones shown in Table 9.1. You can leave the rest of the items at their default values.

Get the GIF

You can download the EARTH-GRID.GIF file from the *Using Visual InterDev 6* home page (see Appendix B for the address).

TABLE 9.1 Setting the *PARAM* values of the sprite object

PARAM	VALUE
SourceURL	Images/earthgrid.gif
AutoStart	1
NumFramesAcross	9
NumFramesDown	2
NumFrames	18
MouseEventsEnabled	0
FrameMap	1,100,,;2,100,,;3,100,,;4,100,,;5,100,,;6,100,,;7,100,,;8,100,,;9,100,,;10,100,,;11,100,,;12,100,,;13,100,,;14,100,,;15,100,,;16,100,,;17,100,,;18,100,,;

The last PARAM is the most interesting of the list. This identifies each frame and how long (in milliseconds) it will be displayed. Of course, the SourceURL PARAM is also pretty important! Be sure it points to the proper place in your Web project. Notice also that the NumFrames, NumFramesAcross, and NumFramesDown properties are used to help the Sprite control understand the contents of EARTHGRID.GIF.

After you've completed your PARAM editing, add an IMG element to the page to display the raw source GIF. The following HTML code can be added right after the </OBJECT> tag of the Sprite control:

```
<p>Source multi-frame GIF file</p>
<img SRC="images/EarthGrid.gif" WIDTH="450" HEIGHT="100">
```

Now save the document, mark it as the startup page, and press F5 to launch the document in your browser. It should look a lot like the document in Figure 9.8.

Moving Graphics with the Path Control

You can use the DirectAnimation Path control to move another object around the page. You can move graphical items, or even text. In this example, you'll move some images around a predefined oval path.

DirectAnimation and MSIE 3

DirectAnimation is part of Microsoft Internet Explorer 4.0 and higher. Internet Explorer 3.0 users are left out in the cold along with Netscape users.

Using the DirectX Animation Controls to Add Advanced Graphics

First, add a new document to the project called PATHCON-TROL.HTM and set its `DefaultClientScripting` property to **Visual Basic Script**. Now, with the document loaded and the Visual InterDev 6 editor in Source mode, drag and drop a DirectAnimation Path control from the Toolbox window onto a blank line in the PATHCONTROL.HTM document. Finally, right-click over the border of the path control and select **Always View As Text** from the context menu.

Use the information in Table 9.2 to edit the path control OBJECT attributes and PARAM values. Note that the first three entries are attributes of the <OBJECT> tag and the next three items are PARAM entries. Finally, the last item must be added to the list of PARAM entries.

Think of paths as a map for sprites

Paths define the movement behavior for sprites. You can use this to create complex actions and movements that otherwise might not be possible without using an extension like Macromedia Flash (`http://www.macromedia.com`).

TABLE 9.2 Editing the path control object

Item Type	Name	Value
OBJECT ATTRIBUTE	ID	ObjPath
	HEIGHT	11
	WIDTH	11
PARAM	Duration	4
	Repeat	-1
	Shape	OVAL(200,10,200,200)

After you've edited the path control, your HTML code should look like the code in Listing 9.6.

LISTING 9.6 Completed Path Control *OBJECT* and *PARAM* Settings

```
1  <!-- path object -->
2  <OBJECT classid="CLSID:D7A7D7C3-D47F-11D0-89D3-
   ➥00A0C90833E6"
3    id=objPath
4    style="LEFT: 0px; TOP: 0px"
5    height=11
6    width=11
7    VIEWASTEXT>
8    <PARAM NAME="Autostart" VALUE="0">
```

continues...

LISTING 9.6 Continued

```
9      <PARAM NAME="Bounce" VALUE="0">
10     <PARAM NAME="Direction" VALUE="0">
11     <PARAM NAME="Duration" VALUE="4">
12     <PARAM NAME="Repeat" VALUE="-1">
13     <PARAM NAME="Target" VALUE="">
14     <PARAM NAME="Relative" VALUE="0">
15     <PARAM NAME="TimerInterval" VALUE="0.1">
16     <PARAM NAME="Shape" VALUE="OVAL(200,10,200,200)">
17 </OBJECT>
```

Now you must add a button element and an image element to the document. The image element will hold the current image, and the button element will be used to toggle the image display.

Listing 9.7 shows the HTML coding needed to complete both the button and image elements for this document.

LISTING 9.7 Adding the Button and Image Elements to the Document

```
1  <input
2      type="button"
3      name="btnImage"
4      value="Toggle Image"
5      style="position:relative">
6  <p>
7  <img
8      src="images/pin.gif"
9      id="imgSource"
10     style="position:relative"
11     WIDTH="39"
12     HEIGHT="126">
```

After you have added all the HTML elements, you're ready to add a touch of Visual Basic Scripting to the page. The Visual Basic Script will initiate the predefined path when the page first loads and will respond to user clicks on the button.

Add a client scripting block (select **HTML**, **Script Block**, **Client** from the main menu) and enter the Visual Basic Script from Listing 9.8 into the code block.

Using the DirectX Animation Controls to Add Advanced Graphics

LISTING 9.8 Adding the Visual Basic Scripting to the Document

```
1  <script ID="clientEventHandlersVBS" LANGUAGE="vbscript">
2  <!--
3  ' shared var
4  Dim intImage
5  intImage=0
6
7  Sub window_onload
8      ' start with pin image
9      btnImage_onclick
10     '
11 End Sub
12
13 Sub btnImage_OnClick
14     ' use pin image
15     objPath.target = "imgSource"
16     if intImage = 1 then
17        imgSource.src = "images/pin.gif"
18        intImage = 0
19     else
20        imgSource.src="images/candle.gif"
21        intImage=1
22     end if
23     objPath.play
24     '
25 End Sub
26 -->
27 </script>
```

The only important code is in lines 15–23 of Listing 9.8. This is where the path control is initiated with the item to move (line 15) and the actual image to display in the `imgSource` element is determined (lines 16–22). Finally, after the image is set, the item is actually put into motion (`objPath.play`) on line 23. The only other code is the line in the `window_onload` event that executes the `onclick` event of the button when the page first loads.

When you are finished adding the Visual Basic Script, save the document, mark it as the startup page, and press F5 to view the document in your browser. The results should look close to those in Figure 9.9.

Scripting complex DirectAnimation events

You can intermix DirectAnimation with both sever- and client-side script. Use server-side script to engineer the interface components and attributes for the client-side DirectAnimation control. One possibility is to use preferences specified by the user that are stored on the server side. These preferences would then modify the behavior of the control on the client.

FIGURE 9.9

Viewing the path control in action.

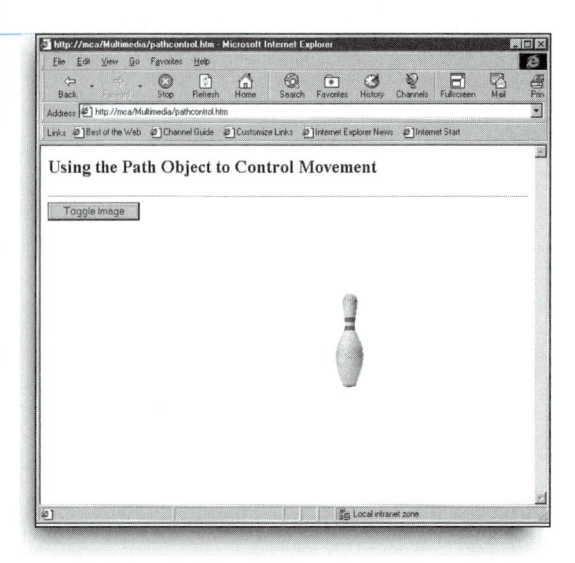

When you press the **Toggle Image** command button, you'll see that the image toggles between the bowling pin and the candlestick. Note that the changing of the image does not disrupt the path of the image.

Drawing Complex Shapes with the Structured Graphics Control

The last DirectAnimation control covered in this chapter is the Structured Graphics control. This control is the most powerful of the three DirectAnimation controls covered here. It is also the most complicated. The Structured Graphics control is designed to give programmers the power to create polygons of various shapes and sizes, color these items as they want, and rotate the items in three-dimensional space.

In this example, you'll learn how to use the Structured Graphics control to build a single item that actually has three shapes inside it. Also, you'll design one of the shapes to rotate with the graphics container. Finally, you'll learn how you can rotate the entire composite graphical item along the X, Y, and Z axes.

Chrome

The next step after the Structured Graphics Control is Microsoft's Chrome package. Chrome is a series of extensions that allow developers to create complex 3-D graphics, as opposed to simple polygons. This comes at a price though—Chrome requires a 300Mhz or higher computer to view the effects.

Using the DirectX Animation Controls to Add Advanced Graphics

Before jumping into the details of programming with the Structured Graphics control (SGC), it will be helpful to get a quick summary of the possible methods you can apply to the SGC. Because the SGC was designed to enable programmers to draw just about any shape needed, there are quite a few methods and properties for programmers to deal with. Table 9.3 lists the important methods of the SGC and a short explanation of their uses.

More information

You can obtain more information on DirectAnimation and Chrome by visiting the Microsoft SiteBuilder's Workshop on the World Wide Web. Point your Web browser (Internet Explorer, of course) to `http://www.microsoft.com/sitebuilder`.

TABLE 9.3 Methods of the Structured Graphics control

Method	Description
`Arc`	Creates a single circular or elliptical arc
`FillSpline`	Creates a closed spline shape, defined by a series of points
`Oval`	Creates an ellipse
`Pie`	Creates an elliptical arc closed at the center of the bounding rectangle to form a wedge (pie) shape
`Polygon`	Creates a closed polygon
`PolyLine`	Creates a segmented line
`PolySpline`	Creates an open spline shape, defined by a series of points
`Rect`	Creates a rectangle
`RoundRect`	Creates a rounded rectangle
`SetFillColor`	Sets the foreground and background colors for graphic fills
`SetFillStyle`	Sets the type of fill
`SetFont`	Sets the font for the control
`SetGradientFill`	Specifies the start- and endpoints for a gradient fill
`SetGradientShape`	Sets the shape of a gradient to be an outline of a polygon shape
`SetHatchFill`	Specifies whether the hatch fill is transparent
`SetLineColor`	Sets the line color for drawing graphics

continues...

TABLE 9.3 Continued

Method	Description
`SetLineStyle`	Changes the line style for the current shape
`SetTextureFill`	Sets the texture source to be used to fill a structured graphics shape
Text	Creates a string with the current font and color

You can see from Table 9.3 that you can draw nine different shapes with the SGC. You also have nine different methods for coloring and shading the shapes. Finally, the SGC can also accept text as the shape to manipulate. This enables you to treat text as a graphic item.

Six other methods you can use with the SGC enable you to manipulate the control during runtime:

- `Clear` clears the control of any current settings.
- `SetIdentity` sets the shape collection to its original (default) state.
- `Rotate` rotates the entire control (including all active shapes).
- `Scale` enables you to scale the shape collection up or down.
- `Translate` enables you to adjust the x, y, and z coordinates of the shape collection.
- `Transform4x4` enables you to set scaling, rotating, and translation values simultaneously.

You will not use all these methods here. However, this will give you a pretty good idea of the power and sophistication of the Structured Graphics control.

Use the Structured Graphics control

1. For this example, add a new HTML document, called SGRAPHICS.HTM, to the current Web.
2. Set the page's `DefaultClientScripting` property to **Visual Basic Script**.

Structured graphic effects

You can achieve remarkable effects that can be combined into your Web site's interface using SGC. The biggest potential lies in incorporating dynamic data, such as user input, to create your effects. Experiment with scripting dynamic data into an SGC and start playing with the possibilities.

Using the DirectX Animation Controls to Add Advanced Graphics

3. Now, with the Visual InterDev 6 editor in Source mode, drag the Structured Graphics control from the Toolbox window over the HTML, document and drop it on a blank line between the `<BODY>` and `</BODY>` tags.

4. Next, right-click on the SGC's border and select **Always View as Text** from the context menu. This will expose the `<OBJECT>` tag of the control.

5. Finally, edit the `OBJECT` tag so that its `ID` and `STYLE` attributes match those shown in Listing 9.9.

LISTING 9.9 Completed Structured Graphics *OBJECT* Tag

```
1  <OBJECT classid="CLSID:369303C2-D7AC-11d0-89D5-
   ↪00A0C90833E6"
2     id=sgShapes
3     style="HEIGHT: 400px;
4            LEFT: 10px;
5            TOP: 100px;
6            WIDTH: 400px;
7            Z-INDEX: -1;
8            POSITION: ABSOLUTE;"
9    VIEWASTEXT>
10   <PARAM NAME="SourceURL" VALUE="">
11   <PARAM NAME="CoordinateSystem" VALUE="0">
12   <PARAM NAME="MouseEventsEnabled" VALUE="0">
13   <PARAM NAME="HighQuality" VALUE="0">
14   <PARAM NAME="PreserveAspectRatio" VALUE="-1">
15 </OBJECT>
```

Next, you must add three buttons to the document. These will be used to toggle the rotation of the X, Y, and Z axes during runtime. Listing 9.10 shows the completed HTML coding for the three buttons. Place this code directly under the SGC `</OBJECT>` tag.

> **Quality and aspect**
>
> Lines 13 and 14 reference two special parameters: **HighQuality** and **PreserveAspectRatio**. You can use these controls to control how the SGC will appear on your visitor's screen. Experiment with different settings so that you can see the results.

LISTING 9.10 Coding the HTML Buttons for the Document

```
1 <!-- toggle buttons -->
2 <input type="button" value="Toggle X" id=btnToggleX
  name=btnToggleX>
3 <input type="button" value="Toggle Y" id=btnToggleY
  name=btnToggleY>
4 <input type="button" value="Toggle Z" id=btnToggleZ
  name=btnToggleZ>
```

Now that all the HTML coding is complete, you're ready to add the Visual Basic Scripting that makes all the magic happen. You will use Visual Basic Scripting to animate the three buttons and perform all the needed work to define and set into motion the structured graphical shapes.

First, you must declare some shared variables and then execute the top-level Visual Basic Scripting that will use the Structured Graphics control to build three shapes and set them into motion. Add a client-side script block to your page and enter the code from Listing 9.11 into the block.

LISTING 9.11 Adding the Top-Level Visual Basic Scripting to Build and Animate the Shapes

```
1 <SCRIPT LANGUAGE="VBScript">
2 '
3 ' shared vars
4 dim dsArea
5 dim sgLibrary
6 dim intX
7 dim intY
8 dim intZ
9 '
10 ' starting values
11 intX=2
12 intY=0
13 intZ=2
14
15 '********************
16 ' main routine
17 '
```

An example of SGC and motion

If you've ever used Microsoft Internet Explorer Active Setup/Update on the World Wide Web to add components to your MSIE installation, you've probably seen SGC in action. As the Web-based Active Setup downloads and installs components, a 3D Internet Explorer logo flies through the background of the page. Great demo, isn't it?

Using the DirectX Animation Controls to Add Advanced Graphics

```
18 Set sgLibrary = sgShapes.Library ' point to library
19 Set dsArea = sgShapes.DrawSurface ' point to
   ➥drawing space
20 '
21 BuildSquare
22 BuildOval
23 '
24 dsArea.SaveGraphicsState() ' save current set
25 '
26 BuildRotatingRectangle
27 '
28 dsArea.RestoreGraphicsState()' restore old set
29 sgShapes.DrawSurface = dsArea ' fetch completed set
30 '
31 RotateAll ' start rendering the images
32 '
33 ' end of main routine
34 '*****************
35
36 </script>
```

Several things in Listing 9.11 deserve comment. First, after declaring (and initializing) several shared variables (lines 3–13), the main routine appears. This routine first gets pointers to the graphics library (line 18) and the drawing space area (line 19) object within the structured graphics control.

Then four things happen. First, methods are called to build the square and oval objects (lines 21 and 22). Next, the method to build a rotating rectangle object is called on line 26. Because you'll be adding animation features to the rectangle, the current drawing state is first saved (line 24) and, after the rectangle is built, restored (lines 28 and 29). Finally, a method is called to start rotating the entire complex graphic (line 31).

After adding the code from Listing 9.11, you must add the code that will build the square and oval objects. Building these objects is quite simple. You first set the color and then execute the square or oval method with the proper sizing values. Listing 9.12 shows the code to do just that. Add this to your HTML document right after the code from Listing 9.11.

Introducing more complexity

It isn't difficult to see after Listing 9.11 that you are beginning to work with more complex scripting than most controls require. To fully realize the potential of DirectAnimation, you will need to work with fairly intricate scripts. This is, of course, a great lead in to Dynamic HTML.

LISTING 9.12 Adding the Visual Basic Scripting to Build the Square and Oval Objects

```
1  Sub BuildSquare
2      '
3      dsArea.fillcolor sgLibrary.blue ' set color
4      dsArea.rect -50,-50,200,200 ' set shape
5      '
6  End Sub
7
8  Sub BuildOval
9      '
10     dsArea.fillcolor sglibrary.silver ' set color
11     dsArea.oval -60,-60, 120, 120 ' set shape
12     '
13 End Sub
```

Next, you must add the Visual Basic Scripting method that will build the rotating rectangle. To do this, you must first use the `transform` method to establish the rotation rate, then set the color, and finally define the rectangle. Listing 9.13 shows the Visual Basic Scripting code that accomplishes this.

LISTING 9.13 Visual Basic Scripting Code to Build a Rotating Rectangle

```
1  Sub BuildRotatingRectangle
2      '
3      dsArea.transform sgLibrary.rotate2rate(5) 'set rotation
4      dsArea.fillcolor sgLibrary.red ' set color
5      dsArea.rect -20, -100, 40,200 ' set share
6      '
7  End Sub
```

The last bit of Visual Basic Scripting code for handling the SGC is the code that will rotate the entire complex graphic in the browser space. To do this, you just need to use the `rotate` method for the control and then execute the `timeout` method in order to repeat the rotation indefinitely. Listing 9.14 shows you how this is done.

LISTING 9.14 Rotating the Entire Graphic in the Browser Space

```
1  Sub RotateAll
2      '
```

Using the DirectX Animation Controls to Add Advanced Graphics

```
3    sgShapes.rotate intX,intY,intZ ' rotate everything
4    window.setTimeout "RotateAll",50 ' repeat loop
5    '
6 End Sub
```

There is just one more set of Visual Basic Scripting code you must add to this document. The `RotateAll` method uses three values for controlling rotation (`intX`, `intY`, `intZ`). These can be toggled between `0` (no movement) and `2` (a slow rate of movement) by pressing the three command buttons on the page. You must add Visual Basic Scripting code that will toggle the values during the button's `onclick` event. Listing 9.15 has the final bits of Visual Basic Scripting code you need to add to this page.

SGC project challenge

After you've completed the example in this chapter with SGC, here's a challenge for you to try. Using SGC and DirectAnimation, build an interactive library of shapes that a user can interact with. Add functionality for users to change shape properties and attributes as they interact with the page. This challenge is a great opportunity to integrate client- and server-side script.

LISTING 9.15 **The Visual Basic Scripting Code to Respond to the Button's *onclick* Event**

```
1  Sub btnToggleX_onclick
2    '
3    if intX=0 then
4        intX=2
5    else
6        intX=0
7    end if
8    '
9  End Sub
10
11 Sub btnToggleY_onclick
12   '
13   if intY=0 then
14       intY=2
15   else
16       intY=0
17   end if
18   '
19 End Sub
20
21 Sub btnToggleZ_onclick
22   '
23   if intZ=0 then
24       intZ=2
```

continues…

LISTING 9.15 Continued

```
25     else
26         intZ=0
27     end if
28     '
29 End Sub
```

Once again: always consider the impact

This can never be repeated too much: Always consider the impact of what you do. Complex SGC pages, as with the rest of DirectAnimation, place a considerable burden on your visitor's Windows operating system. Make sure that you don't strangle the visitor's computer with a routine that is too complex for it to handle.

Now save the document, mark it as the startup page, and press F5 to launch the document in your browser. You will see a screen showing the completed graphic rotating along the X and Z axes. You can affect the rotation by pressing on the command buttons. If you hit the right combination of buttons, you can make the graphic stand still (see Figure 9.10).

SEE ALSO

➤ *Scripting these kinds of events is very similar to Dynamic HTML. When you want to introduce DHTML into your pages, see page 750*

FIGURE 9.10

Viewing the contents of the Structured Graphics control.

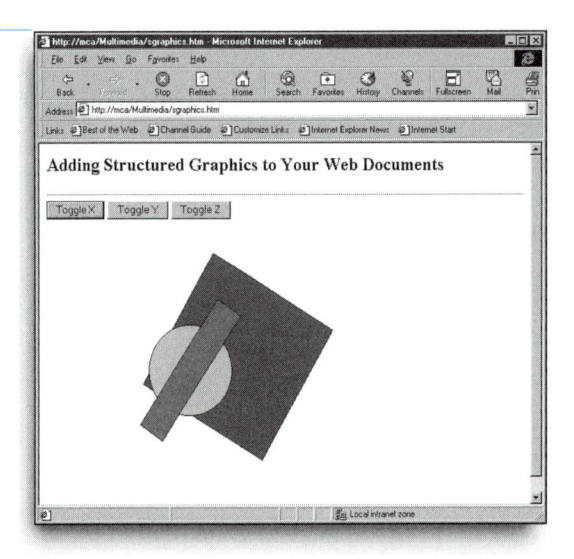

CHAPTER 10

Creating and Using Image Maps

- Learn the theory behind client-side image maps
- Define client-side image maps for your images
- Link URLs to your image mapping

What Are Client-Side Image Maps?

First, an image map is pretty much what you'd think it might be. Specifically, an image map is a graphical image that has a set of two-dimensional coordinates associated with the image. In addition, for each of the coordinates there is an optional URL (Uniform Resource Locator) associated. When users click somewhere on the image within the bounds of one of the coordinates in the set, the browser sends that user to the associated URL.

Another way to think of image map files is that they are a way to mark multiple "hot spots" within a single image and tie those hot spots to URL links that can be used by the browser. This is quite similar to the concept of segmented hypergraphics used by the Windows Help Files.

Originally, image maps were sent to the browser, but after the user clicked somewhere on the image, the coordinates were sent to the server. There, a special routine inspected the coordinates and then returned the associated URL. The most recent version of HTML browsers supports a version of image maps called *client-side* image maps. Client-side image maps send all the details of the image map down to the browser and let the browser determine which URL to link to each of the coordinates in the set. Client-side image maps are much easier to work with and modify, and they are the kind of image maps you'll work with in this chapter.

Advantages of Client-Side Image Maps

The biggest advantage of image maps is that you can present a single graphical image and provide multiple URLs associated with the image. Many Web applications use the image map as a "welcome" screen. This enables you to quickly download a single image to the client and provide several links for the client to work with. This is much faster than sending multiple images, each with its own associated URL.

Second, image maps are easy to maintain and update—especially client-side image maps. Because there is no manipulation of the image itself, you can easily redefine a coordinate region in the

---

Server-side image maps require additional programming

If you want to support server-side image maps instead of client-side maps, you will need additional software running on the server to accept the coordinate values from the client and translate them into new URL addresses. Server-side image map support is not covered in this book.

Creating a Client-Side Image Map   PART II CHAPTER 10

image, add or delete regions, and so on without having to reprocess the image itself.

Finally, because all the URL and coordinate data is simple ASCII text that can be added to any HTML page, you can keep this kind of information in a database and use ASP documents to generate the appropriate coordinates and URLs for each connected client. This makes it easy to generate image maps based on user level or client preferences, too.

SEE ALSO
➤ *To learn how to use images as the Submit button on a form, see page 153*

Client-Side Image Map Drawbacks

The key drawback to using client-side image maps is that some older browsers will not support them. You must test your Web application against several browsers to make sure it will work properly. However, if you are creating a Web application for use inside an organization, you can usually count on browsers that will support image maps (or easily upgrade the clients to versions that do support them).

Another drawback to image maps is that they are invisible. You can't automatically have each coordinate region appear outlined on the image map. This can mislead or confuse some users. Although it is possible to modify the image to include a border that matches the coordinate regions defined in the image map, this is often unpractical and can fall "out-of-sync" with the map coordinates if you are generating the maps dynamically. Usually, you must include some text on the page instructing users to move their mouse over the image to see where the coordinate regions appear.

Creating a Client-Side Image Map

Creating a client-side image map for any graphical image in your Web application is really quite simple. All you must do is drop an image on the page and then use the Source view of the Visual InterDev Editor to add some HTML coding that defines the map and associates it with the image.

Add ToolTips for your image maps

If you add the `TITLE` attribute to your `<AREA>` elements in an image map, most browsers will add a pop-up ToolTip to your image maps when users move their mouse over the image.

Creating and Using Image Maps

For this example, start Visual InterDev and either create a new Web project or load an existing one where you can add a new document. After you have your host Web project loaded into Visual InterDev, add a new document called IMAGEMAP.HTM and bring it up in Design mode.

SEE ALSO
➤ *To learn how to create a new Web project, see page 12.*

Importing an Image File into Your Web Project

Next, load an image into the Web project to use as the basis for the image map. If you don't already have an image available in your Web project, you can use the Project Explorer window to browse your workstation (or any connected network resources) and add an image to your project (see Figure 10.1).

Importing images into your project

1. Right-click over the **Images** folder in the Project Explorer window.
2. Select **Add** from the context menu.
3. Select **Add Item** from the submenu.
4. Select the **Existing** tab to expose the file dialog window.
5. Switch the **Files of type:** pull-down at the bottom of the dialog to display **Image Files**.
6. Use the **Look in:** pull-down to navigate to an area on your workstation that contains a graphical image you want to use in your Web application.
7. When you find the image you want to import, select it and press the **Open** button to add it your Web project.

SEE ALSO
➤ *For more on designing Web documents, see page 57*

Windows filenames are not case-sensitive

The examples in this book show disk filenames in all uppercase letters so you can easily identify the filenames in the text. In the Windows operating system filenames are not case sensitive and any mix of upper- and lowercase letters is treated the same as all upper- or all lowercase.

Creating a Client-Side Image Map | CHAPTER 10

FIGURE 10.1
Importing an image file into the current Web project.

Placing the Image on Your Web Document

The next task is to place the image on your Web document. The easiest way to do this is to simply drag the image from the Project Explorer window and drop it on the page. After you do this, the image will appear on the document ready for you to define an image map.

However, before defining the map for this image, you must do just a bit more HTML coding in the Source view of the Visual InterDev editor. You must add the USEMAP attribute to tell the browser that an image map is associated with this graphical image.

You also should add the optional HEIGHT and WIDTH attributes to control the exact size of display of the image. Although this is not required, failing to do this can result in invalid map coordinates.

Finally, you can add the BORDER=0 attribute to prevent the client browser from painting a border around the image. This is optional, but will help the image look a bit cleaner in the browser window.

Listing 10.1 shows the modified HTML coding for the <IMG> tag that contains the image. Make sure your coding looks like the one in Listing 10.1 (except for the name and location of the image file).

> **Setting image height and width can avoid invalid image maps**
>
> It is a good idea to explicitly set the HEIGHT and WIDTH attributes of the image that will be used in the image map. This can avoid problems with invalid map coordinates if the image file is ever altered or resized.

LISTING 10.1

① This is the line that indicates which <MAP> element is associated with this image.

LISTING 10.1 **Adjusted HTML Coding for the Image File**

```
1 <P align=center>
2 <IMG
3    USEMAP=#MyMAP
4    SRC="images/arrows.gif"
5    BORDER=0
6    WIDTH=400
7    HEIGHT=400>
8 </P>
```

Listing 10.1 shows that the image ARROWS.GIF in the images subfolder will be displayed on the page (line 4). The name and location of your image file might not match this one. That's okay.

The USEMAP attribute (line 3) tells the browser that there is a section in this document with the name MYMAP that contains a set of coordinates and associated URLs. You build this map in the next section.

Lines 6 and 7 tell the browser to display the image in a 400-pixel-by-400-pixel square. For this example, it is important that you use these values for your image. These values outline the boundaries of the image, and these boundaries will be used as part of the coordinates. It is always a good idea to explicitly add the HEIGHT and WIDTH attributes to image mapped images.

Figure 10.2 shows the results of loading the image onto the page.

FIGURE 10.2

Viewing the image file loaded into the document.

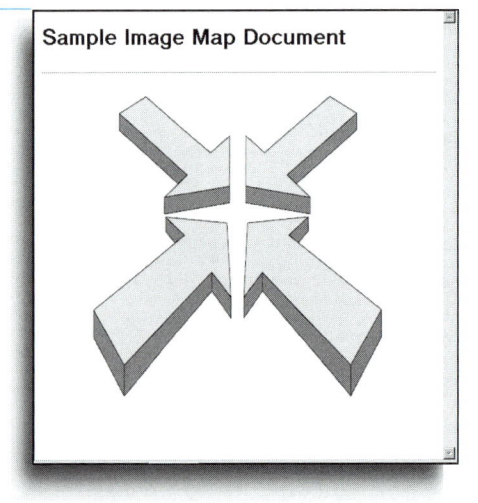

Now that the image is loaded onto the page, you're ready to create a set of map coordinates.

SEE ALSO
➤ *To learn how to control the exact placement of an image in the browser, see page 749*

Adding Map Coordinates to Your Image Files

After you have an image loaded onto your page, you can add the USEMAP attribute to associate the image with a set of map coordinates. These coordinates will contain a shape type, a set of numbers to define the shape, and a URL to associate with the defined region on the map. Each coordinate region is held in an <AREA> HTML tag. The set of defined regions is surrounded by the <MAP> and </MAP> HTML tags.

Understanding the <MAP> and <AREA> HTML Tags

All the magic of client-side image maps occurs within the <MAP> and </MAP> HTML tags. Inside this tag set is a list of <AREA> tags that define each hot spot in the image. It is these hot spots that allow users to click on areas within the image and move to other documents in your Web project.

Listing 10.2 shows the basic HTML coding syntax for building client-side image maps in your HTML documents.

LISTING 10.2 Basic HTML Coding of Client-Side Image Maps

```
1  <MAP name=MyMAP>
2      <AREA
3          SHAPE=RECT
4          COORDS=0,0,200,160
5          HREF="rectangle.htm">
6      <AREA
7          SHAPE=CIRCLE
8          COORDS=10,10,5
9          HREF="circle.htm">
```

LISTING 10.2

① This is the same name you find in the USEMAP attribute of the associated image element.

continues…

LISTING 10.2 Continued

```
10    <AREA
11        SHAPE=POLYGON
12        COORDS=10,50,15,20,20,50
13        HREF="triangle.htm">
14    <AREA
15        SHAPE=DEFAULT                          ❷
16        HREF="default.htm"
17    <AREA
18        SHAPE=RECT
19        COORDS=100,100,150,200
20        NOHREF                                 ❸
21    </MAP>
```

LISTING 10.2 CONTINUED

❷ This will use the entire image as a single clickable region.

❸ Use the NOHREF attribute to explictly document that no URL is associated with this region.

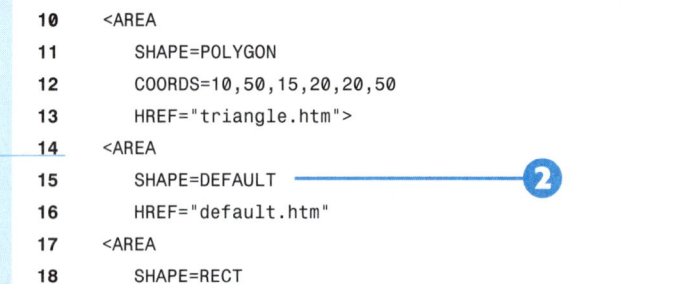

First, note that the name of the map is set with the NAME attribute of the <MAP> tag. This is a required element. This name will be added to the <IMG> element to link the map coordinates with the image file.

In Listing 10.2 several different coordinate regions are defined for the image. You can see that there are four possible values for the SHAPE attribute:

- RECT is any four-sided object. The COORDS values mark the top-left corner (X,Y) and the bottom-right corner (X,Y) of the object.
- CIRCLE is a round map region. The COORDS values define a circle at location X and Y with a radius of Z.
- POLYGON is any irregular shape. The COORDS values define each line segment that marks the outlines of the shape.
- DEFAULT is an entry that can be used to "catch" any mouse clicks in "nondefined" regions. There are no COORDS attributes associated with the DEFAULT shape.

The HREF attribute contains a valid URL that will be used as the navigation target when the user clicks the image within the defined COORDS values. Notice that you can also define a region and use the NOHREF attribute to make sure that no URL is associated with a region.

Adding Map Coordinates to Your Image Files

Finally, notice that the end of the list of `<AREA>` tags is marked by the `</MAP>` HTML tag. This is a requirement.

SEE ALSO
> *For more on how to use the* NAME *attribute of an HTML element in client-side scripts, see page 337*

Defining Your Own Image Map

Now that you know how to define a set of map coordinates for an image, it's time to build an image map for the graphical image you added to your document earlier in this chapter.

In this example, you divide the image into four rectangular regions and associate a URL with each region. The sample image file included in this chapter is a set of four arrows dividing the image into four sections in a rather simple matter. Depending on the image you selected, this might not be the best way to divide the image. However, to get the idea of how image maps work, continue to use the four sections outlined in this example. When you get the hang of things, you can define your own regions to better match your image files.

To define an image map for the loaded image file, switch to Source mode in the Visual InterDev Editor and add the `<MAP>` and `<AREA>` tags that mark the regions. For this example, create four rectangles that outline each of the arrows in the graphical image.

The image in Figure 10.2 shows that the four arrows meet at a point just above the vertical midline and at the horizontal center of the image. Because the `<IMG>` defines the HEIGHT and WIDTH of the image to be 400 pixels, this means that the exact center of the four arrows is around 160 on the X-axis and 200 on the Y-axis. With this information as a starting point, you can now calculate the top-left and bottom-right corners of four rectangles for this image. The results are shown in Table 10.1.

A better way to define map regions

Although computing the map regions for client-side image maps is not impossible, it's a bit of a hassle. There are better ways to do it, too! First, you can use FrontPage to define regions. However, this creates a "web bot" reference that might not be supported in all cases. There are also several freeware or shareware image map editors available on the Internet. They all do about the same thing—enable you to use your mouse to define regions on a graphical image and store the results as standard `<MAP>` and `<AREA>` tags for placement in your HTML documents.

TABLE 10.1 The image map coordinates for the example

Top-Left X	Top-Left Y	Bottom-Right X	Bottom-Right Y
0	0	200	160
0	160	200	400
200	0	400	160
200	160	400	400

The data from Table 10.1 can be converted directly into COORDS attribute values for the image map.

Finally, you must associate a URL for each region in the map. For this example, add PAGE1.HTM, PAGE2.HTM, PAGE3.HTM, and PAGE4.HTM to each of the four defined regions. Although these pages might not exist in your Web project, they will at least complete the map definition properly. You can adjust the URLs later to match real documents in your Web application.

So now, with the IMAGEMAP.HTM document loaded in the Visual InterDev Editor, switch to Source mode and enter the HTML coding from Listing 10.3 into the <BODY> of the document above the <IMG> tag.

LISTING 10.3 Adding the *MAP* and *AREA* Tags to the IMAGEMAP.HTM Document

```
1   <MAP name=MyMAP>
2       <AREA
3           SHAPE=RECT
4           COORDS=0,0,200,160
5           HREF="page1.htm">
6       <AREA
7           SHAPE=RECT
8           COORDS=0,160,200,400
9           HREF="page2.htm">
10      <AREA
11          SHAPE=RECT
12          COORDS=200,0,400,160
```

Adding Map Coordinates to Your Image Files | CHAPTER 10

```
13        HREF="page3.htm">
14     <AREA
15        SHAPE=RECT
16        COORDS=200,160,400,400
17        HREF="page4.htm">
18  </MAP>
```

When you complete your HTML coding, switch to the Design view to see whether your display matches the one in Figure 10.3.

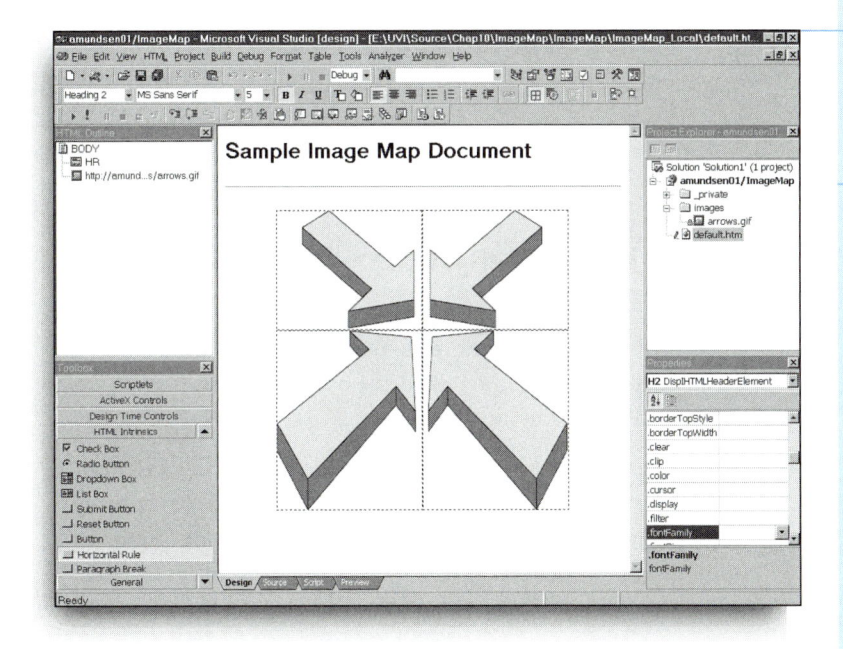

FIGURE 10.3
Viewing the image map in the Visual InterDev Editor Design mode.

Notice that the Visual InterDev Editor uses dashed lines to indicate the defined regions of the associated map file. Although you won't see these in the browser, it is nice to be able to confirm their outlines in the editor before you save the completed HTML document to your production Web.

Adding the Target HTML Documents

In order to test this image map you must add four simple HTML documents that will act as the target for the four HREFs you added in Listing 10.3. You must add PAGE1.HTM, PAGE2.HTM, PAGE3.HTM, and PAGE4.HTM to your Web project.

You can also add an optional heading to each document in the <BODY> section to identify the pages. For example, in PAGE1.HTM, you could add the following HTML coding in the <BODY>:

`<H1>This is Page 1</H1>`

Do this for each of the four pages and then save those pages to your Web project. Now you're ready to test your image map.

Testing the Image Map Document

Now that you have imported the graphical image file into your Web project, loaded it onto the page, defined clickable regions in a client-side map, and added the sample target HTML documents, you're ready to test the page.

Press the **Quick View** tab to view the resulting HTML page and move your mouse over the image. You'll see that it turns into a hand cursor indicating that this is a hot spot or clickable region on the document. If you click anywhere in the region your browser will appear displaying the page associated with the region. You now have an image-mapped document!

SEE ALSO
➤ *For more on using the Quick View pane, see page 36*

PART III

Using Visual Basic Script

11	**Programming with Visual Basic Scripting Language** 247
12	**Expanding Your Scripts with Built-In Methods** 271
13	**Adding Event Handling to Your Visual Basic Scripts** 301
14	**Client-Side Scripting with the MSIE Object Model** 335
15	**Using Server-Side Scripting with the Built-In ASP Objects** 379

CHAPTER 11

Programming with Visual Basic Scripting Language

Store data using VBScript variables

Use program control structures to control the flow of your Web applications during runtime

Understand VBScript basics and how to use VBScript to store and retrieve data

Use VBScript control structures to control the flow of your Web applications

Visual Basic Script Quick Start

In this chapter, you learn how to use Visual Basic Scripting language to animate your Web applications. Visual Basic Scripting language (often referred to as VBScript) is a set of commands and keywords that are interpreted while your application is running. This is why VBScript is called an *interpreted language*. These commands can be used to display text on the client workstation; read data from the server; change fonts, colors, and so on; and even provide simple message box alerts and help-style information when a user clicks in the proper place. In the next several sections you get a quick review of VBScript and its main command and features.

VBScript is similar to the programming language used in Microsoft Visual Basic and all the Microsoft Office applications. In fact, VBScript is a *subset* of Visual Basic. This means that VBScript contains most of the commands of Visual Basic, but not all of them. In fact, the list of commands missing from VBScript is rather short. Although the exact details are not really important here, it is important to remember that VBScript is very powerful and is almost identical to the Visual Basic you might have used with Microsoft Visual Basic or the Microsoft Office products.

Another important aspect of VBScript to keep in mind is that it is an *interpreted* language. This means that the VBScript commands are interpreted while the program is running. Other languages, such as Microsoft Visual Basic or Microsoft C++, are *compiled* languages. The commands for these languages are interpreted when the program is compiled into an executable file (EXE).

Because VBScript is interpreted and not compiled, you can't do things in quite the same way (or quite as quickly) as you can if you were using Microsoft Visual Basic or Microsoft C++.

The compiled versus interpreted war

There are distinctly polarized viewpoints on the interpreted versus compiled languages. Not surprisingly, both opinions have merits. The best way to look at the ideal language is to determine what your overall objective is and how you plan on delivering your code. If you are working in a distributed client/server environment such as the Web and plan on frequent updates, scripting is ideal. It's less complex, easy to implement and maintain, and works well over the Web. However, if you are working with complex interaction, intricate code that will be changed less frequently, and stretching beyond the capabilities of a scripting language it might be time for a compiled language. VBScript is a good segue into development using Visual Basic.

This is important when you begin to write large Web applications. Often, large applications include one or more components built with a compiled language as well as portions written using VBScript to tie things together.

Now that you have a good idea of what VBScript is, you're ready to start diving into the details of VBScript!

Creating a Simple VBScript Application

Creating VBScript applications with Visual InterDev is really easy. It is a lot like using HTML to create Web pages. You start a Visual InterDev Web application, open the starting page, and add some VBScript commands in the Source window.

For example, you can use VBScript to create a single page that has two text boxes and a command button. When you press the command button, information from the text boxes is used to create a message box that will be displayed to the user. Here's a quick step-by-step to create the Web application just described.

Creating a message box for use in future scripts

1. Start Visual InterDev and create a new Web project. Set the Project **Name** to `SimpleVBSDemo`. You can use the same title as the Web name. You can select `<none>` for the **Layout** and **Theme** of this Web project.

2. Add an HTML page to the Web project. Set its name to DEFAULT.HTM. Select **Document** from the **Properties** pull-down and set the `DefaultClientScript` property to `VBScript`.

3. Now lay out a simple page that looks like the one in Figure 11.1. Be sure to use the generic Button object instead of the Submit button or some other one.

4. When you are finished laying out the form, save it before continuing with the VBScript portion of the project.

A poor choice of a name

Scripting languages, by definition, seem to be named poorly. Look at JavaScript—it has nothing to do with Java, it never had anything to do with Java, and isn't going to be Java in the future. It was a name selected for the big "M"—Marketing. VBScript is much the same. The name capitalizes on the familiarity of Visual Basic. But think about it—what's so visual about a scripting language?

What to put in the Source window

Of course, this implies that you have some sort of idea as to what VBScript commands to put in the Source window. But we'll get to that shortly.

Naming your controls

Do yourself a favor: use practical names for your controls. Visual InterDev defaults with a generic name like `textbox1`, `button3`, and so on. Don't fall into the trap of working around these—change their names! Use practical names that mean something. For example, in this chapter's page, use `txt_Message` for the Message text box, `txt_Loops` for the Loops text box, and `btn_Submit` for the command button.

FIGURE 11.1

Laying out the simple VBScript page.

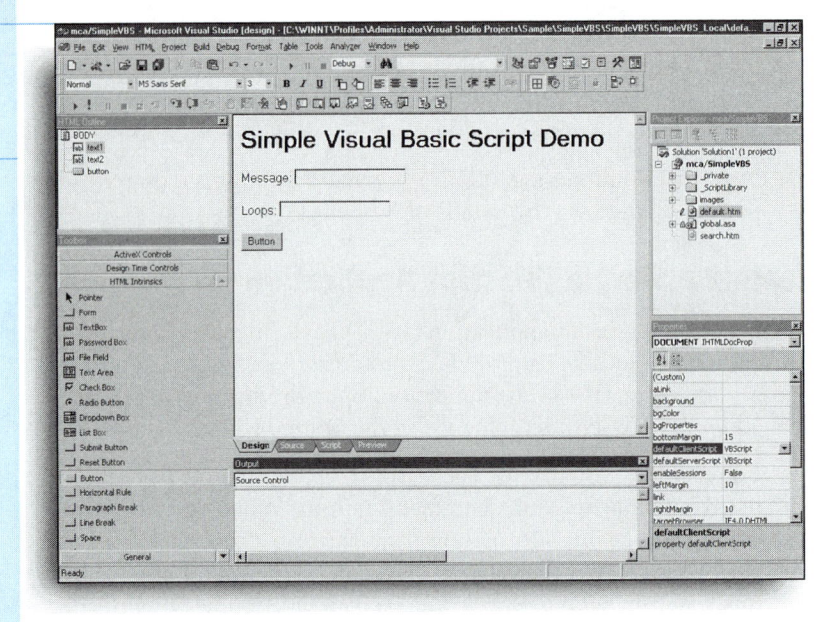

Simplicity itself

Of course I'm not implying that all scripts are this simple. You can use this chapter's examples to build your own complex scripts as you experiment more throughout this book.

Adding VBScript to Your Web Project

Now that the form design is complete, you're ready to add VBScript to the application. Add some code that will use the message entered into the first text box and a number entered into the second text box and, when the user presses the command button, display a message box with the text message repeated as many times as was requested.

In order to complete this task, you use two VBScript variables: one built-in method and one program control structure. You also use the `onclick` event of the command button to know when to display your message.

The next steps show how you can use all the items mentioned previously to create a simple routine with about 10 lines of VBScript.

Creating a simple routine with VBScript

1. Switch to the Source Editor and select the **Script** tab on the editor window to display the script edit space.

Visual Basic Script Quick Start

2. Using the ~~HTML~~ Script Outline window (on the left), select **Client Objects & Events**, **Window**, *Your Button*. If you followed the advice earlier in this chapter, this button will be named `btn_Submit`.

3. Now double-click the `onclick` event to open a code window for the `btn_Submit_onclick` method. Any code you place between the `Sub` and `End Sub` will be executed each time the user clicks the button.

4. Now add the code from Listing 11.1 between the `Sub` and `End Sub`.

5. After adding the code, save the page before continuing.

LISTING 11.1 A Simple VBScript Example

```
1  Sub btn_Submit_onclick
2
3  dim strMessage
4  dim intLoop
5
6  for intloop=1 to txt_Loop.value
7      strMessage = strMessage & txt_Message.value & "!"
8  next
9
10 alert strMessage
11
12 End Sub
```

Testing the SimpleVBSDemo Web Project

Now that you've added all the VBScript and saved the page, you are ready to run the Web project to see your results. To do this, press the Start button on the Visual InterDev toolbar or press F5. An even better way to preview your work is to use the **Quick View** tab, taking advantage of Visual InterDev's "rapid application development" features. You should see your browser appear, display the form, and wait for your input.

PART III Using Visual Basic Script

CHAPTER 11 **Programming with Visual Basic Scripting Language**

Enter `Hello` in the **Message** text box and 3 in the **Loops** text box. When you press the command button, you should see **Hello!Hello!Hello!** in a message box (see Figure 11.2). If your application did not work correctly, check the VBScript to be sure you entered it exactly as it appears in Listing 11.1.

FIGURE 11.2

Viewing the results of the SimpleVBSDemo Web project.

To Quick View, or not to Quick View

You can test your pages in Visual InterDev using two different methods (well, three actually, but that's just nitpicking). The most common method is to preview your Web page in your Web browser by either clicking the Start button in the toolbar or by right-clicking the file in the Project Explorer and choosing **View in Browser** from the context menu. The other method is to click the **Quick View** tab and immediately see results. This saves you overhead of Visual InterDev opening a Web browser to view your page and entering debugging mode. Quick View is not without its faults, however. If you are working with server-side scripting (as you will later in this book), you will not be able to experience most of your script. Quick View is best for client-side scripting tests, while debugging mode is best for server-side. But that could just be my opinion.

Message boxes

The `alert` method is only one of the most common ways to use Windows user interface (UI) elements in your scripts. VBScript supports more complex dialog boxes. For information on this topic, refer to Visual InterDev's online help for the VBScript scripting language.

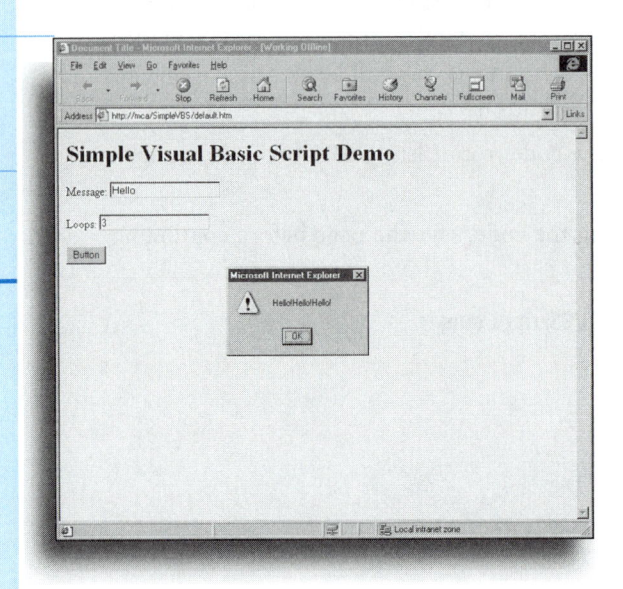

Now that you've completed this simple example, let's take a closer look at some of the details. First, lines 3 and 4 start with the `dim` keyword to declare local storage space, called *variables*. These are use to hold data during the execution of the VBScript.

Next, lines 6 through 8 constitute a program control structure. This controls how the program runs. In this case, the control structure is a `for...next` loop. They are used to repeat one or more lines of VBScript. Line 7 is executed repeatedly and builds the message that will be displayed.

Finally, line 10 of the method starts with the `alert` keyword. This is a built-in method that is used to present message boxes.

In this short example, you've used many parts of VBScript. In the next several sections, you get a more in-depth look at major parts of VBScript.

Using Script Variables

The first two items in the SimpleVBSDemo example you completed in the previous section declared storage space called variables. Variables are used to keep track of simple data values throughout the life of your Web applications. In this section, you learn some details of declaring and using variables with VBScript.

Declaring Variables

The purpose of variables is to store simple data. However, before you can use variables to store information, you should always declare them. Declaring a variable is a way of informing the Web application that you plan on storing a value and that you need some "space" in which to place the value. Although you can often program without declaring variables, this is considered "bad form" in programming—the potential for introducing errors due to poor variable planning is tantamount to committing programming suicide. More structured languages, such as C++, require you to declare all variables before use. This is a wise procedure to adopt even in VBScript to ensure that you are correctly working with the proper variables and not introducing potential flaws.

Declaring variables in VBScript is easy. You simply enter the keyword `dim` followed by a useful name (see Listing 11.2).

LISTING 11.2 Declaring Variables in VBScript

```
1 Dim strCustomerName
2 Dim intCounter
3 Dim lngColumnWidth
4 Dim objFileObject
```

What name you use doesn't really matter as long as you start the name with an alphabetic character (not a number or punctuation mark) and that you keep the name shorter than 32 characters.

> **Code construction: experience makes wise**
>
> There are a lot of "rules to the wise" when developing—declaring variables is just one. As you spend more time developing, you will learn from hardship and experience the right way, and the hard way, to do things. The trick is to turn your mistakes into learning experiences and avoid potential future pitfalls. At the end of the day, you should be saying "You've learned well, grasshopper" to yourself, instead of "Doh!".

The bright history of `dim`

The keyword `dim` was first established for old-style interpreted BASIC language. `dim` is short for dimension. The word dimension was used because the earliest forms of BASIC required programmers to declare all storage spaces as a block of memory. Literally, programmers had to define the dimensions of memory blocks for storage.

Of variants and variables

Many programming languages support variant data types. Although they provide simplicity in programming, they almost always breed bad habits. This is in addition to the overhead involved in using variants. If you use variants (like you do in VBScript), plan carefully. It's easy to confuse variables and compare the wrong types of information (a textual string to a number, for example). A good way to avoid problems is to name your variables for the type of data it contains; for example, `strMyName` or `intExtension`.

Table 11.1 shows some valid and invalid names for VBScript variables.

TABLE 11.1 Valid and invalid VBScript variable names

Valid Variable Names	Invalid Variable Names	Comment
`MyName`	`My Name`	No spaces allowed
`Book7`	`7`[th] `Book`	Can't start names with a number
`ColumnHeader`	`Column.Header`	Punctuation marks not allowed
`SimpleName`	`RatherComplicated AndSomewhatLong Name`	Limit variable names to 32 characters or less
`My_Variable`	`My-Variable`	Special characters (such as +, -, %, /, ? and &) are invalid in variables names

Variable Types in VBScript

If you are used to other programming languages, you might notice something missing in the declarations in Listing 11.2. Most other languages require that you declare a data type when you define a storage location. Basic data types include numeric data and string (or character) data. VBScript does not require you to predeclare a data type when you create your variables. In fact, if you try to do so, you receive an error message.

All VBScript variables are of the same type: *variant*. Variant data types can be numeric or character data. VBScript variables can even change their type during the life of a Web application. The code snippet in Listing 11.3 might cause some computer languages to crash, but VBScript accepts it without a whimper.

LISTING 11.3   Example of Variant Data Types in VBScript

```
1  Sub VBSMethod
2
3      dim MyValue
4
5      MyValue=13
6      alert MyValue
```

```
 7
 8     MyValue="MCA"
 9     alert MyValue
10
11 End Sub
```

Setting the Scope of VBScript Variables

Another major aspect of VBScript variables is called *scope*. The scope of a variable indicates its presence throughout the Web application. VBScript variables have three scoping levels:

- Private (or Local)
- Module
- Public (or Global)

Variables that are declared within a specific routine are *Private variables*. They are created within the routine and are destroyed when the routine completes.

Here's a short example to show you how variable scoping works. First, add a new page to the SimpleVBSDemo project. Name it VARSCOPING.HTM and set the default browser scripting language to VBScript (`defaultClientScript` from the **Document** properties). Add two buttons from the HTML tab labeled **Mike** and **Missing** to the form. Refer to Figure 11.3 as a guide for laying out the form.

Creating the code behind the VARSCOPING.HTM page

1. In the Source Editor, select the **Script** tab to open the script editor window.
2. Use the HTML Outline window to select **Client Objects & Events**, **Window**, **button1** and double-click the `onclick` event to open the method in the code window.
3. Enter the code from Listing 11.4 into the `button1_onclick` event.
4. Now select `button2` in the Script Outline window and double-click the `onclick` event; enter the code from Listing 11.5.
5. Save the page before continuing.

> **Making scope matter**
>
> One of the most common problems introduced in programs is a failure to address the scope of a variable properly. Whenever possible, you should avoid using global variables. That is, variables that are accessible throughout your program's routines and modules. Think of your modules and routines as "black boxes." Predictable information should go in, and predictable information should come out. The rest of your program shouldn't need to understand what goes on inside.

FIGURE 11.3

Laying out the VARSCOPING.HTM form.

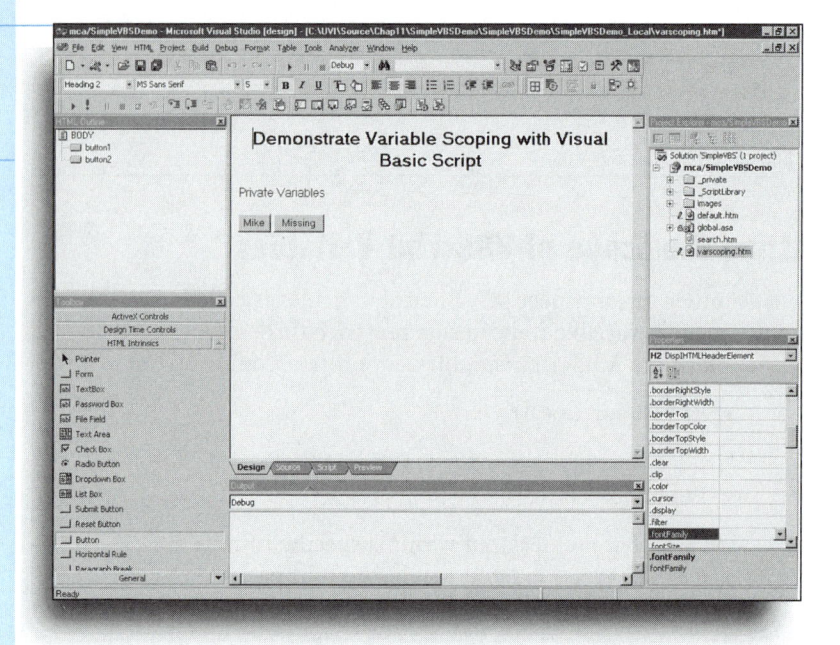

Comment your code

Always comment your code! The best code comments don't detail what your code is specifically doing (for example, `Increment intBlah by 1`; instead it details what you are trying to accomplish. A good example of a comment is `Retrieve the message from the user and store it for future use`. Your code itself should be readable enough so that it acts as its own comment on the logical actions it is taking. The comments act as a roadmap to guide the reader to understand what your code is setting out to do. Comments are an important aspect of development. They improve maintainability, and they force you to have a clearer understanding of what you are trying to do—an important requirement for successful development.

LISTING 11.4 Adding Code to the *button1_onclick* Event

```
1  Sub button1_onclick
2      '
3      ' show private variable scoping
4      '
5      dim strPrivate
6      '
7      strPrivate="Mike"
8      msgbox strPrivate
9      '
10 End Sub
```

LISTING 11.5 Adding Code to the *button2_onclick* Event

```
1  Sub button2_onclick
2      '
3      ' can't find strPrivate!
4      '
5      msgbox strPrivate
6      '
7  End Sub
```

Both routines attempt to display the contents of the variable `strPrivate`. However, when you run the page (press F5), you see that the code from Listing 11.5 shows only a blank message box. This is because the `strPrivate` variable was declared inside the `button1_click` routine. Its scope is limited to that routine alone.

Now let's add some code to show module-level variable scoping. Add two more buttons to the form: **SetValue** and **ShowValue** (see Figure 11.4).

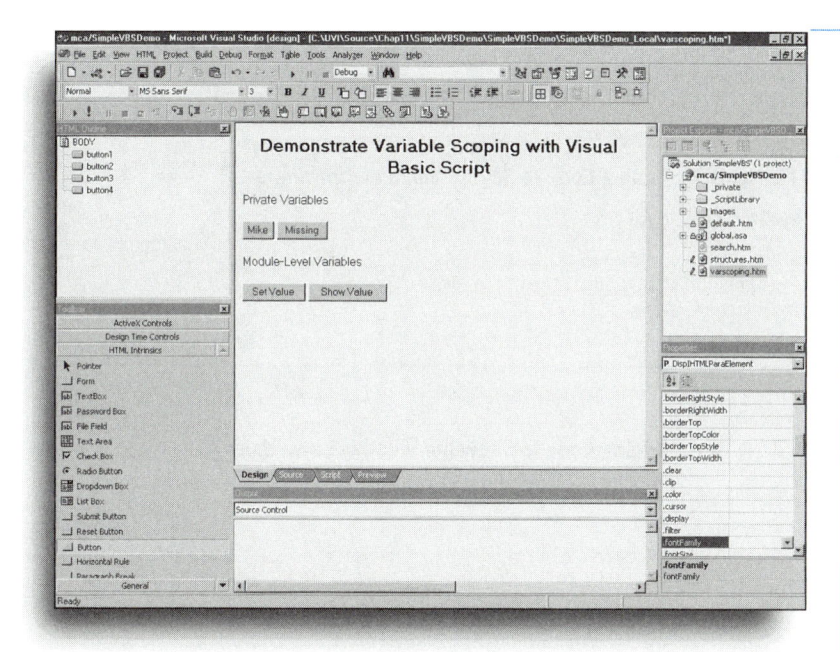

FIGURE 11.4
Adding the **SetValue** and **ShowValue** buttons.

Now while you are in the Source Editor, select the **Script** tab to show the script editor window, and follow the next steps.

Adding module-level variable scoping

1. Move to the top of the VBScript area (marked by `<!---`) and add the code from Listing 11.6. This creates the module-level declaration.

2. From the HTML Outline window, select **Client Object & Events**, **button3**, **onclick** and enter the code from Listing 11.7.

Module-level scope

Maintain consistency when you are using module-level scope. Make sure that you are not duplicating variable names with different purposes between different modules. This only has the potential to confuse you and anyone who might be maintaining your code.

3. Now select **button4**, **onclick** from the Script Outline window and add the code from Listing 11.8 to the page.
4. Save your work before continuing.

LISTING 11.6 **Adding a Module-Level Variable to the Page**

```
1 <SCRIPT LANGUAGE=VBScript>
2 <!--
3 '
4 ' add module-level variable
5 dim strModule
```

LISTING 11.7 **Adding Code to Set the Value of *strModule***

```
1 Sub button3_onclick
2     '
3     strModule=InputBox("Enter a Name:")
4     '
5 End Sub
```

LISTING 11.8 **Adding Code to Show the Value of *strModule***

```
1 Sub button4_onclick
2     '
3     msgbox strModule
4     '
5 End Sub
```

Variable initialization

Variable initialization is an important reason for declaring variables. You should try to initialize variables as close as possible to where the variable was declared. This minimizes the possibility that you will forget the variable's original purpose, and that it has been somehow modified by code between the declaration and the initialization.

Now when you switch to Quick View to view your page, you'll notice that you can set the value of strModule in one routine (button3_onclick) and read the value of strModule from another routine (button4_onclick). Because the variable was declared outside all the routines on the page, it is shared with all of them. This is a module-level variable. Also keep in mind that strModule, as a module-level variable, is not reinitialized each time you click the button. Instead, it stays set until the page is reloaded or it is reinitialized in your code.

There is one more type of variable scope in VBScript: Public (sometimes called Global). You can create variables that can be shared across all the pages and forms in your Web application.

To do this, you must declare these variables in the GLOBAL.ASA file in the home directory of your Web application.

SEE ALSO

▶ You learn about using Public variables in Chapter 15, "Using Server-Side Scripting with the Built-In ASP Objects."

Using Program Control Structures

Along with using variables and accessing methods in your VBScript applications, there are several program control structures you can use when you build VBScript applications. Program control structures are used to control the flow of VBScript programs. In this section, you learn how to use the most common control structures:

- For...Next
- Do...Loop
- If...Then...Else
- Select...Case

Each of these four control structures has its own strengths and disadvantages. The first two are *looping structures*. They are used to create repeating sections in your code. The second two are *decision structures*. They are used to help decide which lines of code will be executed (based on data stored in variables).

Using the *For...Next* Loop Structure

Probably the most common control structure in VBScript applications is the For...Next structure. This is used to mark off one or more lines of code that will be repeated a preset number of times. The basic syntax of the For...Next structure is shown in Listing 11.9.

LISTING 11.9 Basic *For...Next* Loop

```
1 for intLoop=1 to 13 step 1
2   '
3   ' code goes here
4   '
5 next
```

Control structure complexities

Without a doubt, the majority of program errors occur in control structures. When you are designing your control structures, be sure that you have clearly thought out the logic behind it. Plan around unanticipated data so that it doesn't break your structures, and always make sure to keep your structures as simple as possible. No one will congratulate you for a complex and confusing control structure.

The `For...Next` loop in Listing 11.9 will repeat all the code between the `For` and `Next` a total of 13 times. Each time the loop executes, the `intLoop` variable is set to the repeat number. For example, the first time `intLoop=1`; the second time `intLoop=2`, and so on.

The `step 1` part of `For...Next` (line 1) is optional. If you leave it out, each time the loop executes, the variable is incremented by one. However, you can use negative step values to force loops to work in reverse.

As an example, add a new page to the SimpleVBSDemo Web project called STRUCTURES.HTM. Once again, change the default client-side scripting language (`defaultClientScript`) to VBScript. Add a text box and a command button from the **HTML** tab, as shown in Figure 11.5.

FIGURE 11.5

Laying out the STRUCTURES.HTM page.

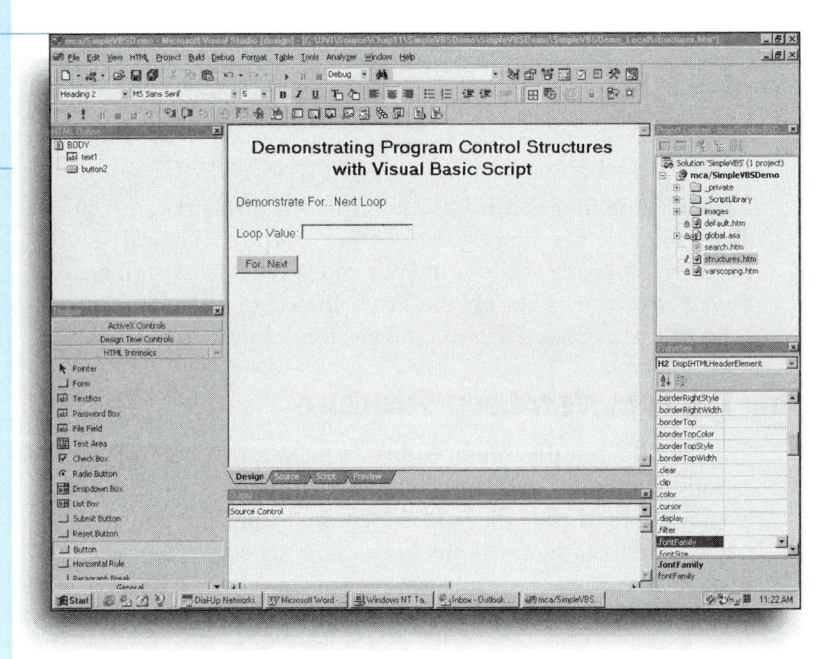

In the Source Editor, switch to the Script window in the editor, use the Script Outline Window to select **Client Objects & Events**, **window**, **button1**, **onclick**, and enter the code from Listing 11.10 into the `button1_onclick` method.

Using Program Control Structures

PART III
CHAPTER 11

261

LISTING 11.10 Coding Example of *For ... Next*

```
1  Sub button1_onclick
2     '
3     ' show for next loop
4     '
5     dim intLoop
6     '
7     for intLoop=1 to text1.value
8        msgbox intLoop,,"Forward"
9     next
10    '
11    for intLoop=text1.value to 1 step -1
12       msgbox intloop,,"Backward"
13    next
14    '
15 End Sub
```

Now save the page and test it by selecting the **Quick View** tab in the editor. When you enter a value in the text box and press the button, you see message boxes count both forward and backward.

SEE ALSO

➤ To learn more about the `Else` condition, see page 264

Using the *Do...Loop* Structure

The `Do...Loop` structure is also a repeating program control structure. However, unlike the `For...Next` structure, the `Do...Loop` structure does not have a predetermined start and stop value. The `Do...Loop` structure repeats until a certain condition is met or as long as a certain condition is true.

There are actually two versions of the `Do...Loop` structure. They are both shown in Listing 11.11.

LISTING 11.11 Examples of Both *Do...Loop* Structures

```
1  do while blnTest=True
2     '
3     ' code goes here
4     '
```

continues...

Plan around the `Else`

A powerful extension to the `For...Loop` control structure is the `Else` and `Else If`. Basically, all control structures support a way of saying "If the situation isn't what is specified here, do this." Many programmers only plan on the certainties. Plan for the uncertainties by using intelligent `Else` statements. Even if your `Else` statement gives you a debugging alert message that says "Hey, you made a boo boo!" it's still better than your entire script behaving oddly or breaking.

PART III Using Visual Basic Script

CHAPTER 11 **Programming with Visual Basic Scripting Language**

Check before or after?

You can modify the `Do...Loop` structure to check the conditional value just before executing the code (as in the examples shown here) or after executing the code. Place the `Until` or `While` portion of the code on the `Do` line (check before) or on the `Loop` line (check after). Most of the time you'll want to check before to prevent code from executing when the condition is true. However, there might be cases in which you want to run the code at least once, even if the condition is true.

LISTING 11.11 Continued

```
5  loop
6
7  do until blnTest=True
8      '
9      ' code goes here
10     '
11     loop
```

As you can see from Listing 11.11, the `Do...Loop` structure checks a condition that must evaluate to TRUE or FALSE to determine whether the loop is completed. Also, there is no variable that gets automatically incremented as in the `For...Next` structure. If you want to increment values, you must add code within the `Do...Loop` itself.

Now let's add some items to the STRUCTURES.HTM page and create a `Do...Loop` example. Add a horizontal rule, a text box, and two command buttons to the page. Refer to Figure 11.6 as a guide in laying out the controls on the page.

FIGURE 11.6

Laying out controls to demonstrate the `Do...Loop`.

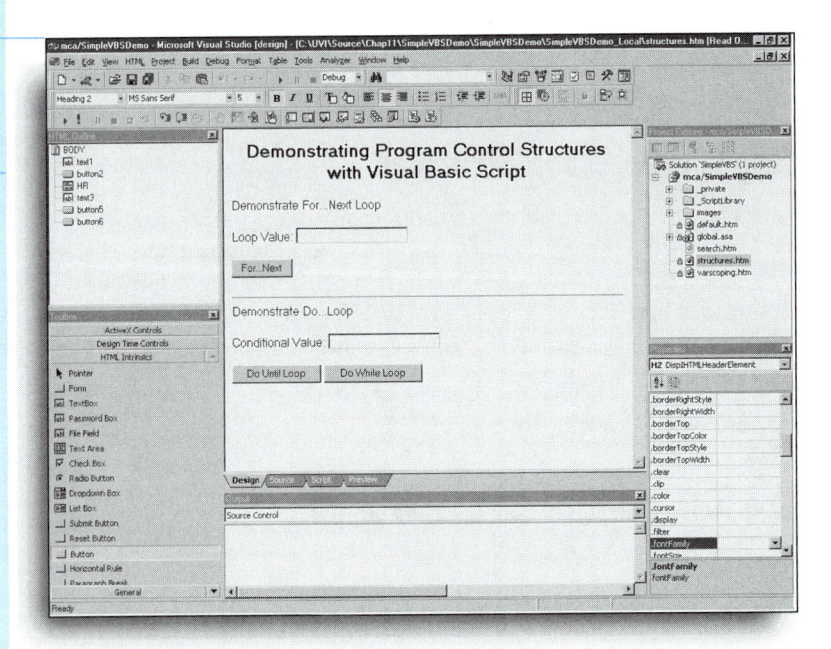

Using Program Control Structures

After laying out the controls on the page, switch to the Source Editor and select the **Script** tab and use the HTML outline control to navigate to the `button2_onclick` event. Double-click this event to add the method to the code window. Next, add the code from Listing 11.12 to the project.

LISTING 11.12 Adding Code to Demonstrate a *Do...Loop*

```
1  Sub button2_onclick
2      '
3      ' show do until loop
4      '
5      dim lngValue
6      dim lngTest
7      '
8      lngValue=0
9      lngTest=cLng(text3.value) 'convert to long integer
10     '
11     do until lngValue>lngTest
12         lngValue=lngValue+5
13     loop
14     '
15     msgbox lngValue,,"Do Until Loop"
16     '
17 End Sub
```

Notice that the method (`cLng`) on line 9 is used to convert the user input into a long integer value. There are several conversion routines in VBScript. They are not covered here, but it is important to know that they exist. You can find more about them by using the online help files.

Listing 11.12 also shows that the `Do` portion of the code (lines 11 through 13) performs a conditional check to see whether the `lngValue` variable contains a value higher than the value stored in the `lngTest` variable. This is the heart of using `Do...Loop` structures.

When you run the project and press the **Do Until Loop** button, you see the first value that is greater than the one you entered into the text box.

Using conversion methods

It's a good idea to use conversion methods on data that you receive from user input. This will help ensure that the data is the proper type before you attempt to use it in your application.

Ugly data creates ugly results

Plan, plan, and plan some more. When a control structure receives malformed or unexpected data, your structure could break or behave in ways you just hadn't planned on. Here's a tip: Use routines that check the validity of data before processing it. The hallmark of a great system is its capability to cope with ugly or unexpected information gracefully. Rather than have your script die by the side of the road because of a user's mistake, let it quietly spit the garbage data aside and resume operations based on some sense of logic.

You can also use the `Do...Loop` with a `While` clause instead of `Until`. Use the HTML Outline window to navigate to the `button3_onclick` event and add the code from Listing 11.13 in the new method.

LISTING 11.13 Adding a *Do...Loop* with the *While* Clause

```
1  Sub button3_onclick
2    '
3    ' show do while loop
4    '
5    dim lngValue
6    dim lngTest
7    '
8    lngValue=0
9    lngTest=cLng(text2.value) 'convert to long integer
10   '
11   do while lngValue<lngTest
12      lngTest=lngTest-5
13   loop
14   '
15   msgbox lngTest,,"Do While Loop"
16   '
17 End Sub
```

Notice that the conditional check on line 11 uses the `While` clause instead of `Until`. Also notice that the comparison operator on the same line is < (less than) instead of the > (greater than) operator used in Listing 11.12. You learn more about comparison operators later in the next section of this chapter.

When you save this project and run it, you see the value -4 appear when you enter a value in the `Do...Loop` text box and press the **Do While Loop** button.

Using the *If...Then...Else* Structure

The most commonly used decision structure in VBScript is the `If...Then...Else` structure. This structure is used to determine whether a set of code lines should be executed at all. The basic form of the `If...Then...Else` structure is shown in Listing 11.14.

Using Program Control Structures   CHAPTER 11

LISTING 11.14   The Basic *If...Then...Else* Structure

```
1 if lngTest=TRUE Then
2    ' some code
3 else
4    ' some other code
5 end if
```

You can see in Listing 11.14 that if the conditional test is TRUE, the section marked some code will be executed. However, if the conditional test is FALSE, the code marked some other code will be executed.

Let's create a simple example. Load the STRUCTURES.HTM page that you have been working on and add a horizontal rule, a text box, and a command button all from the **HTML** tab (see Figure 11.7).

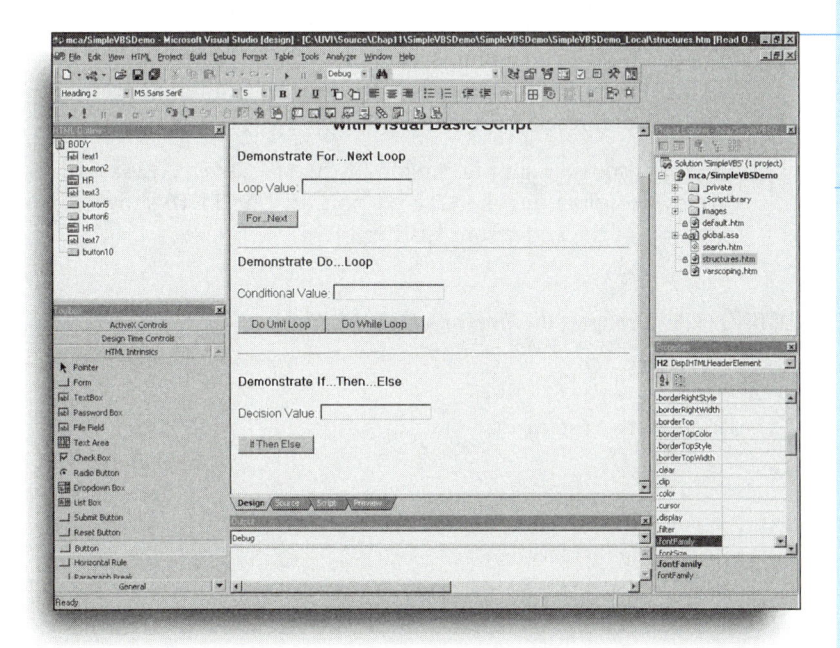

FIGURE 11.7
Laying out the If...Then...Else test page.

Now switch the editor to the Script window and add the code from Listing 11.15. You can use the HTML Outline window to navigate to the button4 control and double-click the onclick event to open the method in the editor.

LISTING 11.15 Coding the *If...Then...Else* Example

```
1  Sub button4_onclick
2      '
3      ' demonstrate if then else
4      '
5      dim lngTest
6      '
7      lngTest=cLng(text3.value)
8      '
9      if lngTest <10 Then
10         msgbox "Less than 10!"
11     else
12         msgbox "Ten or Greater"
13     end if
14     '
15 End Sub
```

End If and the Visual InterDev editor

If you are used to working with Visual Basic or VBA for the Office applications, you might be in the habit of typing **endif** and seeing the editor change that to **End If** (note spaces and capitalization). Unfortunately, the Visual InterDev editor is not "smart" enough to perform this little timesaving feat. When you write code in the Visual InterDev editor, you must be sure to place a space between the words **End** and **if**. Failure to do this will result in an error at runtime.

When you save and run this example, you can enter a value in the text box and if it is less than 10, you see a different message than if you entered a value greater than 10.

You can also use a simple version of the `If...Then...Else` structure by dropping out the `Else` portion. Listing 11.16 shows a variation of the code from Listing 11.15.

LISTING 11.16 Dropping the *Else* from *If...Then...Else*

```
1  Sub button4_onclick
2      '
3      ' demonstrate if then else
4      '
5      dim lngTest
6      '
7      lngTest=cLng(text3.value)
8      '
9      if lngTest <10 Then
10         msgbox "Less than 10!"
11     end if
12     '
13 End Sub
```

Using Program Control Structures

You can place as many lines of code as you want after the `If...Then` line (line 9) and before the `else` or `end if` line (line 11). You can call other methods, even load other pages. However, if you have only one command to execute, it is possible to place the entire structure on a single line as follows:

```
if lngTest<10 then msgbox "Less than 10!" else msgbox
➥"Ten or Greater!"
```

Using the *Select...Case...End Select* Structure

Another very common decision structure in VBScript is the `Select...Case...End Select` structure. This is a bit more flexible than the `If...Then...Else` structure because it allows for more than two options when making a decision. The basic form of the structure is shown in Listing 11.17.

> **Single-line If...Then...Else is a bad idea**
>
> Although VBScript allows the use of single-line `If...Then...Else` structures, it is not a good idea to use them. First, they are harder to read. Second, they are more difficult to debug. Finally, if you ever need to add additional lines of code within the structure, you'll need to expand the code from the one-line form to the multiline form. It is better to start with the multiline form from the beginning.

LISTING 11.17 **Basic Form of *Select...Case...End Select* Structure**

```
1  select case lngTest
2      case IS <10
3          strMessage="Less than 10"
4      case 10
5          strMessage "Exactly 10"
6      case else
7          strMessage "Some other value"
8  end select
```

Unlike the `If...Then...Else` structure that performs the conditional test only once, the `Select...Case...End Select` structure can perform any number of conditional tests on the same value. This allows a greater number of choices and variations.

Now let's build a quick example of the `Select...Case...End Select` structure. Add a horizontal rule, text box, and button from the **HTML** tab to the STRUCTURES.HTM page, as shown in Figure 11.8.

FIGURE 11.8
Laying out the `Select...Case...End Select` controls.

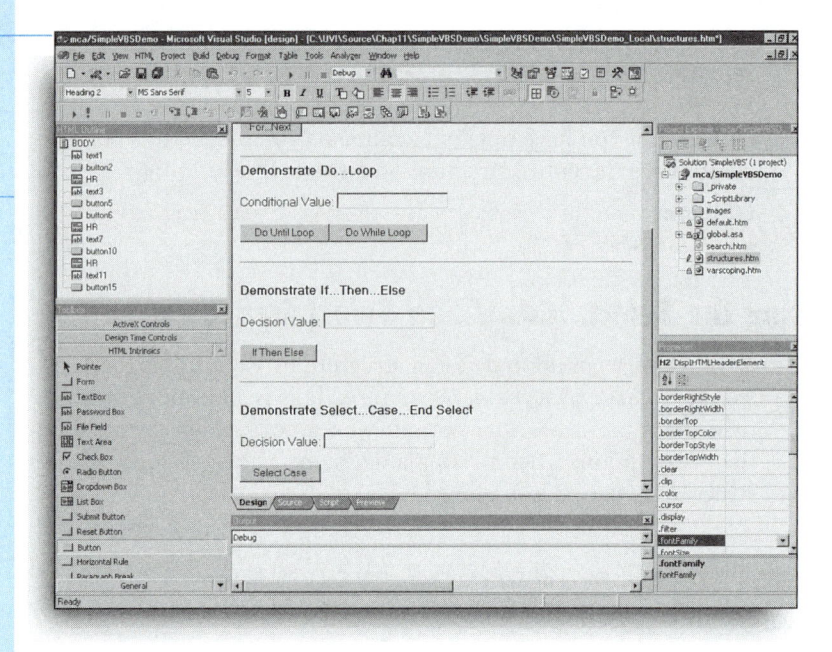

Now move to the script editor window and add the code shown in Listing 11.18.

LISTING 11.18 Coding the *Select...Case...End Select* Example

```
1  Sub button5_onclick
2      '
3      ' demonstrate select case
4      '
5      dim lngTest
6      dim strMessage
7      '
8      lngTest=cLng(text4.value)
9      '
10     select case lngTest
11        case IS <10
12           strMessage="Less than 10"
13        case 10
14           strMessage="Exactly 10"
```

```
15        case else
16            strMessage="Some other value"
17        end select
18        '
19        msgbox strMessage
20        '
21 End Sub
```

Now when you save and run the example you can enter a number of values and get different message boxes in response.

There are several variations you can use within each CASE line. Listing 11.19 shows several possibilities.

LISTING 11.19 **Variations for the *Select...Case...End Select* Structure**
```
1     select case lngTest
2         case Is <10
3             strMessage="Less than 10"
4         case 10
5             strMessage="Exactly 10"
6         case 11,12,13
7             strMessage="11,12, or 13"
8         case 15 to 20
9             strMessage="15 to 20"
10        case 21,23
11            strMessage="21 or 23"
12        case 22
13            strMessage="Exactly 22"
14        case else
15            strMessage="Some other value"
16    end select
```

Modify your code example (from Listing 11.18) to include the options shown in Listing 11.19. Notice that you can include a list of values (11,12,13 and 21,23); a range of values (15 to 20); a logical comparison (<10); an exact match (10 and 22); or use case else to catch any conditions not included in your list.

CHAPTER 12

Expanding Your Scripts with Built-In Methods

Use VBScript methods to add functionality to your Web applications

Use the methods that are built into the VBScript engine to perform math, string, date/time, and other operations

Using the Built-In Methods

Multiple versions of VBScript

There actually are three versions of VBScript. This book covers the features of VBScript 3.0. Microsoft Explorer 1.0 supports only VBScript 1.0. Microsoft Internet Information Server 3.0 supports VBScript 2.0. Microsoft Explorer 4.0+, Microsoft Internet Information Server 4.0, Microsoft Windows Scripting Host 1.0, and Outlook98 all support VBScript 3.0.

If you find that your VBScript Web applications are generating errors on some client machines, those machines might need their version of VBScript or their client browser to be upgraded.

The value of built-ins

Many beginning programmers scoff at the built-in methods provided by many languages (including VBScript). "Bah! When will I need to calculate the logarithm of a number? Never!" Wrong! One of the hallmarks of a great programmer is his ability to use built-in methods to his benefit. It's amazing how many times these built-in methods can be valuable when creating algorithms and routines. Always keep an eye out for how these methods can make your life easier.

In Chapter 11, "Programming with Visual Basic Scripting Language," you learned the basics of scripting using VBScript. In this chapter, you'll delve into more detail using *methods*. Methods are built-in routines that perform an action or return a result. Methods that simply perform an action are often called *subroutines*. Methods are routines that return results and are often referred to as *functions*. You will see all three terms throughout this book.

There are several built-in methods in VBScript. They can be divided into five basic groups:

- Math methods
- String methods
- Date and time methods
- Data conversion methods
- Other methods

In the next several sections, you work through sample Web pages that illustrate the various built-in methods of VBScript. Before going through each section, you must start a new Visual InterDev Web project to hold the examples you'll build.

Create a new Visual InterDev Web project called VBSMethods. Add the DEFAULT.HTM HTML page and, after adding the title (Demonstrate Visual Basic Script Methods), enter four lines of text and their URL links, as shown in Table 12.1 and Figure 12.1.

TABLE 12.1   Adding Text and Links to VBSMethods DEFAULT.HTM

Text	URL Link
Math Methods	MATH.HTM
String Methods	STRING.HTM
Date/Time Methods	DATETIME.HTM
Conversion Methods	CONVERSION.HTM
Other Methods	OTHER.HTM

Using the VBScript Math Methods

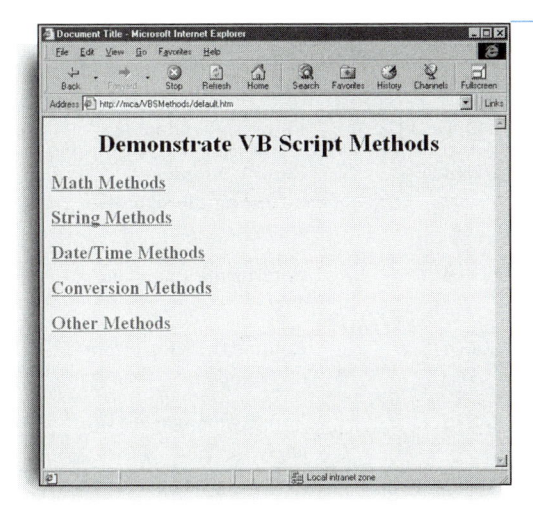

FIGURE 12.1
Laying out the DEFAULT.HTM page of VBSMethods.

Now save the Web project before you continue to the next section.

Using the VBScript Math Methods

VBScript has a handful of built-in math methods you can use in your Web applications. Table 12.2 shows a list of the math methods available, along with a brief description of their use.

TABLE 12.2 **VBScript Math Methods**

Method	Description	Example
ABS(*n.*)	Returns the absolute value of a number	abs(-50)
ATN(*n.*)	Returns the arctangent of a number	atn(3.141)
COS(*n.*)	Returns the cosine of an angle	cos(3.141)
EXP(*n.*)	Returns *e* (the base of natural logarithms) raised to a power	exp(1)
LOG(*n.*)	Returns the natural logarithm of a number	log(100)

continues...

TABLE 12.2 Continued

Method	Description	Example
`RND[(n.)]`	Returns a random *n*.	`rnd`
`SGN(n.)`	Returns an integer indicating the sign of a number	`sgn(-50)`
`SIN(n.)`	Returns the sine of an angle	`sin(3.141)`
`SQR(n.)`	Returns the square root of a number	`sqr(100)`
`TAN(n.)`	Returns the tangent of an angle	`tan(3.141)`

Now let's put together a simple HTML page that demonstrates the VBScript math methods. To do this, build a page that has a table containing the name of the method, a short description, an example, and a test button that shows the results of each example.

First, add a new page to the VBSMethods project called MATH.HTM. Next, add a title and a table with 11 rows each with four columns.

Creating a table with rows and columns

1. Place your cursor on the line where you want the table to start.
2. Select **T**able, **I**nsert **Table** from the Visual InterDev menu.
3. Set the number of rows you want (11).
4. Set the number of columns you want (4).
5. Adjust table and cell attributes as you want.
6. Press **OK** to place the empty table on your page.

After adding the table, enter column headers in the first row of the table:

```
Method
Description
Example
Test
```

> **Your second time around**
>
> After you've completed this example once, you might want to complicate it a little more a second time around. Try to use dynamic numbers and print the results in the Web browser. You learned some of these techniques in Chapter 11.

Using the VBScript Math Methods

After adding the column headers, copy the data from Table 12.2 into the table on the page. For each row, place a button from the HTML tab of the toolbox in the Test column. After placing the buttons, save the page before adding the VBScript.

SEE ALSO
> Remember that Visual InterDev provides more than one kind of button control. For information on the Design-Time control tab's version of a button control, see Chapter 20, "Using Advanced Design-Time Controls."

Now you're ready to add the VBScript to show examples of the math methods. First, however, you must rename the button and assign their IDs to help make the code more readable. For each button in the table, reset the ID tag and the name using the `btn` prefix followed by the name of the math method. For example, `btnABS`, `btnATN`, and so on.

Finally, you're ready to add the VBScript code to execute each math method. Select the **Source** tab of the editor. Be sure the `DefaultClientScript` property of the page is set to **VBScript**. Now use the Script Outline window and select **Client Objects & Events**, **Window** and you'll see a list of all the buttons you created in the previous step, as shown in Figure 12.2.

Hungarian Naming Convention

The `btnName` nomenclature is a standard one for Visual Basic. You use a three-digit abbreviation for the type of object you are creating, followed by its name. This principle is based on the Hungarian Naming Convention, which ironically enough was created by a developer from Hungary.

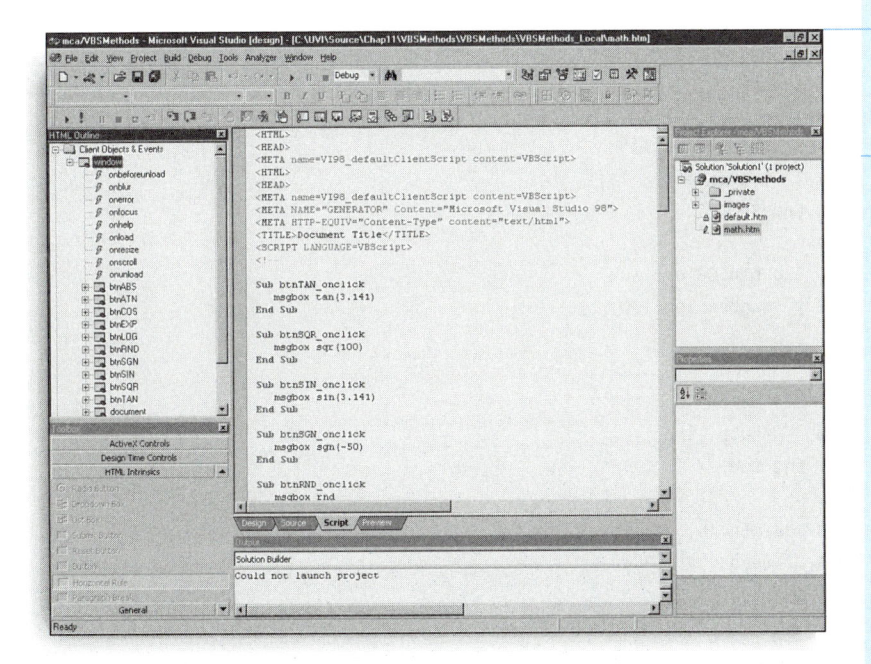

FIGURE 12.2
Viewing the buttons in the Script Outline view window.

Now you can select each button object and click the `onclick` event to expose the code headers for each of the 10 buttons. After you've done this, you can enter the code from Listing 12.1 into the various code headers.

LISTING 12.1 Code to Execute the VBScript Math Methods

```
1  Sub btnTAN_onclick
2      msgbox tan(3.141)
3  End Sub
4
5  Sub btnSQR_onclick
6      msgbox sqr(100)
7  End Sub
8
9  Sub btnSIN_onclick
10     msgbox sin(3.141)
11 End Sub
12
13 Sub btnSGN_onclick
14     msgbox sgn(-50)
15 End Sub
16
17 Sub btnRND_onclick
18     msgbox rnd
19 End Sub
20
21 Sub btnCOS_onclick
22     msgbox cos(3.141)
23 End Sub
24
25 Sub btnLOG_onclick
26     msgbox log(100)
27 End Sub
28
29 Sub btnEXP_onclick
30     msgbox exp(1)
31 End Sub
32
33 Sub btnATN_onclick
34     msgbox atn(3.141)
35 End Sub
```

Using the VBScript String Methods

```
36
37 Sub btnABS_onclick
38   msgbox abs(-50)
39 End Sub
```

> **Try some variety**
>
> You can always experiment with your own numbers in place of those provided in this code listing.

After entering this code, save the page before you run the test. If you get errors, halt the project and check your typing. Your completed page should look like the one in Figure 12.3.

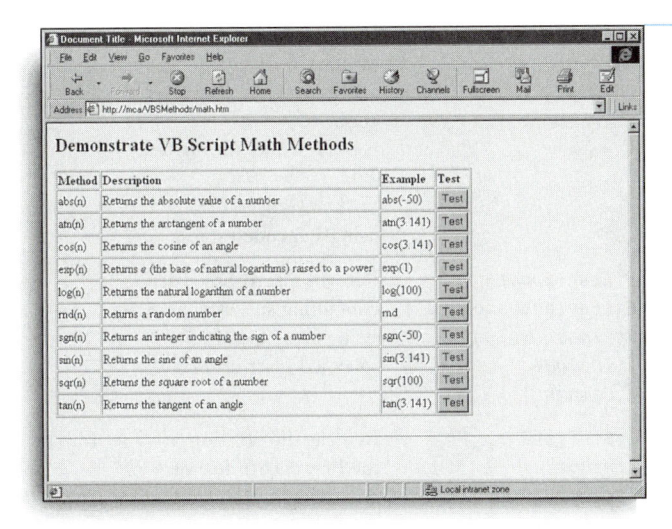

FIGURE 12.3
Viewing the completed Math Methods page.

When you have completed all tests successfully, you can move on to the section on string methods.

Using the VBScript String Methods

You use string methods to perform tasks on string values or turn numeric values into strings. VBScript has 17 different string methods, along with several variations. These methods (and their variants) are listed in Table 12.3.

TABLE 12.3 VBScript string methods

Method	Description	Example

`Asc(string)`
`AscB(string)`
`AscW(string)`
	Returns the ANSI character code corresponding to the first letter in a string
	—`AscB` works with byte data
	—`AscW` returns Unicode value instead of ASCII
		`Asc("A")`

`Chr(n)`
`ChrB(n)`
`ChrW(n)`
	Returns the character associated with the specified ANSI character code
	—`ChrB` works with byte data
	—`ChrW` returns a character using Unicode values
		`Chr(64)`

`Filter(Input`
`Strings, Value`
`[,Include`
`[,Compare]])`
	Returns a zero-based array containing subset of a string array based on a specified filter criteria	`Filter(aryNames,"M")`

`InStr([start, ]`
`string1,`
`string2[,`
`compare])`
`InStrB`
`InStrRev`
	Returns the position of the first occurrence of one string within another
	—`InstrB` works with byte data
	—`InStrRev` starts the search from the end of the string
		`InStr("Find Me","Me")`

`Join(list[,` `delimiter])`	Returns a string created by joining a number of substrings contained in an array	`Join(aryNames,", ")`

`Len(string ¦`
`varname)`
`LenB`
	Returns the number of characters in a string or the number of bytes required to store a variable
	—`LenB` works with byte data
		`Len("My Name")`

Using the VBScript String Methods

Method	Description	Example
LCase(*string*) UCase(*string*)	Returns a string that has been converted to lowercase —Ucase converts to uppercase	LCase("MY NAME")
Left(*string*, *length*) LeftB	Returns a specified number of characters from the left side of a string —LeftB works with byte data	Left("My First Name",2)
Mid(*string*, *start*[, *length*]) MidB	Returns a specified number of characters from a string —MidB works with byte data	Mid("My First Name",4,5)
Right(*string*, *length*) RightB	Returns a specified number of characters from the right side of a string —RightB works with byte data	Right("My First Name",4)
Replace (*expression*, *find*, *replacewith*[, *start*[, *count*[, *compare*]]])	Returns a string in which a specified substring has been replaced with another substring a specified number of times	Replace("My House","House", "Boat")
Space(*number*)	Returns a string consisting of the specified number of spaces	Space(30)
Split (*expression*[, *delimiter*[, *count*[, *compare*]]])	Returns a zero-based, one-dimensional array containing a specified number of substrings	Split("Mike;Mary", ";")
StrComp(*string1*, *string2*[, *compare*])	Returns a value indicating the result of a string comparison	StrComp("mike", "MIKE")

continues...

String manipulation

String manipulation is likely one of the most commonly used groups of methods when developing client- and server-side scripts. You'll use these methods often to handle data for interaction and for storage in a database.

TABLE 12.3　Continued

Method	Description	Example
`String(number, character)`	Returns a repeating character string of the length specified	`String(30,"+")`
`StrReverse (string1)`	Returns a string in which the character order of a specified string is reversed	`StrReverse ("Backward")`
`Trim(string)` `LTrim(string)` `RTrim(string)`	Returns a copy of a string without leading spaces (`LTrim`), trailing spaces (`RTrim`), or both leading and trailing spaces (`Trim`)	`Trim(" Mike ")` `LTrim(" Mike")` `RTrim(" Mike")`

Now it's time to create a Web page that illustrates the VBScript string methods. Add a new page to the VBSMethods Web application called STRING.HTM. After adding a descriptive header, create a table that has 18 rows, each with four columns. To do this, make sure you are displaying your Design window, select **Table**, **Insert Table** from the Visual InterDev menu, and enter 18 rows and 4 columns; then press **OK** to add the table to your page.

Now add headers to the first row of the table:

```
Method
Description
Example
Test
```

After adding the column headers, copy the data from Table 12.3 into the table on the page. For each row, place a button in the `Test` column. After placing the buttons, save the page before adding the VBScript.

Before you add the VBScript to drive the actions behind each button, take a moment to rename all the buttons, using `btn` as the prefix and the method name. For example, the first button would be called `btnASC`, the second one `btnCHR`, and so on.

Intrinsic buttons

Keep in mind we're still using intrinsic HTML buttons here, and not Design-Time controls.

Using the VBScript String Methods

Now you are ready to add the code from Listing 12.2 to your page. Be sure to set the `DefaultClientScript` property of the page to `VBScript` before you start coding.

LISTING 12.2 Adding Code for the VBScript String Methods

```
1  Sub btnTrim_onclick
2      msgbox "¦"& trim(" Mike ") &"¦"
3      msgbox "¦" & ltrim(" Mike")& "¦"
4      msgbox "¦" & rtrim("Mike ") & "¦"
5  End Sub
6
7  Sub btnStrReverse_onclick
8      msgbox StrReverse("Backward")
9  End Sub
10
11 Sub btnString_onclick
12     msgbox String(30,"+")
13 End Sub
14
15 Sub btnStrComp_onclick
16     msgbox StrComp("mike","MIKE")
17 End Sub
18
19 Sub btnSplit_onclick
20     '
21     dim aryNames
22     dim intLoop
23     '
24     aryNames=Split("Mike;Mary",";")
25     '
26     for intLoop=0 to uBound(aryNames)
27         msgbox aryNames(intLoop)
28     next
29     '
30 End Sub
31
32 Sub btnSpace_onclick
33     msgbox "¦" & Space(30) & "¦"
34 End Sub
35
36 Sub btnReplace_onclick
```

continues...

LISTING 12.2 Continued

```
37     msgbox Replace("My House","House","Boat")
38 End Sub
39
40 Sub btnRight_onclick
41     msgbox Right("My First Name",4)
42 End Sub
43
44 Sub btnMid_onclick
45     msgbox Mid("My First Name",4,5)
46 End Sub
47
48 Sub btnLeft_onclick
49     msgbox Left("My First Name",2)
50 End Sub
51
52 Sub btnLen_onclick
53     msgbox Len("My Name")
54 End Sub
55
56 Sub btnLCase_onclick
57     msgbox LCase("MY NAME")
58 End Sub
59
60 Sub btnJoin_onclick
61     '
62     dim aryNames(3)
63     '
64     aryNames(0)="Mike"
65     aryNames(1)="Lee"
66     aryNames(2)="Shannon"
67     '
68     msgbox Join(aryNames,", ")
69     '
70 End Sub
71
72 Sub btnInStr_onclick
```

Using the VBScript String Methods

Long listings

This listing is a whopping 103 lines. Watch out for typos!

```
73     msgbox InStr("Find Me","Me")
74 End Sub
75
76 Sub btnFilter_onclick
77     '
78     dim aryNames(3)
79     dim aryResults
80     dim intLoop
81     '
82     ' build array of names
83     aryNames(0)="Mike"
84     aryNames(1)="Mary"
85     aryNames(2)="John"
86     '
87     ' filter out only those with "M"
88     aryResults=Filter(aryNames,"M")
89     '
90     ' show filtered array
91     for intLoop=0 to uBound(aryResults)
92        msgbox aryResults(intLoop)
93     next
94     '
95 End Sub
96
97 Sub btnCHR_onclick
98     msgbox chr(64)
99 End Sub
100
101 Sub btnASC_onclick
102    msgbox asc("A")
103 End Sub
```

Be sure to save the page and the project before you run it and test it. When you run the Web application and navigate to the String Methods page, your browser should show a page that looks like the one in Figure 12.4.

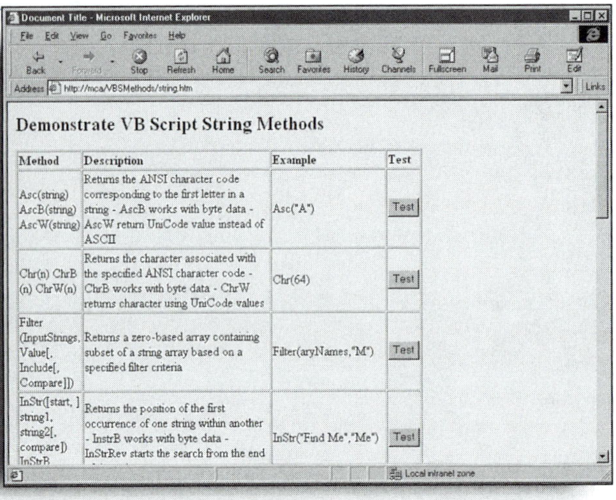

FIGURE 12.4

Displaying the String Methods page.

Using the VBScript Date/Time Methods

VBScript also has several methods for handling date and time values. There are a total of 19 methods available for date/time work. They are listed in Table 12.4.

Date/Time methods

You've likely seen Date and Time methods at work many times. These methods are often used to represent accesses, updates, and control functionality based on time.

TABLE 12.4 VBScript date and time methods

Method	Description	Example
`Date`	Returns the current system date	`Date`
`DateAdd (interval, number, date)`	Returns a date to which a specified time interval has been added. Several settings are possible for the interval value:	`DateAdd("y", 1,"12/31/1999")`
	yyyy Year	
	q Quarter	
	m Month	
	y Day of year	

Using the VBScript Date/Time Methods

Method	Description	Example
	d Day	
	w Weekday	
	ww Week of year	
	h Hour	
	n Minute	
	s Second	
DateDiff (*interval*, *date1*, *date2* [,*firstdayofweek* [,*firstweekof year*]])	Returns the number of intervals between two dates	DateDiff("y", "12/01/1999", "12/31/1999")
DatePart (*interval*, *date*[, *firstdayof week*[, *firstweekofyear*]])	Returns the specified part of a given date	DatePart("d", "12/31/1999")
DateSerial(*year*, *month*, *day*)	Returns a Variant of subtype Date for a specified year, month, and day	DateSerial(1999, 12,31)
DateValue(*date*)	Returns a Variant of subtype Date	DateValue ("12/31/1999")
Day(*date*)	Returns a whole number between 1 and 31, inclusive, representing the day of the month	Day("12/31/1999")
Hour(*time*)	Returns a whole number between 0 and 23, inclusive, representing the hour of the day	Hour("12:15:30")
Minute(*time*) Minute("12:15:30")	Returns a whole number between 0 and 59, inclusive, representing the minute of the hour	

continues...

TABLE 12.4 Continued

Method	Description	Example
`Month(date)` `Month("12/31/1999")`	Returns a whole number between 1 and 12, inclusive, representing the month of the year	

`MonthName(month[,`
`MonthName(12,True)`
`abbreviate])`
	Returns a string indicating the specified month	

`Now`	Returns the current date and time according to the setting of your computer's system date and time	`Now`
`Second(time)` `Second("12:15:30")`	Returns a whole number between 0 and 59, inclusive, representing the second of the minute	
`Time`	Returns a Variant of subtype `Date` indicating the current system time	`Time`

`TimeSerial(hour,`
`TimeSerial(12,15,30)`
`minute, second)`
	Returns a Variant of subtype `Date` containing the time for a specific hour, minute, and second	

`TimeValue(time)`	Returns a Variant of subtype `Date` containing the time	`TimeValue` `("12:15:30")`
`Weekday(date,` `[firstdayofweek])`	Returns a whole number representing the day of the week	`WeekDay` `("12/31/1999")`

`WeekdayName`
`WeekDayName(6,True)`
`(weekday,`
`abbreviate,`
`firstdayofweek)`
	Returns a string indicating the specified day of the week	

`Year(date)` `Year("12/31/1999")`	Returns a whole number representing the year	

Now add a Web page called DATETIME.HTM to the VBSMethods project. Make sure you're in Design mode and, after adding a descriptive header, create a table with 20 rows and

Using the VBScript Date/Time Methods

4 columns. After creating the table, copy the information from Table 12.4 into the first three columns. In the last column, add a command button.

After adding the text and command buttons, switch to the **Source** tab and change the names of all the buttons to match the name of the method, along with a prefix of `btn`. For example, the first button ID would be set to `btnDate`, the second to `btnDateAdd`, and so on.

When you're finished, the page should look like the one in Figure 12.5.

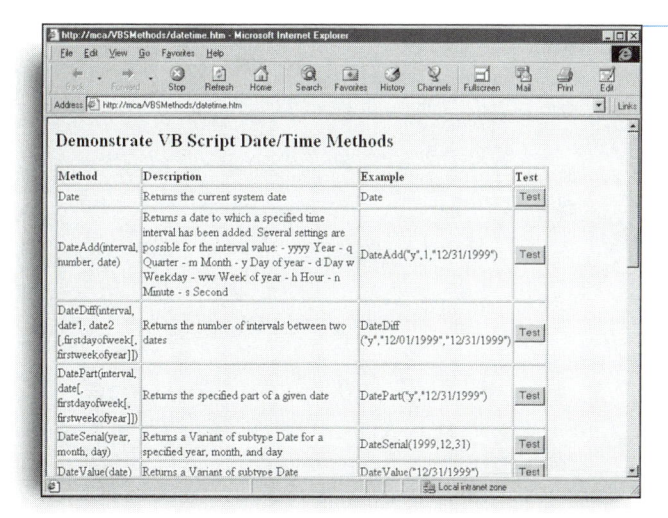

> **Mistaken methods make mistakes**
>
> It is easy to mistype a method and end up with an entirely different result than you expected. The problem lies in that many methods have similar names. Say its late at night and you use `WeekDayName` instead of `WeekDay` as you intended. The result would be completely different than what you wanted. Don't overlook common mistakes!

FIGURE 12.5
Laying out the VBScript Date/Time Methods page.

Now you're ready to add the VBScript that illustrates the date/time methods. Before you begin coding, be sure the `DefaultClientSCript` property of the page is set to **VBScript**. Next, switch to the **Source** tab in the editor to start editing the code. Now use the Script Outline window to locate each button's `onclick` event. Double-clicking the `onclick` event will force Visual InterDev to add the code header and footer for the `onclick` event for that button.

SEE ALSO
▶ In Chapter 14, "Client-Side Scripting with the MSIE Object Model," you will learn more about using the Script Outline window to manipulate scripted events.

Add the code in Listing 12.3 to the page and save the file before running a test.

LISTING 12.3 Coding the VBScript Date/Time Methods

```
1  Sub btnYear_onclick
2      msgbox Year("12/31/1999")
3  End Sub
4
5  Sub btnWeekDayName_onclick
6      msgbox WeekDayName(6,True)
7  End Sub
8
9  Sub btnWeekDay_onclick
10     msgbox WeekDay("12/31/1999")
11 End Sub
12
13 Sub btnTimeValue_onclick
14     msgbox TimeValue("12:15:30")
15 End Sub
16
17 Sub btnNow_onclick
18     msgbox Now
19 End Sub
20
21 Sub btnTimeSerial_onclick
22     msgbox TimeSerial(12,15,30)
23 End Sub
24
25 Sub btnTime_onclick
26     msgbox Time
27 End Sub
28
29 Sub btnSecond_onclick
30   msgbox Second("12:15:30")
31 End Sub
32
33 Sub btnMonthName_onclick
34     msgbox MonthName(12,True)
35 End Sub
36
37 Sub btnMonth_onclick
```

Using the VBScript Date/Time Methods

```
38      msgbox Month("12/31/1999")
39  End Sub
40
41  Sub btnMinute_onclick
42      msgbox Minute("12:15:30")
43  End Sub
44
45  Sub btnHour_onclick
46      msgbox Hour("12:15:30")
47  End Sub
48
49  Sub btnDay_onclick
50      msgbox Day("12/31/1999")
51  End Sub
52
53  Sub btnDateValue_onclick
54      msgbox DateValue("12/31/1999")
55  End Sub
56
57  Sub btnDateSerial_onclick
58      msgbox DateSerial(1999,12,31)
59  End Sub
60
61  Sub btnDatePart_onclick
62      msgbox DatePart("d","12/31/1999")
63  End Sub
64
65  Sub btnDateDiff_onclick
66      msgbox DateDiff("y","12/01/1999","12/31/1999")
67  End Sub
68
69  Sub btnDateAdd_onclick
70      msgbox DateAdd("y",1,"12/31/1999")
71  End Sub
72
73  Sub btnDate_onclick
74      msgbox Date
75  End Sub
```

Using the wrong methods, part 2

You're already aware of how using the wrong method will give you the wrong result. Think about the results of using the wrong parameters or values when using the correct methods. Take care when entering values for methods, ensuring that they are in the proper sequence (if required) and format.

Be sure to test each date/time method before continuing to the next section.

Using the VBScript Data Conversion Methods

VBScript has several methods devoted to converting values from one data type to another. You have already used several of them in the math, string, and date/time sections of this chapter. However, another 13 conversion methods have not yet been covered (see Table 12.5).

TABLE 12.5 **VBScript conversion methods**

Method	Description	Example
Cbool(*expression*)	Returns an expression that has been converted to a Variant of subtype Boolean	Cbool(1>2)
CByte(*expression*)	Returns an expression that has been converted to a Variant of subtype Byte	CByte(255)
CCur(*expression*)	Returns an expression that has been converted to a Variant of subtype Currency	CCur("1750.55555")
CDate(*date*) CDate("12/31/1999")	Returns an expression that has been converted to a Variant of subtype Date	
CDbl(*expression*)	Returns an expression that has been converted to a Variant of subtype Double	CDbl ("4.94065645841247E-324")
CInt(*expression*)	Returns an expression that has been converted to a Variant of subtype Integer	CInt("32767")
CLng(*expression*)	Returns an expression that has been converted to a Variant of subtype Long	CLng ("2147483647")

Using the VBScript Data Conversion Methods

Method	Description	Example
CSng(*expression*)	Returns an expression that has been converted to a Variant of subtype Single	CSng ("3.402823E38")
CStr(*expression*)	Returns an expression that has been converted to a Variant of subtype String	CStr(3.141)
Hex(*number*)	Returns a string representing the hexadecimal value of a number	Hex(255)
Oct(*number*)	Returns a string representing the octal value of a number	Oct(8)
Fix(*number*)	Returns the integer portion of a number	Fix(-8.4)
Int(*number*)	Returns the integer portion of a number	Int(-8.4)

Conversion methods

You can think of conversion methods as the "everything but" group of methods. This group contains many useful, although not easily categorized, methods.

Now add a new page called CONVERSION.HTM to the VBSMethods project. Create a descriptive title and build a table that has 14 rows and 4 columns. Then copy the information from Table 12.5 to the page and add command buttons with a caption of Test in the fourth column. When you're finished, your page should look like the one in Figure 12.6.

Now you're ready to rename the buttons. Be sure the DefaultClientScript property of the page is set to **VBScript** and switch to the **Source** tab. Now locate the ID property of each button and set it to btn plus the name of the method. For example, the first button would be set to btnCBool, the second to btnCByte, and so on.

After renaming the buttons, save the page before adding the VBScript coding. Use Listing 12.4 to add the VBScript to each onclick event. You can type the listing directly or use the Script Outline window to navigate to each button and expose the onclick method.

PART III Using Visual Basic Script
CHAPTER 12 Expanding Your Scripts with Built-In Methods

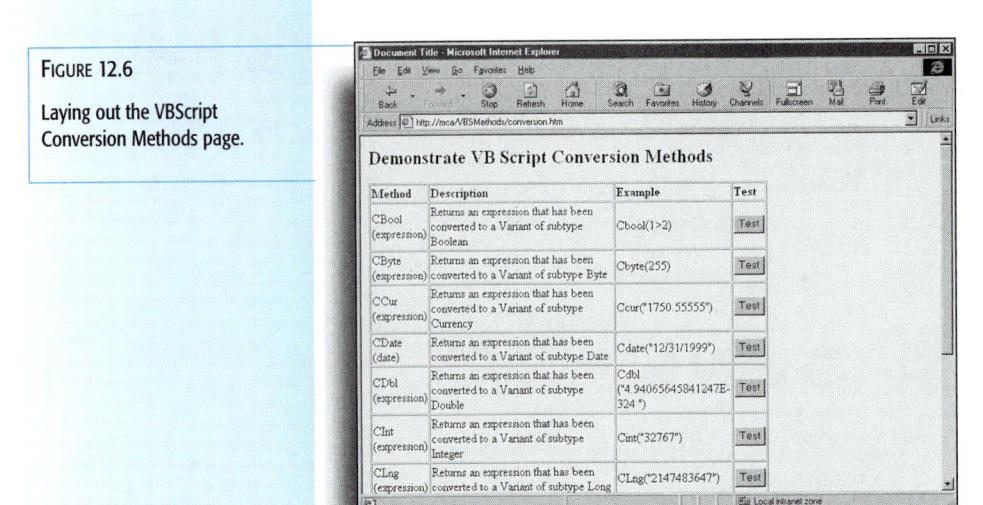

FIGURE 12.6

Laying out the VBScript Conversion Methods page.

LISTING 12.4 Coding the VBScript Conversion Methods

```
1  Sub btnOct_onclick
2      msgbox Oct(8)
3  End Sub
4
5  Sub btnInt_onclick
6      msgbox Int(-8.4)
7  End Sub
8
9  Sub btnHex_onclick
10     msgbox Hex(255)
11 End Sub
12
13 Sub btnFix_onclick
14     msgbox Fix(-8.4)
15 End Sub
16
17 Sub btnCStr_onclick
18     msgbox cStr(3.141)
19 End Sub
20
21 Sub btnCSng_onclick
22     msgbox CSng("3.402823E38")
```

Other VBScript Methods

```
23 End Sub
24
25 Sub btnCLng_onclick
26     msgbox CLng("2147483647")
27 End Sub
28
29 Sub btnCInt_onclick
30     msgbox cInt(32767)
31 End Sub
32
33 Sub btnCDbl_onclick
34     msgbox Cdbl("4.94065645841247E-324")
35 End Sub
36
37 Sub btnCDate_onclick
38     msgbox CDate("12/31/1999")
39 End Sub
40
41 Sub btnCCur_onclick
42     msgbox CCur("1750.55555")
43 End Sub
44
45 Sub btnCByte_onclick
46     msgbox cByte(255)
47 End Sub
48
49 Sub btnCBool_onclick
50     msgbox cbool(1>2)
51 End Sub
```

> **VBScript methods and Visual Basic**
>
> Do you ever get the feeling that Microsoft didn't trim all that much from Visual Basic to make VBScript? Well, you wouldn't be entirely wrong. VBScript is streamlined in comparison to Visual Basic. It contains the methods that you are fundamentally required for any type of programming.

After entering the code, save the page and run a test. Notice that there is a subtle difference between the Fix and Int methods. Fix rounds negative values up, Int rounds them down.

Other VBScript Methods

There are a handful of other VBScript methods that should be mentioned here. These fall into the following categories:

- Output formatting methods
- User Input/Output dialogs

> **Using these methods to your advantage**
>
> The remaining methods can prove handy when you are looking to liven up or enhance your Web application's interactivity. Familiar Windows dialog boxes, for example, can be used for user interaction as opposed to a traditional Web page form.

Each of these categories is covered in the next sections of this chapter.

Using the Output Formatting Methods

There are four methods for producing formatted strings for output in your Web applications. Table 12.6 summarizes these methods.

TABLE 12.6 Formatting methods of VBScript

Methods	Description	Example
`FormatCurrency (Expression[, NumDigitsAfter Decimal [,Include LeadingDigit [,UseParensFor NegativeNumbers [,GroupDigits]]]])`	Returns an expression formatted as a currency value using the currency symbol defined in the system control panel	`FormatCurrency (1750.55555)`
`FormatDateTime FormatDateTime(Now) (Date[,Named Format])`	Returns an expression formatted as a date or time	
`FormatNumber (Expression[, NumDigitsAfter Decimal [,Include LeadingDigit [,UseParensFor NegativeNumbers [,GroupDigits]]]])`	Returns an expression formatted as a number	`FormatNumber (12345678.01)`
`FormatPercent (Expression [,NumDigitsAfter Decimal [,Include LeadingDigit [,UseParensFor NegativeNumbers [,GroupDigits]]]])`	Returns an expression formatted as a percentage (multiplied by 100) with a trailing % character	`FormatPercent (.4555)`

Other VBScript Methods

PART III
CHAPTER 12

295

Now add a new page called OTHER.HTM to your VBSMethods project. Add a title (Other VBScript Methods) and subtitle (Output Formatting Methods). Next, add a table with five rows and four columns and a set of column headers for Method, Description, Example, and Test. Then copy the text from Table 12.6 into the first three columns. Place a command button in the last column. It should look like the page in Figure 12.7.

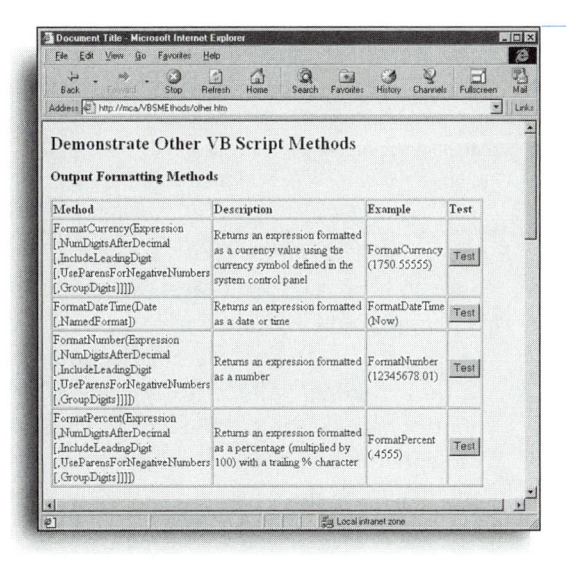

Formatting methods

If you work on many Web applications, you'll likely use the formatting methods provided in VBScript. These methods make it easier to simplify the logic behind the scenes to a user.

FIGURE 12.7
Laying out the Output Formatting Methods table.

Be sure the DefaultClientScript property of the page is set to **VBScript** and switch to the **Design** tab of the editor window. Now change the button ID properties to btn plus the name of the method. For example, the first button would be called btnFormatCurrency.

Save the page before you add VBScript code. Listing 12.5 shows the VBScript code to add to the page.

LISTING 12.5 Adding VBScript for the Output Formatting Methods

```
1  Sub btnFormatPercent_onclick
2      msgbox FormatPercent(.4555)
3  End Sub
4  Sub btnFormatNumber_onclick
5      msgbox FormatNumber(12345678.01)
6  End Sub
7
8  Sub btnFormatDateTime_onclick
9      msgbox FormatDateTime(Now)
10 End Sub
11
12 Sub btnFormatCurrency_onclick
13     msgbox FormatCurrency(1750.55555)
14 End Sub
```

Save and run the page to test the output formatting methods of VBScript. Note that the FormatCurrency method rounds to the nearest fourth decimal place. Also, you should know that all four of these routines will format the values based on the Windows control panel setting of the client. That means that you can use these methods to produce properly formatted currency, numeric, and date/time information for any client in the world.

Using the User Input/Output Methods

There are two commonly used user input/output methods in VBScript. These allow for a simple, consistent way to get user input, display messages, and present images within the client browser. Table 12.7 shows these two methods.

TABLE 12.7 User input/output methods for VBScript

Method	Description	Example
InputBox(prompt [, title][, default][, xpos][, ypos] [, helpfile, context])	Displays a prompt in a dialog box, waits for the user to input text or click a button, and returns the contents of the text box	InputBox("Enter Your Name:","Name","Your Name")

Other VBScript Methods

Method	Description	Example
MsgBox(*prompt*[, *buttons*][, *title*][, *helpfile*, *context*])	Displays a message in a dialog box, waits for the user to click a button, and returns a value indicating which button the user clicked	MsgBox("Ready to Continue?",vbYesNo, "Continue Dialog")

There are several options for the button value in the last entry of Table 12.7:

- vbOKOnly 0 Display **OK** button only.
- VbOKCancel 1 Display **OK** and **Cancel** buttons.
- VbAbortRetryIgnore 2 Display **Abort**, **Retry**, and **Ignore** buttons.
- VbYesNoCancel 3 Display **Yes**, **No**, and **Cancel** buttons.
- VbYesNo 4 Display **Yes** and **No** buttons.
- VbRetryCancel 5 Display **Retry** and **Cancel** buttons.
- VbCritical 16 Display **Critical Message** icon.
- VbQuestion 32 Display **Warning Query** icon.
- VbExclamation 48 Display **Warning Message** icon.
- VbInformation 64 Display **Information Message** icon.
- VbDefaultButton1 0 First button is default.
- VbDefaultButton2 256 Second button is default.
- VbDefaultButton3 512 Third button is default.
- VbDefaultButton4 768 Fourth button is default.
- VbApplicationModal 0 Application modal; the user must respond to the message box before continuing work in the current application.
- VbSystemModal 4096 System modal; all applications are suspended until the user responds to the message box.

Don't go overboard

Don't abuse the MsgBox and InputBox methods. Although they can be used to enhance your application, relying on them too much becomes obtrusive. Most Web site users are not expecting pop-up dialog boxes from a Web page. Instead, they are looking for their activity within the constraints of the Web browser itself. Always use these methods only when you have good reason.

Experimenting with dialog types

Experiment creating different dialog box types using the button values. Using smart design and sound logic, your Web application can mimic a standard Windows application.

There are several possible return values:

- `vbOK` 1 OK
- `vbCancel` 2 Cancel
- `vbAbort` 3 Abort
- `vbRetry` 4 Retry
- `vbIgnore` 5 Ignore
- `vbYes` 6 Yes
- `vbNo` 7 No

As you can see from Table 12.7, `MsgBox` has quite a few options. You can use the `MsgBox` method to display simple messages as well as get user input. This input can be used (along with a decision structure) to determine which VBScript code should be executed.

Now add a horizontal rule to the OTHER.HTM page, along with a table with three rows and four columns. Fill the first column with header names (`Method`, `Description`, `Example`, and `Test`) and copy the data from Table 12.7 into the first three cells in each row. Add a command button in the fourth column and set the button ID properties to `btn` plus the name of the method (`btnInputBox` and `btnMsgBox`). Finally, save the page before adding the VBScript code. It should look like Figure 12.8.

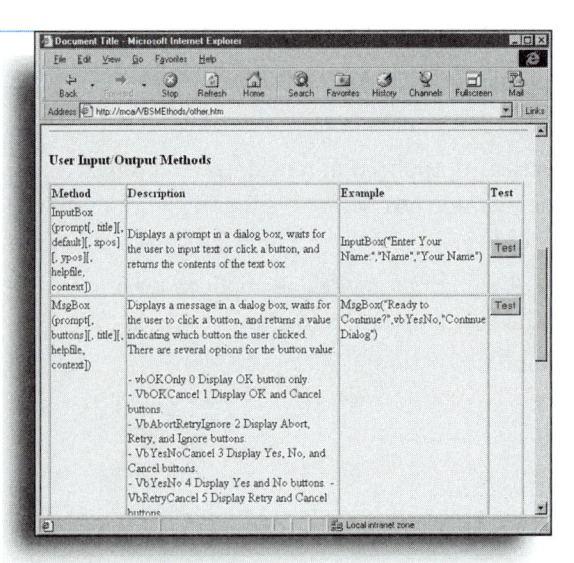

FIGURE 12.8

Laying out the User Input/Output Methods table.

Other VBScript Methods

Before adding code, be sure the `DefaultClientScript` property of the page is set to **VBScript**; then switch to the **Source** tab and enter the code from Listing 12.6.

> **Simplicity in examples**
>
> These examples only outline the most basic uses of dialog boxes. You can probably come up with your own much more practical applications. For example, if your Web application requires a user to log in for authentication and access, you might want to use a login box that resembles a Windows login dialog. This will be familiar to your users.

LISTING 12.6 Adding the VBScript for the User Input/Output Methods

```
1  Sub btnMsgBox_onclick
2     '
3     dim intAnswer
4     '
5     intAnswer=MsgBox("Ready to Continue?",vbYesNo+
       ➥vbQuestion,"Continue Dialog")
6     '
7     if intAnswer=vbYes then
8        msgbox "You selected YES",vbExclamation,"YES"
9     else
10       msgbox "You selected NO",vbCritical,"NO"
11    end if
12    '
13 End Sub
14
15 Sub btnInputBox_onclick
16    '
17    dim strInput
18    '
19    strInput=InputBox("Enter Your Name:","Name","Your
       ➥Name")
20    '
21    msgbox strInput
22    '
23 End Sub
```

The routine for `btnMsgBox_onclick` (lines 1–13) uses the `MsgBox` method in several different ways. First, you see the example that returns the button selected by the user. Then you see two other examples that simply display the message, along with an icon and title.

The `btnInputBox_onclick` routine (lines 15–23) calls upon the `InputBox` method to prompt you for your name. This information is then passed to a standard `MsgBox` method to display your entry.

CHAPTER

13

Adding Event Handling to Your Visual Basic Scripts

Learn how event bubbling provides you with precise control over your events

Create events for windows, documents, and forms

Add events for specific elements

PART **III** Using Visual Basic Script

CHAPTER **13** **Adding Event Handling to Your Visual Basic Scripts**

You can add to your Web applications VBScript that will respond to various events that occur while your application is running. In this chapter, you learn about the various objects that can receive event messages, exactly what those event messages are, and when they occur. In addition to learning about event messages, you also learn the three ways you can link your VBScript to event messages (Intrinsic, Attribute, and Explicit) and the advantages and limitations of each method.

Finally, you learn about the process of event bubbling, which enables event messages from one page element to be received by another, higher-level page element. This allows you to create event links that can receive similar messages from groups of controls (for example, creating event links on a form for all the input controls on that form). This simplifies VBScript coding and makes it easier to maintain your Web applications.

Four objects can receive event messages: Window, Document, Form, and Element. You can also establish an event for the moment when someone clicks on a link item. However, this is a peculiar case and is handled differently from the other four objects.

Events are actually moments during the life of your Web application that are marked by messages broadcast by the browser to the workstation. These messages have specific names and are "attached" to specific objects or elements of your Web application page. When you know how to identify the objects and event names, you can create methods that will be executed whenever the event occurs.

There are lots of possible events, such as loading and unloading windows and documents within your Web application, moving and clicking (or double-clicking) the mouse, pressing keys, and so on. There are also event messages sent whenever a user updates a form element, attempts to submit a form, or presses the F1 key in a request for help services.

When you are finished with this chapter, you'll know how to establish events for the major elements of every Web application page and how to add VBScript to your applications to execute for the selected events.

Event objects and Microsoft Internet Explorer

In this chapter, you learn about the Window, Document, Form, and Element objects. You learn much more about the Microsoft Internet Explorer 4 object model in Chapter 14, "Client-Side Scripting with the MSIE Object Model." For now, just think of each of these four items as relatively independent items. Chapter 14 will show you how these (and other items in the Microsoft Internet Explorer object model) fit together.

For experience

If you are new to VBScript, you might want to start with Chapter 11, "Programming with Visual Basic Scripting Language." This gives you an introduction to VBScript and how to add VBScript to your HTML pages. You might also want to read Chapter 12, "Expanding Your Scripts with Built-In Methods."

Linking Your VBScript to Event Messages   CHAPTER 13

SEE ALSO
- To step into scripting with VBScript, see page 248
- To learn more about scripting, see page 272
- You learn about adding event coding for links on page 331

Linking Your VBScript to Event Messages

Before you can take advantage of the event messages available in your Web application, you must establish a link between the object that reports events and your VBScript code. This can be done in three ways:

- Intrinsic event declaration
- Attribute event declaration
- Explicit event declaration

The details of each of these methods appears in the next three sections.

Using Instrinsic Event Declaration

The first method, Intrinsic event declaration, is the most common method in VBScript. The document is marked for VBScript execution and a page-level HTML tag is included to mark the location of all VBScript code (`<SCRIPT LANGUAGE="VBSCRIPT">` and `</SCRIPT>`). Whenever an event message is reported, it is sent to a method that is named `<object>_<message>` where `<object>` is the name of the object that reports the message and `<message>` is the name of the message that is reported.

For example, the button object reports the `onclick` message whenever someone presses the button. Because each button can receive its own messages, the ID tag is used as the object name for event messages. Using the Intrinsic event declaration method of VBScript, the `onclick` message of `button1` will be sent to a method that looks like Listing 13.1.

LISTING 13.1   **Example of Intrinsic Event Handling for VBScript**

```
1  Sub button1_onclick()
2      alert "Button has been pressed"
3  End Sub
```

If you have marked your HTML documents to use VBScript as the default client script in your page's properties, you just add the proper <object>_<message> method between the <SCRIPT></SCRIPT> tags and you're all set.

Using Attribute Event Declaration

Another common method is Attribute event declaration, in which you declare the name of the event as an attribute in the HTML tag of the element and associate a method name with the event name. In this case, the actual event name is an attribute of the HTML tag. Listing 13.2 shows how this would look on your HTML page.

LISTING 13.2   **An Attribute Event Declaration**

```
1  <INPUT TYPE="button"
2      NAME="Button1"
3      VALUE="PressMe"
4      onClick="pressed"
5      LANGUAGE="VBScript">
6
7  <SCRIPT LANGUAGE="VBScript">
8      Sub pressed
9          alert "Button has been pressed"
10     End sub
11 </SCRIPT>
```

Note that the onclick event has been associated with a method called "pressed" and that the LANGUAGE attribute has been set to "VBScript". This tells the browser that whenever the onclick message is reported by this particular button, there is a method called "pressed" in the "VBScript" area that should be notified.

Linking Your VBScript to Event Messages

The primary advantage of using the Attribute method of event linking is that you can use it in multiple scripting languages for individual elements. For example, some other buttons could be associated with methods in a `"JScript"` or `"PerlScript"` area of the HTML page. Because we are covering VBScript in this book, you'll not see this type of event declaration appear too often.

Also, this method of event declaration will not work for any HTML element that has an `OBJECT` tag. If you are using an item that has an `OBJECT` tag, you must use the Intrinsic or Explicit method of event linking.

Using Explicit Event Declaration

The third method for linking event reports with VBScript methods is to use Explicit event declaration. In this process, you place the VBScript code directly in the HTML definition area instead of in a shared `<SCRIPT></SCRIPT>` area, as in Listing 13.3.

> **Scripting languages**
>
> One of the nicest things about server-side scripting is the capability to use several different scripting languages, such as VBScript, Perl, REXX, and JScript. Unfortunately, client-side scripting (as discussed in this chapter) relies on one of two scripting languages: VBScript or JScript (JavaScript/ECMAScript). Think of your target platform when choosing a scripting language.

LISTING 13.3 An Example of Explicit Event Declaration

```
1  <INPUT TYPE="button" NAME="Button1" VALUE="Click">
2    <SCRIPT FOR="Button1" EVENT="onClick"
   ➥LANGUAGE="VBScript">
3      alert "Button has been pressed"
4    </SCRIPT>
```

Notice that the `<SCRIPT>` tag has been enhanced to include the `FOR` and `EVENT` attributes. These attributes associate the VBScript with the `"button1"` object and the `"onclick"` event message. You are not required to place the code directly next to the `INPUT TYPE` tag, but it is done quite often because it looks nicer than having several `<SCRIPT FOR=...></SCRIPT>` tags sitting in a collection at the top of your HTML document.

Like the Attribute method, the Explicit method enables you to employ multiple scripting languages within the same HTML document. However, the difference between Attribute and

Explicit is that the Explicit method is allowed for elements with an OBJECT tag. In fact, the Explicit method is the only way to associate scripting code with HTML elements that have an OBJECT tag.

About Event Bubbling

IE4 supports a special form of event handling called event bubbling. *Event bubbling* is the capability to pass an event message from the element that reported the message to an element's parent. This means that parent elements can receive (and respond to) event messages aimed toward child elements within the HTML document.

For example, several of the input elements (text box, check box, and so on) have the capability of reporting messages related to data provider updates. When a row of data is updated, the onbeforeupdate message is sent to report that data is about to be sent back to the provider. If all goes well, the onafterupdate message is sent to report that the data has been successfully sent to the provider. However, if an error occurred when sending the data back, the onerrorupdate message is sent instead.

Now here comes the bubbling part. If you want, you can create event links for every data-bound element on a form and write code for each field of the data row. This would, however, take a great deal of time and code maintenance. Instead, you can take advantage of event bubbling and place a single event link on the parent element of the control—the Form object—and receive all data-bound messages there instead. Having one place for all event messages makes it easier to code and easier to maintain, too.

As you work through the event lists for objects in this chapter, you'll see several events that are actually "bubbled" from child elements. They will be marked with a (B) to indicate that they are bubbled events from child elements, not native events for that object.

Bubbling brings power

Through event bubbling you can create complex applications. Bubbling is a familiar concept for programmers who work in Visual Basic or C++. It is new, however, to the world of Web applications. Experiment with bubbling to see how you can improve your program interaction.

Setting Up the VBScript Event Web Project

Before you continue with this chapter, you should start a new Visual InterDev project called VBSEvents. Add an HTML page called DEFAULT.HTM and add a title and link items as defined in Table 13.1.

TABLE 13.1 **Elements to Add to the DEFAULT.HTM Page**

Element	Text	URL
Document header	Demonstrate VBScript Events	
Link	Window Events	Window.htm
	Document Events	Document.htm
	Form Events	Form.htm
	Element Events	Element.htm
	Link Events	Link.htm

After laying out the form, it should look like the one in Figure 13.1.

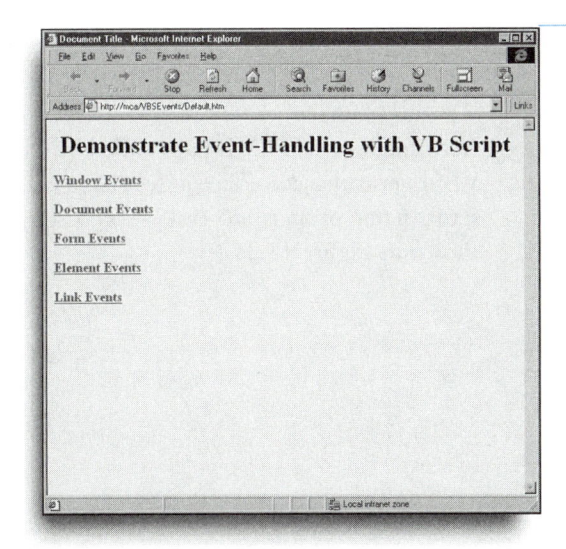

FIGURE 13.1
Laying out the DEFAULT.HTM form of the VBSEvents project.

This page will be the starting point for all the examples in this chapter. Be sure to save the form (DEFAULT.HTM) and the project (VBSEvents) before continuing to the next section.

Using Window Events

The highest-level object that can report events is the *Window*. The Window object represents the current browser window. This window can receive several event messages. They are listed in Table 13.2, along with a short description.

TABLE 13.2 Available Window Messages

Message	Description
Onbeforeunload	Occurs when the window is about to be unloaded
Onblur	Occurs when the window loses focus
Onerror	Occurs when an error occurs within the window
Onfocus	Occurs when the window gains focus
Onhelp	Occurs when the F1 key is pressed in Windows
Onload	Occurs when the window is about to be loaded
Onresize	Occurs when the user resizes the window
Onscroll	Occurs when the user scrolls the window
Onunload	Occurs when the window is actually unloaded

Let's add a new HTML page called WINDOW.HTM to the VBSEvents project. Place a Text Area control on the form and set its name property to `txaEvents`. Also, add some labels, as shown in Figure 13.2.

Keep in mind the object model

Always remember that the Microsoft Internet Explorer object model and the object model for other browsers, such as Netscape, differ greatly. Chapter 14 details the MSIE object model. In this chapter, I'm assuming you're working with Internet Explorer. If you're not, you might get unpredictable results—if any.

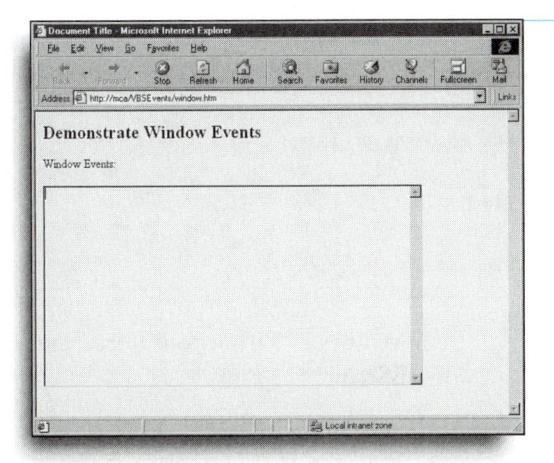

FIGURE 13.2
Laying out the WINDOW.HTM form.

Now you're ready to add some code to respond to the messages. First, make sure the `defaultClientScript` property of the page is set to **VBScript** and then select the **Source** tab in the Visual InterDev editor to expose the coding for the HTML document.

Let's create a custom method to display all event messages in the Text Area control in a numbered list. To do this you must declare a page-level variable outside the method declaration. This variable will be used to keep track of the event count. Then you can add the code that will accept a string as a parameter and add it to the top of the event list in the `txaEvents` Text Area control.

To begin, create the `<SCRIPT>...</SCRIPT>` tags that will identify your scripting code. The easiest way to do this is to double-click an event in the Script Outline window. You can then remove the method code from the listing. For example, if you double-click the `onclick` event for the Document object, the lines shown in Listing 13.4 are added.

Adding Event Handling to Your Visual Basic Scripts

LISTING 13.4 The Code Block Added

```
1 <SCRIPT ID=clientEventHandlersVBS LANGUAGE=vbscript>
2 <!--
3 Sub document_onclick
4
5 End Sub
6 -->
7 </SCRIPT>
```

An easier way to add code blocks

Visual Studio, the interface for Visual InterDev, lets you create complex macros and extensions. You can use these features to create a macro that automatically inserts the code blocks you want, without having to remove unwanted events. The Visual InterDev online help gives more details on this.

Remove lines 2–5 from your document, leaving the handler code for VBScript.

At the top of the `<SCRIPT LANGUAGE="VBScript">` portion of the page (after the `<!--` tag), place the code from Listing 13.5.

LISTING 13.5 Coding the *PostMsg* Method

```
1  '
2  ' page-level variable
3  dim lngCounter
4
5  '
6  ' shared method
7  Sub PostMsg(strMsg)
8     '
9     on error resume next
10    dim strTemp
11    dim strError
12    '
13    lngCounter=lngCounter+1
14    strTemp = cStr(lngCounter) & ": "
15    strTemp = strTemp & strMsg & vbCRLF
16    '
17    txaEvents.value=strTemp & txaEvents.value
18    if err.number<>0 then
19       strError="Err: " & cStr(err.number) & vbCrLf
20       strError=strError & err.description & vbCrLf
21       strError=strError & strMsg
22       msgbox strError,vbCritical,"Scripting Error!"
23    end if
24    '
25 End Sub
```

Built-ins abound

As you learned in Chapter 12, you will use built-ins all over your scripting code. This listing is a good example. How many built-ins can you spot?

Using Window Events   CHAPTER 13

The code in Listing 13.5 contains some lines to handle possible errors. This has been added to prevent the browser from crashing if an error occurs during the execution of the method. You'll learn more about error handling later in the book. For now, just enter the lines as you see them. They'll make more sense later.

Now you can create the event links. For this example, use the Intrinsic event declaration method. You do this by adding method headers that contain the object name (`window`) and the event name (`onbeforeload` and so on) to the VBScript section of the HTML document.

Although you could type it in directly (as in Listing 13.1), you can also use the Script Outline window to expose the event list for the Window object and simply double-click on each event in the list to force Visual InterDev to insert the method header for you.

Adding method headers to the VBScript section of an HTML document

1. Select the **Source** tab to expose Visual InterDev's editing window.
2. In the Script Outline window, select **Client Objects & Events**.
3. Then select **Window** to see the list of events.
4. Double-click on each event, and Visual InterDev will create a method header and footer to match the `<object>_<message>` names.

After you insert the method headers, you must insert a single line of code into each method. Call this line of code the `PostMsg` method and pass the name of the object and event as a string. Listing 13.6 contains the completed code for all nine events for the Window object.

The script outline

The script outline reinforces the object model that Microsoft Internet Explorer and Visual InterDev work by. The relationship between items in the list illustrates their order in the model.

LISTING 13.6   **Coding the Window Object Events**

```
1  Sub window_onunload
2      PostMsg "window_onunload"
3  End Sub
4
```

continues...

LISTING 13.6 **Continued**

```
5  Sub window_onscroll
6      PostMsg "window_onscroll"
7  End Sub
8
9  Sub window_onresize
10     PostMsg "window_onresize"
11 End Sub
12
13 Sub window_onload
14     PostMsg "window_onload"
15 End Sub
16
17 Sub window_onhelp
18     PostMsg "window_onhelp"
19 End Sub
20
21 Sub window_onfocus
22     PostMsg "window_onfocus"
23 End Sub
24
25 Sub window_onerror
26     PostMsg "window_onerror"
27 End Sub
28
29 Sub window_onblur
30     PostMsg "window_onblur"
31 End Sub
32
33 Sub window_onbeforeunload
34     PostMsg "window_onbeforeunload"
35 End Sub
```

Using Window objects smartly

Use of the Window object can greatly enhance your Web application's functionality. You can use the events from the browser's window to drive behaviors in your application. Keep in mind, however, that you should use care when choosing events. Make sure that the actions you are using for an event are warranted. After all, do you want something to happen every time you move your window on a small screen? Don't overdo it!

Now save the page and you'll be ready to test it out. Begin by right-clicking the DEFAULT.HTM page and choose **Set as Start Page** from the context menu. Now run the VBSEvents project (press F5 or select **Debug**, **Start** from the main Visual InterDev menu). When you start the application, you see the DEFAULT.HTM page. Click on the Window Events link to load the WINDOW.HTM page. As soon as the page appears, you see some event messages already in the txaEvents Text Area control.

Using Document Events

If you click your mouse outside the browser window, you see the `window_onblur` message appear. Click on the **Refresh** button to reload the page and you see the refreshed document now contains entries for `window_onbeforeunload` and `window_onload`. If you press the F1 key to request help, you'll see several messages appear, including `window_onhelp`.

Figure 13.3 shows the WINDOW.HTM page in action.

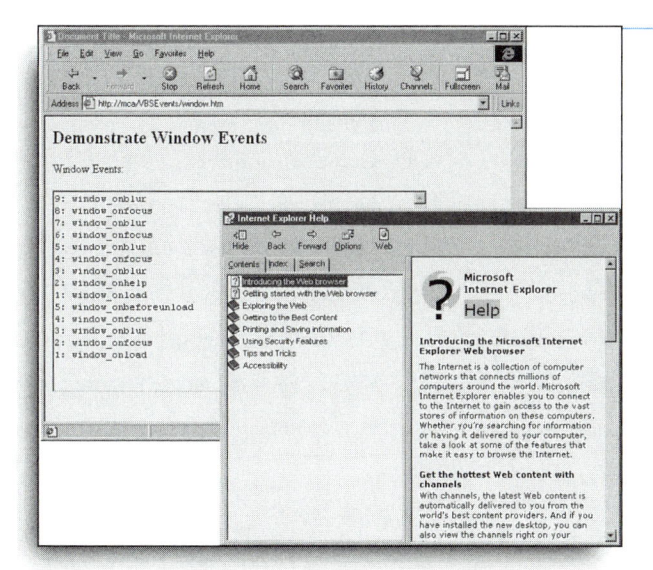

FIGURE 13.3
Running the WINDOW.HTM page.

Using Document Events

The next object that can report messages is the Document object. This object has quite a few more event messages than the Window object, and several of the messages are the same as the Window list. Table 13.3 shows the list of messages and a short description. Remember that the (B) in the description means this is a bubbled event from a child element and not a native event message for the Document object.

Confusing the Document and Window objects

Many beginning programmers confuse the Document object with the Window object. Use this as your key: The Window object reflects the physical window of the Web browser, whereas the Document object reflects everything within that window.

TABLE 13.3 Event Messages for the Document Object

Message	Description
Onafterupdate	(B) Occurs after data has been sent to the data provider
Onbeforeupdate	(B) Occurs just before data is to be sent to the data provider
Onclick	Occurs when the user clicks on the document
Ondblclick	Occurs when the user double-clicks on the document
Ondragstart	Occurs when the user first starts to drag a selected item
Onerrorupdate	(B) Occurs if there is an error sending data back to the data provider
Onhelp	Occurs when the user presses F1
Onkeydown	Occurs when a key is pressed down
Onkeypress	Occurs when a key is pressed
Onkeyup	Occurs when a key that is pressed down is released
Onmousedown	Occurs when a mouse button is pressed
Onmousemove	Occurs when the mouse is moved over the document
Onmouseup	Occurs when the mouse button that was pressed is released
Onreadystatechange	Occurs when the state of a document has changed (just before the onload event of the parent window)
Onrowenter	(B) Occurs when new data is available in a data provider
Onrowexit	(B) Occurs just before the data row is updated
Onselectstart	Occurs when an element on the form is selected

Let's create a page to show the events available for the document object.

Creating the page to illustrate events for the Document object

1. First, add a new HTML document to the project called DOCUMENT.HTM.
2. Open the DOCUMENT.HTM page for editing by double-clicking it in the Project Explorer.
3. Title the page Demonstrate Document Events.

Using Document Events

4. Set the page's `defaultClientScript` to VBScript from the Properties window.
5. Add an event to the page from the Script Outline window, just as you did for the WINDOW.HTM example.
6. Add a Text Area control to the page. You can drag the Text Area control from the toolbox onto your page.
7. Set the ID property of the Text Area control to `txaEvents`.

The page should look the same as the one in Figure 13.2 except that the title should read Demonstrate Document Events.

Next, you must add the same page-level variable and shared method called `PostMsg` from Listing 13.5 to the DOCUMENT.HTM page. This will be used to display messages in the `txaEvents` Text Area control.

Now you're ready to add the event-handling code to the document. Be sure the `DefaultClientScript` property of the page is set to `VBScript`. Use the Script Outline window to select **Client Objects & Events**, **Document** to see the list of events associated with the Document object. Now double-click on each event message to create the method header for each of the 19 events.

Finally, you add a single line of code to each event method that includes a call to the `PostMsg` method along with the name of the object and event. For example, the line for the `onkeypress` event of the Document object would look like this:

```
PostMsg "document_onkeypress"
```

Listing 13.7 contains the completed code for all 19 methods.

> **An example of a shared method's usefulness**
>
> This chapter is a good example of how a shared method can prove useful in your Web applications. You can reuse code throughout your Web application and call upon it for individual events and actions.

LISTING 13.7 Coding the Document Object Event Methods

```
1 Sub document_onselectstart
2     PostMsg "document_onselectstart"
3 End Sub
4
5 Sub document_onrowexit
6     PostMsg "document_onrowexit"
7 End Sub
8
```

continues…

LISTING 13.7 **Continued**

```
 9 Sub document_onrowenter
10     PostMsg "document_onrowenter"
11 End Sub
12
13 Sub document_onreadystatechange
14     PostMsg "document_onreadystatechange"
15 End Sub
16
17 Sub document_onmouseup
18     PostMsg "document_onmouseup"
19 End Sub
20
21 Sub document_onmouseover
22     PostMsg "document_onmouseover"
23 End Sub
24
25 Sub document_onmouseout
26     PostMsg "document_onmouseout"
27 End Sub
28
29 Sub document_onmousemove
30     PostMsg "document_onmousemove"
31 End Sub
32
33 Sub document_onmousedown
34     PostMsg "document_onmousedown"
35 End Sub
36
37 Sub document_onkeyup
38     PostMsg "document_onkeyup"
39 End Sub
40
41 Sub document_onkeypress
42     PostMsg "document_onkeypress"
43 End Sub
44
45 Sub document_onkeydown
46     PostMsg "document_onkeydown"
47 End Sub
48
49 Sub document_onhelp
```

Using Document Events — CHAPTER 13

```
50      PostMsg "document_onhelp"
51 End Sub
52
53 Sub document_onerrorupdate
54      PostMsg "document_onerrorupdate"
55 End Sub
56
57 Sub document_ondragstart
58      PostMsg "document_ondragstart"
59 End Sub
60
61 Sub document_ondblclick
62      PostMsg "document_ondblclick"
63 End Sub
64
65 Sub document_onclick
66      PostMsg "document_onclick"
67 End Sub
68
69 Sub document_onbeforeupdate
70      PostMsg "document_onbeforeupdate"
71 End Sub
72
73 Sub document_onafterupdate
74      PostMsg "document_onafterupdate"
75 End Sub
```

After adding all the code, save the page and view the DEFAULT.HTM page in your browser. When you navigate to the DOCUMENT.HTM page, you see event messages added to the list (see Figure 13.4).

Experiment with the mouse and keyboard to see other messages roll by. Try pressing F1 for help or pressing the **Refresh** button on your browser to see what other messages appear.

SEE ALSO
➤ *To add an event to the page from the Script Outline window, see page 308*

The power of the Document object

When you start working with the Document object you can start to see the power of the object model. Each successive version of the object model, from Internet Explorer 4 to the forthcoming Internet Explorer 5, is expanding the power of the Document object to provide greater functionality, such as drag-and-drop. Soon you won't be able to tell the difference between a traditional application developed in, say C++, and one created using Visual InterDev.

FIGURE 13.4

Running the DOCUMENT.HTM page.

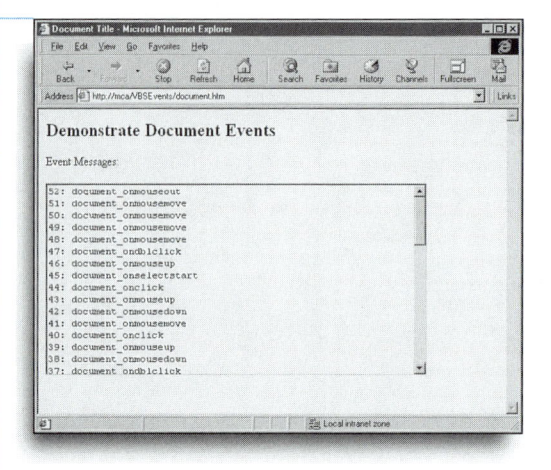

Using Form Events

Using form events for smart database applications

You can use form events to make working with a database even easier. Individual form events can trigger actions behind the scenes, such as populating a field or pushing data to the database. You can also use form events to manipulate data before it is put into the database.

The Form object is also capable of reporting event messages. These event messages include the usual mouse movement and keypress messages, but also include several new messages. A series of database-related messages is available on the form, including some that occur when the data fields are changed and when data sets are updated. There are also some events that occur when the user clicks a page's **Submit** or **Reset** (or equivalent) buttons, and there is even one that occurs when the user attempts to highlight text in a text box within the form. Table 13.4 shows all the event messages available for the Form object.

TABLE 13.4 **Event Messages for the Form Object**

Event Message	Description
Onafterupdate	(B) Occurs after data has been sent to the data provider
Onbeforeupdate	(B) Occurs just before data is to be sent to the data provider
Onclick	Occurs when the user clicks the mouse button within the form
Ondataavailable	(B) Occurs as data arrives for data source objects that transmit their data asynchronously
Ondatasetchanged	(B) Occurs when the data set exposed by a data source object changes

Using Form Events — PART III, CHAPTER 13 — 319

Event Message	Description
Ondatasetcomplete	(B) Occurs when all data is available from the data source object
Ondblclick	Occurs when the user double-clicks a mouse button within the form
Ondragstart	Occurs when the user first starts to drag a selected item
Onerrorupdate	(B) Occurs if there is an error sending data back to the data provider
Onfilterchange	(B) Occurs when a visual filter changes state or completes a transition
Onhelp	Occurs when the user presses the F1 key
Onkeydown	Occurs when the user presses any key
Onkeypress	Occurs when the user presses any key
Onkeyup	Occurs when the user releases a previously pressed key
Onmousedown	Occurs when the user presses a mouse button down
Onmousemove	Occurs when the user moves the mouse over the form
Onmouseout	Occurs when the user moves the mouse out of the form area
Onmouseover	Occurs when the mouse is hovering over the form
Onmouseup	Occurs when the user releases the previously pressed mouse button
Onrowenter	(B) Occurs when new data is available in a data provider
Onrowexit	(B) Occurs just before the data row is updated
Onselectstart	Occurs when the user begins to highlight data within an input control on the form
Onsubmit	Occurs when the user presses the **Submit** button on the form
Onreset	Occurs when the user presses the **Reset** button on the form

Be sure to note the event messages marked with a (B). These indicate bubbled messages from child elements. These messages are not native for this object, but they can be received by the form. This makes it easier to listen for event messages from a set of elements instead of adding code to each element in the set.

Encrypting or hiding information

Which would be the best event to use if you wanted a form to encrypt or hide information for the database after the user has completed filling in the fields? If you guessed `Onbeforeupdate`, you made a good choice. It's not the only method for doing so, but this is a great event for manipulating data just before it is sent to the database.

Let's build a page to illustrate the Form object event messages. Add another document to the VBSEvents Web project called FORM.HTM. This time, use Table 13.5 as a guide in building a simple Web form, along with the message event text box.

TABLE 13.5 Elements for the FORM.HTM Page

Element	Property	Setting
(simple text)	Heading 2	Demonstrate Form Events
`<HR>`		
(simple text)	Heading 4	Sample Form
Text box	ID	`TxtTest`
Submit button	ID	`BtnSubmit`
Reset button	ID	`BtnReset`
`<HR>`		
(simple text)	Normal	Event Messages:
Text Area box	ID	`TxaEvents`

You must add one more element to the page: the `FORM` tags. Because this form will not really be posting anything, you use the **Source** tab to manually type in the HTML `<FORM>` tag that you need. First, select the **Source** tab and then scroll to the first `<HR>` tag. Above this line, add the following HTML tag:

`<FORM id=frmTest name=frmTest>`

Now, scroll to the next `<HR>` tag. Just below this line, add the following HTML tag:

`</FORM>`

This marks the beginning and the end of the `frmTest` form on this page. When you are finished, your document should look like the one in Figure 13.5.

Using Form Events | PART III CHAPTER 13

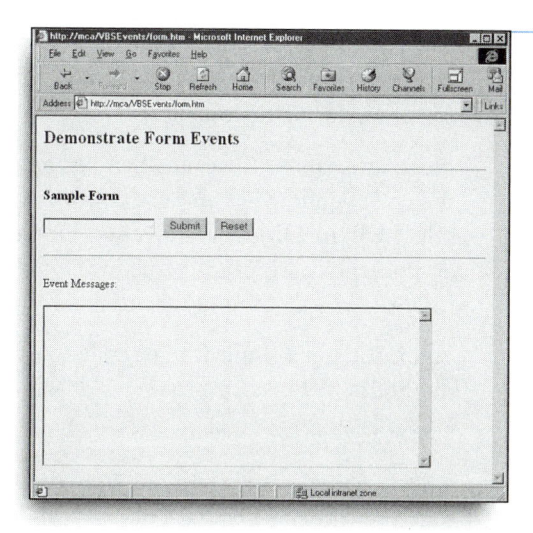

FIGURE 13.5
Laying out the FORM.HTM page.

After making sure the `DefaultClientScript` property of the page is set to `VBScript`, switch to the **Source** tab. The next step is to copy the code from Listing 13.4 into the FORM.HTM page. The easiest way to do this is to perform a copy and paste from the DOCUMENT.HTM page.

Copying code from one page to another

1. Open the page that holds the code to copy (DOCU-MENT.HTM) by double-clicking on it in the Project window.
2. Select the **Source** tab and locate the first line of code to copy.
3. Move to the first character in the line and hold down the Shift button; use the down-arrow key to highlight the area you want to copy.
4. After you paint all the lines you want to copy, press the Ctrl+C keys (or right-click **Copy** from the context menu) to copy the painted text to the Windows Clipboard.
5. Move to the document in which you want to paste the selected text (FORM.HTM).
6. Move the cursor to an open line where the text should be placed (the first line after the `<!--` tag).

Getting creative

Try to enhance this example by combining events from the Form object and the Document object. What would be the best way to make sure that every time a user manipulates any element on the screen or resizes the window, the data is current?

7. Press the Ctrl+V keys (or right-click **Paste** from the context menu) to copy the text from the Windows Clipboard into the selected document.

Next, you expose the event-handler methods in VBScript. With the code window in view, use the Script Outline window to select **Client Objects & Events**, **Document**, **frmTest**; then double-click each event name in the list to force Visual InterDev to create the method header to receive the event messages.

You must add a single line of code to each event-handling method:

`PostMsg <object>_<event>`

where `<object>` is `frmTest` and `<event>` is the name of the message event (that is, `onclick` and so on). Listing 13.8 shows the completed code for FORM.HTM.

LISTING 13.8 Completed VBScript for the Form Object Events

```
1  Sub frmTest_onselectstart
2      PostMsg "frmTest_onselectstart"
3  End Sub
4
5  Sub frmTest_onsubmit
6      PostMsg "frmTest_onsubmit"
7  End Sub
8
9  Sub frmTest_onrowenter
10     PostMsg "frmTest_onrowenter"
11 End Sub
12
13 Sub frmTest_onrowexit
14     PostMsg "frmTest_onrowexit"
15 End Sub
16
17 Sub frmTest_onreset
18     PostMsg "frmTest_onreset"
19 End Sub
20
21 Sub frmTest_onmouseup
22     PostMsg "frmTest_onmouseup"
23 End Sub
```

```
24
25  Sub frmTest_onmouseover
26      PostMsg "frmTest_onmouseover"
27  End Sub
28
29  Sub frmTest_onmouseout
30      PostMsg "frmTest_onmouseout"
31  End Sub
32
33  Sub frmTest_onmousemove
34      PostMsg "frmTest_onmousemove"
35  End Sub
36
37  Sub frmTest_onmousedown
38      PostMsg "frmTest_onmousedown"
39  End Sub
40
41  Sub frmTest_onkeyup
42      PostMsg "frmTest_onkeyup"
43  End Sub
44
45  Sub frmTest_onkeypress
46      PostMsg "frmTest_onkeypress"
47  End Sub
48
49  Sub frmTest_onkeydown
50      PostMsg "frmTest_onkeydown"
51  End Sub
52
53  Sub frmTest_onhelp
54      PostMsg "frmTest_onhelp"
55  End Sub
56
57  Sub frmTest_onfilterchange
58      PostMsg "frmTest_onfilterchange"
59  End Sub
60
61  Sub frmTest_onerrorupdate
62      PostMsg "frmTest_onerrorupdate"
63  End Sub
64
65  Sub frmTest_ondragstart
```

continues…

LISTING 13.8 Continued

```
66      PostMsg "frmTest_ondragstart"
67 End Sub
68
69 Sub frmTest_ondblclick
70      PostMsg "frmTest_ondblclick"
71 End Sub
72
73 Sub frmTest_ondatasetcomplete
74      PostMsg "frmTest_ondatasetcomplete"
75 End Sub
76
77 Sub frmTest_ondatasetchanged
78      PostMsg "frmTest_ondatasetchanged"
79 End Sub
80
81 Sub frmTest_ondataavailable
82      PostMsg "frmTest_ondataavailable"
83 End Sub
84
85 Sub frmTest_onclick
86      PostMsg "frmTest_onclick"
87 End Sub
88
89 Sub frmTest_onbeforeupdate
90      PostMsg "frmTest_onbeforeupdate"
91 End Sub
92
93 Sub frmTest_onafterupdate
94      PostMsg "frmTest_onafterupdate"
95 End Sub
```

Using form events as a fail safe

You can use form events to ensure that everything has been completed properly by the user. You can use these events to validate data, enforce rules, and even act as a "transactional cop" for all information. A good example is the `Onreset` event. You can use this event to make sure everything is cleaned up properly when a form is reset, as opposed to leaving old data behind.

After completing the VBScript code, save the form and run the Web application to test the form events page. You see lots of mouse events roll by every time you move the mouse over the form area. You won't be able to see the `update`, `row`, and `dataset` messages, because they are events that relate to database activity and we have no database connected to this form.

However, you can see messages for the `onsubmit`, `onreset`, and `onstartselect` events. These events are unique for the Form object. The first two events occur when you press the **Submit** or **Reset** buttons. The last event occurs when you select some text in the input text box on the form (you must type some text into the text box first).

Using Element Events

The last object you explore in this chapter is the Element object. The Element object is really an abstract representation of all the controls and visual items that can be placed on a page. For example, all the intrinsic controls (Text Area, Text Box, Radio Button, and so on) are elements. Visual InterDev ships with several design-time controls (DTCs) that also act as Element objects on an HTML page. You can also use ActiveX controls registered on the user's machine as Element objects.

The event messages associated with Element objects vary greatly from one object to the next. In fact, this is the primary advantage of creating and using custom elements in the form of DTCs or ActiveX controls. You can customize behavior and event messages for your objects. However, a set of common messages is associated with almost all Element objects. This list of common events is shown in Table 13.6.

SEE ALSO
➤ You learn more about design-time controls on page 544

Elements or controls?

If you have experience using Visual Basic or Visual Basic for Applications, you are probably used to referring to text boxes and drop-down lists as *controls*. However, it is more common to refer to them as when working with HTML documents. The word *elements* covers all the same items used to build input forms in Windows applications, but it also covers more. Horizontal rules, paragraph markers, even form markers are also elements. Some of these elements can receive messages, too. For this reason, you'll see the word *elements* used where you might expect the word *control*.

TABLE 13.6 Common Event Messages for Element Objects

Event Message	Description
Onafterupdate	Occurs after data has been sent to the data provider
Onbeforeupdate	Occurs just before data is to be sent to the data provider
Onblur	Occurs when the element loses focus
Onchange	Occurs when the data inside the element has been changed
Onclick	Occurs when the user clicks the mouse button within the form

continues...

TABLE 13.6 Continued

Event Message	Description
Ondataavailable	Occurs as data arrives for data source objects that transmit their data asynchronously
Ondatasetchanged	Occurs when the data set exposed by a data source object changes
Ondatasetcomplete	Occurs when all data is available from the data source object
Ondblclick	Occurs when the user double-clicks a mouse button within the form
Ondragstart	Occurs when the user first starts to drag a selected item
Onerrorupdate	Occurs if there is an error sending data back to the data provider
Onfilterchange	Occurs when a visual filter changes state or completes a transition
Onfocus	Occurs when the element gains focus
Onhelp	Occurs when the user presses the F1 key
Onkeydown	Occurs when the user presses any key
Onkeypress	Occurs when the user presses any key
Onkeyup	Occurs when the user releases a previously pressed key
Onmousedown	Occurs when the user presses a mouse button down
Onmousemove	Occurs when the user moves the mouse over the form
Onmouseout	Occurs when the user moves the mouse out of the form area
Onmouseover	Occurs when the mouse is hovering over the form
Onmouseup	Occurs when the user releases the previously pressed mouse button
Onresize	Occurs when the element is resized
Onrowenter	Occurs when new data is available in a data provider
Onrowexit	Occurs just before the data row is updated
Onselectstart	Occurs when the user begins to highlight data within an input control on the form
Onselect	Occurs when the user completes the process of selecting data within an input control

Using Element Events

Notice that none of the event messages is marked with a (B) to indicate that the message is bubbling up from another object. This is because elements are the base objects in the hierarchy. The event messages from an Element object can bubble up to other objects (forms, documents, windows), but not the other way around.

Along with the database-related events and the key and mouse events, a couple of new events are unique to Element objects. Element objects can report event messages when data changes (`onchange`) and when users complete their highlighting of text in an input element (`onselect`). Element objects also report `onresize`, `onfocus`, and `onblur` events like Document and Window objects.

Now let's add another page called ELEMENT.HTM to the VBSEvents project. Add a heading to the page (Demonstrate Element Events) and an intrinsic text box with its ID property set to `txtTest`. Also add a Text Area control and set its ID property to `txaEvents`. When you're finished, your page should look like the one in Figure 13.6.

> **Similarity in events**
>
> The Document, Window, Form, and Element objects all share common events, such as `Onclick`. The difference between the events in the different objects is their scope: what do they effect? You can use this similarity and familiarity in events to control your application on a global scale (using the Document and Window objects), down to a granular level with the individual Element objects.

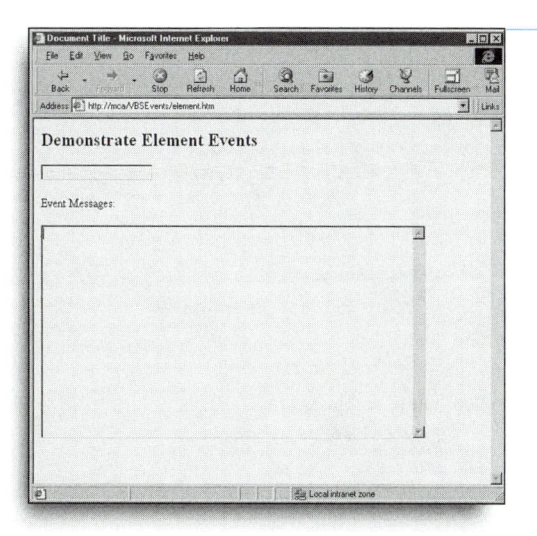

FIGURE 13.6
Laying out the ELEMENT.HTM page.

Now move from the **Design** tab to the **Source** tab (make sure the `defaultClientScript` property of the page is set to `VBScript`) and use the Script Outline window to select **Client Objects and Events**, **document**, **txtTest** to expose the list of events associated with the text box element. Double-click on each event message in the list in order to force Visual InterDev to add the empty event methods to the VBScript portion of the page.

After you've created all the event methods, copy the `PostMsg` method and the page-level variable from WINDOW.HTM to the VBScript area of ELEMENT.HTM. This will be used to post the messages into the `txaEvents` Text Area control.

Now add the following line to each event method:

`PostMsg "<object>_<event>"`

where `<object>` is the element (`txtTest`) and `<event>` is the message (`onblur`)—for example, `"txtTest_onchange"`, `"txtTest_onselect"`, and so on. Do this for each event method in the document. Listing 13.9 has the completed VBScript for all the event messages associated with the text box.

LISTING 13.9 Coding the Event Messages for the *txtTest* Element

```
1  Sub txtTest_onselectstart
2      PostMsg "txtTest_onselectstart"
3  End Sub
4
5  Sub txtTest_onselect
6      PostMsg "txtTest_onselect"
7  End Sub
8
9  Sub txtTest_onrowexit
10     PostMsg "txtTest_onrowexit"
11 End Sub
12
13 Sub txtTest_onresize
14     PostMsg "txtTest_onresize"
15 End Sub
16
17 Sub txtTest_onrowenter
18     PostMsg "txtTest_onrowenter"
19 End Sub
20
21 Sub txtTest_onmouseover
```

```
22      PostMsg "txtTest_onmouseover"
23 End Sub
24
25 Sub txtTest_onmouseup
26      PostMsg "txtTest_onmouseup"
27 End Sub
28
29 Sub txtTest_onmouseout
30      PostMsg "txtTest_onmouseout"
31 End Sub
32
33 Sub txtTest_onmousemove
34      PostMsg "txtTest_onmousemove"
35 End Sub
36
37 Sub txtTest_onmousedown
38      PostMsg "txtTest_onmousedown"
39 End Sub
40
41 Sub txtTest_onkeyup
42      PostMsg "txtTest_onkeyup"
43 End Sub
44
45 Sub txtTest_onkeypress
46      PostMsg "txtTest_onkeypress"
47 End Sub
48
49 Sub txtTest_onkeydown
50      PostMsg "txtTest_onkeydown"
51 End Sub
52
53 Sub txtTest_onhelp
54      PostMsg "txtTest_onhelp"
55 End Sub
56
57 Sub txtTest_onfocus
58      PostMsg "txtTest_onfocus"
59 End Sub
60
61 Sub txtTest_onfilterchange
62      PostMsg ""
63 End Sub
```

continues…

LISTING 13.9 Continued

```
64
65 Sub txtTest_onerrorupdate
66     PostMsg "txtTest_onerrorupdate"
67 End Sub
68
69 Sub txtTest_ondragstart
70     PostMsg "txtTest_ondragstart"
71 End Sub
72
73 Sub txtTest_ondblclick
74     PostMsg "txtTest_ondblclick"
75 End Sub
76
77 Sub txtTest_ondatasetcomplete
78     PostMsg "txtTest_ondatasetcomplete"
79 End Sub
80
81 Sub txtTest_ondatasetchanged
82     PostMsg "txtTest_ondatasetchanged"
83 End Sub
84
85 Sub txtTest_ondataavailable
86     PostMsg "txtTest_ondataavailable"
87 End Sub
88
89 Sub txtTest_onclick
90     PostMsg "txtTest_onclick"
91 End Sub
92
93 Sub txtTest_onchange
94     PostMsg "txtTest_onchange"
95 End Sub
96
97 Sub txtTest_onblur
98     PostMsg "txtTest_onblur"
99 End Sub
100
101 Sub txtTest_onbeforeupdate
102     PostMsg "txtTest_onbeforeupdate"
103 End Sub
104
```

Adding Event Coding to Link Elements

```
105 Sub txtTest_onafterupdate
106     PostMsg "txtTest_onafterupdate"
107 End Sub
108
109 Sub TextBox1_onkeypress
110     PostMsg "TextBox1_onkeypress"
111 end sub
```

After completing the VBScript, save the page and run it to test the events. As an experiment, type some text into the text box, then click the mouse in the `txaEvents` Text Area box. You see the `onchange` event appear in the list just before the `onblur` event. You also notice that events appear only when you are doing something inside the `txtTest` element.

Adding Event Coding to Link Elements

You can also add event coding to link elements on an HTML page. However, the way you do this is different than any other method discussed in this chapter. In order to add event coding for link elements, you must embed the link tag with a call to an existing VBScript method. The basic syntax is as follows:

`<A HREF=`*scriptengine*`:`*scriptcode*`>sample</A>`

Where *scriptengine* is always set to `javascript` and *scriptcode* is the name of the VBScript routine to run when the user clicks on the link.

Listing 13.10 shows how this is done.

> **onchange is not the same**
>
> If you use Visual Basic or Visual Basic for Applications, you might expect the **onchange** event to fire each time the user makes any change to the contents of the element. However, in VBScript, the **onchange** event does not occur until the focus is just about to move to another element on the page.

LISTING 13.10 Sample Link Event Coding

```
1 <SCRIPT LANGUAGE="VBScript">
2 Sub VBSMethod()
3     Msgbox "You Clicked Me!",vbExclamation,"Link Event"
4 End sub
5 </SCRIPT>
6
7 This is a <A HREF="JavaScript:VBSMethod()">link</A>
```

The first thing you notice is that, even though you are calling a VBScript method, you must use the `javascript` keyword as the engine name within the `HREF` element. You can reference a method written in VBScript, JScript, or any other script that is supported, but you must always use `javascript` to accomplish the call.

As an example, load the DEFAULT.HTM page for the VBSEvents project and edit the last link element on the page to match the following one:

```
<A href="JavaScript:VBMethod()">Link Events</A>
```

Also, add a new VBScript method called `VBMethod` to the `<SCRIPT>` section of the page. You learned earlier how to create the `<SCRIPT>...</SCRIPT>` tags. Repeat that process now and use Listing 13.11 as a guide in adding the code.

LISTING 13.11 Adding a Method to Respond to the Link Event

```
1 <SCRIPT LANGUAGE=VBScript>
2 <!--
3
4 Sub VBMethod()
5    msgbox "You clicked me!",vbExclamation,"Link Event"
6 end sub
7
8 -->
9 </SCRIPT>
```

Now save and test the page. You actually run the page in a browser in order for it to work properly. If you attempt to click on the link while in the Visual InterDev preview mode, you get an error when the browser attempts to load a new document called `javascript:VBMethod()`. If all goes well, your browser should look like the one in Figure 13.7.

Adding Event Coding to Link Elements

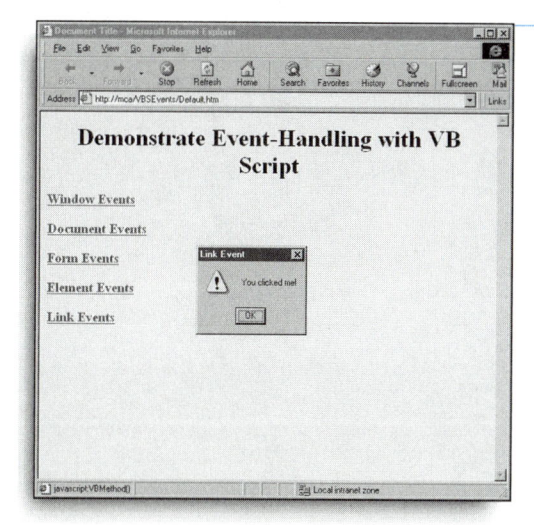

FIGURE 13.7
Testing the link event.

CHAPTER 14

Client-Side Scripting with the MSIE Object Model

Learn the various ways to add and invoke client-side scripts

Learn to program the Microsoft Internet Explorer user interface

Use client-side scripts to explore and manipulate the currently loaded document

What Is Client-Side Scripting?

In this chapter, you learn some of the details of client-side scripting. Two parts of the chapter title need a bit of clarification: *scripting and client-side*.

First, scripting is the process of writing source code that executes various commands and manipulates properties. Typically, scripting code is used to perform tasks that cannot be handled by standard HTML coding.

When you use client-side scripting, you are writing browser script code that will run inside the browser at the client site. In other words, the scripting code is sent to the client browser along with the rest of the HTML document. Then, when appropriate, the scripts are invoked (run) at the client. There is no interaction with the server.

The process of creating the scripts is relatively easy and is covered in other chapters in this book. Along with creating the scripts, there are several different ways to invoke (call) them and a few different ways to actually place them into your HTML documents. You learn more about how to add client-side scripts to your HTML documents in the next section of this chapter.

When you know the various ways to add scripts to your HTML documents, you'll be ready to explore the Microsoft Internet Explorer object model. The Microsoft Internet Explorer object model is a scripting platform that enables you to write client-side scripts to inspect and manipulate the Microsoft Internet Explorer environment. This lets you do things like inspect the browser's history list and review all the anchors or elements in the document. You'll learn how to use the various parts of the Microsoft Internet Explorer object model later in this chapter.

SEE ALSO
- *You learn about scripting on page 248*
- *To learn more detail about scripting, see page 303*

Using Microsoft Internet Explorer and Visual Basic Scripting

This book focuses on using the Microsoft Internet Explorer and Visual Basic Scripting. However, Microsoft Internet Explorer can also use JavaScript to perform client-side scripting. If you are writing scripts that must run in browsers other than Microsoft Internet Explorer, you must use JavaScript instead. However, because this book uses Microsoft Internet Explorer as the browser, you'll find only examples of Visual Basic Scripting here.

Netscape versus Microsoft: The object model wars

Well, you've heard of the browser wars. Welcome to the object model wars. Netscape and Internet Explorer have different object models behind their respective browsers. The key difference lies in Microsoft's strategy. The document object model (DOM) exposes all layers of the browser to programming, whereas Netscape sort of "fakes" an object model. The script you see in this chapter might or might not function properly in Netscape Communicator 4 or higher.

Why Use Client-Side Scripts?

If you are writing high-powered Web applications, you might think that it is best to do without client-side scripting and execute all code at the server instead. In some cases this might be true. Server-side scripts offer the potential of speedy execution and provide a "browser-neutral" scripting solution for your applications. However, there are several cases in which client-side scripting can actually improve your application's speed and responsiveness and even reduce the number of server-side calls needed to successfully complete a series of tasks.

One way in which client-side scripting can improve your Web applications is in performing input validation before forwarding the page to the server for execution. Often you have input fields in a Web form that must be checked for valid date ranges, numeric types, and so on. Although you can do this at the server, it is often much easier to perform basic validation at the client instead. This involves the creation of a client-side validation method and several lines of client script code. If errors are found, you can easily post a message for the users, let them make the change and then, after the input is all within range, send the completed form to the server for processing.

Another common client-side scripting task is handling user interface events, such as mouse movement, keypresses, and requests for online help. This kind of processing can occur only at the client. You cannot handle browser interface events at the server at all. If you want to offer online help, listen for keypresses, or monitor mouse movement in your Web documents, you must use client-side scripting.

Finally, if you have some common calculation routines (interest rates, return on investment, or other math operations), it is usually quicker to include these methods in the client script than to constantly hit the server to get the results of these computations. Many Web applications that enable users to do "what-if" calculations are better served with client scripts than with regular form postings to a distant server.

Mixing server- and client-side scripting

The best Web applications freely mix client-side and server-side scripting. You can use server-side scripting to lighten the load on your client's Web browser, but add client-side scripting to make the interaction between the user, the Web browser, and the server a little smarter.

"Fat" thin clients

The Web browser is known as a *thin* client because it involves very little overhead. As you add client-side scripts, you are making this thin client just a little bit fatter. This isn't a bad thing, but you should always try to keep in mind whether client-side scripting is required.

Adding Client-Side Script Blocks

The first thing you must do when building client-side scripts for Microsoft Internet Explorer is learn how to declare the scripts in the browser. There are actually several ways to do it. The Visual InterDev 6 editor can help you by adding the proper scripting block encoding automatically. However, you might sometimes want to use the alternative methods described in this chapter.

The following are the three main ways to incorporate scripts into your HTML documents:

- The <SCRIPT> tag is a standard method for adding scripts to your documents.
- HTML attributes enable you to address the script method as part of the HTML element's attribute list.
- The FOR...EVENT method enables you to create script blocks that are targeted for a particular event for a specific element in the document.

You can have as many script blocks in your document as you want, and you can place them anywhere in the document. In some cases, these scripts can contain only a single method. However, in the most common cases you can add several scripting methods in a single script block. This makes your client-side scripts easier to read and maintain.

Using the <SCRIPT> Tag

The most common way to add client-side scripts to your HTML documents is to use the <SCRIPT> tag. This HTML tag defines

---

Be safe: add the LANGUAGE attribute to script block declarations

Although it is not required, you should always add the LANGUAGE attribute to your script block declarations (that is, LANGUAGE="vbscript"). If you mix more than one type of scripting language in your document, this will make sure the proper script interpreter is used when executing your client-side script. Even if you use only one type of scripting language in the document now, you might want to add others in the future. Declaring the LANGUAGE attribute now will make it easier for you later.

SEE ALSO
➤ You can start exploring server-side scripting on page 380

Adding Client-Side Script Blocks

the beginning and end of a text block that contains scripting code. Listing 14.1 shows a typical scripting block using the `<SCRIPT>` tag.

LISTING 14.1   **A Typical Client-Side Scripting Block**

```
1 <SCRIPT language=vbscript>
2 <!--
3   document.write "Hello, webmaster!"
4 -->
5 </SCRIPT> tag>
```

The key points to notice are lines 1 and 2 and 4 and 5. These are the minimum portions of a scripting block. Line 3 is the actual scripting code that is executed when the page is loaded.

The easiest way to add a `<SCRIPT>` block to your HTML document is to use the Visual InterDev 6 Editor HTML menu. This menu has an option for adding either a client-side or server-side script block.

Adding a Visual Basic client-side scripting block with the Visual InterDev 6 Editor

1. Load an HTML document in the Visual InterDev 6 Editor.
2. Select the **Source** tab at the bottom of the editor window.
3. Locate the `defaultClientScript` property in the Properties window and set this property to **VBScript**.
4. Move your cursor to the location where you want to add the client-side scripting block.
5. Click **H**TML, **S**cript Block, **C**lient. This will add the code stub to your document (see Figure 14.1).

Save time by setting the project's `defaultClientScript` property

You can save yourself some time and trouble by setting the `defaultClientScript` property of the project to the scripting platform you will be using for all your HTML documents. By doing this, all new documents added to the project will have their own `defaultClientScript` set to match that of the project.

FIGURE 14.1

Adding a client-side script block with the Visual InterDev 6 Editor.

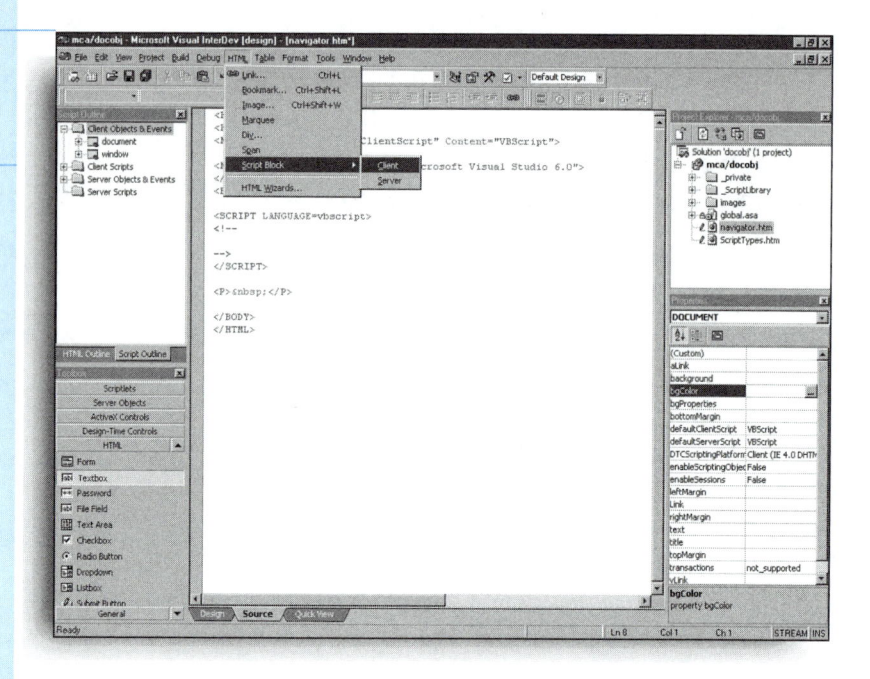

Adding Event-Handling Script Blocks

Finding the Script Outline window

If you don't see the Script Outline window in your Visual InterDev 6 IDE, you might need to add it to your current view. To do this, select **View**, **Other Windows**, **Script Outline** from the main menu. You can also use the shortcut key combination Ctrl+Alt+S.

Another way to add standard client-side scripting blocks to your HTML documents is to use the Script Outline window in the Visual InterDev 6 editor. This window lists all the client-side objects and elements in your document and any events associated with them. You can simply select an item in the list and double-click the event message to add the code block and event method to your HTML document.

One major advantage of using the Script Outline window to add client-side scripting blocks to your documents is that all event-handling methods are added to a single code block in the page. This makes it easier to read and maintain your client-side scripts.

Using the Script Outline window to add client-side script blocks

1. With an HTML document loaded in the Visual InterDev 6 editor, select the **Source** tab at the bottom of the editor window.

Adding Client-Side Script Blocks   CHAPTER 14

2. In the Script Outline window, click the **Client Objects & Events** folder to open it.

3. Click the **Window** item to expand it.

4. Double-click the **OnLoad** event message to add the client-side script block to your document.

5. You can continue to click on other items or messages in the **Client Objects & Events** section of the script outline to add more methods to the same client-side scripting block (see Figure 14.2).

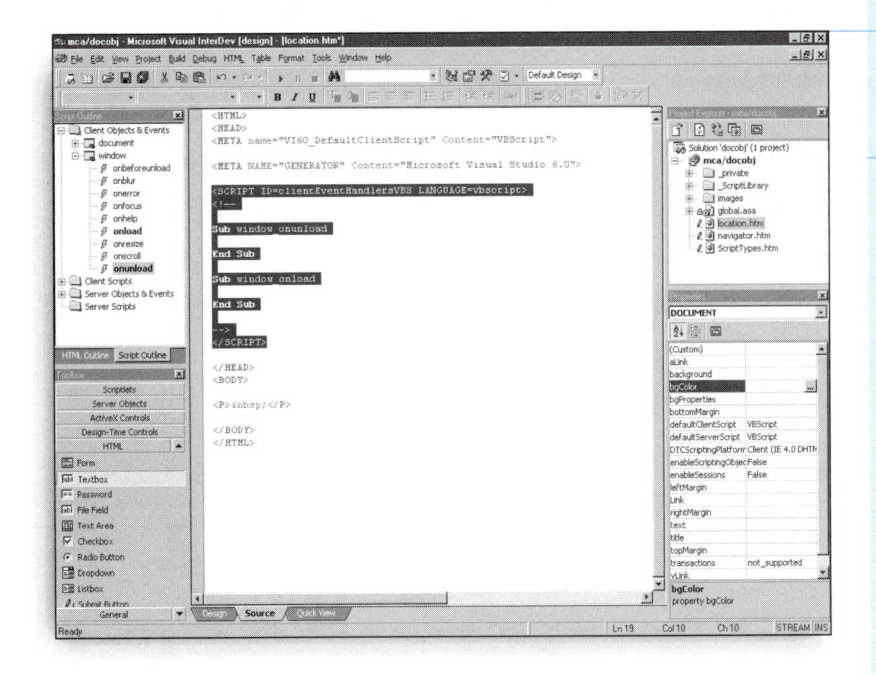

FIGURE 14.2
Using the script outline to add a client-side scripting block.

Adding Scripts via HTML Attributes

In most cases, you use the `<SCRIPT>` tag to declare your client-side scripts. However, you can also add attribute values to an existing HTML element in order to link client-side scripts HTML controls on your page. These are sometimes known as *inline scripts*.

First, build your script block as usual (with the Visual InterDev 6 menu selections **HTML**, **Script Block**, **Client**). Then, add an HTML control to your document (for example, a button control). Finally, add special attributes to the HTML control element that indicate which script methods to execute for various messages received by the control.

Listing 14.2 shows how you could create a button control that listens for the `onclick`, `onmouseover`, and `onmouseout` events.

LISTING 14.2 Using HTML Attributes to Link to Client-Side Scripts

```
1  <P>
2  <INPUT id=btnOnClick name=btnOnClick type=button
   value="OnClick"
3      onclick="showAlert" onmouseover="updateStatus"
   onmouseout="clearStatus"
4          Language="vbscript">
5  </P>
6
7  <SCRIPT LANGUAGE=vbscript>
8  <!--
9  '
10 ' events for btnOnClick button
11 '
12 Sub showAlert
13     alert "You clicked Me!"
14 End Sub
15
16 Sub updateStatus
17     window.status="btnClicker"
18 End Sub
19
20 Sub clearStatus
21     window.status=""
22 End Sub
23
24 -->
25 </SCRIPT>
```

Inline scripts

Inline scripting can often become confusing. One benefit of having all your scripts declared in a single `<SCRIPT>...</SCRIPT>` block is maintainability. This code listing is a good example of this.

Adding Client-Side Script Blocks | CHAPTER 14

You can see that lines 7–25 contain the actual client-side Visual Basic Scripting that is executed for the various events outlined in the button's attributes (line 3). The advantage of this method is that you can easily see all the event-related scripting information as a part of the HTML control declaration. This makes it easy to see just which events this control is ready to deal with. However, if your controls are programmed to listen for several events, this tends to make the control declarations a bit unwieldy and difficult to read.

Using *FOR...EVENT* to Add Scripts

Another way to link your script methods to your HTML controls is to use the FOR...EVENT attributes in the script block declaration. This method enables you to link all the code in a specific script block to a single event for a single HTML control. You can think of this as the opposite approach to using the HTML attributes to list events for an HTML control.

For example, if you want to code the onclick, onmouseover, and onmouseout events for a button using the FOR...EVENT method of declaring code blocks, your code would look like Listing 14.3.

LISTING 14.3 Using *FOR...EVENTS* to Define Client-Side Code Blocks

```
1  <INPUT id=btnForHandler   name=btnForHandler
   ➥type=button value="For Handler">
2
3  <SCRIPT FOR="btnForHandler" EVENT="onClick"
   ➥LANGUAGE=vbscript>
4  <!--
5      alert "ForHandler Click"
6  -->
7  </SCRIPT>
8
9  <SCRIPT FOR="btnForHandler" EVENT="onmousemove"
   ➥LANGUAGE=vbscript>
10 <!--
11     window.status= "btnForHandler"
12 -->
```

continues...

Sharing inline problems

`FOR...EVENT` script blocks share the same problems as inline scripts. These scripts can add up, clutter your document, and make maintenance a headache.

LISTING 14.3 Continued

```
13  </SCRIPT>
14
15  <SCRIPT FOR="btnForHandler" EVENT="onmouseout"
    ➥LANGUAGE=vbscript>
16  <!--
17      window.status= ""
18  -->
19  </SCRIPT>
```

As you look at Listing 14.3, notice that there is a code block for each event method you associate with the HTML control. This greatly simplifies the HTML control declaration (line 1), but adds quite a few script blocks to your page (lines 3–19). However, the advantage of this method is that it is easy to see how each script block is to be used in your document.

About Multiple Script Blocks and Shared Script Blocks

In the preceding three sections, you've seen different ways to declare and use client-side script blocks. Now is a good time to point out that you have a great deal of flexibility in how you use the script blocks in your pages.

Use the `ID` attribute to document your client-side script blocks

It is a good habit to mark each client-side script block with an `ID` attribute to indicate the purpose of the code within the block. This `ID` property is not currently used by the Visual InterDev 6 editor, but does provide an added level of documentation for future reference.

Usually, it is recommended that you use a minimum number of script blocks and place most of your methods inside these few blocks. In other words, share the script blocks with multiple script methods. Listing 14.4 shows an example of an HTML page with only two script blocks to hold all the client-side coding.

LISTING 14.4 Organizing Your Client-Side Script Blocks

```
1  <SCRIPT ID=clientEventHandlersVBS LANGUAGE=vbscript>
2  <!--
3
4  Sub window_onunload
5      '
```

Adding Client-Side Script Blocks

```
 6      alert "Bye!"
 7          '
 8  End Sub
 9
10  Sub window_onload
11          '
12      dim strMsg
13          '
14      intFrames = getFrameCount()
15      strMsg = "frame length: " & cStr(intFrames) &
        ➥chr(13) & chr(13)
16      for x = 0 to intFrames-1
17          strMsg = strMsg & "name: " &
            ➥getFrameName(x) & chr(13)
18          strMsg = strMsg & "url: " & getFrameURL(x) &
            ➥chr(13) & chr(13)
19      next
20          '
21      alert strMsg
22          '
23  End Sub
24
25  -->
26  </SCRIPT>
27
28  <SCRIPT ID=CustomMethods LANGUAGE=vbscript>
29  <!--
30
31  Function getFrameCount
32      getFrameCount = window.frames.length
33  End Function
34
35  Function getFrameName(index)
36      getFrameName = window.frames(index).name
37  End Function
38
39  Function getFrameURL(index)
40      getFrameURL = window.frames(index).document.url
41  End Function
42
43  -->
44  </SCRIPT>
```

In Listing 14.4, you can see that all the event-handing methods are kept in one block (lines 1–26) and all the custom methods for handling local tasks are kept in a separate block (lines 28–44). This is a typical, but arbitrary, way to organize your script blocks. Key points to notice, however, are that it is perfectly legal to place methods in one script block and call them from another. You don't have to place all your methods in a single block.

Another point to notice is the use of the ID attribute to label each code block. This is done for convenience only, but does help to organize your code and make it easier to maintain over time.

Now that you have a good idea of how to declare and organize your client-side code blocks, you're ready to start using client-side scripting to inspect the Microsoft Internet Explorer object model.

Using the Microsoft Internet Explorer Object Model

When creating client-side scripts, you will usually write code to get information about the current window or document or listen for event messages for the HTML controls on the page. In order to get this information, you actually use an object model: the Microsoft Internet Explorer object model. It is the object model that publishes the information about the current document in the browser and about each mouse click and keyboard press that occurs during the session.

Every time you load a document into the Microsoft Internet Explorer, every time you navigate from one page to another, even every time the mouse moves, it is tracked and reported by the Microsoft Internet Explorer object model. You can even use the Microsoft Internet Explorer object model to access the navigation history of the current session.

Although you will probably write customized client-side code to validate user input or perform special calculations based on

Using the object model terminology

The proper term for the Microsoft Internet Explorer object model is the *Document Object Model*. This gets wordy, however, and is often abbreviated to DOM, or just Object Model.

business rules, you usually will employ the client browser object model. This object model is the focus of the rest of this chapter.

The Microsoft Internet Explorer Object Hierarchy

The object model is nothing magical. It's just a way to organize the various parts of the client browser and allow programmers a logical way to access these parts. Like most object models, the Microsoft Internet Explorer is arranged in a hierarchy. The most important objects are listed at the top of the hierarchy, and the other objects are listed as a child object or subobject of the main objects.

Figure 14.3 shows an illustration of the main objects in the Microsoft Internet Explorer hierarchy.

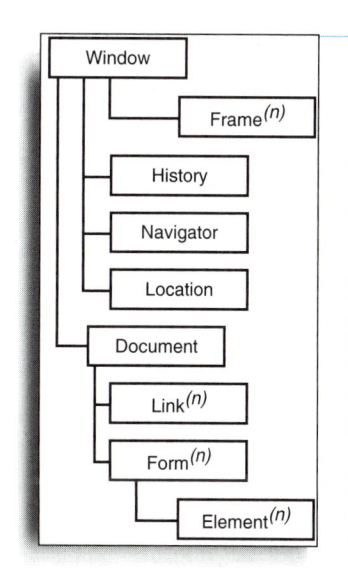

FIGURE 14.3

The Microsoft Internet Explorer object model.

The object model shows that the top object in the hierarchy is the Window object. Actually, both the Window and the Document objects are treated as top-level objects. You can access both of these objects just by entering their names in the script block. Listing 14.5 shows how this looks in Visual Basic Scripting language.

LISTING 14.5 Accessing Both the Window and Document Objects Directly

```
1  <SCRIPT LANGUAGE=vbscript>
2  <!--
3
4  Sub document_onclick
5      alert document.url
6  End Sub
7
8  Sub window_onunload
9      '
10     alert "Bye!"
11     '
12 End Sub
13 -->
14 </SCRIPT>
```

Objects and levels

To have a clearer understanding of the levels in the object model, look at it this way: the Window contains the document, which in turn contains the elements.

Navigator and Microsoft similarities

Because Microsoft wanted Internet Explorer to be basically just as (and more) powerful as Netscape Communicator/Navigator, the Document Object Model inherited several objects from Netscape. The `Navigator` object is a good example. It maintains script compatibility between the browsers when using JavaScript/Jscript.

You can see that even though the Document object is shown as a child object in Figure 14.3, code such as that in line 5 of Listing 14.5 is perfectly legal. For this reason, many refer to both the Window and Document objects as top-level objects in the Microsoft Internet Explorer object model.

Figure 14.3 also shows that four of the objects can have multiple occurrences (see the (n) next to the object name). The Frame, Form, Link, and Element objects can appear multiple times in the same window (frame) or document (form, link, and element). This is also typical of object models. In this way, the Microsoft Internet Explorer object model can easily organize a series of items for you to access via scripting. For example, you might want to view the set of links on a page as an array of items.

Finally, notice from Figure 14.3 that the object model easily divides into two groups. The top group is composed of objects that deal primarily with the browser itself (Window, Frame, History, Navigator, and Location). The second group of objects deals with the document that is currently loaded in the browser (Document, Link, Form, and Element).

Also notice that the Document group has an additional level in the hierarchy. If you have a Form on your page, all the items within the Form will be accessed via the Element object that is a child of the `Form` object. Although it is not critical that you remember the relationships between objects, understanding them helps when you are writing your client-side scripts.

Preparing the DOCOBJ Project

All the examples in the following sections are HTML documents that you can create using Visual InterDev 6. You can hold all these pages in a single project called DOCOBJ. To do this, launch Visual InterDev 6 and create the new project in an appropriate folder on your workstation (or an available network share). Don't worry about applying a theme or layout for this project because you'll just be creating simple HTML documents that test the various properties and methods of the Microsoft Internet Explorer object model.

When you've created your new project, click once on the project name and, using the Property window, set the `DefaultClientScript` property to `VBScript`. This will make sure all new pages you add to your project will default to using VBScript as the client-side scripting language.

Using the *Window* and *Frame* Objects

The top-level object in the Microsoft Internet Explorer hierarchy is the `Window` object. This object has a handful of properties that you can use to learn some general information about the browser window. The main value of the `Window` object is that it has several important methods you can use to launch new pages and display dialog boxes. You can also create a timer loop that will fire at a designated interval. This is handy if you want to set up a screen timeout or regular refresh from some distant URL.

To get an idea of the power of the `Window` object, add a new page called WINDOW.HTM to the current project (DOCOBJ). Next, with the new page loaded in the Visual InterDev 6 editor, switch to Source mode (select the **Source** tab at the bottom of the edit window). Now you're ready to add a little HTML and some client-side script to view some of the properties of the `Window` object.

> **JavaScript**
>
> Again, remember that you can use JavaScript/Jscript (and now ECMA-Script) to access the Document Object Model. This chapter uses VBScript, but the basic principles remain the same between languages.

Listing 14.6 contains the HTML title for the page and a single script block that uses the `write` method of the `Document` object to display a series of window properties. Add this code to the `<BODY>` portion of your document.

LISTING 14.6 Creating a Client-Side Script to Display Properties of the *Window* Object

```
1  <H2>Using the Window Object</H2>
2  <HR>
3  <SCRIPT LANGUAGE=vbscript>
4  <!--
5      '
6      ' show the window object information
7      document.write "<code>"
8      document.write "closed.............: " & _
           window.closed   & "<BR>"
9      document.write "defaultStatus......: " & _
           window.defaultStatus  & "<BR>"
10     document.write "length.............: " & _
           window.length   & "<BR>"
11     document.write "name...............: " & _
           window.name     & "<BR>"
12     document.write "offscreenBuffering.: " & _
           window.offscreenBuffering  & "<BR>"
13     document.write "self...............: " & _
           window.self     & "<BR>"
14     document.write "status.............: " & _
           window.status   & "<BR>"
15     document.write "</code>"
16     '
17 -->
18 </SCRIPT>
```

Depending on your connection to the Web that hosts this page, some of the properties in this list will be left blank. Normally, you will not use many of the `Window` object properties in your scripts.

Next, you must add a series of buttons to your document. These buttons will be used to test the various methods of the `Window`

Consider this listing

This listing is a good example of how you can use the Document Object Model to your advantage. Based on the result of an event, you can tailor the output of your Web page—even other scripting code. You can combine this with server-side scripting to create truly dynamic Web applications.

Using the Microsoft Internet Explorer Object Model

object. Listing 14.7 shows the HTML code for the buttons needed for your page. Add this code right below the script block shown in Listing 14.6.

LISTING 14.7 Adding HTML Buttons to the WINDOW.HTM Document

```
1  <P>
2  <input type="button" value="Alert" id=btnAlert
   ➥name=btnAlert>
3  <input type="button" value="Confirm" id=btnConfirm
   ➥name=btnConfirm>
4  <input type="button" value="Prompt" id=btnPrompt
   ➥name=btnPrompt>
5  </P>
6
7  <P>
8  <input type="button" value="Open" id=btnOpen
   ➥name=btnOpen>
9  <input type="button" value="Navigate" id=btnNavigate
   ➥name=btnNavigate>
10 </P>
11
12 <P>
13 <input type="button" value="Set TimeOut" id=btnSetTO
   ➥name=btnSetTO>
14 <input type="button" value="Clear TimeOut"
   ➥id=btnClearTO name=btnClearTO><BR>
15 </P>
```

The buttons are arranged in three groups. The first group of buttons will be used to call up modal dialog boxes commonly used with input forms. The second group will be used to illustrate the two ways you can load and display new Web documents. The last two buttons will be used to show you how to create a timer event for your Web pages.

Testing the Dialog Methods of the *Window* Object

First, you must add some client-side code to test the first button group. A quick way to add a client-side code block for an

HTML control is to use the Script Outline window to locate the `onclick` event for the control and double-click the event name. See the step-by-step "Using the Script Outline window to Add Client-Side Script Blocks," earlier in this chapter, to see how to do this.

When you have added the first client-side script block, you're ready to enter the Visual Basic Scripting to animate the three buttons. Listing 14.8 shows the code that will display the Alert, Confirm, and Prompt dialog boxes associated with the `Window` object.

LISTING 14.8 Adding Visual Basic Scripting to Display the *Window* Object Dialog Boxes

```
1  Sub btnPrompt_onclick
2      '
3      Dim strAnswer
4      Dim NullCheck
5      '
6      strAnswer=prompt("Are You Ready?","Yes")
7
8      NullCheck = IsNull(StrAnswer)
9
10     if NullCheck = TRUE then
11         alert "Nah!"
12     else
13         alert strAnswer
14     end if
15     '
16 End Sub
17
18 Sub btnConfirm_onclick
19     '
20     if confirm("Really?")=True then
21         alert "Yep!"
22     else
23         alert "Nah!"
24     end if
25     '
```

Using the Microsoft Internet Explorer Object Model

```
26 End Sub
27
28 Sub btnAlert_onclick
29     alert "Hello, webmaster!"
30 End Sub
```

This code demonstrates a good example of checking values to make sure you get what you want. Line 8 carries out a VBScript IsNull function on the results of the Prompt dialog box. If the user clicks the **Cancel** button, a NULL value is returned. If you didn't check for the NULL value, the script would generate an error (try it—remove the check and see what happens). From the results of the IsNull check, you determine if you should display a generic No response or the actual contents of the dialog box.

When you test this page, you'll be able to press the first three buttons to see the different dialog boxes. As you can see from Listing 14.8, the Alert dialog only displays a message. The Confirm dialog box returns a TRUE or FALSE, and the Prompt dialog box returns whatever was entered in the input box, unless the **Cancel** button is clicked.

Testing the *Open* and *Navigate* Methods

Next, you must add some code to exercise the Open and Navigate methods. The Open method enables you to open another document in a new window on the user's screen. You can also control the appearance of the window by turning on or off the toolbars, menu, status bar, and other items. You can even control the size and location of the new window.

To test this, add the code from Listing 14.9 to your current code block.

With power comes a price

The ability to spawn remote windows and control their behavior is incredible. Unfortunately, it also can become painful for the user. Make sure you're popping up windows for a reason. Most users find windows that pop up on their screen because of a Web page intrusive.

LISTING 14.9   Using the *Open* Method of the *Window* Object

```
1 Sub btnOpen_onclick
2     '
3     dim strToolbar
4     dim strLocation
5     dim strDirectories
```

continues...

Client-Side Scripting with the MSIE Object Model

Leave a way out

You might trap a user if you open a window that removes the menu bar and toolbar and doesn't let the user resize the window. Make sure you provide a graceful way out, such as spawning a window with the full controls, just in case they closed the original window.

LISTING 14.9 Continued

```
6   dim strStatus
7   dim strMenubar
8   dim strScrollbars
9   dim strResizeable
10  dim strPosition
11  dim strOptions
12  '
13  strToolbar="toolbar=NO, "
14  strLocation="location=NO, "
15  strDirectories="directories=NO, "
16  strStatus="status=NO, "
17  strMenubar="menubar=NO, "
18  strScrollbars="scrollbars=NO, "
19  strResizeable="resizable=NO, "
20  strPosition="width=400, height=300, top=50, left=50"
21  '
22  strOptions = strToolbar & strLocation
23  strOptions = strOptions & strDirectories & strStatus
24  strOptions = strOptions & strMenubar & strScrollbar
25  strOptions = strOptions & strResizeable &
    ➥strPosition
26  '
27  window.open "http://mca/docobj/location.htm",
    ➥"NewWindow",strOptions
28  '
29 End Sub
```

The code in Listing 14.9 is long because this example sets values for all the different options. Normally, you would not need to adjust all the options in your client-side scripts. Note that you will need to change the URL used in line 27 to match a legal address and page within an accessible Web.

Figure 14.4 shows an example of the `Open` method in action.

By contrast, the `Navigate` method of the `Window` object enables you to load a new document in the current window. This mimics the process of clicking an existing link on a page and then displaying the resulting document in your browser. The code in Listing 14.10 shows how to use the `Navigate` method.

Building your own browser

You can use the `Navigate` method to build your own browser interface without relying on a user to access the conventional user interface.

Using the Microsoft Internet Explorer Object Model | PART III
CHAPTER 14

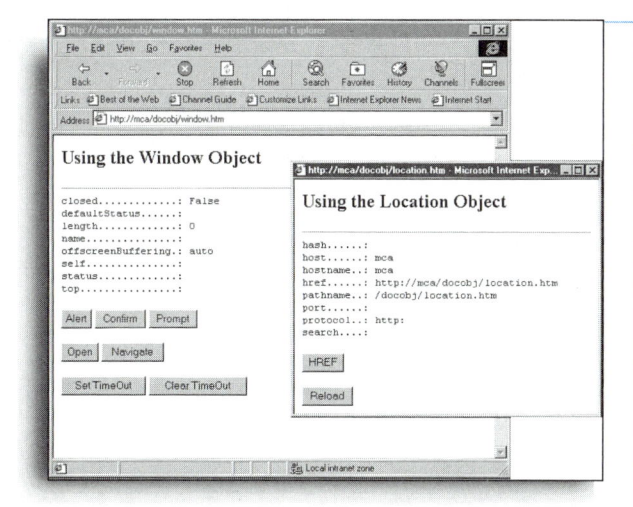

FIGURE 14.4
The results of using the `Open` method of the `Window` object.

LISTING 14.10 Using the *Navigate* Method of the *Window* Object

```
1 Sub btnNavigate_onclick
2   '
3     window.navigate "http://mca/docobj/location.htm"
4   '
5 End Sub
```

Again, you will need to adjust the URL address on line 3 of Listing 14.10 to match a valid location and page for your Web server. When you run this sample code, you'll see the new page appear in the current browser window instead of a new window on the screen.

Using the *setTimeOut* and *clearTimeOut* Methods

You can also use the `setTimeOut` and `clearTimeOut` methods of the `Window` object to create a process that will fire off at some predetermined time. This is good for creating autologoff methods for your Web apps or for building methods that will regularly hit a particular page to pull data from a distant server.

Listing 14.11 shows how to use the `setTimeOut` and `clearTimeOut` methods.

> Use `setTimeOut` and `clearTimeOut` with caution
>
> Make sure you've tested your results. You don't want to have an event firing too often because it might confuse your user or potentially render your system unusable.

The Session object

You can also use server-side ASP objects to create autologoff events for your application using the `Session` object.

LISTING 14.11 Using the *setTimeOut* and *clearTimeOut* Methods of the *Window* Object

```
1  dim timerID
2
3  Sub btnClearTO_onclick
4      '
5      window.clearTimeout timerID
6      '
7  End Sub
8
9  Sub Notice
10     '
11     if confirm("continue time out run?")=true then
12         btnSetTO_onclick
13     else
14         btnClearTO_onclick
15     end if
16     '
17 End Sub
18
19 Sub btnSetTO_onclick
20     '
21     timerID = window.setTimeout("Notice",1000,
       ➥"vbscript")
22     '
23 End Sub
```

Notice that the `setTimeOut` method returns an ID value (line 21 in Listing 14.11). This ID value is used to keep track of the timer loop. Because you can track the ID value, you can create any number of timers in your Web document. For example, you might set a timeout value for logging off the Web and set a timeout value for requesting data from a distant Web site—all on the same page.

You can also see that the `setTimeout` method accepts three parameters: a method name, a wait value (in milliseconds), and an optional language name. In the example in Listing 14.11, the Visual Basic Script method `Notice` will be executed after waiting 10 seconds.

Using the Microsoft Internet Explorer Object Model

It should be pointed out that the `setTimeout` method will fire the `Notice` method only one time. If you want to have the method fire repeatedly (every 10 seconds), you must reexecute the `setTimeout` routine (see lines 11 and 12 in Listing 14.11).

Finally, the `clearTimeout` method can be used to cancel a timer. In this example, line 5 handles this task. Because the current timer fires in 10 seconds, you don't really have time to cancel the timer. However, in an example that sets a timer for several minutes, the `clearTimeout` method can be handy.

SEE ALSO
▶ *For more information on sessions, see page 397*

Testing the *Frame* Object

The `Frame` object is a child object of the `Window` object. This object can be used to inspect the collection of frames defined for a current window. You can access the `Frame` object only from the page that hosts the frames. This is usually a page that has no display components of its own. For this reason, you might not need to use the `Frame` object very often.

However, Listing 14.12 shows how you can write some client-side code that will inspect the frames collection on the page and display a short message to list each frame and the document loaded in the frame.

> **Time in VBScript**
>
> Remember that all time-based actions (`setTimeOut`) are based in milliseconds, not conventional seconds.

> **Frames**
>
> Frames are without a doubt a common element on the Web. You can use the Frame object to manipulate frames, creating a more coherent and interactive Web application when frames are required.

LISTING 14.12 **Testing the *Frame* Object**

```
1  <SCRIPT ID=clientEventHandlersVBS LANGUAGE=vbscript>
2  <!--
3
4  Sub window_onload
5      '
6      dim strMsg
7      '
8      intFrames = getFrameCount()
9      strMsg = "frame length: " & cStr(intFrames) & chr(13)
   ➥ & chr(13)
```

continues...

Relationships between objects

Remember how you learned about the relationships between objects? Here it is again, a little more detailed: The `Window` object refers to the window that contains all elements inside the Web browser. The `Document` object refers to all the elements within the currently loaded document. The `Frame` object is much like the `Window` object, except it lies below the `Window` object in the relationship.

LISTING 14.12 **Continued**

```
10      for x = 0 to intFrames-1
11          strMsg = strMsg & "name: " & getFrameName(x)
            & chr(13)
12          strMsg = strMsg & "url: " & getFrameURL(x) &
            chr(13) & chr(13)
13      next
14      '
15      alert strMsg
16      '
17 End Sub
18
19 -->
20 </SCRIPT>
21
22 <SCRIPT ID=CustomMethods LANGUAGE=vbscript>
23 <!--
24
25 Function getFrameCount
26     getFrameCount = window.frames.length
27 End Function
28
29 Function getFrameName(index)
30     getFrameName = window.frames(index).name
31 End Function
32
33 Function getFrameURL(index)
34     getFrameURL = window.frames(index).document.url
35 End Function
36
37 -->
38 </SCRIPT>
```

The code in Listing 14.12 also shows how you can organize your code into multiple script blocks for easy maintenance.

It should be pointed out that each `Frame` object acts just like a `Window` object. You can get the same properties and methods from a `Frame` object as you get from a `Window` object. In this way, you can think of the `Frame` object as just another window open in the browser space.

Using the *History*, *Navigator*, and *Location* Objects

The `History`, `Navigator`, and `Location` objects each provide additional information about the current browser session. You can use these objects to inspect the history of pages visited during this session and the type and settings of the current browser, and get details about the current server and client locations.

Testing the *History* Object

The `History` object is really quite simple. It contains a list of all the pages visited in this current session thread. The `History` object has three methods:

- `Back` moves backward in the history list to another page.
- `Forward` moves forward in the history list to another page.
- `Go` moves directly to a specific page in the history list.

Listing 14.13 shows a complete page that will display the current history for the session and then enable users to move directly to the first page in the history list.

> **Make your own Web browser**
>
> Try making your own Web browser. Use a combination of the objects you've experimented with in this chapter to make your own Web browser. Try to mimic as much of the functionality as you can, such as an address or location bar, the Back and Forward buttons, and even try working in some personal preferences.

LISTING 14.13 Testing the *History* Object

```
1  <HTML>
2  <HEAD>
3  <META name="VI60_DefaultClientScript" Content="VBScript">
4  <META NAME="GENERATOR" Content="Microsoft Visual Studio">
5  <SCRIPT ID=clientEventHandlersVBS LANGUAGE=vbscript>
6  <!--
7
8  Sub btnHistory_onclick
9      history.back history.length
10 End Sub
11
12 -->
13 </SCRIPT>
14 </HEAD>
15 <BODY>
16 <H2>Using the History Object</H2>
17 <HR>
```

continues...

Use History with caution

Using the `History` object, you can control your user's experience more accurately. One thing you should consider, however, is how the user will perceive your navigational pushes. Make sure that the incorporation of `History` is predictable for the users, so that they don't get confused and try to use the conventional Back and Forward buttons to retrace their steps.

LISTING 14.13 **Continued**

```
18  <SCRIPT LANGUAGE=vbscript>
19  <!--
20      '
21      ' show history object information
22      document.write "<code>"
23      document.write "length..: " & history.length
24      document.write "</code>"
25  -->
26  </SCRIPT>
27  <P>
28  <input type="button" value="History" id=btnHistory
    ➥name=btnHistory>
29  </P>
30
31  </BODY>
32  </HTML>
```

Testing the *Navigator* Object

You can use the `Navigator` object to get detailed information about the browser and workstation that is hosting the document. You can use this information to adjust your page to take advantage of the current browser settings or suppress certain features that are not supported by the current browser.

Listing 14.14 shows a code block that will display a list of information about the workstation and browser.

LISTING 14.14 **Testing the *Navigator* Object**

```
1  <SCRIPT LANGUAGE=vbscript>
2  <!--
3      '
4      ' display the navigator object information
5      '
6      document.write "<code>"
7      document.write "appCodeName.....: " &
       ➥navigator.appCodeName & "<BR>"
8      document.write "appMinorVersion.: " &
       ➥navigator.appMinorVersion & "<BR>"
```

Using the Microsoft Internet Explorer Object Model

```
9     document.write "appName.........: " &
      ➥navigator.appName    & "<BR>"
10    document.write "appVersion......: " &
      ➥navigator.appVersion & "<BR>"
11    document.write "cookieEnabled...: " &
      ➥navigator.cookieEnabled & "<BR>"
12    document.write "cpuClass........: " &
      ➥navigator.cpuClass   & "<BR>"
13    document.write "onLine..........: " &
      ➥navigator.onLine     & "<BR>"
14    document.write "platform........: " &
      ➥navigator.platform   & "<BR>"
15    document.write "systemLanguage..: " &
      ➥navigator.systemLanguage  & "<BR>"
16    document.write "userAgent.......: " &
      ➥navigator.userAgent  & "<BR>"
17    document.write "userLanguage....: " &
      ➥navigator.userLanguage & "<BR>"
18    document.write "</code>"
19    '
20    -->
21    </SCRIPT>
```

Sniffing for information

This code listing illustrates some of the information you can obtain. You can use the Navigation object to empower your scripts. Your scripts, based on the user information, can fine-tune their behavior. For example, perhaps only information relevant to the user's language or system platform will be displayed.

When you add this code block to a new HTML document and run that document, you'll see a display similar to the one shown in Figure 14.5.

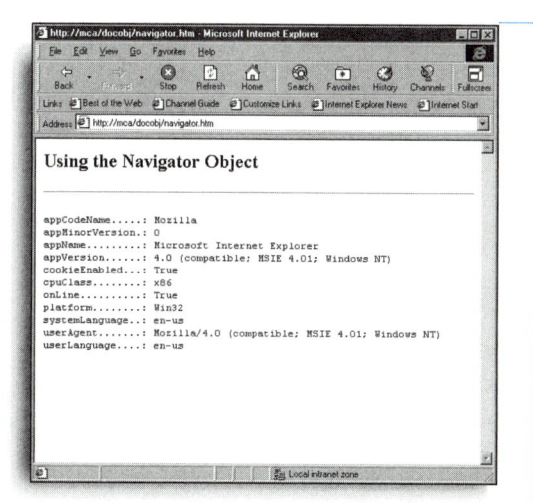

FIGURE 14.5
Displaying the `Navigator` object properties.

Testing the *Location* Object

The `Location` object is the most powerful of the `Window` child objects. You can use the `Location` object to get information about the exact location of the current document at the Web server, the Web server name, and the protocol in use. You can even use it to scan the search (`GET`) string passed to the page.

You can use the `reload` method to refresh the current page via code. There is also an `HREF` method that you can use to force-load any document into the browser. This last method works the same as the `Navigate` method of the `Window` object.

Listing 14.15 shows a complete HTML code page that displays the `Location` object properties and uses both the `reload` and `HREF` methods of the `Location` object. Name this document LOCATION.HTM.

> **Similarity between *History* and *Location***
>
> The same cautionary note about `History` applies to the `Location` object. Make sure you are enhancing your application, not complicating it at the user's expense.

LISTING 14.15 Testing the *Location* Object as LOCATION.HTM

```
1  <HTML>
2  <HEAD>
3  <META name=VI60_defaultClientScript content=VBScript>
4  <META NAME="GENERATOR" Content="Microsoft Visual Studio">
5  <SCRIPT ID=clientEventHandlersVBS LANGUAGE=vbscript>
6  <!--
7
8  Sub btnReload_onclick
9      ' reload this document
10     location.reload
11 End Sub
12
13 Sub btnHREF_onclick
14     ' call a new document
15     location.href="http://mca/docobj/location.htm?user=
       ➥mike"
16 End Sub
17
18 -->
19 </SCRIPT>
20 </HEAD>
```

Using the Microsoft Internet Explorer Object Model

```
21  <BODY>
22  <H2>Using the Location Object</H2>
23  <HR>
24  <SCRIPT LANGUAGE=vbscript>
25  <!--
26      '
27      ' display the location object information
28      document.write "<code>"
29      document.write "hash......: " & location.hash &
        ➥"<BR>"
30      document.write "host......: " & location.host &
        ➥"<BR>"
31      document.write "hostname..: " & location.hostname &
        ➥"<BR>"
32      document.write "href......: " & location.href &
        ➥"<BR>"
33      document.write "pathname..: " & location.pathname &
        ➥"<BR>"
34      document.write "port......: " & location.port &
        ➥"<BR>"
35      document.write "protocol..: " & location.protocol &
        ➥"<BR>"
36      document.write "search....: " & location.search &
        ➥"<BR>"
37      document.write "</code>"
38      '
39  -->
40  </SCRIPT>
41
42  <P>
43  <input type="button" value="HREF" id=btnHREF
    ➥name=btnHREF>
44  </P>
45
46  <P>
47  <input type="button" value="Reload" id=btnReload
    ➥name=btnReload>
48  </P>
49
50  </BODY>
51  </HTML>
```

Use this information

This is a long listing, but it shows just how much information actually is available to you. You can use this information to create more accurate and intelligent Web applications.

When you run the page in your browser, you'll see information about the page location and Web server name. If you press the **HREF** button, you'll execute code that will load the same page with a search string added (`"?user=mike"`). You'll then see this search string appear in the **search** property in the list (see Figure 14.6).

FIGURE 14.6

Results of using the HREF method of the `Location` object.

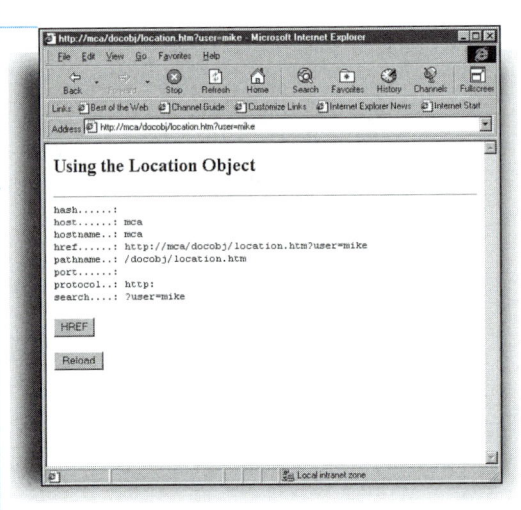

That's the complete set of Window objects associated with the browser and workstation. The next set of objects focus on the loaded document and its contents (links, forms, and elements).

Exploring the *Document* Object

The Document object is the primary object to use when you want to get information about the document that is currently loaded in the browser. You can also use some of the Document object methods to generate new document text and even execute commands against the document, such as selecting and copying data to the Microsoft Windows Clipboard.

Complexity alert

When you start working with the Document object, you're starting to work with the heart of the object model. The Document object is a complex beast, and you should experiment with it before using it in your applications.

Exploring the *Document* Object   CHAPTER 14

In this section of the chapter, you inspect a handful of commonly used Document object properties and then test some of the most often used methods of the object.

Testing the *Document* Object Properties

There are several properties of the Document object that you can inspect to learn more about the document that is currently loaded in the browser. Usually, you'll use these properties to display document information, such as creation and modification dates, size, title, and other properties.

Listing 14.16 shows a script block you can add to a new HTML document. This block can be used to get commonly used properties from the loaded document.

LISTING 14.16 **Inspecting the Document Properties**

```
1  <SCRIPT LANGUAGE=vbscript>
2  <!--
3     '
4     ' show document object information
5     document.write "<code>"
6     document.write "alinkColor.......: " & 
   ➥document.alinkColor & "<BR>"
7     document.write "bgColor..........: " & 
   ➥document.bgColor    & "<BR>"
8     document.write "cookie...........: " & 
   ➥document.cookie & "<BR>"
9     document.write "defaultCharset...: " & 
   ➥document.defaultCharset  & "<BR>"
10    document.write "domain...........: " & 
   ➥document.domain    & "<BR>"
11    document.write "fgColor..........: " & 
   ➥document.fgColor & "<BR>"
12    document.write "fileCreatedDate..: " & 
   ➥document.fileCreatedDate & "<BR>"
13    document.write "fileModifiedDate.: " & 
   ➥document.fileModifiedDate   & "<BR>"
14    document.write "fileSize.........: " & 
   ➥document.fileSize    & "<BR>"
```

continues...

The power of the Document object

The listing demonstrates exactly how much detail you can get from the **Document** object. The power behind the **Document** object is incredible. Remember, not only can you query for information (as you did with this code), you can also use the **Document** object to change properties.

LISTING 14.16 **Continued**

```
15    document.write "fileUpdatedDate..: " &
      ➥document.fileUpdatedDate  & "<BR>"
16    document.write "lastModified.....: " &
      ➥document.lastModified    & "<BR>"
17    document.write "linkColor........: " &
      ➥document.linkColor       & "<BR>"
18    document.write "mimeType.........: " &
      ➥document.mimeType        & "<BR>"
19    document.write "nameProp.........: " &
      ➥document.nameProp        & "<BR>"
20    document.write "parentWindow.....: " &
      ➥document.parentWindow    & "<BR>"
21    document.write "protocol.........: " &
      ➥document.protocol        & "<BR>"
22    document.write "readyState.......: " &
      ➥document.readyState      & "<BR>"
23    document.write "referrer.........: " &
      ➥document.referrer        & "<BR>"
24    document.write "security.........: " &
      ➥document.security        & "<BR>"
25    document.write "title............: " &
      ➥document.title           & "<BR>"
26    document.write "url..............: " &
      ➥document.url             & "<BR>"
27    document.write "vlinkColor.......: " &
      ➥document.vlinkColor      & "<BR>"
28    document.write "</code>"
29       '
30    -->
31    </SCRIPT>
```

When you add this code block to your HTML document and run the page in your browser, you will see results that look something like the ones shown in Figure 14.7.

Exploring the *Document* Object   **CHAPTER 14**   **367**

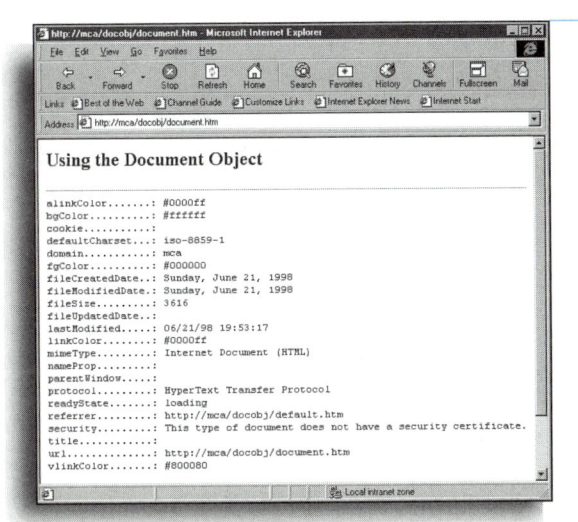

FIGURE 14.7
Results of the Document object properties.

Testing the *Write* and *WriteLn* Methods

Probably the most commonly used methods of the Document object are the Write and WriteLn methods. These methods can be used to generate new HTML lines in the current browser window. The only difference between the two methods is that the WriteLn method actually generates a newline character in the HTML document text. This newline character makes it easier to read the HTML source, but does not affect the way the HTML source is rendered in the browser. It only makes the HTML source easier for humans to read.

To test the Write and WriteLn methods in a document, add two HTML button controls to the page and add Visual Basic Scripting code in a code block to respond to the onclick events. Listing 14.17 shows how that can be done.

> **Using WriteLn makes HTML source easy to read**
>
> If you use the document.write method a lot and inspect the resulting HTML source, you'll see that everything is loaded into the browser as one long line of text. This makes it difficult to read the HTML source after it has arrived in the client browser. If you want to see the HTML source formatted in clean lines, you can use the WriteLn method instead.

LISTING 14.17 Testing the *Write* and *WriteLn* Methods

```
1 <SCRIPT ID=clientEventHandlersVBS LANGUAGE=vbscript>
2 <!--
3
4 Sub btnWriteLn_onclick
5     '
```

continues…

LISTING 14.17 Continued

```
6        ' test writeln method
7        document.clear
8        document.writeln "WriteLn 1<BR>"
9        document.writeln "WriteLn 2<BR>"
10       document.close
11       '
12 End Sub
13
14 Sub btnWrite_onclick
15       '
16       ' test write method
17       document.clear
18       document.write "Write 1<BR>"
19       document.write "Write 2<BR>"
20       document.close
21       '
22 End Sub
23
24 -->
25 </SCRIPT>
26 <P>
27 <input type="button" value="Write" id=btnWrite
    ➥name=btnWrite>
28 <input type="button" value="WriteLn" id=btnWriteLn
    ➥name=btnWriteLn>
29 </P>
30 <P>
31 <input type="button" value="execCommand"
    ➥id=btnExecCmd name=btnExecCmd>
32 </P>
```

Dynamic on-the-fly page generation

Are you starting to think about the possibilities? Using the `Write` and `WriteLn` methods, you can create pages that are modified on-the-fly, depending on the results of your scripts. When you couple this with dynamic page generation from the server side, you are looking toward no two pages ever looking the same.

Notice that the methods that use the `Write` and `WriteLn` methods both use the `Clear` and `Close` methods, too. When generating new documents for the browser window with the `Write` and `WriteLn` methods, it is a good idea to begin the session with a `Clear` method to erase any current text and a `Close` method when you are finished.

Exploring the *Document* Object

To test these two methods, run the page and press the command buttons. The actual resulting page will not be any different. However, if you inspect the HTML source that was generated by each button, you'll see a slight difference. The HTML source generated with the `Write` method looks like this:

```
Write 1<BR>Write 2<BR>
```

And the HTML source generated by the `WriteLn` method looks like this:

```
WriteLn 1<BR>
WriteLn 2<BR>
```

Again, this difference affects only the HTML source code and not the display of the document in the browser.

Testing the *execCommand* and Related Methods

Microsoft Internet Explorer has a very powerful set of methods called the `exec` methods. The `execCommand` method enables you to execute a wide range of operations against the current document. There are actually 48 commands you can execute on the document (see Table 14.1).

> **The execCommand complications**
>
> The `execCommand` method is powerful and provides a lot of capabilities. It also is bordering on the complex. Experiment your `execCommand` uses before you implement them in your Web application.

TABLE 14.1 Possible Command Identifiers for the *execCommand* Method

Command Identifier	Description
BackColor	Sets background color of the current selection.
Bold	Wraps a <B> tag around an object.
Copy	Copies the object to the Clipboard.
CreateBookMark	Wraps a <A NAME=> tag around the object, or edits an existing tag.
CreateLink	Wraps an <A HREF=> tag around the current selection.
Cut	Copies the object to the Clipboard and then deletes it.
Delete	Deletes the object.
FontName	Sets the typeface for the current selection.
FontSize	Sets the font size for the current selection.

continues...

TABLE 14.1 Continued

Command Identifier	Description
`ForeColor`	Sets the foreground of the current selection.
`FormatBlock`	Wraps a block tag as specified around the object.
`Indent`	Indents the selection.
`InsertButton`	Inserts a `<BUTTON>` tag at the insertion point.
`InsertFieldSet`	Inserts a `<FIELDSET>` tag at the insertion point.
`InsertHorizontalRule`	Inserts a `<HR>` tag at the insertion point.
`InsertIFrame`	Inserts an `<IFRAME>` tag at the insertion point.
`InsertInputButton`	Inserts an `<INPUT TYPE=button>` at the insertion point.
`InsertInputCheckbox`	Inserts an `<INPUT TYPE=checkbox>` at the insertion point.
`InsertInputFileUpload`	Inserts an `<INPUT TYPE=fileupload>` at the insertion point.
`InsertInputHidden`	Inserts an `<INPUT TYPE=hidden>` at the insertion point.
`InsertInputPassword`	Inserts an `<INPUT TYPE=password>` at the insertion point.
`InsertInputRadio`	Inserts an `<INPUT TYPE=radio>` at the insertion point.
`InsertInputReset`	Inserts an `<INPUT TYPE=reset>` at the insertion point.
`InsertInputSubmit`	Inserts an `<INPUT TYPE=submit>` at the insertion point.
`InsertInputText`	Inserts an `<INPUT TYPE=text>` at the insertion point.
`InsertMarquee`	Inserts a `<MARQUEE>` tag at the insertion point.
`InsertOrderedList`	Inserts an `<OL>` tag at the insertion point.
`InsertParagraph`	Inserts a `<P>` tag at the insertion point.
`InsertSelectDropDown`	Inserts a `<SELECT TYPE=dropdown>` at the insertion point.
`InsertSelectListBox`	Inserts a `<SELECT TYPE=listbox>` at the insertion point.

Exploring the *Document* Object

Command Identifier	Description
`InsertTextArea`	Inserts a `<TEXTAREA>` tag at the insertion point.
`InsertUnOrderedList`	Inserts an `<UL>` tag at the insertion point.
`Italic`	Wraps an `<I>` tag around the selected object.
`JustifyCenter`	Centers the current selection.
`JustifyLeft`	Left justifies the current selection.
`JustifyRight`	Right justifies the current selection.
`Outdent`	Outdents the selection.
`OverWrite`	Sets the input-typing mode to overwrite or insert (toggle).
`Paste`	Pastes the contents of the Clipboard at the insertion point.
`Refresh`	Reloads the current source document.
`RemoveFormat`	Removes formatting from the current selection.
`SelectAll`	Selects the entire text of the document.
`UnBookmark`	Removes tags from the selection or range.
`Underline`	Wraps a `<U>` tag around the selection.
`Unlink`	Removes a link.
`Unselect`	Clears the selection.

Along with the various commands to execute, there are a series of support methods to help you see whether the selected command is supported, whether it is currently in a ready state, and so on. This last set of commands is part of the `queryExec` series.

In the example in Listing 14.18, Visual Basic Scripting code is used to execute a `SelectAll` and `Copy` to place the contents of the HTML item in focus on the Windows Clipboard.

LISTING 14.18 Testing the *Exec* Methods

```
1 <SCRIPT LANGUAGE="vbscript">
2
3 Sub btnExecCmd_onclick
4     '
```

continues...

LISTING 14.18 Continued

```
5     ' test various exec methods
6     document.clear
7     document.write "<H3>Testing ExecCommand for
      ➥'Copy'</H3><HR>"
8     document.write "<code>"
9     document.write "queryCommandEnabled...: " &
      ➥document.queryCommandEnabled("Copy") & "<BR>"
10      document.write "queryCommandState.....: " &
      ➥document.queryCommandState("Copy") & "<BR>"
11    document.write "queryCommandSupported.: " &
      ➥document.queryCommandSupported("Copy") & "<BR>"
12    document.write "queryCommandIndeterm..: " & document.
      ➥queryCommandIndeterm ("Copy") & "<BR>"
13    document.write "</code><P>"
14    '
15    if document.queryCommandSupported("Copy")=true then
16        document.execCommand "SelectAll",False
17        document.execCommand "Copy",False
18        alert "Item copied to the clipboard."
19    else
20        alert "Copy is not supported!"
21    end if
22    '
23 End Sub
24
25 -->
26 </SCRIPT>
```

The code in Listing 14.18 first lists the status values from the various queryExec methods (lines 6–13) and then attempts to copy the contents of the current HTML control onto the Clipboard (lines 15–21). If the operation fails, you see an alert message instead.

You can test this example by running a page with this code and then checking the Windows Clipboard contents. Load Notepad (NOTEPAD.EXE) and select **Edit**, **Paste** from the menu. This will place the HTML contents into the Notepad editor.

Using the *Link* Object

The `Link` object enables you to inspect a list of all the available URL links in the current document. You can use this information to display a given link, add it to other pages, and even navigate to the selected link in the list.

The `Link` object is really a collection of links. For this reason, you must inspect the `length` property of the object to see how many links are in the list and then use a programming loop to inspect each link in the collection.

Listing 14.19 shows an HTML document that has a set of links and then uses the `Link` object collection to display information about each link on the page.

> **Using the `Link` object**
>
> One potential use for the `Link` object is to maintain an active list of the links available to a user. You can populate a pop-up site map to the user using the `Location` object.

LISTING 14.19 Displaying the *Links* Collection in a Document

```
1  <HTML>
2  <HEAD>
3  <META name="VI60_DefaultClientScript" Content="VBScript">
4  <META NAME="GENERATOR" Content="Microsoft Visual Studio">
5  </HEAD>
6  <BODY>
7  <H2>Using the Link Object</H2>
8  <HR>
9  <A href="history.htm">history.htm</A><BR>
10 <A href="location.htm">location.htm</A><BR>
11 <A href="navigator.htm">navigator.htm</A><BR>
12 <A href="ScriptTypes.htm">ScriptTypes.htm</A><BR>
13 <A href="window.htm">window.htm</A><BR>
14 <A href="default.htm">default.htm</A><BR>
15
16 <P>
17 <SCRIPT language=vbscript>
18 <!--
19     intLinks=document.links.length
20     document.write "<code>"
21     document.write "link length...: " & intLinks &
    ➥"<BR>"
```

continues...

LISTING 14.19 Continued

```
22      for x=0 to intLinks-1
23          document.write "link href.....: " &
            ➥document.links(x).href & "<BR>"
24      next
25      document.write "</code>"
26      '
27  -->
28  </SCRIPT>
29  </P>
30
31  </BODY>
32  </HTML>
```

Notice that the first step in the process is to get the total number of links in the collection (line 19). Then you can use a FOR...NEXT loop to walk through the collection and display the URL for each link. It is important to note that the link collection index starts with 0, not 1. For this reason, the loop counter must start at zero and end at a value one less than the total count of links (see line 22).

Figure 14.8 shows what you would see if you ran the page in Listing 14.19 in your browser.

FIGURE 14.8

Results of using the Link object collection.

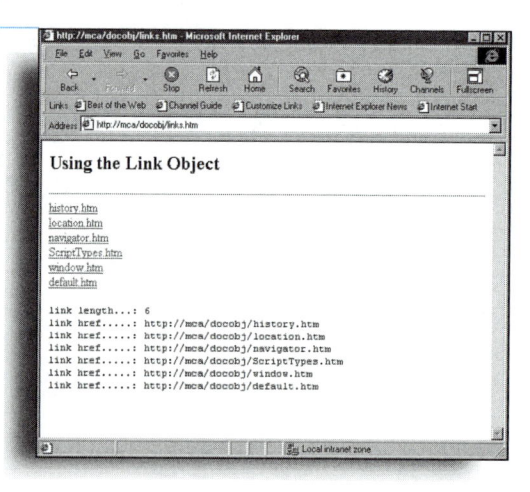

Using the *Form* and *Element* Objects

You use the Form and Element objects to inspect and manipulate the detailed contents of a loaded document. Like the Link object, the Form and Element objects are actually collections. This means that you must first get a count of the total number of items in the collection and then use a loop to access each item in the collection.

A Form object represents the typical HTML form you use to POST or GET data from the client browser to a back-end server. The Element object represents all the HTML controls within a form or document. This includes all the input boxes and buttons, as well as lists, check boxes, and so on. A Document object can have several forms on it (although this is not very common) and each Form or Document object can have many HTML elements (quite common).

You can use the Form and Element collections to view the contents of any loaded HTML document and display the results in the browser. To do this, you must first get the count of all the forms in the document and then, as you work through the forms list, get the count of all the elements in each form and display the information about these elements.

This sounds like a complicated process, but it is actually quite easy. You must write only one Visual Basic Scripting method to handle the listing of all forms and all elements in each form. This code could be added to any HTML document to get the needed information.

Listing 14.20 shows the Visual Basic Scripting code that will display all forms and their elements.

LISTING 14.20 Visual Basic Script Code to Display All Forms and Elements

```
 1  <SCRIPT language=vbscript>
 2  <!--
 3      dim intForms
 4      dim intElements
 5      '
 6      document.write "<code>"
 7      intForms=document.forms.length
 8      document.write "forms length...: " & intForms & "<BR>"
 9      for x=0 to intForms-1
10          document.write "form name......: " &
            ➥document.forms(x).name & "<BR>"
11          document.write "form action....: " &
            ➥document.forms(x).action & "<BR>"
12          document.write "form encoding..: " &
            ➥document.forms(x).encoding & "<BR>"
13          document.write "form method....: " &
            ➥document.forms(x).method & "<BR>"
14          document.write "form target....: " &
            ➥document.forms(x).target & "<BR>"
15          '
16          intElements = document.forms(x).elements.length
17          document.write "element length.: " &
            ➥intElements & "<BR>"
18          for y=0 to intElements-1
19              document.write "element name...: " &
                ➥document.forms(x).elements(y).name
20              document.write ", " & document.forms(x).
                ➥elements(y).value & "<BR>"
21          next
22          document.write "<BR>"
23      next
24      document.write "</code>"
25      '
26  -->
27  </SCRIPT>
```

When you have this code block in your document, you can build any number of forms on the page and then run the page to see the results. Listing 14.21 shows two forms placed on the same page as the code shown in Listing 14.20.

Exploring the *Document* Object

LISTING 14.21 **Placing Two Forms in a Single HTML Document**

```
1  <FORM method=get action="getpage.asp" id=frmFirst
   ➥name=frmFirst>
2  <CODE>
3  <STRONG>FormFirst</STRONG><BR>
4  Name.......<INPUT id=text1 name=text1 value=Dana ><BR>
5  Password...<INPUT type=password id=password1
   ➥name=password1 value=dana><BR>
6  CheckBox...<INPUT type=checkbox id=checkbox1
   ➥name=checkbox1><BR>
7  <INPUT type=hidden value=Hidden id=hidden1 name=hidden1>
8  <INPUT type=submit value=Submit id=submit1 name=submit1>
9  <INPUT type=reset value=Reset id=reset1 name=reset1>
10 </CODE>
11 </FORM>
12 <P>
13 <FORM method=post action="postpage.asp" id=frmLast
   ➥name=frmLast>
14 <CODE>
15 <STRONG>FormLast</STRONG><BR>
16 Name.......<INPUT id=text2 name=text2
   ➥value=Jesse ><BR>
17 Password...<INPUT type=password id=password2
   ➥name=password2 value=jesse><BR>
18 CheckBox...<INPUT type=checkbox id=checkbox2
   ➥name=checkbox2><BR>
19 <INPUT type=hidden value=Hidden id=hidden1 name=hidden1>
20 <INPUT type=submit value=Submit id=submit2 name=submit2>
21 <INPUT type=reset value=Reset id=reset2 name=reset2>
22 </CODE>
23 </FORM>
```

Now when you load the completed document in your browser, you'll see results that look like those in Figure 14.9.

As you can see from Figure 14.9, the Element object can return not only the name of the element in the form, but also the current value in the element. You can use this information to adjust values in HTML controls or inspect them for valid inputs. Notice also that the elements collection exposes even hidden inputs in the form. In this way, you can access inputs that are not even visible to the user.

PART III   Databases and the Web

CHAPTER 14   **Client-Side Scripting with the MSIE Object Model**

FIGURE 14.9

Results of using the `Form` and `Element` objects.

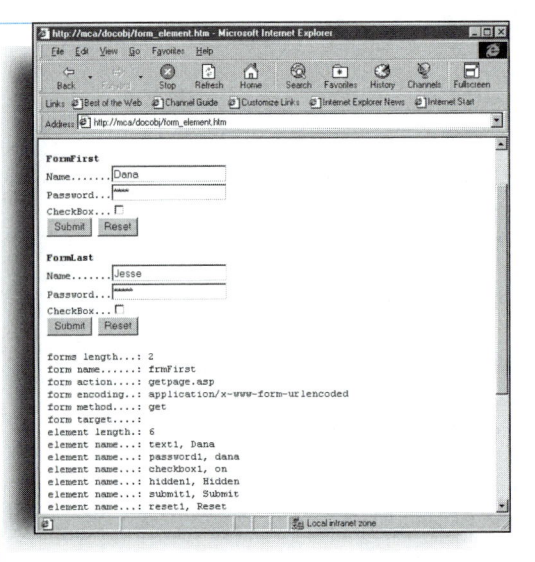

That's the end of the review of the Microsoft Internet Explorer object model. You now know how to use the object model to get detailed information about the browser window and the document loaded in the browser. You can use this information to inspect current values, adjust inputs, and event generate and load new documents—all without making calls to the Web server.

SEE ALSO

▶ To learn how to combine events that trigger actions in the `Form` or `Element` objects, see pages *318* and *325*

▶ After looking at the document object model, also take a look at page *724* to get you started on planning for problems in your Web applications

CHAPTER 15

Using Server-Side Scripting with the Built-In ASP Objects

Learn what server-side scripting is and how it works

Create server-side scripts for your Web applications

Learn how to access and manipulate the five built-in server-side objects

About ASP, server-side script, and VBScript

OK, you've heard about Active Server Pages (ASP), server-side script, and VBScript. What's the difference? Not much, and a whole lot. ASP is really another way of saying server-side script using VBScript. ASP is the marketing name for the technology Microsoft developed for using VBScript as a server-side script language. Because it is quite possible that other languages could be used to perform scripting on the server, ASP is often used to mean server-side script using VBScript. You'll see ASP and server-side script used often throughout this book. Unless otherwise stated, server-side script and ASP are meant interchangeably here.

About the `ScriptingContext` object

There's a sixth built-in server-side object not covered in this chapter: the `ScriptingContext` object. It is used (in conjunction with the Microsoft Transaction Server) to communicate the completion or cancellation of transactions. Microsoft Transaction Server is not covered in this book.

Up to this point, all the chapters in this section have dealt with client-side VBScript. That is VBScript that runs in the client browser at the downstream end of the connection. However, you can also write VBScript that runs only on the Microsoft Internet Information Server that hosts the Web application. This is called *server-side scripting*.

The following are the five built-in server-side objects you will learn about in this chapter:

- The `Server` object is used to access server-related properties and methods.
- The `Application` object is used to share information with all users of the application.
- The `Session` object is used to manage user-specific information for a single session.
- The `Response` object is used to pass information from the server down to the client.
- The `Request` object is used to pass information from the client up to the server.

When you have completed this chapter, you'll have a good understanding of how server-side scripting works, how to create server-side scripts for Web applications, and how to take advantage of the built-in Active Server Pages objects available when you use Microsoft Internet Information Server.

What Is Server-Side Scripting?

The idea behind server-side script processing is rooted in the way the World Wide Web works. The Hypertext Transfer Protocol (HTTP) dictates the way data is passed in conversations between the client (your browser) and the server. Basically, a client contacts a server and requests a page of data. Then the server collects all data for the requested page and ships it to the client. Just what is on the page (including links to other pages and so on) is of no real interest to the server. It can be simple HTML tags, VBScript, Jscript, PERL, CGI, images— whatever.

What Is Server-Side Scripting?

So far, the discussions of VBScript have always assumed that the VBScript you write is sent down to the browser as part of the requested page. This works fine for browsers that are capable of handling VBScript. However, some browsers might not understand VBScript. Also, there might be some tasks you must perform at the server end before you send the page down to the client. That's where server-side script comes in.

When you write your VBScript to run as server-side script, it never reaches the browser. When a client requests a page with server-side script on it, the server loads the page in memory, runs the server-side script and sends the *results* to the client as fulfillment of the page request.

In other words, you can write VBScript routines that read data on the server (access database, read disk files, and so on), then send that information down to the client in the form of an HTML document. The client never sees the VBScript and never knows you were writing VBScript at all.

There are several advantages to employing server-side scripts in your Web applications. First, because the code runs at the server it takes some of the load off the client browser processor. Also, in many cases much less data will be sent over the wire from the server to the client, because only the results of the server-side scripting must be sent to the client.

Another big advantage of using server-side script is that you can do things on the server that just aren't possible on the client. For example, sharing information in an SQL Server database requires the data to be sorted on the server, the connection information to be stored on the server, and the details of selecting and displaying the data to be done at the server before it is sent down to the client browser.

There are other reasons to use server-side script. Here are just a few examples:

- *Improved security.* If you use passwords to access data, you don't want to send them down to the client.

The evolution of server-side scripting

Server-side activation has come a long way. From its humble beginnings in CGI (Common Gateway Interface) programs, Web applications have been relying on the server to do the work. Server-side scripting with ASP takes things to the next level, making it much easier. The advantage with ASP is you aren't locked into one language. This chapter demonstrates how to use VBScript, however you can also use Jscript and even PerlScript with a server-side plug-in.

ASP integration

ASP has great integration with databases using ODBC. For example, you can easily build a Web site that pulls information from a SQL Server or Access database and stores its own data when it's finished.

- *Component reuse.* You can build and use DLLs placed on the server and don't need to send them down to the client.
- *Wire traffic reduction.* Instead of sending several VBScript methods to compute interest rates to every user every time he or she accesses the page, keep the code on the server and send only the results of the calculations.

SEE ALSO
➤ *You'll learn more about using ASP for databases on page 418*

Understanding How Server-Side Scripts Work

Creating server-side script code is easy. There are just a few special rules you must follow to make sure the script runs up on the server instead of down on the client browser. After you get these few rules under your belt, you'll find that writing server-side script is no different than writing client-side script.

First, if you are creating a document that will be running server-side script for Microsoft Internet Information Server, you must add the following line at the top of the document:

```
<% @LANGUAGE="VBScript">
```

This line tells the Microsoft Internet Information Server that the document contains VBScript that must be evaluated and executed before the document is sent downstream to the server. If you fail to place this line at the top of the document, none of the server-side script will be executed, and you will not get the results you expected when the page is finally sent down to the client browser.

Next, all server-side script must be enclosed between the <% and %> markers (see Listing 15.1).

LISTING 15.1 Some Server-Side Script

```
1  <%
2  '
3  ' this code will run at the server
4  '
5  Dim strGreeting
6  '
```

What Is Server-Side Scripting?

```
 7 If Hour(Now)<12 Then
 8     StrGreeting = "Good Morning!"
 9 Else
10     StrGreeting = "Good Afternoon!"
11 End If
12 '
13 Response.Write "<H2>" & strGreeting & "</H2>"
14 '
15 %>
```

These markers identify the server-side script to the Microsoft Internet Information Server. Any VBScript not placed inside these markers will be sent down to the client with the rest of the page.

When the document that contains the server-side script (shown in Listing 15.1) is requested by a client, the server loads the document, evaluates the server-side script, executes the code, and sends the results downstream to the client. In the case of Listing 15.1, the only material that is written to the downstream client (in the mornings) is

`<H2>Good Morning!</H2>`

In other words, the downstream client never sees the server-side script and never knows whether the material sent downstream was pure HTML data or the result of processed server-side script.

This points out another important advantage of using server-side script. Even though you may write your server-side script using VBScript, the downstream client need not understand VBScript. Because the VBScript is all handled on the server side, the client does not need to run a VBScript engine in order to understand the output.

It is also possible to mix server-side script and HTML in the same document. For example, Listing 15.2 shows how you can mix both HTML-tagged text and VBScript running as server-side script to produce the final output to be sent downstream.

The danger of not closing anchors

Anyone who has written a Web page or a script knows how dangerous it can be not to close a tag's anchor. For example, having a <B> and not a </B> means everything on your page following the open anchor will be bolded text. This remains true with server side. Be sure to close your server-side scripting tags (%>), otherwise the rest of your document will be processed on the server side, and likely choked on.

Other scripting languages

Internet Information Server 4.0 supports VBScript and Jscript out of the box. You can also obtain "add ons" or plug-ins that support PERL (or PERLScript) and REXX. This lets you use the scripting language you prefer to develop in.

LISTING 15.2 Mixing HTML and Server-Side Script on the Same Page

```
1  <!-- get instance of CLC -->
2  <%
3  '
4  ' create vars for handling CLC
5  dim objLinker   ' holds CLC
6  dim intLoop     ' counter for items
7  dim strURL      ' holds item URL
8  dim strTitle    ' holds item title
9  '
10 ' get instance of CLC object
11 set objLinker = Server.CreateObject("MSWC.NextLink")
12 %>
13
14 <!-- Insert HTML here --></P>
15 <H2>In This Issue of VID-NC</H2>
16 <HR>
17 <!-- now show articles in this issue -->
18 <%
19 For intLoop=1 to objLinker.GetListCount("cl_data.txt")
20     strURL=objLinker.GetNthURL("cl_data.txt",intLoop)
21     strTitle=objLinker.GetNthDescription("cl_data.txt"
       ➥,intLoop)
22 %>
23 <H4><LI><A href="<%=strURL%>"><%=strTitle%></A></H4>
24 <%Next%>
25 <HR>
```

Using server-side scripts to alter client-side scripts

You can use server-side scripts to populate information and modify scripts that will be used on the client. This is a prime example of the power of taking advantage of both scripting platforms. For example, you could use a query from a database run on the server to populate a script on the client side. This unique data would make the client-side script more applicable.

Listing 15.2 shows the first line as a standard HTML comment line followed by several lines of VBScript marked for server-side execution (lines 2–12). Then in lines 13–17 there are a few more lines of HTML, followed by a block of server-side script (lines 18–22), a line of both HTML and server-side script together (line 23), a line of server-side script (line 24), and one last line of HTML on line 25.

Don't worry if you don't understand what all this HTML and VBScript code is actually doing. The idea here is just to get a notion of how VBScript can be used as a server-side script tool. As you can see, you have a lot of flexibility available to you when you use server-side script.

Now create a simple server-side script page to show how it all works.

Creating a Simple Server-Side Script with VBScript

As a simple example, create a Web page that uses all server-side script with VBScript. This page will use the date and time of the server to determine the greeting you send clients that connect to your Web application.

Before you create this sample ASP page, first start a new Visual InterDev Web project to host all the pages you'll build for this chapter. Start Visual InterDev and create a new project called ServerObjects. Then add a new HTML page called DEFAULT.HTM to the project and a set of links to the page found in Table 15.1.

> **Using debugging**
>
> To really appreciate development of server-side scripts with Visual InterDev, you are going to want to use the debugging features. This requires your Web server to be Internet Information Server 4.0 or higher, and for you to have the Visual InterDev server-side debugging components installed on the server.

TABLE 15.1 Links for DEFAULT.HTM of the *ServerObjects* Web application

Text	Link
Simple ASP example	SIMPLE.ASP
Server Object	SERVER.ASP
Application Object	APPLICATION.ASP
Session Object	SESSION.ASP
Response Object	RESPONSE.ASP
Request Object	REQUEST.ASP

When you're finished, your home page should look like the one in Figure 15.1.

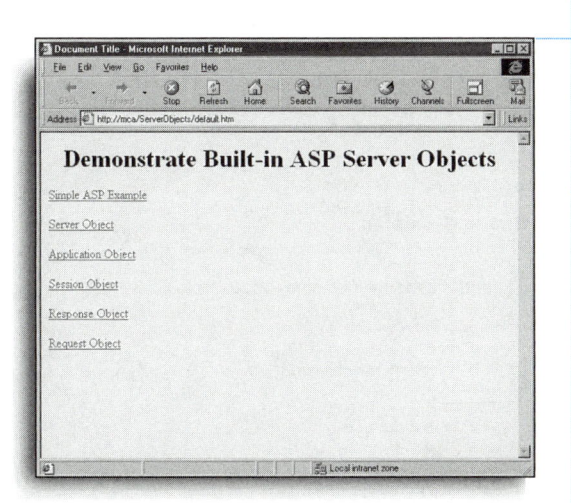

FIGURE 15.1
Layout for the DEFAULT.HTM of the ServerObjects Web application.

Now you're ready to create your first server-side script page using VBScript. To do this, you must add an ASP page to your project.

Adding ASP pages to your project

1. After you load Visual InterDev and access your project, select the project name from the Project Explorer window by clicking on it once with the mouse.
2. Press the right-mouse button and select **Add**, **Active Server Page** from the context menu.
3. When the Add Item dialog appears, enter SIMPLE.ASP into the SIMPLE.ASP **Name** text box. Be sure to use .asp as the final characters in the filename.
4. Press the **Open** button to force Visual InterDev to create the new ASP document in your project and load it into your editor.
5. Now you're ready to start writing your server-side script code!

After you create the SIMPLE.ASP document in your project, you must enter the VBScript that will run at the server. Listing 15.3 shows some very simple server-side script that will create a header for the document and generate a greeting to the client based on the time of day. Add this code within the <BODY></BODY> HTML tags of the document.

LISTING 15.3 **Some Simple Server-Side Script Using VBScript**

```
1 <%
2 '
3 ' simple asp example
4 '
5 dim intHour
6 dim strGreeting
7
8 ' send heading for the document
```

What Is Server-Side Scripting?

```
 9 Response.Write "<H2><CENTER>Simple ASP Example</CENTER>
   ➥</H2><P>"
10
11 ' compute greeting
12 intHour=Hour(Now)
13 Select Case intHour
14    Case 0,1,2,3,4,5,6,7,8,9,10,11
15        strGreeting = "Good Morning"
16    Case 12,13,14,15,16,17
17        strGreeting = "Good Afternoon"
18    Case 18,19,20,21,22,23
19        strGreeting = "Good Evening"
20 End Select
21
22 'send greeting
23 Response.Write "<H4><CENTER>" & strGreeting &
   ➥"</CENTER></H4><P>"
24 Response.Write "<CENTER>Server Date and Time is: "
   ➥& FormatDateTime(Now) & "</CENTER>"
25 '
26 %>
```

> **This listing is a challenge!**
>
> This code is a good example of modifying your page based on a condition. After you've completed this example once, try going back and making it greet you based on the season you're in.

First, notice that the entire block of code is surrounded with the server-side script markers <% and %>. Keep in mind that this is a requirement. Even though the document has <%@ LANGUAGE=VBScript %> as the first line, all server-side script code must still be enclosed in the server-side script markers.

Second, notice that there are three lines (lines 9, 23, and 24) that actually send HTML output downstream. Each of these lines use the Response object. You'll learn more about the Response object later in this chapter. Finally, a single Select Case structure on lines 13–20 is used to determine the current hour of the day and set a variable to the proper greeting.

> **The Response object and the Document Object**
>
> The Response object is much like the Document object on the client side. You can use both objects to dynamically write content to the Web page.

When you have completed this code, save the document and start the Web application (press F5 or select **Debug**, **Start** from the main menu). When you navigate to the SIMPLE.ASP link on the home page, your browser should display a page similar to the one in Figure 15.2.

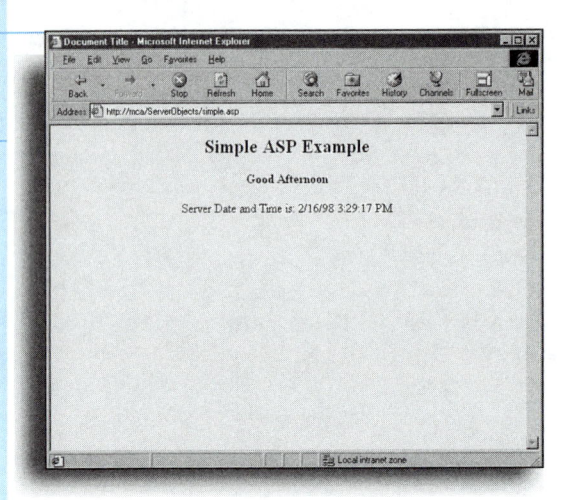

FIGURE 15.2

Displaying the SIMPLE.ASP page.

You can see the exact document sent downstream by selecting **View**, **Source** from the Microsoft Internet Explorer. Listing 15.4 shows the HTML that created the document in Figure 15.2.

Using server-side scripting for protection

You can use server-side scripting to protect sensitive code and information. This is great for not revealing how you did it.

LISTING 15.4 HTML Document Sent by Server-Side Script

```
 1  <HTML>
 2  <HEAD>
 3  <META NAME="GENERATOR" Content="Microsoft Visual Studio">
 4  <META HTTP-EQUIV="Content-Type" content="text/html">
 5  <TITLE>Document Title</TITLE>
 6  </HEAD>
 7  <BODY>
 8
 9  <H2><CENTER>Simple ASP Example</CENTER></H2><P>
10  <H4><CENTER>Good Afternoon</CENTER></H4><P>
11  <CENTER>Server Date and Time is: 2/16/98 3:29:17 PM
12  </CENTER>
13
14  <!-- Insert HTML here -->
15
16  </BODY>
17  </HTML>
```

The exact content of the page or layout of the HTML might not be the same for you, but it should look pretty close to that of Listing 15.4. The main thing to notice is that there is absolutely no trace of VBScript in the HTML document that was sent from the server. Only the result of the server-side script was sent.

That's the basics of server-side script with VBScript. All you're really doing is writing VBScript onto pages that have been marked for executing at the server.

In the next five sections, you create other ASP documents that detail the properties and methods of the built-in ASP objects used in server-side scripting.

Accessing the Host Server with the *Server* Object

The `Server` object gives you access to information available to every Web application running on the host Web server. This enables you to get (and set) information shared by all applications. The `Server` object is the simplest of the built-in ASP objects. The `Server` object has one property and four methods (see Table 15.2).

TABLE 15.2 Properties and methods of the *Server* object

Name	Type	Description	Example
ScriptTimeout	Property	Used to set/get the timeout value for running scripts on the server. Expressed in seconds.	Server.Script Timeout=90
HTMLEncode	Method	Used to convert ASCII text into HTML-safe string.	StrHTML = Server.HTML Encode("<P>")

continues...

TABLE 15.2 Continued

Name	Type	Description	Example
URLEncode	Method	Used to convert ASCII text into URL-safe string.	StrURL=URLEncode(http://www.banick.com/samplepage.asp)
CreateObject	Method	Used to link your server-side script to a COM object at the server.	ObjTemp = Server.CreateObject("MyDLL.MyObject")
MapPath	Method	Used to return the physical disk location of a virtual folder on the Web server.	StrFolder=Server.MapPath("/data")

> **Unpredictable results with the Server object**
>
> If you're not careful when you use the `Server` object, you could get results you hadn't expected. Make sure to test your code thoroughly.

The single property `ScriptTimeout` is used to inspect or set the timeout value for running scripts. This value can be used to prevent server-side scripts from falling into infinite loops and hogging all your server's processing time. The default value is 90 seconds.

Of the four methods, two can be used to encode HTML or URL strings (`HTMLEncode` and `URLEncode`), one can be used to return the disk path of a virtual directory on the server (`MapPath`), and one can be used to create a link between your script and other external objects (`CreateObject`).

Next, you create a new ASP document to show how the `Server` object property and methods work. Add a new ASP file called SERVER.ASP to your ServerObjects project and add the VBScript from Listing 15.5 to the body of the ASP page.

LISTING 15.5 Demonstrating the *Server* Object Property and Methods

```
1  <%
2  '
3  ' show server object properties and methods
4  '
5
```

Accessing the Host Server with the *Server* Object

```
 6  ' document header
 7  Response.Write "<H2>Demonstrate Server Object</H2>"
 8
 9  ' properties
10  Response.Write "<P><H4>Properties</H4><HR>"
11  Response.Write "ScriptTimeout = " & 
    ➥Server.ScriptTimeout & "<BR>"
12
13  ' methods
14  Response.Write "<P><H4>Methods</H4><HR>"
15  Response.Write "MapPath - " & Server.MapPath
    ➥ ("/ServerObjects") & "<BR>"
16  Response.Write "HTMLEncode - " & Server.HTMLEncode
    ➥ ("Show Para Mark: <P>") & "<BR>"
17  Response.Write "URLEncode - " & Server.URLEncode
    ➥ ("http://www.amundsen.com") & "<BR>"
18  Response.Write "CreateObject - used to access
    ➥external objects<BR>"
19
20  '
21  %>
```

The Server and Location objects

The information you can pull out of these two client-side and server-side objects is incredible. Experiment with pulling data from both of them to learn more about the data maintained by the Web server and the Web browser.

Save this document and run your Web application to test the SERVER.ASP page. When you load the page into your browser, you see the current `ScriptTimeout` property displayed along with the actual disk location of your Web application. You also see the encoded URL and what appears to be an unaffected HTML line. However, if you select **View**, **Source** from your Microsoft Internet Explorer, you find that the `HTMLEncode` method has replaced simple `<P>` with `&lt;P&gt;`.

The one method not invoked on this page is the `CreateObject` method. This is used to create links between your Web application and other installed components. You'll learn about this method in later chapters of this book. For now, just remember that `CreateObject` is your way to link to other components.

Sharing Data with All Users with the *Application* Object

The `Application` object is another simple object. Its primary task is to establish values that can be shared with all users that connect to your Web application. For example, you use application-level variables to handle hit counts on your Web pages, connections to databases, and other values that will not be unique for each user session running on your Web application.

The `Application` object has two collections, two methods, and two events associated with it. Table 15.3 shows a summary of the `Application` object.

Application variables

Application variables can be used to track the overall progress of your Web application. The key advantage is that the `Application` object removes the need to manually manipulate this information. This object does it for you. Great, isn't it?

TABLE 15.3   The *Application* object

Name	Type	Description	Example
`Contents`	Collection	Holds the set of application-level variables created at runtime	`IntHitCount= Application. Contents ("HitCounter")`
`StaticObjects`	Collection	Holds the set of shared objects loaded from the GLOBAL.ASA file	`Set LocalCounter= Application. StaticObjects ("MyObject")`
`Lock`	Method	Locks the application contents for update	`Application. Lock`
`UnLock`	Method	Unlocks the application contents after update	`Application. UnLock`
`OnStart`	Event	Occurs when the application is first accessed by a user	`Application_ OnStart`
`OnEnd`	Event	Occurs when the application is shut down	`Application_ OnEnd`

Sharing Data with All Users with the *Application* Object

The two collections give you a predefined way to add, remove, and update any simple or complex data values stored for the application. The Contents collection contains simple data values and objects added during the life of the program (at runtime). The StaticObjects collection contains a list of all the items declared within the GLOBAL.ASA using the <OBJECT></OBJECT> tags in the application. These preloaded COM objects can then be shared by all sessions of the Web application.

The Lock and UnLock methods are used safely to access the Contents collection. Because the collection is available to all users connected to your Web application, you must use Lock before you update an Application.Contents value and use Unlock when you are finished using it. Listing 15.6 shows how this looks in server-side script.

LISTING 15.6 Example of Using the *Lock/UnLock* Methods of the *Application* Object

```
1 <%
2 '
3 ' update hit count
4 '
5 Dim lngHitCount
6 '
7 Application.Lock ' prevent other from updating contents
8 lngHitCount = Application.Contents("HitCount")
9 lngHitCount = lngHitCount + 1
10 Application.Contents("HitCount")=lngHitCount
11 Application.UnLock 'release access to the contents
12 '
13 %>
```

The two events (OnStart and OnEnd) occur when the Web application starts (first session begins) and when the Web application shuts down. The OnStart event is the most common location for making entries in the Application.Contents collection. You can then save any important values related to the Web application in the OnEnd event that occurs when the application is shut down. Actually, these events occur in the GLOBAL.ASA file in your project.

SEE ALSO
➤ *You can learn more about these events on pages 302 and 639*

Coding the *Application* Object Example

Now add a Web page to illustrate the `Application` object.

Creating the APPLICATION.ASP example

1. First, add a new page called APPLICATION.ASP to your ServerObjects project.
2. Open the APPLICATION.ASP page by double-clicking it from the Project Explorer.
3. If you aren't already in Source mode, click the **Source** tab.
4. Next, write some server-side script. Enter the code from Listing 15.7 right after the `<BODY>` tag in the document.

Try to get the variables to change

If you can test this page from more than one browser at once, try to see if you can get the variables to change when they have been locked.

LISTING 15.7 **Creating Entries in the *Application.Contents* Collection**

```
1  <%
2  '
3  ' show application object
4  '
5
6  '
7  ' to pass along errors if found
8  on error resume next
9
10 '
11 ' send out heading
12 Response.Write "<H2><CENTER>Demonstrate Application
   ➥Object</CENTER></H2><P>"
13
14 '
15 ' create some application-level variables
16 Application.Lock
17 Application.Contents("Counter")=12
18 Application.Contents("AppName")="My Web Application"
19 Application.Contents("AppVersion")="1.0"
20 Application.UnLock
21 '
22 %>
```

Sharing Data with All Users with the *Application* Object

You might also notice the appearance of the `on error resume next` line. In some cases, accessing the `Contents` collection at runtime might return an error and stop processing of the server-side script. By adding this line you tell the server-side script to continue processing even after the error is reported.

After sending out a header line that will appear at the top of the document, the main part of the server-side script first locks the `Application` object, then creates three entries in the `Application.Contents` collection before releasing the lock.

The values created here are now available to any other page in the Web application and any other user that currently has a session with this Web application. To test this, add some code to access the `Application.Contents` collection and display it on the page. Listing 15.8 shows you how to do this.

LISTING 15.8 Adding Code to Access the *Application.Contents* Collection

```
1 <%
2 '
3 ' show list of application contents
4 Response.Write "<H4>Contents Collection</H4><HR>"
5 For Each Key in Application.Contents
6    Response.Write Key & " : " & Application.Contents(Key)
     ➥& "<BR>"
7 Next
8
9 %>
```

Notice that Listing 15.8 will work for any number of entries in the `Application.Contents` collection. The `For Each...Next` structure is very handy for creating loops for processes where you don't yet know the total number of items in the collection.

SEE ALSO

> *To learn more about server-side components, see page 598*

Next, add some object declarations in the GLOBAL.ASA file and then view them from the APPLICATION.ASP page.

Creating object declarations in APPLICATION.ASP

1. First, select the GLOBAL.ASA file from the project window and double-click it to open it in the editor.
2. Next, add code that will declare two objects for use throughout the application. To do this, you use the `<OBJECT>` HMTL tag.
3. Add the code shown in Listing 15.9 to your GLOBAL.ASA file.

Placement of the code

Be sure to add these lines after the `</SCRIPT>` tag. If you place the code inside the `<SCRIPT></SCRIPT>` tags, you receive errors when you run the Web application.

LISTING 15.9 Adding Object Declarations to the GLOBAL.ASA File

```
1 <!-- create link to external COM objects -->
2 <OBJECT RUNAT=Server SCOPE=Application ID=appAdRotator
3 Progid="MSWC.AdRotator"></OBJECT>
4
5 <OBJECT RUNAT=Server SCOPE=Application
  ➥ID=appContentLinker
6 Progid="MSWC.NextLink"></OBJECT>
```

Notice that the value used in the `ID` attribute will appear in the Script Outline window in the IDE. This tells you the objects are recognized for your Web application. It is also important to add the `SCOPE` attribute to the declaration. If you fail to include this item, the object will not be available within your Web application.

Now that you have declared the objects, you are ready to add some server-side script to the APPLICATION.ASP file to read the `StaticObjects` collection and report the results. Listing 15.10 has the server-side script you should add right after the code you added from Listing 15.8.

LISTING 15.10 Adding Code to View the *StaticObjects* Collection

```
1 <%
2 '
3 ' show list of app-level objects
4 Response.Write "<H4>StaticObjects Collection</H4><HR>"
5 For Each Key in Application.StaticObjects
```

Tracking User Values with the *Session* Object

```
6  Response.Write Key
7  Next
8  '
9  %>
```

Now save this page and run the project (press F5 or select **Debug**, **Start** from the main menu). When you select the `Application Object` link, you see the list of entries in the `Application.Contents` collection and the `StaticObjects` collection (see Figure 15.3).

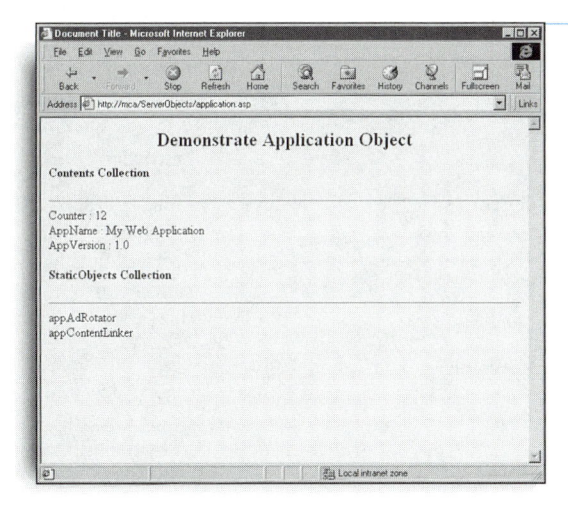

FIGURE 15.3
Displaying the APPLICATION.ASP `Contents` collection.

Remember that these values are usually set in the `Application_OnStart` event that occurs in the GLOBAL.ASA file. The code was placed here just to make it easy to demonstrate the object.

SEE ALSO
➤ *To look more at programming events, see page 303*

Tracking User Values with the *Session* Object

Although the `Application` object enables you to share data with all users who are running a session on your Web application, you can use the `Session` object to store values unique for the current

Using the Application object

The `Application` object can be used to track information that is accessible by all users throughout your Web application, as well as to carry out events and actions in particular cases. For example, when a user first connects to your application, you might want it to establish a database connection that will be used throughout the application's life span. This power gives you a macro level control over your Web application without manually controlling its behavior from every script.

A good use for the `Session` object

A good use for the `Session` object over the `Application` object is individual user data. You wouldn't want individual user information floating around accessible for every individual user. The `Session` object keeps that information unique to a single user's session.

session. This enables you to set up values for each user as he or she starts a session in your Web application, and then carry those values throughout the session until you finally save them to disk or delete them at the end of the user session.

Like the `Application` object, the `Session` object has two collections: `Contents` and `StaticObjects`. The `Session` object has four properties. Two deal with user settings (`LocaleID` and `CodePage`) and two deal with session tracking (`SessionID` and `Timeout`). Finally, there is only one method with the `Session` object: `Abandon`. This can be used to forcibly end a session if needed. Table 15.4 shows a summary of the `Session` object.

TABLE 15.4 The *Session* object

Name	Type	Description	Example
`Contents`	Collection	Holds all the variables declared during runtime for this session.	`Session.Contents ("UserName")="Matt"`
`StaticObjects`	Collection	Holds all the objects declared in the GLOBAL.ASA file using the <OBJECTS> tag.	`Set objTemp = Session.StaticObjects ("YourObject")`
`SessionID`	Property	Holds a unique value that identifies this session for the Web application.	`Response.Write Session.SessionID`
`Timeout`	Property	Used to set/get the timeout value for a session, measured in minutes.	`Session.Timeout = 20`
`LCID`	Property	LocaleID of the current session. Used to determine display of currency, format, and so on.	`Response.Write Session.LCID`

Tracking User Values with the *Session* Object

Name	Type	Description	Example
CodePage	Property	Holds the workstation codepage that will be used to handle character display.	`Response.Write Session.CodePage`
Abandon	Method	Used to end the current session and release all session-level data.	`Session.Abandon`

Adding the Session Sample Page

Now let's add a new page to the `ServerObjects` Web application called SESSION.ASP. After the new ASP file is added to the Web application, you're ready to add some server-side script to the page.

Listing 15.11 shows the code that declares some session-level values. Add this server-side script right after the <BODY> tag in the page.

LISTING 15.11 Adding Code to Create Session Values in the *Contents* Collection

```
1  <%
2  '
3  ' show session object
4  '
5
6  '
7  ' show heading for page
8  Response.Write "<H2><CENTER>Demonstrate Session Object
   ➥</CENTER></H2><P>"
9
10 '
11 ' add some session variables to contents collection
12 Response.Write "<H4>Session Contents</H4><HR>"
13 Session.Contents("sesName")="MySession"
```

continues...

LISTING 15.11 Continued

```
14 Session.Contents("sesStart")=Now
15 Session.Contents("sesPage")="Page 1"
16 '
17 %>
```

Sharing session variables

You can't easily share session variables. Instead, you must store them in some fashion (for example, to the `Application` object) so that other users can access them.

Notice that this code looks almost identical to the code that created application-level entries in the `Contents` collection. However, the values created here are available only to the current session and user. Other users could be connected to this project and see other values in these entries. Notice also that there are no `Lock/Unlock` operations around the `Session` variables in lines 13–15. `Lock` is needed only when more than one user has access to the exact same data. `Session` objects are available only to the current user.

Now add the code to read the `Session.Contents` collection. Listing 15.12 has the code lines to add to the end of the ones in Listing 15.11.

LISTING 15.12 Adding Code to Read the *Session.Contents* Collection

```
1 <%
2 '
3 ' display the session variables
4 For Each Key in Session.Contents
5     Response.Write Key & " : " & Session.Contents(Key) &
➥ "<BR>"
6 Next
7 '
8 %>
```

You can see that this is very similar to the code in Listing 15.8.

After adding the code to display the `Session.Contents`, you must add some code to display the built-in properties of the `Session` object. Add the lines from Listing 15.13 right after the code from Listing 15.12.

Tracking User Values with the *Session* Object

LISTING 15.13 **Displaying the Properties of the *Session* Object**

```
1  <%
2  '
3  ' show current properties
4  Response.Write "<P><H4>Properties</H4><HR>"
5  Response.Write "SessionID : " & Session.SessionID &
   ↪ "<BR>"
6  Response.Write "Timeout : " & Session.Timeout & "<BR>"
7  Response.Write "LCID : " & Session.LCID & "<BR>"
8  Response.Write "CodePage : " & Session.CodePage & "<BR>"
9  '
10 %>
```

Now add code to show the StaticObjects collection at work for the Session object. First, add the lines from Listing 15.14 to the end of the GLOBAL.ASA file. These lines use the <OBJECT> tag to declare objects for the Session.StaticObjects collection.

LISTING 15.14 **Declaring Session-Level Objects in the GLOBAL.ASA File**

```
1  <!-- create session-level link to external COM -->
2  <!-- objects -->
3  <OBJECT RUNAT=Server SCOPE=Session ID=sesAdRotator
4  Progid="MSWC.AdRotator"></OBJECT>
5
6  <OBJECT RUNAT=Server SCOPE=Session ID=sesContentLinker
7  Progid="MSWC.NextLink"></OBJECT>
```

Now save the GLOBAL.ASA file, open SESSION.ASP, and add the code from Listing 15.15 right after the code from Listing 15.13.

LISTING 15.15 **Adding Code to Display the *StaticObjects* Collection**

```
1  <%
2  '
3  ' show list of app-level objects
4  Response.Write "<H4>StaticObjects Collection</H4><HR>"
5  For Each Key in Application.StaticObjects
6    Response.Write Key & "<BR>"
7  Next
8  '
9  %>
```

This displays the preloaded objects within the scope of the session. Note that the two objects declared at the application level (earlier in this chapter) do not appear in this list.

Finally, add the lines from Listing 15.16 to the end of the routine. This executes the `Session.Abandon` method. The `Abandon` method can be used to terminate the current session.

LISTING 15.16 Coding the *Abandon* Method of the *Session* Object

```
1  <%
2  '
3  ' now abandon the session
4  Session.Timeout=20
5  Session.Abandon
6  '
7  %>
```

> **Is there any way back?**
>
> After a session has been abandoned, it is discarded by the server. Information stored in that session is no longer available. Make sure that you don't need any of the session data, otherwise consider moving the data to application variables.

Now save the page and run the Web application to view the SERVER.ASP page. It should look similar to the one in Figure 15.4.

FIGURE 15.4

Viewing the Session Object page.

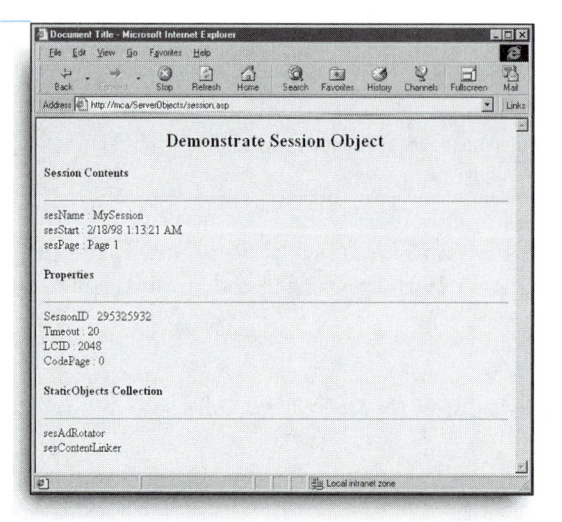

SEE ALSO

➤ *The Content Linking and Ad Rotator objects are explored on pages 601 and 609*

Sending Output to Clients with the *Response* Object

The `Response` object is the most "talented" built-in ASP object in the collection. It is used to send data downstream from the server to client browsers. To do this, several methods and properties of the object deal with the data stream, its contents, and the current state of the communication link between the server and the client.

There is one collection (`Cookies`), five properties, and eight methods for the `Response` object. Half of the properties and half of the methods deal with managing the buffering of data from server to client. Table 15.5 summarizes the `Response` object.

TABLE 15.5 **The *Response* object properties, methods, and collections**

Name	Type	Description	Example
Cookies	Collection	Holds collection of stored values sent from the server and stored on the client.	Response.Cookies ("VID98Site") ("UserName") ="MikeA"
Buffer	Property	Determines whether output is buffered by the server.	Response.Buffer = TRUE
CacheControl	Property	Sets/returns whether proxy servers can cache the page.	CacheControl =private
Charset	Property	Sets/returns character set name sent in page header.	Response. Charset("ISO-LATIN-7")
ContentType	Property	Indicates the HTTP content type for the current response.	Response. ContentType= "text/HTML"

continues...

PART III Databases and the Web

CHAPTER 15 Using Server-Side Scripting with the Built-In ASP Objects

TABLE 15.5 Continued

Name	Type	Description	Example
`Expires`	Property	Sets/returns the amount of time to elapse before the cached page expires. Measured in minutes.	`Response.Expires = 20`
`ExpiresAbsolute`	Property	Sets/returns the date/time when the page expires.	`Response.ExpiresAbsolute="#May 31,1996 13:30:15#"`
`IsClientConnected`	Property	Returns flag indicating client connection status.	`Response.IsClientConnected`
`PICS`	Method	Sends a Platform for Internet Content Selection (PICS) label to the client.	`Response.PICS ("(PICS-1.1 <http://www.rsac.org/ratingv01.html> labels on " & chr(34) & "1997.01.05T08:15-0500" & chr(34) & " until" & chr(34) & "1999.12.31T23:59-0000" & chr(34) & " ratings (v 0 s 0 l 0 n 0))")`
`Status`	Property	Sets/returns the status line sent out by the server.	`Response.Status ="401 - Sorry Document Missing"`
`AddHeader`	Method	Sends an additional header tag to the client.	`Response.Addheader "WWW-Authenticate", "BASIC"`

Sending Output to Clients with the *Response* Object

Name	Type	Description	Example
AppendToLog	Method	Adds text to Web site log (if Extended Logging is enabled).	`Response.AppendToLog "User Logged out " & Now`
BinaryWrite	Method	Sends binary data down to client.	`Response.BinaryWrite jpgDataStream`
Clear	Method	Clears the buffered output from the stream.	`Response.Clear`
End	Method	Terminates the processing of the ASP file.	`Response.End`
Flush	Method	Forces all buffered data to the client.	`Response.Flush`
Redirect	Method	Used to connect browser to another URL.	`Response.Redirect "http://www.newplace.com"`
Write	Method	Sends output down to the client.	`Reponse.Write "Hello world!"`

Adding the *Response* Object Sample Page

Now add a new page called RESPONSE.ASP to the ServerObjects project. When it is added to your project and available in the editor, you're ready to start entering your server-side script.

First, add the server-side script from Listing 15.17 to the top of the document, *before* the <HTML> tag. This sets cookie values on the browser, and it should be taken care of before the HTML tag is sent.

Positioning the script

Where you position the server-side script in the document is important. Consider whether the client will receive the data properly. For example, writing information to the user's screen before the <BODY> tag has been opened will result in the information not being shown.

Part III Databases and the Web
Chapter 15 Using Server-Side Scripting with the Built-In ASP Objects

LISTING 15.17 Adding Server-Side Script to set Cookies on the Client

```
1  <%
2  '
3  ' turn buffering on
4  Response.Buffer=True
5
6  '
7  ' write some cookies to client
8  ' before the header is sent
9  Response.Cookies("UVI")("Title")="Using Visual
   ➥InterDev 6.0"
10 Response.Cookies("UVI")("ISBN")="0-7897-1640-2"
11 Response.Cookies("UVI").Expires=#July 4,1999#
12 '
13 Response.Cookies("Sample")("Date")=Date
14 Response.Cookies("Sample")("Time")=Time
15 '
16 %>
```

In Listing 15.17, notice that line 4 sets the `Buffer` property to `True`. This makes it easier to test the other buffer-related methods later. This line, too, must appear before the `<HTML>` header is sent.

You should also know that the `Cookies` collection is built using the `Key` method. All keys in the same cookie are managed together. Notice also that the `"UVI"` cookie has been set to `Expire`. Keep in mind that you can add properties to cookies.

Now, add some server-side script to display the page heading and then show the items in the `Cookies` collection. To do this, you use the `Request` object because that is how you read cookies from the client. You learn more about the `Request` object in the next section of this chapter, "Accepting Data from the Client with the `Request` Object."

Listing 15.18 has the code you must add right after the `<BODY>` tag in the document.

Cookies are useful

You can use cookies to store data beyond a singular session. Information stored in cookies is still usable only by a single user (unless you take that information and store it in the application object), however it lets data last between sessions. The only real concern is whether the user will remove her cookies before revisiting your site, or if she uses a different machine. Consider adding a method for retrieving information to cookies for the user.

Sending Output to Clients with the *Response* Object

LISTING 15.18 Adding Code to View the *Cookies* Collection

```
1  <%
2  '
3  ' demonstrate response object
4  '
5
6  '
7  ' send heading for document
8  Response.Write "<H2>Demonstrate Response Object</H2><P>"
9
10 '
11 ' now show collection
12 Response.Write "<H4>Cookies Collection</H4><HR>"
13 For Each Cookie in Request.Cookies
14     For Each key in Request.Cookies(Cookie)
15         Response.Write cookie & "(" & key & ") = " &
           ➥Request.Cookies(cookie)(key) & "<BR>"
16     Next
17 Next
18 %>
```

Now list the various properties of the Response object. Listing 15.19 shows the server-side script you must add after the code from Listing 15.18.

LISTING 15.19 Displaying the *Response* Object Properties

```
1  <%
2  '
3  ' show properties
4  Response.Write "<H4>Properties</H4><HR>"
5  Response.Write "Buffer: " & Response.Buffer & "<BR>"
6  Response.Write "CacheControl: " & Response.CacheControl &
   ➥"<BR>"
7  Response.Write "Charset: " & Response.Charset & "<BR>"
8  Response.Write "ContentType: " & Response.ContentType &
   ➥"<BR>"
9  Response.Write "Expires: " & Response.Expires & "<BR>"
```

continues…

PART III Databases and the Web

CHAPTER 15 Using Server-Side Scripting with the Built-In ASP Objects

The End method

If you use the **End** method, remember that anything following it for the **Response** object won't be displayed.

LISTING 15.19 Continued

```
10 Response.Write "ExpiresAbsolute: " &
   ➥Response.ExpiresAbsolute & "<BR>"
11 Response.Write "IsClientConnected: " &
   ➥Response.IsClientConnected & "<BR>"
12 Response.Write "Status: " & Response.Status & "<BR>"
13 '
14 %>
```

Finally, add some server-side script to show the various buffer-related methods of the `Response` object. You've been using the most common method (`Write`) throughout this chapter. Now let's add some code that shows the other buffer methods: `Flush`, `Clear`, and `End`. Add the code from Listing 15.20 right after the code from Listing 15.19.

LISTING 15.20 Adding Code to Illustrate the Buffer Methods

```
1  <%
2  '
3  ' show buffer methods
4  Response.Write "<H4>Methods</H4><HR>"
5  Response.Flush ' force out previous line(s)
6  Response.Write "Sample Line:1"
7  Response.Clear ' drop previous line
8  Response.Write "Sample Line:2"
9  Response.End ' end asp processing and send output
10 Response.Write "Sample Line:3"
11 '
12 %>
```

In Listing 15.20, you see the use of `Flush` in line 5 to force data down to the client, the use of `Clear` in line 7 to cancel a line ready to send, and the use of `End` in line 9 to flush the remaining buffer contents and end ASP processing.

Now save this page and run your Web application (press F5). When you navigate to the `Response` object page, you should see something like the page in Figure 15.5.

Accepting Data from the Client with the *Request* Object

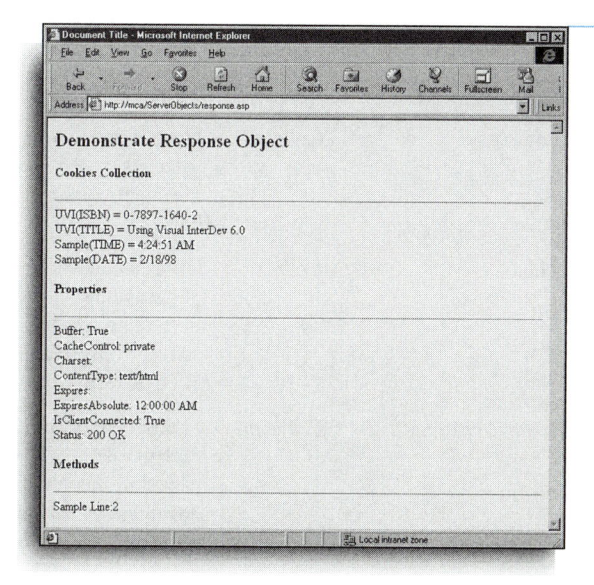

FIGURE 15.5
Veiwing the completed RESPONSE.ASP page.

Accepting Data from the Client with the *Request* Object

The last object to review in this chapter is the Request object. This is the object used to accept data sent upstream from the client to the server. It is most often used to collect cookies or certificate information from the browser or accept data in the form of hyperlink contents (QueryString) or as a collection of items from a posted form (Form collection). Finally, the Request object enables access to several predefined server variables.

The Request object has five collections, one property, and one method. Table 15.6 summarizes the Request object.

The Response and Request objects

The Response object is used to push information out, while the Request object is used to pull information in.

TABLE 15.6 The *Request* object

Name	Type	Description	Example
ClientCertificate	Collection	Holds a collection of values stored in the client certificate	Request.Client Certificate(Key[SubField])

continues...

TABLE 15.6 Continued

Name	Type	Description	Example
`Cookies`	Collection	Holds a collection of values stored in the client cookie file	`Request.Cookies ("MyCookie") ("Name")`
`Form`	Collection	Holds a collection of data values POSTed to the collection from an HTML form	`StrName=Form ("Name")`
`QueryString`	Collection	Holds a collection of data values passed to the document as part of the URL	`StrSearch= QueryString ("DocTitle")`
`ServerVariables`	Collection	Holds a collection of predetermined data values	`Request.Server Variables ("CONTENT_ TYPE")`
`TotalBytes`	Property	Total number of bytes sent upstream from the client to the server	`LngSize = Request. TotalBytes`
`BinaryRead`	Method	Used to read binary data sent upstream from the client to the server	`JpgData= Request. BinaryRead`

> **Certificates and IIS**
>
> If you plan to use client certificates with Internet Information Server, you should look at a copy of *Special Edition Using Internet Information Server 4.0* from QUE Corporation. This book contains comprehensive information on creating and accessing digital certificates.

In order to use the `ClientCertificate` collection, your Web server must be configured to request client certificates. This book does not cover client certificates.

Laying Out the REQUEST.ASP Page

This time, you add several small pages to the project because most `Request` object collections work when data is sent *back* from the client to the server. To illustrate the upstream data process, build a start page for the `Request` object collections and three target pages that will receive the data from the client.

Accepting Data from the Client with the *Request* Object

First, add a page called REQUEST.ASP to the project and lay it out as shown in Figure 15.6 and Table 15.7.

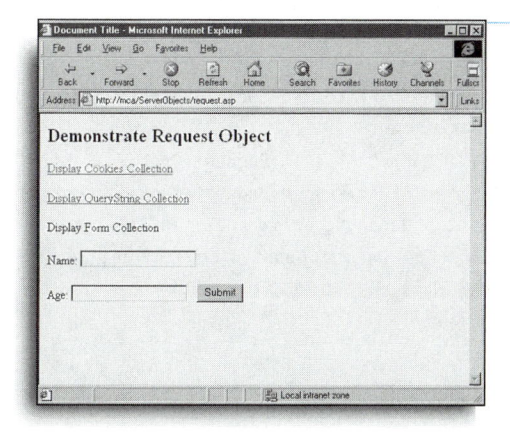

FIGURE 15.6
Laying out the REQUEST.ASP page.

TABLE 15.7 Elements for the REQUEST.ASP page

Element	Attribute	Setting
Display Cookies Collection	HREF	COOKIES.ASP
Display QueryString Collection	HREF	QUERYSTRING.ASP
Display Form Collection		
TextBox	ID	Name
	Name	"Name"
TextBox	ID	Age
	Name	"Age"
SubmitButton	Action	FORM.ASP

After laying out the page, save it before you continue.

Displaying the *Cookies* Collection

Now add a page COOKIES.ASP to the project called and enter the code from Listing 15.21. This shows the cookies added from the `Response` object page. Be sure to add this code after the `<BODY>` tag.

LISTING 15.21 **Coding the COOKIES.ASA Page**

```
1  <%
2  '
3  ' show cookies collection for UVI
4  '
5  Response.Write "<H4>Show Request.Cookies Collection
   ↪</H4><HR>"
6  For Each Cookie in Request.Cookies
7     For Each key in Request.Cookies(Cookie)
8        Response.Write cookie & "(" & key & ") = " &
         ↪Request.Cookies(cookie)(key) & "<BR>"
9     Next
10 Next
11 '
12 %>
```

Save the page and run the project. When you navigate to the COOKIES.ASP page, you see output that looks like this:

```
Show Request.Cookies Collection
UVI(TITLE) = Using Visual InterDev 6.0
UVI(ISBN) = 0-7897-1640-2
```

Displaying the *QueryString* Collection

Now add a page called QUERYSTRING.ASP and enter the code from Listing 15.22 into the <BODY> of the page.

LISTING 15.22 **Coding the *QueryString* Collection**

```
1  <%
2  '
3  ' show contents of the querystring
4  Response.Write "<H4>Request.QueryString</H4><P>"
5
6  '
7  ' unformatted
8  Response.Write "Unformatted QueryString: " & Request.
   ↪QueryString & "<P>"
9
10 '
```

Accepting Data from the Client with the *Request* Object | **CHAPTER 15**

```
11 ' show list of items
12 For Each item in Request.QueryString("N")
13     Response.Write Item & "<BR>"
14 Next
15 '
16 %>
```

When you save and run the project, navigate to the QueryString.asp page and you'll see output that looks like this:

```
Unformatted QueryString: N=Mike&N=Michele&N=MaryAnn
Mike
Michele
MaryAnn
```

Displaying the *Form* Collection

Finally, add a page called FORM.ASP and enter the code from Listing 15.23.

LISTING 15.23 Coding the *Form* Collection Display

```
1  <%
2  '
3  ' show form collection values
4  '
5
6  '
7  ' show heading
8  Response.Write "<H4>Request.Form Collection</H4><P>"
9
10 '
11 ' show unformatted data
12 Response.Write Request.Form & "<P>"
13
14 '
15 ' show items
16 Response.Write "Name: " & Request.Form("Name") & "<BR>"
17 Response.Write "Age: " & Request.Form("Age") & "<BR>"
18
19 '
20 %>
```

> **Using query strings**
>
> You can use the `QueryString` method to add a new level of interactivity to your pages. A single page can contain multiple behaviors based on the information that is fed to it through the URL. For example, if the URL contains `?Beginner`, perhaps your page would describe its usage in more verbose language, while if the URL contained `?expert` it may be very terse and to the point.

When you save and run the project, fill out the Name and Age fields on the form on page REQUEST.ASP and press the Submit button. You should see something like this:

```
Name=Mike&Age=109
Name: Mike
Age: 109
```

PART IV

Databases and the Web

- **16** Accessing Web Databases 417
- **17** Creating Data-Bound Web Forms 439
- **18** Creating Databases for the Web 477
- **19** Using ActiveX Database Objects (ADO) 505

CHAPTER 16

Accessing Web Databases

Learn how to connect your Web project to existing databases

Build and store your own custom database queries

Use the Data view to inspect and update existing data tables

General Tasks for Accessing Web Databases

Many Web applications need access to data stored in databases on the Web server (or some other available server). Visual InterDev 6 makes it easy to connect your project to a remote database using the Data Environment Designer (DED). The DED is part of the Data Tools Utilities that ship with Visual InterDev 6. The Data Tools Utilities use the new ActiveX Data Objects (ADO) and OLE DB data services to link your Web projects to existing data sources. Because Visual InterDev 6 ships with an OLE DB interface that supports ODBC, all your existing ODBC data source names can be used with the new Visual InterDev 6 Data Tools.

The Data Tools enable you to complete major database management tasks for any OLE DB–compatible data source:

- Create live connections to existing databases within the Visual InterDev 6 IDE.
- Add, edit, and delete data from existing database tables.
- Create persistent data command objects that can be stored in your Web application for use at runtime.

If you are connecting to an SQL Server or Oracle database, you can also modify the schema of existing databases. This means you can perform the following additional database administration tasks:

- Add, modify, and delete tables and views to existing databases.
- Add, modify, and delete stored procedures in existing databases.
- Add, modify, and delete table triggers in existing databases.

For most of your Web applications, you will not need to actually create new tables and stored procedures. Database administrators (DBAs) within your organization will usually handle these. If you will be acting as both application designer and DBA for your Web project and you have rights to modify the database schema (tables, views, procedures, and triggers), you'll be able to

---

Visual InterDev 6 can't modify Microsoft Access databases

If you are using Microsoft Access as your remote data source, you will not be able to use Visual InterDev 6 Data Tools to add, modify, and delete tables and query definition objects. You can still add, edit, and delete data within existing databases, however. In fact, You can use Visual InterDev only to really modify the structure of Microsoft SQL Server or Oracle databases.

accomplish this task using the Visual InterDev 6 Data Tools. You'll learn more about performing these tasks in Chapter 18, "Creating Databases for the Web." This chapter focuses on how to use the Visual InterDev 6 Data Tools to create live connections for simple editing and for creating persistent objects to store in your Web projects and access at runtime.

SEE ALSO

➤ *You'll also explore databases and design-time controls on page 552*

OLE DB and ADO

Visual InterDev 6 Data Tools use two new forms of data services: ActiveX Data Objects (ADO) and the OLE Database interface (OLE DB). The ADO model is the object model that is used to give Visual InterDev 6 programs access to the data sources, tables, rows, and columns of your databases. ADO is optimized for access to remote data sources over the Internet. This provides a small object model that is flexible enough to support all kinds of data sources, including RDBMS formats such as SQL Server and Oracle, flat file systems such as Microsoft Access and FoxPro, and even non-SQL data sources such as Microsoft Exchange and the NT Active Directory Services.

Although the ADO model is the program interface, OLE DB is the actual service layer and handles ADO data requests. OLE DB can be thought of as an alternative to the Open Database Connectivity (ODBC) data service used for LAN-connected databases. However, even though it helps to think of OLE DB as another type of ODBC interface, the two are quite different. The biggest difference between the two is that the ODBC requires all data sources to be published as a series of tables with rows and columns. The ODBC interface also requires that all data be accessed using the SQL query language.

OLE DB, however, does not force all data sources to publish as simple tables, rows, and columns. OLE DB data sources also do not have to support the SQL query language (although most still do). This new flexibility makes it easier for OLE DB to support hierarchical data storage formats such as email and directory services.

Incorporating many data sources

You can use ADO to incorporate many data sources that might not otherwise be available through ODBC. The Windows NT Active Directory Services, part of Windows NT 5.0, is a good example.

OLE DB uses providers, not drivers

With the introduction of the OLE DB interface for connecting to remote data, there is also new terminology for the components that perform the actual links between your programs and the database. Under the ODBC system, each component that handles the data requests is called a *driver*. In the OLE DB model, the components that link between your program and the data are called *providers*. The names have changed, but the job is still the same!

SQL Server debugging

Like we said, Visual InterDev 6 doesn't support line-by-line stored procedure debugging for Oracle. To use the debugging features for SQL Server, you must have the SQL Server Debugging components installed on your server.

Jet is powerful

Just because of these limitations, don't think that Microsoft Jet isn't powerful. It is. In fact, Microsoft's groupware/messaging server, Microsoft Exchange, uses a database based on the Jet architecture. How's that for a testimonial?

Because OLE DB is more flexible in its capability to connect to new forms of data storage, OLE DB is the only interface supported by Visual InterDev 6. Luckily, Visual InterDev 6 ships with an OLE DB provider for ODBC data sources, too. This means you'll still be able to connect to all your existing ODBC data sources.

Using SQL Server and Oracle Databases

Visual InterDev 6 was designed to give you complete and easy access to two commonly used databases: SQL Server and Oracle. Visual InterDev 6 ships with OLE DB providers for both these database systems. With SQL Server and Oracle installed, Visual InterDev 6 is able to provide complete DBA service (table and view modification, stored procedures, and triggers). Also, if you are using SQL Server, you can even do line-by-line interactive debugging of stored procedures. For this release, Visual InterDev 6 does not support line-by-line debugging of Oracle stored procedures.

Although the support for Oracle and SQL Server is very strong, there are limits. You cannot use the Visual InterDev 6 Data Tools to manage database security (users, groups, and roles) or to create new databases themselves. These added DBA chores are rarely needed from within a development tool anyway.

Using Microsoft Access Databases

Visual InterDev 6 also does a good job of supporting interaction with Microsoft Access (sometimes called Jet) databases. However, unlike the SQL Server and Oracle OLE DB providers, the Microsoft Jet OLE DB provider does not support DBA tasks, such as creating new tables and stored query definitions. This is a shortcoming of the current OLE DB provider, not of Visual InterDev 6. It is possible that a new version of the Microsoft Jet OLE DB provider will be released soon that will enable you to perform DBA tasks on Microsoft Access databases, too.

Using the Data Environment Designer

The process of creating connections between the remote database and your Web application is handled in the Visual InterDev 6 IDE by creating and managing data environments. This is done with a tool called the Data Environment Designer (DED). The DED is really a series of dialogs that walk you through the process of identifying the server that holds the database and creating the proper information that enables you to link directly to that database from within your Web projects.

After you complete the connection information, the DED stores all this data in your GLOBAL.ASA file in your project. This way, the next time you load the project, all the information needed for connecting to the remote database is ready and waiting. To do this, the DED creates application-level variables in the GLOBAL.ASA file.

While you are creating your persistent data connection information in the GLOBAL.ASA file, the Visual InterDev 6 Data Tools also enable you to use this same information to access the database at design-time. This way you can inspect the tables, modify the records, and so on, and then build Web documents that access and display this new database data.

The DED helps you build two important data objects: the data connection and the data command. The data connection is the object that defines the connection between your Web project and the database server. The data command is the object that defines the rules for requesting data from the database. You will usually build one data connection object for each database your project uses. You will usually build one data command for each data table, stored procedure, or query (view) that is needed in your Web project.

Creating the WEBDB Project

All the database examples in this chapter can be held in a Visual InterDev 6 Web project. You can create this Web project as you create any other Web project. Just load Visual InterDev 6 and,

---

Visual InterDev 6 moves connection data from session to application level

In the previous version of Visual InterDev, all data connection information was stored as session-level variables in the GLOBAL.ASA file. Visual InterDev 6 now stores this information as application-level variables. This enables faster data access and less resource demands on the Web server. When you load Visual InterDev 1.0 projects into Visual InterDev 6, the data connections will automatically be converted from session to application level.

Reducing the need for extra tools

The DED makes Visual InterDev a kind of "one stop shop" for Web application development. You don't need to have all sorts of database tools open to create a database-powered application. However, you still might find that some external tools offer functionality that Visual InterDev does not. To this day, for example, I still often use Microsoft Access to populate data into a SQL Server database while still developing in Visual InterDev.

Data commands

Data commands can be carried out on any database object: tables, views, stored procedures, and synonyms.

when prompted, enter WEBDB as the project name. Connect to an available Web server and accept WEBDB as the Web name. You can skip the Theme and Layout dialogs for this project, too.

After the default project has been built, you're ready to start adding database features to your Web project. However, before you start building your data connection and command objects, you first must make sure you have some ODBC definition information built. This ODBC data will be used by Visual InterDev 6 Data Tools to access the remote databases.

> **ODBC drivers and the server**
>
> Make sure that your Web server has the required ODBC drivers installed before creating a connection.

Internet Data Connections and ODBC

In Visual InterDev 6, the default method for connecting to remote databases is through an ODBC File data source name (DSN). This is a special type of ODBC connection definition that will place all the important data inside the GLOBAL.ASA file for you. Although you use ODBC to build the data source details, Visual InterDev 6 will still use OLE DB to complete the data connection.

Using the Control Panel to Add File DSNs

There are two ways you can build ODBC File DSNs. The first method is to use the Windows ODBC applet in the Control Panel. This method can be used at any time. You do not need to be running Visual InterDev 6 to add an ODBC File DSN from the Control Panel.

> **Of ODBC driver versions**
>
> Often, a new version of an ODBC driver will be released. Sometimes the version of ODBC installed on your workstation or server and the version of the driver will be incompatible. You should always make sure that you are using the most recent version of ODBC. You can check the latest version by visiting Microsoft's Developer Network Web site at http://www.microsoft.com/msdn.

Using the Control Panel to add a new access ODBC File DSN

1. Press the Windows **Start** button.
2. Select **S**ettings from the menu bar.
3. Select **C**ontrol Panel from the submenu.
4. When the Control Panel window opens, locate and double-click the **ODBC** icon (see Figure 16.1).
5. When the Data Source Administrator starts, select the **File DSN** tab and press the **A**dd button to add a new File DSN to the workstation.
6. Select a database driver (in this example, select Microsoft Access) and press the **N**ext button.

PART **IV**

Using the Data Environment Designer   CHAPTER **16**   **423**

FIGURE 16.1

Starting the ODBC Data Source Administrator.

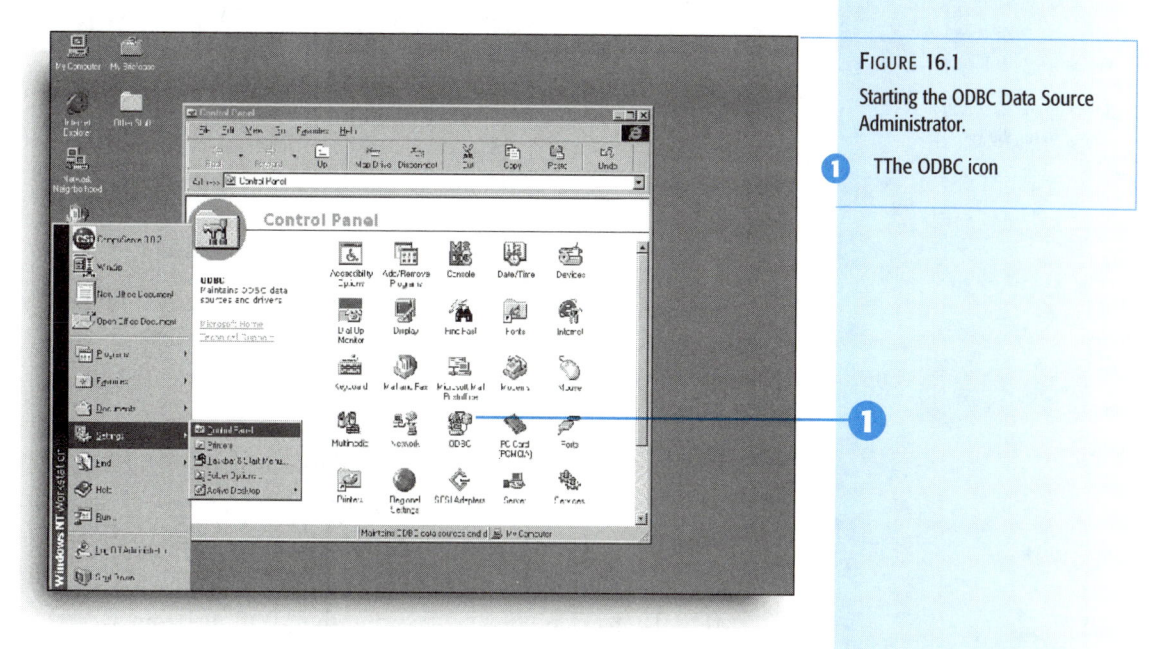

1 TThe ODBC icon

7. Enter a File DSN name (in this example, enter UsingVIJet as the File DSN name) and press the **Next** button.
8. This will display the completed File DSN entry (see Figure 16.2).

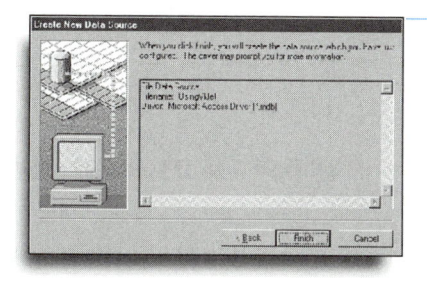

FIGURE 16.2

Completing the File DSN entry.

9. Click the **Finish** button to save the File DSN entry and call up the ODBC Microsoft Access Driver 97 dialog.
10. Select the Microsoft Access database to use for this File DSN. In this example, the BOOKS6.MDB database is selected from the c:\uvi\source\data\ folder (see Figure 16.3).

FIGURE 16.3

Selecting the Microsoft Access database for the File DSN.

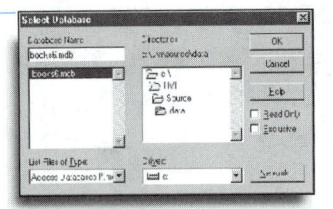

11. Click **OK** to save the database information to the File DSN and return to the ODBC Data Source Administrator.

12. Click **OK** to exit the ODBC Data Source Administrator.

That's all you need to do to add File DSNs to your workstation via the Windows Control Panel. You now have a File DSN that can be used within your Web project.

It is important to note that Microsoft Access File DSNs always store the exact drive letter and directory path used to locate the MDB database. If you are accessing the MDB file from a Universal Naming Convention (UNC) share name (\\machine\sharename\), you won't be able to store the information properly in the File DSN. If you use a mapped drive letter to locate the MDB file, you also must make sure that the same drive letter is used when you run the Web project from your Web server.

SEE ALSO

► You'll learn more about using Microsoft Access databases for your Web projects beginning on page 477

Adding File DSNs with the Data Environment Designer

You can also access the same dialogs from within the Visual InterDev 6 Data Environment Designer interface. This is handy when you want to create a database connection for your Web project but find that there is currently no File DSN available for your database. In this case, all you need to do is begin the process of creating a data connection; but first build a new File DSN instead.

Developer tip

I typically create DSNs for my data sources when I create the database itself. I can then go back and use these DSNs in my development any time I need to.

Using the Data Environment Designer to add a new SQL Server File DSN

1. Right-click over the Web project name in the Project Explorer window.
2. Select **Add Data Connection** from the context menu.
3. When the Select Data Source dialog appears, click the **New** button (see Figure 16.4).

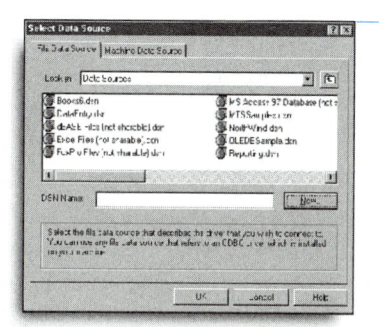

FIGURE 16.4
Adding a new File DSN from the Data Environment Designer.

4. Select a database driver (for this example, select **SQL Server**) and click **Next**.
5. Enter the File DSN name for this entry. For this example, enter UsingVISQL and click the **Next** button.
6. You'll then see the completed File DSN entry (see Figure 16.5). Click **Finish** to save the File DSN entry.

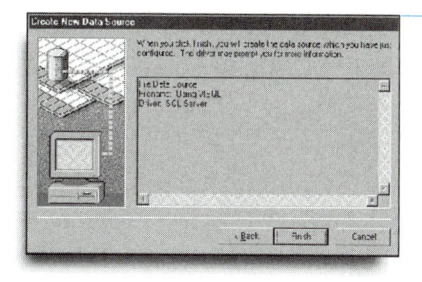

FIGURE 16.5
Completing the SQL Server File DSN entry.

7. When the Create a New Data Source to SQL Server dialog appears, enter the name of the server that holds the database in the **Server** text box and click **Next**.

Authentication and SQL Server

An important thing to understand when developing using SQL Server is how authentication works. When you are developing in Visual InterDev, you are connecting to the database as yourself (your network login). However, visitors to your site will be using the standard Internet Information Server username, `IUSR_MachineName`. You can specify login information for design time and runtime using the Data Connection Properties dialog box.

FIGURE 16.6

Testing the SQL Server File DSN.

Testing the data source

Testing the SQL Server data source only tests that your machine can talk to the SQL Server. It does not test whether you can view data in the database or modify it. That is dependent on your authentication and permissions.

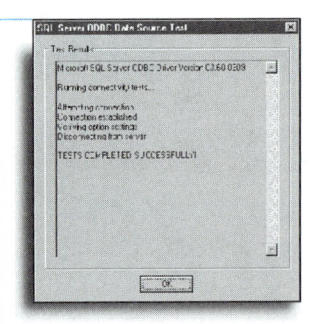

8. Select the authentication method (NT or SQL Server) and, if needed, enter the SQL login ID and password to save with the Web project. Then click the **Next** button.

9. Check the **Change Default Database** box and select a starting database (in this example, select **PUBS** from the list) and click the **Next** button.

10. Click **Next** to skip the next dialog, and then click **Finish** to complete the SQL Server File DSN data entry.

11. You'll see a summary dialog with a **Test Data Source** button. Click the **Test Data Source** button to make sure the File DSN is working properly (see Figure 16.6).

12. Click **OK** twice to exit the ODBC dialogs.

13. Click **Cancel** to exit the Select Data Source dialog and return to your Web project.

You have now completed two File DSNs that you will use in the examples in the rest of this chapter. One will enable you to connect to a Microsoft Access database. The other will connect your Web projects to an SQL Server database.

Now that you have valid File DSNs defined for your Web project, you're ready to build a complete data connection in your project.

Creating Data Connections

The data connection is the object that contains all the information needed to connect your Web project to an existing database.

Using the Data Environment Designer

In most cases, this database will be located on the same machine that is providing the Web services. However, you can also create data connections to existing database servers as long as they are accessible from the Web server. Web server and network administrators are responsible for making sure the Web server and the database servers are communicating properly.

As a minimum, the data connection has three important bits of information:

- The database name (DATA.MDB or SQLServerData)
- The database type (SQL Server, Microsoft Access, and so on)
- The database location (SERVER=mca or DefaultDir=c:\myfolder)

Usually, additional information is also needed, such as user name and passwords and other special settings required by the particular database system. However, the three mentioned here are always present in some form. When you create the data connection object, you're really collecting the preceding data (along with other information).

Adding DSNs to your project

You don't need to add a DSN to your project for it to work. It can stay locally on your machine because Visual InterDev just reads it for the information required to establish the connection.

Adding a Data Connection for a Microsoft Access File DSN

This section demonstrates how to add a data connection object to your Web project.

Adding a data connection object to an existing Web project

1. In the Project Explorer window, right-click over the project name.
2. Select **Add Data Connection** from the context menu.
3. At the Select Data Source dialog, locate and select the **UsingVIJet** entry, and then click **OK** to add this File DSN to your Web project.
4. When the Connection Properties dialog appears, enter a **Connection Name** (in this example, use `conUsingVIJet`). Click **OK** to complete the connection object.

A new window appears in your Visual InterDev 6 IDE: the Data View window. This window gives you direct design-time access to the live database. You can use this window to inspect the contents of the database (tables, views, procedures, and so on) and to perform record adds, edits, and deletes on existing tables (see Figure 16.7).

FIGURE 16.7

Viewing the Data View window.

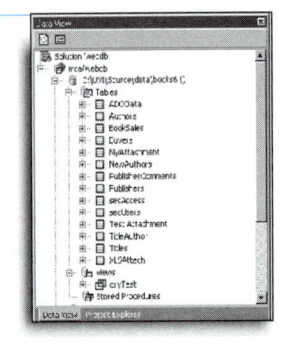

Where's the Data View window?

If you do not see your Data View window, you might need to load it into your current IDE view. To do this select **View**, **Other Windows**, **Data View** from the Visual InterDev 6 menu bar.

You can also see new entries in the Project Explorer window. You should now see a **Data Environment** item underneath the **GLOBAL.ASA** entry and a **conUsingVIJet** connection entry under **Data Environment**. This is how Visual InterDev 6 stores the database connection information in your Web project (see Figure 16.8).

FIGURE 16.8

Viewing new entries in the Project Explorer window.

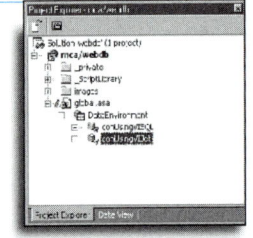

Remember that the Data Environment Designer uses File DSNs to gather the connection data and then copies that information directly into your Web project. After you have created the data connection object in your project, you can actually delete the File DSN (UsingVIJet) from your workstation, and your project will work just fine!

Using the Data Environment Designer

To see why this is true, double-click the **GLOBAL.ASA** entry in your Project Explorer window. This will load the GLOBAL.ASA file and show all the entries in this document. Toward the bottom, you'll see a set of entries that look like the code in Listing 16.1.

LISTING 16.1   File DSN Information Stored in the GLOBAL.ASA File

```
1  <SCRIPT LANGUAGE=VBScript RUNAT=Server>
2  Sub Application_OnStart
3  '==Visual InterDev Generated - startspan==
4  '--Project Data Connection
5  Application("conUsingVIJet_ConnectionString") =
   ➥"DRIVER={Microsoft Access Driver
   ➥(*.mdb)};DBQ=C:\UVI\Source\data\books6.mdb;
   ➥DefaultDir=C:\UVI\Source\data;DriverId=25;
   ➥FIL=MSAccess;ImplicitCommitSync=Yes;
   ➥MaxBufferSize=512;MaxScanRows=8;PageTimeout=5;
   ➥SafeTransactions=0;Threads=3;UserCommitSync=Yes;"
6  Application("conUsingVIJet_ConnectionTimeout") = 15
7  Application("conUsingVIJet_CommandTimeout") = 30
8  Application("conUsingVIJet_CursorLocation") = 3
9  Application("conUsingVIJet_RuntimeUserName") = "admin"
10 Application("conUsingVIJet_RuntimePassword") = ""
11 '-- Project Data Environment
12 Set DE = Server.CreateObject("DERuntime.DERuntime")
13     Application("DE") = DE.Load(Server.MapPath
       ➥("Global.ASA"), "_private/DataEnvironment/
       ➥DataEnvironment.asa")
14 '==Visual InterDev Generated - endspan==
15 End Sub
16 </SCRIPT>
```

Notice that all the information needed to complete the connection between your project and the MDB database is kept in the application-level variables created in lines 5–10. You can also see information about the DED itself is stored here (lines 12–14).

Creating Data Commands

Now that you have a valid data connection object in your project, you're ready to add data command objects. Data command

---

Modifying the GLOBAL.ASA

Although in Visual InterDev 1.0 you needed to manually alter the GLOBAL.ASA often, you don't need to in Visual InterDev 6. Let Visual InterDev deal with your data sources in the GLOBAL.ASA file to avoid potential errors.

Records

Records are a collection of data in a database table. A record is comprised of data in individual columns. Information you store or retrieve from a database is in the form of records. Groups of records are called *recordsets*.

objects hold the rules that govern how a collection of recordsets is built for your Web project. It can be as simple as a table name or as complex as a parameterized custom query that links multiple tables into a single collection of rows.

You usually need only one data connection object for each database your Web project will access. However, you need at least one data command object for each unique table, view, or procedure your Web project will use. In this section of the chapter, you build two data connections: one to connect directly to an existing table in the Microsoft Access database, the other to create a custom SQL SELECT query that provides summary information from an existing table.

Creating a Table Data Command

A very common type of data command object is the table data command. This data command opens up a direct connection between an existing table and your Web project. You can use table data commands as a basis for data entry forms.

Creating a table data command for a Microsoft Access database

1. First, right-click over your Microsoft Access data connection in the Project Explorer (**UsingVIJet**).
2. Select **Add Data Command** from the context menu.
3. When the data command Properties dialog appears, enter `cmdJetAuthors` for the **Command Name**.
4. Set the **Database Object** to **Table**.
5. Set the **Object Name** to **Authors**.
6. Click **OK** to add this data command to your Web project (see Figure 16.9).

FIGURE 16.9

Adding the cmdJetAuthors table data command.

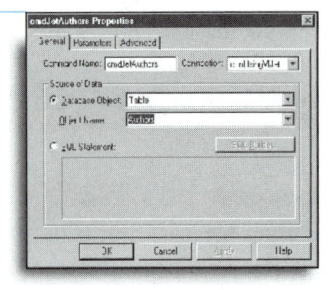

Using the Data Environment Designer

When you exit the data command Properties dialog, you'll see a new entry in the Project Explorer. If you click the plus sign next to the **cmdJetAuthors** data command, you also see a list of all the fields in the data command.

Creating an SQL Statement Data Command

You can also use the Data Environment Designer dialogs to create a custom SQL statement data command. This is a special data command that requests only certain columns from one or more existing tables in the database. These types of data commands are handy for read-only lists, reports, and summary data shown in grids in the Web application.

In the following example, you build a custom SQL statement data command that combines information from three different tables into a single list.

Building a SQL statement data command from three database tables

1. Right-click over the data connection object (**UsingVIJet**) in the Project Explorer and select **Add Data Command** from the context menu.

2. Enter cmdSelectJet as the data command name.

3. Click on the **SQL Statement** radio button and click the **SQL Builder** command button to load the Query Designer Tool (QDT) into the Visual InterDev 6 IDE.

4. With the Query Designer loaded, drag the Authors table from the Data View window and drop it in the gray open space in the QDT. Do the same with the Titles and Publishers tables.

5. You'll see each table appear as a list of columns in the Query Designer. As you add additional tables, the QDT will create links between the tables using common columns.

6. Next, select columns from each table to include in the final SQL Statement. Click the **au_lname** check box in the Authors table, the **Title** check box in the Titles table, and the **pub_name** check box in the Publishers table.

7. You should now see a complete SQL statement appear in the SQL pane and each of the three columns appear in the Grid pane.

> **Going for SQL**
>
> You're not forced to use the GUI interface for database development in Visual InterDev. If you are more comfortable dealing with raw SQL commands, feel free to do so. You can also mix and match the GUI features and SQL to speed your development.

PART IV Databases and the Web
CHAPTER 16 Accessing Web Databases

Does this look familiar?

The Query Builder in Visual InterDev is essentially the same as the interface provided in Microsoft Access. Microsoft has developed this excellent interface that combines graphical database manipulation with the raw speed of SQL commands.

FIGURE 16.10

Using the Query Designer tool to create an SQL statement data command.

8. Now add sorting to your SQL statement by selecting **Ascending** as the **Sort Type** for the **au_lname** column in the Grid pane. This will automatically update the SQL pane.

9. You can test your SQL Statement by pressing the run button (!) in the QDT toolbar. This will produce a list of rows in the Results pane (see Figure 16.10).

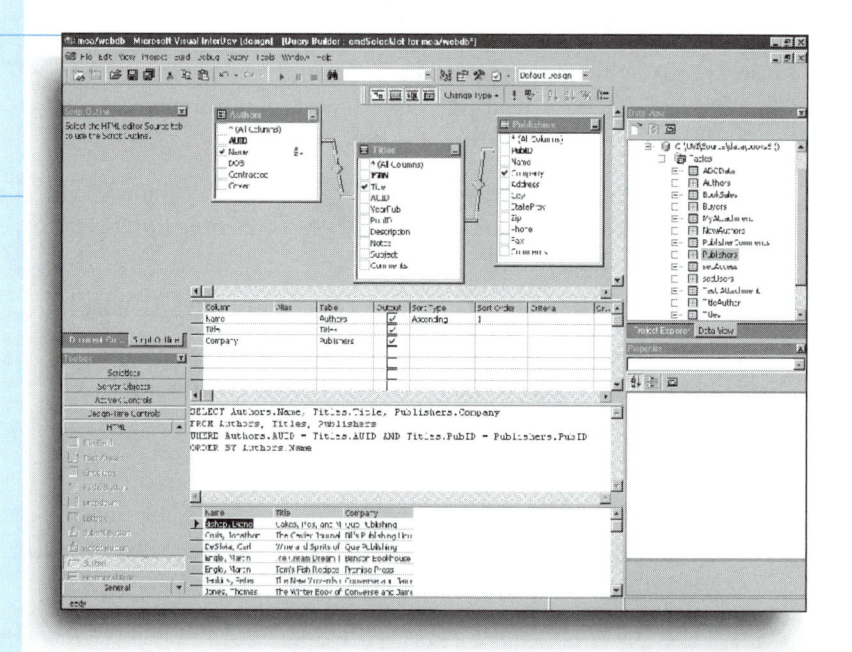

10. You can save the SQL Statement by selecting **File**, **Save** or pressing Ctrl+S.

11. Close the SQL Builder by selecting **File**, **Close** from the menu bar.

When you exit the QDT, you can see the new data command added to the Project Explorer window underneath the data connection. When you click the plus sign next to the **cmdSelectJet** data command, you see that it shows only the three columns you selected in the QDT.

These two data commands are now ready to act as the basis for creating data entry forms and display documents in your Web project. You'll learn how to do this in Chapter 17, "Creating

Editing Database Data with the Query Designer Tool

Data-Bound Web Forms," and Chapter 21, "Adding Reports and Graphs to your Web Applications." For now, just remember that you need to build at least one data connection for each database you use and one data command for each collection of records you use in your Web application.

Now that you have an idea of how to create valid connection and command objects, you're ready to spend a bit more time exploring the Query Designer Tool to see how you can use it to add, edit, and delete records in existing databases.

Editing Database Data with the Query Designer Tool

The Query Designer Tool (QDT), or Query Builder, can be used for more than just creating specialized SQL statements for data commands. You can also use the QDT to perform common data table maintenance tasks, including adding, editing, and deleting records from existing tables. In this section of the chapter, you learn how to use the QDT to create three kinds of SQL queries:

- Update queries—These are used to edit existing records in a table.
- Insert Value queries—These are used to add new records to an existing table.
- Delete queries—These are used to remove existing records from a table.

SEE ALSO
▶ *You learn more about these advanced queries on page 493*

Using the QDT Data Grid to Edit Tables

The simplest way to add, edit, and delete individual records from an existing table is to use the QDT data grid. You can call up the data grid by moving to the Data View window and double-clicking a table in the list of tables. This loads the table (and all its data) into the QDT data grid, ready for your input (see Figure 16.11).

Other advanced queries covered in Chapter 18

There are two more types of queries that you can execute with the QDT. The Append and Make Table queries enable you to transfer records from one table to another—in one case, creating a new table in the process. You'll learn more about these advanced queries in Chapter 18.

Simple is SQL

SQL is at its most basic a very simple language. SQL is comprised of queries. Queries can either display the contents of the database or alter the contents of the database. A good understanding of SQL is a significant asset in Web application development.

FIGURE 16.11

The QDT data grid ready for input.

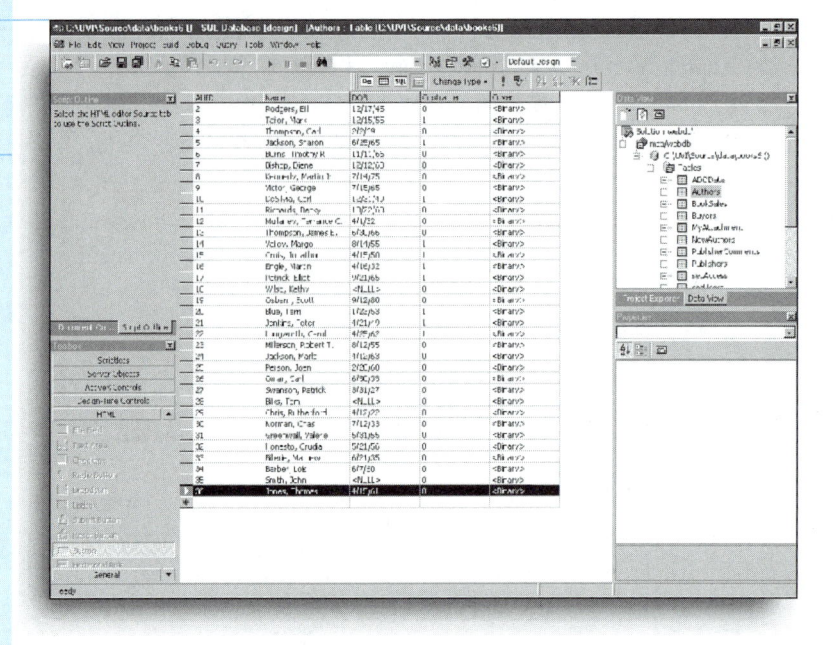

Obeying the rules

Your modifications to a table in the QDT must adhere to the data types specified for the columns. For example, if a column was specified as a **CHAR** character field, it would be treated as a text field. Even if you entered numeric digits into the field, they would be considered a string. You might sometimes receive an error message from Visual InterDev indicating that the modification was not allowed based on the data type or some other rule.

You can add new records to the table by moving your cursor to the blank line at the end of the list (with the * in the left margin) and adding data in each field as needed. When you are finished adding data, you can move your mouse to another row. This forces the QDT data grid to save the new row to the data table.

You can change data in any column in any row just by moving your cursor to that cell in the data grid and editing the contents of the cell. When you move your cursor to another row, the edited data will be saved to the data table.

Finally, you can delete an entire row by clicking once in the left margin of the row (to select the entire row) and then pressing the Delete key on your keyboard. You'll be asked to confirm the deletion before the QDT data grid actually removes the row permanently.

If you just need to fix up a few columns or add or remove a couple records, the QDT data grid is the easiest way to complete the job. If, however, you need to edit a number of records together or add or delete groups of records, the Query Designer offers some powerful custom queries that can do the job instead.

Editing Existing Records with Update Queries

You can programmatically update existing records in your data source through update queries. The UPDATE SQL command is used to modify existing records, but not to create new ones (that's the INSERT command, detailed next). Update queries require several values:

- The table to update
- The columns whose contents you want to update
- The value or expressions to use to update individual columns
- Search conditions to define the rows that you want updated

Say, for example, that you discovered the last name of one of the authors in the Authors table was spelled incorrectly. Follow these steps to update the table with the proper spelling.

Creating an update query for the Authors table

1. From the Query toolbar, set the **Change Type** drop-down menu to **Update**.
2. The Update Table dialog box appears, as shown in Figure 16.12. This dialog box warns you that you can update only one table at a time. From the list, choose the **authors** table and click the **OK** button.
3. The Query Builder display updates to reflect the change in query types. The **Au_Lname** field's check mark changes to a pencil to indicate it has been selected for an update. If it isn't selected, select it now.
4. In the **New Value** column, enter `Banick`. This updates the SQL Query panel with the new value that will be used in the update query.
5. In the Criteria column, enter `Bennet`. This updates the SQL Query panel with the value that will be replaced in the update query.

FIGURE 16.12

You can modify only one table at a time with an update query.

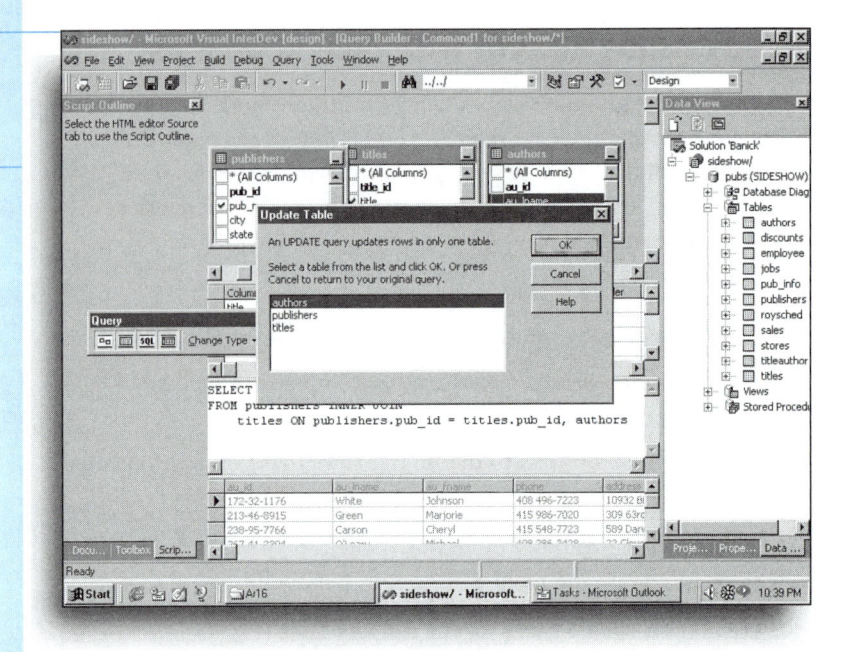

6. Click the Verify SQL Syntax button in the Query toolbar. This will validate your SQL command. Your SQL commands should resemble this:

```
UPDATE authors
SET au_lname = 'Banick'
WHERE (au_lname = 'Bennet')
```

7. Click **OK** to dismiss the confirmation dialog box.

8. Click the Run Query (!) button to execute the update query and replace all instances of `Bennet` in the Authors table with `Banick`. Visual InterDev will report that one row was affected by the query.

9. Now, carry out a `SELECT` query to retrieve the names from the Au_Lname column in the Authors table. You should see that the name `Bennet` has now become `Banick`. Excellent job!

Adding New Records with Insert Values Queries

So what do you do if you want to add new records to the database? `UPDATE` queries can be used only to modify existing data, but `Insert Values` queries can be used to add new records and

Update with care

Use extensive criteria to make sure that you aren't updating the wrong information. More than one table can share the same criteria, although you might not realize it. A good measure is to use two criteria in your expression to ensure that you affect only the records you want to.

Editing Database Data with the Query Designer Tool

values to your database. Not surprisingly, Visual InterDev makes Insert Value queries as easy as SELECT and UPDATE queries. Let's continue with our example with the Authors table. Suppose you want to add a new author to your list of writers. Your new writer's name is Jose Smith. Let's add Jose to the database.

Adding a new author to the Authors table

1. From the Query toolbar, click the **Change Type** drop-down menu and choose **Insert Values**.

2. Because Jose is a new author, you must add all new information for him. Select each column in the Authors table so that they are added to the query.

3. Now, in the **New Value** column, enter Jose's information for each database column. Use the information shown in Table 16.1.

TABLE 16.1 Jose's New Author Information

Database Column	New Value
Au_id	346-94-9132
Au_lname	Smith
Au_Fname	Jose
Phone	403 555-8187
Address	572 Lakewood Road North
City	Atlanta
State	GA
Zip	83201
Contract	1

4. Click the Verify SQL Syntax button on the Query toolbar to confirm the SQL syntax. The results of your SQL commands should resemble this:

```
INSERT INTO authors
    (au_id, au_lname, au_fname, phone, address, city,
    ➥state, zip, contract)
VALUES ('346-94-9132', 'Smith', 'Jose', '403 555-8187',
    ➥'572 Lakewood Road North', 'Atlanta', 'GA',
    ➥'83201', 1)
```

Insert Values queries and typos

This is a good example of why it sometimes is easier to use a GUI than to manually type the SQL behind an `Insert Values` query. The placement of each column is denoted by a comma (,) in the SQL command. If you were to transpose the position of one column, or forget a comma, your input could be incorrect or discarded entirely. If you manually enter your SQL commands in more complex queries like this, use the Verify SQL Syntax button on the Query toolbar to verify your code first. Of course, this will only make sure there are no typos—not that the right data is going into the right column.

5. Click **OK** to dismiss the confirmation dialog box.
6. Click the Run Query (!) button on the Query toolbar. Visual InterDev will add Jose to the Authors table and report that one record was affected.

Deleting Existing Record with Delete Queries

Of course, all data must die, sometime. When you no longer need data in your database, you'll want to delete it. Records can be deleted from the database straight through a DELETE query. Continuing with the example in this section, say that Jose, the great writer that he is, has decided to move on to another publisher that is paying a little better money. Remove Jose from the Authors table.

Using a *DELETE* query to remove Jose from the Authors table

1. From the Query toolbar, click the **Change Type** drop-down menu and choose **Delete**.
2. Select the **Au_Fname** database column in the Grid pane.
3. In the **Criteria** column, enter Jose for our dearly departed writer's first name.
4. Click the Verify SQL Syntax button on the Query toolbar to confirm your SQL command. Your SQL command should resemble this:
   ```
   DELETE FROM authors
   WHERE (au_fname = 'Jose')
   ```
5. Click **OK** to dismiss the confirmation dialog box.
6. Click the Run Query button in the Query toolbar. This instructs Visual InterDev to delete any record in the Authors table that has an Au_Fname column with a value of Jose. Visual InterDev reports that one record was affected.
7. Run a SELECT query on the Authors table to see whether Jose is still part of your group of authors. You'll discover that Jose, along with his vast talent, has moved on to bigger and better things. Good luck Jose!

Delete with care!

After a record has been deleted from the database, that's it. No second chances. As with **UPDATE** queries, it is a good idea to over-qualify your record with multiple criteria.

CHAPTER 17

Creating Data-Bound Web Forms

Learn how to design fast and effective data-bound Web forms

Choose between server- and client-side scripting models

Use design-time controls (DTCs) to build Web forms quickly

Designing Good Data-Bound Web Forms

In this chapter, you learn how to build data-bound Web forms. Data-bound Web forms are input forms that are designed to support the process of viewing, adding, editing, and deleting records in a database. In the past, the tasks required to build data-bound Web forms involved a strong knowledge of database services and heavy HTML and server-scripting coding. Although all these skills are still valuable, Visual InterDev 6 has made it much easier to quickly build quality data-bound Web forms.

In designing good data-bound Web forms with Visual InterDev 6, you deal with three important issues:

- Using data-bound design-time controls (DTCs)
- Selecting client-side and server-side DTC scripting
- Working with the Scripting object model

Visual InterDev 6 has new and very powerful data-bound design-time controls. When you learn how to use these, you'll see how easy it is to build data-bound Web forms.

Another new feature Visual InterDev 6 offers is the capability to choose the method in which DTCs are supported. You now have two options: client-side using DHTML or server-side using ASP. Each has its advantages and drawbacks.

Finally, there are times when you'll need to use another new Visual InterDev 6 feature: the Scripting object model (SOM). The SOM is used when you are creating ASP documents that use design-time controls. You'll see how to use this new feature to enable server-side pages to support client-side events.

When you have a good understanding of these three key points, you'll be ready to build your data-bound Web forms.

SEE ALSO
▶ To learn more about creating databases to suit your needs, see page 477

Exercising magic

Working with data-bound DTCs is really your opportunity to practice magic in Visual InterDev. In the past, database integration required considerably more effort and debugging than it does now. One of the greatest things about DTCs is that they also let you create functional prototypes very quickly.

Using Data-Bound Design-Time Controls

One of the most powerful new features of Visual InterDev 6 is the new crop of data-bound design-time controls. Design-time controls are form elements (buttons, input boxes, lists, grids, and so on) that you define while you are editing a Web document (design-time), but that are actually created and used when clients load your page into their browsers (runtime).

Visual InterDev 1.0 introduced the concept of DTCs. However, the new DTCs in Visual InterDev 6 are much more powerful. The DTCs you'll learn about in this chapter all have the capability to be "bound" to a database table and column. This makes it easy to create forms that have input controls that are automatically tied to an existing field in a database table.

DTCs are a special set of Web controls that appear in their own section in the Visual InterDev 6 Toolbox window (see Figure 17.1).

Other design-time controls

The Microsoft DTC SDK (Software Development Kit) provides information on creating your own design-time controls. You, or other developers, can extend Visual InterDev further by creating your own DTCs that accomplish specifically what you need them to do.

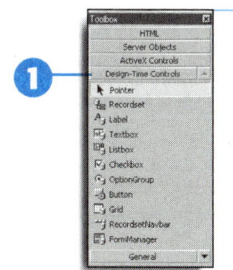

FIGURE 17.1

Viewing the DTCs in the Toolbox window.

❶ Design-time controls.

The names of the DTCs are all familiar (text box, list box, check box, button, and so on). Most of the DTCs have an HTML equivalent, too. However, the DTC version of these familiar controls has several important differences. Primarily, these controls are all created using JavaScript instead of the standard HTML tags. These JavaScript controls have features that enable you to bind them directly to a database—something that is difficult with HTML tag controls. Also, the DTC-type controls can respond to event messages and perform other tasks that HTML tag controls cannot.

A clarification

This isn't to imply that you can't do what we're talking about here without DTCs. In fact, developers have been doing database and event functionality without DTCs up until now. What we're saying is that it is much easier with design-time controls. And who doesn't want things to be easier?

RecordsetNavbar versus Navbar DTC

Don't confuse the `RecordsetNavbar` DTC with the `Navbar` DTC. The `RecordsetNavbar` is used to navigate through a recordset, whereas the `Navbar` DTC is used to navigate through the physical pages in your Web application.

Along with the familiar controls are several other new DTCs that can perform database-related tasks not available in any HTML tag control. These controls include the `Recordset` control (for linking a form to a data table) and the `RecordsetNavbar` control (for moving forward and backward in a data set). You'll learn more about these controls later in the chapter.

SEE ALSO

▶ *To learn more about the* `Recordset` *and* `RecordsetNavbar` *DTCs, see pages 451 and 552*

Even though DTCs use JavaScript to do their work, you do not need to know any of the details of DTCs or about the JavaScript coding they use. In fact, most of the script code they use is kept in a special folder—the _ScriptLibrary folder—in your Web project. This folder stores several read-only scripts that support the work of DTCs at runtime.

To emphasize the fact that Visual InterDev 6 programmers do not need to be concerned with the work of DTCs, the Visual InterDev 6 Editor renders all DTCs as graphical controls instead of showing you the JavaScript that powers them. You can view the script behind the controls by selecting **Show Run-time Text** in the context menu for a DTC (see Figure 17.2).

FIGURE 17.2

Viewing a DTC as text.

Don't alter the _ScriptLibrary folder

The contents of the _ScriptLibrary folder shouldn't be altered. You might "break" the functionality behind Visual InterDev and its DTCs. You might want to extend the contents of this folder with your own code, but don't modify the existing code unless you are extremely confident in what you are doing—and you made a backup.

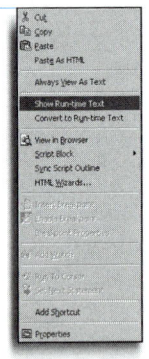

Client-Side Versus Server-Side DTC Scripting

Another new feature Visual InterDev 6 offers is the capability to use client-side or sever-side scripting to support DTCs. This makes it possible to use design-time controls in an ASP document. You can use the DTC scripting options to write Web forms that run on the client but receive event messages on the server. This enables you to build Web-based forms that can support data binding and user events.

If you are building standard HTML documents, the DTCs can use the Microsoft Internet Explorer Dynamic HTML (DHTML) model to receive and respond to user events. This makes your Web forms seem to respond very quickly to user events and provides an optimal experience for users.

This is especially true when you are working with databases on the server. If you use client-side DTC scripting, you'll see a marked increase in responsiveness when updating and editing data. If your application will run with Microsoft Internet Explorer as the client, you'll want to use client-side DTC scripting.

However, if you are not using Microsoft Internet Explorer, the DTCs might not work properly. In this case you must switch from client-side DTC support to server-side. This allows database-related client-side events to be passed from the DTCs to the server for processing. If the server is in charge of handling database events, you can deploy a data-bound DTC ASP document to be hosted in almost any browser. This greatly increases the reach of your solutions.

The drawback of using server-side DTC support is that the server handles all database activity. This includes moving to a new record, as well as updating, adding, and deleting records. The repeated trips to the server can slow your Web application. For this reason, you should use server-side DTC scripting only if you know that your clients will not be using Microsoft Internet Explorer as their browser.

> **Don't bother converting DTCs to text**
>
> You can force Visual InterDev 6 to convert all DTCs to text only. However, this is not needed and is not recommended. You will not need to edit the JavaScript that powers DTCs, so there is no reason to convert them to text. In some cases, converting DTCs to text is irreversible and will reduce the functionality of the DTC at design-time.

> **How does it do it?**
>
> How do DTCs carry out server-side events on the client, and vice versa? Through a complicated combination of passing parameters and information sharing. When you click a button, for example, that has been tied to the server side, the contents of the page are fired back to the Web server for manipulation, and a new page is fired back. Often you will find pages based on DTCs that have a combination of extensive client-side–based actions and server-side–based actions.

> **Server side equals browser neutral**
>
> Whenever you take the burden off the client and put it on the server, you are making your code browser neutral. If you are working in a closed environment (say, an intranet) where you can dictate the browser your users will have, you can rely more on the client-side scripting. When you are working with the balkanized Internet, you will probably push more on to the server.

You can select client-side (DHTML) or server-side (ASP) DTC scripting by setting the `DTCScriptingPlatform` property of a document in the property window of the Visual InterDev 6 Editor (see Figure 17.3).

FIGURE 17.3

Setting the `DTCScriptingPlatform` property.

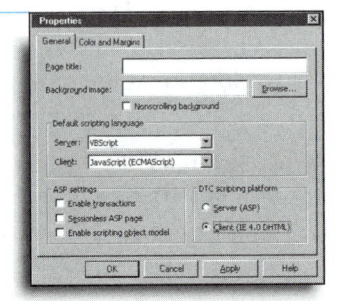

Using the Scripting Object Model

The final item to consider is the new scripting object model. This new Visual InterDev 6 feature enables you to use programming techniques more typical of Visual Basic or Visual C++ instead of relying completely on HTML and ASP in combination. This last point is important when you are building solutions that must run in more than just Microsoft Internet Explorer.

The SOM is a server-side parallel to the document object model (DOM) supported by Microsoft Internet Explorer. This object model enables you to write programs that use properties and methods to automate aspects of the document during runtime. In the past, you had to use a mixture of HTML on the client and ASP on the server. With SOM in place, you can write code that responds to user events by passing them along to the server for processing. This is very much like the server-side DTC model, but not quite the same.

The server-side DTC support affects only DTCs on your page. Adding SOM support to your ASP documents can be done independently and provides its own advantages.

Set the `DTCScriptingPlatform` default for your project

If you will be using the same `DTCScriptingPlatform` for all pages in your project, you can save yourself time by setting the `DTCScriptingPlatform` property of the project itself. When you do this, all new pages will have their `DTCScriptingPlatform` property set to match the project setting.

Creating the DBFORM Project

PART **IV**

CHAPTER **17**

445

The important thing to keep in mind for now is that adding SOM support allows DTCs as well as other controls to send client-side event messages on to the server for processing. For this reason, you must enable SOM support whenever you use data-bound DTCs in an ASP document.

You can turn the SOM support on or off by setting the `ScriptingObjectModel` property of a document using the property box of the page (see Figure 17.4).

Now that you have a good understanding of the new DTCs and the scripting options for Web documents, you're ready to start building a data-bound Web form.

SEE ALSO
➤ You'll learn more about the SOM and DTCs beginning on page 543

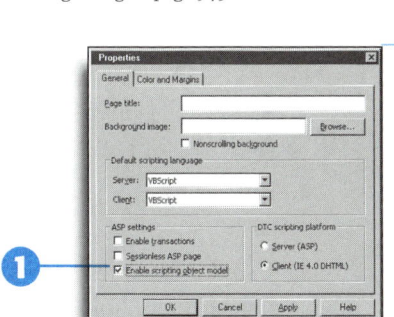

Control your users' interaction

Through the combination of the client-side document object model and the server-side scripting object model, you can control nearly every aspect of a user's interaction with your Web application. This moves your Web application more into the territory of real-time client/server applications made in Visual Basic, Visual C++, or any other conventional language.

FIGURE 17.4
Setting the `ScriptingObjectModel` property.

❶ Set the property here

Creating the DBFORM Project and Adding the Data Connection and Data Command Objects

The first step in building a data-bound Web form is to add the data connection and data command objects to an existing Web project. The data connection is the object that associates your project with an existing database on the Web server. The data command is the object that contains the rules for selecting data from the database and sending it to your Web document.

This chapter's example

The DBFORM project you will create in this chapter is a good example of how you can leverage DTCs and Visual InterDev to create complex Web applications in less time. In a matter of minutes, you will be creating a page that pulls data from the database for you to view, and then you'll be creating an even more elaborate page that lets you modify, add, and even remove data in the database.

Using your own data

If you have your own data sources you would prefer to experiment with, feel free to replace my data source with yours.

The details behind each of these objects is covered in Chapter 16, "Accessing Web Databases." Chapter 16 also covers more information on how data connections and data commands work.

For this chapter, you create a new Web project and connect to and use one of the existing ODBC definitions that you built in Chapter 16. If you haven't built the UsingVISQL or the UsingVIJet DSNs, go back to Chapter 16 and work through those steps before you continue with this project.

Creating the DBFORM Project

Before you can start to build your data-bound Web forms, you must create a new project to hold them. For this example, you build a project called DBFORM that will hold both the database objects and the Web forms.

Creating a new Visual InterDev 6 Web project

1. Start Visual InterDev 6 and select **New Web Project** at the right side of the welcome dialog box or from the menu bar.

2. Enter a project name in the **Name** input box (for example, DBFORM).

3. Use the **Browse** button to locate a folder on your workstation that will hold the source code for your project.

4. Press **Open** to create the project in the selected folder.

5. At the next dialog (Step 1 of 4), select the Web server that will house your project.

6. Select the mode in which you will create the project: **Master** or **Local**. In this example, select **Master** mode. This will give you direct access to the master Web.

7. Click **Next** to move to the next dialog.

8. Enter the **name** of the Web to publish on the Web server. For this example, accept the default (**DBFORM**).

9. Click **Finish** to tell Visual InterDev 6 to build the new Web project. This will skip the Theme and Layout dialogs. You will not need them for this project.

You have just completed the process of creating the Web project. You are now ready to add the data connection and data command objects.

Adding the Data Connection

The data connection object connects your Web project to an existing database on the Web server. Visual InterDev 6 uses predefined ODBC File DSNs as the source for data connection definitions. To complete this step, you must have already defined a File DSN as described in Chapter 16. If you have not done this, go back to Chapter 16 to complete this step.

For this example, you connect to a database that has the SALES table in it. The SALES table is part of the PUBS database that is installed when you install SQL Server 6.5. If you do not have a copy of SQL Server 6.5 available to your Web server, you can use a Microsoft Access database called UVIDB.MDB. This Microsoft Access file contains all the main tables that can be found in the SQL Server PUBS database.

The process of creating the data connection for a Web project includes details for selecting either the UsingVISQL DSN for SQL Server or UsingVIJet for Microsoft Access. Be sure to select the one that fits your working environment.

Adding a data connection to an existing Web project

1. Right-click over the Web project name in the Project Explorer window.
2. Select **Add Data Connection** from the context menu.
3. When the ODBC File DSN dialog appears, locate the existing DSN you want to use. For this example, use the DSNs you created in the last chapter. Select **UsingVISQL** if you have access to SQL Server 6.5. Select **UsingVIJet** if you will be using Microsoft Access as your database for this project.
4. Click **OK** to add this File DSN information to your Web project.
5. If your database server asks you for a login, complete it and click **OK** to continue.

> **Why use PUBS?**
>
> The PUBS database example included with Microsoft SQL Server 6.5 and 7.0 is a great database to develop with. It gives you a variety of data and demonstrates how the interrelationship between data can impact your Web application. If you have your own data source you think would be a better test, go ahead and use it. Otherwise, use the PUBS database to work with a solid foundation.

> **Getting a copy of the UVIDB.MDB access database**
>
> You can get a copy of the UVIDB.MDB file by visiting the home page of the *Using Visual InterDev 6* Web site. You'll find the address for this site in Appendix B, "Online Resources," at the back of this book.

6. At the Connection Properties dialog, select the **General** tab and enter the **Connection** N**ame**. For this example, use cnnUVIData as the connection name.

7. Now select the **Authentication** tab and be sure to fill out information for both the runtime and design-time authentication. Check the **Save** D**esign-time Authentication** and **Save** R**un-time Authentication** boxes to save this information with your project.

8. Finally, click **OK** to save the data connection information to your Web project (see Figure 17.5).

FIGURE 17.5

Adding the data connection object to your project.

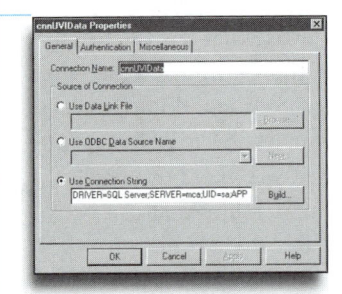

Putting connections in perspective

To better understand the distinction between a data connection and a data command, think of a book. The data connection is the physical container of the book—the spine, the cover, and so on. The data commands are the individual pages inside the book.

You now have a completed data connection object for your project. This will allow any document in your Web project to access the database. However, you need another object in your project before you can actually build a collection of records for use in your pages. You build this object—the data command—in the next section.

Adding the Data Command

In Visual InterDev 6, the data command object holds information on which records to collect from the database described in the data connection object. The data command tells Visual InterDev 6 which table to use and which columns and rows in that table are to be sent to the client browser.

The actual rows and columns are sent as an object called the recordset object. This is not the same as the data command object. The data command object holds the "rules" for collecting records from the database. The recordset holds the actual records collected.

Creating the DBFORM Project | PART **IV** CHAPTER **17** | **449**

Now that you've completed a connection to the PUBS SQL Server database or the UVIDB.MDB Microsoft Access database, you're ready to create a data command object that will pull rows and columns from the SALES table in that database.

Adding a data command to your project

1. Right-click over the existing data connection object in the Project Explorer window. In this case, right-click over the **cnnUVIData** data connection object.
2. Select **Add D<u>a</u>ta Command** from the context menu.
3. When the data command Properties dialog appears, enter a name for the data command. For this example, enter `cmdStores` as the **Command <u>N</u>ame**.
4. Next, select the **<u>D</u>atabase Object** type from the drop-down list. For this example, select **Table** as the database object.
5. Now, select a table name from the **<u>O</u>bject Name** pull-down list. For this example, select **Stores** or **dbo.Stores** from the list.
6. Click **OK** to save your definition to the project (see Figure 17.6).

> **If you're using Access**
>
> If you're developing with Microsoft Access instead of Microsoft SQL Server, you're missing out. I'm not trying to make you feel bad, but understand that there is an exponential world of difference between these two database products. If you can, obtain an evaluation copy of SQL Server to experiment with. You can obtain an evaluation copy by visiting Microsoft's SQL Server Web site at `http://www.microsoft.com/sql`. One of the great things about Microsoft SQL Server 7.0 is that there is a desktop edition that operates on Windows 95, 98, and Windows NT Workstation—not just on Windows NT Server.

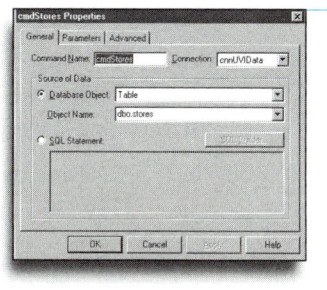

FIGURE 17.6
Adding a data command to the project.

That's all you need to do to build a data command object for Visual InterDev 6. The information in this object will be used to collect records from the Web server. In this case, the information is quite simple: Collect all available records from a table called Stores in the current database. If you had a more complicated request, you could use the SQL Builder from the Data Command dialog box to build a special SQL statement to collect data from the database.

Learn SQL

If you have the time and don't already know it, take some time to learn SQL–the Structured Query Language. SQL is the foundation of almost all databases today. A solid understanding of databases, the SQL language, and database normalization is almost a necessity in today's developer's world.

Diagram, Grid, SQL, and Results

The tried-and-true Diagram, Grid, SQL, and Results panes are common in today's database development tools. You might be familiar with them from Microsoft Access.

Understanding database object references

When you see a reference (such as in step 7) that reads **stores.stor_name** in a database context, it is referring to a table and column pair. Look at it this way: **table.column_name**.

In the next example, you use the SQL Builder to create a special data request that combines information from three different tables and presents the results as a single set of records.

Using the SQL Builder to create a data command

1. Right-click over the data connection in the Project Explorer window. In this example, right-click over the **cnnUVIData** data connection.

2. Select **Add Data Command** from the context menu.

3. When the data command Properties dialog appears, enter the **Command Name**. For this example, enter `cmdStoreSales` as the name.

4. Next, click the **SQL Statement** radio button and click the **SQL Builder** command button.

5. When Visual InterDev 6 starts the Query Builder window, one or more panes appear in the workspace. Make sure the following panes are active: Diagram pane, Grid pane, SQL pane, and Results pane. You can expose these various panes by pressing the appropriate button on the Query Builder toolbar.

6. Bring the Data View window into focus and drag the tables you want to use in the query. For this example, select the following tables from the Data View window and drop them in the Diagram pane of the Query Builder window: **Sales**, **Stores**, and **Titles**.

7. In the Diagram pane, click on the check boxes for each of the fields you want to include in the query. For this example, add the following three columns: **stores.stor_name**, **sales.qty**, and **titles.title**.

8. In the Grid pane, adjust the order of the columns in the results by moving them as needed. To move a column, click the left margin (immediately to the left of the column name) to select the column. Then use the mouse to drag the column name to a new location. For this example, make sure the columns appear in the following order: **Title**, **Qty**, and **Stor_Name**.

Building Data-Bound Entry Forms with DTCs

9. Set the sort order of the collection by clicking in the **Sort** column of one or more lines in the grid. For this example, select the **Sort Type Ascending** for the title column.

10. Now test the grid by pressing the Run Query (!) button to execute the query. Your completed Query Builder should look something like the one in Figure 17.7.

Now that you have built the new project and added a data connection and two data commands, you're ready to start creating your data-bound Web forms.

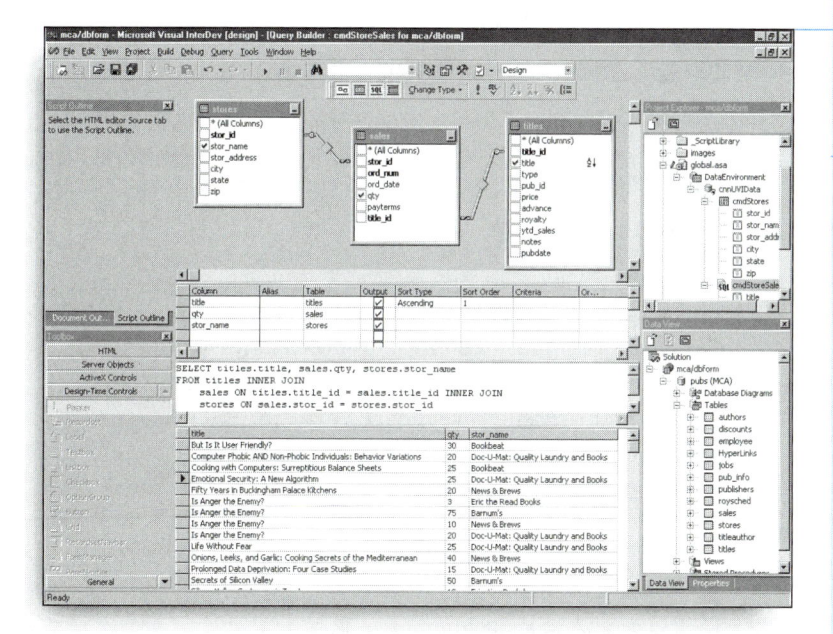

Running the query

One of the great things about Visual InterDev's data environment is that you can test your query before you include it in your Web application. You should always test your query to make sure that you are getting the kind of data that you want (and need).

FIGURE 17.7
Using the Query Builder to create a data command.

Building Data-Bound Entry Forms with DTCs

The process of building data-bound entry forms with Visual InterDev 6 is really pretty easy. In this part of the chapter, you learn how to create two types of data-bound forms:

- An ASP document that uses server-side scripting for DTCs and the scripting object model

- An HTML document that uses client-side (DHTML) scripting to display a read-only version of the SQL statement

It's that easy

If you didn't believe the earlier references to just how easy it is to create data-bound forms that modify the database, read on. You'll be modifying your database in a matter of minutes!

If you need to build data-bound documents that have the widest reach possible or ones that will be loaded by clients other than Microsoft Internet Explorer 4.0, you use ASP documents. If you know you have Microsoft Internet Explorer 4.0 for your clients, use HTML documents with DHTML support for DTCs. This will provide the fastest response time for your data-bound Web forms.

Creating a Simple Data-Bound Grid

The first type of data-bound Web form you'll build is a simple data-bound read-only grid. This will present the results of a data command in an ASP document that is set to support the scripting object model (SOM) and client-side (DHTML) DTC scripting.

This last point is important. Just because you are using ASP documents does not mean you must use server-side (ASP) DTC scripting. If you want to use ASP documents and you know that your client's browsers will support Microsoft Internet Explorer–type DHTML, you can opt to use client-side DTC scripting to improve the responsiveness of the Web document.

Responsiveness

By responsiveness, I mean how quickly things happen. One of the downsides of server-side processing is that the page's data must be sent from the client to the server, and then back. If you have events that trigger a great deal of information sharing, you can have a very slow page.

Here's the process to follow to complete your data-bound grid in a Web document:

1. Add a new ASP document to the project.
2. Add a recordset DTC control to the page that uses the rules in a data command to collect records from the database.
3. Add a grid DTC control to the page that reads the records collected by the recordset DTC and displays them in page format on the Web document.
4. Add any scripting code and HTML to complete the page.

That's all you need to do. Along the way, you'll learn to set many properties that will help the Web document support client-side DTC scripting and the SOM.

Adding a New ASP Document to the Project

The first step is to add a new ASP document to the project. This document will hold all the DTC controls to collect and display the records in the database.

Add a new ASP document, ready to support client-side DTCs and the scripting object model, to the project

1. Right-click over the project name in the Project Explorer window.
2. Select **Add**, **Active Server Page** from the context menu.
3. When the Add Item dialog appears, enter the **Name** for the document. For this example, use `StoreGrid` as the name.
4. After the new document appears in the Visual InterDev 6 Editor, right-click over whitespace near the bottom of the page and select **Properties** from the context menu.
5. When the Properties dialog appears, select the desired DTC scripting platform. For this example, select **Client (IE 4.0 DHTML)**.
6. Next, turn on support for the Scripting Object Model by checking on the **Enable scripting object model** check box in the lower-left of the dialog.
7. Select the appropriate default scripting language for the **Client** drop-down menu. In this example, select **VBScript**.
8. Next, enter the **Page Title** for this document. In this example, enter `Data-Bound Web Grid`.
9. Finally, select the **Color and Margins** tab and set the **Background** color of the page. For this example, select **Silver** from the drop-down list.
10. After all your entries have been added, click **OK** at the bottom of the dialog to save all the property settings for the document (see Figure 17.8).

Using the Properties dialog over the Properties window

You can just as well modify these properties in the Properties window instead of using the Properties dialog box. So why should you? It is often easier to deal with properties in the Properties dialog box–it is less cluttered and confusing. I personally find it is often very easy to lose the property you are looking for in the Properties window. But that could just be me.

You could use JavaScript

Remember that you could just as easily use JavaScript as your client-side scripting language. This chapter builds on VBScript as an example, but there is no technical reason that you should not use JavaScript.

PART **IV** Databases and the Web
CHAPTER **17** **Creating Data-Bound Web Forms**

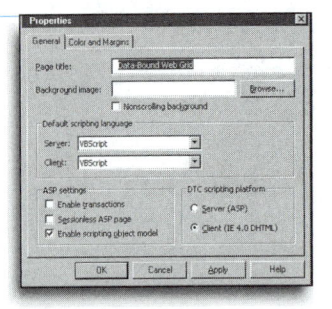

FIGURE 17.8

Setting the document properties.

That's all you need to do to set the document properties to support client-side data-bound DTCs. When you complete the dialog, you'll see several new lines of script code that were added to your document. Note that lines at the top and bottom of the document are marked with a gray background (see Figure 17.9).

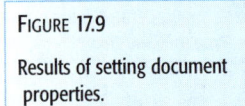

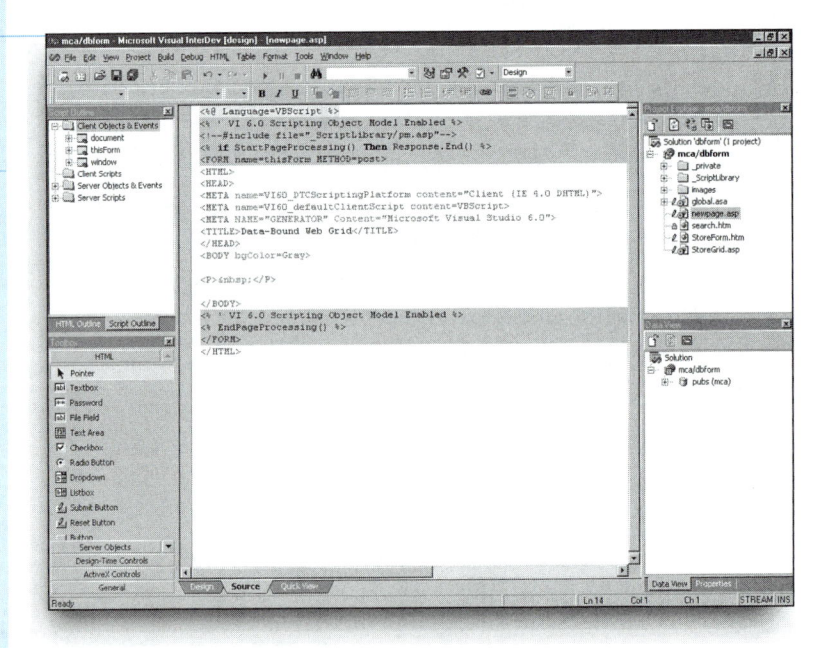

FIGURE 17.9

Results of setting document properties.

This is the code for the SOM support. You should not alter this code in any way. If you do, the SOM support will fail and your page will not operate properly. Notice that the SOM coding actually has a `<FORM>...</FORM>` construct between the top and bottom of the document. This shows you that the SOM support treats your whole page as an HTML form. This is how Visual InterDev 6 is able to pass user events from the client to the server.

Adding the Recordset DTC to Your Document

With the ASP document now prepared, you're ready to add the first of the data-bound DTCs: the recordset.

Adding a recordset DTC to your Web document

1. Be sure the document loaded in Visual InterDev 6 is shown in Source mode (select the **Source** tab at the bottom of the editor window).
2. With the Project Explorer in view, click on the GLOBAL.ASA to expose the **DataEnvironment**.
3. Click the **DataEnvironment** to expose the data connections.
4. Click the data connection (**cnnUDIData**) to expose the data commands.
5. To add the recordset DTC, drag the desired data command (**cmdStoreSales** in this case) from the Explorer window and drop it on the document. Drop it on a blank line at the top of the <BODY> section of the document. When you drop the data command on the page, a recordset DTC will appear with all the proper settings from the data command (see Figure 17.10).

> **Why is the DataEnvironment under the GLOBAL.ASA?**
>
> Although in some ways it makes sense that the DataEnvironment item is located under the GLOBAL.ASA file in the Project Explorer, in others it seems sort of weird. Wouldn't it have been better to have the DataEnvironment in its own node in the Project Explorer tree? Maybe the next version of Visual InterDev will look at that possibility.

By adding the recordset DTC to the page, you have incorporated all the rules from the data command into the Web document. When users load this page into their browsers, the recordset DTC will use the data command rules to collect a set of records from the associated database. However, these records will not be displayed on your document until you place additional DTCs on the page. The recordset DTC only collects the records. In the next step, you'll add a grid DTC to display the records collected by the recordset DTC.

FIGURE 17.10

Adding a recordset DTC to a document.

Controlling the recordset programmatically

Each recordset object has several properties that can be controlled programmatically through your scripts. For example, you can use a script to modify the query used by a recordset based on data provided by the user. How? If your recordset is tied to a SQL query (that is, not a data command itself), the SQL query is retrieved by using the `recordset.getSQLText` method. You can modify the SQL query using the `recordset.setSQLText (SQLCommand)` method. If you modify the query, prompt the recordset to use it by using the `recordset.requery` method.

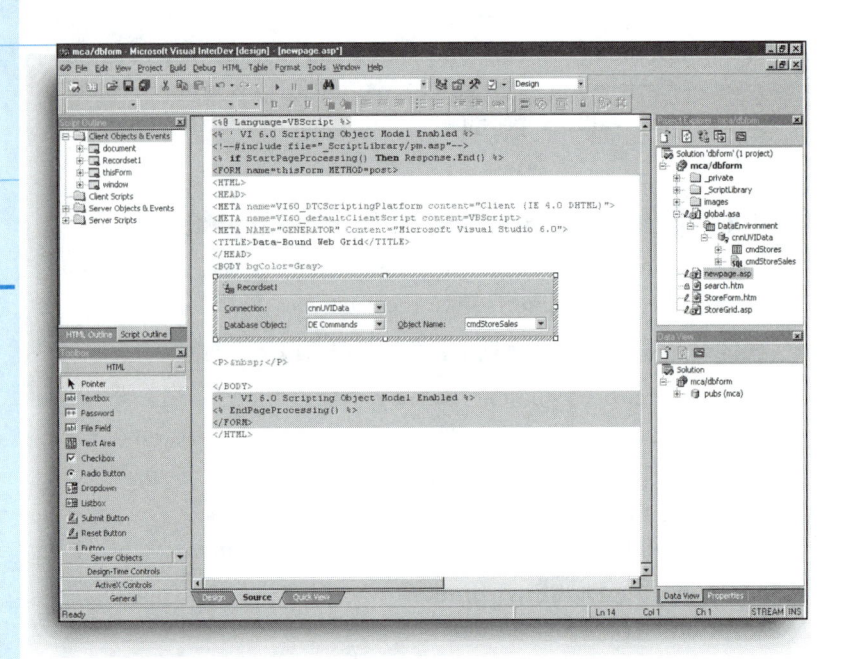

Adding the Grid DTC Control to the Document

The grid DTC will actually display the records collected and delivered by the recordset DTC. You must add this control to the document and link it to the recordset DTC so the grid knows what data to display in the HTML table on the client.

Adding a data-bound grid DTC to your Web document

1. Be sure the document loaded in Visual InterDev 6 is shown in Source mode (select the **Source** tab at the bottom of the editor window).

2. Select the **Design-Time Controls** tab in the Toolbox window.

3. Locate the **Grid** control in the toolbox.

4. To add the grid DTC to your page, drag the item from the toolbox and drop it on a blank line underneath the recordset DTC on the page. The grid appears on your page.

Building Data-Bound Entry Forms with DTCs

5. Click once on the grid to bring it into focus (this adds a wide gray box around the control).

6. Now, use the Property window of the Visual InterDev 6 Editor to locate and click the **Custom** property of the grid DTC. This will bring up the Properties dialog for the grid.

7. In the **General** tab, set the width to **100** and select **Percentage** as the measurement value.

8. In the **Data** tab, set the <u>R</u>ecordset property to **Recordset1** and then click in the check box for each column that appears in the list at the top-right of the tab. This adds columns to the grid display.

9. Click **OK** to save the grid properties. This completes the grid setup for your page (see Figure 17.11).

> **The Grid control**
>
> The Grid control has a lot of flexibility. You can control its appearance (even using several predefined styles), behavior, buttons, and even which particular columns are displayed. Play with the Grid control more after you've finished this chapter's example.

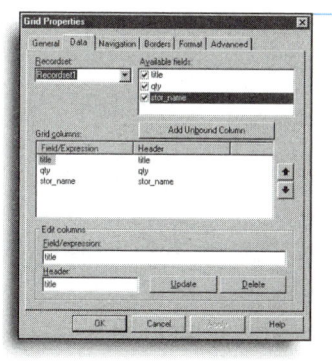

FIGURE 17.11
Setting up the grid DTC.

You now have completed all the steps to add the data-bound DTCs to your document. The last step is to add a small bit of HTML and client-side script to your document.

Adding an HTML Table to the Document

For this example, you'll add an HTML table at the top of the page that will hold the document title and a button. This button will call another data-bound document you'll build in the next section of this chapter.

First, you must add an HTML table to the top of the page. To do this, place your cursor on a blank link directly beneath the `<BODY>` tag. This is where you'll place your HTML table.

Adding an HTML table to your Web document

1. Switch to Source mode in the Visual InterDev 6 Editor.
2. Place your cursor on a blank line where you want the table to appear. For this example, create a blank link directly underneath the `<BODY>` tag in the document.
3. Select **T**a**ble**, **Insert Table** to make the Insert Table dialog box appear.
4. Set the desired number of rows and columns for the table. For this example, set **R**o**ws** to **1** and **Col**u**mns** to **2**.
5. Set the table **W**idth to **100 percent**.
6. Set the background color for the table. For this example, set the **Backgro**u**nd color** to **Gray**.
7. Set the **Border Si**z**e** to **0** to hide the border.
8. Click **OK** to add the new table to your document (see Figure 17.12).

FIGURE 17.12

Adding a table to your Web document.

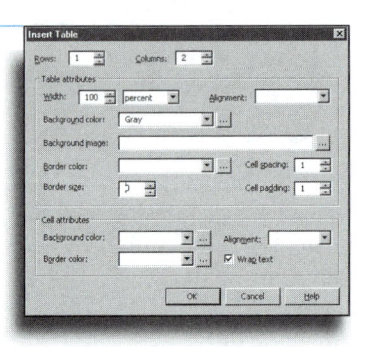

Now you must add the form title to the first cell in the table. To do this, locate the first `<TD>` `</TD>` tag pair and add the text `Store Sales Summary Grid` between the two tags. You also must set the font size to `<H2>`. Next, set the cell width to **50%**. This will make sure the title takes up 5 percent of the document header. Also, set the alignment attribute of the second cell to **Right**. Finally, add a horizontal bar at the bottom of the table. Your table code should now look like the code in Listing 17.1.

Building Data-Bound Entry Forms with DTCs

PART **IV**
CHAPTER **17**

459

LISTING 17.1   **Adding the Document Title to the Table**

```
1  <TABLE bgcolor=Gray WIDTH=100% BORDER=0 CELLSPACING=1
   ➥CELLPADDING=1>
2     <TR>
3        <TD WIDTH=50%><H2>Store Sales Summary View Grid
         ➥</H2></TD>
4        <TD ALIGN=right></TD>
5     </TR>
6  </TABLE>
7  <HR>
```

> **Come up with your own**
>
> You're using the `Store Sales Summary View Grid` title based on this example. If you want to use your own title and data, feel free to change it. Use the general instructions to help you develop your own solution. And maybe you can come up with a better-looking page.

Adding a DTC Button to the Document

The last item to add to the page is a command button in the second cell of the table. Because this is a document that supports DTCs, you'll use the DTC button on this page instead of the standard HTML button control. The DTC button is a bit easier to program, too.

To do this, just drag the Button control from the **Design-Time Control** tab of the toolbox onto the ASP document and drop it directly between the `<TD>` and `</TD>` tags. Next, make sure the button has the focus (click once on it with the mouse), switch to the Properties window, and click on the **(Custom)** property item. This brings up the Properties dialog for the button. Use this dialog to set the **Caption** property to Form and the **Name** property to btnForm (see Figure 17.13).

> **The Name and ID property**
>
> The `Name` property in the Design-Time Control Properties dialog box sets its `ID` property. The `ID` property is used by all your code to refer to the control. The value you use for the `ID` property is also used to identify the control in the Script Outline window.

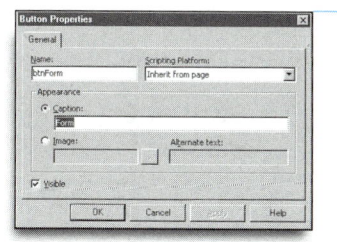

FIGURE 17.13

Setting the DTC button properties.

Now you're ready to add a small bit of client-side Visual Basic Scripting behind the `onclick` event of the button. To do this, locate the Script Outline window and open the tree for the `btnForm` control and double-click the `onclick` event. This will add a client-side script block to your document. You must add a single line of code to this event that will load another page into the client browser. Listing 17.2 has the complete code block. Note that line 5 is the only line you must type. Visual InterDev 6 will supply the rest.

LISTING 17.2 Adding the Client-Side Code Block to Your Document

```
1 <SCRIPT ID=clientEventHandlersVBS LANGUAGE=vbscript>
2 <!--
3
4 Sub btnForm_onclick()
5     window.navigate "StoreForm.htm"
6 End Sub
7
8 -->
9 </SCRIPT>
```

That's all you do to complete the document. Save the document, mark it as the start page, and press F5 to test it in your browser. When you load the page, you'll see an HTML grid appear that has all the records in the recordset defined by the data command `cmdStoreSales`. Your browser page should look like the one in Figure 17.14. If you click the **Form** button, your Web server will give you an error that the page doesn't exist. Don't worry, that's the next step.

Now that you know how to build a simple data-bound display grid form, you're ready to create a complete data entry form that lets users add, edit, and delete records.

SEE ALSO

➤ *To learn how to create reports from database information, see page 574*

PART **IV**

Building Data-Bound Entry Forms with DTCs CHAPTER **17**

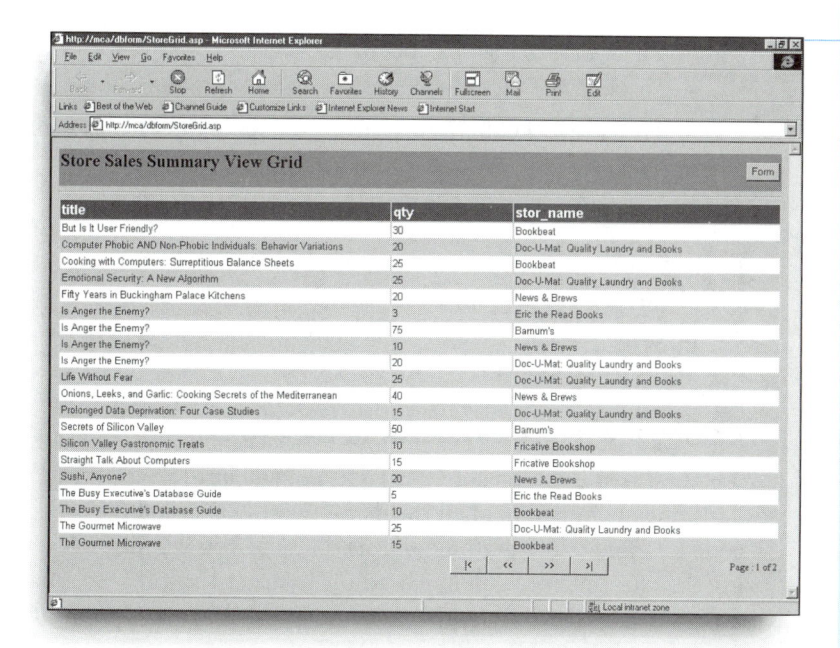

461

FIGURE 17.14
Results of a data-bound grid.

Creating a Complete Data Entry Form

The process of building a complete data entry form using Visual InterDev 6 and the data-bound DTCs is also fairly easy. The process of adding the capability to add, edit, and delete records takes a small bit of scripting code, but not much. The code you add also will be easy to reuse in other data-bound Web forms you build in the future.

For this example, you'll build an HTML document that uses client-side DTC support. Because you'll be using the DHTML features of Microsoft Internet Explorer, you do not need to add SOM support for your data-bound DHTML document.

Here are the key tasks to complete when you create DHTML data-bound forms for Microsoft Internet Explorer 4.0:

- Add a new HTML document to the Web project.
- Add the recordset DTC to load the records into your page.
- Add a set of input boxes to display each record and allow edits and updates.

This might not work in Netscape

There is no guarantee with client-side scripting and DTCs that your application will work in a Netscape Web browser. You can't really fault Microsoft for not going out of its way to make it easier to develop for a competitor's product, but it certainly would be nice if everything were browser-neutral.

- Add a `NavBarRecordset` DTC to allow users to move forward and back in the record collection.
- Add a set of DTC button controls to handle the various edit operations (add, edit, delete, and so on).
- Add client-side code to handle the button events.

When you're finished with the series of tasks, you'll have an HTML document that supports data-bound DTCs and allows complete data entry operations. This form will be optimized for Microsoft Internet Explorer 4.0.

Adding the HTML Document to the Project

The first step is to add a new HTML document to your project. This document will hold all the data-bound DTCs and the script code to animate the button controls. Because you will be building this document to run in Microsoft Internet Explorer 4.0, you do not need to add any support for the SOM. However, you will need to add support for client-side DTC scripting.

Adding a new HTML document to your Web project

1. Right-click over the project name in the Project Explorer.
2. Select **Add**, **HTML Page** from the context menu.
3. Enter the document **Name**. For this example, use `StoreForm.htm` as the name.
4. Click **open** to add the document to your project.
5. Switch to Source mode in the Visual InterDev 6 Editor by selecting the **Source** tab at the bottom on the editor window.
6. Right-click over a blank portion of the document to bring up the context menu.
7. Select **Properties** from the context menu to bring up the Properties dialog.
8. On the **General** tab, set the **Page title** to **Data-Bound Web Form**.
9. Set the **Client** scripting language to **VBScript**.

Why is it so hard to open the Properties dialog?

How many times have you right-clicked a blank portion of the page and selected **Properties** from the context menu only to get the Properties window? It takes a little fine-tuned mouse finagling to open the Properties dialog box. Try right-clicking in the lower portion of the editor, toward the horizontal scroll-bar.

Building Data-Bound Entry Forms with DTCs

10. Switch to the **Color and Margins** tab and set the background color of the page to **Silver**.

11. Click **OK** to save the page properties to the project (see Figure 17.15).

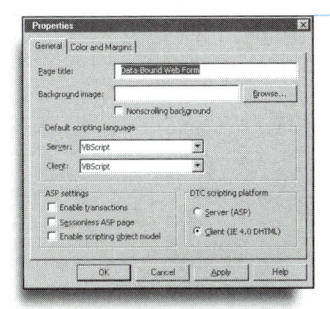

FIGURE 17.15
Setting the properties of the HTML document.

That completes the document definition. Now you're ready to add the data-bound DTCs to the page.

Adding the Recordset DTC to the Document

The first DTC to add to the page is the recordset DTC. This is the DTC that uses the rules in the data command to pull records from the database. The easiest way to add a recordset DTC is to drag the data command from the Project Explorer and drop it on the document. This will force Visual InterDev 6 to add a recordset DTC to the document with all the properties from the data command.

Adding a recordset DTC to an HTML document

1. Make sure the Visual InterDev 6 Editor is in Source view.

2. Locate the desired data command in the Project Explorer under the **GLOBAL.ASA, DataEnvironment, Data Connection** tree. In this case, select the **cmdStores** data command under the **cnnUVIData** data connection object.

3. Drag the selected data command onto the HTML document and drop it on a blank line directly underneath the <BODY> tag on the page. This will force Visual InterDev 6 to add a recordset DTC to the document (see Figure 17.16).

Useful names

You might not have realized it yet, but the choice of names for the data connection and data command items in this chapter have been purposeful. When you are dealing with Web applications that have multiple data connections and potentially dozens of data commands, naming conventions are important. Name your database objects in a clear and understandable fashion so that you won't second guess yourself at four in the morning.

FIGURE 17.16

Adding a recordset DTC to the document.

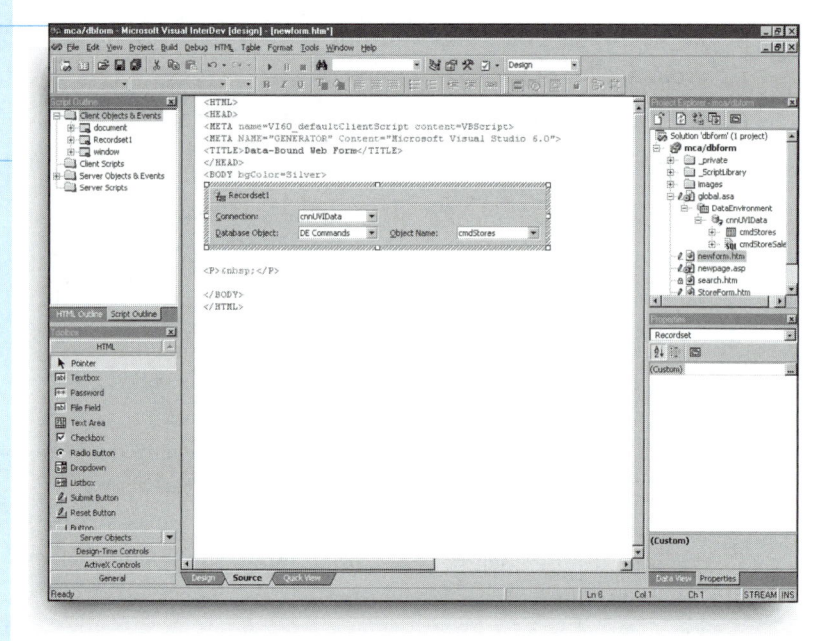

Now your document can collect records from the database. Next, you must add input boxes to the form that will display the fields in the records.

Adding the Data-Bound Input DTCs to the Document

In this step, you add a series of input boxes to the document that will display the contents of each column in records in the database. To do this, you'll use the text box DTCs that ship with Visual InterDev 6. These DTCs look like standard HTML INPUT controls, but are actually unique controls built using JavaScript that can be tied directly to columns in a data collection.

This form of column connection is called data binding. Data binding is the capability to link input controls to a column in the data table in such a way that each time the user views a new record in the collection, the input control automatically displays the column contents. Also, each time the user updates the contents of an input box, the data will automatically be written back to the database. All this is done without writing any script code on the client or the server.

You can use intrinsic elements

You can use intrinsic HTML form elements (such as the text box) and communicate with your recordset, but it requires more work. You must bind the data to the elements through code. And why do that when you can use DTCs?

PART **IV**

CHAPTER **17**

465

Building Data-Bound Entry Forms with DTCs

Adding data-bound input DTCs to your Web document

1. Be sure the HTML document is in Source mode.
2. In the Project Explorer, open the **GLOBAL.ASA**, **DataEnvironment**, **Data Connection**, **Data Command** you want to work with. For this example, select the **cmdStores** data command under the **cnnUVIData** data connection object.
3. Open the data command to expose the list of columns in the data command definition.
4. Click once on the first column item with the mouse.
5. Hold the Shift key down and use the down arrow to highlight all the column names in the list. This is how you select the columns to add to your page.
6. Now use the mouse to drag the highlighted list of columns over to the Web document and drop them on the first blank line beneath the recordset DTC. Visual InterDev 6 adds a table and a set of text box DTCs to the Web document along with column names in text (see Figure 17.17).

Visual InterDev goofs

Occasionally, you might drag and drop a column from a data connection and it won't work. Sometimes the recordset relationship to a DTC is lost. You'll just have to open the Properties dialog box for the DTC and make sure that the correct recordset is selected.

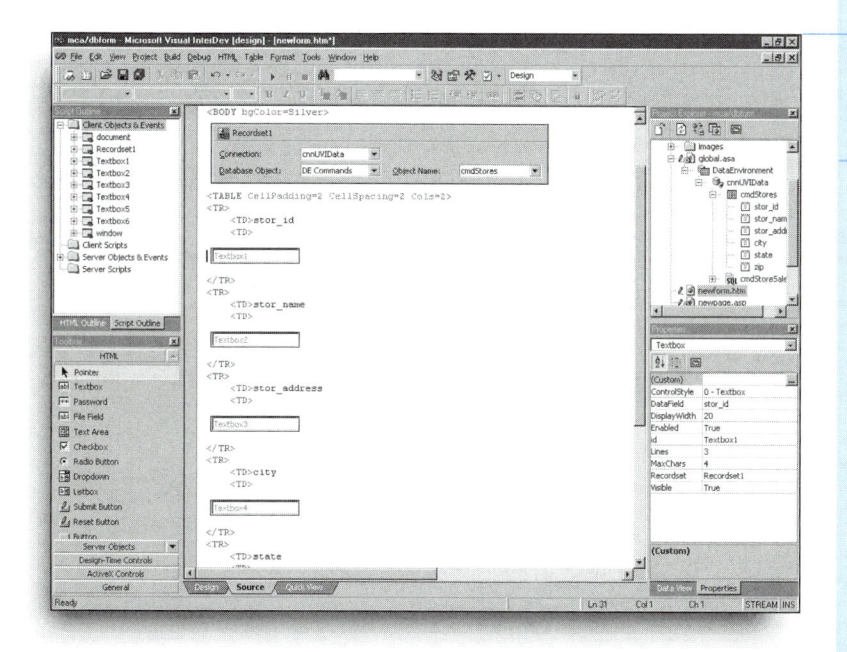

FIGURE 17.17
Adding the data-bound text box DTCs to your document.

You now have a data-bound document that can display all the columns in each record in the collection. However, you must add another DTC to the page to enable users to move from one record to the next in the collection.

Placing a *RecordsetNavbar* DTC on the Document

The next DTC you add will enable users to move forward and backward in the record collection. This process of moving around in the recordset is often call "navigating the recordset." For this reason, the DTC is called the `RecordsetNavbar` DTC. You'll add the `RecordsetNavbar` DTC at the bottom of the page. This will place a four-button control on the document that will enable users to move to the first, previous, next, and last record in the collection.

Adding the *RecordsetNavbar* DTC to your Web document

1. Make sure the document is loaded and displayed in Source view in the Visual InterDev 6 Editor.
2. Click the **Design-Time Controls** tab in the Toolbox window.
3. Locate the `RecordsetNavbar` DTC in the toolbox and drag it over the document in the editor and drop it directly underneath the `</TABLE>` marker after the data-bound input DTCs.
4. Click once on the `RecordsetNavbar` DTC to give it focus (it will have a thick gray bar around the control).
5. Locate the **(Custom)** property in the Properties window and click it to bring up the Properties dialog for the `RecordsetNavbar` DTC.
6. In the **General** tab, set the **Recordset** property to point to the recordset DTC on the page (for this example, use **Recordset1**).
7. Check the **Update on Move** property. This will make sure any changes to the current record are sent to the server when a user moves to a new record.
8. Click **OK** to save the `RecordsetNavBar` properties (see Figure 17.18).

You can customize the `RecordsetNavBar`

You can customize the `RecordsetNavBar` DTC to display custom text for the buttons, or even images. This way you can maintain visual consistency with the rest of your Web application.

The Update on Move property

Use the **Update on Move** property with caution. With this option selected, every time a record is accessed it is updated. This includes the date and time the record was accessed. This involves overhead on the part of both your Web server and the database. Make sure you do indeed need to update the data automatically before you select this.

Building Data-Bound Entry Forms with DTCs

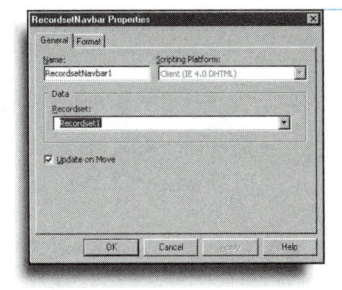

FIGURE 17.18
Setting the RecordsetNavbar DTC properties.

You now have a working HTML document that uses client-side (DHTML) DTC scripting to support data-bound controls. You can display records and move through the recordset, and any changes made to the current record will be written back to the database. However, you must add some buttons to the form to enable users to add and delete records in the table. You'll do that next.

A future project

When you've finished this example, try adding a few new features to the STOREFORM.HTM page. For example, modify the page so that a user can customize the query based on his own input. Earlier in this chapter you might have spotted a note on how to accomplish this.

Adding a Set of Button DTCs in an HTML Table

The next step is to add a set of buttons to the page that will enable users to add and delete records. You'll also add a button to enable users to move to the grid display document you built earlier. Finally, you'll add a title to the form. To do all this, you create an HTML table element to hold the title and the set of DTC button controls.

First, build the HTML table to hold everything.

Adding an HTML table to hold DTC buttons on a document

1. Make sure the page is in Source mode in the Visual InterDev 6 Editor.

2. Place your cursor on the first blank line directly beneath the <BODY> tag on the document. This is where the table will be placed.

3. Select **T**a**ble**, **I**nsert **Table** to bring up the Insert Table dialog box.

4. Set the row and column counts for your table. For this example, set the row count to **1** and the column count to **7**.

5. Set the table **W**idth property. For this example, set it to **100 percent**.

6. Set the **Background color** for the table. Use **Gray** for this table.
7. Set the **Border size** (use **0** for this table).
8. Click **OK** to write the new table to your document (see Figure 17.19).

FIGURE 17.19

Adding a new table to the document.

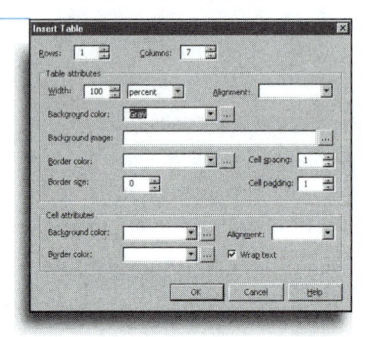

Now that you have built the table, you can add some details. First, set the width attribute of the first cell to **50%**. This cell will hold the title text Store Data Entry Form surrounded by <H2> and </H2> tags. Finally, add a horizontal rule underneath the table. When you're finished, the table HTML coding will look like the code in Listing 17.3.

LISTING 17.3 Modifying the HTML Table Coding

```
1  <TABLE WIDTH=100% BGCOLOR=Gray BORDER=0 CELLSPACING=1
   ➥CELLPADDING=1>
2      <TR>
3          <TD WIDTH=50%><H2>Store Data Entry Form</H2></TD>
4          <TD></TD>
5          <TD></TD>
6          <TD></TD>
7          <TD></TD>
8          <TD></TD>
9          <TD></TD>
10     </TR>
11 </TABLE>
12 <HR>
```

Building Data-Bound Entry Forms with DTCs

Next, add six DTC button controls to the page in each of the remaining six cells of the table. These will be the buttons that will provide the various actions for data entry, including add, update, delete, and list view. Drag a button DTC from the **Design-Time Control** tab of the Toolbox and drop it between the `<TD>` and `</TD>` tags on the page.

After adding all six buttons to the table cells, you must set their `ID` and `Caption` properties. To do this, right-click over the button DTC and select **Properties** from the context menu to bring up the Properties dialog. Use the information in Table 17.1 to set the `ID` and `Caption` properties of each button.

TABLE 17.1 Setting the Button DTC Caption and ID Properties

Old ID	New ID	Caption
Button1	BtnSave	Save
Button2	BtnCancel	Cancel
Button3	BtnUpdate	Update
Button4	BtnDelete	Delete
Button5	BtnNew	New
Button6	BtnList	List

After adding the six buttons and setting their `Caption` and `ID` properties, your document should look like the one shown in Figure 17.20 when you view it in Design mode.

Now that the document layout is complete, you must add client-side scripting to respond to the button click events on the document.

Adding Client-Side Code to the Document

The final step in completing your data entry form is to add client-side scripting code behind the buttons. This is code that will be shipped to the browser and respond to each `onclick` event. Because the target browser for this document is Microsoft Internet Explorer 4.0 and above, you'll use Visual Basic Scripting as the client-side language.

Using buttons instead of Update on Move

Using buttons for saving your changes, as you will do here, is a preferable method over using the **Update on Move** property for the `RecordsetNavbar` DTC. You can also tie more control to the button, letting your scripts carry out more actions each time a button is pressed.

PART **IV**   Databases and the Web
470
CHAPTER **17**   **Creating Data-Bound Web Forms**

FIGURE 17.20

The data-entry form after adding the title and button DTCs.

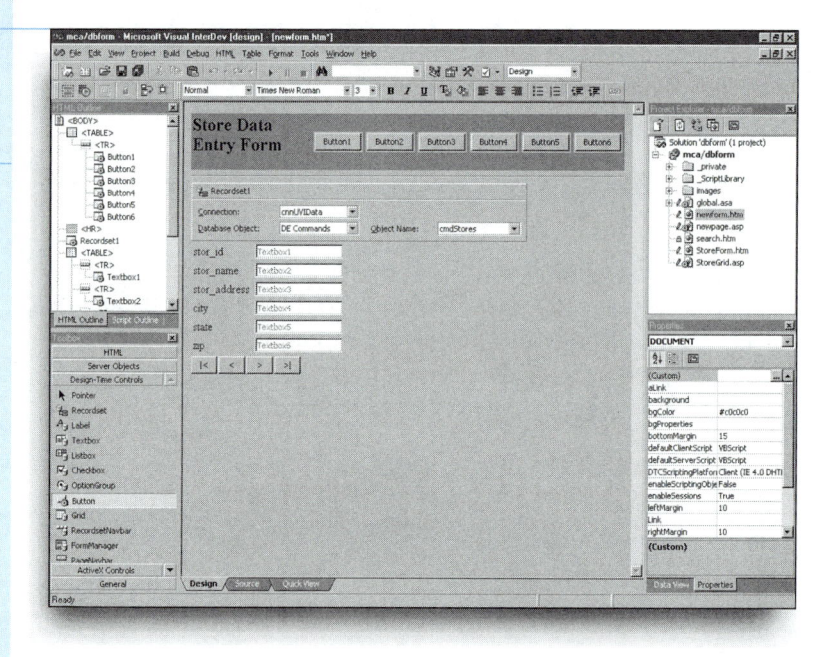

Notice that you have three buttons that perform typical data entry tasks (**Update**, **Delete**, **New**) and two that offer a common choice in data entry (**Save** and **Cancel**). The last button (**List**) will be used to display the Sales form you built earlier.

The **Save** and **Cancel** buttons deserve comment here. What you are actually building is a *multimodal form*. This form has two primary modes: **Add** and **Edit**. You can add new records or you can edit existing ones by changing them or deleting them. The **Save** and **Cancel** buttons will be active during only one of the modes: **Add**. At that time, the **Update**, **Delete**, **New**, and **List** buttons will be inactive. This way, you will be able to help users focus on completing the add operation without making the mistake of pressing the **Delete** button in the middle of an add operation. When it is time to add the client-side code to the document, you'll build a special routine to handle the changes between Edit and Add modes.

Building Data-Bound Entry Forms with DTCs

First you expose the `onclick` events for each of the six buttons. To do this, use the Script Outline window to find each button in the list and double-click the `onclick` event in the list. This will force Visual InterDev 6 to add the various event methods to your document.

You also must add the `window_onload` event to your document. To do this, find the Window object in the Script Outline window and double-click the `onload` event to add the script method to the document. When you're finished adding the event methods to your page, the Visual Basic Scripting code will look like the code in Listing 17.4.

Programming challenge

After you've done this example, try making things more complicated. Add a method to enforce security when a user tries to delete a record, or even modify an existing record. Try using a system of usernames and permissions.

LISTING 17.4 Results of Adding the *onclick* and *onload* Events to the Document

```
1  <SCRIPT ID=clientEventHandlersVBS LANGUAGE=vbscript>
2  <!--
3
4  Sub btnCancel_onclick()
5
6  End Sub
7
8  Sub btnDelete_onclick()
9
10 End Sub
11
12 Sub btnList_onclick()
13
14 End Sub
15
16 Sub btnNew_onclick()
17
18 End Sub
19
20 Sub btnSave_onclick()
21
22 End Sub
23
24 Sub btnUpdate_onclick()
25
26 End Sub
27
```

continues...

LISTING 17.4 Continued

```
28 Sub window_onload
29
30 End Sub
31
32 -->
33 </SCRIPT>
```

Now you're ready to add the actual Visual Basic Scripting code to the document. However, before you build the code for each event, you must add one custom method to handle the switching between Add and Edit modes.

The only purpose of the method will be to enable and disable the proper set of buttons for each mode. In Add mode, the only buttons that should be available are the **Save** and **Cancel** buttons. In Edit mode, these two buttons should be disabled and the rest of the buttons (**Update**, **Delete**, **New**, and **List**) should be enabled. The code in Listing 17.5 shows a method that will handle this. Add this code just above the <SCRIPT> section that holds the event methods.

The Add and Edit modes

You can use modes within your Web applications to enforce rules of behavior. For example, only certain users may be able to enter Edit mode, while everyone can use View mode in your application.

LISTING 17.5 Adding the *SetInputModeTo* Method to the Document

```
1  <SCRIPT LANGUAGE=vbscript>
2  <!--
3
4  Sub SetInputModeTo(Mode)
5      '
6      ' toggle input mode for the form
7      '
8      if uCase(Mode)="EDIT" then
9         blnFlag=false
10     else
11        blnFlag=true
12     end if
13     '
14     btnNew.disabled=blnFlag
15     btnUpdate.disabled=blnFlag
16     btnDelete.disabled=blnFlag
17     btnList.disabled=blnFlag
```

Building Data-Bound Entry Forms with DTCs

```
18    '
19    btnSave.disabled=not blnFlag
20    btnCancel.disabled=not blnFlag
21    '
22 End Sub
23
24 -->
25 </SCRIPT>
```

The method shown in Listing 17.5 accepts one parameter, a string set to either ADD or EDIT. The method checks the parameter and sets a Boolean variable accordingly (lines 8–12). Then this Boolean value is used to set the disabled property of the buttons on or off as needed. Note how the **Save** and **Cancel** buttons are always set to the opposite of the rest of the buttons (lines 19 and 20). In this way, you can use one value to either turn buttons on or turn them off.

After adding the custom method to the project, you're ready to add the code for each event for the document. Listing 17.6 shows the code for the window_onload event. This sets the initial values of the buttons when the user first loads the document in the browser.

LISTING 17.6 Adding Code to the *window_onload* Event

```
1 Sub window_onload
2    '
3    setInputModeTo "edit"
4    '
5 End Sub
```

Next, add code to the **Save** and **Cancel** buttons' onclick events. Listing 17.7 has the code you need to complete these operations.

LISTING 17.7 Adding Code for the Save and Cancel Buttons

```
1 Sub btnSave_onclick()
2    '
3    Recordset1.updateRecord
4    SetInputModeTo "Edit"
```

continues...

PART **IV** Databases and the Web

CHAPTER **17** **Creating Data-Bound Web Forms**

LISTING 17.7 Continued

```
 5      '
 6 End Sub
 7
 8 Sub btnCancel_onclick()
 9      '
10      Recordset1.movefirst
11      SetInputModeTo "Edit"
12      '
13 End Sub
```

Recordset navigation

You can move around in a recordset using several methods. The `recordset.movefirst` method moves you to the first record in the collection. You can use the `recordset.moveabsolute(record)` method to move to a specific record in the recordset. To determine your current position in the recordset, use the `recordset.absolutePosition` property. You can determine how many records total are in the recordset by using the `recordset.getcount` method.

Notice that after each operation, you call the `setInputModeTo` method to update the form's buttons.

Next, add code for the **Update** and **List** buttons. The Update code looks the same as the Save code. The List code just calls the grid ASP document you built earlier in this chapter. Listing 17.8 has all the code you need for these two buttons.

LISTING 17.8 Adding Code for the Update and List Buttons

```
 1 Sub btnUpdate_onclick()
 2      '
 3      Recordset1.updateRecord
 4      SetInputModeTo "Edit"
 5      '
 6 End Sub
 7
 8 Sub btnList_onclick()
 9      '
10      window.navigate "StoreGrid.asp"
11      '
12 End Sub
```

Now you're ready to add the code for the **New** button. This code will prepare the form for input and remind the user to press either the **Save** or **Cancel** buttons to exit the **Add** mode. Enter the code from Listing 17.9 into your document.

Building Data-Bound Entry Forms with DTCs

LISTING 17.9 **Adding Code for the New Button**

```
1  Sub btnNew_onclick()
2      '
3      Recordset1.addRecord
4      SetInputModeTo "Add"
5      '
6      alert "Press the Save or Cancel after filling out form"
7      '
8  End Sub
```

The last bit of code for the **Delete** button is the most involved. When the users press the **Delete** button, they will first see a dialog that asks them to confirm the delete operation. If the answer is **Yes**, the current record is deleted from the database and the record pointer is moved to the first record in the data set. Add the code from Listing 17.10 to your page.

LISTING 17.10 **Adding Code for the Delete Button**

```
1   Sub btnDelete_onclick()
2       '
3       dim blnAnswer
4       '
5       blnAnswer=confirm("Delete this record Permanently?")
6       '
7       if blnAnswer=True then
8          Recordset1.deleteRecord
9          Recordset1.movefirst
10      end if
11      '
12      SetInputModeTo "Edit"
13      '
14  End Sub
```

That is the last of the scripting code for the document. After adding the code from Listing 17.10, be sure to save the document to your Web project. You now have a completely functional data entry Web form that will enable users to add, edit, and delete records from the connected data table.

Data entry made easy

Now do you believe just how easy it is to create data-bound forms in Visual InterDev? You can tie complex actions to elements within your Web application that trigger actions within your database. Imagine the possibilities!

PART **IV**   Databases and the Web

CHAPTER **17**   **Creating Data-Bound Web Forms**

You can test this form by running the document in your Microsoft Internet Explorer Web browser and pressing the various buttons to test the new, update, and delete operations. Figure 17.21 shows a sample session using the new form.

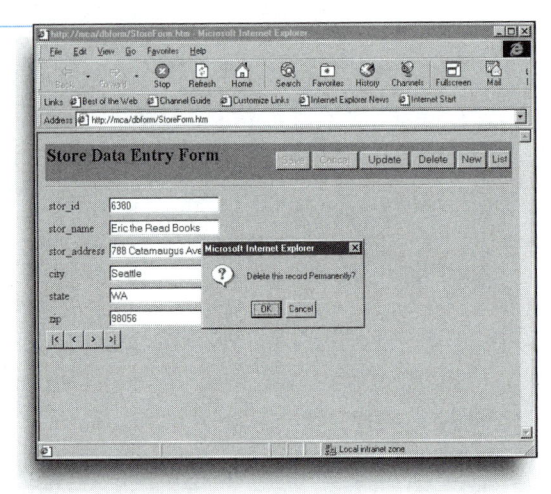

FIGURE 17.21

Testing the data-bound Web form.

CHAPTER 18

Creating Databases for the Web

- Learn to create database projects with Visual InterDev 6

- Add tables, triggers, views, stored procedures, and queries to your database projects

- Define keys and constraints with Visual InterDev 6 data tools

- Modify table content with the Visual InterDev 6 data tools

- Save SQL scripts for execution by SQL Server database administrators

Using Visual InterDev 6 to Create Database Items

One task commonly awarded to the Web programmer is the creation and maintenance of database tables and other related items in the back-end database server. To meet this task, Visual InterDev 6 has very powerful tools built into the editor that enable authorized users to add new tables, views, triggers, and stored procedures to existing databases (see Figure 18.1).

FIGURE 18.1

Using the Visual InterDev 6 Data Tools to create tables in an existing database.

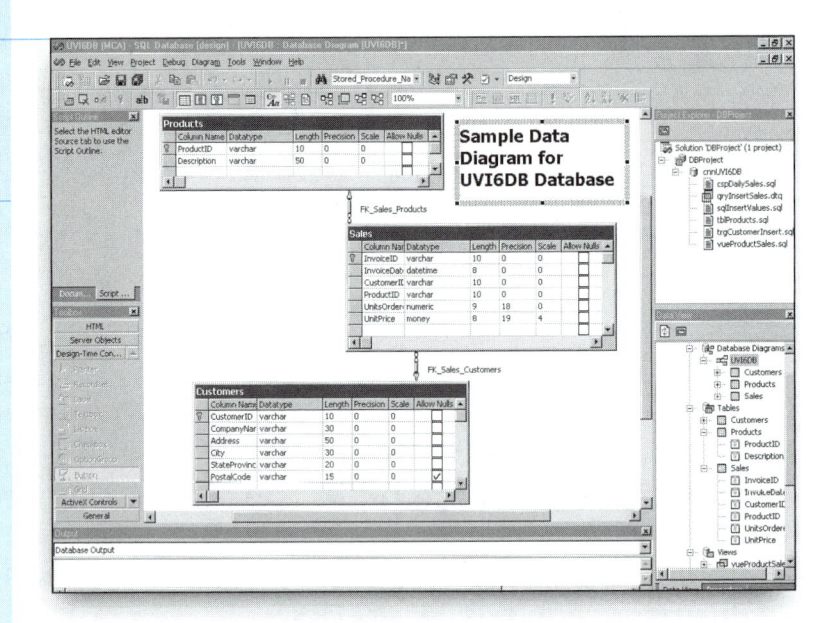

Visual InterDev 6 Enterprise is required for this chapter

The capability to create new database tables, views, and procedures is available only in the Enterprise Edition of Visual InterDev 6. If you do not have the Enterprise Edition, you can still get a lot out of this chapter, even though you will not be able to execute the examples shown here.

Even if you do not have the proper rights to add tables to your Web databases, you can use Visual InterDev 6 to create database scripts that can be delivered to authorized database administrators for execution. You can also use the Data Tools in Visual InterDev 6 to add new rows to existing tables, execute views, and store procedures.

In this chapter, you learn how to use Visual InterDev 6 to create special database projects that hold these scripts and queries and how to use the Data Tools to execute queries and stored procedures on existing databases.

What Is and Isn't Possible with Visual InterDev 6 Data Tools

Before you can use Visual InterDev 6 Data Tools to modify the structure of an existing database, you must have the proper user rights and authorities. If you are working in a large organization, you might need to verify your security rights with your database administrator or network staff. When your rights are properly set, you're ready to begin.

Second, the Visual InterDev 6 Data Tools can provide support only for editing existing SQL Server and Oracle databases. You cannot use Visual InterDev 6 Data Tools to create a new database. If you must create a new database, you must do it outside Visual InterDev 6.

You cannot use Visual InterDev 6 Data Tools to manage users, groups, or roles. These highly sensitive tasks must also be done outside Visual InterDev 6.

Next, Visual InterDev 6 Data Tools cannot be used to add tables or queries to Microsoft Access or any other desktop databases. If you need to create Microsoft Access databases or tables and queries, you can use Microsoft Access itself to do the job.

Having said all that, there are still a lot of tasks you can complete with Visual InterDev 6 Data Tools. You can build new tables and add triggers to these tables. You can create simple queries to store as disk files and recall later for execution. You can also create SQL views and store them in the database. Finally, you can create new stored procedures for your database.

Along with authoring new members for your existing databases, you can use the Visual InterDev 6 Data Tools to insert and delete records in any existing tables and define key constraints and relationships for existing tables.

Finally, all these items can be stored as text files for later recall or for passing along to authors' database administrators for review and execution, if needed.

Using Microsoft SQL Server or Oracle?

This chapter uses examples of database creation techniques for Microsoft SQL Server. In most cases, you'll be able to use the same steps to create valid Oracle database members. However, you should consult your Oracle documentation to verify the exact syntax for all the examples given here.

Keep the Enterprise Manager ready

When you first begin working with databases and Visual InterDev, it usually is a good idea to keep the SQL Server Enterprise Manager within easy reach. You might need to alter the permissions or properties of your database for things to function correctly.

Functionality at a price

Most of this functionality relies on you using a Microsoft SQL Server, Microsoft Internet Information Server 4.0 or higher, and the Visual InterDev extensions for both IIS and SQL Server.

Using ISQL to Create a New Device and Database

In this chapter, you create several database members in a new SQL Server database. Because you cannot use Visual InterDev 6 to create new databases, you must do this using the Microsoft SQL Server Enterprise Manager or via an SQL script file. Before you complete the examples in the book, you should create a new, blank database on a new device in SQL Server for your use. After you finish with this chapter, you can remove the database if you want.

There are several ways to add a new data device and database to SQL Server. First, you can run an SQL script file that contains all the commands you need to complete the task. This script file is available for downloading at the Web site for this book. You can get the Web site address from Appendix B, "Online Resources."

If you do not have the script file from the Web site, you can enter a short script into the ISQL/W query tool that ships with Microsoft SQL Server 6.5. Listing 18.1 shows the complete script you can enter and execute in the ISQL/W editor window.

Microsoft SQL Server 6.5 and 7.0

The material in this chapter is based on Microsoft SQL Server 6.5. SQL Server 7.0 works fine, however some things might be a bit different. For example, SQL Server 7.0 does not require you to create a database device.

ISQL/W

The ISQL/W tool is another useful tool that you might want to keep within reach when developing for databases. Although Visual InterDev's features for databases are great, ISQL/W is better for straight SQL command interaction. Use ISQL/W to test your scripts.

LISTING 18.1 Executing the SQL Create Script Using ISQL/W

```
1 USE MASTER
2 DISK INIT
3    NAME = 'UVI6DEV',
4    PHYSNAME = 'C:\MSSQL\DATA\UVI6DB.DAT',
5    VDEVNO = 255,
6    SIZE = 2560
7 GO
8 CREATE DATABASE UVI6DB ON UVI6DEV = 4
9 GO
```

The script in Listing 18.1 first makes sure the MASTER database is the active database (line 1). Next, a new database device is added to the server called UVI6DEV. Note the physical filename (line 4) and virtual device number (line 5). You might need to alter these values for your server. The physical filename can be any valid name for your server. The VDEVNO value must be

Using Visual InterDev 6 to Create Database Items

between 2 and 255 and unique for your server. When the data device is created, the actual empty 4MB database, called UVI6DB, is built on line 8.

When you enter this into the ISQL/W editor window and press the run arrow, you get a response message that indicates the job has completed successfully:

```
CREATE DATABASE: allocating 2048 pages on disk 'UVI6DEV'
```

After you execute the short script and receive the confirmation message, you are ready to begin using Visual InterDev 6 Data Tools to create your Web database members. However, before you begin, you must first create a new database project with Visual InterDev 6.

Make sure you have space

When creating and working with databases, make sure your database server has the physical storage to hold your data.

Creating a New Database Project with Visual InterDev 6

After you have an existing database to work with, you must create a new Visual InterDev 6 database project to access this database for editing. This process is very similar to the one you use to create a new Web project. In fact, most of the steps are identical.

First, you must confirm that an ODBC File DSN exists for the database you want to access. If not, you must create one. When the File DSN exists, you can use Visual InterDev 6 to create a new database project that uses the ODBC File DSN to connect Visual InterDev 6 to the database.

Create your ODBC File DSN on-the-fly

If you do not have an ODBC File DSN already created on your workstation for the target database, you can still start by creating a new Visual InterDev 6 database project. One of the first steps will ask for an existing ODBC File DSN. If one doesn't exist, Visual InterDev 6 will allow you to create a new one right there.

Creating a new Visual InterDev 6 database project

1. Start Visual InterDev 6 and select **Visual Studio** from the tree view on the left of the Add Project dialog box.
2. Select **Database Projects** from the subtree.
3. Enter a **N**ame for the new project. For this example, use DBProject.
4. Press **O**pen to create the new project on your workstation.
5. When the Select Data Source dialog box appears, select an existing File DSN if one exists. In this case, select the **UVI6DB** DSN if you have one and skip to step 15.

6. If you do not have a **UVI6DB** File DSN, press the **New** button on the dialog box to create a new File DSN.
7. Select **SQL Server** as the database format and press the **Next** button.
8. Enter UVI6DB for the File DSN Name and press **Next** and **Finish**.
9. When the Create New Data Source for SQL Server dialog box appears, enter the SQL Server name and press **Next**.
10. At the next screen, select the appropriate security model and press **Next**.
11. At the next screen, change the default database to the target DB. For this example, use UVI6DB as the target database.
12. Press **Next** repeatedly until you see a **Finish** button and then press it, too.
13. Press **OK** to save the new ODBC File DSN and exit to the Select Data Source dialog box.
14. Locate and select the **UVI6DB** File DSN and click it.
15. Click **OK** to use this ODBC File DSN as your database connection for Visual InterDev 6.

When you add the connection to your database project, you see the Data View window appear in the project showing the contents of the database (see Figure 18.2).

There are four parts to a Visual InterDev 6 database project:

- Database diagrams
- Tables
- Views
- Stored procedures

In the next several sections in this chapter, you learn how to add each of these items to your database.

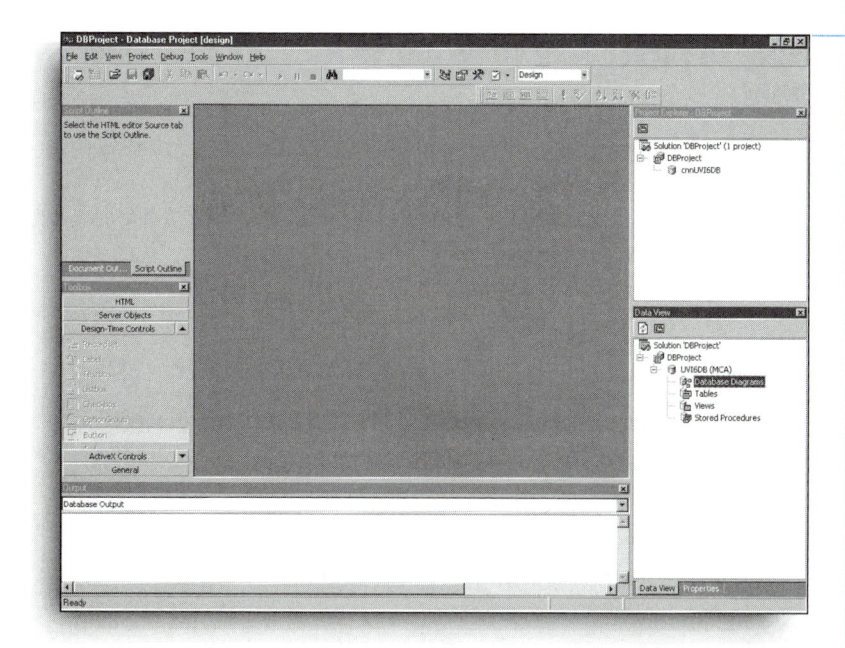

Adding New Tables to an Existing Database | PART IV
CHAPTER 18 | 483

FIGURE 18.2
Viewing a new database project in Visual InterDev 6.

Adding New Tables to an Existing Database

The first thing you must do with a new database is add tables. Visual InterDev 6 has several ways to do this:

- *Use the Database Diagram tool.* This enables you to visually create the table and relate it to other tables in the database.

- *Use the Query Designer tool.* This is very much like the Database Diagram tool except that you cannot create relationships to other tables in the database.

- *Use the Table Script Editor.* This is a simple text script editor that you can use if you are comfortable writing SQL Server scripts. There are now visual aids to help you complete your table definition or relationships.

Database references

If you're looking for comprehensive information on working with databases (SQL Server in particular), check out these two great books from QUE: *Special Edition Using Microsoft SQL Server 6.5 (2nd Edition)* and *Special Edition Using Microsoft SQL Server 7.0*, both by Steve Wynkoop.

Using the Database Diagram to Add the Customers Table

The easiest way to add new tables to an existing database is with the Visual InterDev 6 Database Diagram tool. This is a very visual tool that enables you to add column names in a list and set the primary key for the table, all without writing any SQL code. All you need to do is write the list of column names, data types, sizes, and other values in the New Table grid.

First, you add a new database diagram to the project.

Adding a new database diagram to a Visual InterDev 6 project

1. Right-click over the **Database Diagram** item in the Data View window.
2. Select **New Diagram** from the context menu. A new, blank page will appear in the editor window.
3. Before you add anything to the diagram, save it by selecting **Save Database Diagram** from the **File** menu.
4. Enter a name for the new diagram. For this example, enter UVI6DB as the name.
5. Press **OK** to save the empty diagram.

When you save the new diagram, you'll see it appear in the tree view of the Data View window.

Now with the new diagram already loaded, you're ready to add a new table to the database.

Adding a new table with the Database Diagram tool

1. With a database diagram loaded into the Visual InterDev 6 editor, select **Project** from the menu bar.
2. Select **Add Database Item** from the **Project** menu.
3. Select **Table** from the submenu.
4. **Enter** a name for the new table. For this example, enter Customers.
5. Press **OK** to add the new, empty table to your database diagram (see Figure 18.3).

Database diagrams: what are they?

Think of a database diagram as a map to your database. You can use diagrams to manipulate and organize the structure of your database, as well as to establish relationships between data. Database diagrams are analogous to Visual InterDev's site diagrams for Web sites.

Using diagrams as a starting point

After you create your database, you can use database diagrams as your launching pad for the rest of your database development. You'll likely find yourself spending a great deal of time in database diagrams.

PART **IV**
CHAPTER **18**

Adding New Tables to an Existing Database

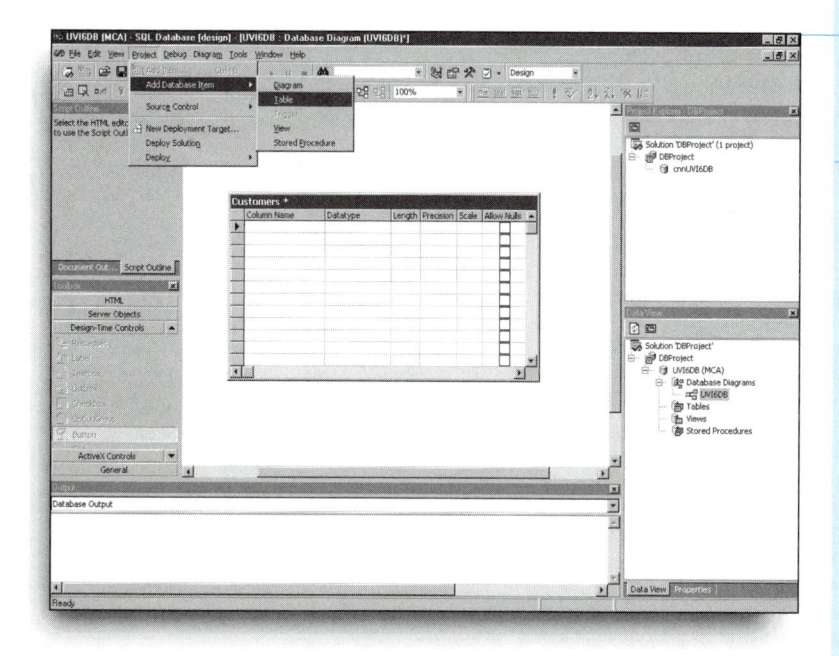

485

FIGURE 18.3
Adding the Customers table using the database diagram.

Now you fill in the various columns of the table grid to create the new database table. Table 18.1 shows the column names and the values you need to add for each column.

TABLE 18.1 **Defining the Customers table**

Column Name	Data Type	Length	Allow Nulls
CustomerID	Varchar	10	OFF
CompanyName	Varchar	30	OFF
Address	Varchar	50	OFF
City	Varchar	30	OFF
StateProvince	Varchar	20	OFF
PostalCode	Varchar	15	ON

After you enter the column information, you declare a primary key for the table. To do this, click the left margin of the CustomerID row to highlight the entire row. Then select **Edit, Set Primary Key** from the main menu (see Figure 18.4).

FIGURE 18.4

Setting the primary key of the table.

Primary keys

The primary key is an important concept behind databases and database indexes. When you search for information in a database, the database server must look at each record in the database. Indexes speed up searches by storing the most frequently accessed information. A primary key is related to indexing by establishing a column of unique data that can be used to identify the rest of the table. This allows you to search for your primary key without having to search for the entire table's contents.

SQL change scripts

At its heart, SQL is very easy. One of the greatest things about working with SQL databases is that you can create your SQL scripts well in advance and use them when you need to. It also makes the structure of databases very portable. If you must re-create the database structure (but not its contents) on another database server, you can use the same scripts. You should get in the habit of holding onto your SQL change scripts as you develop. Keep them as part of your source code so that you can re-create your database if the need arises. Even better, add them to the source control.

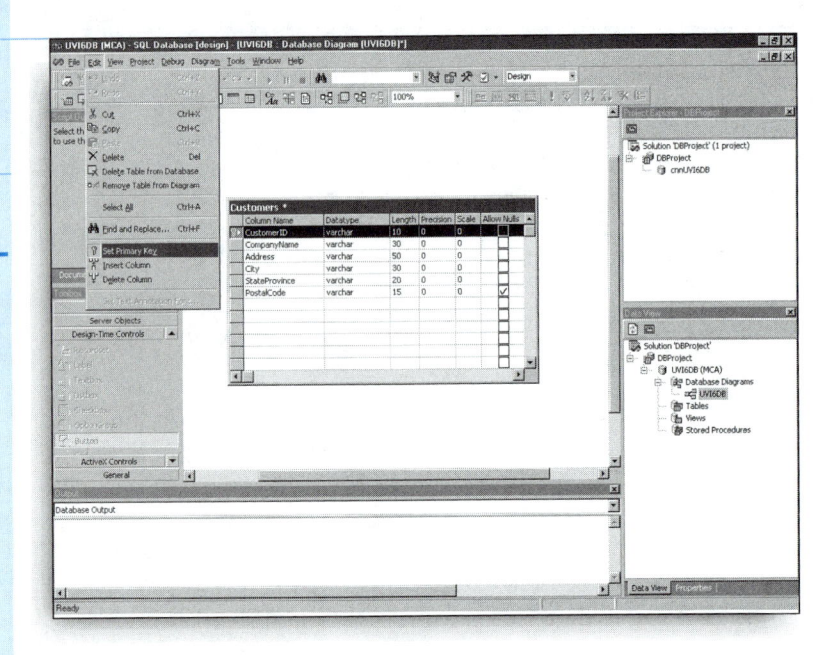

After you complete the table definition, you can close the diagram by selecting **File**, **Close** from the main menu. Be sure to answer **Yes** to save the updated diagram. You can also save the change script for later use if you want.

You now have a new table in your database. In the next step, you add an insert trigger to the Customers table.

Adding a Trigger to the Customers Table

You can use database triggers to execute specialized code whenever someone adds, updates, or deletes a record in the table. The Visual InterDev 6 Data Tools provide you with a trigger script template to help you write your database table triggers. In this section, you write a short trigger that will display a message each time a user adds a new customer record to the database.

Adding New Tables to an Existing Database

Adding a trigger to the Customers table

1. Right-click over the **Connection Name** for your Database Project in the Project Explorer.
2. Select **Add Item** from the context menu.
3. When the Add Item dialog appears, select **Trigger Script** in the right pane and enter `trgCustomerInsert` as the **Name** (see Figure 18.5).

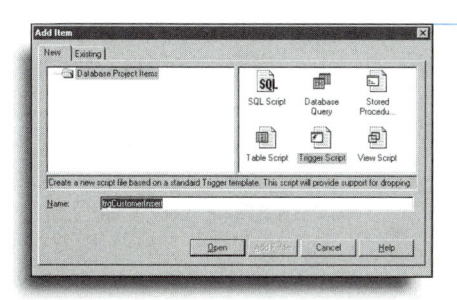

> **Effectively using triggers**
>
> Triggers are a great method for taking the burden off your Web application. You can create database triggers that carry out data manipulation on data you push into the database from a Web page. This saves you from writing the code to manipulate the data as it puts it into the database.

FIGURE 18.5
Adding a new trigger to the project.

4. Press **Open** to open the new trigger template.
5. When the template loads, you'll see several lines of boilerplate script ready for your modification.
6. First, replace `Trigger_Name` with your trigger name (use `trgCustomerInsert` for this example) by selecting **Edit**, **Find and Replace** from the main menu. There are eight occurrences of `Trigger_Name` in the template.
7. Replace the green `/* INSERT TRIGGER ...*/` line with your trigger code. For this example, use the code in Listing 18.2.
8. Save the trigger by clicking the X in the upper-right corner of the editor window. Be sure to say **YES** to save the trigger to the project.

LISTING 18.2 Writing a Simple Message Insert Trigger

```
1 CREATE Trigger trgCustomerInsert
2    ON Customers
3    FOR INSERT
4    AS
5        RAISERROR ('Be sure to notify shipping of the new
         ➥customer.',16,10)
```

Triggers that do something

This example of a trigger is pretty simple; it just raises an error message as visible feedback. You can use triggers to carry out complex SQL actions on your data just as easily.

At this point you've created a trigger script, but it has not been executed yet. If you want the trigger to appear as part of the database you must execute the SQL script you just created. You can do this by right-clicking the script name (`trgCustomerInsert.sql`) in the Project Explorer window and selecting **Execute** from the context menu.

When you execute a script in the Visual InterDev 6 Database project, you see results appear in the Output window at the bottom of the screen. Scripts that do not return rows of data (such as a trigger creation script) return a message similar to the following:

```
No rows affected.
There are no more results
Finished executing script
➥C:\UVI\Source\Chap18\cnnUVI6DB\trgCustomerInsert.sql
```

You now have a completed Customers table. Next, you use the Query Designer to create the Sales table in your database.

Feedback on mistakes

The Database Output window displays all the results of your script execution, including errors. Keep an eye out for any error messages that might indicate a problem with your scripts.

Using the Query Designer to Add the Sales Table

Another way to add a table to your database is to use the Query Designer (QD). This looks a lot like the window you used in Chapter 17, "Creating Data-Bound Web Forms," to create your query statements. However, this window is modified to allow you to create a new table instead.

Using the Query Designer to add a new table

1. In the Data View window, right-click over the **Tables** node.
2. Select **New Table** from the context menu.
3. Enter a name for the new table. For this example, enter Sales and press **OK**.
4. This will bring up the QD add table grid. This looks a lot like the grid in the Database Diagram window. Use the information in Table 18.2 to define the Sales table.

Adding New Tables to an Existing Database

PART IV
CHAPTER 18

489

TABLE 18.2 Defining the Sales table

Column Name	Data Type	Length	Allow Nulls
InvoiceID	Varchar	10	OFF
InvoiceDate	Datetime	NA	OFF
CustomerID	Varchar	10	OFF
ProductID	Varchar	10	OFF
UnitsOrdered	Numeric	NA	OFF
UnitPrice	Money	NA	OFF

After adding all the columns, click the margin next to the `InvoiceID` column name to select the row. Now right-click at the same location and select **Set Primary Key** to make the `InvoiceID` the table's primary key (see Figure 18.6).

You can instantly add this table to the database simply by closing the Query Designer window. Be sure to say **YES** when asked to update the Sales table and save the change script for later use.

You are now ready to add one more table to the database using the Table Script template.

Database data types

Databases, like programming languages, can have values with different types of data. You should refer to the documentation for your database (in this case, SQL Server) for information on the provided data types. If the need arises, you can also create your own data types to accomplish a specific goal.

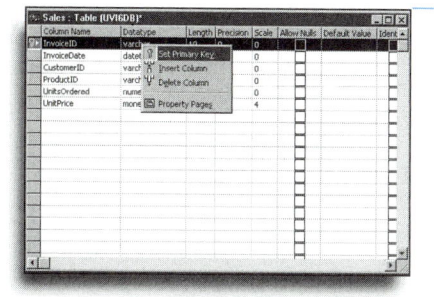

FIGURE 18.6
Using the Query Designer to add the Sales table.

Using the Table Script to Add the Product Table

The last method for adding tables to a database with the Visual InterDev 6 editor is to use the Table Script template. This template is a pure SQL statement method for adding tables to the database. However, even though the template is not very "GUI," it has its advantages.

The SQL script templates

The templates that you are given for SQL scripts encourages organized development. There are provisions for versioning, update notes, and author information. You can use this information to record the purpose of your scripts and encourage maintainability.

First, you actually create a script file to execute later. If you are a Web programmer who does not have rights to add tables directly to the database, you can use this method to build scripts that can be executed by those in your team who have the proper authority to do so.

Also, even if you *do* have rights to add tables yourself, the script template keeps a very handy copy of the creation script in case you need to re-create the database later. This creation script is more portable than the change scripts created by the Query Designer and the Database Diagram windows.

Adding a new table with the Table Script template

1. Right-click over the connection name (**cnnUVI6DB**) in the Project Explorer window.
2. Select **Add Item** from the context menu.
3. Select **Table Script** from the right pane and enter a name for the script. For this example, enter `tblProducts` as the name.
4. Press **Open** to open the Table Template in the Visual InterDev 6 editor.
5. Use the Find and Replace dialog to replace the words `Table_Name` with your desired table name. For this example, use the word `Products` as the new table name. There are seven occurrences of `Table_Name` in the template.

Be careful of typos in SQL

Be careful when modifying SQL scripts. If you make a mistake (a typo) in a script, your script might not function, or worse yet, it might modify data you didn't want to.

6. Enter the table definition details between the parentheses **()** after **CREATE TABLE Products**. Listing 18.3 has the SQL coding to define the Products table. Note you need to enter only lines 3, 4, and 5. The rest are supplied by Visual InterDev 6.
7. After completing the SQL definition, save the script to your project by selecting **File**, **Close** from the main menu. Be sure to say **YES** when asked to save the file.

Adding New Tables to an Existing Database

LISTING 18.3 Defining the Product Table in the Table Template

```
1  CREATE TABLE Products
2  (
3      ProductID varchar(10) NOT NULL,
4      Description varchar(50) NOT NULL,
5      CONSTRAINT PK_Products PRIMARY KEY NONCLUSTERED
       ➥(ProductID)
6
7  )
8  GO
```

Again, since you've built the script, you have not yet executed it. This means the Products table is not yet part of the database. To add the Products table, right-click over the **tblProducts.sql** item in the Project Explorer and select **Execute** from the context menu.

When you execute the script, you'll see status messages appear in the Output window telling you the script has been completed.

You now know three different ways to create tables using Visual InterDev 6 Data Tools. The Data Diagram is the friendliest method. You'll use this again in the next step. The Query Designer can also be used much like the Data Diagram window. However, the Script template is the most detailed and may be preferred by people who already know how to write SQL scripts.

SEE ALSO

▶ On page 486 you saw the results of SQL script output in the Database Output window. Remember to keep your eye open for errors.

Defining Table Relationships with the Database Diagram

After you have added several tables to your database, you can use the Database Diagram window to establish relationships between the tables. This greatly increases the integrity of your databases. To establish relationships, drag your tables from the Data View window onto the Database Diagram window, and then use your mouse to link a column in one table to a similar column in another table. The database diagram will do the rest.

> **Of nulls**
>
> Lines 3 and 4 of Listing 18.3 use `NOT NULL` to indicate that the `ProductID` and `Description` columns cannot contain null data. In databases, all columns must contain some form of information, even if it is a null. Nulls act as a way of saying there's nothing there. The absence of a null (meaning there really wasn't anything there) would break the database and most programming languages. If you do not allow nulls (empty values) in your columns, then you must provide a value when a record is created or modified.

Defining table relationships with the Database Diagram window

1. Double-click on the existing database diagram in the Data View window. For this example, use the **UVI6DB** diagram you built earlier in this chapter.

2. Now make sure all related tables are included in the diagram. For this example, you need the **Customers**, **Sales**, and **Products** tables in the diagram. If any are not there, drag them from the Data View window (under the **Tables** node) and drop them on the Database Diagram window.

3. Simplify your diagram by clicking on each table and pressing the **Show Column Names** button on the Database Diagram toolbar. This will alter the table displays to show only the table names and column names, not the detailed definitions of the columns themselves.

4. Now you can define a relationship between tables by selecting the primary key in one table and linking it to a related field in another table. For example, drag the `ProductID` primary key field from the Products table and drop it on the `ProductID` column of the Sales table. You'll see a dialog box appear showing you the relationships definition between the two tables (see Figure 18.7).

Normalizing relationships

Relationships between data is a fundamental database design goal. In databases, there is a term called *normalization*. Normalization involves removing the redundancy of information in a database and establishing relationships between data in columns. For example, you don't need to store the customer's user information twice—once in the Customers table and once in the Sales table for what they purchased. Instead, you use a relationship between the two tables in the form of the customer ID (CustomerID). Normalization is the goal of every database design.

FIGURE 18.7

Adding relationship definitions to the database.

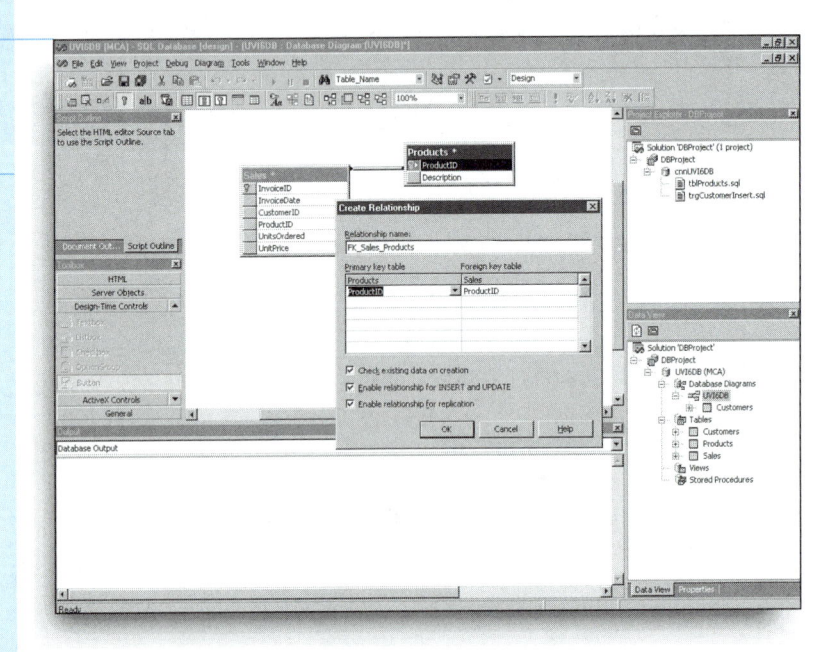

5. Click **OK** to use the relationship.
6. Continue to add relationship definitions as needed. For this example, drag the `CustomerID` primary key column from the Customers table and drop it on the `CustomerID` column in the Sales table. Press **OK** to accept the definition details.
7. To enhance the database diagram view, press the **Show Relationship Labels** button on the Diagram toolbar.
8. Select all the tables by drawing a box around them with your mouse.
9. Press the **Autosize Selected Tables** button and the Arrange Selection button on the toolbar to add the final touches to your diagram.
10. Save the completed database diagram by selecting **File**, **Save** from the main menu. Be sure to say **YES** to update the database and save the change script.

You now have completed three new tables and defined relationships between them. In the next section, you use the Visual InterDev 6 Data Tools to add records to these three tables.

Using the Visual InterDev 6 Data Tools to Add Records to the Database

Usually, you build database tables to enable users to edit them from within your Web applications. However, often you must add test data to existing tables or "prime" base tables with valid values so other data entry forms will work properly. In this section, you learn how to use the Visual InterDev 6 Data Tools to enter records manually and to create INSERT queries that you can run from the Query Designer (QD).

In both cases, you'll see how you can quickly add data to existing tables without having to leave the comfort of the Visual InterDev 6 editor.

Adding records

You can combine the techniques you've learned in Chapter 17, "Creating Data-Bound Web Forms" for adding records and those in this chapter to create smarter applications.

Entering Records Using the Query Designer Grid

The simplest way to add data to your tables is to use the Query Designer grid. This is a simple grid that shows each existing records in the table and has a blank line at the bottom ready for you to add a new record to the table.

You can display the grid by just double-clicking the table name in the Data view window under the **Tables** node. For example, find the Products table in the Data View window and double-click it to open the Query Designer grid (see Figure 18.8).

FIGURE 18.8

Adding records with the Query Designer grid.

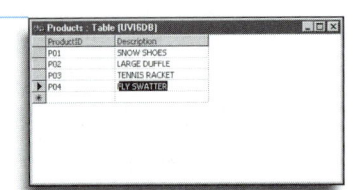

When you have the Products grid open, use Table 18.3 to add some sample data. You'll use this data in the last section of the chapter when you build views and stored procedures.

TABLE 18.3   Adding records to the Products table

Product ID	Description
P01	SNOW SHOES
P02	LARGE DUFFLE
P03	TENNIS RACKET
P04	FLY SWATTER

After adding the records from Table 18.3 into the Products table, you can close the Query Designer grid.

Normalization alert!

The ProductID column is another example of normalization at work. The ProductID column is used for a relationship between the Products table and the Sales table.

Creating an Insert SQL Script with the Script Template

The QD grid is effective for adding short records, but not very convenient if you must add several records to a table. If you must add several rows, you can use the script template to build an INSERT query script. To do this, you can load the generic SQL script template and add your SQL INSERT statements as needed.

Creating and inserting SQL script with the script template

1. Right-click over the connection name (**UVI6DB**) in the Project Explorer and select **Add Item** from the context menu.

2. Select the **SQL Script** in the right pane and enter the script name. For this example, enter sqlInsertValues as the name.

3. Press the **Open** button to load the script template in the Visual InterDev 6 editor. You'll see a blank page ready for your SQL statements.

With the empty script in your editor you can create any type of SQL script you want. Listing 18.4 contains a script that will update both the Customers and the Sales table with data. Enter these SQL statements into the script template in the editor.

LISTING 18.4 **Creating the Insert Values SQL Script**

```
1  /*
2  add customers
3  */
4  INSERT INTO Customers
5     (CustomerID, CompanyName, Address, City, StateProvince,
       ➥PostalCode)
6  VALUES
7     ('C101', 'BASEBALL JESSE', '999 FOUL LINE DRIVE',
       ➥'HIT CITY', 'NJ', '67890')
8
9  INSERT INTO Customers
10    (CustomerID, CompanyName, Address, City,
       ➥StateProvince, PostalCode)
```

continues...

LISTING 18.4 Continued

```
11 VALUES
12    ('C102', 'SHANNONS GYM', '345 POMMEL DRIVE', '
      ➥TEN-OH VILLAGE', 'GA', '34567')
13
14 INSERT INTO Customers
15    (CustomerID, CompanyName, Address, City,
      ➥StateProvince, PostalCode)
16 VALUES
17    ('C103', 'LEES FRESH FOODS', '765 PEACH LANE',
      ➥'HEALTHSBURG', 'CT', '13579')
18
19 /*
20 add sales records
21 */
22 INSERT INTO Sales
23    (InvoiceID, InvoiceDate, CustomerID, ProductID,
      ➥UnitsOrdered, UnitPrice)
24 VALUES ('INV01', '10/10/99', 'C101', 'P01', 35, 15)
25
26 INSERT INTO Sales
27    (InvoiceID, InvoiceDate, CustomerID, ProductID,
      ➥UnitsOrdered, UnitPrice)
28 VALUES ('INV02', '10/10/99', 'C101', 'P01', 35, 15)
29
30 INSERT INTO Sales
31    (InvoiceID, InvoiceDate, CustomerID, ProductID,
      ➥UnitsOrdered, UnitPrice)
32 VALUES ('INV03', '11/11/99', 'C102', 'P02', 45, 25)
33
34 INSERT INTO Sales
35    (InvoiceID, InvoiceDate, CustomerID, ProductID,
      ➥UnitsOrdered, UnitPrice)
36 VALUES ('INV04', '11/11/99', 'C102', 'P03', 55, 35)
37
38 INSERT INTO Sales
39    (InvoiceID, InvoiceDate, CustomerID, ProductID,
      ➥UnitsOrdered, UnitPrice)
40 VALUES ('INV05', '11/11/99', 'C103', 'P04', 65, 45)
41
42 /*
43 eof
44 */
```

Using the Visual InterDev 6 Data Tools to Add Records to the Database

After adding the SQL statements, save the script (select **File**, **Close** and answer **YES** to save). Remember that scripts do not alter any database contents until they are executed. You can do this by right-clicking on the script and selecting **Execute** from the context menu.

When you execute the insert script, you see a response in the output window that looks something like the following:

```
Executing script C:\UVI\Source\Chap18\cnnUVI6DB\
➥sqlInsertValues.sql

[Microsoft][ODBC SQL Server Driver][SQL Server]
➥Notify shipping of the new customer.
[Microsoft][ODBC SQL Server Driver][SQL Server]
➥Notify shipping of the new customer.
[Microsoft][ODBC SQL Server Driver][SQL Server]
➥Notify shipping of the new customer.
Finished executing script C:\UVI\Source\Chap18\
➥cnnUVI6DB\sqlInsertValues.sql
```

Notice that the output window shows the results of the `CustomerInsert` trigger you built earlier in this chapter.

Creating an Insert Query with the Query Designer

You can also use the Query Designer to create a "persistent" insert query. This is one that you can run more than once. The advantage of using the QD to create insert queries is that you can easily rerun the query many times. The disadvantage is that the QD can insert only one record per query.

Using the Query Designer to create an insert query

1. Right-click over the data connection (**UVI6DB**) in the Project Explorer.
2. Select **Add Query** from the context menu.
3. When the Add Item dialog box appears, enter a **Name**. For this example, use `qryInsertSales` as the name.
4. When the QD window appears, drag the Sales table from the Data View window and drop it on the QD diagram pane.

Avoid typing mistakes

With a listing like this, take extra care to avoid typing mistakes. As you learned earlier, a mistake in a SQL script could result in a nonfunction script, or even worse, modification of data that you didn't mean to touch.

Dynamic persistent insert queries

You can use the techniques mentioned in Chapter 17 to create dynamically modifiable persistent queries. For example, your query might insert values into a table. Dynamically you could determine the values to insert into each record based on user input.

5. Use the QD toolbar to change the query type by pressing on the **Change Type** drop-down list and selecting **Insert Values** from the list.

6. When the QD panes change, move your cursor to the grid pane and pull down the column names and enter values for each. Table 18.4 shows the data for this example.

7. After all the data is entered, close the QD window and save the query.

TABLE 18.4 Adding a record in the QD grid

Column Name	New Value
InvoiceID	INV106
InvoiceDate	11/11/99
CustomerID	C103
ProductID	P03
UnitsOrdered	55
UnitPrice	35

You execute stored queries differently than the rest of the scripts. Right-click over the query file (**qryInsertSales**) and select **Open**. This executes the query. If all goes well, you'll see a message telling you how many rows were updated.

Adding New Views to an Existing Database

You can also use the Visual InterDev 6 Data Tools to build and save SQL Server views. Views are a type of definition of how a set of records will be collected. By created and storing views, you can simplify the creation of data-bound Web forms a great deal.

Beware the data type

Make sure you are inserting data using the right data type. If you attempt to use an incorrect data type in a query, the query will break. For example, don't push alphanumeric characters into a numeric column.

Adding New Views to an Existing Database

In this section, you learn two ways to create views: with the Query Designer and with the view script template.

Using the Query Designer to Add the *TotalSales* View

Creating views with the QD window is as easy as pointing-and-clicking. You add a new blank view from the Data View window and then drag-and-drop any required tables into the QD, select the desired columns, and save the resulting view to the database.

Creating a view with the Query Designer window

1. Right-click over the **View** node in the Data View window.
2. Select **New View** from the context menu.
3. When the Query Designer window appears, drag any tables you need from the Data View to the QD window. For this example, drag the **Sales**, **Customers**, and **Products** tables into the Diagram Pane of the QD window.
4. With the tables in view, click the desired columns in the lists in the diagram pane. For this example, select `Description` from the Product table, `CompanyName` from the Customers table, and `UnitsOrdered` and `UnitPrice` from the Sales table.
5. Next, add any computed columns you need for your view. For this example, enter the following formula in the `Column` field of the grid pane: `UnitsOrdered * UnitPrice`. Then enter `TotalSales` in the `Alias` field.
6. Test the resulting SQL query syntax by pressing the **Check SQL Syntax** button on the toolbar. It should announce that the query is verified.
7. Now you can run the query to make sure it returns the values you are looking for. Press the Run Query (!) button to see the records in the result pane (see Figure 18.9).

Views to a savings

Views are a great way to save on time, complication, and overhead. Using views, you can create virtual tables that pull data from multiple tables. As far as your Web application is concerned, a view is just another table. The difference is that this table can share data with many tables.

Step 5

Step 5 is a good example of how you can use SQL to your advantage. Computed columns allow you to obtain information for a view that isn't specifically in another table's columns.

FIGURE 18.9

Using the QD window to build a SQL view.

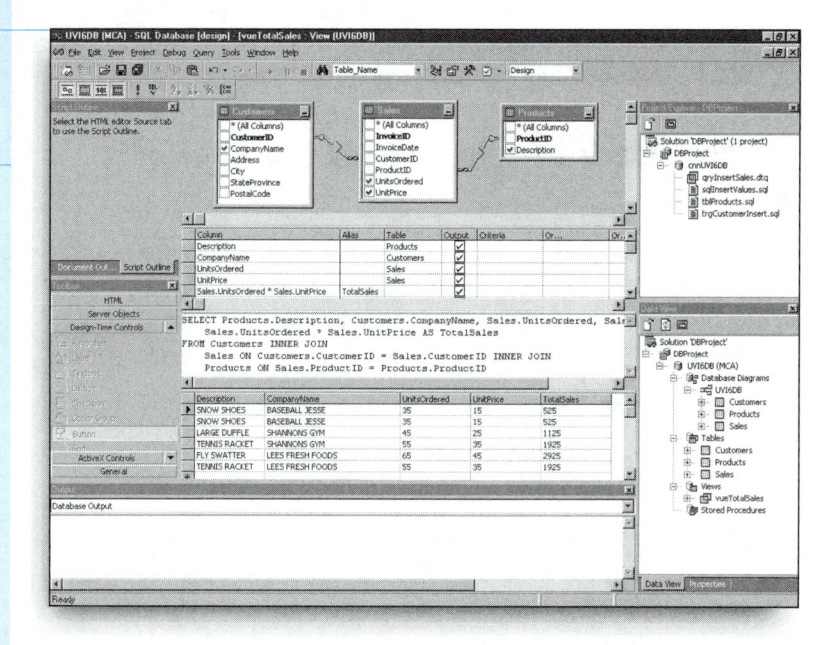

8. Save the View to the database by pressing **File**, **Save** from the menu bar.

9. Enter a name for the saved view. For this example, use `vueTotalSales` and press **OK**.

After you save the query, you'll see it appear in the Views section of the Data View window. You can now close the QD window completely. This saved view is available for others to use.

Using the View Script to Add the *ProductSales* View

You can also use a special View Script to build an SQL view definition for later execution. This is ideal for those who need to create views for the database but who don't have rights to execute scripts.

Creating a view with the View Script template

1. In the Project Explorer, right-click over the connection name (**UVI6DB**) and select **Add Item** from the context menu.

Adding New Views to an Existing Database

2. Select the **View Script** in the right pane of the dialog box.
3. Enter a name for the dialog box. For this example, enter `vueProductSales` as the name.
4. Press the **Open** button to open the template in the Visual InterDev 6 editor.
5. Replace the words `View_Name` with `vueProductSales` in the template. There are seven occurrences of the words `View_Name`.
6. Now enter the actual SQL view statements into the template. Listing 18.5 has the complete SQL code to enter. Note that you enter only lines 4–7. Visual InterDev 6 supplies the rest.
7. After entering the SQL code, close the view template and answer **YES** when asked to save it.

LISTING 18.5 Defining the *ProductSales* View

```
1  CREATE View vueProductSales
2  as
3
4  SELECT Products.Description, Sales.UnitsOrdered
5  FROM Sales INNER JOIN
6       Products ON Sales.ProductID = Products.ProductID
7  GROUP BY Sales.UnitsOrdered, Products.Description
8  GO
9
10 GRANT SELECT ON vueProductSales TO PUBLIC
11
12 GO
```

With the SQL view saved in your project, you can now actually add the view to your database by right-clicking over the view and selecting **Execute** from the context menu. You'll see some status messages appear in the Output window indicating the execution ran successfully.

After the view script is executed, you can see the view appear in the Data View window under the **Views** node. You might have to refresh the Data View window first.

Refreshing the Data View

Visual InterDev only periodically refreshes the Data View (or the Project Explorer, for that matter). If something has changed the structure on the server, you will usually need to refresh the view to see the changes.

That's how you add stored views to an SQL server database. The last item you'll work with in this chapter is adding a stored procedure.

Adding a Stored Procedure to an SQL Server Database

You can use Visual InterDev 6 to add special routines to SQL Server databases called *stored procedures*. Stored procedures—sometimes called *sprocs* (pronounced sprocks)—are short methods that run within SQL Server. They can have input parameters and output parameters and even perform looping and other common programming constructs. For this example, you build a simple sproc that accepts a data as input and returns a recordset containing all the sales for that day.

Stored procedures versus triggers

Which is the one to use? Triggers are used to carry out an action based on an event. For example, a user updates a record on your database, so you fire an action to update the last accessed column. Stored procedures are more of a programmatic extension to conventional database objects. They let you pass a set of information to themselves so that they can complete an action, and usually return a result. For example, a stored procedure could be used to take input from a user, modify several tables at once and manipulate data, and then return the results. You can also combine triggers and stored procedures. A trigger can call a stored procedure, and a stored procedure could be the event that launches a trigger's action.

You can use the QD window or a script template to create your sprocs. However, the QD window does not give you a visual drag-and-drop interface for building your procedure. Instead, it offers a simple text editor screen similar to the script template. For this reason, the more complete script template is probably a better way to create your stored procedures for SQL Server databases.

Creating a stored procedure with the script template

1. Right-click over the data connection (**UVI6DB**) in the Project Explorer.
2. Select **Add Item** from the context menu.
3. In the Add Item dialog box, select the **Stored Procedure** template in the right pane.
4. Enter a **Name** for the script. For this example, enter `cspDailySales` for the name.
5. Press **Open** to load the template in the Visual InterDev 6 editor.
6. Use find and replace to replace the words `Stored_Procedure_Name` with your desired name. For this example, use `cspDailySales`. There are seven occurrences of `Stored_Procedure_Name` in the template.

Adding a Stored Procedure to an SQL Server Database

7. Now enter the actual SQL stored procedure code. Listing 18.6 has all the code you need to enter. Note that you type only lines 3–8. The rest is supplied by Visual InterDev 6.

8. After you enter all the SQL text, close the editor and answer **YES** when asked to save the template.

LISTING 18.6 **Coding the SQL Stored Procedure**

```
1  CREATE Procedure cspDailySales
2
3      @pSalesDate datetime
4
5  AS
6      SELECT Sales.*
7      FROM Sales
8          WHERE InvoiceDate = @pSalesDate
9
10 GO
```

With the script completed, you're ready to execute the script to add it to the database. Right-click over the script in the Project Explorer window and select **Execute**. The results will appear in the Output window at the bottom of the page.

Now that the sproc is added to the database, you can use the Visual InterDev 6 Query Designer to run it and get a recordset in return.

Executing a Stored Procedure with Visual InterDev 6 Data Tools

To run an existing sproc in your database, right-click on it in the Data View window (under the **Stored Procedures** node), supply any requested input parameters, and then view the results in the Output window.

Running a stored procedure in Visual InterDev 6

1. Right-click on the desired stored procedure in the Data View window. For this example, select **cspDailySales**.

2. Select **Execute** from the context menu to run the sproc.

Debugging stored procedures

Because developing stored procedures can be an involved process, Visual InterDev provides facilities for debugging them. Unfortunately stored procedure debugging isn't on a line-by-line process (maybe in the next version of Visual InterDev). Refer to the Visual InterDev online documentation for information on using the debugging features. They do require components to be installed on your server to function.

FIGURE 18.10

Entering the input parameters for a sproc.

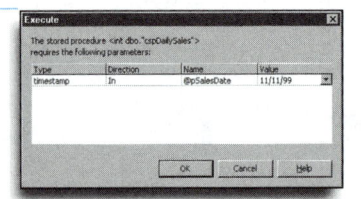

3. When the Execute dialog box appears, enter the requested input parameters. For this example, enter 11/11/99 (see Figure 18.10).

4. Press **OK** to run the procedure.
5. The results of the sproc appear in the Output window. If the query returns records, you see them listed in the window. Listing 18.7 shows a typical result set from the `cspDailySales` sproc.

LISTING 18.7 Typical Results of the *cspDailySales* Sproc

```
 1 Running dbo."cspDailySales" ( @pSalesDate = 11/11/99 ).
 2
 3 InvoiceID    InvoiceDate         CustomerID    ProductID
   ➥UnitsOrdered            UnitPrice
 4 INV03        11/11/99            C102          P02
   ➥45                      25
 5 INV04        11/11/99            C102          P03
   ➥55                      35
 6 INV05        11/11/99            C103          P04
   ➥65                      45
 7 INV06        11/11/99            C103          P03
   ➥55                      35
 8 (4 row(s) returned)
 9 No rows affected.
10 There are no more results
11 RETURN_VALUE = 0
12 Finished running dbo."cspDailySales".
```

You now know how to define database diagrams, new tables, table triggers, views, insert queries, and stored procedures using the Visual InterDev 6 Data Tools.

CHAPTER 19

Using ActiveX Database Objects (ADO)

Learn about ADO models and properties

Create ADODB for the Web and your pages

Connect databases to the Web

Work with parameter queries

The Basics of ActiveX Data Objects (ADO)

The Microsoft ActiveX Data Objects (ADO) are a set of programming objects that you use to build applications that can connect to remote databases and retrieve records for use in your Web project. For the basic needs of most Web applications (data entry forms, displays, and reports) you can use the Design-Time Controls (DTCs) along with Data Connection and Data Command objects. In fact, the DTCs actually use the ADO library to provide their database services.

However, if you need to do some special database work (performing update queries, mass insert or delete queries, and so on), you might want to code your Web pages manually using the ADO library. The advantage of ADO coding is that you are in complete control of all aspects of data connection and retrieval. The drawback of ADO coding is that you must provide all the code needed to complete the connection to the remote database; set the rules for collecting records; perform the actual recordset requests; and after modifying any records in the set, return the modified set back to the server for update.

The ADO library contains all the objects, methods, and properties you need to do all this work. However, in order to use ADO properly you must understand some of the more complex aspects of database service for remote clients over the Internet (or intranet). To do this, you should understand the ADO library model and several of the key properties that control how the ADO library connects to the database, how it decides where records will be sent, and how they will be returned.

The ActiveX Data Object Model

ActiveX Data Objects are supplied to your Web project through the component object model (COM) service interface. COM service defines a process for publishing objects and their methods and properties to other, external programs—such as your

Work ahead!

Working with ADO translates into more work, in comparison to design-time controls (DTCs). There are many advantages to using DTCs for your database development—speed and simplicity are the prime reasons. However, there comes a time when ADO is a better choice. Any time you are carrying out complex programmatic control of your database and information, ADO is likely the best way to go.

The Basics of ActiveX Data Objects (ADO)

Web project. The way in which COM objects are published is referred to as the *object model*. This model is an organized way to view the collection of objects in a COM component. The ActiveX Data Object model is very lean. It is designed to allow easy access to a set of records from the data source as quickly as possible. Because speed and simplicity are key objectives of ADO, the model is designed to enable you to create a recordset object without having to create and navigate numerous other intervening objects along the way.

If you're a programmer who has used other Microsoft database object libraries, such as Database Access Objects (DAO) or Remote Data Objects (RDO), you'll be surprised to find that the ADO model is quite a bit smaller than its older cousins. In fact, there are only three key objects in the model:

- The Connection object represents the actual database connection.
- The Command object is used to execute queries against the data connection.
- The Command object represents the set of records collected from the query issued via the Command object.

The Connection object has a collection child object called Errors to hold any error information associated with the connection. The Command object has a child object collection called Parameters to hold any replaceable parameters for queries. The Recordset object has a child collection object called Fields to hold information about each field in the recordset. Finally, the Connection, Command, Recordset, and Fields objects all have a Properties collection to hold detailed information about the object.

Figure 19.1 shows a simple version of the ADO model. A set of properties collections has been left out of the diagram for clarity. These extra collections add flexibility to the model, but are not of real importance for our discussion.

There are few frills to ADO development

There aren't really any frills to ADO development. It is still easier than manually coding database connections through a CGI or ISAPI program; however, it isn't "point, click, drag, and drop."

If you find ADO limiting

You always have the option to create an ISAPI or CGI program that communicates with your database through other means, rather than using ADO or design-time controls. Unfortunately, that is beyond the scope of this book.

FIGURE 19.1

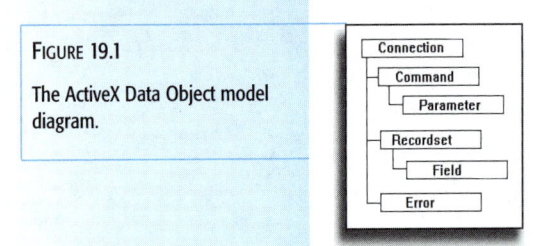

The ActiveX Data Object model diagram.

Special ADO Properties

The ADO model has several unique properties not encountered with other Microsoft database object models. These properties control how the dataset is generated, movement of the pointer within the set, and your access rights within the data connection. Seven unique properties of the ADO model are covered here:

- `ConnectionString`
- `CommandText`
- `CommandType`
- `CursorLocation`
- `CursorType`
- `LockType`
- `Mode`

In the following sections you learn what each of these properties is and how it is used when accessing data using the ADO model.

ConnectionString

The ADO model uses the `ConnectionString` property to indicate the OLE DB provider to use to connect to the data store, along with all the details needed to complete the data connection. A typical connection string has two parts:

`Provider=<provider name>;Data Source=<source details>`

For example, the following is a valid connection string for connecting to a Microsoft Access database:

`Provider=Microsoft.Jet.OLEDB.3.51;Data Source=C:\UVI\`
➥`Source\data\UVIDB.mdb`

Special ADO Properties | PART IV CHAPTER 19

Some data sources can have additional required or optional values as part of the <source details> portion of the connection string. The following is a valid connection string for an SQL Server database that uses additional values:

```
Provider=SQLOLEDB.1;User ID=sa;Initial Catalog=pubs;
➥Data Source=MCA
```

The exact format of the detail section of the connection string is governed by the provider.

CommandText

The CommandText property of the ADO model is the property that holds the actual data request query. The syntax of this data request depends on the provider you are using. For example, the following request is valid when using the OLE DB Jet 3.51 provider:

```
TRANSFORM SUM(Sales)
    SELECT Title FROM Booksales GROUP BY Title
PIVOT SalesRep
```

The following request will work with the SQL Server provider:

```
CALL spMyProc(35,15)
```

It is important to keep in mind that OLE DB providers do not need to use SQL syntax as their query language. You might need to consult the documentation that ships with your provider files in order to learn the query syntax required for that provider.

SEE ALSO

▶ *You also learn how to manipulate database connections and data commands through design-time controls on page 445.*

CommandType

You use the CommandType ADO property to tell ADO what type of query you are using to execute a data request. The default value is adCmdUnknown. In some cases you can execute data requests without setting the CommandType property. However, the ADO provider might not understand how to interpret the request or might execute the request more slowly if you do not specify a

---

Three ways to connect to databases

There are actually three ways to build valid database connection strings. You can use the OLEDB format shown here, or you can use what are called DSN-less connection strings or DSN-based ODBC connection strings.

The command text

The command text is where you get down to the nitty gritty programmatic manipulation of your data. You can use your scripts to modify the command text as your code requires.

`CommandType`. Table 19.1 shows the list of valid settings for the `CommandType` property.

Command type confusion

If you use a `CommandType` that isn't quite what you wanted, you'll get odd results. As with all database interaction, always make sure you're working with the right data types and command types.

TABLE 19.1 **Valid settings for the *CommandType* property**

Setting	Value	Description
`AdCmdText`	1	Evaluates `CommandText` as a textual definition of a command.
`AdCmdTable`	2	Evaluates `CommandText` as a table name in a generated SQL query returning all columns.
`AdCmdStoredProc`	4	Evaluates `CommandText` as a stored procedure.
`AdCmdUnknown`	8	Default. The type of command in the `CommandText` property is not known.
`AdCommandFile`	256	Evaluates `CommandText` as the filename of a persisted recordset.
`AdCmdTableDirect`	512	Evaluates `CommandText` as a table name whose columns are all returned.

CursorLocation

The ADO model enables you to request client-side or server-side cursor management for your recordset. In ADO a *cursor* is the collection of records that is returned to your program in response to a data request. You can use the ADO `CursorLocation` property to control where this collection of records is kept. Table 19.2 shows the valid settings for this property.

TABLE 19.2 **Valid settings for the *CursorLocation* property**

Setting	Value	Description
`AdUseClient`	3	Uses client-side cursors supplied by a local cursor library. Local cursor engines often will allow many features that driver-supplied cursors might not, so using this setting can provide an advantage with respect to features that will be enabled.
`AdUseServer`	2	Default. Uses data-provider or driver-supplied cursors. These cursors are sometimes very flexible and enable additional sensitivity to changes others make to the data source. However, some features of ADO might not be available with server-side cursors.

Special ADO Properties

Setting	Value	Description
AdUseClientBatch	3	This is the same as `AdUseClient` and is included for backward compatibility only. You should not use this value in your Visual InterDev 6 projects.
AdUseNone	1	No cursor services are used. This constant is obsolete and appears solely for the sake of backward compatibility. Do not use this in your Visual InterDev 6 projects.

Notice that even though there are four possible values for the ADO `CursorLocation` property, only the first two (`AdUseClient` and `AdUseServer`) are valid. The other two are provided only for backward compatibility with earlier versions of ADO and should not be used with your new Visual InterDev 6 projects.

CursorType

The ADO `CursorType` property is used to indicate the type of recordset that will be returned by the data provider. There are four valid settings for the `CursorType` property. These are shown in Table 19.3.

> **Cursor location**
>
> The cursor location determines your ADO connection's behaviors. For most Web applications, the default is fine.

TABLE 19.3   Valid settings for the *CursorType* property

Setting	Value	Description
AdOpenForwardOnly	0	This provides a forward-only cursor recordset. You can only scroll forward through records in the collection. This improves performance in situations in which you must make only a single pass through a recordset. This is the default.
AdOpenKeyset	1	This provides a Keyset cursor recordset. This recordset has a changing membership. Edits by other users are visible. Records that other users delete are inaccessible from your recordset. Records that other users add are not available.
AdOpenDynamic	2	Dynamic cursor. This recordset has a changing membership. All adds, edits, and deletes by other users are visible.
AdOpenStatic	3	This provides a Static cursor recordset. This is a static copy of a set of records that you can use to find data, move forward and back, and so on. Any adds, edits, or deletes by other users are not visible.

> **AdOpenDynamic costs**
>
> Using an `AdOpenDynamic` dynamic cursor type causes overhead. This involves a lot of work for your database and application. Use it only when it's required.

There are a couple of important things to keep in mind when choosing a `CursorType` for your recordset. First, if you are using a client-side cursor (`CursorLocation=adUseClient`), `adOpenStatic` is the only valid value for the `CursorType` property.

Another major issue when selecting a cursor type is knowing what the data provider supports. It is possible that the cursor type you request is not supported by your data provider. In this case, the data provider might return a recordset with a different cursor type. If you are selecting a cursor type and expecting a certain behavior (such as the capability to see changes), you should check the `CursorType` property after completing your data request to see what type of cursor was returned by the provider.

LockType

The ADO `LockType` property can be used to indicate how you want to manage locking during edit sessions with your recordset. Table 19.4 shows the four valid options for lock types.

TABLE 19.4 Valid settings for the *LockType* property

Setting	Value	Description
`AdLockReadOnly`	1	Default. Read-only. You cannot alter the data.
`AdLockPessimistic`	2	Pessimistic record locking. This usually means the provider will lock records at the data source immediately upon editing.
`AdLockOptimistic`	3	Optimistic record locking. The provider will lock records only when attempting to update the record.
`AdLockBatchOptimistic`	4	Optimistic batch locking. This means the provider will lock the entire batch when you attempt to use the `UpdateBatch` method on the recordset.

Your provider might not support the locking method you request. If this is the case, the provider will substitute another locking method instead. You can inspect the `LockType` property after the recordset is returned to see the actual locking method selected by the provider.

Unpredictable locking

If you choose a method for locking that your data provider does not support, your application could exhibit odd behaviors. Be sure to read up on what your data source provides before implementing locking.

Locking wisdom

Consider the amount of traffic you anticipate for your Web application when you choose a locking type. If you think you'll see a lot of data interaction, it is probably best to use `AdLockPessimistic`. However, if you expect few simultaneous accesses, move more toward the optimistic locking methods.

Special ADO Properties

If you are using a client-side cursor (`CursorLocation=adUseClient`), you cannot use pessimistic locking (`LockTyp=adLockPessimistic`).

Mode

You can use the `Mode` property to instruct the provider to limit access to the data store while you have an open recordset. Table 19.5 shows the valid settings for the ADO `Mode` property.

TABLE 19.5 **Valid settings for the ADO *Mode* property**

Setting	Value	Description
AdModeUnknown	0	Default. Indicates that the permissions have not yet been set or cannot be determined.
AdModeRead	1	Open the recordset with read-only permissions.
AdModeWrite	2	Open the recordset with write-only permissions.
AdModeReadWrite	3	Open the recordset with read/write permissions.
AdModeShareDenyRead	4	Prevent others from opening the connection with read permissions.
AdModeShareDenyWrite	8	Prevent others from opening the connection with write permissions.
AdModeShareExclusive	12	Prevent others from opening the connection.
AdModeShareDenyNone	16	Prevent others from opening the connection with any permissions.

If you need only a read-only recordset, you can increase the performance of your Visual InterDev 6 project by setting the `Mode` property to `adModeRead`.

Now that you have a good understanding of the various special properties used to build valid database connections with the ActiveX Data Objects, you're ready to create a Visual InterDev 6 project that does just that.

Using modes and lock types together

By combining locking types and methods you can enforce the integrity of your data source. Keep in mind, however, that you are impacting how other users access the database. Make sure that your Web application isn't speeding along only to have your user run into a brick wall because of locking or methods. Plan around your user's loads.

PART **IV**   Databases and the Web

CHAPTER **19**   **Using ActiveX Database Objects (ADO)**

Setting Up the ADODB Web Project

For the rest of this chapter, you create and execute ASP documents that use ADO coding to perform database operations. In order to make testing each ADO example easier, you can build a sample Visual InterDev 6 Web project and add some include files that can be linked to all your sample pages.

When you start your new Visual InterDev 6 project and add the two include files described here, you'll be ready to start building ASP documents to test the ActiveX Data Objects.

Building the ADODB Project

The first step is to build a new Visual InterDev 6 project to hold all the examples in this chapter. To do this, start Visual InterDev 6 and select **File**, **New Project** from the main menu.

Enter ADODB as the folder name for your source code. Select an available Web server to host the project and accept **ADODB** as the default Web name. You can skip applying a layout or theme to this project.

After you create the empty Web project, you're ready to add two include files to the project.

Using the ADOVBS.INC Include File

Using include files reduces the amount of coding needed for your project. One handy use of an include file is to store all the commonly used constants and variables for your Web project. The ActiveX Data Object library has several predefined constants that you'll use when you write your ADO scripts. To make it easy to remember and write your ADO code, you can add a reference to an include file that holds all the predefined values needed for the ADO library. Microsoft supplies just such a file: the ADOVBS.INC file. You can find a version of the ADOVBS.INC file at the Web site home page mentioned in Appendix B, "Online Resources," in the back of this book.

If you want to, you can create a new ADOVBS.INC file in your project and add the code from Listing 19.1 to the file. This includes all the values from the master ADOVBS.INC that you'll use in this chapter.

Comparing database access methods

While you're going through the examples in this chapter, compare it to how you interacted with a database in Chapter 16, "Accessing Web Databases," and Chapter 17, "Creating Data-Bound Web Forms." You can see two different schools of thought in Web design. These two approaches need not be polar opposites, however—the two approaches can be combined for more effective development.

Choosing your own project name

If you have your own project name you would prefer to use, or if you'd like to continue off of an existing project, feel free. Be sure to translate any instructions to your new project, however.

Setting Up the ADODB Web Project

PART **IV**
CHAPTER **19**

515

LISTING 19.1   **Selected Values from the ADOVBS.INC Master File**

```
1  <%
2  '---- CursorTypeEnum Values ----
3  Const adOpenForwardOnly = 0
4  Const adOpenKeyset = 1
5  Const adOpenDynamic = 2
6  Const adOpenStatic = 3
7
8  '---- LockTypeEnum Values ----
9  Const adLockReadOnly = 1
10 Const adLockPessimistic = 2
11 Const adLockOptimistic = 3
12 Const adLockBatchOptimistic = 4
13
14 '---- CursorLocationEnum Values ----
15 Const adUseServer = 2
16 Const adUseClient = 3
17
18 '---- DataTypeEnum Values ----
19 Const adEmpty = 0
20 Const adTinyInt = 16
21 Const adSmallInt = 2
22 Const adInteger = 3
23 Const adBigInt = 20
24 Const adUnsignedTinyInt = 17
25 Const adUnsignedSmallInt = 18
26 Const adUnsignedInt = 19
27 Const adUnsignedBigInt = 21
28 Const adSingle = 4
29 Const adDouble = 5
30 Const adCurrency = 6
31 Const adDecimal = 14
32 Const adNumeric = 131
33 Const adBoolean = 11
34 Const adError = 10
35 Const adUserDefined = 132
36 Const adVariant = 12
37 Const adIDispatch = 9
38 Const adIUnknown = 13
39 Const adGUID = 72
40 Const adDate = 7
41 Const adDBDate = 133
42 Const adDBTime = 134
```

continues...

PART IV Databases and the Web
CHAPTER 19 Using ActiveX Database Objects (ADO)

LISTING 19.1 **Continued**

```
43 Const adDBTimeStamp = 135
44 Const adBSTR = 8
45 Const adChar = 129
46 Const adVarChar = 200
47 Const adLongVarChar = 201
48 Const adWChar = 130
49 Const adVarWChar = 202
50 Const adLongVarWChar = 203
51 Const adBinary = 128
52 Const adVarBinary = 204
53 Const adLongVarBinary = 205
54
55 '---- AffectEnum Values ----
56 Const adAffectCurrent = 1
57 Const adAffectGroup = 2
58 Const adAffectAll = 3
59
60 '---- ParameterDirectionEnum Values ----
61 Const adParamUnknown = &H0000
62 Const adParamInput = &H0001
63 Const adParamOutput = &H0002
64 Const adParamInputOutput = &H0003
65 Const adParamReturnValue = &H0004
66
67 '---- CommandTypeEnum Values ----
68 Const adCmdUnknown = &H0008
69 Const adCmdText = &H0001
70 Const adCmdTable = &H0002
71 Const adCmdStoredProc = &H0004
72 %>
```

About this listing

Listing 19.1 demonstrates just how long and consuming ADO connections can be in code. This is why it is a good idea to reuse whatever you can through server-side includes. This way you don't need to add the same code to every page you work with.

Keep in mind that this is just a part of the master ADOVBS.INC document. If you plan to do extensive ADO coding, you should get the complete file for your Web projects.

SEE ALSO
➤ *You'll learn more about server-side includes on page 652*
➤ *Server-side includes are also used on page 738*

Creating the ADO Programming Objects in the ADOSTUFF.INC File

You can also use include files to hold common variables and objects for your Web project. In this example, you build a new document called ADOSTUFF.INC that will hold a set of predefined connection strings and a set of ADO programming objects that you'll use in your examples for this chapter.

Create a new document called ADOSTUFF.INC and add the connection strings in Listing 19.2 to the document.

LISTING 19.2 Adding Connection Strings to the ADOSTUFF.INC Document

```
1 <%
2 ' various valid connections
3 strJetDSNLess = "DRIVER={Microsoft Access Driver (*.mdb)}
   ➥;DBQ=c:\uvi\source\data\uvidb.mdb;"
4 strJetOLEDB = "Provider=Microsoft.Jet.OLEDB.3.51;Data
   ➥Source=C:\UVI\Source\data\UVIDB.mdb;"
5 strSQLDSNLess = "Driver={SQL Server};SERVER=mca;UID=sa;
   ➥PWD=;DATABASE=pubs"
6 strSQLOLEDB = "Provider=SQLOLEDB.1;User ID=sa;Initial
   ➥Catalog=pubs;Data Source=MCA"
7 %>
```

These four connection strings offer different ways to connect to a Microsoft Access (Jet) database and an SQL Server database. Be sure your Microsoft Access (Jet) strings are pointing to the correct location for the UVIDB.MDB database. This is a copy of the PUBS database from SQL Server.

Also be sure to update the SERVER and Data Source values in the SQL Server connection strings to point to a valid server in your network.

After adding the connection strings, you must add four lines of code that will create instances of ADO programming objects. Add the code from Listing 19.3 to the same ADOSTUFF.INC document.

Database locations

Keep in mind that these paths are the physical paths to the database on your Web server, not your workstation. Make sure that you've set up your paths exactly how your Web server will see it.

LISTING 19.3 Adding Code to Create ADO Programming Objects

```
1  <%
2  ' ADO objects for use
3  Set objConn = Server.CreateObject("ADODB.Connection")
4  Set objCmd = Server.CreateObject("ADODB.Command")
5  Set objParam = Server.CreateObject("ADODB.Parameter")
6  Set objRst = Server.CreateObject("ADODB.Recordset")
7  %>
```

You now have an include file that contains predefined instances of ADO programming objects and a set of valid connection strings. Next, you must add two custom methods to ADOSTUFF.INC to support your work in the other examples in this chapter.

Adding Support Methods to the ADOSTUFF.INC File

To make it easy to complete the ADO examples in this chapter, you must add two customer methods to the ADOSTUFF.INC document. The first method will display all the ADO programming object properties in a table in the browser. The second method will display the name and contents of the first field in a collected recordset in a table. After you have these two "helper" methods built, you'll be ready to start creating ADO sample documents.

First, add the code from Listing 19.4 to the ADOSTUFF.INC document. This code will display all the built-in properties of a given ADO programming object.

Building your own "helpers"

As you develop, you'll likely find several routines and methods you use on a regular basis. The best thing to do is create a library of your own scripts that can act as "helpers" in other applications and pages. Reuse this code through server-side includes to save yourself work on each page.

LISTING 19.4 Adding the *ShowProperties* Method to the ADOSTUFF.INC Document

```
1  <%
2  Sub ShowProperties(adoObject,Title)
3     '
4     ' display table of all properties
5     Response.Write "<H3>" & Title & "</H3><HR>"
6     Response.Write "<TABLE>"
7     For Each objProp in adoObject.Properties
8        Response.Write "<TR>"
```

Setting Up the ADODB Web Project

```
9         Response.Write "<TD>" & objProp.Name & "</TD>"
10        Response.Write "<TD>" & objProp.Value & "</TD>"
11        Response.Write "</TR>"
12    Next
13    Response.Write "</TABLE>"
14    '
15 End Sub
16 %>
```

Finally, you must add the ShowRecords method to the ADOSTUFF.INC document. This method will display the first field in the collected set of records. You'll use this several times in this chapter (see Listing 19.5).

LISTING 19.5 Adding the *ShowRecords* Method

```
1  <%
2  Sub ShowRecords(Records,Title)
3      '
4      ' show records in the collection
5      Response.Write "<H3>" & Title & "</H3><HR>"
6      Response.Write "<TABLE>"
7      Do While Records.EOF=False
8          Response.Write "<TR>"
9          Response.Write "<TD>" & Records.Fields(0).Name &
           ➥"</TD>"
10         Response.Write "<TD>" & Records.Fields(0).Value
           ➥ & "</TD>"
11         Response.Write "</TR>"
12         Records.MoveNext
13     Loop
14     Response.Write "<TABLE>"
15     '
16     Response.Write "Records in Table: " & cStr(Records.
       ➥RecordCount)
17     '
18 End Sub
19 %>
```

After adding these two methods to the ADOSTUFF.INC document, save it and close it completely. You'll not need to work with this file directly for the rest of the examples. However, you'll "include" it in every ADO example you code.

SEE ALSO

▶ In Chapter 15, "Using Server-Side Scripting with the Built-In ASP Objects," you learned how to use the Response object. Flip to page 403 if you want to re-read that section for this code.

Connecting to a Database with the *Connection* Object

The first step in using ADO programming is to connect to an existing database on the Web server. The ADO Connection object is used for this purpose. The Connection object has two key properties you must use and understand:

- The ConnectionString property contains the information that defines the connection.
- The CursorLocation property determines where recordsets will be stored (client or server).

The Connection string has two main parts: Provider Name and Data Source. This describes the most commonly used Connection string—the one that connects your Web project to a database using the OLEDB provider set for that target database.

However, you can also use connection strings that simply address the physical location of the database and use the OLEDB ODBC provider. This generic provider sometimes has different features and capabilities than other, custom-built OLEDB providers.

Listing 19.2 shows examples of OLEDB provider-based and generic OLEDB ODBC-based connections strings. You'll use these in your examples in this chapter.

Finally, you can also use the existing data environment designer (DED) data connection object data stored in the GLOBAL.ASA file to complete your data connections. The advantage of using

---

ADO connections get lengthy

Between the ConnectionString and the CursorLocation, your ADO connections can get pretty lengthy to code. Wherever possible, use shortcuts and predictable paths to minimize extra work.

Connecting to a Database with the *Connection* Object

DED-based connections is that any changes to the connection information is reflected in any ASP documents that use that connection definition.

If, for example, you used the DED to create a data connection called cnnSQLPubs, you can access the connection string for this data connection with the following bit of ASP code:

```
StrMyConnectString = Application("cnnSQLPubs_
➥ConnectionString")
```

Note that you use an application-level variable to represent the connection string. When you use the DED to add a data connection to your Web project, you are actually adding a set of application-level variables to your GLOBAL.ASA file. Listing 19.6 shows the portion of a GLOBAL.ASA file that contains the results from adding a cnnSQLPubs data connection to the project.

> **The GLOBAL.ASA file: a window to your Web application**
>
> The GLOBAL.ASA file stores all the session- and application-level information for your Web application. This includes database connections, variables, and behaviors.

LISTING 19.6 Data Connection Details Stored in the GLOBAL.ASA File

```
1  Sub Application_OnStart
2  '==Visual InterDev Generated - startspan==
3  '--Project Data Connection
4      Application("cnnSQLPubs_ConnectionString") =
       ➥"DSN=SysDSN_SQLPubs;User Id=sa;PASSWORD=;
       ➥Description=SQL Pubs Database;SERVER=mca;
       ➥UID=sa;APP=Microsoft
       ➥Development Environment;WSID=MCA;DATABASE=pubs"
5  Application("cnnSQLPubs_ConnectionTimeout") = 15
6  Application("cnnSQLPubs_CommandTimeout") = 30
7  Application("cnnSQLPubs_CursorLocation") = 3
8  Application("cnnSQLPubs_RuntimeUserName") = "sa"
9  Application("cnnSQLPubs_RuntimePassword") = ""
10 '-- Project Data Environment
11 Set DE = Server.CreateObject("DERuntime.DERuntime")
12 Application("DE") = DE.Load(Server.MapPath("Global.ASA")
   ➥, "_private/DataEnvironment/DataEnvironment.asa")
13 '==Visual InterDev Generated - endspan==
14 End Sub
15 </SCRIPT>
```

PART IV   Databases and the Web

CHAPTER 19   Using ActiveX Database Objects (ADO)

Application versus session code

Where you locate your code depends on when you want it to run. Application code is executed each time the application is started (typically by a user who is the first person to access your application since it was restarted). Session code refers to code that is executed for a single user's time using your application. Think of it in terms of scope: Application code affects everyone using your application, while session code affects only the session user.

The actual details of the data connection will vary from one Web project to the next. The important thing to understand is that you can use the data connections already in your Visual InterDev 6 Web project as the source for connection strings in your ADO-coded ASP documents.

SEE ALSO
➤ *The GLOBAL.ASA file is covered on page 641*

Using Server-Side ADO to Open a Data Connection

Now that you understand how the ADO `Connection` object is used, you're ready to build an ASP document that completes a database connection and then displays several properties of the ADO object. To do this, add a new page to your Web project called CONNECTION.ASP and enter the code shown in Listing 19.7 into the `<BODY>` of the document.

LISTING 19.7   **Using ADO to Create a *Connection* Object**

```
1  <BODY>
2
3  <!-- add some include files -->
4  <!--#include file="adovbs.inc"-->
5  <!--#include file="adostuff.inc"-->
6
7  <SCRIPT LANGUAGE=vbscript RUNAT=server>
8  '
9  ' create connection and show properties
10 '
11 objConn.ConnectionString=strSQLOLEDB
12 objConn.CursorLocation=adUseClient
13 objConn.Open
14 '
15 ShowProperties objConn,"Connection Properties"
16 '
17 </SCRIPT>
18
19 </BODY>
```

Connecting to a Database with the *Connection* Object

Be sure to add the references to the include files (lines 4 and 5) to the document. This will make sure all the code you built earlier will be included when the page is downloaded to the client.

There is really not much to this page. First, you set the connection string (line 11) using a predefined string from the ADOSTUFF.INC file. Next, you indicate that the data connection should place any collected records on the client machine (line 12). This is not important for this document, but it is a good habit to get into. Finally, you use the `Open` method (line 13) to actually open the database for use. Line 15 calls a method in the ADOSTUFF.INC document that displays a long list of properties and their values for this connection (see Figure 19.2).

> **Watch out for typos**
>
> Be particularly careful to avoid typos when you are working with ADO connections. Because you are working with the raw text accessing your database, the potential for mistakes is great. You could accidentally return data you don't need, or worse, alter data that you don't want to. Double-check your code when working with databases.

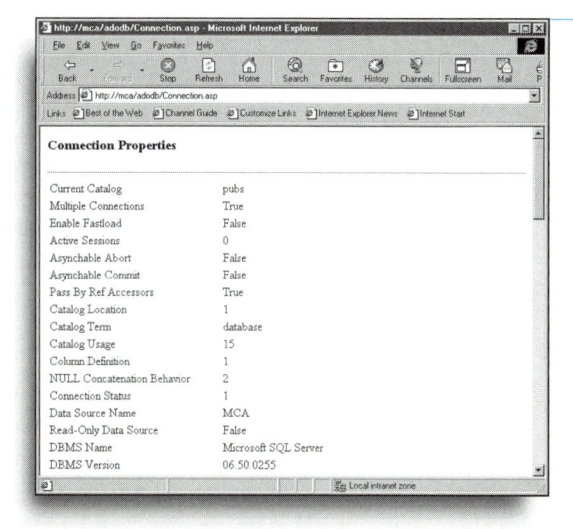

FIGURE 19.2
Viewing the properties of an ADO `Connection` object.

The actual properties listed in the browser and their values can be different depending on the connection type and the target database. The key thing to remember is that you use three simple steps to create and use valid ADO `Connection` objects:

- Set the `ConnectionString`
- Set the `CursorLocation`
- Use the `Open` method

Retrieving Records with the *Recordset* Object

Although the ADO `Connection` object is used to open a database connection within your Web project, it still does not actually collect records and place them in a page for you. In order to do that, you must use another ADO object: the `Recordset` object. The `Recordset` object will hold all the records you request from the database.

There are two basic ways you can use the ADO `Recordset` object to collect records from the server:

- The standalone recordset uses only the ADO `Recordset` object to collect records.
- The connected recordset uses an ADO `Connection` object (and possibly an ADO `Command` object) to collect records.

The first method of creating a valid recordset enables you to populate a recordset without using any other ADO objects. This is a quick way to create a data collection without the need for other ADO objects. This is an advantage if you don't need any advanced features of the ADO object model (that is, using parameter queries and so on).

The second method of creating the ADO `Recordset` object uses intervening objects such as the `Connection` and `Command` object. The advantage of doing this is you can share `Connection` and `Command` objects with several ADO recordsets. You can also use the `Command` object to inspect and update parameters for SQL stored procedures or Microsoft Access QueryDef objects.

Using Text Recordsets

It's easy to build a standalone ADO recordset. All you must do is prepare a valid `Connection` string and SQL `SELECT` statement. Then use these two strings as parameters with the `Recordset`

ADO and DTC

Behind the scenes, design-time controls are actually using ADO to interact with the database. DTCs, however, act as your "front end" to the ADO connection and recordset objects. The same concepts apply, however. In fact, you can alter the properties of most DTCs to behave just as if you were coding the ADO connection properties yourself.

What is a QueryDef?

A QueryDef (or `CdaoQueryDef`) represents a query definition typically saved in one database. Loosely put, it is an object that contains the SQL statement that made up the query and its properties. This allows the query to be reused. QueryDefs are saved in a collection for reuse.

Retrieving Records with the *Recordset* Object

Open method. To see how this works, create a new ASP document in your Web project called RECORDSETTEXT.ASP and add the code from Listing 19.8 to the `<BODY>` of the document.

LISTING 19.8 Testing a Standalone ADO *Recordset* Object

```
1  <BODY>
2  <!-- add includes -->
3  <!--#include file="adovbs.inc"-->
4  <!--#include file="adostuff.inc"-->
5
6  <SCRIPT LANGUAGE=vbscript RUNAT=Server>
7  '
8  ' create a text-based recordset
9  '
10 strSQL = "SELECT title, pub_name FROM titles, publishers
   ➥ WHERE titles.pub_id=publishers.pub_id"
11 '
12 objRst.open strSQL,strSQLOLEDB,adOpenStatic,
   ➥adLockOptimistic
13 '
14 showRecords objRst,"Sample Recordset"
15 '
16 </SCRIPT>
17
18 </BODY>
```

QueryDef contents

A QueryDef can be any kind of query: a **SELECT**, **UPDATE**, **INSERT**, **INSER VALUES**, or **DELETE** query. Think of a QueryDef as your bookmark to a query, while the QueryDef collection is your card catalog.

As you can see from Listing 19.8, the only important line of code you need to build a valid standalone ADO recordset is the one in line 12. Notice that two additional parameters (`asOpenStatic` and `adLockOptimistic`) were used to establish the cursor type and lock type of the dataset. The current settings ensure that the dataset can be updated (`adOpenStatic`) and safely accessed by more than one person at a time (`adLockOptimistic`).

When you run this example in your browser, you see a set of recordsets appear in a table showing the contents of the first column of the resulting dataset (see Figure 19.3).

FIGURE 19.3

The results of a standalone ADO recordset.

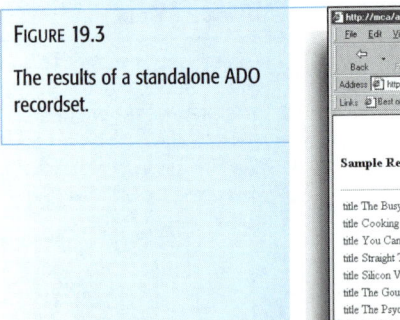

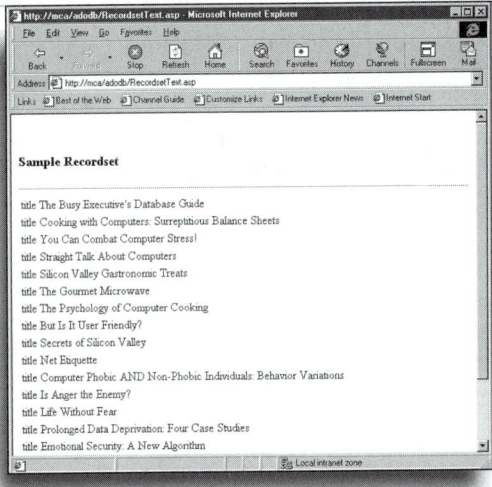

Using a Table Command Type

You can also use the more traditional method of creating a valid ADO `Recordset` object. This uses the existing ADO `Connection` object and, possibly, the ADO `Command` object to provide the connection information and the record collection rules. The advantage of using this method is that you can create several ADO `Recordset` objects from the same `Connection` or `Command` objects. This speeds execution in many cases.

In addition to using the `Connection` and `Command` objects, you can also access existing tables, views, or stored queries in the database instead of having to build SQL statements each time you need some records. This is done using the `CommandType` property of the `Command` object. You'll learn more about the `Command` object in the next section. For now, remember that you can directly access tables to build ADO recordsets.

Listing 19.9 shows you how you can use the `Connection` and `Command` objects to provide all the information needed to populate an ADO `Recordset` object. Create a new document in your Web called RECORDSETTABLE.ASP and add the code from Listing 19.9 to the `<BODY>` of the document.

ADO power

The capability to directly access the database structures, and not just recordsets, makes ADO very appealing to power developers.

Retrieving Records with the *Recordset* Object

LISTING 19.9 **Testing the ADO Recordset from *Connection* and *Command* Objects**

```
1  <BODY>
2
3  <!-- add includes -->
4  <!--#include file="adovbs.inc"-->
5  <!--#include file="adostuff.inc"-->
6
7  <SCRIPT LANGUAGE=vbscript RUNAT=Server>
8  '
9  ' open a table and view recordsets
10 '
11 objConn.ConnectionString = strSQLOLEDB
12 objConn.CursorLocation = adUseServer
13 objConn.Open
14 '
15 objCmd.ActiveConnection = objConn
16 objCmd.CommandType = adCmdTable
17 objCmd.CommandText="Authors"
18 '
19 Set objRst = objCmd.Execute
20 '
21 ShowRecords objRst,"Authors Table"
22 '
23 </SCRIPT>
24
25 </BODY>
```

Notice that the code to create the `Connection` object is identical to the code you used in Listing 19.7 (lines 11–13). The code to create a valid `Command` object (lines 15–17) will be covered in more detail in the next section. All you're doing there is passing the connection information to the `Command` object (line 15) and setting the object's `CommandText` property to access the Authors table (lines 16 and 17). Finally, the recordset is created by telling the `Command` object to execute the contents of the `CommandText` property (line 21) and store the resulting dataset in the ADO recordset.

When you run this document in your Web project, you see a set of records appear in a table in your browser (see Figure 19.4).

Document your code

There are several good habits to get into when working with databases. To begin, always clearly document your code when working with a database. This makes maintainability easier. This is particularly important if your database structure is not clear or easy to understand at first glance.

FIGURE 19.4

The results of a traditional `Recordset` object.

Use clear variable names

Another good habit to get into when working with databases is to use clear and easily understood variable names for objects and collections. When you are working with many different objects and queries, it is best to keep your code understandable and the intent clear.

Close your connections

Always close your connections. Don't leave your database connections hanging when you're finished with them. Close them promptly after your last involvement with them is complete. Parallel to this is as soon as you open a connection, use it. Keep the code that interacts with a connection and the actual connection management code close together. This makes the code more maintainable and easier to debug.

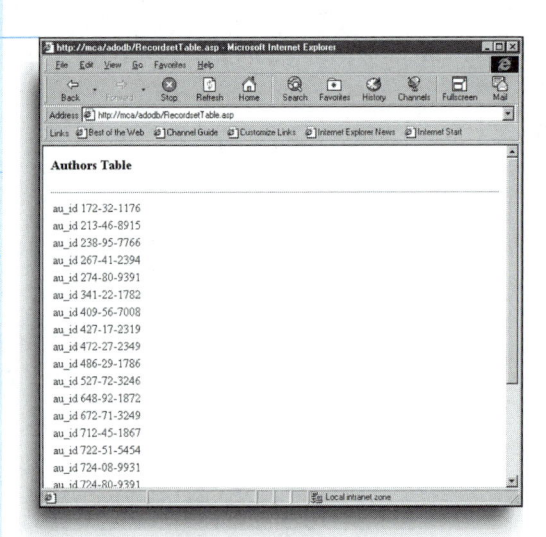

Setting Execution Rules with the *Command* Object

You can use ADO `Command` objects to supply information for creating simple record collections (as in Listing 19.9). However, the real power of the ADO `Command` object is to execute advanced SQL statements and run SQL stored procedures. It can also run Microsoft Access QueryDefs that require input parameters or supply output parameters instead of typical recordsets.

In this section, you learn how to use the ADO `Command` object to execute the advanced SQL statements UPDATE, DELETE, and INSERT. There are times when you'll want to use these types of queries in your Web projects instead of requiring users to manually update data or remove or add individual records in tables.

Creating *UPDATE* Queries with the *Command* Object

In the first command execution example you create an SQL statement that will automatically update all the store discount values by increasing them 10 percent (it's been a good year!). To do this, you first open a valid ADO `Connection` object, then fill a `Command` object with the proper SQL statement to complete the

Setting Execution Rules with the *Command* Object

update operation, and execute the command. Because you won't be downloading any records for viewing, you do not need an ADO `Recordset` object for this task.

Create a new ASP document in your project called COM-MANDUPDATE.ASP and enter the code from Listing 19.10 into the `<BODY>` section of the document.

Have an escape plan if something goes wrong

When you are working with important data, it is important to have an escape plan in case something goes wrong. Although it is outside the scope of this book, Microsoft Transaction Server can act as your safety office in database interactions. Using MTS, you can ensure that an action completes in its entirety before the data is modified. This prevents accidental modification of some data and not the rest when something breaks or does not work quite right.

LISTING 19.10 Executing an *UPDATE* Query with an ADO *Command* Object

```
1  <BODY>
2
3  <!-- add includes -->
4  <!--#include file="adovbs.inc"-->
5  <!--#include file="adostuff.inc"-->
6
7  <SCRIPT LANGUAGE=vbscript RUNAT=Server>
8  '
9  ' open connection and execute UPDATE Query
10 '
11 strSQL="UPDATE discounts SET discount = discount * 1.10"
12 '
13 Response.Write "<H3>Command Object SQL Update Query</H3>
   ➥<HR>"
14 Response.Write "<P>Executing the following SQL
   ➥Statements:</P>"
15 Response.Write "<P><code>" & strSQL & "</code><P>"
16 '
17 ' open connection
18 objConn.ConnectionString=strSQLOLEDB
19 objConn.CursorLocation=adUseClient
20 objConn.Open
21 '
22 Response.Write "Connection Open.<BR>"
23 '
24 ' execute UPDATE command
25 objCmd.ActiveConnection=objConn
26 objCmd.CommandType=adCmdText
27 objCmd.CommandText=strSQL
28 objCmd.Execute
29 '
30 Response.Write "SQL UPDATE Completed.<BR>"
```

continues...

LISTING 19.10 Continued

```
31 '
32 </SCRIPT>
33
34 </BODY>
```

Most of the code in Listing 19.10 should be familiar by now. Many lines also deal with sending text to the browser instead of completing the database operation. Lines 18–20 create the valid Connection object. The real work is accomplished in lines 25–28. This is where the UPDATE query (from line 11) is added to the Command object and then executed (line 28). Note that you never see an ADO Recordset object in this script. It is not necessary to use an ADO Recordset object when you are executing an SQL query that does not return records.

Creating *INSERT* and *DELETE* Queries with the *Command* Object

You can also use the ADO Command object to delete and insert records into existing tables—all without ever opening the table in an ADO recordset. This is done the same way the UPDATE example was accomplished (see Listing 19.10)—by loading the ADO Command object with SQL statements and executing them one at a time.

Add a new page to your Web called COMMANDINSERT.ASP and enter the code from Listing 19.11 to the <BODY> of the new document.

LISTING 19.11 Using the ADO *Command* Object to Execute *DELETE* and *INSERT* Queries

```
1 <BODY>
2
3 <!-- add includes -->
4 <!--#include file="adovbs.inc"-->
5 <!--#include file="adostuff.inc"-->
6
7 <SCRIPT LANGUAGE=vbscript RUNAT=Server>
```

> **Keep similar things together**
>
> Try to order your database involvement. It's not always possible, but try to keep queries together, updates together, and so on. Sometimes this is impractical, but it helps you keep track of the flow of your database connection more reliably.

> **Saving on the recordset**
>
> In not using a Recordset object in Listing 19.10, you're reducing overhead on your application. Always be conscious of overhead that could impact your database, your Web application, or both.

Setting Execution Rules with the *Command* Object

```
 8  '
 9  ' open connection and execute INSERT Query
10  '
11  strSQLInsert="INSERT INTO stores "
12  strSQLInsert=strSQLInsert & "(stor_id, stor_name,
    ➥stor_address, city, state, zip) "
13  strSQLInsert=strSQLInsert & "VALUES "
14  strSQLInsert=strSQLInsert & "('9876', 'Byte City', '123
    ➥Chip Street', 'Silcon Valley', 'CA', '12345')"
15  '
16  strSQLDelete="DELETE FROM stores WHERE stor_id='9876'"
17  '
18  Response.Write "<H3>Command Object SQL Statement
    ➥Execution</H3><HR>"
19  '
20  Response.Write "<P>Executing the following SQL
    ➥Statements:</P>"
21  Response.Write "<P><code>" & strSQLDelete & "<P>" &
    ➥strSQLInsert & "</code><P>"
22  '
23  objConn.ConnectionString=strSQLOLEDB
24  objConn.CursorLocation=adUseClient
25  objConn.Open
26  Response.Write "Connection Open.<BR>"
27  '
28  objCmd.ActiveConnection=objConn
29  objCmd.CommandType=adCmdText
30  '
31  ' delete rec if it exists
32  objCmd.CommandText=strSQLDelete
33  objCmd.Execute
34  Response.Write "Deleted existing record.<BR>"
35  '
36  ' insert replacement record
37  objCmd.CommandText=strSQLInsert
38  objCmd.Execute
39  Response.Write "Inserted new record.<BR>"
40
41  </SCRIPT>
42
43  </BODY>
```

Be careful entering code lines for this listing

Be particularly careful entering the code on lines 16–18. This listing is a good example of how much you can interact with a database with raw SQL queries. The potential for mistakes is large. However, this is why we chose to use a server-side include file to manage the database connection information rather than typing it in each time.

Parameter queries

Think of parameter queries as methods for your database code. They always require a parameter and return a result.

As in Listing 19.10, much of the code in Listing 19.11 deals with sending text to the browser and initializing the SQL statement strings. The `Connection` object is created in lines 23–25 and the `Command` object is established in lines 28 and 29. The `Delete` statement is loaded and executed in lines 32 and 33, and the `Insert` statement occurs in lines 37 and 38.

You can create ASP documents that insert and delete as many records as you want. After the connection is open and the `Command` object is prepared, you can continue to feed valid SQL statements into the system as needed.

Running Parameter Queries with the *Parameter* Object

The last type of ADO operation you learn in this chapter is executing parameter queries. A parameter query is a special type of query that has either input parameters or output parameters or both. These parameters are needed to complete the query, but are undetermined at the time the query is first created.

Here is an example of a parameter query:

`SELECT * FROM Authors WHERE au_id = ?`

The ? is the parameter. When you fill an ADO `Command` object with the SQL statements shown above, the ADO `Command` object will "know" that an additional bit of information (in this case the author ID value) is needed to complete the query statement.

You can supply the missing value in three ways:

- Pass the parameter in the `Execute` method of the `Command` object.
- Fill the `Parameters` collection array of the `Command` object.
- Append a complete `Parameter` object to the `Command` object.

In the first method, you just need to include the missing value as an added parameter in the `Execute` method of the `Command` object:

`Set objRst = objCmd.Execute(adAffectAll,"172-32-1176")`

Running Parameter Queries with the *Parameter* Object

The value "172-32-1176" is the missing value that will be used by the Command object to complete the SQL query.

In the second method, you use the existing Parameters collection of the Command object to hold the missing value:

```
objCmd.Parameters(0).Value = "172-32-1176"
objCmd.Parameters("au_id").Value = "172-32-1176"
```

You can see from the code that using either the parameter number or name is valid. The advantage of this method is that you can inspect the list of parameters in the query before you fill in the details.

Finally, the most involved method for supplying parameter values is to use the ADO Parameter object to build a complete parameter object and then append this completed object to the Command object:

```
objParam.Name = "percentage"
objParam.Type = adInteger
objParam.Direction = adParamInput
objParam.Value = 50
objCmd.Parameters.Append objParam
```

The advantage of this last method is that you have greater control of the details of the parameter properties.

Executing a Text Parameter Query Statement

A very common type of parameter query is a simple SQL SELECT statement that that has one or more replaceable parameters represented as a ?. These queries are easy to build and easy to execute, too. You create the query in advance (that is, in an ASP variable in the document) and then allow users to supply the missing value at runtime.

To test this, create a new ASP document in your Web project called PARAMETERTEXT.ASP and enter the code from Listing 19.12 in the <BODY> section of the document.

Be careful with parameters

As with any data type, be careful what kind of information you are passing a parameter query. Make sure you are indeed handing it the kind of information it needs to complete its action.

Using ActiveX Database Objects (ADO)

LISTING 19.12 **Executing a Text Parameter Query**

```
1  <BODY>
2
3  <!-- include some files -->
4  <!--#include file="adovbs.inc"-->
5  <!--#include file="adostuff.inc"-->
6
7  <SCRIPT LANGUAGE=vbscript RUNAT=Server>
8  '
9  ' execute text-based parameter query
10 '
11 strSQL="SELECT * FROM Authors WHERE au_id = ?"
12 '
13 objConn.ConnectionString = strSQLOLEDB
14 objConn.CursorLocation = adUseClient
15 objConn.Open
16 '
17 objCmd.ActiveConnection = objConn
18 objCmd.CommandType = adCmdText
19 objCmd.CommandText = strSQL
20 '
21 ' execute command w/ parameter
22 Set objRst = objCmd.Execute(adAffectAll,"172-32-1176")
23 '
24 showRecords objRst, strSQL
25 '
26 </SCRIPT>
27
28 </BODY>
```

Use constants

Most programmers are familiar with constants. Constants make database development easier as well, allowing you to update a constant's value in one location rather than a variable or parameter value throughout your code. Constants are particularly useful when dealing with parameter queries.

In Listing 19.12, you'll find that lines 13–19 look very familiar. The important parts of this code are on lines 11 and 22. In line 11, the parameter query is built (notice the use of the ?). In line 22, the Execute method is used along with two additional values. The first value (adAffectAll) is optional, but using it is a good idea. The second value is the missing string that will replace the ? in the SQL statement.

The results of running this query are shown in Figure 19.5.

Running Parameter Queries with the *Parameter* Object

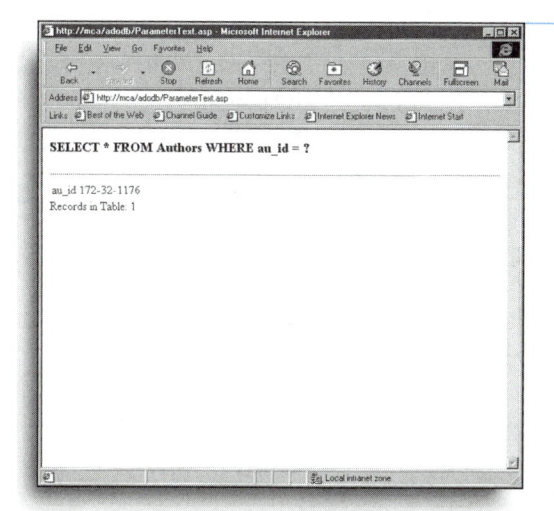

FIGURE 19.5
Viewing the results of a text parameter query.

Executing a Microsoft Access Parameter QueryDef

You can also use ADO to execute parameter queries that are stored in a Microsoft Access database. These special types of queries are called *QueryDefs* in Microsoft Access language. QueryDefs contain a declaration of parameters followed by the SQL statement that uses the parameters. Listing 19.13 shows a parameter QueryDef that appears in the UVIDB.MDB database used in this (and other) chapters.

LISTING 19.13 A Sample Parameter QueryDef in Microsoft Access

```
1  PARAMETERS pRoyalty Long;
2  SELECT *
3      FROM roysched
4          WHERE Royalty >= pRoyalty;
```

Notice that the first line in the QueryDef declares a single parameter of type LONG called pRoyalty. This is an input parameter that will be supplied when you run the ADO command. In this example, you use the Parameters collection of the ADO Command object to supply the missing parameter for the QueryDef.

Add a new page to your Web project called PARAMETER-SQD.ASP and enter the code form Listing 19.14 into the `<BODY>` section of the document.

LISTING 19.14 Using the *Parameters* Collection of the *Command* Object

```
1  <BODY>
2
3  <!-- add includes -->
4  <!--#include file="adovbs.inc"-->
5  <!--#include file="adostuff.inc"-->
6
7  <SCRIPT LANGUAGE=vbscript RUNAT=Server>
8  '
9  ' execute MS Access Parameterized QueryDef
10 '
11 objConn.ConnectionString = strJetDSNLess ' not OLEDB!
12 objConn.Open
13 '
14 objCmd.ActiveConnection = objConn
15 objCmd.CommandType = adCmdStoredProc
16 objCmd.CommandText = "byRoyalty"
17 '
18 ' update parameter collection
19 objCmd.Parameters.Refresh
20 objCmd.Parameters("pRoyalty").Value = 20
21 '
22 objRst.Open objCmd,,adOpenStatic
23 '
24 showRecords objRst,"MS Access QueryDef pRoyalty >= 20"
25 '
26 </SCRIPT>
27
28 </BODY>
```

There are a few important points to cover in Listing 19.14. First, you should notice that the ConnectionString property of the objConn Connection object uses an alternative method of defining the connection (line 11). Instead of using the default OLEDB connection, the DSN-less version is used. This uses the default OLEDB ODBC provider instead of the Jet OLEDB provider.

Running Parameter Queries with the *Parameter* Object

At the time this book was released, the Jet OLEDB provider was not handling parameter QueryDefs properly.

Next, notice the `CommandType` property is set to `adCmdStoredProc` (line 15). This will tell the `Command` object that it is executing a Microsoft Access QueryDef instead of a regular SQL `SELECT` statement. You also see how the `Parameters` collection is first refreshed and then the declared parameter value is set to 20 (lines 19 and 20). This is how you can use the `Parameters` collection to pass values to the query.

Finally, notice that line 22 looks a bit different from previous examples. This is an alternative method for using the information in the ADO `Command` object to fill the ADO recordset.

When you run this page, you'll see a list of book title IDs in your browser (see Figure 19.6).

SEE ALSO

➤ *Interacting with databases and views is discussed on page 498*

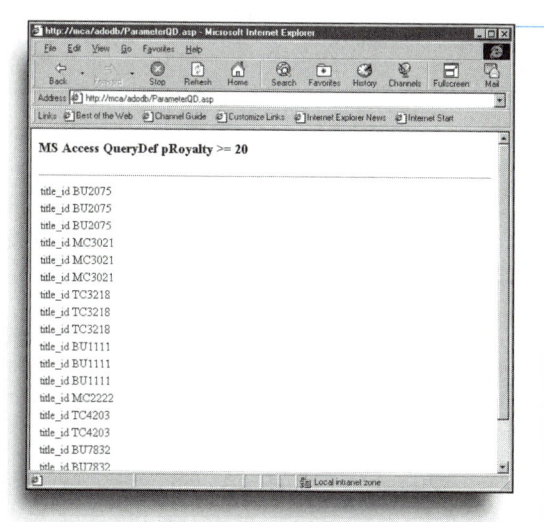

> **Use views**
>
> Use views. Database views let you have more control over the data you are pulling from tables. This saves you from managing many connections to different tables. Centralize all the similar information you need in one query from a single view.

FIGURE 19.6
Results of using the `Parameters` collection of the `Command` object.

Executing a Microsoft SQL Server Parameter Stored Procedure

You can also use ADO objects to execute a Microsoft SQL Server stored procedure, including one that requires input parameters. SQL Server stored procedures (sometimes called *sprocs*) are very similar to Microsoft Access QueryDefs. However, sprocs can do quite a bit more than execute simple SELECT statements. In fact, a single sproc can create new accept input parameters, create new tables, add and delete records, and even perform backup and restore operations.

In this example, you use a sproc that already exists in the PUBS database that ships with Microsoft SQL Server 6.5: the byRoyalty sproc. Listing 19.15 shows the source code for this stored procedure. Compare this to Listing 19.13.

LISTING 19.15 Viewing a Microsoft SQL Server Stored Procedure

```
1 CREATE PROCEDURE byroyalty
2     @percentage int
3 AS
4     select au_id
5        from titleauthor
6           where titleauthor.royaltyper = @percentage
```

You can see that an SQL Server stored procedure looks very much like a QueryDef in Microsoft Access.

In the final ADO coding example for this chapter, you execute the byRoyalty sproc using the ADO `Parameter` object. You build the `Parameter` object and then append it to the `Command` object before execution.

Add one more ASP document to your Web project called PARAMETERSSP.ASP and copy the code from Listing 19.16 into the `<BODY>` of the document.

LISTING 19.16 Using the *Parameters* Object with the *Command* Object

```
1 <BODY>
2
3 <!-- include stuff -->
```

Running Parameter Queries with the *Parameter* Object

```
 4 <!--#include file="adovbs.inc"-->
 5 <!--#include file="adostuff.inc"-->
 6
 7 <SCRIPT LANGUAGE=vbscript RUNAT=Server>
 8 '
 9 ' execute SQL Server stored procedure
10 '
11 objConn.ConnectionString = strSQLOLEDB
12 objConn.CursorLocation = adUseClient
13 objConn.Open
14 '
15 objCmd.ActiveConnection = objConn
16 objCmd.CommandType = adCmdStoredProc
17 objCmd.CommandText = "byRoyalty"
18 '
19 ' build parameter object
20 objParam.Name = "percentage"
21 objParam.Type = adInteger
22 objParam.Direction = adParamInput
23 objParam.Value = 50
24 objCmd.Parameters.Append objParam
25 '
26 Set objRst = objCmd.Execute
27 '
28 showRecords objRst,"ByRoyalty SP Percentage=50"
29 '
30 </SCRIPT>
31
32 </BODY>
```

The only new code in this example is the code in lines 20–24. This is the code that uses the ADO `Parameter` object to set the `Name`, `Type`, `Direction`, and `Value` properties before adding the new `Parameter` object to the `Command` object's `Parameters` collection.

When you execute this ASP document, you see a list of author ID codes (see Figure 19.7).

SEE ALSO
➤ *Stored procedures are discussed on page 502*

PART **IV**   Databases and the Web

540

CHAPTER **19**   **Using ActiveX Database Objects (ADO)**

FIGURE 19.7

Viewing results of executing a Microsoft SQL Server stored procedure.

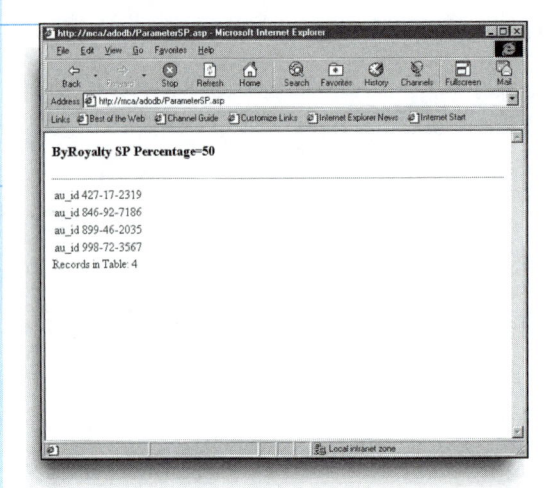

PART V

Using ActiveX Technologies

20	Using Advanced Design-Time Controls 543
21	Adding Reports and Graphs to Your Web Applications 569
22	Adding Active Content to Your Web Application 597
23	Adding Active Documents to Your Web Projects 617

CHAPTER 20

Using Advanced Design-Time Controls

Learn about design-time controls

Bind DTCs to communicate with data sources

Use DTCs to enhance your pages

Introducing Design-Time Controls (DTCs)

With the power that Visual InterDev and Internet Information Server give you, you can create dynamic and intricate Web sites. Of course, the one caveat is that this can require a great deal of effort on your part. In this chapter, you learn how Visual InterDev's design-time controls (DTCs) can simplify your development. DTCs are very much at the heart of Visual InterDev's "rapid application development" approach to Web application engineering. This chapter provides you with the information you need to understand DTCs and use them for your benefit.

Design-Time Controls Versus Other Components

As a Web developer, you're likely familiar with different component types, such as ActiveX controls. DTCs are similar in many respects to these other types of components, making it easier for you to learn how to use them. DTCs are objects that have been designed to encapsulate functionality that can be added to your Web page with a visual interface. Much like ActiveX controls, they possess properties, methods, and (sometimes) events. Where DTCs differ is in their purpose.

Unlike ActiveX controls that are used to extend a Web page, DTCs are used to simplify the development of dynamic Web applications. DTCs represent blocks of scripting code, known as *runtime text*. When you manipulate the properties and position of a DTC in your Web page, you are actually modifying the script behind the DTC. This is analogous to working in Visual Basic, where you manipulate a control or a form to engineer the code behind the scenes.

Why use them? What's the big deal? Consider this: In Chapters 17, "Creating Data-Bound Web Forms," and 18, "Creating Databases for the Web," you learned how to use Visual InterDev to create database interaction via a Web interface. Each of the interactions with the database required scripting code to carry out individual actions. DTCs accomplish the same task; however, they require considerably less code because most of the code is written for you as you modify the DTC properties with the graphical interface. Figure 20.1 demonstrates the simplicity of customizing DTCs.

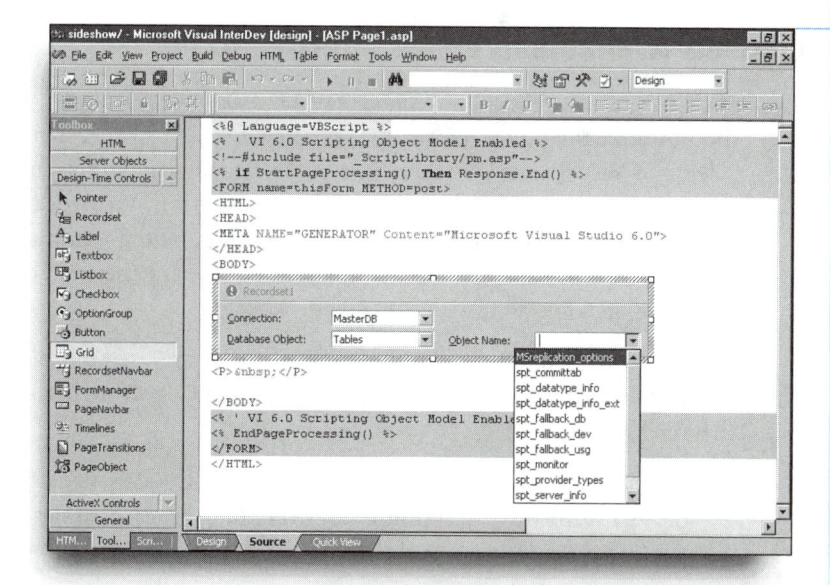

FIGURE 20.1
Design-time controls let you easily modify properties and attributes for the runtime text.

These controls also resemble wizards or builders; you set a series of options, and they generate the appropriate code. DTCs differ from wizards and other similar tools in that they stick around. When using a wizard, you get one chance to make your choices; and if you decide later to change those choices, you generally must start over or attempt to make the change manually. DTCs enable you to make changes to their properties at any time, and the changes directly modify the generated code.

SEE ALSO
➤ You also used DTCs on page 451

The Advantage of Design-Time Controls

The key advantage to using DTCs over ActiveX controls or Java applets is their platform independence. Although an ActiveX component or Java applet might offer similar functionality, DTCs exist only at design time. During runtime (when a user accesses your Web page), they are replaced with the customized runtime code behind the control. This makes the control platform independent for the client—regardless of what browser the user opens your page in.

DTC platform independence

A design-time control is platform independent but the script it generates might not be. No restriction is placed on that generated text. It can use any controls or technologies the creator of the DTC wants to give it, such as Dynamic HTML, and become dependent on a specific browser as a client.

Controls Available in Visual InterDev 6

DTCs were introduced in Visual InterDev 1.0; however, they did not offer the potent power that the new DTCs provide. This release of Visual InterDev represents a fundamental evolution in terms of DTCs. In addition to greatly improving how you work with them, more of them are also available. Many of these new controls are also capable of generating either client- or server-side code, making them two controls in one.

Visual InterDev 6's DTCs can be grouped together based on the functions they perform. The main groups of DTCs provided in this release are

- Form controls—The first and largest group, these controls deal with the display and input of data. This group includes familiar controls such as the ListBox, CheckBox, TextBox, and so on.
- Data controls—These controls facilitate connecting and working with a database. The Recordset control, the RecordsetNavbar, and the Grid control all fall into this category.
- Multimedia controls—These controls, the Page Transitions control and the Timeline control, are placed together because they are used to produce graphic effects.
- Miscellaneous controls—As is common in any method of categorization, some items do not fall neatly into any specific group and are grouped together for the sake of convenience. These controls include the Visual InterDev 1.0 controls (or "legacy controls," as Microsoft calls them).

Before covering the controls in detail though, the next section takes you through the mechanics of inserting and manipulating DTCs in your Web pages.

Incorporating DTCs into Your Pages

Using DTCs in your Web pages requires little effort on your part. You can easily add a DTC to a page from the Toolbox window (you knew it was good for something). Shown in Figure 20.2, the Toolbox window contains several tabs that group similar objects together. The **Design-Time Controls** tab (as shown in the figure) displays several different DTCs that can be placed in your Web page.

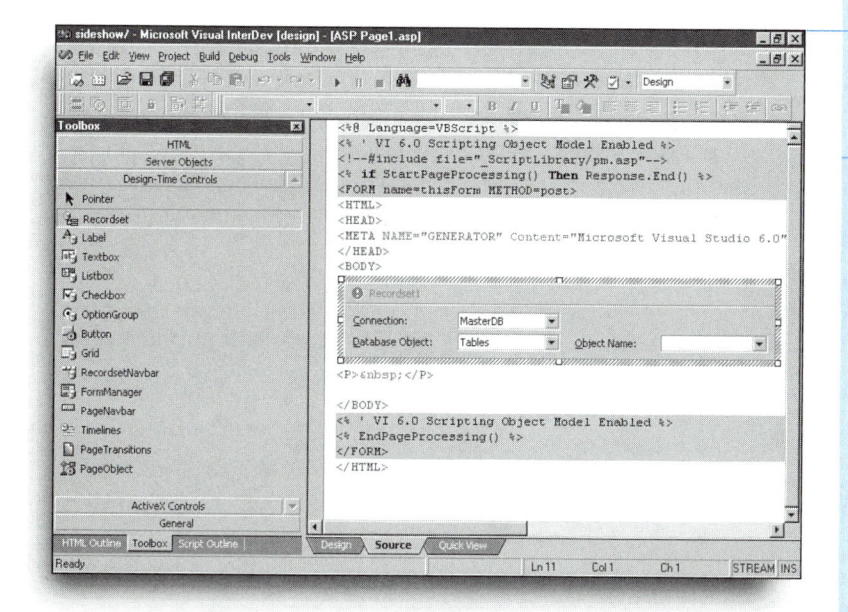

FIGURE 20.2
Design-time controls are located in the Toolbox window.

DTCs can be added to your document in the same way as controls in Access or Visual Basic forms. You can either click and drag them onto the page, or double-click the control to place it at the current cursor position on your page.

As an example, drag a Recordset DTC from the toolbox onto your page.

Understanding the Scripting Object Model

The first time you insert a DTC onto a Web page, you are typically prompted by the dialog box shown in Figure 20.3. This dialog box informs you that the scripting object model is required to use the control.

FIGURE 20.3

The scripting object model is required for most controls.

Not enabling the scripting object model

If you do not enable the scripting object model, you will not be able to use most design-time controls. Enabling the model involves very little overhead for your page, and is in your better interest. In fact, you might want to enable the scripting object model even if you don't use DTCs–the model will expose additional programmability in your page for your own scripts.

Another method of enabling the scripting object model

Another method for adding the scripting object model's runtime code to your page is to use the Properties dialog box. If you choose **True** for **Enable Scripting Object Model** from the document's properties, the runtime code is inserted without the need of a DTC. You can disable the object model by choosing **False** if you decide it is no longer needed.

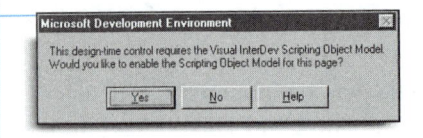

To use the control, click the **Yes** button. In doing so, you are instructing Visual InterDev to insert the required pieces of run-time code to use the control. This code, shown in Listing 20.1, acts as a "wrapper" around the normal processing of your page, so that the events, properties, and objects in your page can be manipulated and accessed. This wrapper also enables you to use a standard event-driven approach to coding, which traditionally could not be done in a Web page.

LISTING 20.1   ASP PAGE1.ASP   Your Page After the Scripting Object Model Code Is Inserted

```
1  <%@ Language=VBScript %>
2  <% ' VI 6.0 Scripting Object Model Enabled %>
3  <!--#include file="_ScriptLibrary/pm.asp"-->
4  <% if StartPageProcessing() Then Response.End() %>
5  <FORM name=thisForm METHOD=post>
6  <HTML>
7  <HEAD>
8  <META NAME="GENERATOR" Content="Microsoft Visual
   ➥Studio 6.0">
9  </HEAD>
10 <BODY>
11
12 <P> </P>
13
14 </BODY>
15 <% ' VI 6.0 Scripting Object Model Enabled %>
16 <% EndPageProcessing() %>
17 </FORM>
18 </HTML>
```

Manipulating Control Properties

With your control in place, you're ready to get down to work. Each control that you add to your page appears as an independent object that can be selected and manipulated. Unlike

Incorporating DTCs into Your Pages PART V
CHAPTER 20   549

conventional HTML elements (say, an intrinsic form field), DTCs appear as objects in both the Design and Source Editors. To preview your page without the controls, you should open your page in a Web browser. Figure 20.4 illustrates a control in a Web page, ready for modification.

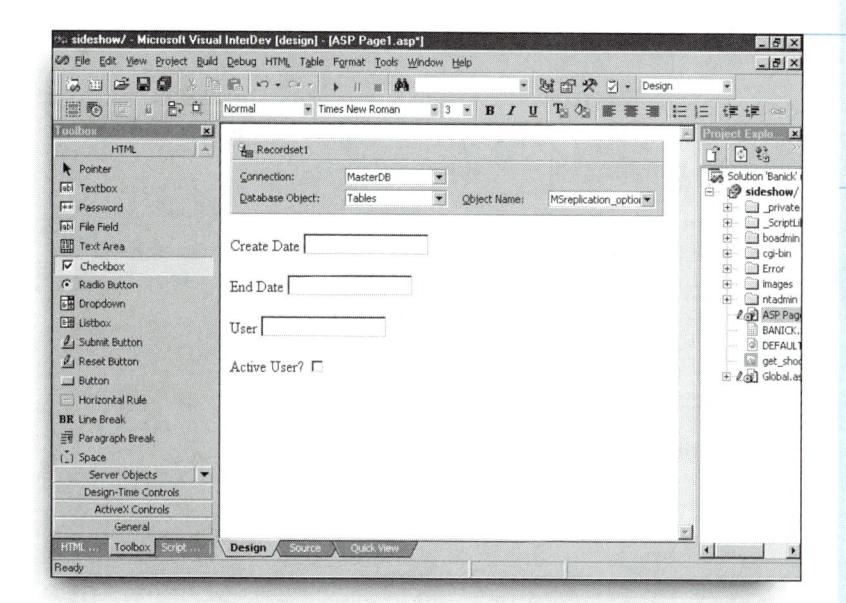

FIGURE 20.4

You can move, resize, and manipulate a control from the Source or Design Editor.

Like all objects, when your control is selected it updates the Properties window with a list of attributes. Unlike most other objects, however, you can manipulate many DTC's properties directly in the editor. You can also modify the properties of a DTC by right-clicking it and choosing **Properties** from the context menu. This is shown in Figure 20.5. Try this yourself with the Recordset DTC you added.

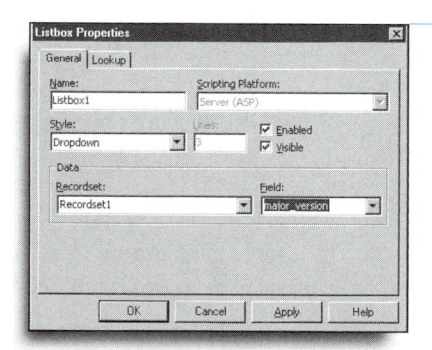

FIGURE 20.5

Most design-time controls can be customized using the Properties dialog box or the Properties window.

SEE ALSO
➤ *You'll explore how to manipulate the properties of individual controls on page 552*

Viewing Runtime Text

As you read earlier, a DTC acts as a visual "front-end" to runtime script on the server or client side. This visual interface is your shield from the complex scripts that carry out the DTC functionality. However, just because Visual InterDev tries to hide this complexity from you, nothing is preventing you from digging into the code—or at least taking a glance.

To view the runtime text that makes up the DTC script, right-click on the DTC. From the context menu, choose **Show Runtime Text**. Below your control, a block of scripted code appears on a gray background, as shown in Figure 20.6.

FIGURE 20.6

Visual InterDev can't hide the underlying code from you if you don't want it to.

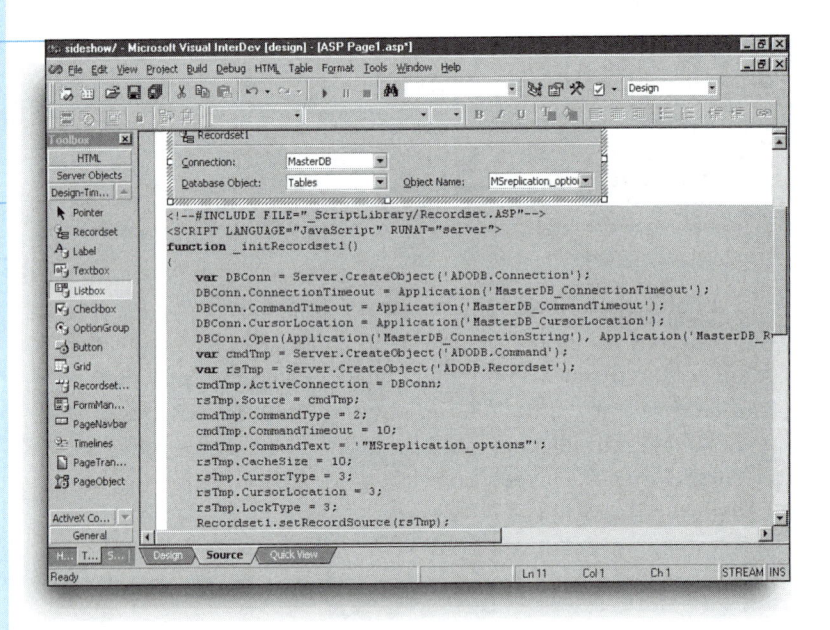

As long as the runtime text is on a gray background, the code cannot be directly modified—that's what the graphical interface of the control is for. If you would prefer to work with the raw script code, as opposed to the DTC, you can choose to convert the control to runtime text. To do so, right-click on the same control and choose **Convert to Run-time Text** from the

Incorporating DTCs into Your Pages

context menu. Listing 20.2 displays a sample of converted runtime text.

LISTING 20.2 ASP PAGE1.ASP   Runtime Text for a Recordset DTC

```
1  <!--#INCLUDE FILE="_ScriptLibrary/Recordset.ASP"-->
2  <SCRIPT LANGUAGE="JavaScript" RUNAT="server">
3  function _initRecordset1()
4  {
5      Response.Write('Recordset DTC error: Failed to get
       ➥connection string');
6      var cmdTmp = Server.CreateObject('ADODB.Command');
7      var rsTmp = Server.CreateObject('ADODB.Recordset');
8      cmdTmp.ActiveConnection = DBConn;
9      rsTmp.Source = cmdTmp;
10     cmdTmp.CommandType = 2;
11     cmdTmp.CommandTimeout = 10;
12 //Recordset DTC error: Failed to get command text
13     cmdTmp.CommandText = '';
14     rsTmp.CacheSize = 10;
15     rsTmp.CursorType = 3;
16     rsTmp.CursorLocation = 3;
17     rsTmp.LockType = 3;
18     Recordset1.setRecordSource(rsTmp);
19     Recordset1.open();
20     if (thisPage.getState('pb_Recordset1') != null)
21     Recordset1.setBookmark(thisPage.getState(
       ➥'pb_Recordset1'));
22 }
23 function _Recordset1_ctor()
24 {
25     CreateRecordset('Recordset1', _initRecordset1, null);
26 }
27 function _Recordset1_dtor()
28 {
29     Recordset1._preserveState();
30     thisPage.setState('pb_Recordset1', Recordset1.
       ➥getBookmark());
31 }
32 </SCRIPT>
```

SEE ALSO

▶ *A good example of comparing runtime text to a DTC is with ActiveX Data Objects (ADO). You learned ADO on page 520*

Convert runtime text with caution

When you choose to convert a DTC to runtime text, Visual InterDev prompts you to confirm your choice. Visual InterDev warns you that you will use some functionality with the conversion—and you will. After you convert a DTC to runtime text, you must manually (programmatically) modify the code behind the DTC because the DTC itself disappears.

Convert a DTC to runtime text only if you want to work with the raw script yourself. If you plan to modify the script and would prefer to work with the DTC interface, don't convert it—view the runtime text if you want to look at it instead.

Using Data-Bound DTCs in Forms

Arguably the most appealing DTCs are *data-bound controls*. A data-bound control acts as an intermediary between your Web page and a data source (presumably a database). The key appeal to DTC data-bound controls is in just how easily you can integrate a database into your pages. Conventional database connections with Active Server Pages rely on manual coding to create a database connection and code to populate form fields. Visual InterDev's data-bound form DTCs take care of the hassle for you: Drag, drop, click, and voila! You have a database connection.

Adding the Recordset

At the heart of all data-bound controls is the *recordset*. A recordset acts as your "host" when working with databases. It handles all the chores of connecting to the database, authenticating who you are, and labeling itself as a data source to your page. Subsequent data-bound controls on your page can use this recordset as their data source.

Before you can use a data-bound control, you need a recordset DTC present on your page. The first step to adding a recordset to your page is selecting what data command you want to use.

SEE ALSO
▶ To learn how to create a data connection and data commands for use in your pages, see page 418

Adding a recordset

1. From the Project Explorer, locate the data command that you want to use as your recordset.
2. Drag and drop the data command from the Project Explorer into the desired position on your Web page. The Recordset DTC will appear on your page, as shown in Figure 20.7.
3. Right-click on your new recordset and choose **P**roperties from the context menu. This opens the Recordset Properties dialog, as shown in Figure 20.8.

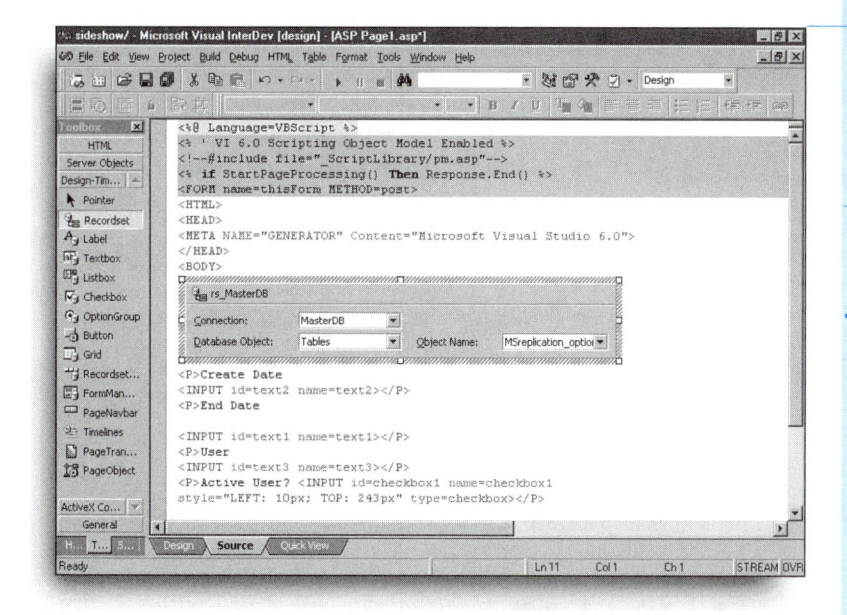

Using Data-Bound DTCs in Forms

PART V
CHAPTER 20

553

FIGURE 20.7
The physical location of your recordset control doesn't really matter—it won't appear on your finished Web page.

Another method of adding recordsets

You can also add recordsets to your pages by dropping the Recordset control on a page from the toolbox. Using the design-time control's visual interface, you can then specify the database connection to use, the type of database object the recordset is accessing, and its name.

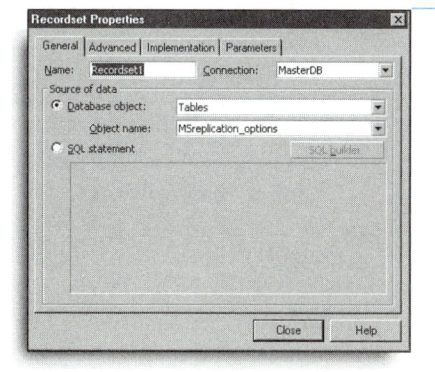

FIGURE 20.8
You can alter your recordset's source of data, as well as other attributes, from this dialog box.

A word of advice on naming recordsets

I highly recommend renaming your recordsets from the default `Recordset1`, `Recordset2`, and so on approach. I personally name recordsets in a standard `rs_RecordSet_Name` format for readability. When you are working with multiple recordsets on the same page, it is very easy to confuse the different recordsets in scripts and controls. By adopting a clear and consistent naming scheme for recordsets, you can avoid potential confusion and problems in your scripts. This practice can be extended throughout your development.

4. In the **Name** text box, enter the name you want your recordset to be referred to—for example, `rs_MasterDB_Logins`.

5. Click the **Close** button to return to your page in the editor.

After the recordset has been added to your page, it is available for other DTCs (and ASP script).

SEE ALSO

➤ *You also learned recordsets on page 524*

Binding Form Controls to the Data Source

With your recordset in place, it's time to start working with the data. Forms are the most common (and convenient) method for interacting with databases in a Web page. Different form elements enable you to control how data is displayed to your users. Visual InterDev provides you with several DTCs specific to data-bound forms:

- Textbox—The standard form text box is used to display or modify data from the data source.
- Checkbox—Check boxes are an ideal way to represent a binary (TRUE/FALSE) state with data.
- OptionGroup—When a selection might be more than a TRUE/FALSE state, the OptionGroup control can be used to create radio button sets to select a specific option.
- Listbox—Drop-down menus and list boxes are both represented by the Listbox DTC. These lists can be bound to another recordset to determine the list contents, or they can contain static menu items.
- Label—Although not a "form element" per se, the Label control can be used to display data from a data source as inline read-only text.

Instructions for incorporating these controls are essentially identical; however, each has its own unique properties. Regardless of which control you use, use the following steps to add a data-bound form control.

Adding a data-bound form control

1. Drag the control you want to use from the toolbox into position on your page. For example, drag a text box field onto your page.
2. Right-click on your DTC and choose **Properties** from the context menu. This opens the Properties dialog box for your control. Figure 20.9 illustrates the Textbox Properties dialog box.

Using Data-Bound DTCs in Forms | PART V
CHAPTER 20

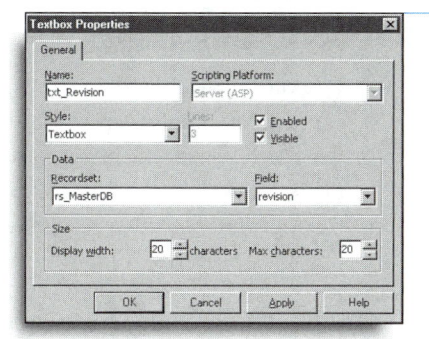

FIGURE 20.9
Each DTC has its own Properties dialog box.

3. Locate the **Recordset** drop-down menu in the **Data** panel. From this menu, choose the recordset that you have added to the page that contains the data.

4. From the **Field** drop-down menu, choose the data field that the DTC represents.

5. In the **Name** text box, enter a name for your DTC—for example, `txt_LoginName`.

6. Click the **OK** button to close the dialog box and return to your page in the editor.

Play with data-bound DTCs by adding a control of each type, bound to your database. Experiment with the properties of each control. Consider these points:

- If you set a control as **Visible** in the Properties dialog box, the control isn't visible on a page. This also means the control cannot be updated or modified, even programmatically.

- Listbox and OptionGroup controls either can display static menu items or be bound to a data source. You can choose the value to be displayed on the menu and the value that is actually inserted in the database.

- Label controls can be formatted to display your data in a particular way. You can even determine that the field contains HTML tags to be displayed.

SEE ALSO
➤ This is your refresher on DTCs and forms. You can see page 451 for more information.

A convenient method for adding text box fields

Visual InterDev is replete with convenient shortcuts for developers. One convenient one can be used to add Textbox DTCs to your page. From either the data command in the Project Explorer or from Data view, drag and drop individual fields onto your page. This adds the DTC to your page, ready for you to customize.

Introducing Recordset Navigation

Of course, there isn't much use in a data-bound Web page that can display only one record. Visual InterDev solves moving between records with the RecordsetNavbar control. This control provides your users with a convenient means of navigating through the recordset, and you with a simple means of customizing its appearance. One powerful feature of the RecordsetNavbar control is its **Update on Move** property. With this property selected, your recordset is automatically updated whenever a user moves between records, enabling transparent database updates with user-modified data (assuming that the users have made a change in the form).

Adding a RecordsetNavbar control to your page

1. Drag and drop the RecordsetNavbar DTC from the toolbox into position on your page. The control is added to your page, as shown in Figure 20.10.

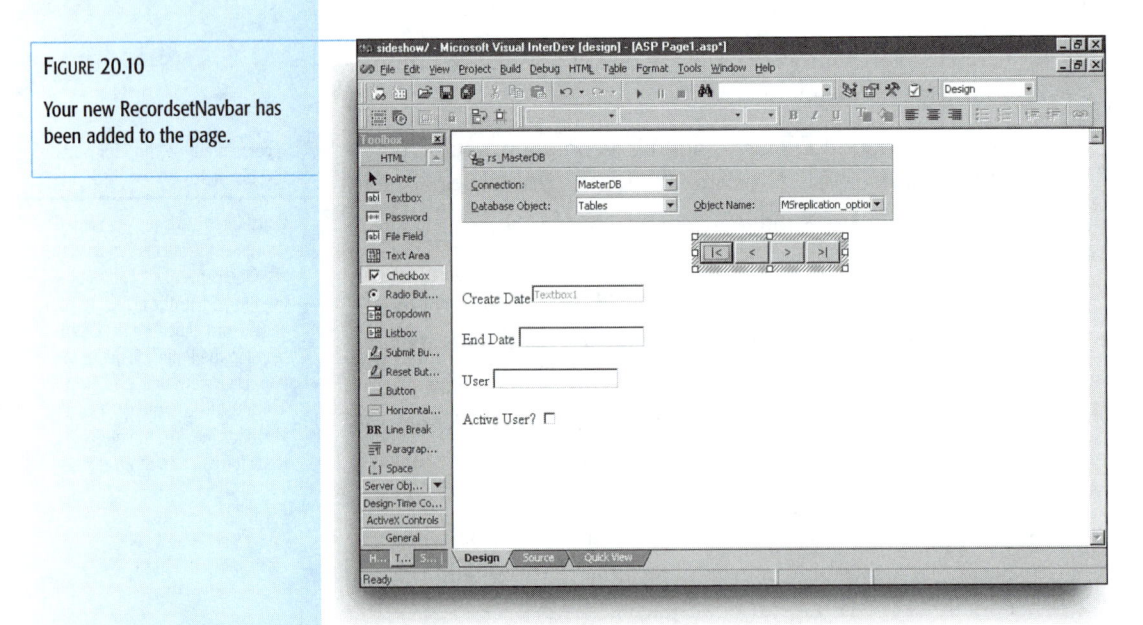

FIGURE 20.10

Your new RecordsetNavbar has been added to the page.

2. Right-click the control and choose **Properties** from the context menu. This opens the RecordsetNavbar Properties dialog box, shown in Figure 20.11.

Using Data-Bound DTCs in Forms

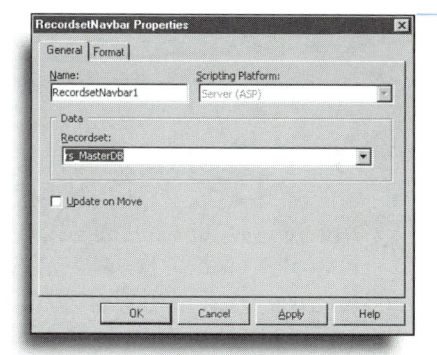

FIGURE 20.11
Your navigational bar must have the recordset specified.

3. From the **Recordset** drop-down menu in the **Data** panel, choose the recordset you want to navigate.

4. In the **Name** text box, enter the name for your RecordsetNavbar—for example, `rsnav_MasterDB`.

5. If you want the recordset fields automatically updated when moving between records, select the **Update on Move** check box.

6. Click the **Format** tab. This displays the page shown in Figure 20.12.

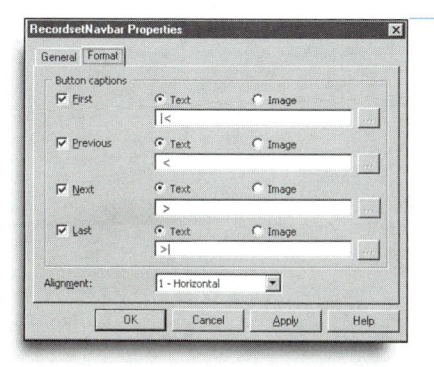

FIGURE 20.12
The **Format** tab lets you specify the text or images used for the navigational bar.

7. Customize the buttons that you want visible in your navigational bar. You can also specify the text used for each button or choose an image.

8. Select the alignment for your navigational bar from the **Alignment** drop-down menu. Alignment can be either **Horizontal** or **Vertical**.

Exercise caution with update on move

Keep in mind that when you update your records on each move, you are increasing database overhead and impacting performance. Also remember that your data will not be massaged or checked on the client side before update—if you must do client-side manipulation, don't use this option! (Well, this isn't entirely true, but it's a better way of doing things.)

9. Click the **OK** button to commit your changes and return to your page.

Adding Buttons

You can use programmatically controlled DTC buttons to control form actions and behaviors. DTC buttons are not exclusively used for forms; however, they are an ideal extension to a forms interface. Buttons can be used to create new records, update existing records, or even delete records. The advantage to using a button for these actions over the RecordsetNavbar control is programmability. You can tie several actions, such as data massaging, along with the database action itself. This enables you to carry out several actions on the data before it is saved to the database.

Adding a DTC button to your form

1. Drag and drop the Button DTC from the toolbox into position on your page.
2. Right-click on the **Button** control and choose **Properties** from the context menu. This opens the Button Properties dialog box, shown in Figure 20.13.

FIGURE 20.13

A button can appear as text or an image.

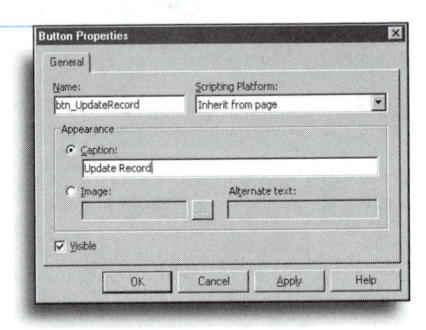

3. Enter a name for your button in the **Name** text box—for example, `btn_UpdateRecord`.
4. Customize how your button appears on your page in the **Appearance** panel. You can customize the **Caption** text or choose an image to be displayed in the button's place.

Using Data-Bound DTCs in Forms

5. Click the **OK** button to commit your changes and return to the page.

With your button in place, you write the code behind its action. Of particular interest in data-bound forms are these recordset methods:

- `updateRecord` updates the current record.
- `addRecord` creates a new record.
- `moveAbsolute(Record)` moves the recordset cursor to a specific record.
- `deleteRecord` deletes the current record.

Creating the script for the button

1. If you're not already there, switch to the Source Editor.
2. In the **Script Outline** tab, locate the **Server Objects & Events** folder. Expand this folder and locate the name of the button you just created (**btn_UpdateRecord**).
3. Double-click the name of your button to expand it. This should display the `onClick` event.
4. Double-click the `onClick` event. This inserts the script block for your button when it is clicked. The script code should look something like the code shown in Listing 20.3.

LISTING 20.3 ASP PAGE1.ASP   The *onClick* Event for a DTC Button

```
1 <SCRIPT ID=serverEventHandlersVBS LANGUAGE=vbscript
 ➥RUNAT=Server>
2 Sub Button1_onclick()
3
4 End Sub
5 </SCRIPT>
```

5. Insert the code for your button's action in this handler. For example, to insert the current date and time into a field and then save the record, add the code in Listing 20.4.

LISTING 20.4   **ASP PAGE1.ASP**   **The Complete *onClick* Event for a DTC Button**

```
1 <SCRIPT ID=serverEventHandlersVBS LANGUAGE=vbscript
  ➥RUNAT=Server>
2 Sub Button1_onclick()
3 txt_LastLogin.value = now
4 rs_MasterDB.updateRecord
4 End Sub
5 </SCRIPT>
```

6. Save your page by choosing **File**, **Save**.

7. Preview your page in the browser by right-clicking your page in the Project Explorer and choosing **View in Browser**. Be sure to test your button.

SEE ALSO

➤ *For more information on scripting events in your pages, see page 303*

Using the Grid Control

Often, the best method for displaying and modifying data is the Grid control. The Grid control displays all data from a recordset in a column format, much like Microsoft Access or Microsoft Excel. A sample Grid control is shown in Figure 20.14.

FIGURE 20.14

The Grid control is familiar to most Microsoft Access users.

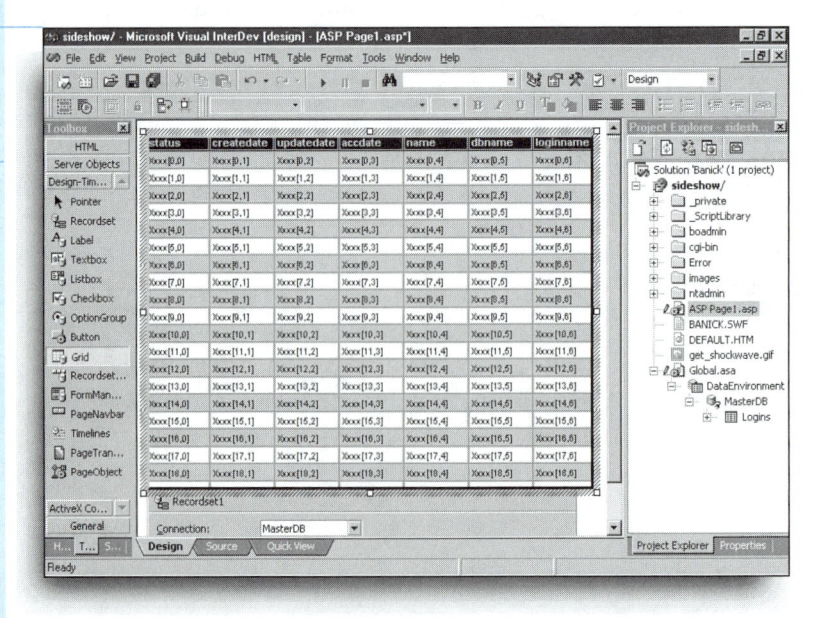

Using Data-Bound DTCs in Forms CHAPTER 20 561

The Grid control is easily added to your page, and can be customized to suit your needs. The Grid control can be autoformatted to a particular style, or you can customize the format and borders. The contents of the grid itself can be customized from available fields and can use expressions to determine the displayed data.

Adding a Grid control

1. From the toolbox, drag and drop the Grid control into position on your page.
2. Resize the control to occupy the relative space you want it to occupy on the page.
3. Right-click the control and choose **Properties** from the context menu. This opens the Grid Properties dialog box, shown in Figure 20.15.

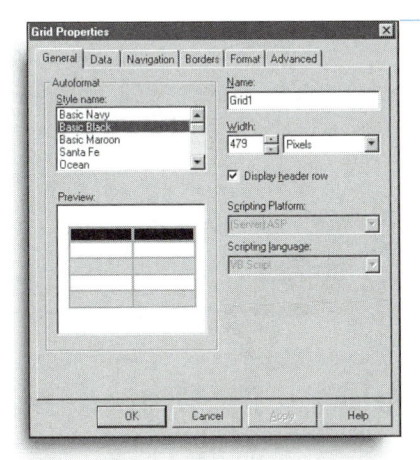

FIGURE 20.15
You can have Visual InterDev autoformat a style for your grid.

4. Enter a name for your grid in the **Name** text box—for example, `grd_DBLogins`.
5. Click the **Data** tab at the top to display the page shown in Figure 20.16.
6. From the **Recordset** drop-down menu, choose your recordset.
7. In the **Available Fields** list box, select the fields you want to display. This updates the **Grid columns** list box with the currently selected fields and header.

FIGURE 20.16

The **Data** tab is used to select fields for your grid columns.

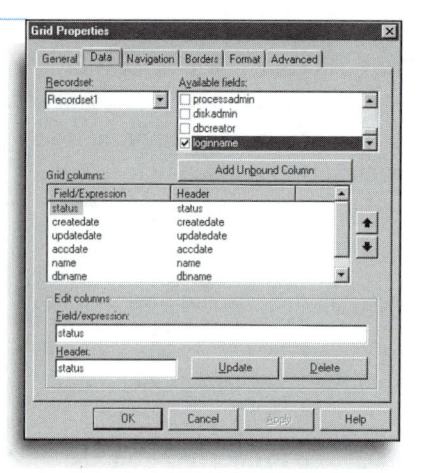

8. Use the **Edit columns** panel to customize the individual columns. As you select columns you can specify a custom header and the order in which the columns appear by using the arrows on the right side of the dialog box.

9. Click the **OK** button to commit your changes and return to the page.

Preview your Grid control in a Web browser. Now experiment with different navigational options and formats.

SEE ALSO
➤ *You also used the Grid control on page 451*

Adding Multimedia DTCs

Although the majority of Visual InterDev's DTCs are geared toward data-bound interactivity, Microsoft wisely included two other powerful DTCs that can be categorized as "multimedia." These controls can be used to alter the appearance of your pages and offer a more rich experience to your users.

By providing these controls, Microsoft is removing the learning curve from some Dynamic HTML (DHTML) and making it quick and easy to use. It is likely that someone, either Microsoft or a third-party developer, will produce more DHTML-oriented DTCs, and over time, most of the capabilities of this powerful tool will be accessible through an easy-to-use interface.

The Page Transitions Control

The Page Transitions control enables you to create visual effects when the user moves between the pages of your site or from a page in your site to some external URL. If you are familiar with video editing or even with Microsoft PowerPoint, you will be used to the concept of placing fades, sweeps, and dissolves between slides or clips to provide a transition. This control serves the same purpose.

Place the Page Transitions control anywhere on your Web page and then bring up its Properties dialog box, as shown in Figure 20.17. Both tabs, **Site Transition** and **Page Transition**, are nearly identical. For each, you have two events to control: `Exit` and `Enter`. Set the combo box to the type of transition you want and then click **Preview** to see a simulation of the transition. Adjusting the duration controls how long the effect takes and, therefore, how much of it the user will see.

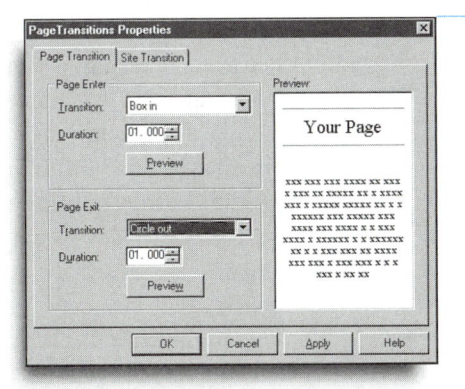

FIGURE 20.17

The Properties dialog box for the Page Transitions control enables you to preview effects such as an animation.

The `Page Enter` and `Exit` events occur whenever someone arrives at this page from another page within your Web site, and when this user leaves this page to go to another page within your Web site. In contrast, the `Site Enter` and `Exit` events occur during a visitor's arriving and leaving this page, but from a URL that is not within your Web site. Remember that this control affects only this page. If you want a certain transition to take effect whenever someone arrives at or leaves your entire Web site, this Page Transitions control must be present on every page.

Using duration for good and not for evil

The Page Transition control provides a **Duration** setting for each of its effects; be sure to use this setting wisely. The most important part of a Web site is the content on the pages, not the navigation between them. If users must wait through a 10-second dissolve every time they move to a different page, they will quickly tire of the experience and leave the site for good.

The Timeline Control

The Timeline control, like the Page Transitions control, is client-side only. It depends on certain features of Dynamic HTML that enable scripting functions to be called based on time intervals. The possibilities for using this control are endless, but a common use is animation. You can set up a timeline that calls a series of 15 events (or the same event 15 times), once per half-second. Then in your client-side event handler, you can move through the frames of an animation on your page. You can set up this timeline to start as soon as the page loads, or you can control it from script (using the `play`, `pause`, and `stop` methods). Imagine the interesting effects you can generate by starting a timeline playing based on selections from a form.

Setting up the control is completely visual; you use its Properties dialog box, as shown in Figure 20.18. The combo box and buttons along the top enable you to work with multiple timelines. A Web page can have only one Timeline control, but you can set up (using the **New** button) as many individual timelines as you want. When you create a new timeline, a dialog box is displayed, as shown in Figure 20.19, enabling you to specify the name and choose whether the timeline starts when the page is loaded. If you want to change this setting or the timeline's name later, you can use the **Edit** button to bring this dialog box up again.

FIGURE 20.18

The Timeline control has a detailed graphical interface in its Properties dialog box.

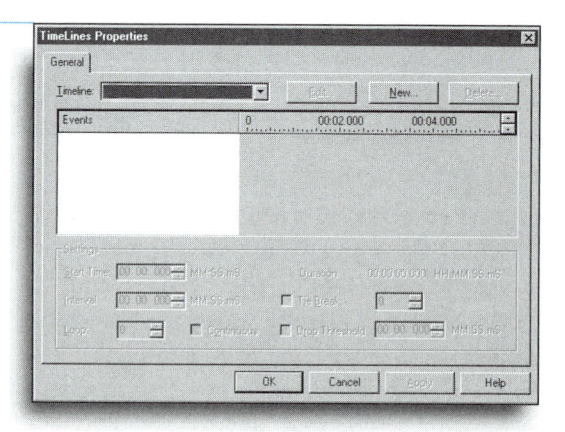

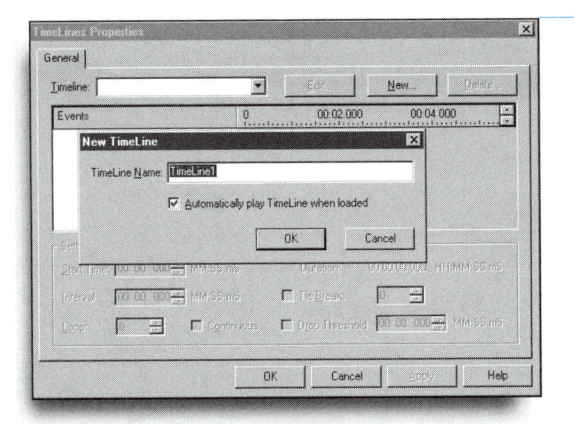

FIGURE 20.19
When adding a new timeline, you can choose to have it start automatically when the page is loaded.

After you select a timeline, adding events is just a matter of clicking the last item in the events list. A new event starts as a Discrete event, signifying one that just fires once at a single point in time. You can add the same event name several times to the list and therefore cause it to fire multiple times. You can change when the event fires both graphically and numerically, either by dragging the small diamond (for a Discrete event) or by changing the value in the **Start Time** field.

Events can be set as discrete, continuous, or looping. The type is controlled by the setting of three fields in the Properties dialog box. The **Continuous** check box specifies that the event fires once per *interval* units of time for the entire time the timeline is playing (starting at the time set in the **Start Time** field). The timeline is active until the user leaves the page, or until it is stopped through script. Looping events are created by increasing the **Loop** value to greater than one. If this is the case, the **Interval** property becomes enabled, allowing you to specify the time between loops. The total duration of the event is, therefore, until all loops have been completed and can be calculated as follows:

(loops – 1) * the interval value

In Figure 20.20, you can see three events. **Event1** is a discrete event that will fire once, one second into the timeline. **Event2** (selected) will fire three times (**Loop = 3**), with one second between each occurrence, causing it to execute at two seconds, three seconds, and four seconds. The display-only **Duration** field gives the overall duration of the selected event. **Event3**, which is another discrete event, will fire only once, at three seconds into the timeline.

FIGURE 20.20

Three events are set up for the Main timeline.

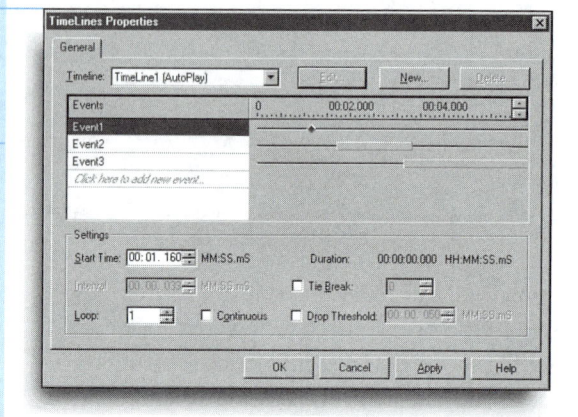

In the preceding example, both Event2 and Event3 will fire at the three-second point, but both events cannot occur simultaneously. The remaining two properties in the dialog box, **Tie Break** and **Drop Threshold**, deal with multiple events occurring at once. The **Tie Break** value, if specified, determines which of two or more events should occur first. Lower values are considered of higher priority and are always executed first, with a value of zero (0) being the highest priority and 10 being the lowest. If **Tie Break** is disabled (unchecked), the event always occurs last.

In the case of some events firing before others, an event might not be executed exactly at the right time. For example, in the preceding example, Event2 and Event3 are both set to execute at three seconds. If you know that the **Tie Break** value of Event2 is **2** and the value for Event3 is **4**, Event2's event procedure executes before Event3's. If Event2's procedure contains code that takes approximately 30 milliseconds (ms) to execute, Event3 doesn't fire until 30ms after the three-second mark. In most cases, this wouldn't really matter, but if your code is time-sensitive, you can prevent late events from firing. You can set the **Drop Threshold** property to prevent execution if the

Adding Multimedia DTCs   CHAPTER 20

intended time is exceeded by more than the specified amount. If this property is not enabled, the event will fire regardless of how late it occurs.

You can easily code against the Timeline control by using the **Script Outline** tab. Each of the Timeline objects (not the Timeline control itself) appears as an object, and each event appears as an event under that object. Remember that they are client-side objects only and, therefore, appear under that branch of the **Script Outline**.

SEE ALSO
➤ *You can experiment more with DHTML on page 750*

Including scripts for all events

Note that you must include scripts for all the events of all the Timeline objects you create, even if they do not do anything. If you do not, you receive a notice stating that an error appears in your page at Line 1, Char 1. This message is misleading because nothing is wrong with that section. The error is that some of the DTC-generated code is attempting to call functions that do not exist in the page. Simply double-click all the Timeline events in the Script Outline to ensure that at least a scripting stub exists for each function.

CHAPTER 21

Adding Reports and Graphs to Your Web Applications

Learn how to use HTML tables to produce columnar reports

Use the REPORT.ASP document to create tabular reports

Install the ASPChart DLL component

Use ASPChart to create 3D graphical displays of data

The Advantages of Reporting Formats

In this chapter, you learn how to publish data from your databases into useful report formats. Although there are as many different report designs as there are programmers, they usually fall into three basic groups:

- *Columnar reports* look similar to index cards and are usually designed to display one data record per page.
- *Tabular reports* look much like spreadsheets and are usually designed to display one data record per line.
- *Graph reports* are 2D or 3D visual displays of data and are designed to display a summary of the entire data collection on one single page.

There are advantages and drawbacks to each type of report format. In the next few sections, you learn the features of each format and the situations in which each report format can be used. When you complete this review of data formats, you move on to create examples of each report using HTML and VBScript.

Using Columnar Reports

The columnar report is the simplest of all the formats discussed in this chapter. The columnar report format presents each column of data as a single line on the page and, usually, one page represents one record in the data collection. For example, Figure 21.1 shows a columnar report format for the Authors table of the SQL Server Pubs database.

You can see that the names of the columns in the table appear down the left side of the document (shown in bold) and the actual contents of the columns appears on the right side of the page. This is typical columnar report format.

If you've used Microsoft Excel

If you've spent any time in Microsoft Excel then you will likely know exactly what you're looking for in a report. Your business needs will usually drive the kind of report that you want to use, based on the information being presented.

The Advantages of Reporting Formats

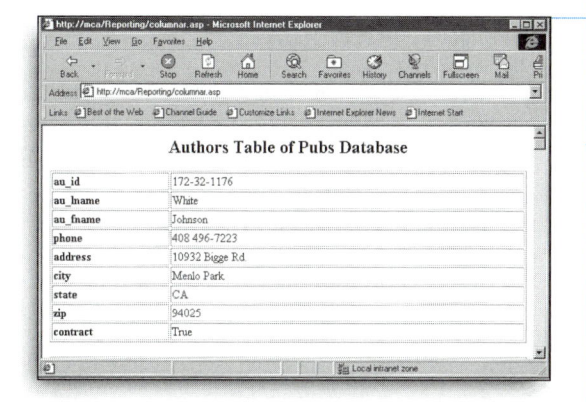

FIGURE 21.1
Viewing a columnar report for the Authors table.

Columnar reports are very handy when you must print items such as

- Mailing labels
- Index cards
- Completed form letters
- Partially completed user entry documents

Although the first three items in the list are commonly considered prime candidates for columnar reports, the last item is the one that is the most useful. You might find that you must produce printouts that contain customer request data, employee personal information, and other application data. These forms can then be turned over for review and editing before the final version is uploaded into the company database.

Often, columnar formatted reports are easier to edit and correct than tabular forms. For this reason, columnar format is often the preferred report style for creating data entry forms for editing.

However, because columnar reports tend to consume a lot of paper (typically one piece of paper for each record in the report), you should use this format sparingly.

Assessing the impact of your reports

Evaluate what type of report would be best for presenting your information. Make sure your report does not interfere with the information. Instead, your report should make the information easily accessible and understood by anyone reading it. Reports are there to make it easier to understand raw data, so it shouldn't be insurmountable.

Columnar reports

Columnar reports are a lot like the classified advertisements in your newspaper. They present a lot of information but require careful attention when reading.

Using Tabular Reports

The tabular report is probably the most commonly used report format. A tabular report presents each column of table data as a column on the page and each record in the table as a line on the page. This spreadsheet-style report can be very efficient for displaying a large amount of data.

Figure 21.2 shows an example of a tabular report. This is taken from the Northwind Microsoft Access database.

FIGURE 21.2
Tabular report of order information.

You can see the table field names appear along the top of the page in this example. And each line of text in the HTML table represents a single record in the data table. This is typical tabular formatted data.

Tabular data format is most effective when you must display long lists of data in a small amount of space. Another reason to use tabular format is that it works very well when you must produce totals or subtotals of data columns. Printing the data in neat columns, followed by totals or subtotals, has become the standard practice for almost all data-intensive reports.

The Advantages of Reporting Formats

However, as powerful and familiar as the tabular data format is, it has some drawbacks. First, tabular data reports are rather boring to look at and sometimes even difficult to read. The constant droning of columns and columns of figures can sometimes leave readers lost. In some cases, tabular reports can make it hard for the reader to understand the importance of the data. This can usually be remedied by creating a summary report or (as you'll see in "Using Graphical Chart Reports") a graphical display of the data.

Although tabular reports are common, if your report is primarily to be used to summarize data or inform the reader of overall trends, you might want to produce a graphical report format instead.

The tabular format report

Tabular format reports are probably the most common type of report you will see in a business. It is ideal for representing a mass of information in a clear and structured form.

Using Graphical Chart Reports

The last reporting style covered in this chapter is the graphical chart report format. In this format, the report is designed to summarize key information from one or more tables into a single display. Unlike the columnar format, which presents one record a page, or the tabular format, which presents one record per line, the graphical format presents the entire table (or its summary) in a single image (see Figure 21.3).

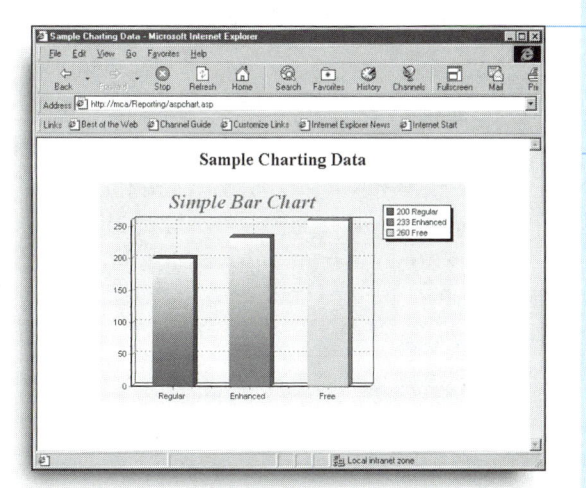

FIGURE 21.3
Viewing a sample graphical chart report.

Graphical reports

In the day of media, graphical reports are popular. Newspapers, magazines, and television all use graphical reports to report information and statistics to an audience. Graphical reports have the advantage of being able to represent a quick snapshot without requiring a great deal of understanding on the part of the audience.

The primary advantage of the graphical chart format is that the reader can quickly see significant trends or comparisons without having to wade through several pages of numbers. If the stated aim of the report is to summarize data or highlight trends in the data, you should consider using a graphical chart format for your report. However, because the graphical report format often does not show a great deal of detail, you should not use this format if your readers are primarily interested in the data *behind* the trends.

Preparing for the Reporting Examples

Now that you've learned a bit about each of the primary data reporting styles, you're ready to start building your own sample reports. In order to complete the examples in this chapter, you need the following two items:

- The REPORT.ASP tabular report document
- The ASPChart.DLL graphical chart component

Both these items are available at the *Using Visual InterDev 6* home page. You can find the address of the home page in Appendix B, "Online Resources." REPORT.ASP is a free Active Server Page document. ASPChart.DLL is a trial version of an IIS4 component that creates graphical charts.

Reporting components

There are many other reporting components that you can purchase. Look for the component that best suits your needs and budget.

You can still get a lot out of this chapter if you do not download the two components. However, you will not be able to complete the programming exercises covered here without them.

So, before continuing, log onto the Internet and pick up your components. Don't worry about installing them yet. You learn how to do that later in the chapter. Just make sure you have them copied to your workstation and ready for your use.

SEE ALSO

▶ *For information on several URLs and starting points for components, see page 792*

Using HTML Tables to Produce Formatted Columnar Reports

The first working example you'll create is a columnar-style report. In this example, you create an ADO DB data connection and an ADO DB recordset object in an ASP document and then write VBScript to generate columnar tables for each record in the recordset.

You learn how to build the columnar ASP document so that you can use it with just about any recordset you encounter. In other words, you create a reusable ASP document you can add to any other Web application you are working with.

The process of creating a columnar report using ASP script is really pretty simple. There are only three key tasks you must complete:

1. Open the desired database and get a valid set of records.
2. Create the method that loops through the entire data set to create columnar output.
3. Create the method that actually reads the data columns and produces the detail output.

Before you start coding, create a new Web project called Reporting. This project will hold all the documents you create in this chapter. After the project is created, add a new ASP document called COLUMNAR.ASP to the Web project and load it in the editor in Source mode.

Now you're ready to begin.

Adding a Data Connection

Before you can start coding your columnar report, you first must create a valid data connection to the database. The easiest way to do this is to use the Visual InterDev editor to create a data connection object. When you do this, you can use the information stored in the GLOBAL.ASA file as part of your COLUMNAR.ASP document.

> **Reduce! Reuse! Recycle!**
>
> In the spirit of environmentalism, get in the habit of reducing the amount of work you have to do with each project you start. Reuse and recycle as much material as you can. This is one of the advantages of Web development with Visual InterDev—it encourages you to learn the lessons that Visual Basic and Visual C++ programmers learned about reusing code long ago.

Work with your own data

If you would prefer to work from your own data source, feel free to replace the DSN created here with your own.

Database access

Make sure that your Web server username (typically `IUSR_MachineName`) has access to your database.

In this example, you create a new data source name (DSN) for SQL Server data. After that, you set the data connection object values for your Web project. Because you'll be creating a new DSN, there are quite a few steps to go through. Don't let it intimidate you! Creating DSNs is really pretty simple when you get the hang of it.

Creating a data connection object

1. Right-click over the project name in the Project Explorer window (**Reporting**).
2. Select **Add Data Connection** from the context menu.
3. When the Select Data Source dialog appears, press the **New** button to create a new data source.
4. At the next dialog, select the proper database driver (for this example, select **SQL Server**) and press **Next**.
5. On the next page of the dialog, enter the name of the data source (`Reporting`) and press **Next**.
6. Confirm that the entries are correct and press the **Finish** button to complete the new data source.
7. The Create a New Data Source to SQL Server dialog asks you for information about the SQL Server data source. Skip the **Description** field, but select a **Server** name from the drop-down list (if none appears, select (**localhost**)) then press **Next**.
8. Choose the proper security authentication. If you are publishing data for intranet users and have SQL and NT security integration, select **With Windows NT authentication using the network login ID**. If you are publishing data for anonymous users, you should select **With SQL Server authentication using a login ID and password entered by the user** and enter the proper SQL Server user ID and password to gain access to the data. Then press **Next**.
9. Check the **Change the default database** check box and select the proper database. For this example, use the **Pubs** database.

10. Press **Next** for each dialog to accept the default settings until you see the **Finish** button. Press the **Finish** button to complete the Data Source definition.

11. At the final ODBC Microsoft SQL Server Setup dialog, press the **Test Data Source** button to confirm all the settings are correct. You should see a message box that says **TESTS COMPLETED SUCCESSFULLY!**

12. Press **OK** to dismiss the test dialog, and press **OK** again to save the Data Source definition.

13. At the Select Data Source dialog, select the **Reporting** DSN and press **OK**.

14. When asked to log into the SQL Server, enter the proper user ID and password.

15. Visual InterDev will connect to the SQL Server and present the Data Connection Properties dialog box.

16. Enter a valid connection name (for this example, use `cnnReporting`) and press **Apply** to save the name.

17. Press the **Authentication** tab and check **Save Design-Time Authentication**; press **Apply** to save the settings.

18. Press **OK** to close the dialog.

Although there are a lot of steps in the process, you just completed a very valuable task! By defining the data connection object in this way, Visual InterDev has actually stored all the important connection information in your GLOBAL.ASA file for this project. Now, any time in this project, you can refer to this data connection using application-level variables stored in the GLOBAL.ASA file.

Using VBScript and ASP to Access SQL Server Data

Now that the data connection is defined, you can use the stored information in your Visual Basic Script to create an active database connection. To do this you must use two server-side objects:

- `ADODB.Connection`
- `ADODB.Recordset`

ADO DB connections

ADO connections are a bit different than the database connections you learned in Chapter 16, "Accessing Web Databases." The fundamentals remain the same, but you're not using design-time controls to handle your database here.

These two server objects are all you need to create a complete connection and retrieve records from the database.

You can find these two objects on the **Server Objects** tab of your Toolbox window. Drag them from the toolbox onto the <BODY> of your loaded ASP document.

Adding server objects to your ASP document

1. Be sure the document is in Source mode (select the **Source** tab in the editor).
2. Click on the **Server Objects** tab of the Toolbox window to open the list.
3. Locate the **ADO Connection** object in the list and drag it from the toolbox up to the ASP document. Drop it on a blank link right under the <BODY> tag.
4. Set the ID property of the **ADO Connection** object to objConn.
5. Locate the **ADO Recordset** object in the list and drag it from the toolbox to the ASP document. Drop it right under the **ADO Connection** object.
6. Set the ID property of the **ADO Recordset** object to objRS.

When you're finished placing the Connection and Recordset objects on your page and editing the ID attributes, your ASP document should look like the document in Listing 21.1.

LISTING 21.1   Adding the ADODB Connection and Recordset Objects

```
1 <OBJECT RUNAT=server PROGID=ADODB.Connection id=objConn>
   ➥ </OBJECT>
2 <OBJECT RUNAT=server PROGID=ADODB.Recordset id=objRS>
   ➥</OBJECT>
```

Now you're ready to add some server-side script to use these objects. Place your cursor on the line below the two object definitions and select **HTML**, **Script Block**, **Server** from the main menu. This will place a server-side script block in your document. Now add the code shown in Listing 21.2.

Using HTML Tables to Produce Formatted Columnar Reports

LISTING 21.2 Adding Server-Side Script to Connect to a Database

```
1  <SCRIPT LANGUAGE=vbscript RUNAT=Server>
2
3  Sub OpenDatabase
4     '
5     ' open data using available connection
6     '
7     Dim strConn
8     Dim strSource
9     '
10    strConn=Application("cnnReporting_ConnectionString")
11    strSource="SELECT * FROM Authors"
12    '
13    objConn.Open strConn,"sa",""
14    objRS.Open strSource,objConn
15    '
16 End Sub
17
18 </SCRIPT>
```

The OpenDatabase method declares two variables and fills them with values. Notice that the strConn variable (line 10) is loaded with the connection string created for the cnnReporting database connection object. This was the sole reason for creating the connection object to provide easy access to the database. The strSource variable is filled with a simple SQL SELECT statement (line 11) that will retrieve data from the Authors table. Finally, the objConn object and objRS on lines 13 and 14 are used to open the connection and recordset, respectively.

That's all there is to connecting your ASP document to live data. The next step is to create a method that will read all the records in the selected table.

SEE ALSO
➤ *To learn about design-time controls in detail, see page 544*

Traditional database interaction

ADO is the traditional method that Web application developers have used to interact with databases and Active Server Pages. You can easily control your SQL queries directly in the code, as opposed to manipulating design-time controls. The trade off, however, is more work.

SQL queries

You can carry out any kind of SQL query in your code: SELECT, INSERT, INSERT VALUES, DELETE, and UPDATE. This gives you the flexibility to totally interact with the database in your code.

Creating the Report Heading and Print Loop

Now that you have a live data connection, you use server-side script to create a method that will read every record of the data table and prepare to create the columnar output. However, this routine's job is not to actually read the records and output data. Instead, you use this routine to loop through all the records in the recordset. This routine will handle the report heading, too.

Add a new server-side code block to the project and enter the code from Listing 21.3 in your document.

LISTING 21.3 Adding the *PrintDatabase* Method

```
1  <SCRIPT LANGUAGE=vbscript RUNAT=Server>
2
3  Sub PrintData
4     '
5     ' send each record as a page of columns
6     '
7     Response.Write "<CENTER><H2>"
8     Response.Write "Authors Table of Pubs Database"
9     Response.Write "</H2></CENTER>"
10    '
11    objRS.MoveFirst
12    do while objRS.EOF<>True
13       PrintRecord
14       objRS.MoveNext
15    loop
16    '
17 End Sub
18
19 </SCRIPT>
```

The first important action in this code is in lines 7–9. This code defines the report title that will be displayed at the top of the page. Next, the record pointer is positioned at the start of the recordset (line 11) and the loop (lines 12–15) continues to read each individual record, calling another method (you'll get to that in a minute) and moving ahead one record to do it all over again. This is the part of the application that ensures all the records in the collection are reported.

Moving around the recordset

Notice that in lines 11 and 14 you're directly moving around the recordset. You can use navigation through the recordset to interact with your database more accurately.

Displaying Data Detail with HTML Tables

Now, for the most important part of the code—the method that actually writes the data! Add another server-side script block and enter the code from Listing 21.4. As you type the code, be sure to pay attention to how the HTML <TABLE> elements are being used.

LISTING 21.4 Adding the *PrintRecord* Method to the COLUMNAR.ASP Document

```
1  <SCRIPT LANGUAGE=vbscript RUNAT=Server>
2     Sub PrintRecord
3     '
4     ' send out a record
5     '
6     Dim intCols
7     Dim intLoop
8     '
9     intCols=objRS.Fields.count
10    ' start table
11    Response.Write "<TABLE WIDTH=100% BORDER=1>"
12    ' add rows & cols
13    for intLoop=0 to intCols-1
14       ' column name
15       Response.Write "<TR>"
16       Response.Write "<TD WIDTH=25%>"
17       Response.Write "<STRONG>"
18       Response.Write objRS.Fields(intLoop).Name
19       Response.Write "</STRONG>"
20       ' column data
21       Response.Write "<TD WIDTH=75%>"
22       Response.Write objRS.Fields(intLoop).Value
23       Response.Write "</TR>"
24    next
25    ' end table
26    Response.Write "</TABLE><P>"
27    '
28    End Sub
29 </SCRIPT>
```

The grid DTC

Another method you could use for this is the Grid design-time control. The Grid control can be customized to suit your display's needs. It also outputs your data in an HTML table that can be customized.

Is it a TABLE or a Table?

It's easy to confuse the <TABLE> HTML element with the word Table used to define a physical database storage medium. It's even more bewildering when you deal with columnar reports, because the idea is to use the HTML <TABLE> for every *record* in the database table! To help keep things straight, throughout this book the HTML version is spelled <TABLE> and the database version is spelled Table.

Reusing the code

You could create a library of code just like this and reuse it throughout your Web application. Server-side includes let you create the code once and use it in several places. Check out Chapter 24, "Looking at ASP Behind the Scenes."

You can see from Listing 21.4 that a complete HTML table is created for each record of the data set. This is the essence of building columnar data reports with HTML. You can think of each record in the data set as a table of data to present to the user.

There's just one tiny bit of code left to add. Now that you have all methods and objects properly defined, you must add some high-level server-side script to call them all together. Add one more server-side script code block to the top of the page (under the <OBJECT> elements) and add the code from Listing 21.5.

LISTING 21.5 Adding the High-Level Call Method to the COLUMNAR.ASP Document

```
1 <SCRIPT LANGUAGE=vbscript RUNAT=Server>
2 '
3 OpenDatabase
4 PrintData
5 '
6 </SCRIPT>
```

The code from Listing 21.5 first calls the `OpenDatabase` method to open the active connection. Then the `PrintData` method is used to "walk" through all the records in the data set.

After adding this last bit of code, save the document, mark it as **Set As Start Page**, and press F5. The Web application will start, complete the database connection, and load all the records into the browser (this might take some time—be patient). If all goes well, your screen will look much like the one in Figure 21.1.

SEE ALSO

▸ *You learn about the Grid design-time control on page 445*
▸ *SSI is covered starting on page 652*

Building Tabular Reports with the REPORT.ASP Document

The next report style you build in this chapter is the tabular report. The tabular report presents data records as lines on the page and each data field as a column in the line. The output looks very similar to a spreadsheet (refer to Figure 21.2).

The process of creating tabular reports is a bit more involved than that for columnar reports. Although the basic output of the fields and rows is not too complex, most tabular reports also contain two additional features not found in columnar reports:

- Column totals—One or more of the displayed columns is totaled and the results displayed at the end of the report.
- Group break—A column is selected as the "break column" and subtotals are reported.

The details of defining and tracking column totals and group breaks can get rather complex, depending on the report requirements. For this example, you don't need to worry about these details. Instead, you use an ASP document that already has all the details worked out for you: the REPORT.ASP document.

Simply download the REPORT.ASP document from the *Using Visual InterDev 6* Web site and copy it into your Web project.

Copying a document into an existing Web project

1. With the target Web project loaded in Visual InterDev 6, minimize the Visual InterDev editor by clicking on the _ button at the top-right of the window.
2. Use your File Explorer to locate the REPORT.ASP document you downloaded from the *Using Visual InterDev 6* Web site.
3. When you locate the REPORT.ASP document, right-click over it and select **Copy** from the context menu.
4. Minimize the File Explorer and switch to the Visual InterDev editor (use Alt+Tab to move between windows on your desktop).

> **Get the REPORT.ASP document**
>
> The REPORT.ASP document is free and can be found at the *Using Visual InterDev 6* home page. The address is in Appendix B. If, however, you don't have the REPORT.ASP document, you can still learn a lot from the chapter by reading through the example.

5. With the Visual InterDev editor in focus again, right-click over the project name in the Project Explorer window (**Reporting**).

6. Select **Paste** from the context menu (look toward the bottom) to drop the REPORT.ASP document in your project.

7. Select **Project** from the main menu, then **Web Project**, then **Synchronize Files** to make sure that the new document is added to both the Local and Master version of your Web project.

Now that the REPORT.ASP document is added to the project, you're ready to learn how to use it to create tabular reports.

A Quick Tour of REPORT.ASP

The REPORT.ASP document is really a complete tabular report library in one file. REPORT.ASP has several very nice features you can use with any Visual InterDev 6 application. This document does the following:

- Works with any database format (SQL Server, Oracle, Microsoft Access, FoxPro, and so on)
- Enables you to add a title and subtitle to the top of the report
- Enables you to optionally add up to two image files to the report header (left and right of the title)
- Enables you to establish a list of columns that should be totaled for the report
- Enables you to designate one column as the "BreakOn" column. This column will be used to subtotal any declared total columns
- Enables you to control the width of the report space and the thickness (or visibility) of the table borders
- Enables you to define each report in a report information file for easy reloading of complex report definitions

Building Tabular Reports with the REPORT.ASP Document

PART V
CHAPTER 21

You use REPORT.ASP by creating a report information file (RIF) that contains all the parameters needed to generate a tabular report. After you create the RIF, you can call REPORT.ASP using the following HTML link syntax:

```
www.mywebserver/mywebproject/report.asp?ReportInfoFile=
➥myreport.rif
```

Optionally, you can create an HTML `<FORM>` that lists several reports from which the user can select and "submit" to REPORT.ASP (see Figure 21.4).

Note that the variable name must always be in the form `ReportInfoFile=<your report file>` when you use this method to call the REPORT.ASP document.

The `<FORM>` element for the example shown in Figure 21.4 looks like the one in Listing 21.6.

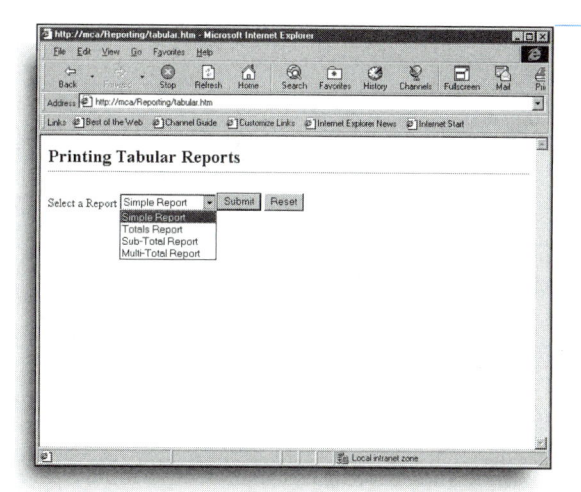

> **REPORT.ASP reusability**
>
> The REPORT.ASP file can be reused in your applications. You might want to customize it to suit your own needs, but the basics can apply to any application that needs to do reporting.

FIGURE 21.4
Submitting a report to REPORT.ASP.

LISTING 21.6 Sample Submit Form Using REPORT.ASP as the Target URL

```
1  <FORM action=report.asp id=frmReport method=get
   ➥name=frmReport>
2    <P>Select a Report <SELECT id=ReportInfoFile
     ➥name=ReportInfoFile>
3    <OPTION selected value=simple.rif>Simple Report
4    <OPTION value=totals.rif>Totals Report
```

continues...

LISTING 21.6 Continued

```
5     <OPTION value=subtotal.rif>Sub-Total Report
6     <OPTION value=multitot.rif>Multi-Total Report
7  </SELECT>
8
9     <INPUT id=submit1 name=submit1 type=submit
   ➥value=Submit>
10    <INPUT id=reset1 name=reset1 type=reset value=Reset>
11    </P>
12 </FORM>
```

Again, notice that the HTML element that returns the name of the report information file is always called `ReportInfoFile`. In the case of Listing 21.6, the drop-down `<SELECT>` element is set to `ReportInfoFile` (line 2).

Now that you have an idea of how to call the REPORT.ASP document to create a report, you're ready to build your report information file.

Building Your Report Information File

The process of building a valid report information file (RIF) is pretty simple. The RIF file is a simple ASCII text file that contains information on the database, recordset, totals and break columns, titles, images, and table attributes for your report. The only tricky part is that you must be sure to account for all the parameters—even if they are left blank.

Listing 21.7 shows a sample report information file, and Table 21.1 explains what each entry means.

LISTING 21.7 Sample Report Information File

```
1 DRIVER=SQL Server;SERVER=(local);User Id=sa;PASSWORD=
  ➥;DATABASE=pubs;
2 admin
3 mypassword
4 SELECT * FROM Orders ORDER BY CustomerID,OrderID
5 Monthly Orders Report
6 Multi-Totals Version
7 Freight;EmployeeID;ShipVia;
```

Building Tabular Reports with the REPORT.ASP Document

PART V
CHAPTER 21

```
 8 CustomerID
 9 images/leftimage.gif
10 images/rightimage.gif
11 100%
12 1
```

TABLE 21.1 Report information file format

Name	Required?	Description	Example
DBConnection	Yes	Complete database connection string.	DRIVER=SQL Server; SERVER=(local); Use Id=sa; PASS-WORD=; DATABASE=pubs;
UserID	No	Valid database ID.	Admin
Password	No	Valid database password.	Mypassword
SQL SELECT	Yes	Valid SQL SELECT statement.	SELECT * FROM MyTable
ReportTitle	Yes	Title to display on the page.	Monthly Report
SubTitle	No	Title to display under main title on the page.	Sorted by Customer
TotalColumns	No	List of columns to track for totals. Separate multiple columns with a semicolon (;).	Units;Cost; ExtAmount;
BreakOnColumn	No	Column to use for subtotal break. All columns in the TotalColumns list will be subtotals and printed each time the BreakOn Column changes.	CustomerID
LeftImage	No	Image to appear left of the title.	companylogo.gif

continues...

TABLE 21.1 Continued

Name	Required?	Description	Example
RightImage	No	Image to appear right of the title.	departmentlogo.gif
TableWidth	Yes	Width of table in percent or pixels.	100% -or- 800px
BorderWidth	Yes	Thickness of cell border, used to remove cell borders.	1

As shown in Table 21.1, there are 12 possible parameters for REPORT.ASP. Five of them are required parameters (DBConnection, SQL SELECT, ReportTitle, TableWidth, and BorderWidth). The rest are optional. However, if you want to skip the optional parameters, you must include a blank line where the parameter would usually appear. In other words, every RIF will have 12 lines, and some of them may be blank.

Now that you know how the report information file looks, you're ready to create your own. Add a new document to your project called TEST.RIF.

Adding a new report information file to your project

1. Right-click over the project name in the Project Explorer window.
2. Select **Add** from the menu.
3. Select **Add Item** from the submenu.
4. Enter the name of the file to add (TEST.RIF) and press **Open** to add the file to the project.
5. When the file appears in your editor, remove any existing text. You're ready to edit your RIF.

For this example, you use the same database connection that you used to create the COLUMNAR.ASP document. However, you must actually copy the connection string from the GLOBAL.ASA file into your RIF document.

Flat-file databases

A *flat-file* database refers to data that is stored in a text or resource file as opposed to a formal database format, such as Microsoft Access, or a structured database server like Microsoft SQL Server.

Building Tabular Reports with the REPORT.ASP Document

Listing 21.8 shows a completed RIF document that will display the Authors table in the SQL Server Pubs database. You can copy this data directly into your own TEST.RIF document. You might also need to edit the user ID and password for your site. You might want to skip the image references if you do not have any available in your Web project.

LISTING 21.8 Sample TEST.RIF Report Information File

```
1 DRIVER=SQL Server;SERVER=(local);DATABASE=pubs;User
 ➥Id=sa;PASSWORD=;
2 sa
3
4 SELECT au_id,au_lname,au_fname,city,state,'1' AS cnt
 ➥FROM Authors ORDER BY state
5 Authors Report
6 By state
7 cnt
8 state
9 images/report.gif
10 images/report.gif
11 100%
12 0
```

Now you can create a very simple HTML document called TABULAR.HTM that has a single button. After adding the button, add the following client-side Visual Basic Script to execute when a person presses the button (see Listing 21.9).

Skipping parameters

If you skip any of the parameters shown in Listing 21.9, be sure to include a blank line in its place (see line 3).

LISTING 21.9 Using Simple Visual Basic Scripting to Call REPORT.ASP

```
1 <SCRIPT LANGUAGE=vbscript>
2 <!--
3 Sub button1_onclick
4    window.navigate "report.asp?ReportInfoFile=test.rif"
5 End sub
6 -->
7 </SCRIPT>
```

PART V   Using ActiveX Technologies

CHAPTER 21   **Adding Reports and Graphs to Your Web Applications**

Save the document, mark it as the startup page, and press F5 to run it. When you click on the button, you see something that looks like Figure 21.5.

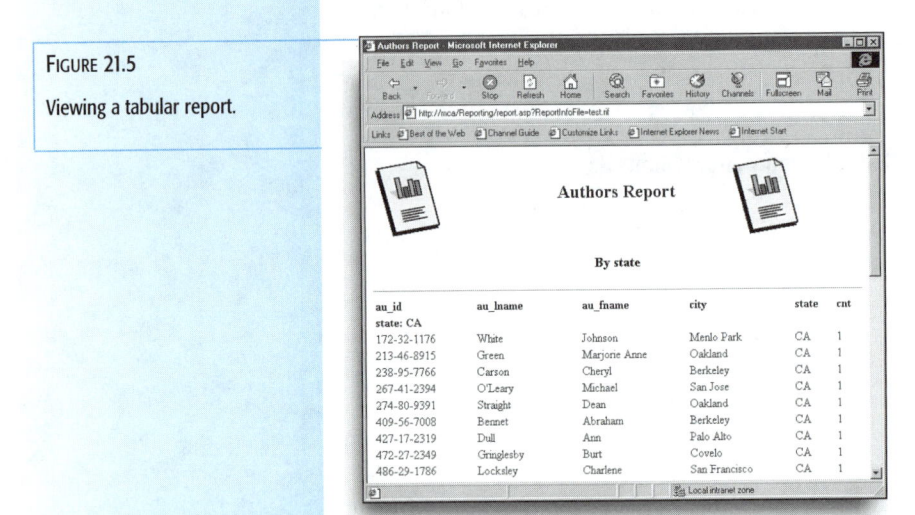

FIGURE 21.5

Viewing a tabular report.

Now you can create columnar and tabular reports from database recordsets. Even better, you can use both these documents in other Web applications with very little alteration.

Using ASPChart to Display Database Recordsets

The last type of reporting covered in this chapter is graphical chart reports. Chart reports are a very effective way to focus the reader's attention on just the important aspects of the data. By using colors, bars, and other shapes, you can summarize the relationship of a great deal of data in one quick image.

Although chart reports are very handy, creating them is a challenge with Visual InterDev 6, because Visual InterDev 6 does not ship with an Internet-aware graphing component.

Using ASPChart to Display Database Recordsets

However, there is a very good component, called ASPChart, available via the Internet. Also, the makers of ASPChart have agreed to allow readers of this book to download a 30-day trial copy of their product for use with the exercise. You can visit the *Using Visual InterDev 6* home page to find the link for downloading your trial copy of ASPChart.

If you haven't done this yet, take a few moments to log onto the Internet, visit the *Using Visual InterDev 6* home page, and download the ASPChart component. When you have a copy of the download package, you can continue with the chapter. You get step-by-step instructions on installing and registering the DLL on your Web server in the next section of this chapter.

Don't have ASPChart? That's OK!

If you do not have a copy of ASPChart available and can't install it on the server you are using with this book, that's OK. You can still learn a lot by reading through the exercise.

SEE ALSO

▶ *The Using Visual InterDev 6 Web site has a link to download ASPChart. For the URL, flip to page 791*

Installing ASPChart

ASPChart is a simple server-side component in the form of a DLL (dynamic link library). The download package that contains the ASPChart DLL also contains several sample scripts and documentation.

You must do two things in order to complete the installation of the ASPChart component:

1. Copy the file ASPCHART.DLL to a shared folder on the Web server (usually \WINNT\SYSTEM32\ or \WINDOWS\SYSTEM\).
2. Register the DLL using REGSVR32.EXE.

To perform the last step, exit to the operating system (DOS), move to the folder where you copied the ASPCHART.DLL file, and type the following:

REGSVR32 ASPCHART.DLL<return>

You should then see a dialog that tells you the DLL has been successfully registered.

Administrator rights required

In order to complete these steps you must have administrator's rights on the Web server. For Windows NT machines, it is not good enough to be a member of the Domain Administrator group. You must be a member of the Administrator group for that machine.

Register the DLL!

If you don't register the component using **REGSVR32**, the component will not function!

Other components

As mentioned earlier in this chapter, other components are used for reporting and charting. ASPChart is a simple start into reporting, but it might not suit your needs. Use it to get your feet wet and evaluate your needs, then look for a replacement.

After you have the ASPCHART.DLL installed and registered, you're ready to create an ASP script that calls the graphing component.

Creating the CHARTING.ASP Document

Now add a new ASP document to the Web project called CHARTING.ASP. This document will be used to create an instance of the ASPCHART.DLL and send it information so that it will create a 3D bar chart.

Programming the ASPChart component is relatively simple. No matter what type of data you want to display, you still go through the same basic steps.

Programming the ASPChart component

1. Create an instance of the ASPChart component for your use.
2. Add the data values to display in the chart.
3. Add the chart titles.
4. Set the final image output size.
5. Set any additional features (colors, backgrounds, and so on).
6. Generate the image to disk.
7. Call up the image and display it to the user.

It might seem like a lot to cover, but it's not too bad. First, you create a shared object variable, some default values, and a set of top-level calls to methods that cover the previous list.

In the <BODY> section of your ASP document, add the code shown in Listing 21.10.

LISTING 21.10 Adding Top-Level Code to the CHARTING.ASP Document

```
1 <SCRIPT LANGUAGE=vbscript RUNAT=Server>
2 Dim Chart
3
4 cNone   = 0
```

Using ASPChart to Display Database Recordsets

```
 5 cBar     = 1
 6 cRectGradient =6
 7 '
 8 Set Chart = Server.CreateObject ("ASPChart.Chart")
 9 '
10 AddChartData
11 AddChartTitles
12 AddChartFeatures
13 SetImageSize
14 SaveChartImage
15 Set Chart = nothing
16 </SCRIPT>
```

As mentioned earlier, the code in Listing 21.10 follows closely the steps outlined above the code listing. Note line 7. This is where the instance of the charting object is created. Note also that the last line of the listing (16) is where the charting object is released from memory.

Now add a new Visual Basic Scripting sub method that will add some data to the chart (see Listing 21.11).

LISTING 21.11 Adding Data to the Chart

```
 1 Sub AddChartData
 2    '
 3    ' add some data points to the chart
 4    '
 5    Chart.AddSeries (cBar)
 6    Chart.AddValue 200, "Regular", vbBlue
 7    Chart.AddValue 233, "Enhanced ", vbRed
 8    Chart.AddValue 260, "Free", vbGreen
 9    Chart.BarStyle = cRectGradient
10    '
11 End Sub
```

The next step is to add titles to the chart. This is shown in Listing 21.12.

> **Keep it in bounds**
>
> All the code in this example is Visual Basic Script code. That means it should appear within `<SCRIPT>` and `</SCRIPT>` boundaries. The first listing in this group shows the script tags, but the rest do not. This was done for clarity. You can enclose each Visual Basic Script block within a `<SCRIPT>...</SCRIPT>` set or place the entire Visual Basic Scripting code listing with the same `<SCRIPT>...</SCRIPT>`.

LISTING 21.12 Adding Titles to the Chart

```
1  Sub AddChartTitles
2    '
3    ' add titles
4    '
5    Chart.ChartTitleAdd ("Simple Bar Chart")
6    Chart.ChartTitleFont.Size = 20
7    Chart.ChartTitleFont.Name = "Times New Roman"
8    Chart.ChartTitleFont.Italic = true
9    Chart.ChartTitleFont.Bold = true
10   '
11 End Sub
```

Next, you can add additional values to control the way the image appears in the browser (see Listing 21.13).

LISTING 21.13 Adding Extra Features to the Chart

```
1  Sub AddChartFeatures
2    '
3    ' Remove the OuterBevel, add a gradient fill to
4    ' chart panel
5    '
6    Chart.BevelOuter = cNone
7    Chart.GradientVisible = true
8    Chart.GradientStartColor = vbWhite
9    Chart.GradientEndColor = vbYellow
10   '
11 End Sub
```

Next, you set the final size of the chart image that will be created (see Listing 21.14).

LISTING 21.14 Setting the Chart Image Size

```
1  Sub SetImageSize
2    '
3    ' Set the Width and Height of the image
4    '
5    Chart.Height = 300
6    Chart.Width = 500
7  End Sub
```

Using ASPChart to Display Database Recordsets

The last high-level routine saves the chart as a JPG file and then displays the file to users (see Listing 21.15).

LISTING 21.15 Adding the *SaveChartImage* Method

```
1  Sub SaveChartImage
2    '
3    ' Set the filename, save the image and write the
4    ' image tag
5    '
6    dim strSaveName
7    dim strFolder
8    dim strFullName
9    '
10   strFolder=FolderOnly("charting.asp")
11   strSaveName="charting.jpg"
12   strFullName=strFolder & strSaveName
13   '
14   Chart.FileName = strFullName
15   Chart.SaveChart
16   Response.Write "<img src=" & chr(34) &
     ➥strSaveName & chr(34) & ">"
17   '
18 End Sub
```

Because you must save the file to a local drive, you need one more routine that can read the current HTTP URL and convert it into a valid local file folder for use by the Web server. Add the FolderOnly() method to the ASP document (see Listing 21.16).

LISTING 21.16 Adding the *FolderOnly* Method

```
1  Function FolderOnly(FileName)
2    '
3    ' get current folder
4    '
5    dim strPath
6    dim intPos
7    '
8    strPath=Server.MapPath(Request.ServerVariables(
     ➥"PATH_INFO"))
```

continues...

LISTING 21.16 Continued

```
9     intPos=inStr(uCase(strPath),uCase(FileName))
10    FolderOnly=Left(strPath,intPos-1)
11  '
12 End Function
```

That's the end of the code for the CHARTING.ASP document. Save the document, mark it as the startup page, and press F5 to see the 3D image appear on your screen. If all goes as expected, your video display will look like the one in Figure 21.3.

The ASPChart component has lots of features and possibilities. You can review the examples that ship with the trial version of the component to get an idea of its possible uses. Be sure to review the documentation for updates and fixes, too.

CHAPTER 22

Adding Active Content to Your Web Application

Use date- and time-based content

Create pages that use external sources for part of their composition

Use three of the active content components that are installed with Microsoft Internet Information Server

Design Web applications that can use other active content components

PART V   Using ActiveX Technologies

CHAPTER 22   **Adding Active Content to Your Web Application**

Harnessing the Power of Active Content

Anyone who has started a Web page knows how important it is to keep it updated and accurate. Creating Web applications and Web sites can be a time-consuming task—so time-consuming that by the time the process is finished, some of the content can already be out of date! Although it is possible (and quite common) that Web authoring can be a constant series of updates without any release date, there is a better way: active content.

Microsoft developed the active content idea to combat the very problem mentioned here—outdated content in a Web application. The idea is really quite simple: Develop a model that allows Web authors to design Web documents that act as "frameworks" for changing content. In other words, build some tools that allow authors and programmers to plug in updated content at any time without having to change the Web documents themselves.

To do this, Microsoft put together a set of components that cover some of the most common active content scenarios, such as

- Banner advertisement rotation
- Table of contents linking

SEE ALSO
➤ *For information on adding Microsoft Office documents to your Web, see page 621*
➤ *For information on adding Visual Basic ActiveX documents to your Web see page 627*

Designing to Take Advantage of Active Content

The key to harnessing the power of the active content model is to alter the way you begin to design a Web solution. Instead of thinking about how to collect and present the desired content, it is better to think first about how to create a document (or documents) that represent an "abstracted" version of the solution. This helps focus the design on the creation of a framework without specific content. When the framework is in place, you can then insert the content any time you want. Because the solution

---

Just the start of active content

Several other active content–related objects are available with Microsoft Internet Information Server. There are also new components available every month. You can even build your own active content component using Visual Basic or Visual C++. In this chapter, you explore two commonly used components (Ad rotator and Content Linker) in order to give you a good idea of how the active content model works and how you can take advantage of active content programming in your Web applications.

involves a clear separation between presentation and content, changing the content will not require extensive change to the presentation portion of the solution itself.

Consider the following example: You've been given the task of putting together an online magazine for a client. The client has all the content but needs help building an online presence for the material. After consulting with the client, you realize that it wants to update this online magazine every month. The client needs a simple Web application that will allow it to easily add new articles to the magazine without having to re-author any existing pages in the application.

At the same time, the client needs a central table of contents for the magazine to act as a home page for visitors. This should have a basic masthead with some art (supplied by the client), along with a list of the most recent articles available online. However, the client does not want to have to edit this list every time a new article is added or removed from the collection. Instead, this table of contents should be designed to be dynamic. It should automatically present only the material deemed current or available by the client staff. And adding or deleting article references from this page should be simple.

SEE ALSO
➤ *For more on desgning Web forms and documents, see page 111*

Using the Active Content Solution Framework

You can easily build a Web solution that allows for changes in content by using the server-side active content objects. Because the client is providing the content documents, all you must do is build a framework to display the current documents available to readers. To do this, you can use server-side script to connect to one of the Microsoft active content components, have it read a simple text file that contains a list of available articles, and present them as links in the home page of the Web application.

Then, as new articles are added or removed the client staff can simply update the text file without having to touch the actual

More active content means more hits

The single most important thing you can do to increase your hit count at your Web sites is to continually update the content. Using active content components like the ones covered here is a good way to design constantly changing content.

Web page seen by visitors. When the text file is updated, that will be reflected in the contents of the home page in the Web application.

In the next several sections of this chapter, you learn how to build the magazine solution and two other common active content Web applications: building an advertisement rotator and checking the capabilities of client browsers.

Preparing the Active Content Project

The three active content components discussed in this chapter can be created as standalone solutions or as a single solution with three separate documents and a home page. This section of the chapter shows you how to build a single home page for the project, which can jump to each of the three solutions you'll build.

First, start a new Visual InterDev Web project called ActiveContent and add a new HTML page called DEFAULT.HTM. After you add the page to your Web application, be sure to mark it as the startup page.

Marking a document as the start page

1. Use the Project Explorer to select the page you want to mark.

2. After selecting the desired page (click once), right-click over the page to view the context menu.

3. Select the **Set as Start Page** item from the menu to mark the page.

After marking the DEFAULT.HTM page as the startup page, you must add a heading and two hyperlinks to the document. Table 22.1 shows the heading text, the link titles, and associated URLs for each item. Add these elements in the **Design** tab of the Visual InterDev editor. You can refer to Figure 22.1 as a guide in laying out this page.

Add active content to an existing project

You can add active content to any existing project. Just add the control files, the ASP page to host the active content, and the other documents that will be the target URLs, and you're set.

Building an Online Magazine with the Content Linker Objects | PART **V**, CHAPTER **22** | **601**

TABLE 22.1 **Laying out the ActiveContent start page**

Text	Link
Demonstrate Active Content	NA (this is the title)
The Content Linking Component	`Contentlink.asp`
The Ad Rotator Component	`Adrotator.asp`

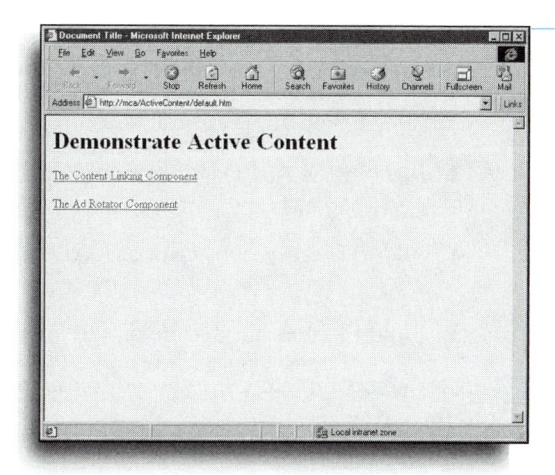

FIGURE 22.1
Viewing the DEFAULT.HTM page of the ActiveContent Web.

Now save the project and run it (press F5 or select **Debug, Start**) from the main Visual InterDev menu. When you are sure the page is working fine, you're ready to start adding the active content portions of the Web application.

SEE ALSO
- *For more on creating new projects with Visual InterDev 6, see page 7*
- *To learn how to add new pages to an existing project, see page 33*

Building an Online Magazine with the Content Linker Objects

The first active content solution you'll build uses the Content Linker object. This object enables you to create a simple text file that associates a friendly title with a URL (Uniform Resource

Locator). This URL can be a document in the current Web application, a downloadable binary file, an image file, or even a link to another Web server somewhere. The Content Linker object is perfect for building solutions that must present lists of references to a user when the reference list changes frequently.

For this example, you build a page that reads a text file containing the URL and the title of articles that are stored somewhere on the Web. This page will act as the table of contents for a fictitious online magazine called *VID News Central*.

Creating a Web application like this requires three basic steps:

1. Lay out the ASP page that will host the Content Linking Component (CLC).
2. Add the server-side script that will activate the Content Linker.
3. Build the text file that holds the pointers to content pages.

After you complete these simple steps, you are ready to test your online magazine!

SEE ALSO
> For information about Active Server Pages (ASP), see page 379

> **Content links can point to other content links**
> You do not have to use only HTM documents in your content linking control file. You can use any valid URL including external Web pages, downloadable files, and even other ASP documents that use additional control linker control files to present a table of links.

Laying Out the *VID News Central* Contents Page

The first step is to create an Active Server Page (ASP) that will act as the table of contents for your online magazine. To do this, load the ActiveContent project and add a new ASP page called CONTENTLINK.ASP.

Adding an ASP page to the current project

1. Select the project name in the Project Explorer window (**ActiveContent**).
2. Right-click over the name and click **Add** in the context menu.
3. Next, select Acti**v**e Server Page from the context menu.
4. When you see the Add Item dialog, enter the name of your new Active Server Page in the **Name** field and press **Open**. In this example, enter the name of the new document (for this example enter CONTENTLINK.

Building an Online Magazine with the Content Linker Objects

PART **V**
CHAPTER **22**

603

5. You'll then see the new ASP page appear in the Project Explorer window and in your Visual InterDev Editor window with the **Source** tab as the active tab.

Now that you have a new ASP document in your project, switch to the **Design** tab in the Visual InterDev Editor to add the visual elements to your page.

You must add a table with one row and three columns to the top of the page. This will hold a graphic, the main title, and the current date and time. That is all you must do visually. The rest of the content (the list of articles) will be added using server-side script. Refer to Table 22.2 and Figure 22.2 as a guide.

> **You can't execute ASP documents in Quickview**
>
> Even though you can use Design view to see how your standard HTML elements look on an ASP document, you cannot use the **Quickview** tab to see how the final ASP document will appear in client browsers. This is because the **Quickview** tab does not preprocess ASP code. Only a Web server can do that.

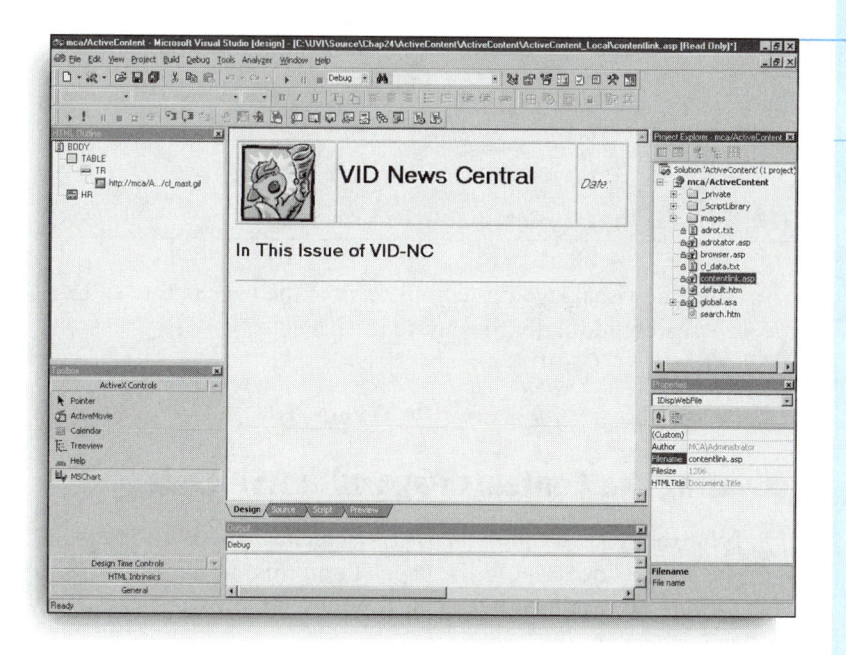

FIGURE 22.2
Laying out the online magazine.

TABLE 22.2 Elements of the *VID News Central* contents page

Element	Property	Setting
Table	Rows	1
	Columns	3
	Width	100 percent

continues...

TABLE 22.2 Continued

Element	Property	Setting
Image	`ALIGN`	Left
	`ALT`	Masthead
	`SRC`	CL_MAST.GIF
(Text)		VID News Central
	(Style)	H2
	(Placement)	Column 2 of Table
		Date:
	(Style)	ADDRESS
	(Placement)	Column 3 of Table
		What's New in This Issue
	(Style)	H4
	(Placement)	Below Table
Horizontal Bar	(Placement)	Below subheading

After the visual layout is complete, save the page before adding the server-side script to activate the page.

SEE ALSO
► *For more on using HTML intrinsic controls, see page 133*

Activating the Contents Page with ASP Code

Now that you've added the visual elements, you're ready to add the server-side script to the page. To do this, switch from the **Design** tab to the **Source** tab. You must add two server-side script items to the project.

First, you must add the current date and time to the last cell in the table. To do this you must add a small bit of server-side script code to the page. Locate the word **Date:** in the last column of the table and modify the HTML code to look like the code in Listing 22.1.

Where are the graphics?

The graphics items used throughout this book can be replaced with any images you have on hand. They are used for layout only and their content is not important. However, if you'd like, you can download the complete set of images by visiting the *Using Visual InterDev 6* Web site. The address of the Web site is in Appendix B in the back of this book. You'll find links for the graphics, the source code, and other material related to Microsoft Visual InterDev.

Building an Online Magazine with the Content Linker Objects

LISTING 22.1 **Adding ASP Code to Send the Current Date/Time**

```
1  <ADDRESS>Date: 
2  <%=Now%> <!-- added ASP Code -->
3  </ADDRESS>
```

LISTING 22.1

❶ The <% and %> mark the start and end of ASP code.

Next, you must add the server-side script that will create an instance of the Content Linking component, read the contents of the text file, and send that information down to the client in the form of an HTML table. You do this in a couple of steps.

First, you add the server-side script that will create an instance of the Content Linking component. In the **Script** tab of the editor window, move to the first empty line after the </TABLE> HTML tag and add the first set of server-side script. Listing 22.2 has the code you need to add at this point. Note that the server-side script always starts with a <% and ends with a %>.

LISTING 22.2 **Adding the Server-Side Script to Start the CLC**

```
1   <!-- get instance of CLC -->
2   <%
3   '
4   ' create vars for handling CLC
5   dim objLinker ' holds CLC
6   dim intLoop ' counts items to display
7   dim strURL ' holds item URL
8   dim strTitle ' holds item title
9   '
10  ' get instance of CLC object
11  set objLinker = Server.CreateObject("MSWC.NextLink")
12  %>
```

LISTING 22.2

❶ This is the line that creates an instance of the Content Linker COM component for use in the ASP script.

The next code you must add displays the URL and title pairs to the user in a table format. This code piece combines both server-side script and HTML. This is a common practice. Although you could write the entire routine using server-side script only, it would take more time and the results would be no different.

So, move your cursor to the first empty line after the horizontal bar (<HR>) element. This is where you want the content items to appear. Listing 22.3 has the code you must add at this point.

PART V Using ActiveX Technologies

CHAPTER 22 Adding Active Content to Your Web Application

> **LISTING 22.3**
>
> ① Notice that this line is outside the <% and %> markers. This is just plain HTML code with two ASP snippets inside the HTML line.

LISTING 22.3 Adding the Code to Display the URL/Title Pairs

```
1  <!-- now show articles in this issue -->
2  <%
3  For intLoop=1 to objLinker.GetListCount("cl_data.txt")
4      strURL=objLinker.GetNthURL("cl_data.txt",intLoop)
5      strTitle=objLinker.GetNthDescription("cl_data.txt"
       ➥,intLoop)
6  %>
7  <H4><LI><A href="<%=strURL%>"><%=strTitle%></A></H4>  ──①
8  <%Next%>
9  <HR>
```

This piece of code deserves a bit of comment. First, notice that the first three lines are pure server-side script surrounded by <% and %> markers. This code starts a For...Next loop (lines 3–6) that uses the CLC to read each item in the text file, pull out the associated URL and title for each item, and place them in VBScript variables.

Line 7 is mostly HTML with a few server-side script items mixed in to complete the process. Notice how the line that produces the article entry uses the server-side script variables strURL and strTitle as parts of the HREF tag. This is active content in action!

Finally, line 8, or <%Next%>, completes the server-side script For...Next loop, and the <HR> visual marks the end of the list in line 9.

> **Breaking up ASP script is perfectly legal**
>
> You do not have to keep all your ASP script in a single script block or within one set of <% and %> tags. In fact, it is quite common to use multiple script sections in the same ASP document.

That's the end of the coding for this document. Be sure to save the page before continuing to build the CL_DATA.TXT file.

SEE ALSO
▶ For details about how ASP pages work, see page 636

Adding the Text File to Control Online Content

The final task is to create a simple text file that contains the URL and titles for all the articles for this issue of *VID News Central*. First, you must add a text document to the project. Then you can use the Visual InterDev Editor to create the CLC entries.

Building an Online Magazine with the Content Linker Objects

Adding a text file to your project

1. Select the project name in the Project Explorer window by clicking it once.
2. Press the right mouse button over the project name and select **Add** from the context menu.
3. Now select **Add** **I**tem... from the submenu.
4. When the Add Item dialog appears, enter the filename in the **N**ame input box (CL_DATA.TXT); then press the **O**pen button.
5. The document will appear in the Project Explorer and in the Visual InterDev Editor with an initial set of HTML header and footer codes.
6. Remove all the default text to start with a clean text document.
7. After editing the document, you can save it as you would any other project document.

After adding the CL_DATA.TXT file to your project and deleting all the default text, you must add entries to fill in the magazine contents page. Each line in the text file must be in the following form:

<URL><tab><Title>

where

- <URL> is a valid Uniform Resource Locator. subfolder/page3.htm or http://www.myserver.com/myweb/subfolder/page3.thm.
- <tab> is a tab (ASCII character 9) that acts as a separator.
- <Title> is a friendly title to display on the page, such as Amundsen Web Site or Mail Support Request.

You do not need to use special characters such as quotes or commas to mark the text in any way. The <tab> character is the only important character recognized by the Content Linking Component.

Associating your favorite text editor

When you open a text type document, Visual InterDev 6 uses NOTEPAD.EXE as the editor. If you have another ASCII editor you prefer to use, you can install it into Visual InterDev 6 by right-clicking over the loaded text file and selecting **Open With**. Follow the prompts to add a new editor to your list.

Using relative and absolute URL addressing

When adding pointers to other Web documents, you can use two forms of URL addressing: Relative and Absolute. Absolute addressing uses the complete URL, such as http://myserver/myweb/mypage.htm. Relative addressing is the most flexible because it calculates the location of a another Web document based on the current document's location. For example, the URL somefolder/page3.htm tells the browser to move to a subfolder one level down from the current location and load page3.htm.

PART **V** Using ActiveX Technologies
CHAPTER **22** **Adding Active Content to Your Web Application**

Table 22.3 shows the entries you should make in the CL_DATA.TXT file. When you are finished, it should look like Listing 22.4.

TABLE 22.3 Entries in the CL_DATA.TXT file

URL	Title
fpnews.htm	FrontPage News
vidid.htm	Visual InterDev InDepth
ichit.htm	Image Composer a Hit
wish.htm	Using VID a Bestseller!

LISTING 22.4 Contents of the Completed CL_DATA.TXT File

```
1   fpnews.htm    FrontPage News
2   vidid.htm     Visual InterDev InDepth
3   ichit.htm     Image Composer a Hit
4   wish.htm      Using VID a Bestseller!
```

After completing the CL_DATA.TXT file, save it and run the project (press F5) to test your online magazine. When the project first starts, you'll see the DEFAULT.HTM page showing the two links. Select the **Content Linking Component** item. If you find errors, you can halt the run and fix them. When your page is able to run without errors, it should look like the one in Figure 22.3.

FIGURE 22.3

Running the *VID News Central* online magazine.

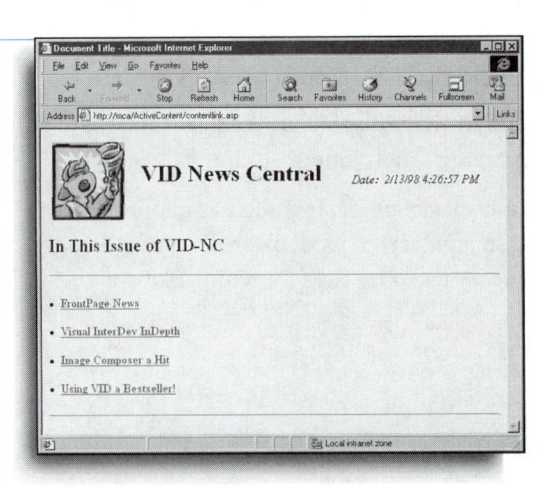

Creating Rotating Banner Ads with Ad Rotator Component

Of course, at this point the various links will report errors because there are no HTML documents to match the entries. However, you could easily modify this example to contain links to valid content within your Web application or anywhere on the Internet.

SEE ALSO
➤ For more on using the Visual InterDev 6 editor, see page 33

Creating Rotating Banner Ads with Ad Rotator Component

A very common element of Web sites is the rotating banner advertisements that appear at the top of Web pages. These ads usually attempt to convince the reader to click within their borders in order to be transported to another site somewhere on the Internet. However, not only are the ads meant to compel readers to click on them, most hosting Web sites actually count the number of times the ads get clicked. The Ad Rotator Component that ships with Microsoft Internet Information Server is a simple way to add this functionality to your Web pages.

The Ad Rotator Component requires very little server-side script code to implement. Listing 22.5 shows the entire code segment needed in order to place rotating ads on your Web pages.

> **Be sure to use tabs instead of spaces**
>
> The Content Linker component looks for a tab (character 9) to separate the URL item from the title. If you use spaces instead of a tab to separate the two items, the Content Linker will not report an error; it will simply stop processing your list.

LISTING 22.5 Minimum Script Needed to Activate the Ad Rotator

```
1  <%
2  '
3  ' get instance on add rotator and show ads
4  '
5  Dim objAd ' holds object
6  '
7  ' connect to object
8  Set objAd = Server.CreateObject("MSWC.AdRotator")
```

> **LISTING 22.5**
>
> ❶ This is the line that gets an instance of the Ad Rotator for your use.

continues...

LISTING 22.5 Continued

```
9    ' display the ad
10   Response.Write objAd.GetAdvertisement("adrot.txt")
11   '
12   %>
```

② This is the line that uses the control file to display the next add in the rotation.

As you can see in Listing 22.5, only three lines of server-side script (5, 8, and 10) are needed to complete a rotating ad banner for a page. You must declare an object variable, link that variable to an instance of the Ad Rotator component, and use the `Response` object to write out the current ad banner found in a text file.

The Text File that Runs the Ad Rotator

The server-side script coding of the ad rotator component is simple because all the important stuff is stored in a text file in the Web project. This text file contains information about how to display ad images in general, including

- The width and height of the banner space on the page
- The thickness of the border placed around each banner ad
- An optional URL to use as a redirect page in order to centrally log ad clicks by users

The text file also includes detailed information about each banner, including

- The image file to display
- The URL associated with the image
- The text to display in case images are turned off by the browser
- The number of times each image should be included in the rotation (expressed as a percentage)

To add banner ads, collect the advertisement images and information, add a few lines of server-side script to your Web page, create the text file to control the rotation, and (optionally) set up a redirect page to log user clicks.

So let's do it.

Creating the Ad Banner Display Page

The first step is to create an ASP file that will display the collected banner advertisements. To do this, add a new ASP document called ADROTATOR.ASP to the ActiveContent Web project. After adding the page to the project, you must add a little HTML and a few lines of server-side script.

Listing 22.6 shows all the code you need to enter into the ADROTATOR.ASP document. Enter this code at the first empty line after the <BODY> tag.

LISTING 22.6 Adding Code to the ADROTATOR.ASP Document

```
1   <H2>Ad Rotator Sample</H2><br>
2
3   <%
4   '
5   ' get instance on add rotator and show ads
6   '
7   Dim objAd ' holds object
8   '
9   ' connect to object
10  Set objAd = Server.CreateObject("MSWC.AdRotator")
11  ' display the ad
12  Response.Write objAd.GetAdvertisement("adrot.txt")
13  '
14  %>
```

By now this code should look pretty familiar. Line 7 declares a variable that will hold the pointer to the Ad Rotator object. Line 10 is the code that actually creates the instance of the pointer in your script. Line 12 reads the text file (ADROT.TXT) and displays one of the banner ads on the page.

That's all the coding you need to do for this page. Save it before you go on to the next task.

SEE ALSO

➤ *For information on adding new ASP documents to your Web page, see page 33*

Adding a Hit Check Page to Monitor Ad Usage

Next, let's add another ASP document to the project called ADCHECK.ASP. This document will act as a gateway from this Web project to all the URLs associated with the banner ads. By creating this additional document, you can add server-side script that will log user clicks to various sites. This will also give you a chance to run other server-side script code like updating counters, and so on before you send your visitors on to the next location.

After adding the ADCHECK.ASP document to your Web project, you must add some server-side script to it in order to handle the redirection information you will be receiving from the ADROTATOR.ASP document. Listing 22.7 shows all the code needed to handle basic click-through logging and redirection on the target site.

> **About counting click-throughs**
>
> The example shown here shows you how to capture what are known in the business as "click-throughs" from your site to other sites. Many companies use this information as a method for charging advertisers who use their sites. However, the example shown here is very rudimentary. Additional coding, including error handling and storing counters in text files on the Web server, is needed before this routine would be ready for production use.

LISTING 22.7 Adding Code to Handle Logging Click-Throughs and URL Redirection

```
1   <%
2   ' *************************************
3   ' handle redirect from ad rotator
4   ' *************************************
5   '
6   ' note:
7   ' you must do this *before* the
8   ' <HTML> header tag is sent to the browser
9   '
10  strURL=Request.QueryString("url") ' get URL from line
11  Response.AppendToLog "AD HIT: " & strURL ' update log
12  Response.Redirect strURL ' send user off
13  '
14  %>
```

It is important to note that this code must be added at the top of the ASP document, right after the `<@ LANGUAGE="VBScript">` and just *before* the `<HTML>` tag. If you add this code after the `<HTML>` header has been sent, you will receive errors.

Creating Rotating Banner Ads with Ad Rotator Component

The ability to provide URL redirection in an ASP document is very powerful. It also has its problems. First, any redirection information must be processed at the server *before* the HTML header data (the HTML code at the top of every page) is sent to the browser. The idea of redirection is to force the browser to "go somewhere else" instead of displaying this page.

Listing 22.7 shows three lines of server-side script that perform all the operations needed to log the click-through and redirect the user to the target URL. First, the URL is pulled from the command line using the `.QueryString` method of the `Response` object (line 10). Next, the `.AppendToLog` method is used to write that URL (along with some added text) to the Web site's log file (line 11). Finally, that same URL is used by the `Redirect` method to forward the user to the target site (line 12).

After adding the code from Listing 22.7 to the ADCHECK.ASP document, save it before continuing to the next task.

> **Another way to redirect users**
>
> You can also use the HTML tag `<META HTTP-EQUIV="REFRESH" CONTENT="15; URL=http://www.amundsen.com/staging/">` with the `<HEAD></HEAD>` portion of an HTML document to perform redirection. This works differently than the server-side script version because it happens at the client (downstream) end of the connection. The `Response.Redirect` method occurs at the server (upstream) end of the connection.

SEE ALSO
➤ For details on how to use `response.redirect` in ASP documents, see page 405

Building the Ad Rotator Control File

The last task needed to implement the Ad Rotator component is the creation of the control file that is read by the ad rotator. This control file contains all the required information about how to display each ad in the banner space. Although this is a simple text file, the layout of the file is rather peculiar. If it is not built correctly, if one line is out of place, the ad rotator component will fail.

The control file is divided into two parts: the banner description information and the list of ads to display in the banner. The banner description information can include up to four lines of text in the following form:

```
redirect <URL>
width <n>
height <n>
border <n>
```

where `<URL>` is a valid location to be used to log click-throughs and send the user to the target location. This is an optional line. The remaining three lines (`width`, `height`, and `border`) are all required.

A single asterisk (*) on a line separates the banner description information and the list of ads to display.

The display ad section must be laid out in the following form:

```
<image URL>
<target location URL> or "-"
<text version of the banner>
<n>
```

The first line contains a URL that points to the location of the banner image to display (that is, `images/compost.gif`, and so on). The second line contains the target URL to which the user will be sent (that is, `http://www.compost.com`). The third line is used to hold the alternative text displayed when the image is not available or turned off (for example, `Dig into some fun at COMPOST.COM`).

Finally, the fourth line contains a number from 1 to 100 to indicate the percent of rotations this ad gets overall. For example, an entry of 30 instructs the ad rotator component to display the associated ad 30 percent of the time the page is sent downstream.

There can be as many ad entries in the list as you like. However, the total percentage of display time should always add up to 100. For example, if you have four ads to display and want to display them each an equal number of times, each ad should be assigned the value 25 to represent 25 percent.

Now that you know how the ad rotator control file is constructed, add a new text file to the Web project called ADROT.TXT. Delete any HTML data that appears in the page when it first is loaded into the editor and copy the data from Listing 22.8 in the document.

Creating Rotating Banner Ads with Ad Rotator Component

PART V
CHAPTER 22
615

LISTING 22.8 Building the Ad Rotator Control File ADROT.TXT

```
1   redirect adcheck.asp
2   width 400
3   height 100
4   border 1
5   *
6   images/ar_compost.gif
7   compost.htm
8   Dig into the fun - Visit Compost.com!
9   30
10  images/ar_dingbat.gif
11  dingbat_air.htm
12  Confused? - Fly Dingbat Airlines!
13  40
14  images/ar_fred.gif
15  fred_ld.htm
16  Talk Fast - You're using Fred's Long Distance!
17  20
```

LISTING 22.8

① This marks the end of the banner description information and the beginning of the display ad information.

② This is the last line of information for the first display ad.

Notice that the data in Listing 22.8 refers to image files that were used to build the original project covered in this book. You can use any images you want as you test your own example. The content of the images is not important.

After completing the ADROT.TXT control file, save it and test-run your Web project (select F5). After viewing the main page, select **Ad Rotator Component** and you will see something that looks like Figure 22.4 appear in your browser.

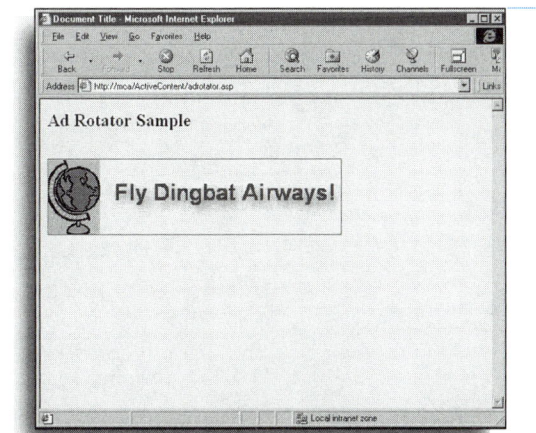

FIGURE 22.4
Viewing the Ad Rotator page.

While you are viewing the Ad Rotator Sample page, select **View**, **Source** from the Microsoft IE4 menu to display the HTML source sent from the server down to the client. Where you wrote the three lines of server-side script to display the banner ad (see Listing 22.5), you'll now see simple HTML (see Listing 22.9).

LISTING 22.9

❶ Notice the use of the redirection to `adcheck.asp` with the `url` and `image` parameters.

LISTING 22.9   The HTML Output of the Ad Rotator Component

```
1  <A HREF="adcheck.asp?url=dingbat_air.htm&image=
2     images/ar_dingbat.gif" ><IMG SRC="images/ar_dingbat.gif"
3     ALT="Confused? - Fly Dingbat Airlines!" WIDTH=400
4     HEIGHT=100 BORDER=1></A>
```
❶

Notice that the HREF portion of the tag includes the redirect document name (ADCHECK.ASP) followed by the two named parameters (`url` and `image`). These parameters are available via the `Response.QueryString` method and are used in the ADCHECK.ASP document to log the hit and forward the user to the target URL.

Now you know how to include banner ads as active content in your Web applications.

CHAPTER 23

Adding Active Documents to Your Web Projects

Learn the definition of an active document

View Excel and Word files in the Microsoft Internet Explorer browser

Install and distribute Visual Basic ActiveX documents from your Web project

What Are Active Documents and Why Should You Use Them?

If your Web project is accessed by users who already have Microsoft Internet Explorer and Microsoft Office installed on their workstations, you can greatly enhance your project by taking advantage of *active documents*. Active documents are document files that can be loaded into the Microsoft Internet Explorer and viewed within the browser instead of being viewed in a separate window. The ability to load active documents in this way is called *active document hosting*. Microsoft Internet Explorer is an active document host.

Microsoft Office Active Documents

Almost all the document formats created by Microsoft Office are active documents. This includes Excel spreadsheets (.XLS), Word documents (.DOC), and PowerPoint presentations (.PPT). If your Web project must provide access to data in any of these document formats, you do not have to convert them into HTML format before you can use them.

As long as the people accessing your Web project are using Microsoft Internet Explorer, they can directly open any active document and it will appear in the browser, as would standard HTML documents. Figure 23.1 shows the Microsoft Internet Explorer viewing a Microsoft Word 97 document.

Although viewing Microsoft office documents in their native format is very handy, there is an even bigger advantage to using active document access to Microsoft Office files. Microsoft Internet Explorer not only enables you to view active documents, but also enables you to edit them.

When you load an active document into Microsoft Internet Explorer you'll notice that the menu bar changes. It now includes menu items related to the document that is currently loaded. You will also notice that a new button appears on the Microsoft Internet Explorer toolbar: the **Tools** button. You can view all the currently loaded toolbars by toggling the **Tools** button (see Figure 23.2).

What about Microsoft Access?

You might have noticed that Microsoft Access files (.MDB) were not included in the list of active documents produced by Microsoft Office. The Microsoft Access files are actually databases instead of documents. This means that you cannot open MDB files directly from within Microsoft Internet Explorer. However, you can access the data within MDB files using the data connection and data command objects from Visual InterDev.

What Are Active Documents and Why Should You Use Them? PART **V**
CHAPTER **23**

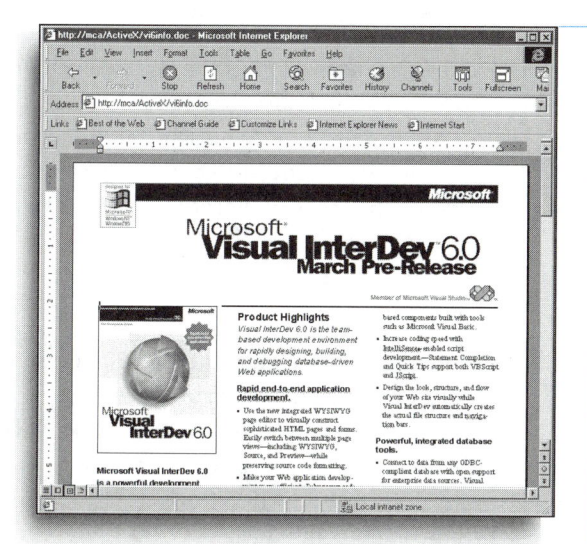

619

FIGURE 23.1
Viewing a Microsoft Word97 active document with Microsoft Internet Explorer.

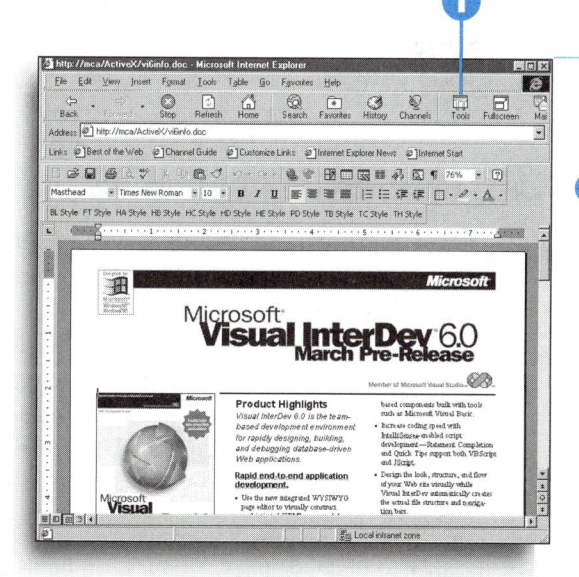

FIGURE 23.2
Using the **Tools** button to view the document toolbars.

1 The **Tools** button.

You can see the Microsoft Word toolbars when you load a Word document because Microsoft Internet Explorer is actually "communicating" with Microsoft Word when the DOC file is loaded. In fact, by loading the Microsoft Word document, you are actually loading Microsoft Word *inside* the Microsoft Internet Explorer. This is a key point. Active documents are really documents that include information that enables the active document host to locate and load the associated executable that understands the document format. This means that, in order for Microsoft Internet Explorer to successfully host an active document, the workstation that is running Microsoft Internet Explorer must also have a local copy of the executable that understands the document format.

For example, if you add a link to a Microsoft Word document to your Web project and a visitor uses Microsoft Internet Explorer to navigate to the Word document link, Microsoft Internet Explorer will automatically download the document and then make a call to load MSWORD.EXE from the local workstation. If there is no copy of MSWORD.EXE registered for the local workstation, Microsoft Internet Explorer will prompt the user to download the file rather than view it.

SEE ALSO
➤ For more on active content, see page 597
➤ For more on using Microsoft Access with Visual InterDev 6, see page 417

Visual Basic ActiveX Documents

Along with the Microsoft Office documents, you can also take advantage of special files called *ActiveX Documents*. These are DLL or EXE files that contain one or more standard Microsoft Windows dialog boxes. This dialog collection is published within the DLL or EXE using the same technology that is used to publish Microsoft Office documents. This means that the dialogs stored in the ActiveX Document DLL or EXE can be hosted by Microsoft Internet Explorer (see Figure 23.3).

The ActiveX Document package (DLL or EXE) can include any number of dialogs. These dialogs can be linked together, called as standard windows, or even mixed between Windows dialogs and standard HTML documents. The key thing to keep in mind is that programmers who write Microsoft Windows applications can, without too much trouble, publish the same windows

---

Viewing Microsoft Office documents without installing Microsoft Office

If you or your Web clients do not have Microsoft Office installed on your workstation, you can still view Office documents in your Web browser. To do this, you must download the appropriate viewer EXE from the Microsoft Web site at `http://www.microsoft.com/office/office/viewers.asp`.

Visual Basic ActiveX documents are Window applications

Because Visual Basic ActiveX documents are really complete Windows applications, you can run them only in Microsoft Internet Explorer browsers that run on the Windows operating system. This means you cannot execute Visual Basic ActiveX documents on a Mac computer running Microsoft Internet Explorer 4.x.

Adding Microsoft Office Documents to Your Web Project

dialogs in ActiveX Document packages (DLLs or EXEs). These packages can then be installed to an existing Web project and published to visitors who are using Microsoft Internet Explorer as the browser.

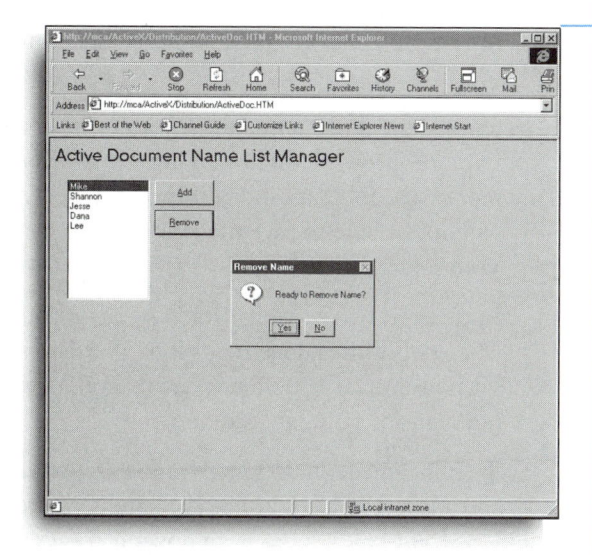

FIGURE 23.3
Viewing a Visual Basic ActiveX Document.

In fact, Microsoft originally created the ActiveX Document package as a way to help Windows programmers migrate their existing Windows-only applications to the Internet. For example, Microsoft Visual Basic includes a special wizard that will convert any existing Windows dialog form into an ActiveX Document form.

Now that you have an idea of how active documents work, you're ready to use Visual InterDev 6 to add them to your Web projects.

ActiveX documents work best in an intranet

Although you can use ActiveX documents for both Internet and intranet Web projects, they work best in an intranet environment where the Web server is connected to your clients via high-speed lines instead of over telephone lines.

Adding Microsoft Office Documents to Your Web Project

Adding Microsoft Office documents to your Web project is really easy. You simply copy the documents into the project, add a link to an HTML document, and you're set.

The key thing to keep in mind is that support for active documents is determined by the software on the client, not on the server. In other words, the client machine must have a registered version of the software that created the document. In the case of Microsoft Word documents, the client must have a copy of Microsoft Word installed on his or her own machine.

As long as the client has the associated EXE installed, the client will see the document appear within the Microsoft Internet Explorer browser window. The user will also be able to access menus and toolbars and edit the document. However, the user will not be able to save the altered document back up to the Web server.

In the next two sections, you'll see how you can import Microsoft Office documents into an existing Visual InterDev 6 Web project. If you do not have a Web project loaded, take a moment to create or load one now.

The documents mentioned in this section include an Excel spreadsheet (ACOUNTS.XLS) and a Microsoft Word document (VI6INFO.DOC). You can download these documents from the *Using Visual InterDev 6* home page (see Appendix B, "Online Resources," for the address), or use any Excel or Word documents you have available to your workstation.

Adding an Excel Spreadsheet

The first item you add to your Web project is an Excel spreadsheet. To do this, you must first start Visual InterDev 6 and load the Web project you want to use to hold the active document. Then, add a new page to the Web project called ACTIVE-DOCS.HTM. You'll use this document to hold the links to all the active documents you use in this chapter.

Importing an Excel spreadsheet into your Visual InterDev 6 Web project

1. Right-click on the project name in the Visual InterDev 6 Project Explorer window.
2. Select **Add** from the context menu.
3. Select **Add** **I**tem from the submenu.

The Save menu option is disabled

For security reasons, you cannot download an active document from the Web server, edit it, and save it back to the Web server. You can, however, use the Save As option for most documents and save a local copy for your own use.

Adding Microsoft Office Documents to Your Web Project

4. When the Add Item dialog box appears, select the **Existing** tab.
5. Select **All Files** from the **Files of type** pull-down list in order to see the .XLS file type.
6. Navigate to the location on your workstation (or shared folder) that holds the target excel spreadsheet (ACCOUNTS.XLS).
7. Click once on the target file and press **Open** to add the file to your Web project.

Now that you have the Excel document added to your Web, you can treat it like any other Web document in the project. For example, you can double-click on the item to load it into the Visual InterDev 6 editor. That's right—Visual InterDev 6 is an active document host, too! (See Figure 23.4.)

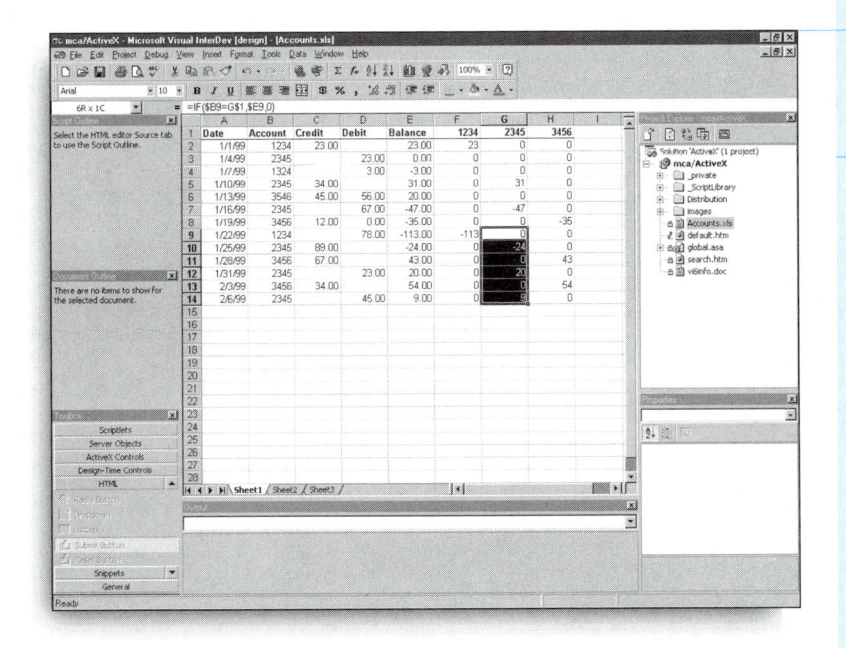

FIGURE 23.4
Using Visual InterDev 6 to edit an Excel spreadsheet.

After you have added the Excel document to your Web project, you can create a link on any HTML (or ASP) document that will allow Microsoft Internet Explorer users to load the Excel document in their browsers.

To do this, all you must do is add a standard HTML-formatted HREF link. However, it's easier to just drag the document from your Project Explorer window onto an HMTL document in the editor.

Adding links via drag-and-drop

1. Load an HTML document into the Visual InterDev 6 editor (for example, DEFAULT.HTM). This is the document that will display the link to the target URL.

2. With the document in Design mode, move your cursor to the Project Explorer window and locate the target document to which you want to link.

3. Press the left mouse button on the target document and drag it over onto the HTML document in the Visual InterDev 6 editor window.

4. Position the cursor on the line where you want the link to appear, and release the left mouse button.

5. The link and link text will appear in the document (see Figure 23.5).

FIGURE 23.5

Results of performing drag-and-drop document linking.

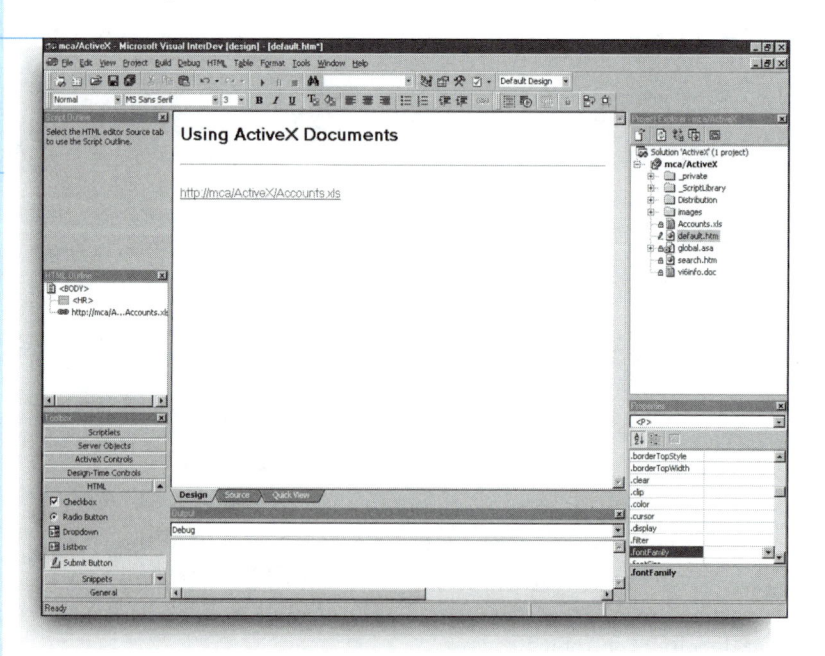

Adding Microsoft Office Documents to Your Web Project | PART V, CHAPTER 23

You can now test your Excel link (if you have Excel registered on your machine) by marking the HTML document (DEFAULT.HTM) as the startup page and pressing F5 to launch your browser. After the browser is loaded with the HTML document, you can click on the ACCOUNTS.XLS link to see the Excel document appear in your browser. The resulting view should resemble Figure 23.6.

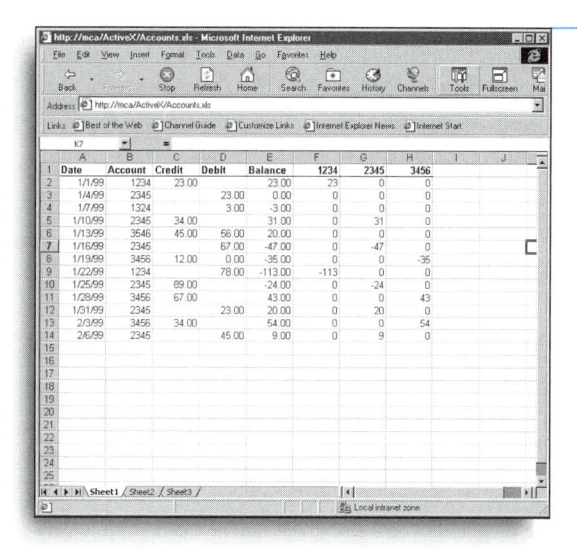

FIGURE 23.6
Viewing the ACCOUNTS.XLS document in the Microsoft Internet Explorer browser.

SEE ALSO
➤ For more on adding links to your Web documents, see page 33

Adding a Word 97 Document

Adding a Microsoft Word 97 document is just as simple as adding an Excel document. The first step is to locate the document and import it into your Web project. Then just add the link to an HTML document and you're all set.

Adding a Microsoft Word Document to your Web Project

1. Right-click the project name in the Project Explorer window.
2. Select **Add** from the **Connect** menu.

Links dropped in Source view and Design view differ

When you perform a drag-and-drop link from the Project Explorer to the Design view page, you'll see the complete URL address appear for the anchor text. When you do the same task in Source view, you'll see only the simple document name as the anchor text. In both cases, only the relative path of the document is used as the HREF.

3. Select **Add Item** from the submenu.
4. Select the **Existing** tab.
5. Select **All Files** from the **Files of type** pull-down list in order to see the .XLS file type.
6. Navigate to the location on your workstation (or shared folder) that holds the target Microsoft Word document. In this example you can use the VI6INFO.DOC file that is available at the Visual InterDev 6 home page.
7. Click once on the target file and press **Open** to add the file to your Web project.

After adding the document to your Web project, load the HTML document that will hold the link, drag the Word document over the HTML document, and drop it on a blank line. You'll see the new link appear on the page (see Figure 23.7).

FIGURE 23.7

Dropping the Microsoft Word document link on an HTML page.

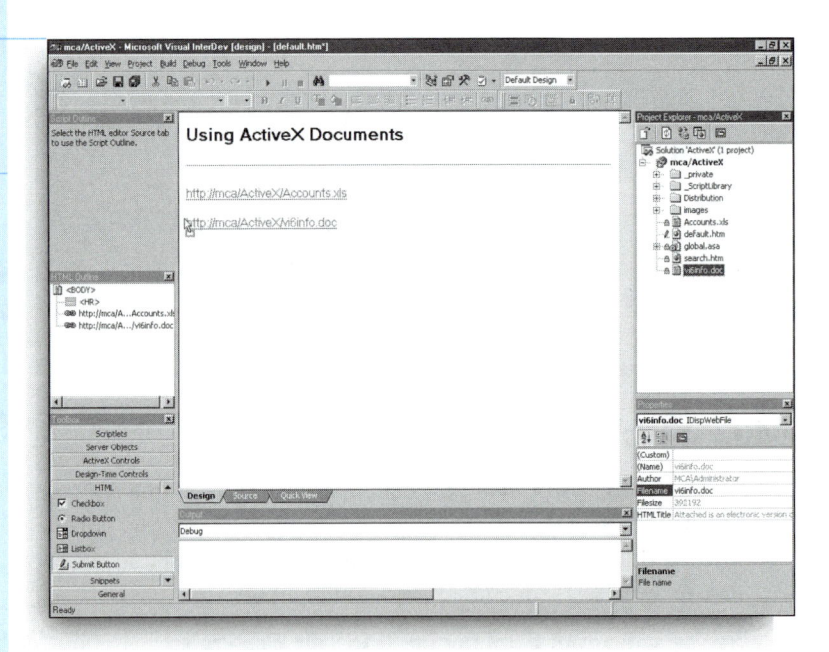

When you run the Web project, you'll be able to click on the Microsoft Word link and see the DOC file appear in the browser. It will look like Figure 23.1 (if you used the VI6INFO.DOC file in this example).

Adding Visual Basic ActiveX Documents to Your Web Project

You can use the same basic technique for adding custom-built Visual Basic ActiveX Documents to your Web projects. Visual Basic ActiveX Documents are, however, not quite the same as the active documents of Microsoft Office. Unlike the Microsoft Office documents, your users will not need a copy of the Visual Basic development tool in order to view Visual Basic ActiveX Documents.

Because Visual Basic ActiveX Documents are actually complete programs that have Windows dialogs in the package, your users will need all the files necessary for running the Windows program. Several standard Visual Basic runtime files must exist on the user's workstation. Numerous additional Visual Basic and third-party components might also be needed, depending on what features and services are included in the ActiveX Document itself.

In order to allow Microsoft Internet Explorer users to access Visual Basic ActiveX Documents, you add a complete set of ActiveX Document installation files to your Web project. This is not as difficult as it sounds. Fortunately, the programmers who create the Visual Basic ActiveX Document will be able to build the complete installation package for you.

You merely add the package to your Web project and add a link to the starting document for the ActiveX Document itself. When a user accesses the ActiveX Document link on your site, the installation routine will automatically check to see whether the proper files are located on the user's station. If not, they will be downloaded and installed before the ActiveX Document is shown.

ActiveX Documents and Browser Security

Downloading and installing software from the Internet is a potential security risk. Some users might have their browser security set to disallow the downloading of your ActiveX

Supplying Visual Basic runtimes to your users

When you add Visual Basic ActiveX documents to your Web project you will need to supply the complete Visual Basic runtime file set to all your visitors. By default, the Visual Basic Setup Wizard will construct an Internet download package that searches the Internet for these files. If you deploy your ActiveX documents in an intranet, you'll need to place these runtime files somewhere on your Web server instead.

Document package. Others might have their security set so tightly that they will not even see the option to download and will simply see a blank page.

If you will be using ActiveX Documents for your Web project, you should try to warn your visitors ahead of time that they might need to loosen their security settings in order to successfully access the ActiveX Documents.

SEE ALSO
➤ *For more on Web and browser security issues, see page 691*

The VB ActiveX Document Installation Package

> **Make sure your users are able to download your ActiveX documents**
>
> If you are building a Web application that uses ActiveX documents (AXD), you must make sure all users have their security settings tuned to accept AXD downloads. If security settings are too high, users will not be notified that an AXD exists.

As mentioned previously, users must have all the necessary runtime and support files in order to access Visual Basic ActiveX Documents from your Web project. There are several files that you need to add to your Web project and some that can be accessed from the Microsoft Web site. Just what you do depends on how your Web project is installed and how your users will access the Web project.

First, the Visual Basic programmers who build the ActiveX Document will be able to provide you with a set of basic installation files. These files should be added to your Web project as a complete set. Table 23.1 shows the list of files and folders that are created for the typical Visual Basic ActiveX Document project, along with a short description of each document.

TABLE 23.1   Typical Visual Basic ActiveX document install files

Filename	Example	Description
CAB File	ActiveDoc.CAB	The Microsoft cabinet file that contains a compressed version of the DLL or EXE that holds the ActiveX Documents.
HTML Start Page	ActiveDoc.HTM	An HTML document that contains a reference to the startup file for the ActiveX Document.

Adding Visual Basic ActiveX Documents to Your Web Project

Filename	Example	Description
Dialog Start File	MyDialog.VBD	The startup file for the active document itself. There can be more than one of these in the folder.
Download data file	Support/ActiveDoc.DDF	This file contains information used to uncompress the CAB file.
ActiveX DLL or EXE file	Support/ActiveDoc.DLL	The component that contains all the ActiveX Documents themselves.
Setup Information File	Support/ActiveDoc.INF	This file contains details needed to complete the automated Internet setup of the ActiveX Documents. It might also include references to Microsoft Web sites or other Internet addresses where the needed components can be found.

Note that Table 23.1 shows that three files appear in a subfolder (Support). This is very important. When you add the installation package to your Web project, you must maintain the SUPPORT subfolder and keep it one level "down" from the main installation files.

About the Setup Information File

Most information in these files is of no real interest to you as the Web project developer. However, one file in the package contains some very important information: the INF or Setup Information file. This file contains details on how the component will be registered on the user's machine and where certain support files are located in case they need to be added to the user's workstation.

For any Visual Basic ActiveX Document, at least two DLLs (not counting the actual ActiveX Document file) must be present and

Don't worry if this is all 'GEEK' to you

If all this talk of INF, CAB, DDF, VBD, and DLL files is a big mystery to you, don't worry about it. The Visual Basic programmers understand all this stuff so you don't have to. Just make sure all these files are present and that they are in the right subfolders within your Web application.

registered on the user's machine before the Visual Basic ActiveX Document will run:

ASYCFILT.DLL
MSVBVM50.DLL

By default, the installation package adds entries to the INF file that direct the browser to navigate to a Microsoft Web site to download those files if they are needed. This is no problem if your Web project (and its users) will be connected to the Internet when accessing your ActiveX Document pages. However, if your Web project is located on an intranet, your users might not have access to the Microsoft Web site to download the needed files.

Luckily, Microsoft thought of this. When creating the installation package for the ActiveX Document, the Visual Basic programmers have an option to indicate an alternative location for the ASYCFILT.DLL and MSVBVM50.DLL files. If your project will not have access to the Internet, be sure to confirm that the ActiveX Document project has been created with this in mind. You might also need to locate copies of the ASYCFILT.CAB and MSVBVM50.CAB files somewhere on your own Web server in order to support ActiveX Documents for your Web projects.

Now that you know a bit more about Visual Basic ActiveX Documents and how they differ from the standard Microsoft Office Active Documents, you're ready to add a Visual Basic ActiveX Document to your Web project.

Including ActiveX Documents in Your Web Project

For this example you'll use a Visual Basic ActiveX Document project called ActiveDoc. You can get a copy of this project from the *Using Visual InterDev 6* home page (see Appendix B for the address). If you want, you can use any other valid Visual Basic ActiveX Document package.

After you have the Visual Basic ActiveX Document package that will be used in your project, you first import it into the Web project while it is loaded in Visual InterDev 6. This is done very

Establishing an AXD DLL site for your intranet

If you will be supporting ActiveX documents within an intranet setting, you'll need to create a Web site that holds all the support DLLs needed for the AXDs. You can use the contents of the INF file created by the Visual Basic install routine as a guide in setting up your own local mirror of the Microsoft site.

Adding Visual Basic ActiveX Documents to Your Web Project

much the same way as with standard Microsoft Office active documents. However, because there are several files to work with, it is best if you create a separate folder for each download package you will have in your project.

Usually, the Visual Basic ActiveX Document is loaded into a folder that has a subfolder called SUPPORT. You can use this folder or create a new one in your project. For this example, create a new folder called Distribution in the Visual InterDev 6 project.

Creating folders in your Visual InterDev 6 project

1. In the Project Explorer window, right-click over the project name.
2. Select **New Folder** from the context menu.
3. Enter the name of the new folder you want to add (Distribution).
4. Press **OK** to add the folder to the project.

After you have added the folder, you can add the Visual Basic ActiveX Document installation files to your project. This time, instead of using the Visual InterDev 6 Add Item dialog, you can drag items from the Windows File Explorer directly into the new folder you created in the Visual InterDev 6 project.

Using drag-and-drop from the Windows File Explorer to add documents to your Web project

1. With Visual InterDev 6 loaded, reduce the window size so that you can see most of the workstation desktop.
2. Load a copy of the Windows File Explorer. To do this, select **Start** from the Windows task bar. Then select **Programs** from the menu. Finally, select **Windows Explorer** from the submenu and reduce its size so you can see both Visual InterDev and the File Explorer side-by-side.
3. Use the Windows File Explorer to navigate to the folder that holds the CAB, HTM, and VBD files, along with the SUPPORT subfolder for the ActiveX Documents.
4. Select the CAB, HTM, and VBD files and the SUPPORT subfolder by highlighting them with your mouse.

> **If you don't have a Visual Basic ActiveX Document package**
>
> If you do not have a valid Visual Basic ActiveX Document package to work with, you can still get a lot out of the chapter by following the example.

5. Now drag those items across the Windows File Explorer, over Visual InterDev, and drop them directly on the target folder in the project (**Distribution**).

6. An Adding Files dialog will appear while Visual InterDev 6 imports the selected files into the Web project (see Figure 23.8).

FIGURE 23.8

Importing the ActiveX Document package using drag-and-drop from the Windows File Explorer.

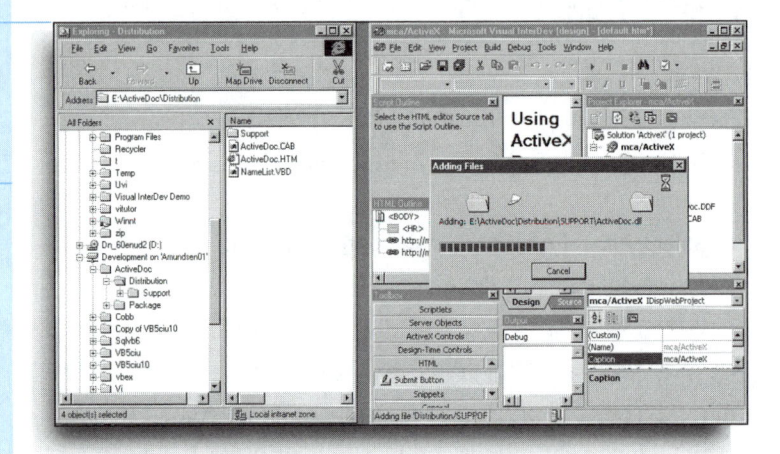

You now have all the files needed to allow users to access the Visual Basic ActiveX Documents from your Web project.

The final step in the process is to add a link to the HTM file from the ActiveX Document package to your Web page. You can do this by dragging the HTM document in the Distribution folder from the Project Explorer onto the loaded HTML document in the Visual InterDev 6 editor. This will automatically add the link to your document.

Inspecting the ActiveX Document Startup HTML Page

The startup HTML page that ships with the Visual Basic ActiveX Document installation package includes an object reference to the ActiveX Document DLL (or EXE) and a FRAMESET that will automatically load the first dialog in the package.

Adding Visual Basic ActiveX Documents to Your Web Project

This is an HTML document that is created by the Visual Basic installation utility. Listing 23.1 shows the HTML source for this document.

LISTING 23.1 Viewing the ActiveX Document Startup HTML Page

```
1   <HTML>
2   <OBJECT ID="NameList"
3   CLASSID="CLSID:676AABD6-DEA1-11D1-8B54-00A0C9897944"
4   CODEBASE="ActiveDoc.CAB#version=1,0,0,0" VIEWASTEXT>
5   </OBJECT>
6
7   <SCRIPT LANGUAGE="VBScript">
8   Sub Window_OnLoad
9       Document.Open
10      Document.Write "<FRAMESET>"
11      Document.Write "<FRAME SRC=""NameList.VBD"">"
12      Document.Write "</FRAMESET>"
13      Document.Close
14  End Sub
15  </SCRIPT>
16  </HTML>
```

Actually, Listing 23.1 is not what you normally will see in the Visual InterDev 6 editor **Source** tab. The OBJECT tag is actually rendered in the Visual InterDev 6 editor to show the general shape and content of the Windows dialog that will appear in the user's browser (see Figure 23.9).

The dark areas in the object will be filled in with other Windows controls (buttons, list boxes, and so on) at runtime. If you attempt to view the ActiveX Document in Design mode, you receive a notice from Visual InterDev 6 telling you that elements of the page cannot be rendered in Design mode and that Source mode will be used.

If you attempt to view the document in Quick View mode, Visual InterDev 6 will attempt to display the Active Document dialog and, if necessary, will initiate auto-download in order to install the object on your workstation.

ActiveX Document start HTML files break browse buttons

The default HTML document created as the host for the ActiveX Document uses the <FRAMESET> element instead of the <BODY> element. This makes it easy to host ActiveX Documents in the browser, but often renders the Forward and Back buttons useless. Microsoft calls this *behavior by design*.

FIGURE 23.9

Viewing the ActiveX Document startup HTML page in the Visual InterDev 6 Editor **Source** tab.

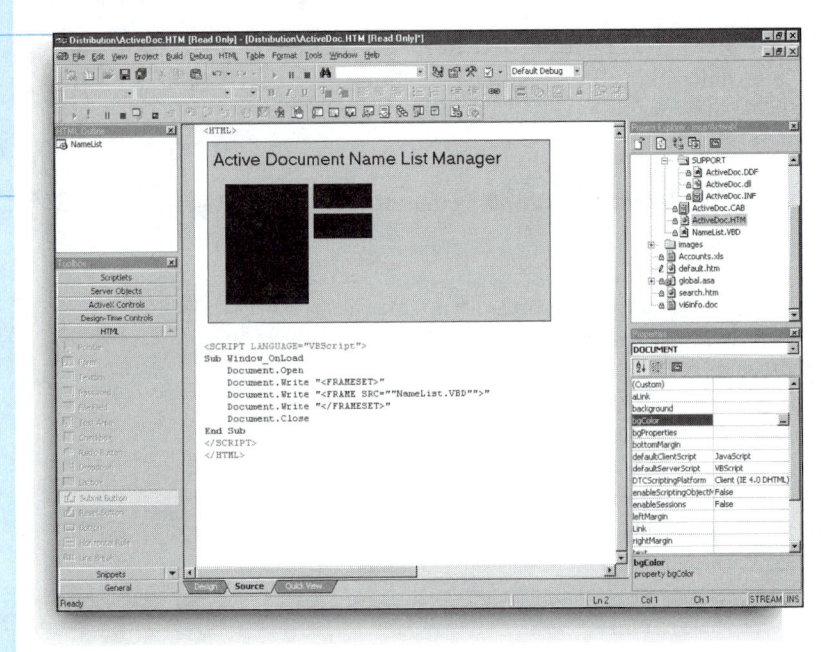

SEE ALSO
➤ *For more on how to use the Visual InterDev 6 editor, see page 33*

Testing the Visual Basic ActiveX Document Automatic Installation

After the package has been added to your Web project and a link to the starting HTML page has been added, you're ready to test the automatic installation of the ActiveX Document.

Start the Web project by pressing F5 and, when the startup page appears, click on the link to the ACTIVEDOC.HTM document. This loads the HTML page that has the OBJECT reference to the first dialog. When this happens, Microsoft Internet Explorer checks to see whether the ActiveX Document has been installed on this workstation and that all the needed components are available. If not, you see the ActiveX installation dialog warning appear asking you to confirm the installation of the ActiveX Document (see Figure 23.10).

Adding Visual Basic ActiveX Documents to Your Web Project

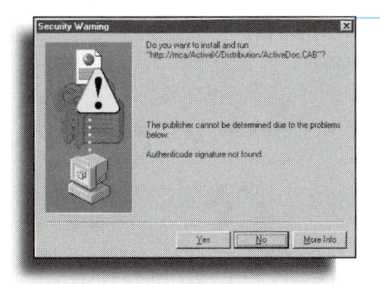

FIGURE 23.10
ActiveX installation dialog warning.

If you answer yes to this dialog, Microsoft Internet Explorer installs the needed files on your workstation and, after registering the ActiveX Document, displays the first dialog in the browser. Figure 23.3 shows an example of the dialog after the user presses the **Remove** button.

First timers must be patient

The first time a user downloads an ActiveX Document, he or she might need to add as much as 2MB in support files. This can take quite a bit of time, depending on the user's connection to the Web server. However, after the ActiveX Document is installed, downloading it will take much less time (usually just a few seconds).

PART VI

More Active Server Programming

24 **Looking at ASP Behind the Scenes** 639

25 **Managing Files with ASP** 663

26 **Adding Security to Your Web Applications** 691

27 **Using Program-Based Security** 707

28 **Adding Error Handling to Your Web Application** 723

29 **Using DHTML to Dynamically Alter HTML Content and Positioning** 749

CHAPTER 24

Looking at ASP Behind the Scenes

Understand and use the GLOBAL.ASA file

Take advantage of server-side include files (SSIs)

Use server variables to learn more about connected clients

This chapter contains a handful of topics that deal with some of the behind-the-scenes details of programming with Active Server Pages (ASP). In this chapter, you learn to take advantage of some of the more technical aspects of ASP and Web application programming.

Setting Up the BehindTheScenes Web Application

Throughout this chapter, you build several examples of code that give you a "behind-the-scenes" look at ASP and Microsoft Internet Information Server. Before you start, let's build the basic framework for the Web application that will house these examples.

First, create a new Web project called BehindTheScenes. Next, add two new folders to the Web application. These will hold several additional documents for the application.

Creating new folders for your Web application

1. Load or create the target Web application (BehindTheScenes).
2. Select the project name in the Project window.
3. Right-click the mouse on the project name and select the **New Folder** menu option.
4. When the New Folder dialog appears, enter the name of the folder (`includes`) and press **OK**.
5. When the dialog is dismissed, you see the new folder appear in the Project window.

You'll use this folder later in this chapter.

Now add a new HTML document to the project called DEFAULT.HTM. Table 24.1 shows the elements you must add to this page. Refer to Figure 24.1 for the final layout of the page.

The BehindTheScenes project

You can continue to use your existing project in this chapter rather than create a new one. We recommend creating a new project, however, to make sure that you're working from the same page we are.

Using GLOBAL.ASA in Your Web Applications
CHAPTER 24

TABLE 24.1 Elements of DEFAULT.HTM

Element	Attribute	Setting
Demonstrate Asp Behind the Scenes	H2	
The GLOBAL.ASA File	HREF	Globalasafile.asp
Server Side Include Files	HREF	Includefiles.asp
Server Variables	HREF	Servervariables.asp

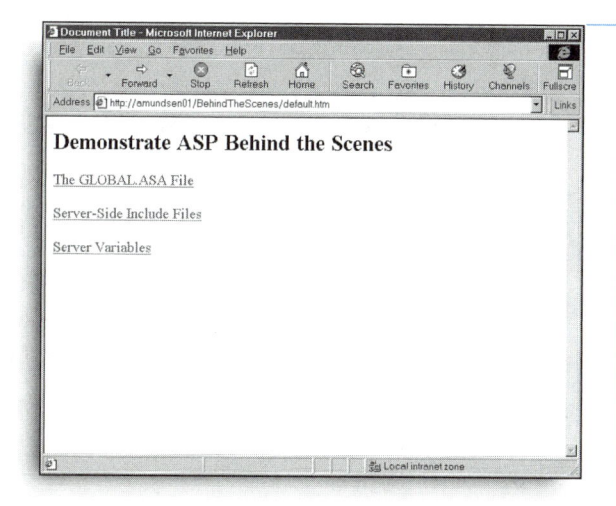

FIGURE 24.1
The layout of the DEFAULT.HTM page.

Now that the Web application is laid out, you're ready to begin!

Using GLOBAL.ASA in Your Web Applications

One of the most important files in your Web application is the GLOBAL.ASA file. This file contains valuable information about shared data and object pointers that can be used throughout your entire Web application. Often, you can add entries to the GLOBAL.ASA file that can speed your application's processing and simplify data manipulation for your program.

The GLOBAL.ASA file has three primary functions:

- Receive event messages when the Web application starts and stops
- Receive event messages when a client browser starts and stops a session
- Declare and manipulate COM objects and simple data values to be shared at the application and/or session level

In this section, you learn how to write code that runs when your Web application starts and when a new session starts, and how to declare storage to be shared among all the pages in your application.

SEE ALSO
▶ *You explore data connections and how to make them on page 418*

The Life of GLOBAL.ASA

The GLOBAL.ASA file has just a few tasks to do, but they are very important tasks. Four event messages are received within the GLOBAL.ASA file. There are also three ways in which you can declare and manipulate storage and COM object pointers within the GLOBAL.ASA file.

First, let's review the chronology of the GLOBAL.ASA file:

1. The `Application_OnStart` event occurs when the first client requests any page in your Web application. Any server-side script that resides within the event method is executed.

2. The `Session_OnStart` event occurs when a new client requests any page in your Web application. Any server-side script that resides within the event method is executed.

3. If this is the first time the GLOBAL.ASA file has received an event message (the `Application_OnStart`), any other `<OBJECT>` or `<METADATA>` tags that reside within the GLOBAL.ASA file are scanned and executed.

4. The `Session_OnEnd` event occurs when a client terminates the session. Session termination occurs when the client browser unloads the last page from its cache or if the `Session.Timeout`

The GLOBAL.ASA connection

The GLOBAL.ASA file is also used by Visual InterDev to establish your data connections for the application. Try adding a database connection, and then look at the GLOBAL.ASA's contents.

Using GLOBAL.ASA in Your Web Applications

value is exceeded (default 20 minutes). At this time, any server-side script that resides within the `Session_OnEnd` event is executed.

5. The `Application_OnEnd` event occurs when the Web application is unloaded from the Web server. This can occur when the Web application is forcibly stopped or when the Web server process is halted. At this time, any server-side script that resides within the `Application_OnEnd` event is executed.

You can see from the summary that there are several places where you can add server-side script that will be executed for your Web application.

Sharing Data and COM Objects with the GLOBAL.ASA

Even more important than the execution chronology, you have the power to declare and release data storage and COM object pointers at key moments within the life of the GLOBAL.ASA. These declared storage and object pointers can be shared with all the pages within a session and among multiple sessions within the application.

There are several ways in which the sharing of data and COM object pointers can occur within the GLOBAL.ASA:

- *Application-level sharing.* Any server-side script executed during the `Application_OnStart` or `Session_OnStart` event that uses the `Application.Contents` collection can create and modify data storage and COM object pointers that can be seen by all sessions running your application.

- *Session-level sharing.* Any server-side script executed during the `Session_OnStart` event that uses the `Session.Contents` collection can create and modify data storage and COM object pointers that can be seen from all pages running in the same session.

- *`<OBJECT>` tags.* Any `<OBJECT>` tags that are added to the GLOBAL.ASA file can be marked with a `SCOPE` attribute of `Application` or `Session`. These pointers to COM objects can then be accessed via the `Application.StaticContents` or `Session.StaticContents` collections.

> **The GLOBAL.ASA file is not meant for HTML**
>
> The GLOBAL.ASA file is used to control the application and session events, it is not intended for HTML authoring. Make sure that you have only event script within the GLOBAL.ASA file.

Your application's starting point

Think of the GLOBAL.ASA as your Web application's starting point. Every time your Web application is accessed by a new user, this file is read. If the user is the first to use your application, it carries out the actions tied to that event. If the user is just starting her own session, those events are also carried out.

- *`<METADATA>` tags.* Any `<METADATA>` tags that are added to the GLOBAL.ASA file can be used to access type libraries on the Web server. These libraries are available at the application-sharing level.

The Difference Between Storing Pointers in the *Contents* Collections

You can store two types of information in the `Contents` collections: simple data and COM object pointers. It is important to understand the differences between these two items and the steps needed to store and retrieve them.

You add strings and numeric values using the format shown in Listing 24.1.

LISTING 24.1 **Storing Simple Data Values in the *Contents* Collections**

```
1 Application.Contents("MyName")="Shannon"
2 Application("YourName")="Dana"
3 Session.Contents("MySize")=13
4 Session("YourSize")=9
```

As you can see from Listing 24.1, you can use the explicit form of declaration:

`<object>.Contents(<name>)=<value>`

or the implicit form of declaration:

`<object>(<name>)=<value>`

Declaring variables in the GLOBAL.ASA

Declaring your session and application variables in the GLOBAL.ASA is preferable over doing it inside your application's code elsewhere. You can easily modify and update these variables from one central point.

Both forms are valid. Usually, it is a good idea to use the explicit form. This is especially true if you use the `StaticContents` object to store data as `StaticContents` collection instead of the `Contents` collection.

You can also insert COM object references into the `Contents` collection by using the code snippets in Listing 24.2.

PART **VI**
CHAPTER **24**

645

Using GLOBAL.ASA in Your Web Applications

LISTING 24.2 **Storing COM Object Pointers in the *Contents* Collections**

```
1 Set Application.Contents("MyObject")=Server.
  ↪CreateObject("myPackage.MyObject")
2 Set Session.Contents("YourObject")=Server.
  ↪CreateObject("yourPackage.yourObject")
```

The difference in the code from Listing 24.1 and 24.2 is slight, but important. Whenever you want to store a COM object reference, you must use `Server.CreateObject(<package.Object>)` to retrieve the object pointer. You also must use the `Set` keyword to place the object pointer into the `Contents` collection. If you fail to use this format, you receive errors when you attempt to store and retrieve COM pointers from the `Contents` collections.

Using the GLOBAL.ASA Events

Now let's add some entries to the GLOBAL.ASA file that will add information to the `Application` and `Session` `Contents` collections. Then you build a Web page that accesses these values and displays them to the user.

Adding code to the GLOBAL.ASA file

1. First, open the GLOBAL.ASA file for editing. To do this, click once on the GLOBAL.ASA file in the Project window; then right-click the mouse to bring up the context menu. Select **Get Working Copy**. Double-click the item to load it in the Visual InterDev editor.

2. Add the code from Listing 24.3 to the file right after the comment section.

Comments and the GLOBAL.ASA

You see several lines of comment code that explain the possible uses of the GLOBAL.ASA file. You can ignore them for now.

LISTING 24.3 **Adding Code to Store Data in the *Contents* Collections**

```
1 Sub Application_OnStart
2   '
3   ' update app-level shared item
4   Application.Contents("appStart")=Now()
5   '
6 End Sub
7
```

continues...

PART **VI**   More Active Server Programming

CHAPTER **24**   **Looking at ASP Behind the Scenes**

Understanding the listing

Listing 24.3 declares two storage items—once each for the `Application` and `Session` objects (lines 1–6 and 8–13, respectively). The application-level item is initialized with a date and time (line 4) when the Web application is accessed by the first user. The session-level item is initialized with the date and time of the most recent user to connect to the application and start a session with the Web server (line 11).

LISTING 24.3   **Continued**

```
8  Sub Session_OnStart
9      '
10     ' update session-level shared item
11     Session.Contents("sesStart")=Now()
12     '
13 End Sub
```

3. To see how these values can be retrieved and displayed, let's add a new page to the project called GLOBALASAFILE.ASP.

4. Add the server-side script code from Listing 24.4 to the `<BODY>` section of the page.

LISTING 24.4   **Adding Code to View the *Contents* Collection Values**

```
1  <%
2  '
3  ' initial heading
4
5  Response.Write "<H3>GLOBAL.ASA Values</H3>"
6
7  %>
8
9  <%
10 '
11 ' access app and session storage
12
13 appStart=Application.Contents("appStart")
14 sesStart=Session.Contents("sesStart")
15 '
16 Response.Write "<H4>App and Session Storage</H4><HR>"
17 Response.Write "appStart=" & appStart & "<BR>"
18 Response.Write "sesStart=" & sesStart & "<BR>"
19
20 %>
```

Understanding this listing

The code in Listing 24.4 first displays a simple heading for the page (line 5), then copies the items from the `Contents` collections to local variables (lines 13 and 14) and finally displays those variables on the page (lines 16–18).

5. Save and run this project and then navigate to the GLOBALASAFILE.ASP page. You should see something like the display in Figure 24.2.

Using GLOBAL.ASA in Your Web Applications | CHAPTER 24

FIGURE 24.2
Viewing the `Contents` collection values.

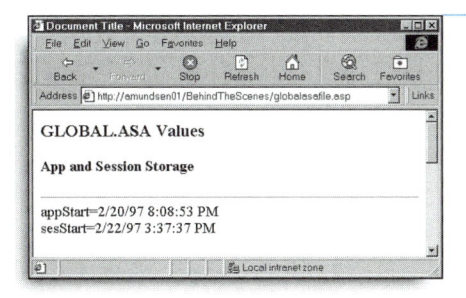

Adding <*OBJECT*> Tags

You can also add entries to the GLOBAL.ASA file that create a static reference to an external COM object. These references are made using the HTML <OBJECT> tag instead of server-side script. Listing 24.5 shows an example of this method of connecting to external COM objects. Add this code to your GLOBAL.ASA file.

LISTING 24.5 **Using the <*OBJECT*> Tag to Connect to COM Objects**

```
1 <!-- Add Link to External COM object -->
2 <OBJECT RUNAT=Server SCOPE=Application
3    ID=MyContent PROGID="MSWC.NextLink">
4 </OBJECT> tag to connect to COM objects>
```

There are a few important things to understand about using the <OBJECT> tag to link to COM objects. First, because it is an HTML tag, you do not place this item within the <SCRIPT></SCRIPT> tags. Also, it is important to add both the RUNAT=Server and SCOPE=Application (or SCOPE=Session) attributes to the tag.

After this entry is added to the GLOBAL.ASA file, you can access the COM object by addressing the StaticObjects collection of the appropriate scoping object (Application or Session). Listing 24.6 shows the code to do this. Add this code to your GLOBALASAFILE.ASP page right after the code from Listing 24.4.

Understanding the changes

The first time you run this Web application, both the appStart and sesStart values are the same. However, users that access this Web application later will see different times displayed in the HTML document sent down to the client.

Referencing external COM objects

Remember that you're referencing external server-side COM objects, not client-side COM objects like client-side scriptlets or ActiveX controls. These server-side COM objects could be Active Server components (ActiveX controls for the server) or even server-side scriptlets.

Understanding scope

Understanding the scope of a component or variable is very important when developing complex applications. Make sure you know how you want your data to move. Ideally, your information should be in the smallest scope possible to avoid accidental modification.

LISTING 24.6 Accessing COM Objects Using the *StaticObjects* Collection

```
1  <%
2  '
3  ' access pre-defined COM Object
4
5  Response.Write "<H4>Access Pre-Defined COM Object</H4>
   ↪<HR>"
6
7  Set objContent=Application.StaticObjects("MyContent")
8  lngCount=objContent.GetListCount("asafile.txt")
9
10 Response.Write "MyContent.Count=" & lngCount & "<P>"
11
12 %>
```

ASFILE.TXT

Of course, this file could be any name, just be sure to update any references in the provided listings.

The code in Listing 24.6 attempts to open a text file within your project called ASFILE.TXT. You can create this by following the next step-by-step.

Creating a text file for use in your project

1. Select the project name from the Project window.
2. Right-click the mouse over the project name and select **Add** from the context menu.
3. Select New Active Server Page from the submenu.
4. In the Name text box, enter `asafile.txt` as the filename.
5. Press Open to create the new file.
6. When the file appears in your Visual InterDev editor, remove all the existing text that was added for the ASP page.
7. Now you're ready to edit your text document.

After opening the text file, add the two lines from Listing 24.7 to the file. Be sure to separate the two items on each line with a <TAB>—not spaces.

LISTING 24.7 Contents of the ASAFILE.TXT Text File

```
1  asafile1.asp      File1
2  asafile2.asp      File2
```

Using GLOBAL.ASA in Your Web Applications | PART VI, CHAPTER 24 | 649

After adding the two lines in the text file, save it to the Web application.

Now run the Web application and view the results of the GLOBALASAFILE.ASP changes you added in Listing 24.6. When you run the application and navigate the GLOBAL.ASA page, you should see the same display shown in Figure 24.3.

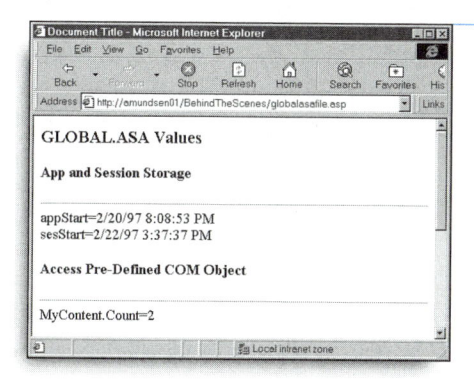

FIGURE 24.3
Viewing the results of accessing the `StaticObject` collection.

You can see from Figure 24.3 that the COM object defined in the `<OBJECT>` tag of the GLOBAL.ASA file was accessed and the `GetListCount` of that object was executed to display the count of items in the list.

Referencing Type Libraries

You can also add references to type libraries to the GLOBAL.ASA file. By adding references to type libraries, you can import predefined constants for use in your Web application. Using predefined constants instead of literal values makes it easier to read and understand your Web application.

You use the `METADATA` tag to declare the reference. This is similar to using the `<OBJECT>` tag. Listing 24.8 shows you how this is done. Add this to your GLOBAL.ASA file.

LISTING 24.8 Adding a *METADATA* Type Library Reference to the GLOBAL.ASA File

```
1 <!-- Add reference to installed type library -->
2 <!-- METADATA TYPE="TypeLib"
3 <!-- ' point to file on your system -->
4    FILE="C:\Winnt.SBS\System32\STDOLE2.TLB"
5 -->
```

Development tip: keep your files in order

Try to keep your files in a predictable location when working with them from a Web application. Obviously, system files won't be easy to control, but your own data files should be located in a common location.

Constants

Predefined constants are a valuable tool when developing. When you use a constant in your code, you can modify the value behind the constant in one place, as opposed to changing every instance of that value.

You must adjust the FILE attribute to point to the actual location of the STDOLE2.TLB file on your system. You can use the **Find** option of your **Start** menu (Win95/98 and WinNT4/5) to locate this file. Be sure to enter the value correctly to avoid errors when you attempt to start your Web application.

When you make this entry in your GLOBAL.ASA file, you are actually importing the contents of the library into your Web application. It turns out that the STDOLE2.TLB file contains a set of predefined values for rendering images. These predefined constants are shown in Table 24.2.

TABLE 24.2 The Predefined Constants in the STDOLE2.TLB File

Name	Value
Default	0
Checked	1
UnChecked	0
Monochrome	1
Color	4
VgaColor	2
Gray	2

When you add the type library to your Web application, you can use the names to represent the values. To show you

Using GLOBAL.ASA in Your Web Applications

how this works, add the code from Listing 24.9 to the GLOBALASAFILE.ASP document right after the code from Listing 24.6.

LISTING 24.9 Accessing Constants from the STDOLE2.TLB Type Library

```
1  <%
2  '
3  ' report constants from the STDOLE2.TLB
4
5  Response.Write "<H4>STDOLE2.TLB TypeLib Values</H4><HR>"
6
7  Response.Write "Default=" & Default & "<P>"
8
9  Response.Write "Checked=" & Checked & "<BR>"
10 Response.Write "UnChecked=" & UnChecked & "<P>"
11
12 Response.Write "Monochrome=" & Monochrome & "<BR>"
13 Response.Write "Color=" & Color & "<BR>"
14 Response.Write "vgaColor=" & vgaColor & "<BR>"
15 Response.Write "Gray=" & Gray & "<P>"
16
17 %>
```

Notice that the server-side script in Listing 24.9 does not use any numeric values, but instead uses the names of the constants imported from the STDOLE2.TLB type library. When you save and run this page, you see the numeric values associated with these names (see Figure 24.4).

You now know how to store and retrieve values using the Contents collections of the Application and Session objects, how to use <OBJECT> tags to add object entries to the StaticObjects collections, and how to use the METADATA tag to import type libraries into your Visual InterDev Web applications.

FIGURE 24.4

Viewing the type library constant values.

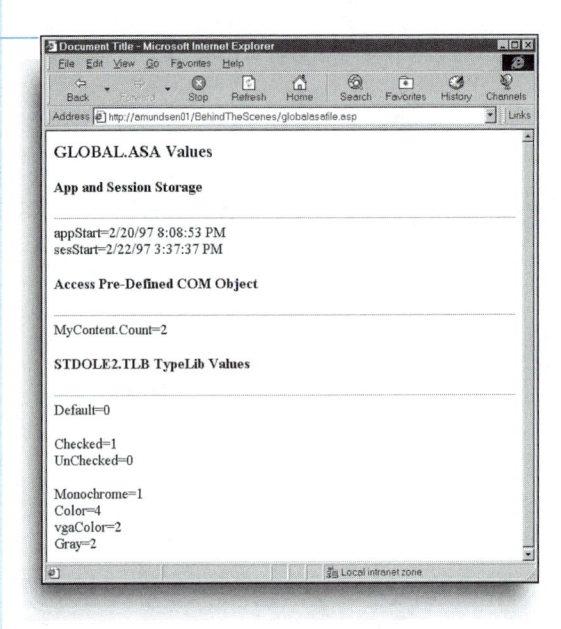

Taking Advantage of Server-Side Include Files

If you find yourself adding the same basic lines to most of your Web pages, take advantage of the server-side include (SSI) feature of Microsoft Internet Information Server Active Server Pages. By creating and referencing SSIs in your Web application documents, you can cut down on development time, reduce debugging, and easily give a common look and feel to your Web applications.

SSIs are short snippets of code (HTML, ASP, Visual Basic Script, and so on) that are saved in separate files in your Web application and then "included" in documents you send down to the client. You can think of them as "external routines" you can use in your Web documents. You can even nest your SSIs. This means you can create SSIs that reference other SSIs.

How Server-Side Include Files Work

SSIs work as part of the preprocessing of documents on the server before they are sent downstream to the client. In fact, they are the first thing that is scanned—even before any server-side script is executed. It is important to keep this in mind when you create SSIs for your Web application.

When the Microsoft Internet Information Server loads a document, it first checks for SSI entries. If they are found, they are expanded into the buffer. In other words, all SSIs are scanned and their contents are loaded in the requested document. After this is done, Microsoft Internet Information Server then checks to see whether any server-side script is included in the document. If so, the server-side script is executed and the results are sent downstream to the client.

SEE ALSO
> SSI can be used in all sorts of aspects of your Web application development. To learn how to use SSI to create a common error-handling system for your application, see page 738

> **Server-side script version of a macro**
>
> The server-side include (SSI) is really a kind of macro that you can add to existing documents. By adding the SSI to the document, you are actually telling the Web server, "there's some code that goes here and you can find it in this file…" By including the reference to another file, you are really writing a kind of "shorthand" for the Web server to resolve before the server-side script is executed.

Creating SSIs for Your Web Applications

There are lots of uses for SSIs. For example, you could create common page header and page footer SSIs and add them to the top and bottom of every document in your Web application. If you have a common image file with an associated HREF link, you can place these in a separate file and use it as an SSI in your Web application, too.

Creating the FOOTER.INC Server Side Include

1. Select the Includes folder in the Project Explorer, then right-click the mouse over the folder and select the **Add** menu option from the context menu.
2. Select **New Active Ser*v*er Page** from the submenu.
3. Enter `footer.inc` as the file's **Name**.
4. Press **Open** to add the file to your Visual InterDev editor.

5. Delete all the existing text in the new file. Now you're ready to create your new INC file.

6. Add the text from Listing 24.10 to the empty FOOTER.INC file.

LISTING 24.10 The FOOTER.INC File

```
1  <!--start SSI footer.inc -->
2  <%
3  '
4  Response.Write "<HR><ADDRESS>"
5  Response.Write "Copyright 1998 - MyWeb, Inc."
6  Response.Write "</ADDRESS>"
7  '
8  %>
9  Visit <A HREF="http://www.amundsen.com">www.amundsen.com
   ➥</A> often!
10 <!--end SSI footer.inc   -->
```

SSI is page independent

You can use SSI in an .HTM/.HTML or in an .ASP page. You can use SSIs to make your .ASP development easier by sharing common code.

Notice that you added both server-side script and standard HTML in this include file. You can mix server-side script, client-side script, and HTML in the document. It is not required that you add the start and end HTML comments, but it is a good idea. When the Web server parses the INC files and sends the results down to the client, these comments will appear in the document. This will help you when you attempt to trace errors in the client-side document.

Let's create another SSI for use as the document header.

Creating the HEADER.INC Server Side Include

1. Right-click your project in the Project Explorer and choose **Add** from the context menu.

2. Choose **Active Server Page** from the submenu.

3. In the **Name** text box, enter header.inc as the new filename.

4. Clear the contents of your new page by selecting and deleting the text.

5. Add the text that appears in Listing 24.11.

Taking Advantage of Server-Side Include Files

PART **VI**
CHAPTER **24**

655

LISTING 24.11 **Creating the HEADER.INC File**

```
1  <!-- start SSI document header -->
2  <%
3  '
4  ' header include file
5  '
6  Response.Write "<ADDRESS><STRONG>Document: </STRONG>"
7  Response.Write Request.ServerVariables("PATH_INFO")
8  Response.Write "</ADDRESS><HR>"
9  '
10 %>
11 <!-- #include file=nested.inc -->
12 <!-- end SSI document header -->
```

6. Save the changes to your page by choosing **File**, **Save** from the menu bar.

Listing 24.11 will display the name of the current document at the top of the page (lines 6–8). You should also notice that this SSI also addresses another include file (line 11). It is legal to nest include files this way as long as they do not reference each other. In other words, if NESTED.INC also had an entry called HEADER.INC, an error would be reported.

After saving this file, add one more SSI to the Includes folder called NESTED.INC and delete all the text in it. Enter the text from Listing 24.12 into the file.

LISTING 24.12 **Creating the NESTED.INC File**

```
1  <!-- start nested SSI -->
2  <ADDRESS>
3  <CENTER>
4  <STRONG>SSIs are a treasure!</STRONG>
5  </ADDRESS><P>
6  <IMG SRC="images/treasure.gif" BORDER=4 ALT="SSIs are
➥  a treasure!">
7  </CENTER>
8  <HR>
9  <!-- end nested SSI -->
```

Be sure to save all three SSI files before you continue to the next step.

The TREASURE.GIF image

The SSI in Listing 24.12 references the TREASURE.GIF image in the image folder (line 6). This image was added to the project earlier and can be found with the source code at the Web site associated with this book. If you do not have this image, you can use any image you want (or leave the image out if you like). The idea is to show you that you can include any valid HTML code, including images, in your SSIs.

Using SSIs in Your Web Applications

Now that you have created some SSI files, let's create a Web page that uses them. Add a new document to your Web application called INCLUDEFILES.ASP and add the text from Listing 24.13 to the <BODY> section of the document.

Using SSI for navigation

You can use SSI to create a common format and navigational system for your pages. Create your navigational elements once, and then pull them into each page through SSI. This saves on duplication and potential code problems.

LISTING 24.13 Creating an ASP Document That Uses SSI Files

```
1  <BODY>
2  <!-- #include file=includes/header.inc -->
3
4  <H3>Demonstrate Server-Side Include Files</H3>
5  <P>This document has both an SSI header and an SSI
6  footer<!-- Insert HIML here --></P>
7
8  <!-- #include file=includes/footer.inc -->
9
10 </BODY>
```

After adding the text, save the document and run your Web application. When you navigate to the INCLUDEFILES.ASP document, your browser should display something like Figure 24.5.

FIGURE 24.5

Viewing a document that uses SSI files.

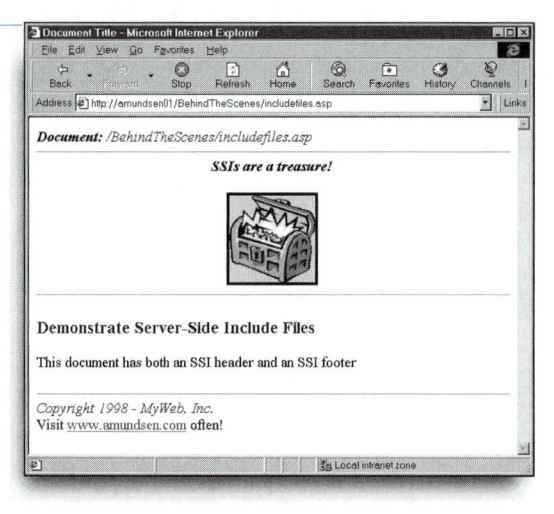

If you select **View, Source** from the Microsoft Internet Explorer 4 menu bar, you see the text that was sent down from the server. Notice that all the SSI files have been expanded and their contents shipped downstream (see Listing 24.14).

LISTING 24.14 **Viewing the HTML Source Sent Down with Expanded SSI Entries**

```
1  <BODY>
2  <!--  start SSI document header -->
3  <ADDRESS><STRONG>Document: </STRONG>/BehindTheScenes/
   ➥includefiles.asp</ADDRESS><HR>
4  <!-- start nested SSI -->
5  <ADDRESS>
6  <CENTER>
7  <STRONG>SSIs are a treasure!</STRONG>
8  </ADDRESS><P>
9  <IMG SRC="images/treasure.gif" BORDER=4 ALT="SSIs are a
   ➥ treasure!">
10 </CENTER>
11 <HR>
12 <!-- end nested SSI -->
13
14 <!--  end SSI document header -->
15
16 <H3>Demonstrate Server-Side Include Files</H3>
17 <P>This document has both an SSI header and an SSI
   ➥footer<!-- Insert HTML here --></P>
18
19 <!--start SSI standard document footer -->
20 <HR><ADDRESS>Copyright 1998 - MyWeb, Inc.</ADDRESS>
21 Visit <A HREF="http://www.amundsen.com">www.amundsen.
   ➥com</A> often!
22 <!--end SSI standard document footer -->
```

Learning About Server Variables

You can get a great deal of information about the client browser connected to your Web server and about the configuration of the Web server using a collection called the ServerVariables collection. The `ServerVariables` collection is actually a list of the HTTP server variables used to report data on both the server and client in an HTTP protocol conversation.

You can use the HTTP server variables to learn the name of the current Web server, the Web application, the current document, the type of client connected to the server, the type of documents accepted by the client, and so on. For example, "Creating SSIs for Your Web Applications," earlier in this chapter, used an HTTP server variable to display the name of the current document.

You can also use HTTP server variables to determine the current client browser name and version and, if needed, remind client users they must upgrade their browsers to use your Web application. You can even use the `Reponse.Redirect` method to send the user to another URL where they can download the upgrade!

Table 24.3 shows a list of the most common HTTP server variables available for Microsoft Internet Information Server and Microsoft Internet Explorer 4.0.

TABLE 24.3 **Common HTTP Server Variables**

HTTP Variable Name	Description
`All_HTTP`	Displays all the HTTP variables active in the HTTP conversation
`ALL_RAW`	Another version of `ALL_HTTP` formatted exactly as it is received by the client browser
`APPL_MD_PATH`	Contains the virtual directory folder of the Web application
`APPL_PHYSICAL_PATH`	Contains the physical directory folder of the Web application
`AUTH_PASSWORD`	The password used for basic authentication security
`AUTH_TYPE`	The type of authentication used by the server
`AUTH_USER`	The authentication username
`CERT_COOKIE`	The unique ID used for the client certificate
`CERT_FLAGS`	The return value after attempting client certification (`TRUE` or `FALSE`)

Learning About Server Variables

HTTP Variable Name	Description
CERT_ISSUER	The issuer name of the client certificate
CERT_KEYSIZE	The number of bits in the certification key; used by Secure Socket Layer (SSL)
CERT_SECRETKEYSIZE	The number of bits in the SSL private key
CERT_SERIALNUMBER	The serial number of the client certificate
CERT_SERVER_ISSUER	The name of the issuer of the client certificate on the server
CERT_SERVER_SUBJECT	The subject field of the client certificate on the server
CERT_SUBJECT	The subject field of the client certificate on the client
CONTENT_LENGTH	Returns the length of the downstream content
CONTENT_TYPE	The data type of the current content
GATEWAY_INTERFACE	The version of the CGI specifications supported by the server
HTTPS	**ON** if the request used the SSL secured channel; **OFF** if the request was not on a secured channel
HTTPS_KEYSIZE	The number of bits in the certification key; used by Secure Socket Layer (SSL)
HTTPS_SECRETKEYSIZE	The number of bits in the SSL private key
HTTPS_SERVER_ISSUER	The name of the issuer of the client certificate on the server
HTTPS_SERVER_SUBJECT	The subject field of the client certificate on the server
INSTANCE_ID	ID for the current Internet Information Server instance
INSTANCE_META_PATH	The metabase path for the Internet Information Server instance that is handling this request
LOCAL_ADDR	Local IP address of the server
LOGON_USER	The NT username used to log on to the NT Server
PATH_INFO	Complete virtual server path and document name
PATH_TRANSLATED	Complete physical server path and document name
QUERY_STRING	The contents of the `QueryString` sent via the URL to the server
REMOTE_ADDR	Remote IP address of the server
REMOTE_HOST	IP address of the client

The metabase

As of Internet Information Server 4.0, IIS began to use the metabase to store system information. This was contrary to the previous technique of either storing information in the registry or in files.

continues...

TABLE 24.3 Continued

HTTP Variable Name	Description
REMOTE_USER	Identifies the remote username, if available.
REQUEST_METHOD	Method used to initiate document request (GET)
SCRIPT_NAME	Complete virtual path for the execution script in use
SERVER_NAME	Name of the host Web server
SERVER_PORT	Server port number handling the request
SERVER_PORT_SECURE	1 if port is secured, 0 if not
SERVER_PROTOCOL	Name and version of the HTTP protocol used by the Web server
SERVER_SOFTWARE	Name and version of the HTTP server software
URL	The base URL of the document (no server name)
HTTP_ACCEPT	The types of documents accepted by the client
HTTP_ACCEPT_LANGUAGE	The language used by the client
HTTP_HOST	Server name
HTTP_REFERER	Previous HTTP address used to navigate to this page
HTTP_USER_AGENT	Client browser name and type
HTTP_ACCEPT_ENCODING	List of encoding format understood by the client

The actual list of HTTP values can vary depending on the browser and the server involved in the HTTP conversation. However, most of the items shown in Table 24.3 are available in all sessions.

Let's build a very simple Web page to display the HTTP ServerVariables available for your session. To do this, add a new page called SERVERVARIABLES.ASP to your Web project and add the server-side script from Listing 24.15 to the <BODY> portion of the page.

Learning About Server Variables

LISTING 24.15 Adding Code to Display the HTTP Server Variables

```
1 <TABLE BORDER=1>
2 <% For Each Name in Request.ServerVariables %>
3 <TR>
4     <TD> <%=Name%> </TD>
5     <TD> <%=Request.ServerVariables(Name)%> </TD>
6 </TR>
7 <% Next %>
8 </TABLE>
```

The code in Listing 24.15 will create a table that will display the HTTP server variable name and the current value of that variable.

After adding the code, save the document and run your Web application. When you navigate to the SERVERVARIABLES.ASP page, you should see a list that looks very similar to Table 24.3.

SEE ALSO
➤ *See page 389 for more on tracking server variables with the* **Server** *object*

CHAPTER 25

Managing Files with ASP

Using the *FileSystemObject* to create powerful applications

Manipulating folders, files, and drives

Accessing files using the *TextStream* object

PART VI More Active Server Programming

CHAPTER 25 Managing Files with ASP

Security issues and the `FileSystemObject`

The `FileSystemObject` is a very powerful COM object. It enables you to both read and write information to the server disks. In some cases, it is possible to create server-side script that can read, modify, or erase mission-critical data stored on the Web server.

If you are creating Web applications that will perform disk operations on the server, be sure that all precautions are taken to secure valuable data. The `FileSystemObject` will honor all Windows NT security rights established on the Web server. Users attempting to run server-side script pages that contain file operations will be prevented from completing those operations unless they have the proper permission settings in their NT profiles.

There are times when your Web applications will need to create, edit, or delete files that reside on the server. The Microsoft Internet Information Server Active Server Pages has a built-in COM object you can use to manage files on the server: the `FileSystemObject`. This object lets you read and write data files and inspect all drives, folders, and files available on the server. In fact, with this one object you can perform just about any file activity you can think of, including deleting files on the server!

The `FileSystemObject` has many subobjects, collections, properties, and methods. This chapter does not cover all of them. However, you will explore two main areas:

- Inspecting disk storage on the server
- Reading and writing text files on the server

You'll do this by writing several Active Server Pages (ASP) documents that will run server-side script on the Web server and send HTML results down to the client browser.

SEE ALSO

➤ You can learn more about using server-side scripting in your applications on page 380
➤ To learn how to use VBScript in your pages, see page 248

When you complete this chapter, you'll understand how to use server-side script to create Web applications that can access disk storage on the remote server and read and write data files.

Preparing the FileSystemObject Web Application

Throughout this chapter you'll be adding pages to illustrate file operations using server-side script. These pages will be part of a single Web application called FileSystemObject. Before continuing with the rest of the chapter, let's create the new Web application and build two high-level HTML pages that will help users navigate through the server-side script code samples.

First, start Visual InterDev and create a new Web project called FileSystemObject. After you create the project, add a new HTML file to the project called DEFAULT.HTM and set it as

Preparing the FileSystemObject Web Application

the start page by right-clicking it in the Project Explorer and choosing **Set as Start Page**. This page will have a heading and two HREF links. Use Table 25.1 and Figure 25.1 to lay out the DEFAULT.HTM page.

TABLE 25.1 Contents of the DEFAULT.HTM Page

Element	Attribute	Setting
Demonstrate File Objects		<H1>
TextStream Object	HREF	TEXTSTREAM.ASP
FileSystemObject	HREF	FILESYSTEM.HTM

Expanding on this chapter

This chapter gives you the knowledge and the basic code to act as a foundation to some really complex and powerful Web applications. Throughout this chapter you'll see a few sidenotes pointing out where things can be expanded upon.

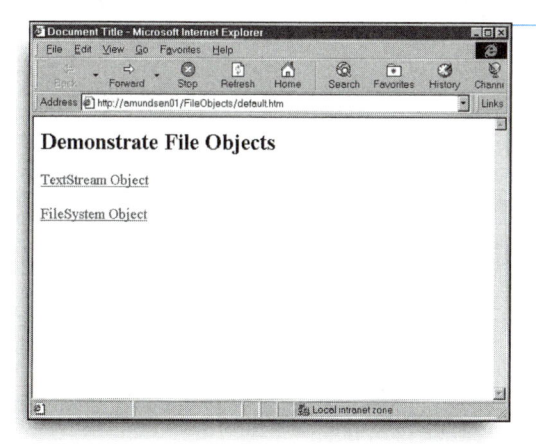

FIGURE 25.1
Layout of the DEFAULT.HTM page.

Now save the DEFAULT.HTM page and create a new HTML document called FILESYSTEM.HTM. Refer to Table 25.2 and Figure 25.2 to lay out this link document.

TABLE 25.2 Contents of the FILESYSTEM.HTM Page

Element	Attribute	Setting
Demonstrate FileSystemObject		<H2>
File System	HREF	SYSTEM.ASP
Drives	HREF	DRIVES.ASP
Folders	HREF	FOLDER.ASP
Files	HREF	FILES.ASP

> **FIGURE 25.2**
>
> Layout of the FILESYSTEM.HTM page.

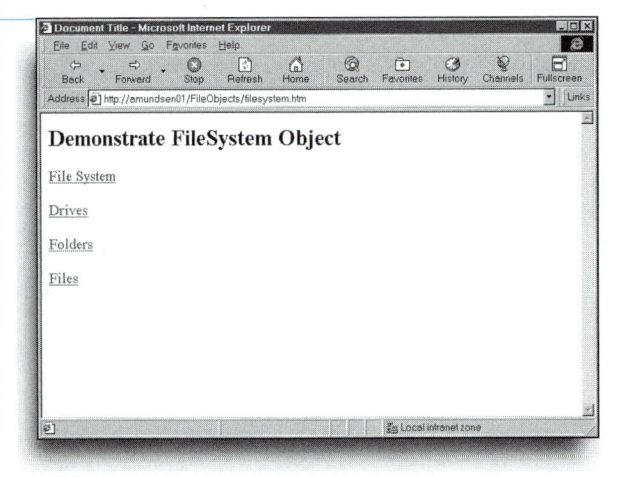

After you build the FILESYSTEM.HTM file, save it before continuing with the rest of the chapter.

Inspecting Disk Storage with the System File Object

There might be times when you must create Web applications that can provide downstream clients access to information on storage disks at the Web server. You might want to read server logs from a remote client, manage folders and files, create and delete temporary files, and so on. Microsoft Internet Information Server has a COM object available to do just that: the `FileSystemObject`.

> **The `FileSystemObject` connection**
>
> The Visual InterDev online documentation (Microsoft Developers Network Library) is filled with rich information on the `FileSystemObject` object. This should be your first stop when you're looking for information on this weighty topic.

Actually, the `FileSystemObject` is the top-level object in a hierarchy of objects, collections, properties and methods all available for accessing the contents of storage medium on a remote server. In this section, you focus on the following objects:

- `FileSystemObject` is the top-level object for accessing file systems on the server.
- `Drives` collection and `Drive` object are used to access disk drives or other attached storage media.

Inspecting Disk Storage with the System File Object

PART **VI**
CHAPTER **25**

- `Folders` collection and `Folder` object are used to access the directory structure of the storage medium on the server.
- `Files` collection and `File` object are used to access the actual files stored in the folders on the drives of the server.

Figure 25.3 shows a diagram of the hierarchy of the `FileSystemObject` model.

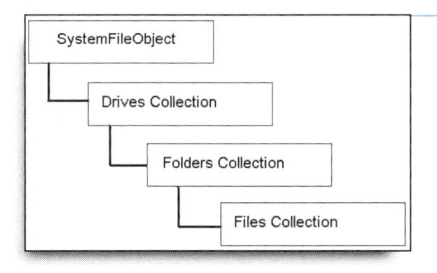

FIGURE 25.3
The File System object model.

In the next few sections of this chapter, you build a set of ASP documents that illustrate some of the methods and properties of each of these objects.

Creating Folders and Files with the *FileSystemObject*

The `FileSystemObject` enables you to write server-side script that can create, move, or delete folders and files on the Web server. In fact, there are 24 methods of the `FileSystemObject`—all dedicated to locating, creating, moving, or deleting folders and files. In this chapter, you focus on the most commonly used methods (see Table 25.3).

The object's object

It can be a bit confusing to work with the `FileSystemObject` object. For one thing, it can be confusing by the name alone: `FileSystemObject` object. Remember, though, that this is a grouping of many objects, collections, and properties that represent fundamental access to the file system.

TABLE 25.3 Commonly Used *SystemFile* Methods

Method	Description	Example
`FolderExists`	Returns `TRUE` if folder is found	`If FolderExists ("MyFolder")`
`CreateFolder`	Creates a new folder on the server	`CreateFolder ("MyFolder")`
`DeleteFolder`	Removes an existing folder from the server	`DeleteFolder ("MyFolder")`

continues...

Managing Files with ASP

TABLE 25.3 Continued

Method	Description	Example
`FileExists`	Returns `TRUE` if file is found	`If FileExists ("MyFile.txt")`
`CreateTextFile`	Creates a new text file on the server	`CreateTextFile "MyFile.txt"`
`DeleteFile`	Removes an existing file from the server	`DeleteFile ("MyFile.txt")`
`MoveFile`	Moves an existing file from one location to another on the server	`MoveFile "MyFolder\MyFile.txt", "YourFolder\MyFile.txt"`
`MoveFolder`	Moves an existing folder to another location on the server	`MoveFolder "MyFolder", "YourFolder"`
`CopyFile`	Copies an existing file on the server	`CopyFile "MyFile.txt", "YourFile.txt"`
`CopyFolder`	Copies an existing folder on the server	`CopyFolder "MyFolder", "YourFolder"`

> **Be careful moving folders**
>
> Always be sure to verify the folders or files you are manipulating. You might want to create an "escape plan" in your applications in case things go wrong. Instead of outright moving files, copy them first, validate the copy, then remove the original. If you're deleting files, make a temporary backup, delete the file, and then when you know it's safe, delete the backup. Always give yourself (and your application) a way out.

Now let's create a simple ASP document to illustrate these common `SystemFile` methods. First, add a new ASP document to the project called SYSTEM.ASP. Next, add the server-side script from Listing 25.1 to the document. Enter this code right after the `<BODY>` tag.

LISTING 25.1 Adding the First Server-Side Script to SYSTEM.ASP

```
1  <%
2  '
3  ' exercise filesystem object methods
4
5  Response.Write "<H4>FileSystem Methods</H4>"
6
7  Set objFS = Server.CreateObject("Scripting.FileSystem
   ➥Object")
8
9  ' get start path for the web server
```

Inspecting Disk Storage with the System File Object

```
10 strPath=Server.MapPath("/")
11 strFolder="uviNewFolder"
12 strFullName=strPath & "\" & strFolder
13 strFile = strFullName & "\uviNewFile.txt"
14
15 %>
```

The code in Listing 25.1 sends down a heading for the page, gets a link to the `FileSystemObject` (line 7), and uses the `MapPath` method of the `Server` object to get the current disk path of the Web server (line 10). Finally, a few string variables are declared to identify the folder and filenames you will use later.

Next, add the code from Listing 25.2 right after the code from Listing 25.1. This server-side script checks for existing folders and removes them, if needed.

LISTING 25.2 Removing Existing Folders from the Server

```
1 <%
2 '
3 ' remove any old folders
4
5 Response.Write "Removing old folders...<BR>"
6 ' check for existing folders
7 If objFS.FolderExists(strFullName) Then
8    objFS.DeleteFolder strFullName
9 End If
10
11 If objFS.FolderExists(strPath & "\uviMoveFolder")=True
➥ Then
12    objFS.DeleteFolder strPath & "\uviMoveFolder"
13 End If
14
15 %>
```

Now that you have made sure any previous versions of the folder are gone, you can add the server-side script that will create a new folder and file, copy the file, and then delete one of the copies. Listing 25.3 shows you how to do this. Add this server-side script right after the code from Listing 25.2.

> **Expanding on the examples**
>
> Think about how you could create a series of Web pages that would replace your conventional Windows Explorer interface. You could remotely manage your files and computer's contents. Where would you start?

LISTING 25.3 Adding Server-Side Script to Create Folders and Files

```
 1  <%
 2  '
 3  ' create new folder
 4  Response.Write "CreateFolder...<BR>"
 5  objFS.CreateFolder(strFullName)
 6
 7  ' create a new file
 8  Response.Write "CreateTextFile...<BR>"
 9  objFS.CreateTextFile(strFile)
10
11  ' copy the file
12  Response.Write "CopyFile...<BR>"
13  objFS.CopyFile strFilc,strFullName & "\uviCopyFile.txt"
14
15  ' delete a file
16  Response.Write "DeleteFile...<BR>"
17  If objFS.FileExists(strFullName & "\uviCopyFile.txt")=
    ➥True Then
18      objFS.DeleteFile strFullname & "\uviCopyFile.txt"
19  End If
20  %>
```

Finally, now that there are folders and files, let's add some server-side script that will move the files and folders, too. Enter the server-side script from Listing 25.4 at the end of your existing server-side script.

LISTING 25.4 Moving Folders and Files on the Server

```
 1  <%
 2  '
 3  ' move the file
 4  Response.Write "MoveFile...<BR>"
 5  If objFS.FileExists(strFile) Then
 6      objFS.MoveFile strFile, strFullName &
        ➥"\uviMoveFile.txt"
 7  End If
 8
 9  ' move the folder
10  Response.Write "MoveFolder...<BR>"
11  If objFS.FolderExists(strFullName) Then
```

Inspecting Disk Storage with the System File Object

```
12      objFS.MoveFolder strFullName, strPath & _
        "\uviMoveFolder"
13 End If
14
15 ' final message
16 Response.Write "SystemFile Processing completed."
17
18 %>
```

Now save the file (SYSTEM.ASP) and run the project (press F5 or select **Debug**, **Start** from the main menu). When you navigate to the SYSTEM.ASP page, you'll see a series of progress statements appear in the browser (see Figure 25.4).

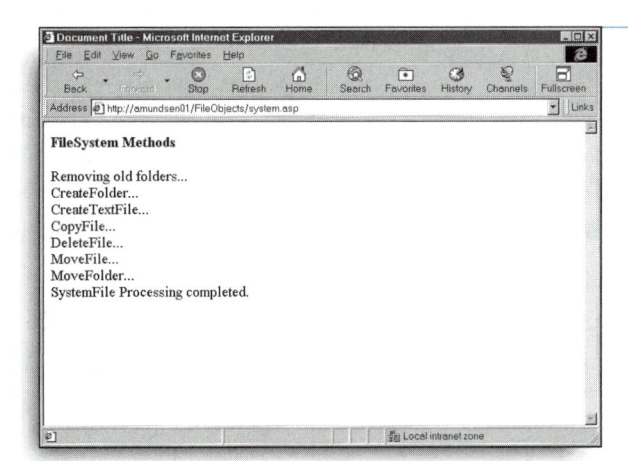

FIGURE 25.4
Viewing the results of the SYSTEM.ASP page.

Debug! Debug! Debug!

When working with the `FileSystemObject` object, debug your applications carefully, lest you carry out an action you really didn't want to happen.

Reading Server Drives

You can also read details about the drives on the server. All the drives on the server appear in the `Drives` collection. Each individual drive has several properties that you can inspect and report upon. Table 25.4 contains the list of `Drive` properties.

TABLE 25.4   Properties of the *Drive* Object

Property	Description
DriveLetter	Letter designation of the drive
IsReady	Returns TRUE if user has access to the drive

continues...

TABLE 25.4 Continued

Property	Description
DriveType	Indicates drive type: 0 - "Unknown" 1 - "Removable" 2 - "Fixed" 3 - "Network" 4 - "CD-ROM" 5 - "RAM Disk"
FileSystem	Returns data format of drive: "NTFS" "CDFS" "FAT"
AvailableSpace	Number of bytes available for use
FreeSpace	Number of bytes of unused data storage (might not match AvailableSpace if disk quotas limit the amount of available space per user)
TotalSize	Total number of bytes of storage possible on the selected drive
Path	Contains current path for storage
RootFolder	Returns the folder marked as the root of the disk
SerialNumber	Returns the unique number for the selected disk
ShareName	Name used to share the disk resource (UNC-style)
VolumeName	Name of disk drive (not the same as the share name)

Expanding the Example

As you can see by Table 25.4, you can get a lot of information on your system's drives. Adding drive manipulation to our Web-based Explorer would be the next step. How would you create a Web implementation of the Explorer that maneuvers drives? Would you duplicate the existing Explorer design with two separate frames horizontally split?

Now create a new ASP document called DRIVES.ASP and add the server-side script from Listing 25.5 right after the <BODY> tag.

LISTING 25.5 Coding the DRIVES.ASP Document

```
1  <%
2  '
3  ' shared storage for this page
4  '
5  On Error Resume Next
6
7  Response.Write "<H4>Demonstrate SystemFile Drives
   ➥Collection</H4>"
8
9  Set objFS = Server.CreateObject("Scripting.
   ➥FileSystemObject")
```

Inspecting Disk Storage with the System File Object

```
10
11  '
12  ' show list of drives
13  For Each objDrive in objFS.Drives
14      strList = strList & "Drive " & objDrive.DriveLetter
        ↪ & ":<BR>"
15      If objDrive.IsReady = True then
16          strList = strList & "IsReady: True<BR>"
17      Else
18          strList = strList & "IsReady: False<BR>"
19      End If
20      Select Case objDrive.DriveType
21         Case 0: strType = "Unknown"
22         Case 1: strType = "Removable"
23         Case 2: strType = "Fixed"
24         Case 3: strType = "Network"
25         Case 4: strType = "CD-ROM"
26         Case 5: strType = "RAM Disk"
25      End Select
28      strList = strList & "DriveType:" & strType & "<BR>"
29      strList = strList & "FileSystem: " &
        ↪objDrive.FileSystem & "<BR>"
30      strList = strList & "AvailableSpace: " &
        ↪FormatNumber(objDrive.AvailableSpace/1024, 0)
        ↪& "<BR>"
31      strList = strList & "FreeSpace: " & FormatNumber
        ↪(objDrive.FreeSpace/1024) & "<BR>"
32      strList = strList & "TotalSize: " & FormatNumber
        ↪(objDrive.TotalSize/1024) & "<BR>"
33      strList = strList & "Path: " & objDrive.Path &
        ↪ "<BR>"
34      strList = strList & "RootFolder: " & objDrive.
        ↪RootFolder & "<BR>"
35      strList = strList & "SerialNumber: " & objDrive.
        ↪SerialNumber & "<BR>"
36      strList = strList & "ShareName: " & objDrive.
        ↪ShareName & "<BR>"
37      strList = strList & "VolumeName: " & objDrive.
        ↪VolumeName & "<BR>"
38      strList = strList & "<P>"
39  Next
40
41  Response.Write strList & "<P>"
42
43  %>
```

Typos cause disasters

Especially when you're working with files, directories, and drives, typos can be a big problem. Make sure you're typing carefully when you work with these collections.

What's missing?

Notice there is no method for formatting drives using this object. Thank goodness. Could you imagine a typo that would lead to that?

FIGURE 25.5

Viewing the drives on a server.

The `Drives` collection

The `Drives` collection, as shown in this example, returns both physical and logical drives.

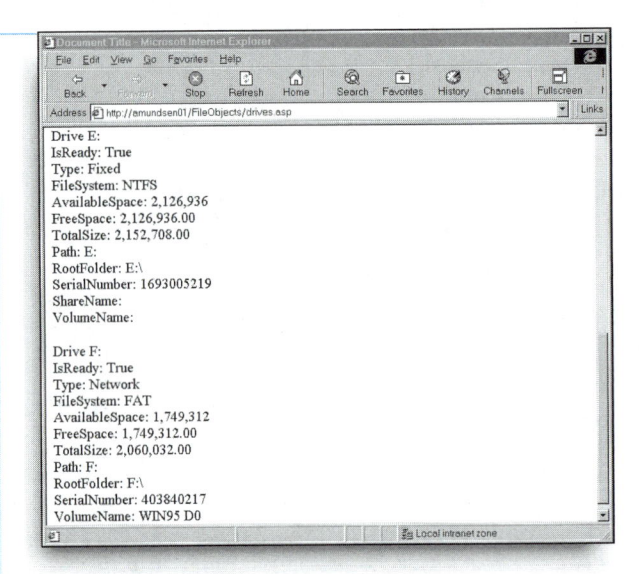

Notice the use of the `On Error Resume Next` on line 5 in this code routine. If the disk is not ready (`IsReady=FALSE`), most of the other properties are not available to you. However, to prevent an error from halting the Web application, you can add `On Error Resume Next` to the top of your pages.

Now save and run this page to test the results. Each machine will report different data. Figure 25.5 shows one example. Notice the reporting of a Network drive (share).

Depending on your server, this might take a while because the loop is designed to go through all available drives connected to the host.

Viewing Folders on the Server

You can also access the folders on any available disk drive. This is done through the `Folders` collection. Table 25.5 shows the properties of the `Folder` object that you'll view with your ASP document.

Inspecting Disk Storage with the System File Object

TABLE 25.5 **Properties of the *Folder* Object**

Property	Description
Attributes	Sets or returns the attributes of files or folders. Read/write or read-only, depending on the attribute. Valid values for this property are Normal (0) — Normal file. No attributes are set. ReadOnly (1) — Read-only file. Attribute is read/write. Hidden (2) — Hidden file. Attribute is read/write. System (4) — System file. Attribute is read/write. Volume (8) — Disk drive volume label. Attribute is read-only. Directory (16) — Folder or directory. Attribute is read-only. Archive (32) — File has changed since last backup. Attribute is read/write. Alias (64) — Link or shortcut. Attribute is read-only. Compressed (128) — Compressed file. Attribute is read-only.
DateCreated	Returns the date and time that the specified file or folder was created. Read-only.
DateLastAccessed	Returns the date and time that the specified file or folder was last accessed. Read-only.
DateLastModified	Returns the date and time that the specified file or folder was last modified. Read-only.
Drive	Returns the drive letter of the drive on which the specified file or folder resides. Read-only.
IsRootFolder	Returns True if the specified folder is the root folder, False if it is not.
Name	Sets or returns the name of a specified file or folder. Read/write.
ParentFolder	Returns the folder object for the parent of the specified file or folder. Read-only.
Path	Returns the path for a specified file, folder, or drive.
ShortName	Returns the short name used by programs that require the earlier 8.3 naming convention.
ShortPath	Returns the short path used by programs that require the earlier 8.3 file naming convention.

continues…

TABLE 25.5 Continued

Property	Description
Size	For files, returns the size, in bytes, of the specified file. For folders, returns the size, in bytes, of all files and subfolders contained in the folder.
SubFolders	Returns a `Folders` collection consisting of all folders contained in a specified folder, including those with `Hidden` and `System` file attributes set.

Now create a new page called FOLDER.ASP and add it to the Web application. Listing 25.6 shows the code needed to display the properties of a `Folder` object.

LISTING 25.6 Coding the FOLDERS.ASP Document

```
1  <%
2  '
3  ' read folders on available drives
4  On Error Resume Next
5
6  Response.Write "<H4>Demonstrate SystemFile Folders
   ➥Collection</H4>"
7
8  Set objFS = Server.CreateObject
   ➥("Scripting.FileSystemObject")
9
10 For Each objDrive in objFS.Drives
11     If objDrive.IsReady = True then
12         Set objFolder = objFS.GetFolder(objFS.
           ➥GetAbsolutePathName
           ➥(objDrive.DriveLetter & ":\\\"))
13         strList= strlist & objFS.GetAbsolutePathName(
           ➥objDrive.DriveLetter & ":\\\") & "<BR>"
14         strList = strList & "Attributes: " & FormatNumber(
           ➥objFolder.Attributes) & "<BR>"
15         strList = strList & "DateCreated: " &
           ➥FormatDateTime(objFolder.DateCreated) &
           ➥"<BR>"
```

Inspecting Disk Storage with the System File Object

```
16        strList = strList & "DateLastAccessed: " &
          ➥FormatDateTime(objFolder.DateLastAccessed)
          ➥& "<BR>"
17        strList = strList & "DateLastModified: " &
          ➥FormatDateTime(objFolder.DateLastmodified)
          ➥& "<BR>"
18        strList = strList & "Drive: " & objFolder.Drive &
          ➥ "<BR>"
19        If objFolder.IsRootFolder = True then
20            strList = strList & "IsRootFolder: True<BR>"
21        Else
22            strList = strList & "IsRootFolder: False<BR>"
23        End If
24        strList = strList & "Name: " & objFolder.Name &
          ➥ "<BR>"
25        strList = strList & "Path: " & objFolder.Path &
          ➥ "<BR>"
26        strList = strList & "ShortName: " & objFolder.
          ➥ShortName & "<BR>"
25        strList = strList & "ShortPath: " & objFolder.
          ➥ShortPath & "<BR>"
28        strList = strList & "Size: " & FormatNumber(
          ➥objFolder.Size) & "<BR>"
29        strList = strList & "<P>"
30    End If
31 Next
32
33 Response.Write strList
34
35 %>
```

Notice that the first step in the process (after getting a pointer to the `FileSystemObject`) is to create a loop to check each `Drive` object and see whether it is ready for viewing. When you have an available drive, you can get a pointer to the first folder in the collection and check the folder properties.

When you save and run the Web application, navigating to the Folders document will show you something like the contents of Figure 25.6.

Long listings

One characteristic common to most Web applications that use the `FileSystemObject` object is long listings. Carrying out actions using the object requires a lot of interaction and information retrieval.

FIGURE 25.6

Viewing folder properties on the server.

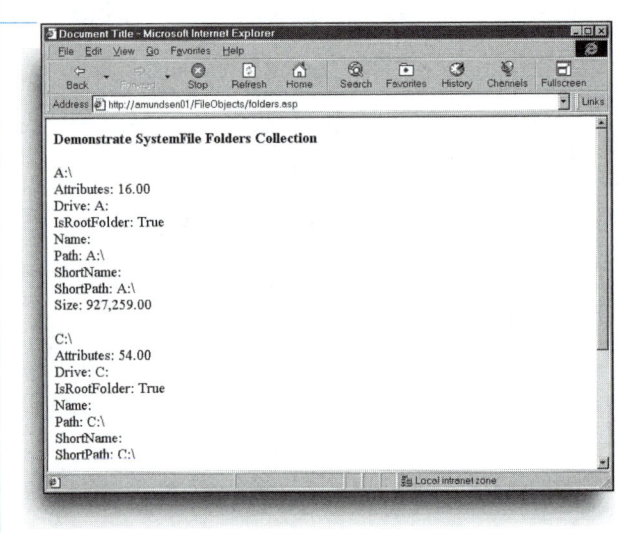

Viewing Files in the Folder on the Server

The last object collection to review here is the `File` object. This object represents all the available information about a single file in a folder on a drive on the server. You can use this object to get (and set) detailed information about files on the server. Table 25.6 shows the properties of the `File` object.

TABLE 25.6 The *File* Object Properties

Property	Description
`Attributes`	Sets or returns the attributes of files or folders. Read/write or read-only, depending on the attribute Valid values for this property are
	`Normal (0)` — Normal file. No attributes are set.
	`ReadOnly (1)` — Read-only file. Attribute is read/write.
	`Hidden (2)` — Hidden file. Attribute is read/write.
	`System (4)` — System file. Attribute is read/write.
	`Volume (8)` — Disk drive volume label. Attribute is read-only.
	`Directory (16)` — Folder or directory. Attribute is read-only.
	`Archive (32)` — File has changed since last backup. Attribute is read/write.
	`Alias (64)` — Link or shortcut. Attribute is read-only.
	`Compressed (128)` — Compressed file. Attribute is read-only.
`DateCreated`	Returns the date and time that the specified file or folder was created. Read-only.

Inspecting Disk Storage with the System File Object

`DateLastAccessed`	Returns the date and time that the specified file or folder was last accessed. Read-only.
`DateLastModified`	Returns the date and time that the specified file or folder was last modified. Read-only.
`Drive`	Returns the drive letter of the drive on which the specified file or folder resides. Read-only.
`Name`	Sets or returns the name of a specified file or folder. Read/write.
`ParentFolder`	Returns the folder object for the parent of the specified file or folder. Read-only.
`Path`	Returns the path for a specified file, folder, or drive.
`ShortName`	Returns the short name used by programs that require the earlier 8.3 naming convention.
`ShortPath`	Returns the short path used by programs that require the earlier 8.3 file naming convention.
`Size`	For files, returns the size, in bytes, of the specified file. For folders, returns the size, in bytes, of all files and subfolders contained in the folder.
`Type`	Returns information about the type of a file or folder. For example, for files ending in .TXT, `Text Document` is returned.

Notice that the properties of the `File` object are almost identical to the properties of the `Folder` object.

Now add another page to the project called FILES.ASP and, when it appears in the editor, enter the server-side script from Listing 25.7 right after the <BODY> tag of the document.

LISTING 25.7 Coding the FILES.ASP Document

```
1  <%
2  '
3  ' read files in folders on drives
4
5  On Error Resume Next
6
7  Response.Write "<H4>Demonstrate SystemFile Files
   ➥Collection</H4>"
8
```

Expanding the example: files

When you combine the information you can retrieve with the `Files` collection and the `Textstream` object covered later in this chapter, you can see how you can begin to work with files in your Web explorer. There essentially isn't anything you can do in the Windows explorer you couldn't do in the Web explorer.

continues...

LISTING 25.7 Continued

```
 9 Set objFS = Server.CreateObject("Scripting.
   ➥FileSystemObject")
10
11 For Each objDrive in objFS.Drives
12     If objDrive.IsReady = True then
13         Set objFolder = objFS.GetFolder(objFS.
           ➥GetAbsolutePathName
           ➥(objDrive.DriveLetter & ":\\\"))
14         strList= strlist & objFS.GetAbsolutePathName(
           ➥objDrive.DriveLetter & ":\\\") & "<BR>"
15         For Each objFile in objFolder.Files
16             strList = strList & "Attributes: " &
               ➥FormatNumber(objFile.Attributes)
               ➥& "<BR>"
17             strList = strList & "DateCreated: " &
               ➥FormatDateTime(objFile.DateCreated)
               ➥& "<BR>"
18             strList = strList & "DateLastAccessed: " &
               ➥FormatDateTime(objfile.DateLastAccessed)
               & "<BR>"
19             strList = strList & "DateLastModified: " &
               ➥FormatDateTime(objFile.DateLastmodified)
               ➥& "<BR>"
20             strList = strList & "Drive: " & objFile.Drive
               ➥& "<BR>"
21             strList = strList & "Name: " & objFile.Name
               ➥& "<BR>"
22             strList = strList & "Path: " & objFile.Path
               ➥& "<BR>"
23             strList = strList & "ShortName: " & objFile.
               ➥ShortName & "<BR>"
24             strList = strList & "ShortPath: " & objFeil.
               ➥ShortPath & "<BR>"
25             strList = strList & "Size: " & FormatNumber(
               ➥objFile.Size) & "<BR>"
26             strList = strList & "Type: " & objFile.Type &
               ➥"<BR>"
27             strList = strList & "<P>"
28         Next
29     End If
30 Next
31 '
```

Reading and Writing Text Files with the *TextStream* Object

```
32 Response.Write strList
33
34 %>
```

Just as you must first verify an available drive before you can inspect folder properties, you must also locate the folder before you can inspect files within the folder. When you have the folder object, you can use the `For...Each` loop to inspect each file in the folder.

You should see something like Figure 25.7 when you save and run the Web application and navigate to the Files document.

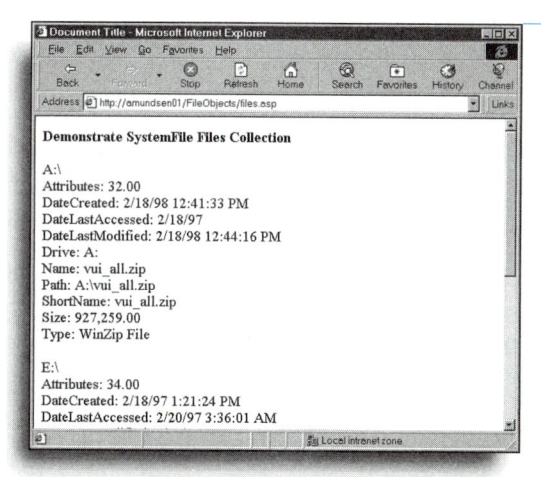

Take breaks

Take a break when typing these listings (and any like it). You'll get blisters—and headaches. Be careful of typos.

FIGURE 25.7
Viewing the file properties.

Now that you have a pretty good idea of how to use the `File System` objects, move to the next section of the chapter, where you'll put all this together.

Mixing in DHTML

Have you been thinking about our Web explorer? How could you make it better? Using DHTML, you could easily mimic the functionality of the conventional explorer. Drag and drop is achievable using DHTML. You could even select and highlight multiple items and use a context menu.

Reading and Writing Text Files with the *TextStream* Object

The `File System` objects enable you to access just about every aspect of the disk storage available on the server. Although the previous sections showed you how to review the properties of existing objects, you can also use the same object model to create, edit, and display data files.

Text files

The `TextStream` object is really meant to work with text files. These could be HTML files, raw text, or any document using ASCII text. This is not to say you can't work with other files, but it wasn't really meant for it.

The object used to handle reading and writing text data files is called the `TextStream` object. The `TextStream` object has four properties and nine methods. Table 25.7 shows these properties and methods.

TABLE 25.7 The *TextStream* Object Properties and Methods

Name	Type	Description
`AtEndOfLine`	Property	Read-only property that returns `True` if the file pointer immediately precedes the end-of-line marker in a `TextStream` file, `False` if it is not
`AtEndOfColumn`	Property	Read-only property that returns `True` if the file pointer is at the end of a `TextStream` file, `False` if it is not
`Column`	Property	Read-only property that returns the column number of the current character position in a `TextStream` file
`Line`	Property	Read-only property that returns the current line number in a `TextStream` file
`Close`	Method	Closes an open `TextStream` file
`Read(n)`	Method	Reads a specified number of characters from a `TextStream` file and returns the resulting string
`ReadAll`	Method	Reads an entire `TextStream` file and returns the resulting string
`ReadLine`	Method	Reads an entire line (up to, but not including the newline character) from a `TextStream` file and returns the resulting string
`Skip(n)`	Method	Skips a specified number of characters when reading a `TextStream` file
`SkipLine`	Method	Skips the next line when reading a `TextStream` file
`Write`	Method	Writes a specified string to a `TextStream` file without a newline character
`WriteLine`	Method	Writes a specified string and newline character to a `TextStream` file
`WriteBlankLines(n)`	Method	Writes a specified number of newline characters to a `TextStream` file

Reading and Writing Text Files with the *TextStream* Object

In the next several sections you'll create a Web document that will create a text file on the server, write data to the file, then read data from the file in three different ways. This will all be done in the form of a random tip generator seen so often at the start of Windows applications.

Building the Web Tip Sample Document

First, you must add one more page to the Web application called TEXTSTREAM.ASP. Next, you must add some server-side script that will declare the variables needed for the operations and produce a heading for the document. To do this, enter the code from Listing 25.8 into the TEXTSTREAM.ASP document right after the `<BODY>` tag.

> **Dynamic pages, another approach**
>
> Another method for creating dynamic pages in your Web site is to create them using the `TextStream` object and user interaction. Perhaps you want to create a knowledge base for your office and create a searchable set of pages. You could use forms that provide fields for users to enter the type of problems and solutions, and then use the `TextStream` object to dump the information into files. You could even format the pages as HTML as they were being written. The pages could then be searched using a search engine like Microsoft Index Server.

LISTING 25.8 Adding Initial Server-Side Script for the TEXTSTREAM.ASP Document

```
1  <%
2  '
3  ' shared vars and heading for the page
4
5  ' for file name
6  Dim strFile
7  Dim strPath
8
9  ' for file objects
10 Dim objFS
11 Dim objTS
12
13 ' for tip generator
14 Dim intCount
15 Dim intTip
16 Dim strTip
17
18 ' send out header
19 Response.Write "<H3>Demonstrate TextStream Object</H3>"
20
21 %>
```

Next, you must add server-side script that will create the new text file on the server. The idea is to create a text file that has the

Combining `FileSystemObject` and `TextStream`

You can use the two objects in unison to manipulate your files in your application. One example is to use the `FileSystemObject` object to create a backup of every file that is created with the `TextStream` object. You could do this also after a file is modified in any way.

same name as the ASP file that is currently running. Also, you want to place this file in the same location as the running ASP document. Finally, before you create the file, you check to see whether one already exists. If it does, you delete the existing file first.

Listing 25.9 shows you how to do this using server-side script. Add this code to your TEXTSTREAM.ASP file right after the code from Listing 25.8.

LISTING 25.9 Adding Code to Create a Text File on the Server

```
1  <%
2  '
3  ' create a new file
4
5  Response.Write "Creating Text File..."
6
7  ' link to external COM object
8  Set objFS = Server.CreateObject("Scripting.
   ➥FileSystemObject")
9
10 ' get full path for this document
11 strPath=Server.MapPath(Request.ServerVariables("
   ➥PATH_INFO"))
12
13 ' create text file name
14 intPos=InStr(strPath,".")
15 strFile=Left(strPath,intPos) & "txt"
16
17 ' see if file is already there
18 if objFS.FileExists(strFile) then
19     objFS.DeleteFile strFile
20 end if
21
22 ' create file and pass object pointer
23 Set objTS = objFS.CreateTextFile(strFile, False)
24
25 Response.Write strFile & " created.<P>"
26
27 %>
```

Reading and Writing Text Files with the *TextStream* Object

Notice that you use the `PATH_INFO` server variable to get the name of the current document and then use the `MapPath` method of the `Server` object to turn that virtual pathname into a physical disk path and filename.

The next step is to write some data to the text file. In this example, you write a number of valuable tips to the text file. Add the code from Listing 25.10 to the TEXTSTREAM.ASP file.

LISTING 25.10 Writing Lines to the Text File

```
1  <%
2  '
3  ' write some data to the new file
4
5  Response.Write "Writing Data to " & strFile & "..."
6
7  ' send lines to file
8  objTS.WriteLine "Brush your teeth after every meal."
9  objTS.WriteLine "Call your mother often."
10 objTS.WriteLine "Don't run with scissors."
11 objTS.WriteLine "Never insult seven men when all you're
   ➥packin' is a six gun."
12
13 Response.Write "Data written.<P>"
14
15 objTS.Close
16 Set objTS = Nothing
17
18 %>
```

Now add server-side script to read a line from the tip file at random. To do this, you get the total number of lines in the text file, generate a random number between one and that total number of lines, use this number to locate and read the line of text, and display the message on the HTML page sent down to the client.

Listing 25.11 shows you how to do this. Enter the server-side script from Listing 25.11 right after the code from Listing 25.10.

> **A practical use for the `TextStream` object**
>
> One use for the `TextStream` object is for error management and recovery. Perhaps your Web application could be improved to carry out an audit trail of its actions. This would allow you to track down where things might break. You could also use it to record a page's state or information when it "crashes." The "dump" file could then be analyzed to see where your code went wrong.

LISTING 25.11 Reading a Random Line from the Text File

```
1  <%
2  '
3  ' read data from the data file
4
5  ' get total lines in file
6  Set objTS = objFS.OpenTextFile(strFile)
7  Do While objTS.AtEndOfStream <> True
8      objTS.SkipLine
9      intCount=intCount+1
10 Loop
11 objTS.Close
12
13 ' get a random number for tip
14 Randomize
15 intTip = Int((intCount - 1 + 1) * Rnd +1)
16
17 ' get tip from file
18 Set objTS = objFS.OpenTextFile(strFile)
19 For intLoop = 1 to intTip-1
20     objTS.SkipLine
21 Next
22
23 strTip = objTS.ReadLine
24 Response.Write "<H4>Today's Tip</H4><HR>"
25 Response.Write strTip & "<P>"
26
27 objTS.Close
28 Set objTS = Nothing
29
30 %>
```

Notice that the last two lines of server-side script in Listing 25.11 are used to close the open text file and set the pointer to the TextStream object pointer to Nothing. After closing the text file, it is important to set the object pointer to Nothing in order to free up memory used by the object. If you fail to do this, you will eventually run out of free memory space on your server.

It is also possible to read the contents of a text file all in one step. This is valuable for small files, but can be inefficient for

Reading and Writing Text Files with the *TextStream* Object

large files because it can take up quite a bit of memory on the server.

Add the server-side script from Listing 25.12 to your document.

LISTING 25.12 Reading Text Files in One Step

```
1  <%
2  '
3  ' read entire file in one line
4
5  Response.Write "<H4>ReadAll</H4><HR>"
6
7  Set objTS = objFS.OpenTextFile(strFile)
8  strTip = objTS.ReadAll
9  Response.Write "<P>" & strTip & "</P>"
10
11 objTS.Close
12 Set objTS = Nothing
13
14 %>
```

> **Choking the server**
>
> If you read large files all at once into memory, you could very well down your Web server, or at least slow it down some.

You can also read text files one byte at a time. In some cases, it might be easier for you to read the file in this manner. Listing 25.13 shows you how to do this. Add this server-side script to your document, too.

LISTING 25.13 Reading Data Files One Byte at a Time

```
1  <%
2  '
3  ' read file in chunks
4  Response.Write "<H4>Read</H4><HR>"
5  Set objTS = objFS.OpenTextFile(strFile)
6  Do While objTS.AtEndOfLine <> True
7      strTip = strTip & objTS.Read(1)
8  Loop
9  Response.Write strTip & "<BR>"
10 objTS.Close
11 Set objTS = Nothing
12
13 %>
```

Reading files slowly

Another advantage to reading files one line at a time is that it enables you to manipulate the input. Your text file could be raw text that you want to format for display. You could use line-by-line reading to format the incoming data, perhaps based on the type of information contained on a single line.

Finally, after you have finished all work with the `File System` object, you should release the memory used by the `SystemFileObject` reference. To do this, add the server-side script from Listing 25.14 to the end of your document (right after the code from Listing 25.13).

LISTING 25.14 Releasing the Reference to the *SystemFileObject*

```
1 <%
2 '
3 ' release FS object
4
5 Set objFS = Nothing
6
7 %>
```

That's the end of the coding for this document. After saving the document, run the Web application. When you navigate to the TEXTSTREAM.ASP page, you should see something like the contents of Figure 25.8.

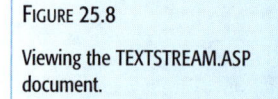

FIGURE 25.8

Viewing the TEXTSTREAM.ASP document.

Reading and Writing Text Files with the *TextStream* Object

That's a quick lesson in building a random tip generator using the `TextStream` object. You can use this basic code to create your own (much more fancy) random tip generator for your Web applications.

SEE ALSO
- *To learn about server variables in more detail, see page 657*
- *The* `MapPath` *and server-side scripting is covered on page 389*

Evolving the Example

How many ideas have you come up with for your new Web explorer? Have you thought about creating a simple editing program so that you can create and modify text files or your Web pages right from a browser? Using other components, such as the Microsoft DHTML Editing Component (available at `http://www.microsoft.com/sitebuilder`), you could create a complex WYSIWYG editor right within a Web page. Good-bye, bulky applications!

CHAPTER 26

Adding Security to Your Web Applications

Define security requirements

Use operating system security

Secure an application folder

Defining Security Requirements

There will be times when you must add security features to your Web application. There are basically two reasons to add security features to your Web applications:

- Authority Access
- Membership Access

The two access types have different goals. *Authority Access* is security access designed to enable or disable application features based on the authority level of the user. *Membership Access* is security access designed to limit access to the application based on a list of members that can run the application.

Understanding Authority Access

In the case of Authority Access, you want to limit access to your Web application based on the user's authority to perform such actions as reading, writing, creating, and deleting data. Note that there is more to the security model than just allowing users to run your application. The idea is to design a scheme that can also limit the actions of users while they run your application.

Here are typical examples of Authority Access applications:

- Accounting applications
- Personnel systems
- Purchase order systems
- Bank account transfer systems

The systems mentioned here usually have large groups of users with differing responsibilities. For example, in accounting or banking systems you might have users authorized to add new entries in the bank accounts, but not authorized to edit the existing amounts or transfer the amount from one account to another. In personnel systems, you might have several people authorized to edit basic employee data, but only a few that have the power to view or edit salary data.

Authority Access security schemes are usually managed using existing operating system security features. Usually authority

Defining Security Requirements

security is enabled by first defining valid users at the operating system level. For example, Visual InterDev and Microsoft Internet Information Server Web applications can use NT Server user and group definitions as a first line of defense. By defining all the users and adding them to the appropriate groups, you can add extremely powerful security to a Web application.

Depending on the type of actions you must monitor, you might also need to add a security layer within your Web application source code. This usually involves getting user names (either from the operating system or from a login dialog box within your application) and limiting access to certain functions (Print Salary Report, Delete Bank Account, and so on) based on the user name.

In addition to the operating system and code-based security, you might want to take advantage of security features built into the database system used to store the vital data. For example, Microsoft SQL Server enables you to define users within the database and set their rights within the database. If your Web application takes advantage of information stored in simple documents such as Word or Excel files, you can also add security to your system by including passwords within the documents themselves.

Keep in mind the key things about Authority Access:

- It is based on limiting the tasks users can perform within the application.
- It usually takes advantage of operating system security features.
- Depending on the action you want to limit, you might need to add code within your application to check users' access to certain actions.
- It might also take advantage of additional security features of the database or stored documents.

Understanding Membership Access Security

Unlike Authority Access, Membership Access security is designed to limit access to the application to only those who are

Authority access is best handled by operating system security

Because Authority Access often involves sensitive information or critical actions, it is best to use as much operating system security features as possible.

in the membership list. After the user is given access to the Web application, there is usually no further checking of rights. The user is free to view and execute all available portions of the application. In other words, Membership Access models validate the user when he first arrives at the Web application site and, after the user is determined to be a valid member, no further security levels are used within the Web application.

This is a typical security model for simple Web sites and Web applications. Here are examples of Web application that can take advantage of this model:

- Private topic newsgroups
- Webs built to support project teams or departments
- Software customer support site for registered users

Under the Membership Access model, when a user attempts to access some part of the Web application the user is instead redirected to a login form that asks for a valid username and possibly a password. This login data is checked against a control file and, if the login is valid, the user is directed to the requested page of the Web application.

Membership Access can be implemented easily using the operating system security features. By simply building a list of usernames within a single group, you can give the group the proper access to the folder that holds the Web application.

Membership can be handled within your program

Because some aspects of membership security can involve access to selected documents within a Web, you can use program-based security to prompt users for login information within your Web application.

You can also build a Membership Access security model in program code. You can build a simple login dialog box to collect data and compare it to the control file. Then add a small code fragment to perform user validation on each page of the Web application. This last step is very important. Because users might gain access to any page of your Web application, you must check for a valid user on almost every document in your Web application.

Here are the key aspects of the Membership Access security model:

- Its primary role is to screen users' access to the site, not limit their activities within the application.

Using Operating System Security

- You can use operating system users and group security to implement Membership Access.
- You can also use program code to authorize users when they first attempt to view documents within the Web application.

SEE ALSO
➤ *To learn about adding program-based security, see page 707*

Using Operating System Security

Whether you implement Authority or Membership Access models, you can use the built-in operating system security to enforce your Web application's security rules. Adding operating system security has several advantages and only a few downside considerations.

The process of securing your Web application using operating system security involves setting permissions for the folder on the Web server that holds the Web application documents. If your Web application uses more than one folder (for example, several subfolders), you must consider adding permissions for each of the folders involved.

If your application is running on a private intranet, you probably have all the needed users already defined. In many cases, you can define one or more groups, add the existing users to these groups, and simply add the group to the permission list for the application folder. If you build the application for a public Web server, you must add users to the operating system database before you can add them to any defined groups. In some cases, you might define a small set of users and share the user and password data with a large group of application users. This technique of sharing usernames within a group prevents the list of defined users from getting too large and difficult to manage.

After the users and groups are defined and applied to the Web application folder, any attempts to access any of the documents in the Web application result in the appearance of a login dialog box (see Figure 26.1).

Intranet-only Webs should use operating system security

If you are building an intranet-only Web where all the users already have defined accounts within the network, you should use operating system security whenever possible. This reduces maintenance and increases security with the network.

PART **VI**   More Active Server Programming
CHAPTER **26**   Adding Security to Your Web Applications

FIGURE 26.1

Attempting to access documents under operating system security.

If the user is not authorized to view the document at the requested URL, the Web server returns an error page similar to the one shown in Figure 26.2.

FIGURE 26.2

Viewing the Logon Failed page from the Web server.

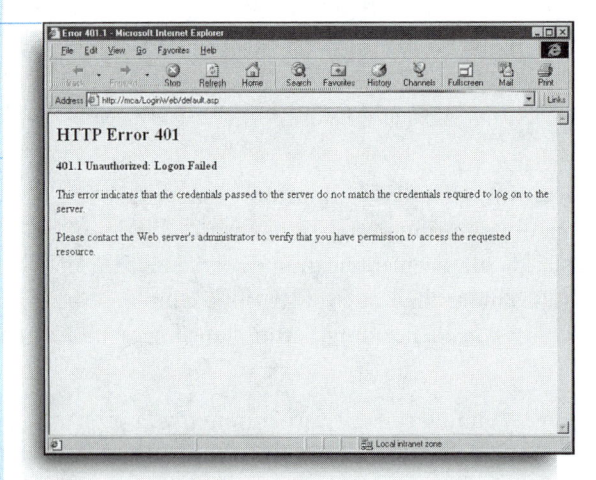

Advantages of Operating System Security

The built-in security of the features of the operating system offer several advantages:

- It's easy to add security to your Web application.
- If you build a Web application for a private Web host, the required users—and possibly the groups—are already defined.
- It's easy to add or remove users and groups from within the operating system dialog boxes.
- If your Web application requires only Membership Access security, operating system security might be all you need.

First, it's easy to add operating system security to your Web application. By setting the permission for the folder that holds the Web application, you have effectively added your security system.

Second, if you build a Web application for a private Web host or company intranet, you probably have all the users predefined in the operating system database. You might even have the required groups in place as well. By taking advantage of existing users and groups, you can minimize the setup required to implement your security scheme.

Third, after the system is in place, adding and removing users or groups is relatively easy. Because the operating system has all the dialog boxes needed to manage user and group definitions, you don't need to add any source code to your Web application to support this part of the process.

Finally, if your Web application requires only Membership Access security, you might not need to add any additional security. Because all users will be met with the login dialog box no matter which document they attempt to view within the Web application, you can be assured that membership will be verified for all users attempting to run the application.

The Downside of Operating System Security

As you might expect, there is a downside to using the operating system as an integral part of your Web application security scheme.

- The user list can become unwieldy if you build a Web application for a public Web server.
- If you support a remote server, you might not have access to the user and group database.
- If your application requires Authority Access security, you might need to add additional security checks in your program anyway.

The biggest drawback to using operating system security is that the list of users can become quite large—especially if your Web application is hosted on a public Web server. You can limit this exposure by sharing user definitions among a group of people who use your Web application. However, this might pose an unacceptable security compromise.

Another major drawback is that your access to the user and group database of the host server might be restricted. For example, if you create a Web application that is placed on a server for which you do not have administrative rights, you must rely on others to manage the user and group records for your application. This is especially difficult when your Web application is placed on a public Web server. It is quite possible that the administrators of a public Web server have no desire to pollute their user database with a long set of names just so you can add security to your applications.

Finally, if your Web application requires more than Membership Access security, you probably need to add program code to check usernames at several points within your application. In this case, using the operating system provides only limited security.

Securing an Application Folder

Now that you know the advantages and disadvantages of using the security features of the operating system, you're ready to add this level of security to a Web application.

The rest of this chapter is dedicated to adding and editing security rights to an existing Web application. Throughout this chapter, the Web application LoginWeb is used as the sample Web application. This is available from the home Web site for this book (http://www.amundsen.com/books/uvi6/default.htm). You can, however, use any existing Web application as the target for these exercises.

The process of establishing operating system security is relatively simple. At most, there are three steps to applying operating system security to your Web application:

- Make sure all the needed users are defined for your Web application.
- Define a group to contain all the users for your Web application.

Public Internet-only Webs can use program-based security

If you are maintaining a highly trafficked, public Web that exists on the Internet, you can consider using program security to validate visitors to your site. This reduces user account maintenance in an environment in which the user list changes often.

Using Operating System Security

- Set the permissions for the folder that contains your Web application.

All this action happens on the server that is hosting your Web application. This means you need administrator rights on the Web server to complete these tasks.

Adding Users to the Windows NT Workstation Database

First, you must make sure that the operating system database contains the list of needed users for your application. To do this, you must view the current list of users in the database and add any that are missing. The following exercise is a set of steps for viewing the user database on a Microsoft Windows NT Workstation 4.0.

Viewing the users in the Windows NT Workstation database

1. From the **S**tart menu, select **P**rograms, **Administrative Tools (Common)**, and **User Manager**.
2. You see the list of defined users on the top of the form and the list of defined groups at the bottom (see Figure 26.3).

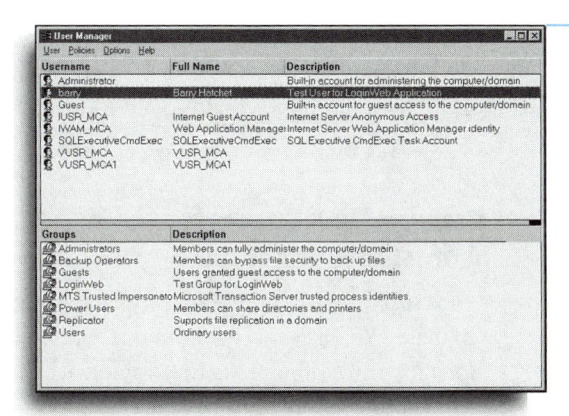

NT Server 4.0 is similar

If you are using an NT Server 4.0 operating system, most of these screens will look similar. You might see additional lists or dialog boxes, but you will also find all the inputs and dialog boxes mentioned here.

FIGURE 26.3
Viewing the users and groups in the NT Workstation database.

If you find that users must be added, you can use the same program to edit the list of users. You can also use the User Manager program to define a new group that can be associated with your application.

Adding a user to the NT Workstation database

1. After loading the User Manager, select **User** from the menu bar and then select **New User...** (see Figure 26.4).

FIGURE 26.4

Adding a new user to the NT Workstation database.

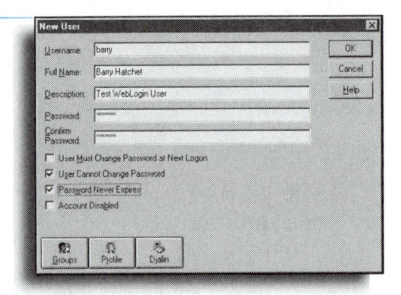

2. Enter the **Username** (in this case barry).
3. Enter the **Full Name** (Barry Hatchet).
4. Enter the user **Description** (Test WebLogin User).
5. Enter the **Password** (hatchet). Enter the same value in the **Confirm Password** field.
6. Clear the **User Must Change Password at Next Logon** box.
7. Check the **User Cannot Change Password** box.
8. Check the **Password Never Expires** box.
9. Press **OK** to save the new record to the database.

Defining New Groups for the Windows NT Workstation Database

Now you're ready to add a new group definition to the security database. You use this group name when you define the permissions for the Web application folder. It's a good idea to only allow defined groups to have access to your application. Managing security groups is much easier than managing individual user's access to your Web application. All you must do is create a new group and add users from the database to the group.

Defining a New NT Workstation group and adding users

1. After loading the User Manager, select **User** from the menu bar and then choose **New Local Group**. The New Local Group dialog box appears (see Figure 26.5).

Don't let your dedicated Web user passwords expire

It is a good idea to set the **Password Never Expires** flag to **True** when defining remote, dedicated usernames for Web applications. Usually these remote users will not have access to update their user profiles on the server and will not change their password if requested. Failure to change the password disables the account and prevents them from accessing the Web application.

Using Operating System Security

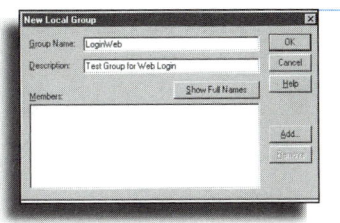

FIGURE 26.5
Adding a new local group.

2. Enter the **Group Name** (for this example, `LoginWeb`).
3. Enter the **Description** (`Test Group for Web Login`).
4. Press the **Add** button to add users to the group.
5. When the Add Users and Groups dialog box appears, select a user (`barry`) and press the **Add** button. The user's name appears in the list at the bottom of the dialog box. Do this for each user you want to add to the group. Note, be sure to select the proper machine in the **List Names from** drop-down list (see Figure 26.6).

> **Simplify membership access with NT user groups**
>
> If your primary task is to design a Membership Access security scheme, you can consider building different groups to handle different levels of security or tasks within your Web app such as GuestGroup, DataEntryGroup, and AdminGroup.

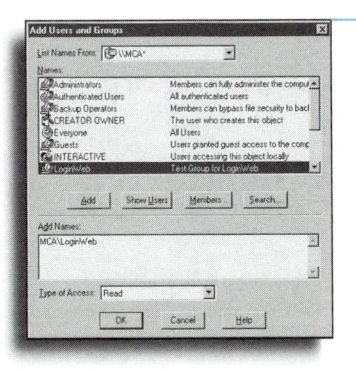

FIGURE 26.6
Adding users to the group.

6. Press **OK** on the Add Users and Groups dialog box to save the user list.
7. Press **OK** on the New Local Group dialog box to save the group definition.

Adding New Security Permissions for Your Web Application

Now that you have defined the users needed for your Web application and completed the group definition that contains the users, you're set to finally define the security permissions for your Web application. In this step, you must do a few things:

- Add the new group to the permission list for your Web application folder.
- Set the permission flags to enable users to read and execute your Web application documents.
- Remove some existing permissions to prevent other users and groups from accessing the folder.

When you first create the Web application for Microsoft Internet Information Server (or Personal Web Server), the default access setting for the Web application is read and execute rights for all users. This means that, after adding permission to your newly defined group, you must remove permissions for these default groups.

Adding permissions for an existing Web application

Be sure to assign permissions for your new group

It is not enough to create the new group and assign it to the folder. You must also assign that group the proper permissions for that folder.

1. Load the Windows File Explorer by pressing the **Start** button from the **Start** menu and then selecting **Programs** and **Windows Explorer** (or **Windows NT Explorer**).
2. Navigate to the folder that contains your Web application. For this example, you can select any existing Web application or the wwwroot folder of the c:\InetPub folder to secure the entire Web server.
3. After selecting the Web application folder, click the right mouse button to display the Context menu. Then select **Sharing** (see Figure 26.7).
4. Select the **Security** tab on the Properties dialog box and then press the **Permissions** button.
5. Be sure both the **Replace Permissions on Subdirectories** and **Replace Permissions on Existing Files** options are checked (see Figure 26.8).
6. Press the **Add** button to add a new group to the list.
7. When the Add Users and Groups dialog box appears, first be sure you have selected the correct machine from the **List Name From** drop-down list. Next, locate and double-click the group you want to add (for this example use **LoginWeb**) so that it appears in the list at the bottom of the dialog box (see Figure 26.9).

Using Operating System Security

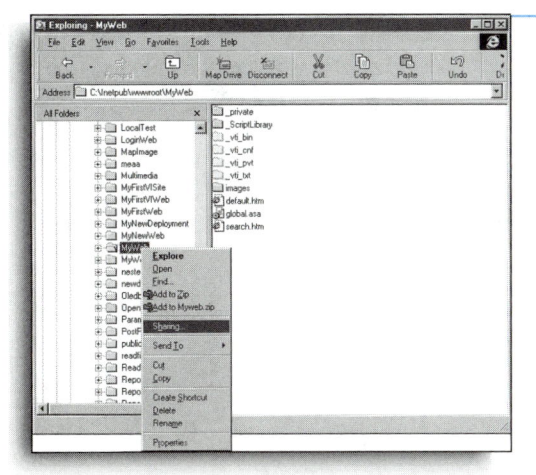

FIGURE 26.7
Selecting the **Sharing** tab.

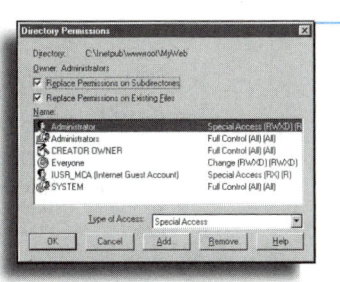

FIGURE 26.8
Setting directory permissions.

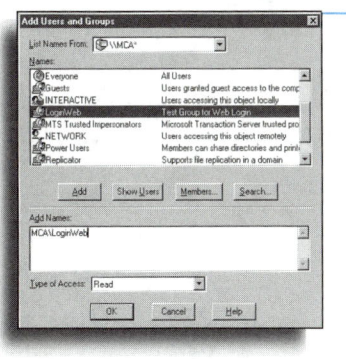

FIGURE 26.9
Adding a group to the permissions list.

8. Press **OK** to save the group list and return to the Directory Permissions dialog box.

PART **VI**   More Active Server Programming

CHAPTER **26**   **Adding Security to Your Web Applications**

9. Now select the group again (**LoginWeb**) and select **Special Directory Access** from the **Type of Access** drop-down list at the bottom of the dialog box (see Figure 26.10).

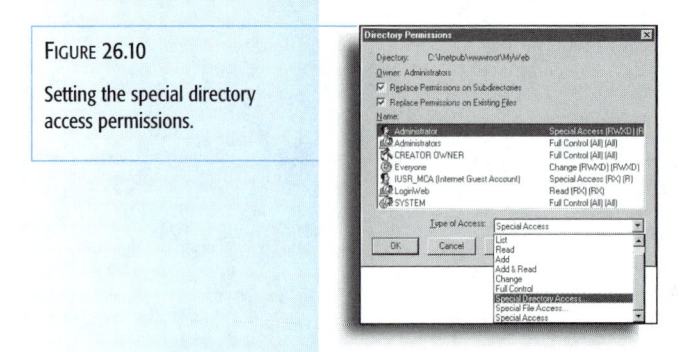

FIGURE 26.10

Setting the special directory access permissions.

10. When the Special Directory Access dialog box appears, select the **Other** radio button and then check the **Read** and **Execute** boxes on the form before pressing **OK** to save the directory permissions and return to the Directory Permissions dialog box (see Figure 26.11).

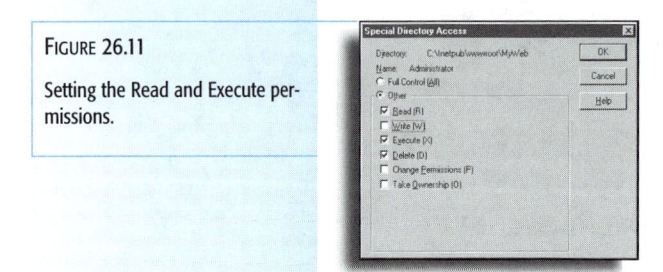

FIGURE 26.11

Setting the Read and Execute permissions.

11. With the group still highlighted (**LoginWeb**), select **Special File Access** from the **Type of Access** drop-down list.

12. With the **Other** radio button selected, check the **Read** and **Execute** boxes; then press **OK** to return to the Directory Permissions dialog box.

13. Press **OK** to complete the permission changes and exit to the File Explorer.

Removing Existing Permissions for Your Web Application

Now that you have added the new group to the permission list for the Web application folder, you must remove permissions for some existing groups. At least four groups exist that must have their permissions reviewed in order to properly secure your Web application:

- The Everyone group should be removed.
- The Administrator group should be given limited permissions.
- The Local Administrator user should be given limited permissions.
- The IUSER_<machinename> user should be given limited permissions.

It is possible that there are other groups that have already been given access to your Web application folder. You might need to also adjust their rights in order to completely secure your Web application.

Removing existing permissions for an existing Web application

1. Load the Windows File Explorer by pressing the **Start** button from the **Start** menu and then selecting **Programs** and **Windows Explorer** (or **Windows NT Explorer**).
2. Navigate to the folder that contains your Web application. For this example, be sure to select the same Web application folder that you used when you added the LoginWeb group to the permission list.
3. After selecting the Web application folder, click the right mouse button to display the context menu and select the **Sharing** menu option (see Figure 26.6).
4. Select the **Security** tab on the Properties dialog box; then press the **Permissions** button to display the Directories Permissions dialog box.
5. Select the **Everyone** group from the list and press the **Remove** button. This prevents all defined users from accessing the Web application.

> **Be sure to remove permissions for default groups**
>
> It is not enough to define a new group and assign permissions to that group. You must also remove permissions for any existing groups that have access to the folder.

6. Select the **Administrators** group and select **No Access** from the **Types of Access** drop-down list at the bottom of the form. This prevents anyone in the administrators group from accessing the Web application.

7. Select the **Administrator** user and select **No Access** from the **Types of Access** drop-down list at the bottom of the form. This prevents the local Web server administrator from accessing the Web application.

8. Select the **IUSER_<machinename>** user and select **No Access** from the **Types of Access** drop-down list at the bottom of the form. This prevents any remote anonymous Web user from accessing the Web application.

9. Press **OK** to save the permission changes, and press **OK** to close the Properties dialog box.

You have now completed the process of applying operating system security features to your Web application. To test this, you can open your Microsoft Internet Explorer and navigate to the secured Web site. You should see the login dialog box that appears in Figure 26.1 earlier in this chapter.

CHAPTER 27

Using Program-Based Security

- Learn the advantages of program-based security
- Learn the downside of program-based security
- Build a program-based security system
- See a blueprint for creating your own program-based security

In several cases you might need to use program-based security to limit access to your Web application. In the example in this chapter, you learn how to create a series of ASP documents for your Web application that can read a data file that can hold the list of users and their passwords. Along with creating these ASP documents and the control list, you see how you can add a few lines of ASP code to every document that you want to secure within the Web application in order to verify users who attempt to request documents from within your Web application. This added code validates the logged in user every time someone sends a request for a document from your Web application.

It is also important to note that, in our example, all user verification routines must run at the server, before any document is sent to the client. This means that all secured documents must be stored as ASP documents on the server. It's an added security bonus that most uninvited users are unlikely to request documents with the .asp suffix.

Trust and verify

Because most Web applications enable users to directly request any document within the application, you must add user verification code to every document you want to secure. If you fail to do this, anonymous users have the power to gain access to one or more of the documents within your Web application.

SEE ALSO
➤ *For more on creating Active Server Page (ASP) documents, see page 379*

Advantages of Program-Based Security

Some real advantages exist to using program-based security to your Web application:

- You can build a security list without having access to the host Web server user database.
- You can create a list of secure users without complicating the existing security files of the host server.
- You can customize your security scheme to include various levels and access checks that go beyond typical operating system security schemes.
- You can still use security features of databases such as SQL Server and documents such as Word or Excel files.

One of the biggest advantages of program-based security schemes is that they are not tied to the host server user and group database. Because you are not using the built-in security data files, you can define users without having administrator rights to the server. You can also create your user list from a remote location. This means that Web programmers mounting Web applications on distant public Web hosts (such as Internet service providers) can still create and manage user security.

Even for Web applications that are placed on private, local Web servers, you might want to use program-based security instead of using the built-in operating system security database. First, using program-based security frees the Web server administrator from managing user lists for possibly numerous Web applications. Second, as user lists grow, the process of managing these multiple Web applications and their users and groups can become complicated and possibly result in compromising server security.

It is also important to note that you can use program-based security to build a more flexible security scheme than can be built using the operating system database. You can build your own user lists, groups, and access levels (print, read, add, edit, delete, create, and so on) to meet the needs of your Web application.

Finally, even when you use the program-based security model, you can still use the operating system security features as a "first line of defense." This means you can create a list of valid members for the application and then add additional control files to limit actions within the Web application itself.

Simple security for public Webs

If you are in charge of maintaining a public Web on the Internet and want to create a section within the Web site that can be accessed only by selected users, program-based security can be an excellent option.

SEE ALSO
> *For more on using Microsoft Word and Excel documents in your Web projects, see page 618*

The Downside of Program-Based Security

Along with the advantages, there are a few disadvantages of program-based security schemes. Carefully consider the disadvantages when you evaluate your Web application security options.

- Securing the user list can be difficult.
- You will be limited to using ASP documents when securing your Web application.

- Adding program-based security can conflict with the existing operating system security permissions.
- Program-based security might not be as effective or adaptable as the operating system's security model or might increase risk due to improper operation or design.
- Program-based security takes additional support and maintenance from programmers and technicians.

First, if one of your goals is to allow distant Web application managers to access and edit the user list for the Web application, it might also be possible for unwanted visitors to locate and edit the user list. The least secure files are simple text files stored in a directory that anonymous users can scan from remote browsers. You can use unusual filenames and encrypt the text to thwart most nosey users. It is even better to store the user information in database files on the server but these, too, might be susceptible to hackers.

Second, because program-based security checks must be executed at the server (before the document is sent to the user), you must rely on server-side script to perform the user verification. In the case of Microsoft Internet Information Server, this means you must store all secured documents as Active Server Pages (ASP) documents. This can complicate Web application management if users expect to request standard HTM files. In some cases, authors that rely heavily on HTML editors such as Microsoft FrontPage might have some difficulties dealing with the ASP documents.

Also, it's possible that your program-based security scheme will attempt to grant permissions to users that conflict with their defined rights on the Web server. This is especially true for intranet or privately hosted Web servers where all your Web application users already have a security profile defined on the server. In some cases, you might define a permission to create a data file within your Web application when the logged-in user does not have rights defined for that folder. This can cause confusion and frustration for users, Web programmers, and server administrators.

Consider it public

Although you can do many things to discourage unwanted intruders from seeing your files, you should always operate from the idea that anything you place on a public Web server could potentially be downloaded or viewed. If you don't want anyone to see it, remove it from the Web server.

Use program-based security as a gatekeeper

Instead of trying to duplicate the security features of the operating system, use program-based security as an added gatekeeper at the entrance to your Web site. This can slow potential hackers without compromising system security.

Another important consideration is the possibility that any program-based security system might be obsolete if the operating system changes. If you base your security design on existing operating system behaviors, and these behaviors change or no longer exist in future versions of the operating system, your security model can be compromised. Even worse, this security compromise can occur without you even knowing it. This leaves your application, Web server, or possibly your entire network open for security violations.

Finally, the very act of designing, implementing, testing, and supporting program-based security can be daunting. In large organizations, the maintenance and implementation of program-based security can easily consume one or more full-time staff members. You should carefully assess your needs and resources before deciding to implement a program-based security scheme.

SEE ALSO
➤ *For more on operating system security, see page 691*

Building a Program-Based Security System

Now that you understand the pros and cons of program-based security, you're ready to see how to put one into action. In this section, you learn how to create the needed ASP documents and the user list control file, and how to add code to each secured document so that you can enforce your program-based security model.

The basic tools of this program-based security system are listed here:

- GETUSER.ASP. An ASP document that contains a form that prompts for a username and password.
- VERIFYUSER.ASP. An ASP document that compares the data entered in the GETUSER.ASP form against an existing list of valid users.
- CHECKUSER.INC. A special SSI (server-side include) file to be added to each secured document.

> **Get to the source (code)**
>
> All the material discussed in this chapter is included in a test project called LoginWeb. The project source code is available at the book's Web site (see Appendix B).
>
> **Session variables are private**
>
> Session variables exist only for the currently connected user. Each user has his own set of session variables. You cannot share them with another user or view another user's session variables.

- USERLIST.TXT. A text file that contains the list of usernames and passwords.

All the preceding documents are stored in a subfolder of the Web application called login.

Also, two session-level variable definitions are added to the GLOBAL.ASA file in order to keep track of the current user and the requested secured document (see Listing 27.1). These variables will be used throughout the session and hold the validated username and, when needed, the initial secured document requested by the new user.

LISTING 27.1 Session-Level Variables in GLOBAL.ASA

```
1 Sub Session_OnStart
2     '
3     ' start with blanks for new user
4     Session.Contents("User")=""
5     Session.Contents("RequestedURL")=""
6     '
7 End Sub
```

Here's how you can enter these values into the GLOBAL.ASA file.

Adding code to the GLOBAL.ASA file

1. Right-click the mouse over the GLOBAL.ASA document in the Project Explorer window.
2. When the GLOBAL.ASA document loads into the editor, locate the `Session_OnStart` method. If it does not exist, add it to the file by typing **Sub Session_OnStart** on one line and **Sub End** on the next.
3. Add any code you want to execute in between these two lines. For this example, add the code from Listing 27.1.
4. Close the GLOBAL.ASA document and save the changes.

Finally, a short bit of code will be added to all secured pages in order to check for a valid user and, if needed, request the user Log-in dialog box to prompt new users to enter their ID and password. Listing 27.2 shows the code piece added to all documents.

Building a Program-Based Security System

LISTING 27.2 Code Added to Every Secure ASP Document

```
1  <%@ LANGUAGE=VBScript %>
2  <%
3  Response.Buffer=True
4  %>
5  <!-- #include file=login/checkuser.inc -->
6
7  <HTML>
```

Note that Listing 27.2 shows that the added code is inserted between the `<%@ LANGUAGE=VBScript %>` line and the `<HTML>` line. This code first makes sure the server buffers all output to the client followed by a single line that calls an SSI (server-side include) file. It is this file that contains the server-side script that checks to see whether the user has completed a valid login dialog box.

For example, you can create a document called DEFAULT.ASP and add the buffer code and include statement to the top of that document (see Listing 27.3).

LISTING 27.3 Sample DEFAULT.ASP File with Security Code Added

```
1  <%@ LANGUAGE=VBScript %>
2  <%
3  Response.Buffer=True
4  %>
5  <!-- #include file=login/checkuser.inc -->
6
7  <HTML>
8  <HEAD>
9  <META NAME="GENERATOR" Content="Microsoft Visual
   ÂStudio 98">
10 <META HTTP-EQUIV="Content-Type" content="text/html">
11 <TITLE>Document Title</TITLE>
12 </HEAD>
13 <BODY>
14 <H1>Demonstrate Program-Based Security</H1>
15 <P><A href="sample.asp">Visit Sample
16 Page</P>
17
```

ASP documents required for program-based security

Because the security routines will run on the server and use server-side memory (session variables), you must use Active Server Pages documents to test for the presence of the user ID and password.

continues...

Using Program-Based Security

LISTING 27.3 Continued

```
18  </BODY>
19  </HTML>
20
```

SEE ALSO
▶ *For more on using session variables, see page 397*

Checking for Valid Users

After you define the server-level variables and add the security code at the top of the document, you're ready to complete the CHECKUSER.INC server-side include file. This file will be stored in the LOGIN folder (see Listing 27.4).

LISTING 27.4 The Contents of the CHECKUSER.INC File

```
1  <!-- SSI CheckUser Start -->
2  <%
3  '
4  Dim strRequest
5  '
6  ' get requested page (me!)
7  strRequest = "http://"
8  strRequest = strRequest & Request.ServerVariables(
   ➥"SERVER_NAME")
9  strRequest = strRequest & Request.ServerVariables(
   ➥"PATH_INFO")
10 '
11 If Session.Contents("User")="" Then
12     Session.Contents("RequestedURL")=strRequest
13     Response.Redirect "login/getuser.asp"
14 End If
15 %>
16 <!-- SSI CheckUser End -->
```

Server-side include files are expanded at the server

When you use server-side include (SSI) files, you are really just using a form of shorthand to tell the Web server that there is additional code to include in this document before you send it to the client. You must place the SSI files exactly where you would normally type the code that the SSI file contains.

The CHECKUSER.INC file has two main tasks. The first task is to place the name of the requested document into the session-level variable called `RequestedURL`. This will be used to direct the valid user to the originally requested document.

Building a Program-Based Security System | CHAPTER 27

The second task is to see whether the user has already successfully logged into the Web application. If the session-level variable, User, is empty, the user is redirected to the GETUSER.ASP file to complete the login dialog box.

SEE ALSO
➤ *For more on using the* ServerVariables *collection, see page 657*

Collecting User Login Data

The first dialog box a new visitor to the Web site sees is the form in the GETUSER.ASP document (see Figure 27.1). Listing 27.5 shows the details of the GETUSER.ASP file that collects the data.

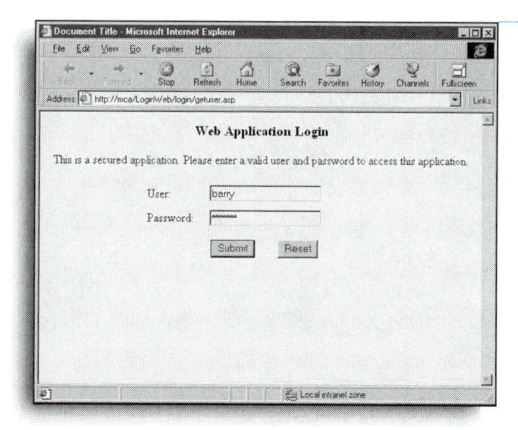

FIGURE 27.1
Viewing the new user login dialog box from GETUSER.ASP.

LISTING 27.5   Source Code for GETUSER.ASP File

```
1  <%@ LANGUAGE=VBScript %>
2  <%
3  Response.Expires=0 ' prevent caching
4  %>
5  <html>
6  <head>
7  <meta name="VI98_defaultClientScript" content="VBScript">
8  <meta NAME="GENERATOR" Content="Microsoft Visual Studio 98">
9  <meta HTTP-EQUIV="Content-Type" content="text/html">
10 <title>Document Title</title>
```

continues…

LISTING 27.5 Continued

```
11
12  </head>
13  <BODY>
14
15  <FORM method=post action=verifyuser.asp>
16  <H3 align=center>Web Application Login</H3>
17  <P align=center>This is a secured application. Please
18  enter a valid user and password to access this
19  application.</P> <P>
20  <TABLE align=center border=0 cellPadding=1 cellSpacing=1
    ➥height=116   width=316>
21    <TR>
22      <TD>User:
23      <TD>
24              <INPUT id=text1 name=txtUser>
25    <TR>
26      <TD>Password:
27      <TD>
28              <INPUT id=password2 name=pswPassword
                  ➥type=password>
29    <TR>
30      <TD>
31      <TD>
32              <TABLE border=0 cellPadding=1 cellSpacing=1
                  Âheight=38 width=175>
33        <TR>
34          <TD><INPUT id=submit3 name=btnSubmit
              ➥type=submit value=Submit>
35          <TD><INPUT id=reset4 name=btnPassword
              ➥type=reset value=Reset</TD>
36        </TR>
37      </TABLE>
38      </TD>
39    </TR>
40  </TABLE>
41  </FORM></P>
42
43  </BODY>
44  </html>
45
```

The form dialog box in GETUSER.ASP collects two pieces of data, `txtUser` and `pswPassword` (lines 24 and 28), and passes them to the final ASP file called VERIFYUSER.ASP (line 15). It is the VERIFYUSER.ASP file that actually reads the stored user list and compares it to the data entered into the form.

SEE ALSO
➤ For more on creating input forms, see page 111

Validating the Logged-In User

The final ASP document in the login folder is VERIFYUSER.ASP. This document collects the `txtUser` and `pswPassword` form values and compares them to data stored in the USERLIST.TXT data file. If the pairs match, the user is directed to the requested document. If not, the user is asked to log in again with a valid user and password pair.

The USERLIST.TXT file in this example is a simple ASCII text file in the following format:

`<username><tab><password><cr>`

Listing 27.6 shows a sample USERLIST.TXT control file.

LISTING 27.6 A Sample USERLIST.TXT Control File

```
1 chicken<tab>hawk
2 foghorn<tab>leghorn
3 barry<tab>hatchet
```

One advantage of this simple data file format is that it is exactly the same format used by the Content Linker Component already installed with the Active Server Pages features of Microsoft Internet Information Server. This makes it easy to create an ASP document that can read the USERLIST.TXT data file.

The heart of the VERIFYUSER.ASP file is in three private methods that perform the following tasks:

- Collect the data entered into the GETUSER.ASP form.
- Compare that data to the stored user/password list.

The password INPUT control is not secure

Even though the password **INPUT** control echoes only asterisks (*) to the user, the actual content of the **INPUT** control is stored, and transmitted, as plain text.

Plain text is dangerous

If you plan to implement a program-based security scheme that uses a stored list of users and passwords, consider encrypting the file to make it harder to read by unauthorized users. A simple method is to add a displacement value to each ASCII character stored. For example, adding the value **3** to each ASCII value changes the string **ABC** (ASCII values 64, 65, and 66) into **DEF** (ASCII values 67, 68, and 69).

- After getting the results of the compare, direct the valid user to a requested document and ask the invalid user to try again.

Listing 27.7 shows these three methods in the VERIFYUSER.ASP file.

LISTING 27.7   The VERIFYUSER.ASP File that Performs the User Validation

```
1  <%
2  '
3  ' verify user login
4  '
5
6  ' shared vars
7  Dim strUser
8  Dim strPassword
9  Dim strFile
10 Dim strURL
11
12 '
13 ' call private methods
14 GetData
15 CheckLogin
16 SendResults
17
18 '
19 ' set data values for processing
20 Sub GetData
21     '
22     ' set user file
23     strFile = "userlist.txt"
24
25     ' get items from input form
26     strUser = Ucase(Request.Form("txtUser"))
27     strPassword = Request.Form("pswPassword")
28
29     ' get requested URL
30     strURL = Session.Contents("RequestedURL")
31     If Trim(strURL)="" Then
32         strURL="default.asp"
33     End If
34     '
```

Building a Program-Based Security System

```
35   End Sub
36
37   '
38   ' perform lookup and set session var
39   Sub CheckLogin
40      '
41      Dim objCLC
42      Dim intUserCount
43      Dim intLoop
44      Dim strRUser
45      Dim strRPassword
46      '
47      ' open content link file
48      Set objCLC = Server.CreateObject("MSWC.NextLink")
49      intUserCount = objCLC.GetListCount(strFile)
50
51      ' clear any old value
52      Session.Contents("User")=""
53
54      ' look for user/password
55      For intLoop = 1 to intUserCount
56         ' get pair from file
57         strRUser = UCase(objCLC.GetNthURL(strFile, intLoop))
58         strRPassword = objCLC.GetNthDescription(strFile,
            ↪intLoop)
59         ' check against input
60         If strRUser = strUser And strPassword =
            ↪strRPassword Then
61            Session.Contents("User") = strUser
62         End If
63      Next
64      '
65   End Sub
66
67   '
68   ' ship results downstream
69   Sub SendResults
70      '
71      If Session.Contents("User")="" Then
72         Response.Write "<H4>Invalid Login!</H4><HR>"
73         Response.Write "Press the back button on your browser"
```

continues…

LISTING 27.7 Continued

```
74      Else
75          Response.Write "<H4>Welcome " & strUser & "!
            ↪</H4><HR>"
76          Response.Write "Click here to continue...<BR>"
77          Response.Write "<A HREF="&chr(34)&strURL&chr(34)
            ↪&">" &    strURL & "</A>"
78      End If
79          '
80  End Sub
81
82  %>
83
```

Although Listing 27.7 has several lines of code, the basic tasks are simple. First, the `GetData` method (lines 20–35) is used to get the name of the user control file, the two form variables (`txtUser` and `pswPassword`), and the name of the requested document from the session-level variable (`RequestedURL`).

Next, the `CheckLogin` method (lines 39–65) creates a pointer to the `MSWC.NextLink` COM object (line 48), gets a count of the users in the file (line 49), and then reads each user/password pair until a match with the form variables is found (lines 55–63). If a match is found, the session-level variable `User` is set with the user's valid name (line 61). If not, this value is left blank.

The `SendResults` method (lines 69–80) determines whether the `User` variable has been filled. If it has not, a warning message is sent and the user is directed to try again (lines 71–73). If the `User` variable has been filled, the user is shown a welcome message and directed to the requested document (lines 75–77) (see Figure 27.2).

SEE ALSO

▶ *For more on using the Content Linker component, see page 601*

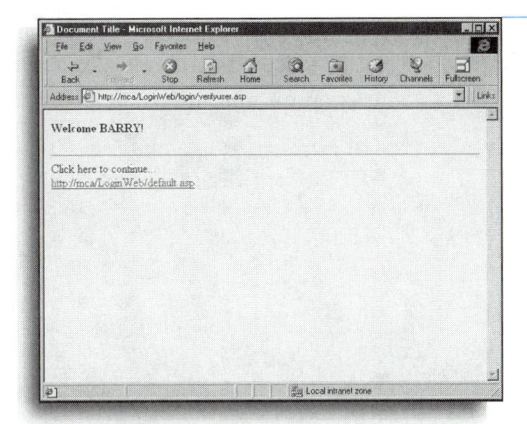

FIGURE 27.2
Confirmation of a valid user.

A Blueprint for Creating Your Own Program-Based Security

This completes the program-based security example. The example was kept very basic in order to focus on the key tasks required to complete a useful program-based security model. You can use the example shown here to add the most basic security to your Web application. Or you can use these key tasks as a basic outline for building your own advanced security implementation.

As a quick review, here are the highlights of the process:

- Define two session-level variables (in the GLOBAL.ASA file) for the application that holds the validated username and the URL of the requested secured document.
- Create a control file (USERLIST.TXT) that holds names and passwords. In this example, the data was stored in plain ASCII text. However, it's safer to encrypt the data to keep it from being easily read by uninvited users.
- Create a login form (GETUSER.ASP) that collects username and password and passes this data to a verification script.
- When the form is submitted, call an ASP document (VERIFYUSER.ASP) that compares the input to a stored control list and redirects the user to the proper location.

- Create an SSI file (CHECKUSER.INC) that can be added to all secured documents along with the ASP statement that turns on output buffering.

CHAPTER 28

Adding Error Handling to Your Web Application

Understand error handling with Visual InterDev

Learn how Visual InterDev reports errors

Create an error trap include file

Understanding Error Handling with Visual InterDev

Error handling is an important aspect of building quality Web applications. No Web application should go into production without adequate error-handling code. However, error handling can be a tricky business. In fact, error handling for Web applications is actually a bit more complicated than it is for standard Windows applications. For this reason, it is important that you have a good understanding of how errors occur and how they are reported within your Visual InterDev Web applications.

The idea behind error handling is to add code that checks for expected error conditions and remedies the process during runtime. This kind of error handling prevents the application from halting unexpectedly, and can potentially prevent the loss of vital data. To do this, you must understand the various types of error conditions that can occur in a Web application and how you can plan for and hopefully prevent errors from happening.

There are basically three types of errors that can occur in a Web application:

- Syntax errors—These errors are caused by programmer mistakes when the Web application is first constructed. Syntax errors are code segments that are unrecognizable by the compiler (or in this case, the Web browser or system component). Most errors are caused by a typographical error.
- Web-related errors—These are errors that occur due to problems among the inter- or intranet itself. This can be due to hardware difficulties, broken links, and so on.
- Code-related runtime errors—These errors are usually caused by user input or some other data values added during the execution of your Web application.

Cleaning Up Syntax Errors

The first category of errors, syntax errors, occur when the code pages are written incorrectly. These errors occur when the programmers type mistakes in the Web documents. Most of these

Understanding Error Handling with Visual InterDev

errors are caught when you attempt to execute the page. Listing 28.1 shows a typical syntax error that is reported by the Web server attempting to process an ASP document.

LISTING 28.1 **Sample Syntax Error Reported from an ASP Page**

```
1  Microsoft VBScript compilation error '800a03ea'
2  Syntax error
3  /TrapErrors/savedata.asp, line 29
4  response.write strName & <BR>"
5  ------------------------^
```

As you can see from Listing 28.1, the Visual Basic Script engine recognizes an error on line 29 of the document (line 3 of the listing), stating the line that needs to be corrected. If this application were placed into production on the Internet, people all over the world would see that you missed a quote mark on line 29 (as you can see from the code snippet on line 4).

Although the Visual Basic Script engine reports syntax errors when they are found, the HTML engine is not quite so intelligent. Take a look at Figure 28.1 and see if you can determine the problem.

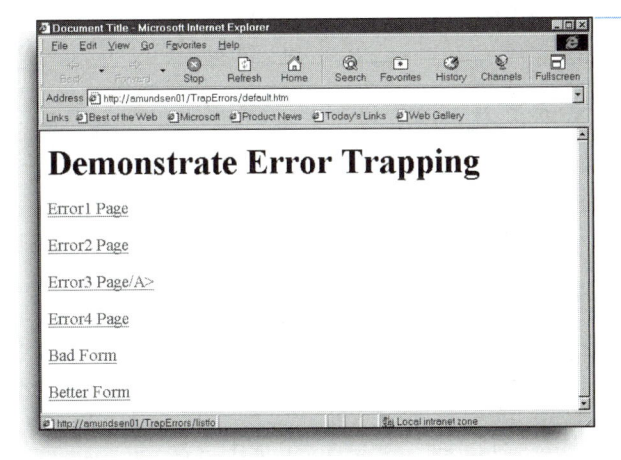

FIGURE 28.1
A problem HTML document.

You might notice that the `Error3 Page` link has an added `/A>` at the end. This happened because a less-than sign (<) was left out of the `HREF` line:

```
<A href="error3.asp">Error3 Page/A> <!-- an error -->
<A href="error3.asp">Error3 Page</A><!-- an fixed! -->
```

So, although Visual Basic Script errors will be reported whenever you attempt to download a broken document, HTML errors are rarely reported. Instead, the HTML engine does its best to render the document for the client and ignore any parts that it does not understand. For this reason, it's important to thoroughly test all the documents in your Web application.

Syntax errors can be prevented only through rigorous testing and review of the application before it is placed into production. The Visual InterDev editor gives you a great deal of help in the initial stages of coding the various objects, methods, and properties of your application. However, nothing takes the place of a good round of testing.

The reason this step is so important is that Web applications operate in an "interpreted" mode. If you usually build applications for Windows with Visual Basic, Visual J++, or Visual C++, you compile your code before testing. This compiling process reviews the entire code base for syntax errors and (usually) prevents completion of the compile until all syntax errors are corrected.

Because Web applications depend on VBScript, JScript, Active Server Pages, and HTML, you can't compile your Web application into a single package. This means that you must perform the review step usually covered for you by the language compiler.

Remember these key points when testing your Web code:

- Be sure to click every button and test every entry field on every form of every page of the entire Web application.
- Test forms with entry fields empty as well as with live data.
- If your scripting code has several branches (`IF..THEN..ELSE`, `SELECT...CASE`, and so on), be sure to test all possible branches of your code.

- Be sure to test all Web links in your application, including the Web links that are created during runtime (that is, HTTP:// and strURL).
- Test your input fields with multiple data types and unconventional data. Often programs will break due to input the programmer just didn't expect.

Dealing with Web-Related Errors

The next type of error with which you must consider is the Web-related error. A Web error usually occurs due to some unforeseen condition on the inter- or intranet. This can be due to hardware problems (servers are down or responding too slowly) or due to changes in the contents of the Web itself.

Here are typical examples of hardware problems:

- Servers on the net are down at the moment.
- Servers are swamped with requests and responding too slowly.
- Communications lines between sites are temporarily down.

Here are typical content-related problems:

- Links to distant servers are broken because the document author has altered the target URL.
- Data in databases is missing or the storage format has been changed.
- Access rights to requested documents has been changed or revoked.

Unfortunately, no sure-fire method exists for protecting your Web application from Web-related errors. The very nature of the Web network prevents this kind of protection. If your Web application depends on several distant resources (other servers, databases, distant communications, and so on) you must be prepared for situations in which your Web application can't operate as planned.

Fortunately, Web users are accustomed to these types of errors. When presented with a screen that tells them the server is not responding, users are ready to select another link in your Web. However, sometimes the lack of unavailable resources causes problems with your Web application. In those cases, you must design your Web applications to handle the error "gracefully."

For example, you might design a form that accepts data from users and then, when the user presses the Submit button, sends that data to a distant server to update a database. If the database server is unavailable or the communication lines are faulty, your Web app will receive a notice saying the server or document is unavailable (see Figure 28.2).

FIGURE 28.2

Web-related error display.

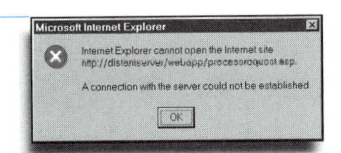

In cases in which unexpected things might happen, you can create your user forms with added protection by placing helpful messages that at least show the user you understand the possible trouble spots and can help the user make a decision on how to handle the situation. Figure 28.3 shows one such approach.

FIGURE 28.3

Displaying a warning message when users can't complete transactions.

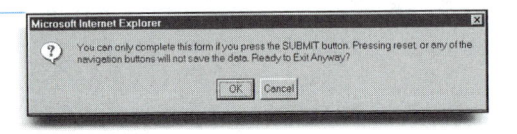

This particular message was generated during the onbeforeUnload event of the browser window. By adding some client-side script to display the message, you can warn users of potential trouble in advance.

Because the very nature of the Web prevents you from predicting all possible errors that can occur outside your own Web application, there is little you can do to prevent them from happening. The best you can do is plan ahead and try to build interfaces that reduce the possibilities of Web-related errors and help users recover in cases where they do come up.

Handling Code-Related Runtime Errors

The last of the three error types typical in Web applications is the code-related runtime error. These are errors that occur due to unexpected data values from either the user or from other sources such as databases or other input documents used throughout the course of the execution of your Web application.

Like syntax errors, code-related errors occur within the execution moments of the application. However, unlike syntax errors, code-related runtime errors often can't be caught by simply inspecting and testing the documents in your Web application. Code-related errors are often tied closely to data inputs that can't be easily predicted or verified during testing.

A typical example of a code-related error is shown in Figure 28.4.

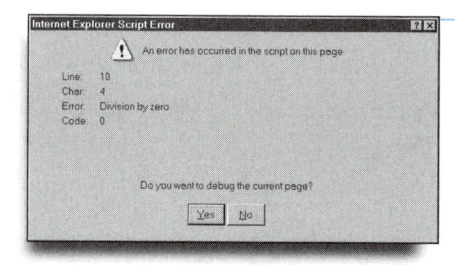

FIGURE 28.4
A typical code-related runtime error.

In this case, the user entered two values that result in a divided-by-zero error. This error occurred because the user entered unexpected values. This kind of error is quite common and can be even more obvious, too. What if the user entered text values into the same field and pressed OK?

There is another variety of code-related runtime errors. This type of error occurs when a COM object fails to properly initialize or when your code attempts to access invalid methods or properties of COM objects. As an example, review the Active Server Page (ASP) code shown in Listing 28.2.

LISTING 28.2 Runtime Error Due to Improper COM Object Method

```
1  <%
2  ' call bogus method
3  =Response.Junk
4  %>
```

Although it is obvious in this example that there is no `Junk` method of the `Response` COM object, other examples are not as easy to spot. This type of code is usually caught in testing but might not always be cleaned up before an application code goes into production.

An even better example would be valid code that somehow fails to execute due to registration problems with the COM object; for example, attempts to use a custom COM object that was properly registered on the test server but was not added to the production server when the Web application was installed. In both cases, the code from Listing 28.2 results in a runtime error, displaying the same alarming dialog box seen in Figure 28.4.

Because most runtime errors are caused by unexpected data or unforeseen component problems, the possibility for a runtime error occurring in your Web application is quite high. Fortunately, Visual InterDev has a powerful built-in COM object that can report these errors to you at runtime, so you can deal with them before the user sees the dreaded error dialog box.

The next major section of this chapter explains this COM object and how you can use it. But first, there is one more aspect of error handling to consider: application design.

The Best Defense Is a Good Design

The most powerful error-handling method is a good application design. A well-designed form or group of forms can eliminate the potential for most errors. Before you even consider adding code to your Web applications to handle errors, review the basic design of your application to look for potential situations in which users can create situations that might cause application errors.

Understanding Error Handling with Visual InterDev

PART **VI**
CHAPTER **28**

731

For example, the form shown in Figure 28.5 asks for user input on two fields.

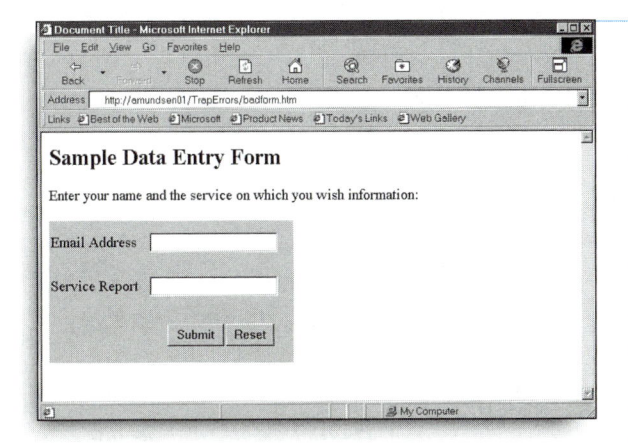

FIGURE 28.5
A sample form design with potential for errors.

The first is the person's email address. The second field must be the name of the service report desired. For this system, you have only three possible valid service reports: WholeSale, Commercial, and Retail. Right now, the user has no way of knowing this, and a faulty entry in this field will cause the confusing runtime error shown in Listing 28.3.

LISTING 28.3   **Confusing Runtime File Error**

```
1  Server object error 'ASP 0177 : 80070057'
2  Server.CreateObject Failed
3  /TrapErrors/savedata.asp, line 31
4  The operation completed successfully.
```

What actually happened is that the data filename was invalid and the `OpenTextFile` method of the `FileSystemObject` failed. Users will not get this kind of detailed information, however.

You might think that the first step is to add code that checks the filename before attempting the `OpenTextFile` method. But there's a better answer. Instead of adding code, you can redesign the form to allow users to select only one of the valid filenames. Figure 28.6 shows the new form layout with a drop-down list box with all the valid report names.

FIGURE 28.6

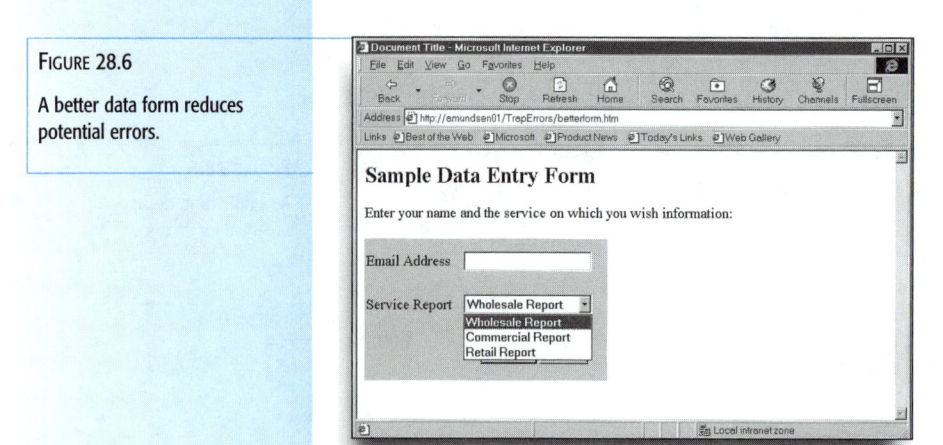

A better data form reduces potential errors.

This is a simple illustration of one of the basic rules of error handling: *Most runtime errors occur because of bad design—not bad users*. Always review your form design to hunt down potential trouble spots for users. The best Web application is designed so well that users are prevented from making mistakes.

How Visual InterDev Reports Errors

Now that you understand the types of errors that can occur in the Web application and how you can plan for them in the initial design, it is time to get down to the details of how Visual InterDev reports runtime errors and how you can use Visual InterDev to respond to them.

There is a built-in COM object in Visual InterDev called the `Err` object. This object has two methods:

- `Clear`—Clears out any previous values in the `Err` object properties.
- `Raise`—Generates your own custom error codes within the script code.

The `Err` object also has five properties. The first three are used quite often. The last two are more rarely used in Web applications.

- `Number`—This is the code number of the error that has most recently occurred.

How Visual InterDev Reports Errors

- `Description`—This is the text description associated with the error code.

- `Source`—This is the name of the COM object or process that reported the error (usually the Visual Basic Script runtime engine).

- `HelpFile`—This holds the name of a help file that contains information associated with the error code.

- `HelpContext`—This holds the help context ID number of the help topic that is associated with the error code.

When an error occurs in your Web application code, the runtime engine receives an error number and places it in the `Number` property of the `Err` object. You can retrieve the current error condition at any time during the life of your Web application by simply inspecting the `Number` property. If the property is set to `0`, no error has been reported. Any nonzero value means that an error has occurred.

Listing 28.4 shows a bit of ASP code that performs an operation and then checks the error status.

LISTING 28.4 Checking the Error Status in ASP Code

```
1  <%
2  '
3  ' using the err object in a program
4
5  ' clear any old values
6  Err.Clear
7
8  ' call important routine
9  Call SaveVitalData(myDataList)
10
11 ' check to see if an error was reported
12 If Err.Number=0 Then
13    alert "Data Saved to the Database"
14 Else
15    alert "Error Code " & Err.Number & " occurred while
   ➥ saving the data."
16 End If
17 '
18 %>
```

Each time an error occurs, the error code, description, and source information is loaded into the Err object. The Err object can store only one set of error data at a time. As each error is reported, the previous error data is removed from the object. For this reason, it is important to check the contents of the Err object frequently in order to catch any reported errors.

Accessing the Built-In *Err* Object

Unlike other COM objects that must first be initialized, the Err object already exists and is ready for your use the moment you first run a line of Visual Basic Script or Active Server Page script. In other words, you do not need to declare a variable and use a Set statement in order to begin using the built-in Err COM object. Listing 28.5 shows both the usual and atypical way to access the Err COM object.

LISTING 28.5 Standard and Atypical Ways to Access the *Err* Object

```
1  <%
2  '
3  ' not needed to access the built-in Err object
4  Dim MyErrObj
5  Set MyErrObj = Err
6  alert MyErrObj.Number
7
8  '
9  ' the usual method for accessing the Err object
10 alert Err.Number
11
12 %>
```

It is worth noting that both methods work equally well. There are some cases in which you might want to get an instance of the current Err object and pass it to another routine. However, it is much more common to simply use the built-in Err object and access its properties and methods directly.

Turn On Error Handling with *Resume Next*

Even after adding the script code that checks error conditions, you will still see error dialog boxes appear in your program such as the ones in Figure 28.7. In fact, the only way you can suppress these dialog boxes is to first add the following line of code to the script sections of your documents:

On Error Resume Next

This line of code tells the runtime engine to stop reporting errors to the user. Now that the reports have been suppressed, you can add your own code to check the Err.Number property and react accordingly. It is important to note that this line of code must be added to every method of every document in which you plan to check for errors. It is not enough to place this line in the GLOBAL.ASA file or some other single location.

Listing 28.6 shows a typical client-side error-handling routine for an onclick method of a button.

All errors are local

Every Err object exists as a local COM object on the page that is executing the script code. If you want to check error status and react within your script code, you must add error-handling routines (including the On Error Resume Next line) to every method on every page that might produce an error. If you fail to do this, errors that occur within "unprotected" routines will result in error dialog boxes sent to the client browser.

LISTING 28.6 Adding Error-Handling Code to a Client-Side *onclick* Event

```
1  <SCRIPT LANGUAGE=VBScript>
2  <!--
3  Sub button3_onclick
4  '
5  On Error Resume Next
6  '
7  alert Text1.value*Text2.value
8  If Err.Number<>0 Then
9  alert "Error Code: " & Err.Number & chr(13) &
     ➥ "Description: " & Err.Description
10 End If
11 '
12 End Sub
13 -->
14 </SCRIPT>
```

Adding Error Handling to Active Server Pages

The rules for error handling are slightly different when you use server-side scripting with Active Server Pages. Because ASP documents are preprocessed at the server before they are sent downstream to the client browser, you can create error-handling code that will work for the entire document. This greatly simplifies error handling for your Web application.

However, there are a few important additions to the ASP documents that you must make before error handling will work properly. First, you must add the lines of code shown in Listing 28.7 to the top of all ASP documents that will handle errors.

LISTING 28.7 **Required Entries at the Top of ASP Documents That Will Handle Errors**

```
1  <%@ LANGUAGE=VBScript %>
2
3  <%
4  ' added to support error trapping
5  Response.Expires=0
6  Response.Buffer=True
7  On Error Resume Next
8  %>
```

The three important lines from Listing 28.7 are lines 5–7. Line 5 forces the document to expire immediately upon receipt from the browser (`Response.Expires=0`). Line 6 forces the server to completely process all ASP code before sending the document downstream (`Response.Buffer=True`). And line 7 turns off the error reports from the runtime engine (`On Error Resume Next`). When these three lines are in place, you can add your typical error-checking code throughout the document. Listing 28.8 shows a sample ASP document that uses this technique.

LISTING 28.8 Adding Error-Handling Code to ASP Documents

```
1   <%@ LANGUAGE=VBScript %>
2
3   <%
4
5   Response.Expires=0
6   Response.Buffer=True
7   On Error Resume Next
8   %>
9
10  <HTML>
11  <HEAD>
12  <META NAME="GENERATOR" Content="Microsoft Visual Studio
    ➥ 6.0">
13  <META HTTP-EQUIV="Content-Type" content="text/html">
14  <TITLE>Document Title</TITLE>
15  </HEAD>
16  <BODY>
17
18  <!-- Insert HTML here -->
19
20  <%
21  ' force a divide by zero error
22  Response.Write 3/0
23  If Err.Number<>0 then
24  Response.Write "Err.Number=" & Err.Number & "<BR>"
25  Response.WRite "Err.Description=" & Err.Description &
    ➥ "<BR>"
26  Response.Write "Err.Source=" & Err.Source
27  End If
28  %>
29
30  </BODY>
31  </HTML>
```

Figure 28.7 demonstrates an example of the output from ASP error-handling.

FIGURE 28.7

An example of the ASP error-handling output.

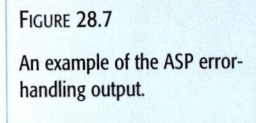

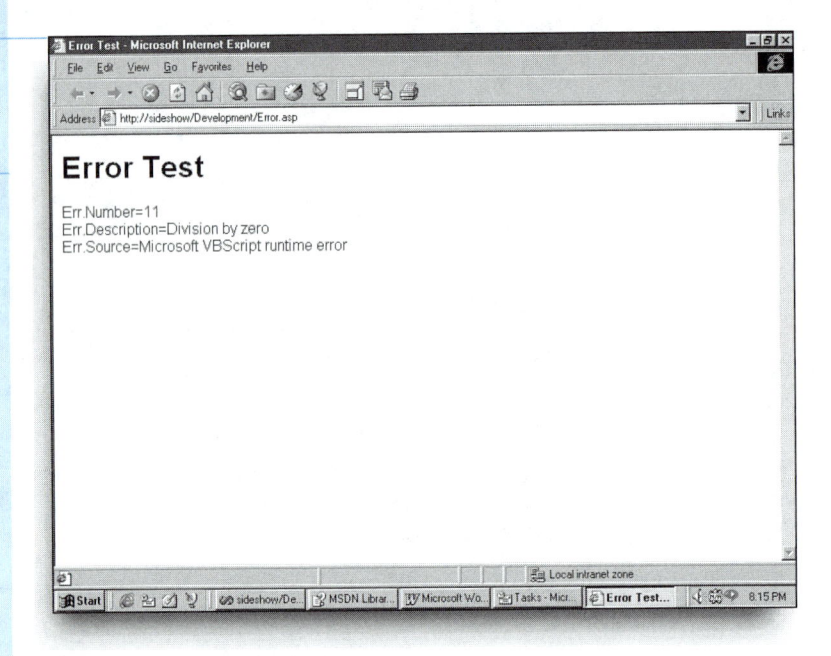

Creating an Error Trap Include File

Adding error-handling code to all your Web documents can become tedious and time-consuming. Luckily, you can reduce your efforts greatly by creating SSI (server-side include) files that hold most of the important error-handling code. By adding these SSI files to your documents, you can speed Web application development without sacrificing application safety.

In this example, you learn how to build an SSI file that can act as the generic error handler for all your ASP documents. You can use the same basic technique to add error-handling code to your server-side documents, too.

When you are designing a generic error handler for ASP documents, you must plan for the following possibilities:

- The error occurred in a document directly accessed by the client (by typing `http://myweb/badpage.asp`).
- The error occurred in a document that was the target of a navigation action in the browser (user pressed a Submit button or some other link on a page).

- The error occurred in a self-referring document (user pressed the Submit button on a page whose action target is set to itself).

In each of these cases, you must handle the error report slightly differently. If at all possible, automatically refer the users away from the error-prone page back to a previous document. If that is not possible, redirect them to move to some other page manually.

After the navigation method is understood by the server, you can format the error information in a display table and send that error document to the client. This document reports the error number, description, and source. It also instructs the user on how to return to a previous page in the Web. Figure 28.8 shows what a completed error display looks like.

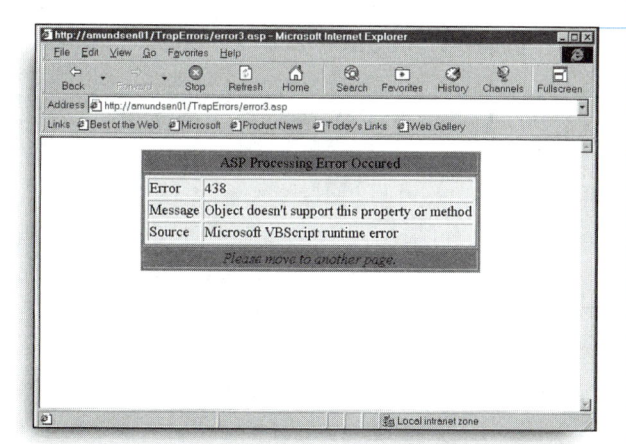

FIGURE 28.8
Viewing an error report document from the SSI file.

Building the SSI File to Handle ASP Errors

The actual file that can handle the ASP errors is a bit lengthy but not too complicated when you understand the process. There are three important steps:

- Determine whether a runtime error occurred processing the ASP code.

- If it did, determine how the user arrived at the page (referred or direct). If the user was referred from another page, compose a header that automatically returns the user to the previous document; otherwise, prepare a document with no special header.
- Collect the Err object data and format it into an easy-to-read table and send the document to the client browser.

Now create the file.

Creating the ERRORTRAP.INC file

1. Right-click your project name in the Project Explorer. From the context menu, choose **Add**, **HTML Page**. This opens the Add Item dialog box.
2. In the **Name** text box, enter the name for this document: errortrap.inc.
3. Click the **Open** button to create the document. Your basic HTML page is created and opened in the Source Editor.
4. Delete the contents of the page. Because this document will be included inside your pages, you don't need to repeat the common HTML page tags, such as <BODY>.
5. Duplicate the contents of Listing 28.9 in the editor. Be careful not to make any typographical errors because this is a long listing.

LISTING 28.9 The Complete Generic Error-Handler for ASP Documents

```
1  <!-- SSI Start errortrap.inc -->
2  <%
3  ' Generic Error Trapping Code for ASP Pages
4  '
5  ' top-level vars
6  Dim strHeaderColor
7  Dim strBodyColor
8  Dim strRefreshWait
9
10 ' top header of error display
11 strHeaderColor="bgcolor=red"
```

Creating an Error Trap Include File

```
12  ' inner body of error display
13  strBodyColor="bgcolor=yellow"
14  ' refresh wait for returning to referer
15  strRefreshWait="3"
16
17  ' check for an ASP error on this page
18  ' if yes, do this work, else skip it all!
19  If Err.Number <> 0 then
20  ProcessError
21  End If
22
23  '
24  ' do error processing
25  Sub ProcessError
26  '
27  Dim strHeader
28  Dim strMessage
29  '
30  ' dump all previously buffered output
31  Response.Clear
32  '
33  ' see if HTTP_REFERER  exists
34  If VarType(Request.ServerVariables("HTTP_REFERER"))<>0
    ➥ Then
35     ' if HTTP_REFERER exists, who is it?
36     If SelfRef=False Then
37        ' not myself
38        strHeader=MakeHeader
39        strMessage="...returning to referring page."
40     Else
41        ' referred by myself
42        strHeader="<HTML>"
43        strMessage="Please press the BACK button on your
           ➥ browser."
44     End If
45  Else
46     ' directly navigated by the user
47     strHeader="<HTML>"
48     strMessage="Please move to another page."
49  End If
50  '
```

continues…

LISTING 28.9 **Continued**

```
51  ' format and send results
52  ReportError strHeader, StrMessage
53  '
54  End Sub
55
56  '
57  ' build page header
58  Function MakeHeader()
59  '
60  Dim strTemp
61  '
62  strTemp = strTemp & "<HTML><HEAD><META HTTP-EQUIV=
    ➥ REFRESH "
63  strTemp = strTemp & "CONTENT=" & chr(34) &
    ➥ strRefreshWait & ";"
64  strTemp = strTemp & "URL=" & Request.ServerVariables
    ➥("HTTP_REFERER")
65  strTemp = strTemp & chr(34) & "></HEAD>"
66  '
67  MakeHeader=strTemp
68  '
69  End Function
70
71  '
72  ' check for self-referencing page
73  Function SelfRef()
74  '
75  Dim strRefer
76  Dim strSelf
77  '
78  strRefer = Request.ServerVariables("HTTP_REFERER")
79  strSelf = "HTTP://" & Request.ServerVariables(
    ➥"SERVER_NAME")
80  strSelf = strSelf & Request.ServerVariables(
    ➥"PATH_INFO")
81  '
82  If UCase(strRefer) = UCase(strSelf) then
83      SelfRef = True
84  Else
85      SelfRef = False
86  End If
```

Creating an Error Trap Include File

```
87  '
88  End Function
89
90  '
91  ' send out error display in a colorful table
92  Sub ReportError(strHeader,strMsg)
93  '
94  Dim strTemp
95  '
96  ' add document header first
97  strTemp=strTemp & strHeader
98  '
99  ' start document body
100 strTemp=strTemp & "<BODY>"
101 ' define outer table
102 strTemp=strTemp & "<TABLE " & strHeaderColor & _
103 " align=center border=1 cellPadding=1 cellSpacing=3
    ➥ width=0>"
104 ' add first cell for outer table
105 strTemp=strTemp & "<TR><TD><CENTER>ASP Processing
    ➥ Error Occurred _
106    </CENTER><TR><TD>"
107 ' define inner table
108 strTemp=strTemp & "<TABLE " & strBodyColor & "
    ➥ border=1 cellPadding=1 _
109    cellSpacing=3 width=100" & chr(asc("%")) & ">"
110 ' add first row to inner table
111 strTemp=strTemp & "<TR><TD>Error"
112 strTemp=strTemp & "<TD>" & Err.Number & "<TR>"
113 ' add second row to inner table
114 strTemp=strTemp & "<TD>Message"
115 strTemp=strTemp & "<TD>" & Err.Description & "<TR>"
116 strTemp=strTemp & "<TD>Source"
117 strTemp=strTemp & "<TD>" & Err.Source & "</TR>
    ➥</TABLE>"
118 strTemp=strTemp & "<TR>"
119 ' add last cell in outer table
120 strTemp=strTemp & "<TD><CENTER><ADDRESS>" & strMsg & _
121    "</ADDRESS></CENTER></TR></TABLE>"
122 '
123 ' close out document
124 strTemp=strTemp & "</CENTER></BODY></HTML>"
```

continues...

LISTING 28.9 Continued

```
125 '
126 ' send it all downstream to client
127 Response.Write strTemp
128 '
129 End Sub
130 %>
131 <!-- SSI End errortrap.inc -->
```

> **Long listing alert!**
>
> There is a great deal going on in this single file. However, after you complete this ASP document you can add solid error handling to all your other ASP documents by adding just a few short lines of code.

6. Save your changes by choosing **File**, **Save errortrap.inc** from the Visual InterDev menu bar.

Let's analyze this listing, as there is a lot going on here. First, after declaring some shared variables and setting their values (lines 5–8), the `Err.Number` value is checked on line 19. If it is not zero, the top-level routine (`ProcessError`) is called in lines 17–21.

The `ProcessError` method in lines 25–54 first clears out the document buffer (line 31) and then checks to see whether the user arrived at this page through a referrer document (lines 34–39) or if the user directly typed the URL into the browser (lines 40–43).

If the user was referred to the page, the reference is checked against the current document name by calling the `SelfRef` method (lines 73–88). This method compares several server variables to see whether the current document and the referrer document are the same. The results are reported back to the `ProcessError` method for use in composing the final HTML to be sent down to the client.

> **The advantage of using errortrap.inc**
>
> The key advantage to entering this huge listing and using it in your Web applications is that you must do it only once. This file will be used by every page in your application through Server Side Includes. This saves you from creating this sort of error handling in every document. Who said Web development doesn't have shortcuts?

If the user arrived at the page by reference and the reference document is not the same as the current document, you can automatically return the user to the previous page by adding a `META` tag to the header of the document. This special header is built in the `MakeHeader` method (lines 58–69).

After the header is determined, it (along with an added message) is sent to the `ReportError` method (lines 85-123) that composes the body of the document and finally sends it downstream to the client. This method looks quite involved, but it is not. The use of nested tables and colors to format the page for easy viewing is only for cosmetic purposes. The important lines in this routine are lines 92–129 where the `Err.Number`, `Err.Description`, and `Err.Source` information is added to the document. Line 121 sends the entire document to the client.

Using the ERRORTRAP.INC File in Your ASP Documents

Now that you have the ERRORTRAP.INC file completed, you only need to add a few lines of code to your ASP documents in order to add error-handling services to your Web application. First, you must add the lines from Listing 28.10 to the top of the ASP document.

LISTING 28.10 **Error-Handling Header Code for All ASP Documents**

```
1  <%@ LANGUAGE=VBScript %>
2
3  <%
4  ' added to support error trapping
5  ' include file (see end of doc)
6  Response.Expires=0
7  Response.Buffer=True
8  On Error Resume Next
9  %>
10
11 <HTML>
```

Note that the important ASP code (lines 3–9) is added between the `<%@ LANGUAGE=VBScript %>` line and the `<HTML>` line. Failure to add this code in this exact location breaks the error-handling features of the document.

Next, you must add one line at the very bottom of the document, after the `</HTML>` line.

```
</HTML>

<!-- #include file=errortrap.inc -->
```

Make this part of your template

If you use a common template to create your pages, consider adding the code from Listing 28.10 to it. This will save you from adding it every time.

The second line in the previous code snippet does the real work. It calls the SSI file shown in Listing 28.9 and adds it to the document during the preprocessing phase of the ASP page. If an error is noted, only the error information (from the ERRORTRAP.INC file) will be sent to the browser.

Listing 28.11 shows a simple ASP document that uses the generic error-handling code described here. Note lines 3–9 and line 24.

Improving ERRORTRAP.INC

How could you make ERRORTRAP.INC better? There are many ways. One improvement could be to provide navigational buttons within the page. Rather than encouraging your site visitor to use their browser's Back button, why not hook into the `History` object of the browser and move from there? Brainstorm on other ways to improve this error page. This is only the beginning!

LISTING 28.11 Using the Generic Error Handler for ASP Documents

```
1  <%@ LANGUAGE=VBScript %>
2
3  <%
4  ' added to support error trapping
5  ' include file (see end of doc)
6  Response.Expires=0
7  Response.Buffer=True
8  On Error Resume Next
9  %>
10
11 <HTML>
12 <HEAD>
13 <META NAME="GENERATOR" Content="Microsoft Visual Studio
➥ 98">
14 <META HTTP-EQUIV="Content-Type" content="text/html">
15 <TITLE>Document Title</TITLE>
16 </HEAD>
17 <BODY>
18
19 <!-- Insert HTML here -->
20
21 <%
22 ' good object & method, bad data file
23 Set objCLC=Server.CreateObject("MSWC.NextLink")
24 objCLC.GetListCount("temp.txt")
25 %>
26
27
28 </BODY>
29 </HTML>
30
31 <!-- #include file=errortrap.inc -->
```

Creating an Error Trap Include File | CHAPTER 28

The results of an error encountered on this page are shown in Figure 28.9.

SEE ALSO
➤ *For more information on the* `History` *object and using client-side scripting, see page 346*

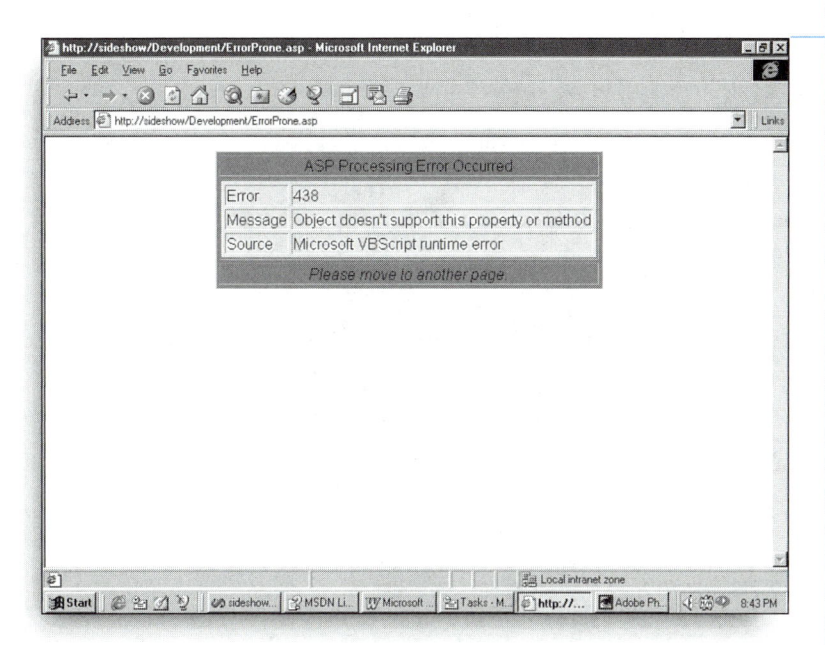

FIGURE 28.9
ERRORTRAP.INC in action—no more disastrous error messages.

CHAPTER 29

Using DHTML to Dynamically Alter HTML Content and Positioning

Learn about DHTML and how to add dynamic content to your Web site

Understand event bubbling

Use the mouse to move graphics in the browser space

Create and work with drag-and-drop interfaces

What Is Dynamic HTML?

Dynamic HTML is really more "dynamic" than it is HTML. Most commands that you use to provide DHTML services are extensions of the standard HTML language and not new HTML commands. In fact, HTML itself is not a programming language. The letters HTML stand for Hypertext Markup Language. HTML was originally designed as a tool for formatting text on the screen.

However, as HTML becomes more popular and more common on workstations that host the Windows interface, expectations for the language have increased. Now it is common for users to expect many of the same features available on personal computer operating systems to be available on thin-client browsers. To meet this challenge, HTML has been expanded in ways that once were not even contemplated. The result is called Dynamic HTML or DHTML.

Although there are several ways in which DHTML adds power and new features to HTML browsers, there is a core set of functionality that gives DHTML its own distinct flavor. The following are the key components of DHTML:

- Event handling—DHTML defines a set of standard event messages (keypresses, mouse movements, loading and unloading of documents, and so on) that can be trapped using script coding. Now you can execute scripts when certain events occur.

- Document object model—DHTML defines a collection of objects that have methods, properties, and events. You can use the hierarchy of objects to gain access to all parts of the loaded document and to the browser that contains the document.

- Element naming—DHTML introduces the concept of adding NAME attributes to virtually any element in the document (paragraphs, controls, images, event whole document sections). This enables document developers to associate methods and properties to any portion of the document— including the actual content itself.

In order to accomplish the tasks of adding DHTML features to your Web documents, you must grasp the following techniques:

- Listening for and responding to event messages
- Using the STYLE attribute to control content display at run-time
- Marking large document sections with HTML DIV and SPAN elements

Each of these topics is covered in the next three sections of this chapter. When you get the hang of these three techniques, you'll spend the rest of the chapter exploring examples that enable you to create visually rich user interfaces and dynamic documents.

Microsoft Internet Explorer 4.x is required for DHTML support

The flavor of DHTML covered here requires Microsoft Internet Explorer 4.x or higher. If you plan to use DHTML in your Web documents, be sure all your users have Microsoft Internet Explorer 4.x or greater.

Listening for Events

One of the most important features of DHTML is the addition of event messages. Event messages are notifications from the browser that occur whenever certain predefined actions take place during a client session. Each time one of these predefined events occurs, a message is sent by the browser. As a programmer, you can "listen" for these messages and add scripting code to your HTML page that will run each time the message is sent. This kind of programming is the basis for the Windows operating system.

There are lots of event messages. Each element in the browser document object model (DOM) has its own associated events. For example, the Window object has the following events:

- onbeforeunload occurs just before the document is loaded into the window.
- onblur occurs when the window loses focus.
- onerror occurs when an error is reported by the browser.
- onfocus occurs when the window gains focus.
- onhelp occurs when the user presses the F1 key.
- onload occurs when a document loads into the window.

Events are always happening

The Windows operating system is designed to send event messages even when no one is listening. You do not have to do anything special to make events happen—they are always occurring. You just need to add code to "listen" for the messages that interest you.

- `onresize` occurs when the user resizes the window.
- `onscroll` occurs when the user scrolls the document in the window.
- `onunload` occurs when the document is unloaded from the window.

Event messages are associated with the window, the document, even elements in the document such as `<INPUT>` controls and paragraph markers (`<P>`). This means that there is a potential for hundreds of messages to occur within a single document loaded in a window.

SEE ALSO
> *To learn more about event handling, see page 301*
> *To learn more about events in Microsoft Internet Explorer, see page 335*

Listening for Messages

To keep track of the events, the DOM defines a method for reporting the events in the format of a Visual Basic Script message header. This message header has the following format:

```
<SCRIPT Language=VBSCript>
<!--
Sub <elementname>_<eventname>

End Sub
-->
</SCRIPT>
```

For example, if the `onclick` event occurs for a button element with the name `btnShow`, the actual event script header would be

```
<SCRIPT Language=VBSCript>
<!--
Sub btnShow_onclick

End Sub
-->
</SCRIPT>
```

What Is Dynamic HTML?

After you define the Visual Basic Script message header, you can add code within the script block that will run each time the event message is received. For example, to show a message box each time the user clicks the **Show** button, you could add the following code to your HTML page:

```
<SCRIPT Language=VBSCript>
<!--
Sub btnShow_onclick
    Alert "You clicked me!"
End Sub
-->
</SCRIPT>
```

The Magic of Event Bubbling

Another rather powerful feature of DHTML is called *event bubbling*. Event bubbling is the process of passing event messages up through the hierarchy of the document object model. With event bubbling, event messages that are sent for one element in the HTML page can be received by all the elements "above" the element to which that message was addressed. In other words, if the `onclick` message of the `btnShow` button is sent (when a user clicks on the button), the `onclick` event of the button occurs and the `onclick` event of the document that holds the button occurs. To see how this actually works, look at the code in Listing 29.1.

> **Events with Visual Basic Script differ from JavaScript**
>
> The reporting of event messages for JavaScript is slightly different than the method for Visual Basic Script. JavaScript is not covered in this book.

LISTING 29.1 Example of Event Bubbling

```
 1  <SCRIPT LANGUAGE=VBScript>
 2  <!--
 3  Sub document_onclick
 4    alert "You Clicked Something!"
 5  End Sub
 6
 7  Sub btnShow_onclick
 8     alert "You Clicked Me!"
 9  End Sub
10  -->
11  </SCRIPT>
```

LISTING 29.1

❶ You are "listening" for the `onclick` event message.

❷ When the `onclick` event message is heard this line of code will be executed by the browser.

In Listing 29.1, you can see two Visual Basic Script event messages headers. When the user clicks the button named `btnShow`, the `onclick` event message is sent to `btnShow` (line 7). In addition, the `onclick` event message is also sent to the `document` (line 3) object, because the button appears within the document object. The `onclick` event "bubbles up" the object hierarchy. This is event bubbling.

Event bubbling is unique to the DHTML object model and can come in quite handy. For example, if you want to fire the same message when the user clicks on any element in the document, you only must write code for the `document_onclick` event. Under the Windows event model, you would have to write code for every event message of the individual controls on the form—much more code!

Canceling Event Bubbling

Even though event bubbling is powerful, it can get in the way at times. In Listing 29.1, you can see that clicking on a button on the document actually causes two Visual Basic Script code blocks to execute. This might not be what you want to happen. For example, you might want the `document_onclick` event to fire only if the user actually clicks somewhere on the document face, not on one of the defined controls on the document. To do this, you must suppress the event bubbling for the button element.

To suppress event bubbling, you can set the `CancelBubble` property to TRUE. Listing 29.2 shows a modified version of Listing 29.1 that includes the canceling of event bubbling.

Reduce code with event bubbling

If you must write event-handling code that will convert every keypress into uppercase characters for every input box on the form, you can reduce your coding by only writing code for the `document_keypress` event and letting event bubbling send all the keypress events from the input controls up to the document.

Cancel events in your handler

It is a good idea to use the `cancelBubbling` method only in the script section that handles the event. This way you will not be looking all over the document to see who cancelled your important event.

LISTING 29.2

① If the `cancelBubble` property is set to `True`, this line will never be executed.

② This line cancels event bubbling for the `onclick` message of this button.

LISTING 29.2 Canceling Event Bubbling

```
1  <SCRIPT LANGUAGE=VBScript>
2  <!--
3  Sub document_onclick
4      alert "You clicked on the document"         ①
5  End Sub
6
7  Sub btnShow_onclick
8      alert "You clicked the Show button"
9      window.event.cancelBubble=True              ②
```

```
10  End Sub
11  -->
12  </SCRIPT>
```

You'll use both event messages and event bubbling often when you create DHTML documents.

SEE ALSO
➤ *For more on using events in Visual Basic Scripting, see page 303*
➤ *For information on events in the Microsoft Internet Explorer document object model, see page 335*

The Power of the *STYLE* Attribute

A key item in the creation of DHTML documents is the STYLE attribute. The STYLE attribute enables you to add DHTML features to most of the HTML elements. Several parameters can be used with the style attribute. Listing 29.3 shows a typical setting for the STYLE attribute of an image (IMG) element.

LISTING 29.3   **Typical *STYLE* Attribute Settings**

```
1   <IMG
2      NAME=imgCoins
3      ID=imgCoins
4      ALT=Coins
5      SRC="images/coins.gif"
6      WIDTH=88
7      HEIGHT=101
8      STYLE="POSITION: absolute;
9             LEFT: 134px;
10            TOP: 200px;
11            HEIGHT: 64px;
12            WIDTH: 64px;
13  >
```

The STYLE attribute in Listing 29.3 can be found in lines 8 through 13. Note that all the settings appear inside double quotes and that each setting name and value is separated by a colon (:). In Listing 29.3, the STYLE attribute establishes the absolute position of the image on the document.

The settings of the STYLE attribute can also be accessed using Visual Basic Script. However, Visual Basic Script treats the settings as properties of the style object of an element. Listing 29.4 shows how to set the absolute position of an image element using Visual Basic Script.

LISTING 29.4

This is the script equivalent of using the STYLE="TOP: 200" attribute in the Coins IMG element.

LISTING 29.4 Using Visual Basic Script to Modify *STYLE* Settings

```
1  <SCRIPT LANGUAGE="VBScript">
2  <!--
3  Sub btnDefault_onclick
4      '
5      window.imgCoins.style.posLeft=134
6      window.imgCoins.style.posTop=200
7      '
8  End Sub
9  -->
10 </SCRIPT>
```

Be sure to use : and not = with STYLE settings

It is a common mistake to use the equal sign (=) when working with STYLE attributes instead of the colon (:). Doing this will not return an error, but will cause the browser to ignore the settings completely.

Although the most common use of the STYLE attribute is in establishing the size and location of elements, it is also used to alter the visibility of elements (window.imgCoins.style.visibility= "hidden"). The STYLE attribute can also be used to apply visual filters to an element.

You'll learn more about visual filters later in the chapter. The key point to remember is that the STYLE attribute can be applied to almost any HTML element, and it enables you to control the position and appearance of elements in the document.

Using the *DIV* and *SPAN* HTML Elements

The final concept to discuss here is the use of the DIV and SPAN HTML elements. These two HTML elements enable you to mark sections of the document and apply style and other DHTML features to the marked section. The only difference between the SPAN and DIV elements is that the SPAN element is a text-level element and the DIV element is a block-level element.

What Is Dynamic HTML?

In other words, SPAN can be applied only within a text element (that is, a paragraph or heading), but DIV can be applied to a set of elements (that is, to several paragraphs).

For example, you can use the SPAN element to create a defined area on the document that will contain text. Because the SPAN element can accept the STYLE attribute, you can create a text section in the document of a fixed width and height that holds an absolute position in the document. Listing 29.5 shows an example of how this can be done using DHTML features.

> **Use DIV before SPAN**
>
> Because DIV elements can be applied to entire blocks of text, they are preferred over SPAN. If you have only one or two words to work with, SPAN is better. However, if you have a paragraph or more that must be marked as a section, use SPAN instead.

LISTING 29.5 Using *SPAN* to Create an Absolute Text Area in a Document

```
1  <SPAN
2      NAME=spnMain
3      ID=spnMain
4      STYLE="POSITION: absolute;
5              HEIGHT: 200px;
6              LEFT: 100px;
7              TOP: 100px;
8              WIDTH: 200px" >
9  This text appears within the SPAN Element.
10 </SPAN>
```

> **LISTING 29.5**
>
> ① The ABSOLUTE setting will make sure other text does not shift this SPAN further down the page.

Listing 29.5 shows a small area on the document where text will appear. If the text line is longer than the defined area (the width attribute in line 8), it will automatically wrap to fit the space. If the wrapped text extends beyond the bottom of the defined area (the height attribute in line 5), the extended text will be hidden from view. In other words, the SPAN element enables you to define a type of "window" within the document where you can place any text or image. You use SPAN and DIV to create areas of the document where DHTML STYLE attributes can be applied.

Now that you have a pretty good idea of how the key elements of DHTML work, you're ready to apply them to real-life documents. In the next several sections you create Web pages that use events, STYLE attributes, and some other DHTML features to create dynamic HTML documents.

PART **VI** More Active Server Programming

CHAPTER **29** Using DHTML to Dynamically Alter HTML Content and Positioning

Creating the DHTML Web Project

All the pages in this chapter will be added to a single Web project. Before you continue, start Visual InterDev and create a new Web project called DHTML. Don't apply any theme or layout information to the project when you build it. You'll add the fancy stuff later.

SEE ALSO
➤ *To learn how to create a new Web project, see page 12*

Altering HTML Content at Runtime

You can use DHTML commands to create documents that have changing content during runtime. Essentially, these documents contain hidden text that can be viewed using client-side Visual Basic Script triggered by events. In this section, you build a document that has simple headers and, when the user moves the mouse over the headers, displays additional text associated with the headers.

To start, create a new HTML document called MOUSEOVER.HTM and, when it appears in the WYSIWYG editor, add the text shown in Figure 29.1.

FIGURE 29.1

Laying out the MOUSEOVER.HTM document.

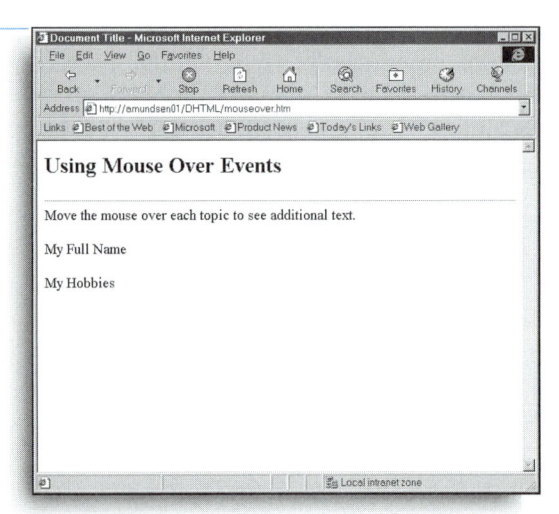

Altering HTML Content at Runtime — CHAPTER 29

After you add the text in WYSIWYG mode, switch to Source mode and set the NAME and ID properties of the <P> elements of each of the subtitles, as shown in Listing 29.6.

LISTING 29.6 Setting the *NAME* and *ID* Attributes of *<P>* Elements

```
1 <P NAME=MyName ID=MyName>
2 My Full Name
3 </P>
4
5 <P NAME=MyHobbies ID=MyHobbies>
6 My Hobbies
7 </P>
```

Here you are creating a NAME and ID handle that can be used with Visual Basic Script to address this part of the document. Then you can read and set the various properties of the paragraph using Visual Basic Script.

You want to make additional text appear in the document whenever the user positions the mouse pointer over the header. This means you must listen for the proper event and execute Visual Basic Script accordingly.

Using the *ONMOUSEOVER* Event and the *innerHTML* Property

You can listen for the onmouseover event message to see when a user moves the mouse over any area that has a NAME and ID attribute. In this case, you want to add a Visual Basic Script code block for the onmouseover event and execute Visual Basic Script code when it occurs.

When the event message is received, you want to add new text to the selected paragraph. You can do this by using the innerHTML property of the paragraph. This enables you to alter the text within the HTML tag.

Listing 29.7 shows the completed Visual Basic Script for the MyName_onmouseover event. Add this to your document.

> **Using NAME and ID attributes**
>
> It is a good idea to keep the NAME and ID attributes of an element the same. Some scripting methods use the NAME attribute. Most HTML operations use the ID attribute. Keeping them both the same makes maintaining and debugging your documents easier.

LISTING 29.7

① Don't let the onmouseover event pass to any other elements on this document.

LISTING 29.7 Adding the *MyName_onmouseover* Event Script

```
1  <SCRIPT LANGUAGE=VBScript>
2  <!--
3
4  Dim strHeader
5  Dim strDetail
6
7  Sub MyName_onmouseover
8      '
9      strHeader="<B>My Full Name</B><BR>"
10     strDetail="<I>Franklin Lee Fransworthy, III</I>"
11     '
12     window.MyName.innerHTML=strHeader & strDetail
13     window.event.cancelBubble=true                    ①
14     '
15 End Sub
16
17 -->
18 </SCRIPT>
```

Notice that lines 4 and 5 of Listing 29.7 declare two document-level variables. Although this is not required, it makes reading the Visual Basic Script code easier. You also use these same variables later in the script. Declaring them outside the scope of any `sub...end sub` ensures they can be shared among all the methods in the page.

Note that you use the `innerHTML` property to alter the contents of the named paragraph. Because you are using the `innerHTML` property, you can also include any valid markup elements (that is, the `<B>` and `<I>` elements).

Notice that the method ends by canceling event bubbling (line 13). Again, it is not required, but it's a good idea to cancel event bubbling unless you know you will be using it somewhere else in the document.

Now add the code from Listing 29.8 to your document. This alters the text of the `MyHobbies` paragraph.

Using the `innerHTML` and `innerTEXT` scripting properties

If you need to insert only plain text into a section, you can use the `innerTEXT` property. This property leaves all the HTML formatting within the `SPAN` or `DIV` intact. The `innerHTML` property replaces all the HTML format elements within the `DIV` or `SPAN`.

Altering HTML Content at Runtime — PART VI, CHAPTER 29 — 761

LISTING 29.8 Altering the Contents of the *MyHobbies* Paragraph

```
1  <SCRIPT LANGUAGE=VBScript>
2  <!--
3  Sub MyHobbies_onmouseover
4     '
5     strHeader="<B>My Hobbies</B><BR>"
6     strDetail="<I>Reading, Puzzles, and Knitting</I>"
7     '
8     window.MyHobbies.innerHTML=strHeader & strDetail
9     window.event.cancelBubble=true
10    '
11 End Sub
12 -->
13 </SCRIPT>
```

LISTING 29.8

❶ When the mouse moves over the MyHobbies section, dislay the header and detail information.

There are no real surprises here. Notice that the `strHeader` and `strDetail` variables are used here, but do not appear inside the `SCRIPT` block. Because they were declared earlier (refer to Listing 29.7) you don't need to redeclare them here.

Finally, you must add Visual Basic Script that will remove the added text when the user moves the mouse off the named header. Listing 29.9 shows the code to do this.

LISTING 29.9 Visual Basic Script to Remove Added Text

```
1  <SCRIPT LANGUAGE=VBScript>
2  <!--
3  Sub document_onmouseover
4     '
5     if window.event.srcElement.id<>"MyName" then
5        window.MyName.innerHTML="My Full Name"
7     end if
8     '
9     if window.event.srcElement.id<>"MyHobbies" then
10       window.MyHobbies.innerHTML="My Hobbies"
11    end if
12    '
13 End Sub
14 -->
15 </SCRIPT>
```

LISTING 29.9

❶ When the document receives the `mouseover` message from some element and it is not the `MyName` element, set the contents of that element to the plain heading text.

As you can see from Listing 29.9, each time the `onmouseover` event message is received for the document, the Visual Basic Script checks to see whether the current element is not one of the two named elements (lines 5 and 9). If the expression evaluates to TRUE (that is, the current element is not one of the named elements), the `innerHTML` property is returned to the original format. This is how you can remove content at runtime.

After completing this document, save it and view it in the **Quick View** tab. When you move the mouse over the headers, you will see the added text (see Figure 29.2).

FIGURE 29.2

Testing the ONMOUSEOVER.HTM document.

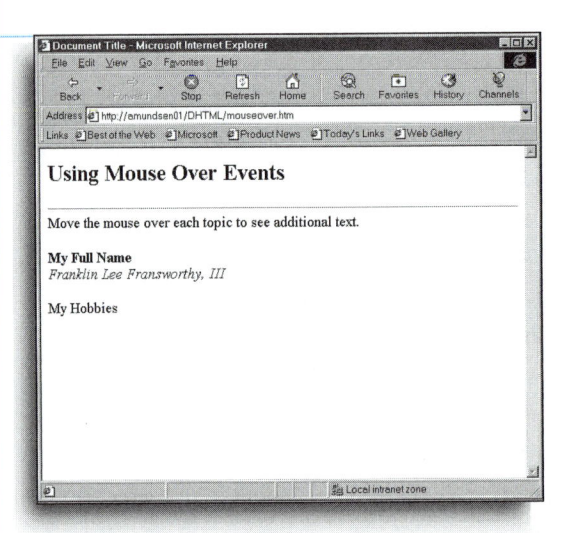

Creating Visual Drag-and-Drop Interfaces

You can also use DHTML to create a drag-and-drop type of interface for HTML documents. In this case, you want to listen for mouse up and down events and also keep track of the X and Y coordinates of the mouse. Finally, you want to use the X and Y data to alter the positions of graphic images on the page. This will give the appearance that the user can "pick up" and "move" graphic images on the browser page.

Creating Visual Drag-and-Drop Interfaces

PART VI
CHAPTER 29

763

Laying Out the REPOSITION.HTM Document

The first step is to add a new document called REPOSITION.HTM to your Web project. When it is loaded in the editor, you must add a single button to the page (and some heading text). Figure 29.3 shows how you should lay out the top part of the document.

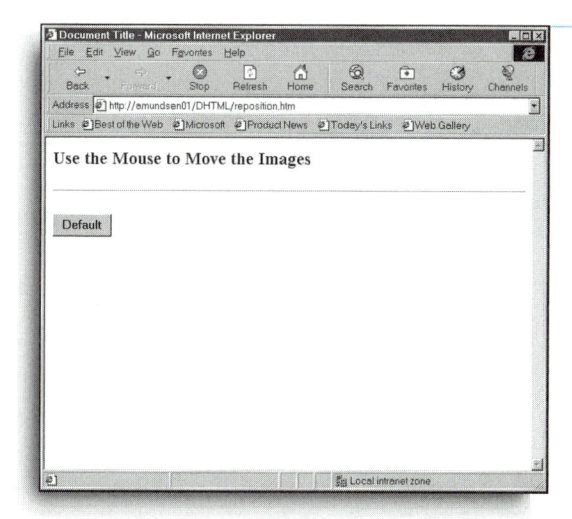

FIGURE 29.3
Laying out the REPOSITION.HTM document.

Set the NAME and ID attributes of the button to btnDefault and the VALUE to Default. Listing 29.10 shows how the HTML code will look after you complete these changes.

LISTING 29.10 **Modifying the Attributes of the Button Control**

```
1  <H3>Use the Mouse to Move the Images</H3>
2  <HR>
3
4  <P>
5  <INPUT
6      TYPE=button
7      NAME=btnDefault
8      ID=btnDefault
9      VALUE=Default>
10 </P>
```

In this next step, you import four images from somewhere else on the disk into your current Web project. For this, you must locate some GIF or JPG images somewhere on your workstation or local network.

Where are the images?

If you want, you can download the images shown here from the *Using Visual InterDev 6* Web site. Check Appendix B for the exact location of the Web site.

Importing images into your project

1. Click the Images folder in the project window.
2. Right-click to bring up the context menu.
3. Select **Add** from the menu.
4. Select **Add Item** from the submenu.
5. When the Add Item dialog box appears, select the **Existing** tab.
6. Select **Image Files** in the **Files of type:** pull-down menu at the bottom of the dialog box.
7. Navigate to the folder that holds the graphics you want to import into your Web project (for example, e:\my images).
8. Select one or more items from the folder to import. You can select multiple items by pressing the Ctrl key while clicking on each item with the mouse (see Figure 29.4).

FIGURE 29.4

Adding images to your Web project.

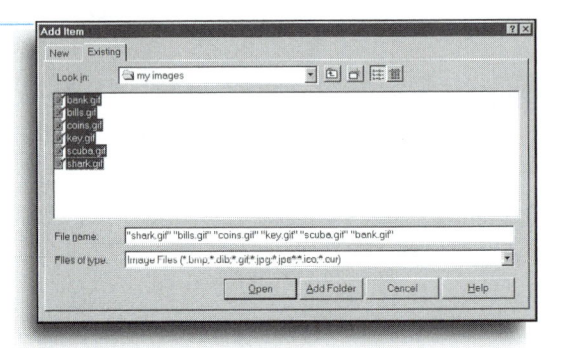

9. When you've selected all your images, press the **Open** button to add them to your Web project.

After the images are added to your project, you can add them to your document. Because you want to use absolute positioning and track the movement of the images on the page, it will be easier to hand-code the image elements instead of using the Visual InterDev menu options to place images.

Differences between local Web and master Web

If you have your project open in Local mode, a blue flag appears next to all the added images. This means the images are in the Local project only. To add them to the Master Web, select all the images, right-click to view the context menu, and select **Add to Master Web**.

Creating Visual Drag-and-Drop Interfaces | CHAPTER **29**

For this example, you want to place the images side-by-side underneath the button. You also want to mark them for absolute positioning and indicate the exact size of the images. This last step will make it much easier to place and manipulate the images at runtime. Listing 29.11 shows the HTML code to add four images side-by-side in the document.

Use this as a guide when you add your own images. Even if you are using some other images, be sure to use the exact same attributes, as shown in Listing 29.11. This will make it much easier to work through the Visual Basic Script code later in this section.

LISTING 29.11 Adding Four Images to the REPOSITION.HTM Document

```
1  <P>
2  <IMG
3     NAME=imgBank
4     ID=imgBank
5     STYLE="HEIGHT: 64px;
6            LEFT: 0px;
7            POSITION: absolute;
8            TOP: 200px;
9            WIDTH: 64px;
10           ZINDEX: -1"
11    alt=Bank
12    src="images/bank.gif"
13    WIDTH=100
14    HEIGHT=100
15  >
16 </P>
17
18 <P>
19 <IMG
20    NAME=imgBills
21    ID=imgBills
22    STYLE="HEIGHT: 64px;
23           LEFT: 66px;
24           POSITION: absolute;
25           TOP: 200px;
26           WIDTH: 64px;
```

LISTING 29.11

① Use the ZINDEX setting to control which item should appear on top of others when they are dragged over each other.

continues...

LISTING 29.11 **Continued**

```
27              ZINDEX: -2"
28      alt=Bills
29      src="images/bills.gif"
30      WIDTH=100
31      HEIGHT=100
32  >
33  </P>
34
35  <P>
36  <IMG
37      NAME=imgCoins
38      ID=imgCoins
39      STYLE="HEIGHT: 64px;
40              LEFT: 134px;
41              POSITION: absolute;
42              TOP: 200px;
43              WIDTH: 64px;
44              ZINDEX: -3"
45      alt=Coins
46      src="images/coins.gif"
47      WIDTH=88
48      HEIGHT=101 >
49  </P>
50
51  <P>
52  <IMG
53      NAME=imgKey
54      ID=imgKey
55      STYLE="HEIGHT: 64px;
56              LEFT: 202px;
57              POSITION: absolute;
58              TOP: 200px;
59              WIDTH: 64px;
60              ZINDEX: -4"
61      alt=Key
62      src="images/key.gif"
63      WIDTH=100
64      HEIGHT=100 >
65  </P>
```

Creating Visual Drag-and-Drop Interfaces | PART VI CHAPTER 29 | **767**

Notice that each image has been given a NAME and ID attribute. These will be used in the Visual Basic Script to address the image and reposition it based on the movement of the mouse.

Figure 29.5 shows how the page will appear after adding the HTML code from Listing 29.11.

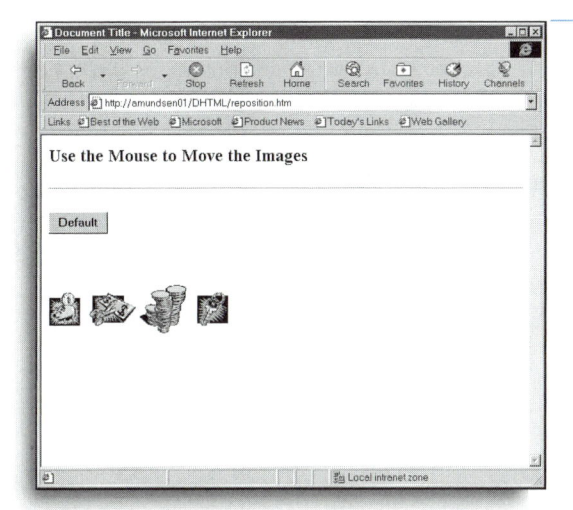

FIGURE 29.5
The completed layout of the REPOSITION.HTM document.

SEE ALSO
➤ To learn more about adding images to your Web project, see page 57

Using the *event* Object to Enable Drag-and-Drop for Web Documents

Now it's time to write the Visual Basic Script that will track mouse movements and reposition the images as requested. There are three key things you must keep track of within the Visual Basic Script:

- Has the user pressed the mouse button?
- Did the user press the mouse button over an IMG element?
- Has the user moved the mouse since pressing the mouse button?

PART VI More Active Server Programming

CHAPTER 29 Using DHTML to Dynamically Alter HTML Content and Positioning

You can use a single object of the document object model to determine all this: the `event` object. You add code to the `onmousedown` event of the document and then check for the condition of the mouse, the `IMG` elements, and the movement.

Listing 29.12 shows all the code needed to do this work. Although the listing seems long, it's not really too complicated when you understand the idea behind it. Copy this Visual Basic Script code into your document; the following paragraphs review the code in greater detail.

LISTING 29.12 Adding Visual Basic Script to the *document_onmousemove* Event

> **LISTING 29.12**
>
> ① This line checks the hidden TAG attribute to see whether it is set to IMG.
>
> ② This line updates the location of the left side of the image on the document.

```
1  <script LANGUAGE="VBScript">
2  <!--
3  Sub document_onmousemove
4    '
5    Dim lngleft
6    Dim lngTop
7    Dim lngX
8    Dim lngY
9    Dim objElement
10   '
11   ' get current mouse position
12   lngX=window.event.x
13   lngY=window.event.y
14   '
15   ' is mouse button depressed?
16   if window.event.button=1 then
17     '
18     ' get a copy of the selceted object
19     Set objElement=window.event.srcElement
20     ' is it one of the images?
21     if objElement.tagname="IMG" then                  ①
22       '
23       ' update the x position of the image
24       lngLeft=lngX-(objElement.style.posWidth/2)
25       If lngLeft<0 then
26         lngLeft=0
27       end if
28       objElement.style.posLeft=lngLeft                ②
29       '
```

```
30              ' update the y position of the image
31              lngTop=lngY-(objElement.style.posHeight/2)
32              if lngTop<0 then
33                  lngTop=0
34              end if
35              objElement.style.posTop=lngTop
36              '
37              ' kill event messages
38              window.event.returnValue=false
39              window.event.cancelBubble=true
40              '
41          end if ' tagname=IMG
42      end if ' button=1
43      '
44  End Sub
45  -->
46  </script>
```

LISTING 29.12

3 This line updates the location of the top of the image on the document.

There are several things to review in Listing 29.12. First, note that lines 12 and 13 get the current mouse position and store it in local variables. Line 16 checks to see whether the left mouse button was pressed. Line 19 retrieves the element that was clicked and stores it in a variable. Line 21 checks to see whether the selected element is an IMG element (you want that!).

Next, lines 24–28 and 31–35 use the mouse position (X and Y) to update the IMG element position. Again, notice that the STYLE attribute of the elements is used throughout these lines of code.

Finally, lines 38 and 39 cancel any possible return value or event bubbling that might occur. This will make sure that the browser will ignore unwanted event messages while the user is positioning the images on the document.

You must add one more method to the document, the btnDefault_onclick method that will fire when the user clicks the **Default** button. The Visual Basic Script in Listing 29.13 shows you how to use the style object to fix the positions of images on a page. Add this code to your document.

LISTING 29.13 Adding Visual Basic Script to Set Image Positions

```
1  <script LANGUAGE="VBScript">
2  <!--
3  Sub btnDefault_onclick
4      '
5      ' reset graphics to original position
6      '
7      window.imgBank.style.posLeft=0
8      window.imgBank.style.posTop=200
9      '
10     window.imgBills.style.posLeft=66
11     window.imgBills.style.posTop=200
12     '
13     window.imgCoins.style.posLeft=134
14     window.imgCoins.style.posTop=200
15     '
16     window.imgKey.style.posLeft=202
17     window.imgKey.style.posTop=200
18     '
19 End Sub
20 -->
21 </script>
```

As you can see from Listing 29.13, all you must do is set the posLeft and posTop properties of the style attributes for each image element in the document. Now save the document and view it in Quick View mode. You will be able to click on each image in the page and, with the mouse still pressed down, move that image and drop it anywhere else on the page.

SEE ALSO
▶ *For more on handling mouse events with Visual Basic Script, see page 302*

PART VII

Appendixes

- **A** Using Microsoft FrontPage and FrontPage Server Extensions 773
- **B** Online Resources 791
- **C** Glossary 795

  Index 821

APPENDIX A

Using Microsoft FrontPage and FrontPage Server Extensions

- Integrate Microsoft FrontPage and Visual InterDev 6
- Install Microsoft FrontPage Server Extensions properly
- Troubleshoot FrontPage and Visual InterDev 6 problems

Advantages of Mixing Microsoft FrontPage and Visual InterDev 6

There are several reasons why you might want to be able to use FrontPage and Visual InterDev 6 to edit the same Web project. For example, FrontPage has a very friendly user interface and has very powerful tools for generating common Web page templates and managing a large Web site. Visual InterDev 6, however, has excellent database-handling features and offers some excellent design-time controls that can be used to build sophisticated Web forms in a very short amount of time.

Another reason you might want to mix FrontPage and Visual InterDev 6 to edit the same Web is to allow people with varying talents and responsibilities to manage the same site. Those with primary responsibility for database, server-side scripting, and component integration can use Visual InterDev 6 as a primary editing tool for the site. Those people whose primary directives are to maintain the contents of static pages, image files, site maps, and other content-based tasks might be more familiar with the Microsoft Office–like look and feel of FrontPage.

Finally, there might be times when a developer or Web administrator must access an existing Web to perform a simple update or fix and has only FrontPage or only Visual InterDev 6 available to do the job. In most cases, either tool will be successful.

Mixing FrontPage and Visual InterDev 6 editors on the same project is possible, but there are some warnings and cautions that you should keep in mind. First, you must properly install Visual InterDev 6 and FrontPage on both the client and server machines to make sure they can cooperate properly. Second, when the installation is successful, there are some general guidelines to follow when using FrontPage to edit Visual InterDev 6 projects and Visual InterDev 6 to edit FrontPage projects. Finally, there are some typical errors and troubleshooting activities that you can watch for when mixing FrontPage and Visual InterDev 6.

Don't mix FrontPage and Visual InterDev 6 unless needed

Microsoft FrontPage and Visual InterDev 6 are both great products, but they are geared toward different audiences. FrontPage is designed to be a great Web *site* tool. Visual InterDev 6 is designed to be a great Web *application* tool. Although you can use them both to complete the same project, it is best to stick with a consistent tool as much as possible.

After you have the details ironed out and have given developers the proper warnings, you can safely and effectively use both FrontPage and Visual InterDev 6 to manage the same Web projects.

SEE ALSO
➤ *Page 34 gives you a start in using the editing features of Visual InterDev.*

Recommended Installation Steps

If you want to integrate the use of Microsoft FrontPage with Visual InterDev 6, you must be sure to install the two packages properly. Although the two systems work well together, there are a few glitches that you must overcome when installing FrontPage and Visual InterDev 6 on the same machine.

The key to the whole process is to install all the components in the proper sequence. If you want to integrate FrontPage and Visual InterDev 6 on the same machine, the best approach is to

1. Remove FrontPage from the developer workstation.
2. Remove FrontPage Server Extensions from the developer workstation.
3. Install Visual InterDev 6 workstation components.
4. Install the NT/IIS4 Option Pack Web server components on the developer workstation.
5. Install the FrontPage Server Extensions on the developer workstation.
6. Install the FrontPage client tools on the developer workstation.

By following these steps, you'll get the right mix of client and server components from both Visual InterDev 6 and FrontPage.

The following sections present a series of recommended installation steps that will help you make sure both FrontPage and Visual InterDev 6 can work well on the same machine. These steps apply to both client-side and server-side installations.

Always check the README files

Just about every Microsoft software product comes with one or more files named README. These files contain details on how to make the installation go smoothly, and often have corrections that appeared too late to be included in the printed documentation. Always read the README files before beginning an installation.

Remove FrontPage from the Client

If you already have Microsoft FrontPage installed, it is best to remove it before you install Visual InterDev 6. The FrontPage package was originally designed to run on machines that had no Web server software. To do this, FrontPage does several things that convince the workstation that a Web server exists. Some of the things FrontPage does can confuse Visual InterDev 6 about the location of the Web host server.

To avoid confusion, run the FrontPage uninstall from the Windows control panel Add/Remove Programs applet. This will not remove any existing FrontPage Webs that you have already created or delete any FrontPage source code you have on the workstation. It will remove only the FrontPage edition tools and several DLLs that are involved in making FrontPage communicate with the Web server.

Remove FrontPage Server Extensions—Twice

If you have installed the FrontPage Server Extensions on the workstation, these should be removed as well. The Server Extensions can cause quite a bit of trouble for Visual InterDev 6.

Use the Control Panel Add/Remove Programs applet to locate and uninstall the Microsoft FrontPage Server Extensions. After you have completed the install, check the Control Panel applet again to see whether it still exists on the list. This is very important. You usually must uninstall the SFP Server Extensions *twice*. You might receive a message the second time saying that the uninstall could not be completed. That's OK. Just be sure to check and recheck the items in the list of installed software and make sure that the Microsoft FrontPage Server Extensions are no longer on the list.

At this point, you can fire up your Visual InterDev 6 installation CD-ROM and start working through the installation.

Removing FrontPage will not remove the Webs

Uninstalling Microsoft FrontPage will not delete the Webs on the machine. You will still be able to browse to the Webs created by FrontPage even after FrontPage has been deleted. If you install FrontPage again on the same machine, the old FrontPage Webs will be available for editing.

Twice might not be enough

You might need to uninstall the FrontPage Server Extensions multiple times in order to remove the entry from the list of installed software. Be sure to check the list each time to make sure the entry has been removed from the list.

Install the Option Pack Without FrontPage Server Extensions

When installing the server-side components of Visual InterDev 6, there are some special steps you must take to make sure Visual InterDev 6 and FrontPage work well together. The key task is to not install the Microsoft FrontPage Server Extensions that are included in the NT/IIS4 Option Pack. Instead, you want to install the Microsoft FrontPage Extensions separately, after the NT/IIS4 Option Pack has already been installed. This will make sure that both FrontPage and Visual InterDev 6 can use the FrontPage extensions properly.

When you install the NT/IIS4 Option Pack, select the **Custom** install option and uncheck the box that will install the Microsoft FrontPage Server Extensions. You can then make any other install adjustments you want and complete the NT/IIS4 Option Pack installation.

Install the FrontPage Server Extensions Separately

After you have completed the NT/IIS4 Option Pack installation, you can safely install the FrontPage Server Extensions. There should be an option to install them from the Visual InterDev 6 Server-Side Component list.

If you don't see them on the installation list, you can install them manually from the Visual InterDev 6 CD-ROMs. Just look for the folder FP98EXT on one of the Visual InterDev 6 CD-ROMs and double-click the SETUP.EXE file to run the installation.

Install Microsoft FrontPage Without the Personal Web Server

After you have successfully installed the NT/IIS4 Option Pack and the FrontPage Extensions, you can safely add the Microsoft FrontPage client installation. You can use the Visual InterDev 6 installation Wizard to install FrontPage or locate the FRONTPAGE folder on the Visual InterDev 6 installation CDs and use that instead.

When it comes to running the install, don't be typical

Even if you have no plans to modify the list of installed components, don't select the "typical" install when running Microsoft installation routines. Almost always, you can press the **Custom** button and see the typical items listed in detail, along with the opportunity to change the list of installed components. Even if you do not change anything on the lists, at least you'll have a better idea of just what components have been added to the target machine.

It is important that you do not install the FrontPage Personal Web Server when you install FrontPage. Be sure to use the Custom installation and uncheck the option to install FrontPage Personal Web Server (PWS). Installing the FrontPage PWS might cause Visual InterDev 6 to report that it is unable to locate the Web server whenever you attempt to use that machine as the Web host for your Visual InterDev 6 projects.

If, while you are installing FrontPage, you are prompted to install the server extensions, answer NO. The proper extensions are already installed, and you do not want to install the default set over them.

You now have a workstation that can support both FrontPage and Visual InterDev 6, including the proper server-side components.

> **You don't need the FrontPage personal Web Server**
>
> The FrontPage Personal Web Server is included for those who are not using any other Web server products or development tools from Microsoft. This is handy for people who want to use FrontPage but don't use any other Web authoring software. However, Visual InterDev 6 needs the advanced features of the NT/IIS4 Option Pack version of Microsoft PWS in order to support the new design-time controls and other advanced features.

Sharing Projects Between Microsoft FrontPage and Visual InterDev 6

One of the greatest benefits of using FrontPage and Visual InterDev 6 together is that you can open the same project with two different editors and use the strengths of each tool. For example, you can use FrontPage's visual editor to quickly build static Web documents and use Visual InterDev 6's powerful database connection and server-side scripting tools to add the dynamic portions of your Web site.

Sharing a project between Visual InterDev 6 and FrontPage is really easy. Because FrontPage and Visual InterDev 6 have different project control requirements, each tool has its own special set of files that must exist before the project can be managed by both tools. However, even though different files are required, these files are not incompatible. You just need to get them all together in the same Web project and you're all set.

Sharing Projects Between Microsoft FrontPage and Visual InterDev 6

PART **VII**
APPENDIX **A**

779

Connecting to Existing FrontPage Webs with Visual InterDev 6

If you want to use Visual InterDev 6 to connect to an existing FrontPage Web project, you have three important tasks to keep in mind:

- You must create your own local Visual InterDev 6 project to manage the FrontPage Web.
- When creating the project files, don't create a new Web on the host server; instead, select the existing FrontPage Web.
- When you first build the Visual InterDev 6 project, you must also upload a set of support documents to the FrontPage Web to allow Visual InterDev 6 to work properly.

The next three sections explain these tasks in more detail.

Creating a New Visual InterDev 6 Project

The process of opening a FrontPage Web page from within Visual InterDev 6 means that you really need a local Visual InterDev 6 project from which to start. So you must first create a new Visual InterDev 6 project, because Visual InterDev 6 manages all its documents from within a local project.

When you create your new Visual InterDev 6 project, you can select any local disk drive as the source code location. You can also give the Visual InterDev 6 project any name you want. The only thing you must remember is that the local Visual InterDev 6 project is used by Visual InterDev 6 to create the connection to the FrontPage Web. You cannot use Visual InterDev 6 to connect directly to the FrontPage Web; you need a local project first.

SEE ALSO
▶ *To learn how to create a new Visual InterDev 6 project, see page 8*

Selecting an Existing Web

After selecting a location for the Visual InterDev 6 project and establishing its name, you must select the Web server that hosts the FrontPage Web as the master Web server for the Visual InterDev 6 project. For example, if the FrontPage Web is running on your own workstation (called MyStation), you would select **MyStation** as the Web server to host the Visual InterDev 6 project.

Next, when asked to either create a new Web on the Web host server or connect to an existing Web, you must select **Connect to an existing web**. When you do this, you see a drop-down list of all the Webs published on the selected server. Now you need to locate the FrontPage Web you want to manage from within Visual InterDev 6. When you select this Web, you have connected your local Visual InterDev 6 project to the FrontPage Web (see Figure A.1).

FIGURE A.1

Connecting a new Visual InterDev 6 project to an existing FrontPage Web.

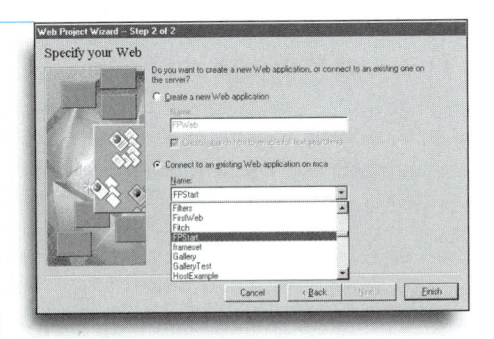

Again, you must connect the Visual InterDev 6 project to the Web server that hosts the FrontPage Web and connect your project to the existing FrontPage Web.

Installing the Visual InterDev 6 Script Library

The last task you must complete in order to allow Visual InterDev 6 to properly manage an existing FrontPage Web is to add the Visual InterDev 6 Script Library to the FrontPage Web. This will allow Visual InterDev 6 to properly support any design-time controls that you use when designing the Visual InterDev 6 pages for the FrontPage Web.

If it's big, it might take some time

The first time you connect your new Visual InterDev 6 project to an existing Web on the host server, Visual InterDev 6 will download all the documents from the remote Web and place them in your local Web on your workstation. If the remote Web is large and the connection speed is slow, this might take a while. This happens only the first time you connect your project to the remote Web.

Sharing Projects Between Microsoft FrontPage and Visual InterDev 6

When you are creating the new Visual InterDev 6 project and connecting to the FrontPage Web for the first time, you'll see a dialog box pop up suggesting that you add the Script Library files to the Web. Although you are given an option to say **NO**, you should answer **YES** unless you are absolutely sure that you will never use DTCs in this Web project. Because they do not take up much space, answer **YES**.

SEE ALSO
➤ *For more on Visual InterDev 6 and design-time controls, see page 544*

Viewing the FrontPage Documents from Within Visual InterDev 6

After you have connected your Visual InterDev 6 project to an existing FrontPage Web, you can use Visual InterDev 6 to edit existing pages and add new pages to the Web. There are a few things to keep in mind when using Visual InterDev 6 to edit a FrontPage Web.

FrontPage and Visual InterDev 6 use entirely different tools for creating site diagrams. You cannot edit a FrontPage site diagram from within Visual InterDev 6. If you are using FrontPage to build your layouts and site diagrams, you should not use Visual InterDev 6 to build a site diagram. This will confuse both you and the Web server!

If you create a FrontPage project that uses navigation bars and then open the project with Visual InterDev 6 and add a new page, that new page will not contain the correct FrontPage theme and border meta tags. That is because FrontPage adds this information when the document is first created and does not add it later. You can easily fix this by added the following two lines to the <HEAD> section of documents built in Visual InterDev 6 that need to participate in FrontPage themes and borders:

```
<meta name="Microsoft Theme" content="none, default">
<meta name="Microsoft Border" content="none, default">
```

Finally, because FrontPage uses a different method for creating themes and borders, you will not see the FrontPage themes and borders when you view the FrontPage-generated document

---

Don't edit the Script Library

After adding the Script Library to the existing FrontPage Web, you must be careful not to edit these files from within FrontPage. This might cause your Web project to crash and be rendered permanently inoperable (a bad thing!).

Don't mix navigation bar sets

If you used FrontPage to create your navigation bars for the Web, do not try to build a site diagram using Visual InterDev 6, too. FrontPage will not understand it, and existing navigation bars on other pages might break, too.

within the Visual InterDev 6 Editor. However, when you submit the page to the host Web server, the themes and borders will appear as they should. Figures A.2 and A.3 show how the FrontPage page looks in the Visual InterDev 6 Editor's quick view and how it looks in the client's browser.

FIGURE A.2

Viewing a FrontPage-generated document in the Visual InterDev 6 Editor Quickview.

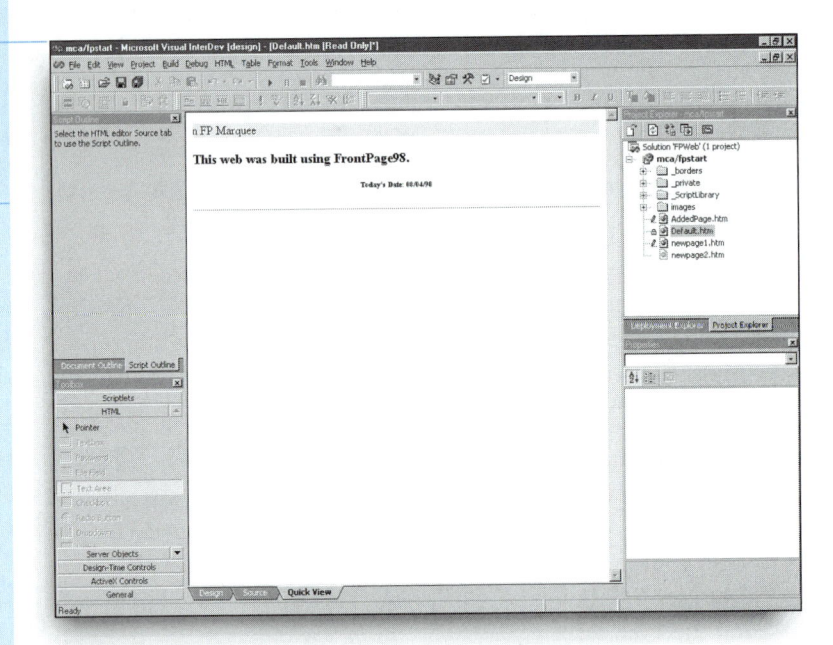

FIGURE A.3

Viewing a FrontPage-generated document in the client's browser.

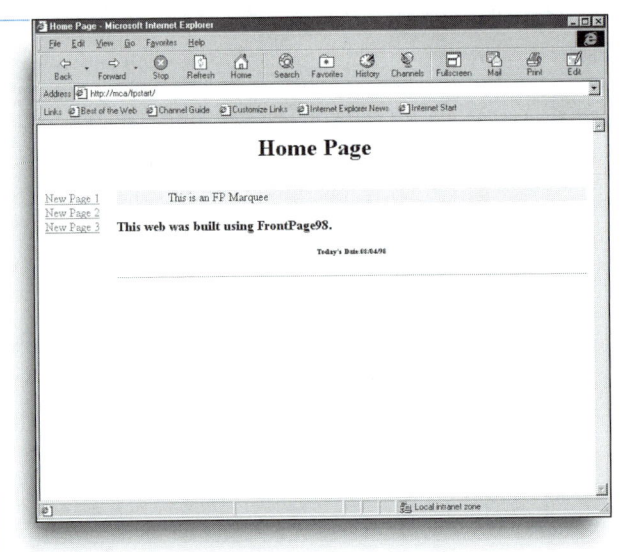

SEE ALSO
➤ *For more on using themes and layouts in Visual InterDev 6, see page 24*

Connecting to Existing Visual InterDev 6 Webs with FrontPage

Connecting your FrontPage editor to an existing Visual InterDev 6 project and editing its documents is easy: Open the existing Web on the master Web server using the FrontPage Explorer. This will automatically create a new FrontPage Web project that you can use to access the Web documents.

After you open the Visual InterDev 6 Web in FrontPage, you can edit the existing documents or add new ones as needed.

Opening the Visual InterDev 6 Web with FrontPage Web

To prepare FrontPage for managing a Web created with Visual InterDev 6, fire up the FrontPage Explorer and open the existing Visual InterDev 6 Web on the host Web server. It is important that you do not create a new FrontPage Web. Instead, use FrontPage to open the existing Web.

Using FrontPage to open a Web created with Visual InterDev 6

1. Start the FrontPage Explorer.
2. Select **Open FrontPage web** from the **File** menu.
3. When the Getting Started dialog box appears, press the **More Webs** button.
4. When the Open FrontPage Web dialog box appears, select the Web host server that contains the Visual InterDev 6 master Web and press the **List Webs** button.
5. When the list box is filled with all the available FrontPage-compatible Webs on the selected server, select the Visual InterDev 6 Web you want to open in FrontPage (see Figure A.4). FrontPage will then dismiss the dialogs and load the completed Web into the FrontPage Explorer.

FIGURE A.4

Selecting a Visual InterDev 6 Web to load into FrontPage.

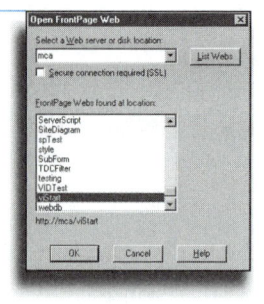

You now have created a valid FrontPage project that links to an existing Visual InterDev 6 Web.

Viewing the Visual InterDev 6 Documents from Within FrontPage

When you load Visual InterDev 6–generated pages in the FrontPage Editor, you'll see several things that look quite different from the Visual InterDev 6 Editor. In most cases, these differences are only cosmetic. However, in some cases, the differences can "break" Visual InterDev 6 functionality if not handled correctly.

Leave the GLOBAL.ASA alone

When you open a Visual InterDev 6 project in FrontPage, you'll see the GLOBAL.ASA file in a list of FrontPage files. Do not attempt to load or edit this file using FrontPage. Visual InterDev 6 uses this to manage key aspects of each user session, and changes to this file can crash your Web project.

First, all the Visual InterDev 6 design-time controls (DTCs) appear as pure text, not as rendered graphic controls as in Visual InterDev 6. Figures A.5 and A.6 show the differences when viewing the source code of a page in FrontPage and Visual InterDev 6.

One nice feature is that when you create the Visual InterDev 6 project and apply a Visual InterDev 6 site diagram to the project, any navigational changes made in FrontPage will be reflected in the Visual InterDev 6 project. In other words, FrontPage understands Visual InterDev 6 site diagram files.

However, how the themes and borders are generated in the FrontPage editor is slightly different than how they are generated in the Visual InterDev 6 editor. For example, when you use FrontPage to add a new document to a Visual InterDev 6–generated project, the Visual InterDev 6 themes and borders material will not be added to the FrontPage document. However, this is easily fixed by reloading the document in Visual InterDev 6 and applying the proper theme and border information.

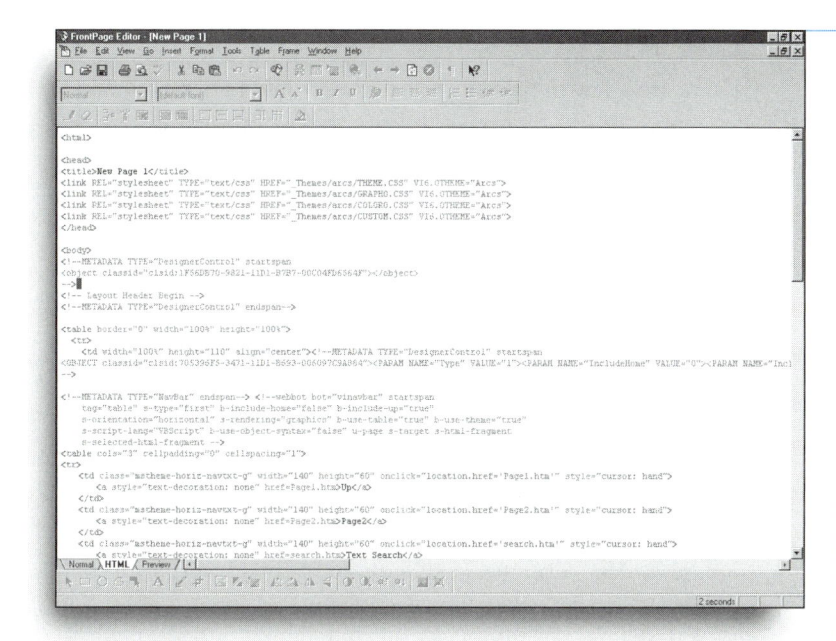

Sharing Projects Between Microsoft FrontPage and Visual InterDev 6   APPENDIX A   785

FIGURE A.5
Viewing a Visual InterDev 6 page with DTCs in FrontPage.

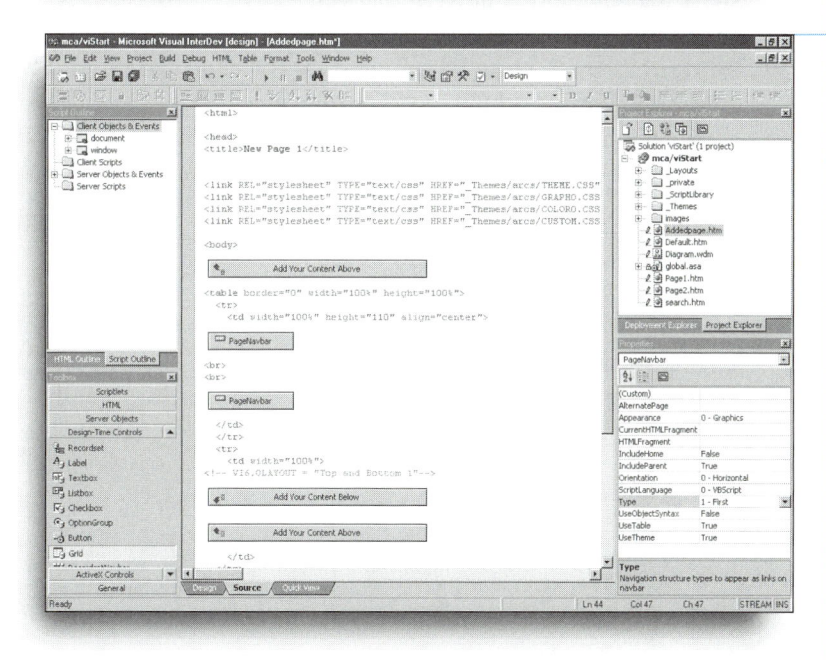

FIGURE A.6
Viewing the same page in the Visual InterDev 6 editor.

FrontPage cannot edit Visual InterDev 6 site diagrams

Although FrontPage honors the information stored in Visual InterDev 6 site diagrams, FrontPage cannot edit the existing Visual InterDev 6 site diagram. Any attempt to do so will render the site diagram useless.

SEE ALSO

> *For more on data-bound DTCs, see page 440*

Some Other Issues to Keep in Mind

There are a few other things that you should understand and remember when you use FrontPage to edit an existing Visual InterDev 6 project. As long as you keep the following items in mind, you should have no problem moving between FrontPage and Visual InterDev 6 project editors.

First, you should not edit any Visual InterDev 6 design-time control (DTC) information while in FrontPage. FrontPage does not understand this DTC information, and changes made while in FrontPage might render the DTC controls useless when they are later opened in Visual InterDev 6.

Next, how FrontPage and Visual InterDev 6 operate on project files is quite different. Visual InterDev 6 enables developers to work in a "local mode" that protects the master Web from updates unless developers explicitly tell Visual InterDev 6 to update the master Web. However, FrontPage does not work in quite the same way. The Web that you edit with FrontPage is just that: a Web. FrontPage does not understand the difference between a local Web and a master Web. If you plan to do a lot of FrontPage/Visual InterDev 6 mixing, you must be sure to remember that FrontPage developers could easily change items in the master Web and that others working in Visual InterDev 6 local mode will not see these changes.

Finally, whether you are in FrontPage or Visual InterDev 6, developers should get in the habit of updating their projects from the master Web server frequently. This will make sure any changes made to the Web are brought into the developer's version of the project and reduce the chance of overwriting another person's work from a previous session.

SEE ALSO
➤ *For more on site diagrams, see page 17*

Editing design-time controls can break them

The Visual InterDev 6 Editor expects the details of design-time controls to appear in a particular order on the page. If you change this order, Visual InterDev 6 will not be able to render the graphic images in the Visual InterDev 6 Editor. If this happens, you might not be able to use the design-time dialogs anymore and might have to delete the DTCs and start again.

Troubleshooting FrontPage and Visual InterDev 6 Problems

Although several possible problems might arise when you mix FrontPage and Visual InterDev 6 on the same machine, two problems continually appear in the Internet newsgroups and come up in training and workshops on Visual InterDev 6. Because they come up so often, it is worthwhile to take a few moments to cover them here.

Cannot Locate Web Server

The first problem comes up quite a bit: You install Visual InterDev 6, following the directions on the CD-ROM and README files to the letter. You even accept the "typical" installations, skipping any custom options that might mess up your machine. Still, after hours of installation headaches, each time you attempt to create a new project with Visual InterDev 6, you get a message telling you that either the selected Web server does not exist or that you cannot connect to the Web server selected.

There are several reasons for getting this error. Here's a troubleshooting list you can start with to solve this problem:

- Be sure that you can connect to the target machines without using Visual InterDev 6. For example, if it is a machine on your local network, try to map a drive to the machine or attempt to connect to an existing Web on that machine with your browser. If it is a remote machine, see whether you can use Telnet, FTP, or some other way to log onto the machine.

- If you know the machine exists, be sure you have rights to access it. You might need to contact the network administrator for this.

- Be sure the machine name is correct. If you are attempting to connect to a Web server that is a UNIX machine, be sure to use the proper upper- and lowercase letters, too.

Windows 95/98 machines are more likely to cause problems

The Visual InterDev 6 developer tool was built with Windows NT in mind. Although it is supported on Windows 95 and 98, several features of Visual InterDev 6 expect to use the NT operating system. If you are having trouble with your Win95 or 98 installation, you might see whether the same problems occur from a WinNT workstation. You might have troubles with Win95 and not Visual InterDev 6.

- If the machine really exists, make sure it has the most recent version of FrontPage Server Extensions installed. You can find these at the Microsoft FrontPage Web site.
- If the machine is a Windows NT workstation or Windows 95/98 machine, make sure that it is using the version of Personal Web Server from the NT/IIS4 Option Pack. If you are not sure, follow the steps outlined in the first part of this chapter to remove FrontPage and any Personal Web Server and install the NT/IIS4 version instead.
- If you know that the NT/IIS4 version of PWS was installed, be sure that subsequent installations of FrontPage did not install their own WPS over the NT/IIS version. The best way to test this is to uninstall FrontPage and the FrontPage Server Extensions, as described earlier in this chapter.
- If you are attempting to contact a Windows NT Server machine, make sure it is using the NT/IIS4 version of Web server and the latest version of FrontPage Server Extensions.

The most common reason for this problem is that the target machine is not running the NT/IIS4 version of the Web server software. If none of the previous suggestions helps, you can visit the Visual InterDev 6 and FrontPage newsgroups on the Internet (see Appendix B) or contact Microsoft for help.

Visual InterDev 6 VINAVBAR Component Broken

Another typical problem is that the Visual InterDev 6 navigation bars created with the theme and layout selections and the site diagram fail to show up properly. Instead, you see only the following text in the client browser:

[Frontpage vinavar component]

This problem occurs when the Web server cannot properly respond to the theme and layout information stored in the Visual InterDev 6 Web. There are two main ways to fix this problem. The first is to simply use the FrontPage admin tools to recalculate the location and contents of the subfolders used to create the navigation bars on pages. The second is to fix an improperly installed set of FrontPage Server Extensions.

Troubleshooting FrontPage and Visual InterDev 6 Problems

First, use FPSRVADM.EXE to fix up internal links to the navigation information. This program is run from the command line and can usually be found in the following folder:

`\Program Files\Microsoft FrontPage\version3.0\bin`

When you run this program, select option **#8** (recalculate links) and leave the Web name blank. This forces the utility to update all FrontPage Webs on that server.

If this does not work (about 50 percent of the time), you probably have a bad set of FrontPage Server Extensions (FPX) installed on the machine. They might be out of date or might be the ones installed with FrontPage instead of the ones that should be installed with Visual InterDev 6. There are details on how to properly install the FPX files in the first section of this chapter.

Keep in mind the following key bits of information when dealing with the FPX sets:

- If FrontPage is installed on the same machine, you should not use the FPX set that ships with FrontPage. Instead, use the FPX set that ships on the Visual InterDev 6 CD-ROMs.
- If FrontPage is not installed on the same machine (for example, on an NT Server), you should not install the FPX set when you are installing the NT/IIS4 Option Pack. Instead, use the FPX set that ships on the Visual InterDev 6 CD-ROMs.

In both cases, it is important to install the FPX set after you have installed the NT/IIS4 Option Pack. When you install FrontPage (if at all) is not important. It is important only that you install FrontPage without installing the FPX set at the same time.

Again, if these fixes don't help, you can visit the Visual InterDev 6 and FrontPage newsgroups in the Web (see Appendix B) or contact Microsoft for assistance.

VINAVBAR problems are usually caused by bad FrontPage Extension installations

The most common reasons for seeing the `[FrontPage VINAVBAR Component]` error is that the proper FrontPage Server Extensions set was not installed. Be sure to read through the suggestions on how to install FrontPage and Visual InterDev 6 on the same machine, earlier in this chapter.

APPENDIX B

Online Resources

Using Visual InterDev 6 Web Site

The official home page for *Using Visual InterDev 6* is

http://www.amundsen.com/uvi6

This site has lots of material to help you get more out of *Using Visual InterDev 6*, including

- Downloadable versions of all the source code in the book
- The latest updates and fixes for the text
- Additional articles and tutorials
- All the links, newsgroup references, and mailing lists mentioned here

Along with the official Web site, there are several other related Web sites, newsgroups, and mailing lists you can access to learn more about Visual InterDev and related issues.

Online Resources

Related Web Sites

Table B.1 lists several Web sites that support Visual InterDev programming and other forms of Web authoring with Microsoft tools. You'll find the most up-to-date version of this list at the official *Using Visual InterDev 6* Web site.

TABLE B.1 Related Web sites

Web Site Address	Comments
www.15seconds.com	A very popular Web site for Active Server Pages technology
www.activeserverpages.com	Devoted to ASP and related programming
www.amundsen.com/vinterdev/default.htm	A general site covering Visual InterDev 6
www.asphole.com	Includes lots of tutorials
www.aspalliance.com	A site devoted to linking fellow ASP sites in an easy-to-navigate "ring"
www.clubsbn.net	A Web server supporting all aspects of Microsoft Web authoring technologies
www.zdjournals.com	Ziff-Davis/*Cobb Journal* site supporting Visual InterDev 6, ASP, Microsoft Internet Explorer, and other technologies
www.genusa.com/asp/	A site dedicated to ASP programming
www.microsoft.com/data	Microsoft site supporting various data connection technologies, including ADO and RDS
www.microsoft.com/frontpage	Microsoft site for news and information on FrontPage Web authoring tool
www.microsoft.com/ie	Visit this site to get the latest on Microsoft's Internet browser tool
www.microsoft.com/scripting	Microsoft site for Visual Basic scripting and Java scripting support and information
www.microsoft.com/vinterdev	Microsoft's official home page for Visual InterDev 6
www.microsoft.com/vstudio	Microsoft main Web site for all the Visual Studio products, including Visual InterDev 6

Web Site Address	Comments
www.microsoft.com/sitebuilder	Microsoft site dedicated to all aspects of building and maintaining Web sites
www.banick.com	Author's Web site for Steven Banick, contributor on this book and author of other Visual InterDev references

Related Newsgroups

There are several newsgroups you can monitor to learn more about Visual InterDev 6 and related topics. Table B.2 shows a list of some of the more active newsgroups. You'll find a more updated list at the *Using Visual InterDev 6* Web site.

TABLE B.2 Related newsgroups

Newsgroup Name
Microsoft.public.ado.*
Microsoft.public.ado.rds
Microsoft.public.inetserver.*
Microsoft.public.inetsdk.programming.scripting.*
Microsoft.public.vinterdev.*
Microsoft.public.inetexplorer.*

Cobb Web sites (www.zdjorunals.com) also host discussion forums for many of the same topics. There are also several private newsgroup servers that cover Visual InterDev 6–related material, including

- news.clubsbn.net for selected SiteBuilder members
- www.devx.com for subscribers of *Visual Basic Programmer's Journal* and other related publications

Related Mailing Lists

You can also sign up to receive discussion postings in your email box. Table B.3 shows some of the various Visual InterDev 6–related lists you can join. The most updated list can be found at the *Using Visual InterDev 6* Web site.

TABLE B.3 Related mailing lists

Title	Subscription Address	Other Info
VI6News	www.amundsen.com/ vinterdev/join/ default.htm	
ASP Free For All	Listserv@mailexperts.com	Write subscribe aspfreeforall [*Your Name*] in the BODY of the message.
ASP Newbies ListServ	Majordomo@bcpub.com	Write subscribe aspnewbie [*your@email*] in the BODY of the message.

About Other Online Resources

The list of available online resources for Visual InterDev 6 information is constantly changing. If you see items in these pages that are no longer active or see that an item is missing from these pages, feel free to send your suggestions and updates to vi6_resources@amundsen.com.

APPENDIX C

Glossary

This glossary contains terms related to Visual InterDev and the Internet. Even though acronyms with the Internet and Microsoft change on a daily basis, this glossary includes as many as possible. Cross-references for acronyms direct you to the correct entries. Cross-references to related topics (shown in boldface) are listed at the ends of the definitions.

1-Bit Color The number of colors per *pixel* a particular graphics file can store. Having 1-bit color means that each pixel is represented by one bit, which has only one of two states or colors. The 1-bit pixels are either black or white. (See also **Color Depth**.)

8-Bit Color/Grayscale Having 8-bit color means that each pixel is represented by eight bits, which can have 256 colors or shades of gray (as in a *grayscale* image). (See also **Color Depth** and **Grayscale**.)

24-Bit Color A 24-bit color provides 16.7 million colors per *pixel*. The 24 bits are divided into 3 bytes: one each for the red, green, and blue components of a pixel. (See also **Color Depth**, **True Color**, and **Channel**.)

2B+D The ISDN Basic Rate Interface (BRI) that consists of a single ISDN circuit divided into two 64Kbps digital channels for voice or data and one 16Kbps channel for low-speed data and signaling. 2B+D is carried on one or two pairs of wires. (See also **BRI** and **ISDN**.)

3D Graphics   The process of creating three-dimensional models within the computer's memory, setting up lights, and applying textures. After the computer is told from which angle to view the 3D scene, it generates an image that simulates the conditions defined in the scene. Three-dimensional animation involves the same steps but sets up the choreography, or movement, of the 3D objects, lights, or cameras. (See also **Texture Mapping**.)

Access   (See **Microsoft Access**.)

Active Server Application (ASA)   An Active Server Page (.ASP) containing global session settings and information. This file is used for maintaining global behaviors and attributes for a Web application. Typically used for establishing database connections and maintaining session controls. (See also **Active Server Page (.ASP)**.)

Active Server Page (.ASP)   A Web page or file that includes server-side script executed by Microsoft Internet Information Server. The .ASP extension alerts the server that the file should be processed before sending it to the client's browser. After it is processed, it is delivered to the browser in the same manner as an HTML file. (See also **Active Server Application**.)

ActiveMovie   A Microsoft technology for streaming video content across the Internet.

ActiveX Control Container   A program capable of running an ActiveX control.

ActiveX Controls   Small software components used by larger applications to accomplish a specific task. These controls can be downloaded and installed on-the-fly as needed. They have .OCX filename extensions. ActiveX controls can be written in virtually any language such as Java, C++, or Visual Basic. (See also **OLE Control**.)

ActiveX Data Objects (ADO)   A cross-language technology for accessing data based on an object model that incorporates data connection objects, data command objects, and recordset objects. (See also **Data Command**, **Data Connection**, **Data Environment**, and **Recordset**.)

Advanced Data Connector (ADC) A distributed data access technology for the Web. Microsoft's Advanced Data Connector provides data manipulation over retrieved data, client-side caching, and integration with data-aware ActiveX controls.

Advanced Data TableGram Streaming Protocol (ADTG) An application protocol for streaming database data over HTTP. It defines a concept for a tablegram, a self-describing data blob that supports transport of any type of data.

Alpha Channel An additional piece of information stored for a pixel that represents the pixel's transparency. An image, composed of many *pixels*, often has a separate channel for red, green, and blue. (See also **Pixel** and **Channel**.)

Animation The illusion of movement caused by the rapid display of a series of still images. When each image differs slightly, and the images are viewed at speeds of over 10 per second, the eye perceives motion.

Antialiasing The process of smoothing edges where the individual pixels are visible. Antialiasing removes the stair-stepping effect caused by large square pixels that the eye can see.

Applet A Java program that can be embedded within an HTML page and run within a Java-enabled browser.

Argument Data passed to a procedure.

Array In programming, a fundamental data structure consisting of a single or multidimensional table that the program treats as one data item. Any information in the array can be referenced by naming the array and the location of the item in the array. Each piece of information in the array is called an *element*.

ASCII Character Set American Standard Code for Information Interchange. A standard code that assigns a unique binary number to each character in the English alphabet along with other special characters. The first 128 characters (0 through 127) in the ANSI character set are identical to those in the ASCII character set.

Aspect Ratio   The height-to-width ratio of an image. (The standard for a television frame is 4:3.)

Automation Object   Microsoft's new term to describe objects exposed to other applications or programming tools through Automation interfaces.

B Channel   An ISDN communication channel that carries voice, circuit, or packet conversations. The B channel is the fundamental component of ISDN interfaces and carries 64,000 bits per second in either direction. (See also **ISDN**.)

Backbone   A high-speed network for networked computers.

Bandwidth   The amount of data that can be sent through a connection, usually measured in bits per second (bps).

Binary   Having only two states, On and Off, or 0 and 1. A light switch could be considered a *binary* switch because it is either on or off, and no other settings are possible.

Bit   A *binary* unit of storage that can represent only one of two values: On and Off, or 0 and 1 (BInary digiT).

Bitwise Comparison   A comparison of two numeric expressions made by examining the position of their bits. (See also **Bit** and **Byte**.)

Blurring Filter   A special effects filter that simulates an out-of-focus photograph.

BMP   A BitMaP file. A graphics file format used as a standard for the Microsoft Windows GUI. It stores *raster graphics* images. (See also **File Format** and **Raster Graphics**.)

Boolean Expression   An expression that evaluates to either True or False.

Bounding Box   A square box created by clicking and dragging the mouse. Often used in graphical user interfaces to select an object or group of objects on the screen.

BRI (Basic Rate Interface)   The most common ISDN interface available. It uses two B channels, each with 64Kbps capacity, and a single D channel (16Kbps) for signaling. (See also **ISDN**.)

Brightness   A component of the HSB (Hue, Saturation, and Brightness) color model. For RGB pixels, the largest component value is the brightness. (See also **HSB** and **RGB**.)

Browse   To navigate the World Wide Web. Also known as cruising and surfing the Web.

Burning   Darkening specific areas of a photograph. Originally used in the darkroom with traditional photographic equipment, this process is now simulated by all image-editing programs. (See also **Dodging** and **Painting Tool**.)

By Reference   A method of passing the address of an argument to a procedure instead of the value. This capability allows the procedure to change the variable's actual value. (See also **Argument** and **By Value**.)

By Value   A method of passing the value of an argument to a procedure instead of the address. This capability allows the procedure to access a copy of the variable without changing the variable's actual value. (See also **Argument** and **By Reference**.)

Byte   A unit of storage composed of eight *bits*. It can store a numeric value from 0 to 255 (decimal) or one letter. (See also **Bit**.)

Cascading Style Sheets   A set of tags that describe the appearance of HTML tags. Style sheets can describe the font, color, alignment and other attributes for common HTML tags such as headings, paragraphs, and lists. Style sheets can be defined in a Web page, in a tag, or in a separate CSS file. Style sheet information is used only by browsers that support the standard.

CGI   Common Gateway Interface. A standard that describes how Web servers should access external programs that can return data in the format of a Web page. CGI programs are commonly called scripts.

Channel   One piece of information stored with an image. *True Color* images, for example, have three *channels*: red, green, and blue.

Character Code   A number used to represent a character in a set, such as the ASCII character set. (See also **ASCII Character Set**.)

Chatting Talking in real-time to other network users from any and all parts of the world, either through text or multimedia-based methods.

Class In programming, a formal definition of an object's properties and methods. It acts as the template from which an instance of an object is created at runtime. (See also **Object**, **Methods**, and **Properties**.)

Class Module The definition of a class' properties and methods. (See also **Object, Class**, **Methods**, and **Property**.)

Client/Server Architecture A design model for applications running on a network in which the bulk of the back-end processing—such as performing a physical search of a database—takes place on a server. The front-end processing, which involves communicating with the user, is handled by smaller programs distributed to the client workstations. This architecture is commonly used for database systems. (See also **Database** and **Structured Query Language**.)

Clone Tool A popular tool in image-editing programs that allows small groups of pixels to be copied from one location to another. (See also **Painting Tool**.)

CMYK The four colors used for color printing: Cyan, Magenta, Yellow, and Black.

Collection A special type of object that contains a set of other objects. (See also **Object**.)

Color Correction The process of correcting or enhancing the color of an image.

Color Depth The amount of color stored in an image expressed in *bits*. An image with a 24-bit color depth can have 16.7 million colors. An image with 8-bit color depth can have only 256 colors or shades of gray. (See also **1-Bit**, **8-Bit**, and **24-Bit**.)

Color Model A method of describing color. (See also **HLS**, **HSB**, and **RGB**.)

Color Similarity A description of how close two different colors are to each other within the respective color model being used. (See also **Color Model**.)

Comment Information added to a program to document how the code works.

Comparison Operator (See **Relational Operator**.)

Compositing The process of merging two or more images together digitally.

Compression A means by which the amount of data required to store a computer file is reduced. (See also **File Format, Fractal Compression, Lossey Compression, JPEG, Huffman Compression,** and **LZW**.)

Computer Generated Created on or by the computer. Any image that was not scanned in from an existing original.

Control (See **ActiveX Controls, Object,** and **OLE Control**.)

Constant A variable in a program that always remains the same. Constants make programming easier because a name can be used to refer to a value instead of the value itself. For example,

```
Const MyForm = Window.Document.Form("DataCollection")
```

Cookie A small piece of data used to store persistent information on the user's computer in the form of a file.

Cropping Tool A tool that simulates the traditional method of cropping or trimming photographs. (See also **Painting Tool**.)

Custom Filter A special image filter that can be defined by the user. Values are entered on a matrix grid. Those values, in turn, determine how the filter affects each pixel in an image.

D Channel An ISDN communication channel for sending information between the ISDN equipment and the ISDN central office switch. (See also **ISDN**.)

Data Binding Using data-aware ActiveX controls to directly manipulate databases.

Data Command An object in the data environment used to access a database object (such as a table, stored procedure, script, or view). Commands are used within Web pages to interact with databases. (See also **ActiveX Data Object (ADO), Data Connection, Data Environment,** and **Recordset**.)

Data Connection   A collection of information used by a Visual InterDev project to communicate with a database. The collection includes a data source name (DSN) and logon information. (See also **ActiveX Data Object (ADO)**, **Data Command**, **Data Environment**, and **Recordset**.)

Data Diagram   A graphical representation of any portion of a database schema. (See also **Schema**.)

Data Environment   A repository in Visual InterDev projects that holds database access information in the form of data connections and data commands. (See also **ActiveX Data Object (ADO)**, **Data Command**, **Data Connection**, and **Recordset**.)

Data Ranges   The allowable range of data that a particular variable can accept.

Data Type   A classification for both programming variables and database fields. Common data types include numeric, string, date, and so on.

Database   A collection of related information stored in a structured, organized way. Using this structured collection, standard methods of retrieving data can be used. (See also **Table**, **Record**, and **Field**.)

Date Expression   Any type of value that can be interpreted as a date. It can be a string or number that represents a date. Dates are usually stored as part of a floating-point number with the values to the left of the decimal representing the date and the values to the right of the decimal representing the time.

Default Setting   Typically used in computer programs to set any variables or values to a common setting or setting that is most likely to be used.

Despeckle Filter   A special filter that removes any specks from the image. It actually blurs the entire image except for any edges.

Dialog Box   Any type of screen in a graphical user interface that displays or requests information from the user.

Diffusion Dithering   A method of dithering that randomly distributes pixels instead of using a set pattern. (See also **Dithering**.)

Digital   A form of representation in which information or objects (digits) are broken down into separate pieces. Numbers are examples of *digital* information. *Digital* is the opposite of *analog* information, such as sound and light waves.

Digital Painting   Creating artwork on a computer directly as opposed to using traditional media and scanning the artwork.

Digital Signature   A security technique consisting of attaching a code to a software component that identifies the vendor of the component.

Digital-to-Analog Converter (DAC)   A tool that converts *digital* information, such as numeric data, into analog information, such as a sound waves.

Digitizing   The process of converting analog information into a digital format. Recording sound into a computer and capturing video or pictures on a computer are considered digitizing.

Directories   Electronic areas on a computer disk for storing data files—similar to storing letters in a folder. A directory can be considered an electronic folder. (See also **File**.)

Dithering   A method of simulating many colors with only a few. If a limited number of color dots are placed closely together, the eye blends them into a new color. (See also **Diffusion Dithering**.)

Dodging   Lightening specific areas of a photograph. Originally used in the darkroom with traditional photographic equipment, this process is now simulated by all image-editing programs. (See also **Burning**.)

Domain Name   (See **Domain Name Service**.)

Domain Name Service (DNS)   A program that runs on an Internet-connected computer system (called a DNS server) and provides an automatic translation between domain names (such as netst.com) and IP addresses (such as 207.199.32.76). The purpose of this translation process, called resolution, is to allow Internet users to use simple domain names to reference computers as opposed to IP addresses.

DPI   Dots Per Inch. A resolution for scanning and printing devices.

Dynamic HTML (DHTML)   An extension to HTML that allows all elements in a Web page to be treated as scriptable objects. Using DHTML, the appearance, content, and behavior of a Web page can be directly altered by a client-side script.

Emboss   A common image processing filter that simulates the look of a picture that is embossed on paper or metal.

Empty   A value that indicates that no beginning value has been assigned to a variable. Empty variables are 0 in a numeric context or zero-length in a string context.

Encryption   The process of converting information into codes that cannot be deciphered.

EPS   An Encapsulated PostScript graphics file. This format can store both *raster* and *vector* graphics. (See also **File Format**, **Raster Graphics**, and **Vector Graphics**.)

Equalization   A method of enhancing an image by evenly distributing the color or gray values of pixels throughout the image.

Error Number   A number representing the current error condition of a program. A property of the Error Object. (See also **Error Object**.)

Error Object   A common programming object used to trap errors. (See also **Error Number**.)

Event   When a user clicks or otherwise manipulates objects in a Web page or ActiveX control, an event is generated. The program or script can then respond to this event. For example, when a button object is used, the process of actually clicking the button triggers a "click" event.

Expression   A line of instructions in a program to accomplish a given task.

Extranet   An area of a Web site accessible only to a set of registered visitors beyond the internal network. (See also **Intranet**.)

Eye Dropper Tool   An image-editing tool used to select a color from the current image.

Fade   In film or video, the smooth transition from one sequence to another. Often fades are made to a solid color such as black.

FAQ (Frequently Asked Questions)   A list that attempts to answer the most-asked questions on a given topic. Many FAQs are transmitted monthly over Usenet and are archived on the Internet.

Field   A space reserved for a particular type of information stored in a database. For example, if the telephone book were a database, the fields would be Name, Address, and Phone. A field also is a column of a data table. (See also **Database**, **Table**, and **Record**.)

FIF   The Fractal Image Format. A method of storing *raster graphics* and compressing them with *fractal transform* formulas. (See also **File Format** and **Raster Graphics**.)

File   A collection of data organized on some type of storage media such as a hard disk or a floppy disk.

File Format   The specific type of organization a given file uses. Some file formats are strictly for word processing documents (such as DOC files), whereas others are for graphics or images (such as BMP, GIF, JPG, and so on). Most file formats support some form of data compression to save storage space. (See also **Compression**.)

Fill Tool   A common painting tool used to fill a solid area with color. (See also **Painting Tool**.)

Firewall   A security procedure that sets up a barrier between an internal LAN and the Internet. Commonly implemented by software on a network server, it prevents hackers from gaining access to an internal network.

Floating Palettes   Groups of icons grouped together that perform functions. Palettes can be freely positioned anywhere on the screen with a *graphical user interface*. (See also **Icons**.)

FoxPro   (See **Microsoft Visual FoxPro**.)

Fractal Compression   A compression method developed by Michael Barnsley. It reduces images to a series of fractal-based formulas for very high compression levels. (See also **File Format**, **FIF**, and **Compression**.)

Function   A group of program instructions stored under a name so that it can be executed as a unit and return a value. (See also **Procedure**.)

Gamma   A measure of contrast that affects the middle tones in an image.

Gaussian Blur   A blurring filter that can be adjusted to provide very high levels of blurring. (See also **Blurring Filter**.)

GIF   The Graphics Interchange Format. A common graphics format for storing *raster graphics*. This format was made popular by the CompuServe online service and is supported by a number of *hardware* platforms. (See also **File Format** and **Raster Graphics**.)

Gigabyte   A unit of computer storage representing one billion *bytes*. (See also **Byte**.)

Gradient Fill   An enhancement to the Fill tool that fills an area with a gradual transition from one color to another.

Gray/Color Correction   The process of adjusting the gray or color levels of an image to enhance its quality.

Gray/Color Map   A method of adjusting the gray or color levels in an image. A 2D line graph represents the incoming and outgoing brightness or color values.

Grayscale   An image that contains continuous tones from white to black.

GUID (Globally Unique ID)   A sequence of letters and numbers that uniquely identify each OLE component registered on a computer system. When OLE objects are embedded in Web pages, this ID specifies which objects are to be used. These IDs are stored in the Windows 95 or Windows NT system registries.

Halftone   The *screening* of a continuous-tone image into small dots of varying sizes. (See also **Screening**.)

Highlight   The lightest areas of an image.

HLS (Hue, Lightness, and Saturation)   A color model based on the hue, lightness, and saturation of a color. (See also **Color Model**, **Hue**, **Saturation**, and **Lightness**.)

Home page   The first Web page of a Web site.

HSB (Hue, Saturation, and Brightness) A color model based on the hue, saturation, and brightness of a color. (See also **Color Model**, **Hue**, **Saturation**, and **Brightness**.)

HTML (Hypertext Markup Language) The language used to create conventional Web pages.

HTTP (Hypertext Transfer Protocol) The native communications scheme of the World Wide Web, initially used to transfer hypertext documents.

HTTP Server Hypertext Transfer Protocol Server; a computer (server) that serves HTML documents.

Hue Another term used to describe color. Hue usually represents the color without its brightness or *saturation*.

Huffman Compression A method of compressing data developed by David Huffman in 1952. Commonly used to compress graphics files. (See also **File Format** and **Compression**.)

Hyperlink A reference in HTML to another hypertext segment.

Hypertext A system of writing and displaying text that enables the text to be linked in several ways. Hypertext documents can also contain links to related documents, such as those referred to in footnotes. Hypermedia can also contain pictures, sounds, and video.

Icons Small graphics symbols used to represent programs, data, or other functions within a *graphical user interface*.

Image Processing The capture and manipulation of images in order to enhance or extract information.

Imagemap A graphic image embedded within a Web page that supplies different links, based on where the cursor is clicked within its borders.

Internet A worldwide system of linked computer networks for data communication services such as remote login, World Wide Web, electronic mail, file transfer, and newsgroups. The Internet provides a way of connecting existing computer networks that greatly extends the reach of each participating system. Originally designed to withstand a nuclear attack, today the Internet spans almost every national border on the Earth. (See also **Intranet**.)

Intranet   An internal network designed around existing Internet standard protocols such as HTTP. (See also **Internet**.)

Intrinsic Constant   A constant parameter built into an application. (See also **Constant**.)

Invert Filter   A filter that inverts the pixel values of an image, creating a negative.

IP (Internet Protocol)   In TCP/IP, the standard that describes how an Internet-connected computer should break down data into packets for transmission across the network, and how those packets should be addressed so they arrive at their destination.

ISAPI (Internet Server Application Programming Interface)   A standard method to write programs that communicate with Web servers through OLE.

ISDN (Integrated Services Digital Network)   A digital telephone network that carries voice, data, and video information over the existing telephone wiring. It offers up to 10 times the speed of normal analog data transmission.

Jaggies   The jagged "stair-stepping" effect often seen in images in which the *resolution* is so small that the individual *pixels* are visible. (See also **Antialiasing**.)

Java   A development language that allows Web developers to create applications for the Internet. Java is based on the C++ development language, and the resulting applications can be executed on any computer platform: Macintosh, PC, or UNIX.

JavaScript   A language created by Netscape that can be used to expand the capabilities of a Web page. Like VBScript, JavaScript instructions are embedded within an HTML document for a page. JavaScript is based on the Java language, which is similar to C++. (See also **JScript**.)

JScript   The Microsoft implementation of JavaScript. Although fundamentally the same as JavaScript, it does have some differences and compatibility problems. Most conflicts arise out of JavaScript features that are not present in JScript. (See also **JavaScript**.)

JPEG A file format and compression method for storing images named after the committee that developed it (Joint Photographic Experts Group). The JPEG compression algorithm is a *lossey* compression technique. (See also **File Format** and **Lossey Compression**.)

Keyword A reserved word or symbol in a programming language.

Kilobyte A unit of storage that represents one thousand *bytes*. Often referred to as KB, as in 640KB. (See also **Byte**.)

Lightness A component of the HLS color space. It is determined by taking the average maximum and minimum values in each RGB channel. Sometimes called Luminance. (See also **HLS**, **Color Model**, and **Channel**.)

Local Mode The state of a Web project that allows a developer to modify copies of files on the local workstation without affecting the master Web files. (See also **Master Mode**.)

Lossey Compression A method of compressing images by throwing away unneeded data. JPEG is a lossey compression method. (See also **File Format** and **JPEG**.)

LPI Lines Per Inch. A measure of resolution, often used to describe screens. (See also **Resolution** and **Screening**.)

LZW (Lempel Ziv Welch) A compression algorithm based on work done by Abraham Lempel, Jacob Ziv, and Terry Welch. Commonly used for compressing graphics files. (See also **File Format** and **Compression**.)

Magic Wand A painting tool that selects any range of similar, adjoining colors. Most magic wand tools include a similarity or tolerance setting. (See also **Painting Tool**.)

Mask A special type of image that can be used as a stencil or mask for any painting operation that might be made.

Master Mode The state of a Web project that allows a developer to directly modify the master Web files on the Web server as changes are made. (See also **Local Mode**.)

Megabyte   A unit of storage that represents one million *bytes*. Often referred to as a "Meg." (See also **Byte**.)

Menu Bar   In *graphical user interfaces*, a bar that organize groups of commands in *menus* along the top of a program's window. (See also **Menus**.)

Menus   Groups of related commands provided in a list that drops down from a *menu bar*. Used in *graphical user interfaces*. (See also **Menu Bar**.)

Metafile   A type of file format for graphics that stores both *raster* and *vector* graphics. (See also **File Format**.)

Methods   The actions that can be taken against an object. For example, to add a new item to a `list box` object, the `additem` method can be called. (See also **Object** and **Property**.)

Microsoft Access   Microsoft's entry-level database management system that ships with Microsoft Office Professional. (See also **Database**, **Microsoft Visual FoxPro**, and **Microsoft SQL Server**.)

Microsoft Developer Studio   Microsoft's integrated development environment. Used for Visual InterDev, Visual C++, and Visual J++. (See also **Microsoft Visual InterDev**, **Microsoft Visual C++**, and **Microsoft Visual J++**.)

Microsoft FrontPage   Microsoft's entry-level Web site publishing tool. It is compatible with Web sites built with Visual InterDev. (See also **Microsoft Visual InterDev**.)

Microsoft SQL Server   Microsoft's high-end, client/server database application. (See also **Database**, **Client/Server Architecture**, **Microsoft Access**, and **Microsoft Visual FoxPro**.)

Microsoft Visual C++   Microsoft's C++ language development environment that runs in Developer Studio. (See also **Database**, **Java**, and **Microsoft Developer Studio**.)

Microsoft Visual FoxPro   Microsoft's mid-level database management system. (See also **Database**, **Microsoft Access**, and **Microsoft SQL Server**.)

Microsoft Visual InterDev   A rapid application development tool for building data-driven Web sites. (See also **Database**.)

Microsoft Visual J++   Microsoft's Java language development environment that runs in Developer Studio. (See also **Database**, **Java**, and **Microsoft Developer Studio**.)

MIME (Multipurpose Internet Mail Extension)   A method for transmitting binary files across the Internet.

Name Server   A computer that provides translation between alphabetical Internet domain names and numerical IP addresses. (See also **Internet**, **Domain Name**, and **IP**.)

NI1 (National ISDN 1)   A common standard specification for ISDN phone lines. (See also **ISDN**.)

Noise Filter   An image *filter* that adds random noise (pixels) to an image to simulate a grainy look.

Nothing   A value that, when assigned to an object variable, removes it from its object. (See also **Object**.)

NT-1 (Network Termination 1)   A device required to connect ISDN terminal equipment to an ISDN line.

Null   A value that represents no valid data.

Object   A modular, self-contained program that can be included in larger projects or combined with other objects to create an application. Objects have both methods and properties. Methods allow the object to perform an action, and properties store data related to the object. (See also **ActiveX Controls** and **OLE Control**.)

ODBC   Open Database Connectivity. A standard protocol for database servers. If a database has an ODBC driver, it can be connected with almost any industry standard database tool. (See also **Database**.)

OLE Control   Small software components that accomplish a specific task, such as provide a radio button, command button, or combo box. These controls greatly simplify the task of writing software for complex graphical user interfaces. (See **ActiveX Controls** and **Object**.)

Paint Palette   An electronic version of an artist's palette. It allows the user to select from a wide variety of colors or even mix new ones.

Paintbrush   A *painting tool* that simulates painting with a paintbrush. (See also **Painting Tool**.)

Painting Tool   A command or function of an image-editing program that simulates a traditional art or photographic tool. The *Paintbrush tool* is an example of a painting tool that simulates paintbrush strokes.

PC PaintBrush Format (PCX)   A graphics file format that stores *raster* graphics. Made popular by Zsoft's PC PaintBrush program. (See also **File Format**.)

PCD   The Photo CD format. Kodak uses this graphics file format to store images on Photo CDs. (See also **File Format**, **Raster Graphics**, and **Photo CD**.)

PCX   The graphics file format created by Zsoft's PC PaintBrush program. This graphics file format stores *raster graphics images*. (See also **File Format** and **Raster Graphics**.)

Pencil Tool   A *painting tool* that simulates drawing with a sharp pencil. (See also **Painting Tool**.)

Photo CD   A new technology developed by Eastman Kodak to scan high-resolution 35mm or professional-quality images and write them to a CD-ROM. The resulting PCD (Photo CD) can be viewed with consumer players that attach to televisions. They can also be viewed on personal computers that have multisession-compatible CD-ROM drives.

Photoshop   An image-editing program available from Adobe Systems.

Pixel   A picture element. The smallest element of an image that has been *digitized* into a computer. The more pixels per square inch, the higher the resolution of the image will be.

Pixellization   The effect when the *pixels* making up an image are so large that they are visible.

Private   A procedure or variable that is visible only to its current procedure. (See also **Scope**, **Public**, and **Procedure**.)

Procedural Textures   The use of shaders, or small pieces of programming code, for describing 3D surfaces, lighting effects, and atmospheric effects.

Procedure   A group of program instructions stored under a name so that it can be executed as a unit. (See also **Function**.)

Process Color   The four color pigments used in color printing. (See also **CMYK**.)

Property   Data associated with an object. For example, a label object has a `caption` property, which stores the text displayed as the label's caption. (See also **Object** and **Methods**.)

Proxy Server   An intermediary server that acts as a security barrier between an internal network and the Internet.

Public   A procedure or variable that is visible to all parts of a program. Variables declared using the `Public` statement are visible to all procedures in all modules in all applications. (See also **Scope**, **Private**, and **Procedure**.)

Raster Graphics   Computer graphics in which the images are stored as groups of *pixels*, as opposed to *vector graphics*, which are stored as groups of lines. (See also **File Format** and **Vector Graphics**.)

Record   A collection of related data in a database. For example, if the telephone book were a database, a record would be all the information about a single person. (See also **Database**, **Table**, and **Field**.)

Recordset   An ActiveX Data Object used by Visual InterDev to display information from a data command in a Web page. (See also **ActiveX Data Object (ADO)**, **Data Command**, **Data Connection**, and **Data Environment**.)

Registry   A database within the Windows 95 and Windows NT operating systems that contains information about a computer and its configuration.

Relational Operator   A symbol used to specify a relationship between two pieces of data. The result of using a calculation with relational operators is always a Boolean (True or False).

Render   To create a new image based on a transformation of an existing one or a three-dimensional scene.

Resize   To alter the resolution or the horizontal or vertical size of an image.

Resolution For computer displays, their height and width in pixels; for images, the height and width in pixels; and for output devices, the dots-per-inch they can produce.

Reverse Cropping The process of artificially extending the boundaries of an image to obtain more space. Performed by duplicating existing elements in the image.

RGB (Red, Green, and Blue) A color model that describes color based on percentages of red, green, and blue. Commonly used by computers and television to produce or simulate color. (See also **Color Model**, **HLS**, and **HSB**.)

Ripple Filter A filter that creates fluid ripples in an image, simulating waves in water.

Runtime In programming, the time when a program is running.

Runtime Error A programming error that manifests itself only while the program is running.

Saturation The degree to which color is undiluted by white light. If a color is 100 percent saturated, it contains no white light. If a color has no saturation, it is a shade of gray.

Scan Rate A measurement of how many times per second a scanner samples an image; also, a measurement for the speed that a monitor's electron beam scans from left to right and top to bottom.

Scanline A single line of pixels displayed on a computer monitor to be scanned in by a *scanner*. (See also **Scanner**.)

Scanner A hardware device for converting light from a source picture or transparency into a digital representation.

Schema A description of a database to the database management system.

Scope The visibility of a variable, procedure, or object. Scope is either public or private. (See also **Private**, **Public**, and **Procedure**.)

Screening   The process of converting a grayscale image to patterns of black and white dots that can be printed commercially. In the case of color images, the color is split into primaries, and they, in turn, are individually screened. Those screens are then printed in their respective primary colors, and the original color image reappears.

Script Level   Any scripting code located outside a procedure.

Selection   An area of computer data that is currently chosen to perform some type of operation.

Selection Border   An option used to select only the border of the current selection. (See also **Selection**.)

Server   A software package connected to a network that supplies information or services based on the requests of a connecting client program.

Session   The course of a visit by a user to a Web site.

Shadow   The darkest area of an image.

Shareware   Computer software that is copyrighted but still made available for anyone on a trial basis. If the user decides to keep and use the software, he or she is expected to pay a registration fee to the author.

Sharpening   A process that increases contrast between pixels, with the end result of a more defined-looking image. (See also **Smoothing**.)

Shockwave   An extension for the Web that allows users to view multimedia content originally authored with Macromedia tools such as Director, Authorware, and Flash.

Slider   A method of entering numeric values used in graphical user interfaces. If the slider is moved back and forth, numeric values can be adjusted.

Smoothing   A process that averages pixels with their neighbors, thus reducing contrast and simulating an out-of-focus image. (See also **Sharpening**.)

Solorization The photographic effect of reducing the number of colors in an image. This effect is also simulated by many image-editing programs.

Solution A Visual Studio container that holds the elements that comprise multiple projects. These projects may be Web applications or database connections. (See also **Web Application**.)

Sphere Filter A special effects filter that simulates wrapping the current image around a three-dimensional sphere.

SPID (Service Profile Identifier) A unique identification number for each ISDN modem. (See also **ISDN**.)

SQL (See **Structured Query Language**.)

SQL Server (See **Microsoft SQL Server**.)

S/T Interface Used with a four-wire ISDN circuit, it connects an ISDN line that connects to the terminal equipment or ISDN modem. (See also **ISDN**.)

Status Bar An information bar common in graphical user interfaces. Status bars display important information about the current status of the document or file in use.

String A data type for containing alphanumeric characters.

Structured Query Language (SQL) In database management systems, an IBM-developed query language widely used in mainframe and minicomputer systems. It's also gaining acceptance on PC-based local area networks (LANs). SQL is an elegant and concise query language with only 30 commands. The four basic commands (SELECT, INSERT, UPDATE, and DELETE) correspond to the four basic functions of data manipulation (data retrieval, data insertion, data modification, and data deletion, respectively). SQL queries approximate the structure of the English natural-language query. A data table consisting of columns (corresponding to fields) and rows (corresponding to records) displays a query's results. (See also **Database**, **Record**, **SQL Server**, and **Field**.)

T1 A high-bandwidth telephone trunk line that can transfer 1.544 megabits per second (Mbps) of data. (See also **T3**.)

T3 A very high-bandwidth telephone trunk line that can transfer 44.21 megabits per second (Mbps) of data. (See also **T1**.)

Table A group of related information in a database. Tables are collections of rows of records storing a particular type of data. (See also **Database**, **Record**, and **Field**.)

Tagged Image File Format (TIFF) A common file format that can store both *raster* and *vector* graphics information. (See also **File Format**, **Raster Graphics**, and **Vector Graphics**.)

Targa Format (TGA) A file format originally designed for storing video images. Since then, it has been enhanced to include high-resolution images in *raster* format. (See also **File Format**.)

TCP/IP (Transmission Control Protocol/Internet Protocol) The set of communications protocols the Internet uses to communicate.

Texture Mapping The process of applying a 2D image to a 3D object defined within the computer. Similar to wrapping wallpaper around the object. This process allows computer artists to simulate items such as wood by scanning in an image of wood grain and having the computer texture map the wood to a 3D model of a board. Developed by Ed Catmull in 1974. (See also **3D Graphics**.)

Theme A set of combined graphics, fonts, and elements that create a consistent visual design for a Web site or page.

Title Bar The top bar across any window in a graphical user interface. The title bar usually includes the name of the program or data file currently in use. The active window can be moved by clicking and dragging a title bar.

Trace Contour A filter that looks for edges and then traces them while making all the different solid colors in the image the same color. This has the effect of simulating a drawing.

Transaction A server operation that succeeds or fails as a whole, even if the operation involves many sub-steps. This process is usually monitored using a Transaction Server. (See also **Transaction Server**.)

Transaction Server A server component that is used to monitor and evaluate the completion of transactions, such as ordering or billing. Determines whether the complete transaction has succeeded and how to resolve incomplete transactions. (See also **Transaction**.)

True Color Color that has a color depth of 24 bits (16.7 million colors). (See also **Color Depth** and **24-Bit**.)

U Interface A two-wire ISDN circuit, the most common ISDN interface.

Undo Option A command that undoes the last operation performed.

URL (Uniform Resource Locator) The site- and file-addressing scheme for the World Wide Web.

Variable A storage location of data assigned to a meaningful name. This allows the program to alter and reference the data regardless of what it is.

Vector Graphics Graphics that are based on individual lines from point A to point B. Vector graphics represent line drawings well but cannot represent photographs. For photographs, *raster graphics* are required. Early computer graphics displays used vector graphics. (See also **File Format** and **Raster Graphics**.)

Virtual Root The directory that appears to be a subfolder to a Web server, although it may physically reside on a different file system or server.

Web Application A collection of elements (Web pages, database objects, and so on) that make up a complete Web site or distinct portion of a Web site under a virtual root.

Web Project A collection of files that comprise a Web application. Web projects are stored on both the server and the local machine. A Web project is part of a larger container called a solution. (See also **Solution** and **Web Application**.)

Wipe A transition from one scene to another. Wipes come in many different forms; the new scene can appear top to bottom, left to right, from the center out (in the case of a circular wipe), and many other ways.

WWW (World Wide Web) A popular hypertext-based system of transmitting textual and multimedia-based information through the Internet.

Zoom Tool A tool for magnifying the current image being worked on.

Index

Symbols

2B+D, 795

3D graphics, 796

8-bit color, 795

16-bit color, 795

24-bit color, 795

: (colon), HTML syntax, 756

* (asterisks), displaying in place of passwords, 141-142

= (equal sign), HTML syntax, 756

<%...%> notation, 605

A

Abandon method (Session object), 399, 402

Abs method, 273

absolute positioning, 128

absolute URL addressing, 607

accepting data from users, 409-414

Access (Microsoft), 810
    Data Tools Utilities, 418
    database access, 420
    File DSNs, 424, 427-429
    QueryDefs, 535-537

access control
    Authority Access, 692-693
    Membership Access, 693-695

accessing
    databases. *See* connecting databases
    Err object, 734
    hosts (Server object), 389-391

ACTION attribute (<FORM> tag), 119

active content, 598
    adding to Web projects, 600
    design issues, 598-599
    documents, *See* active documents
    online magazine project (VID News Central), 601-602
        contents page layout, 602-604
        server-side scripting, 604-606
        text files, 606-609
    rotating banner ads, 609
        banner display pages, 611
        control files, 613-616
        hit counters, 612-613
        server-side script, 609-610
        text files, 610
    solution framework, 599-600

active documents, 618
    ActiveX documents. *See* ActiveX documents
    hosts, 618
    Microsoft Office
        adding to Web projects, 621-622
        editing, 618-620
        Excel spreadsheets, 622, 625
        viewing, 618-620
        Word97 documents, 625-626

Active Server Page command (Add menu), 121, 453

Active Server Pages. *See* **ASPs**

ActiveMovie control, 212, 796
    adding to toolbox, 215
    HTML coding syntax
        <OBJECT> tag, 213-214
        PARAM attributes, 216

ActiveX controls, 544
    ActiveMovie, 212, 796
        adding to toolbox, 215
        HTML coding syntax, 213-216
    container, 796
    DirectAnimation controls, 216-217
        advantages, 217
        browser compatibility, 217

Index

ActiveX controls

installing, 217-218
Path control, 220-224
Sprite control, 218-220
Structured Graphics control, 224-232

ActiveX Data Objects. *See* ADO

ActiveX documents, 620-621

adding to Web projects, 627, 630-632
browser security, 627-628
download speed, 635
installation package, 628-629
intranets, 621
platform support, 620
setup information files, 629-630
startup HTML page, 632-633
testing, 634-635

Ad Rotator component, 609

control files, 613-616
instantiating, 609-610
rotating banner ads
banner display pages, 611
hit counters, 612-613
text files, 610

ADC (Advanced Data Connector), 797

Add Database Item command (Project menu), 484

Add HTML Page command (Add menu), 117

Add Item command (Add menu), 764

Add Item dialog box, 764

Add menu commands

Active Server Page, 121, 453
Add HTML Page, 117
Add Item, 764
HTML Page, 462
Style Sheet, 182

Add Users and Groups dialog box, 701

addHeader method, 404

addRecord method, 559

ADO (Active Data Objects), 506, 514

adding to ASPs, 578
advantages, 506
COM, 507
Command object, 507, 528, 538-539
delete queries, 530-532
insert queries, 530-532
update queries, 528-530
Connection object, 507, 520-523
ConnectionString property, 520
CursorLocation property, 520
connections, 577-578
server objects, 578
server-side script, 578-579
Data Tools Utilities, 419
design-time controls, 506, 524
development, 507
drawbacks, 506
include files
ADOSTUFF.INC, 517-520
ADOVBS.INC, 514-516
library, 506

model, 419, 507-508
CommandText property, 508-509
CommandType property, 508-510
ConnectionString property, 508-509
CursorLocation property, 508-511
CursorType property, 508, 511-512
LockType property, 508, 512-513
Mode property, 508, 513
Parameter object, 538-539
parameter queries, 532-537
Recordset object, 507, 524-527
SQL Server stored procedures, 538-539
typos, 523

ADOSTUFF.INC include file, 517-520

ADOVBS.INC include file, 514-516

ADTG (Advanced Data TableGram Streaming Protocol), 797

Advanced command (Edit menu), 44-45

advertisements (rotating banner ads), 609

banner display pages, 611
control files, 613-616
hit counters, 612-613
server-side script, 609-610
text files, 610

alert method (VBScript), 252

Index

ASPs (Active Server Pages)

alignment. *See also* **CSS (Cascading Style Sheets)**
  images
    HTML coding syntax, 756, 765-766
    VBScript, 769-770
  tables, 61, 128-132
All_HTTP HTTP server variable, 658
All_RAW HTTP server variable, 658
alpha channels, 797
anchors (HTML tags), 383
animation (DirectAnimation controls), 216-217, 797
  advantages, 217
  browser compatibility, 217
  installing, 217-218
  Path control, 220-224
  Sprite control, 218-220
  Structured Graphics control, 224-232
antialiasing, 797
Appearance tab (Project Properties dialog box), 16
AppendToLog method, 404
APPL_MD_PATH HTTP server variable, 658
APPL_PHYSICAL_PATH HTTP server variable, 658
applets, 797
Application object
  Contents collection, 392-397
  Lock method, 392-393
  OnEnd event, 392-393, 643

OnStart event, 392-393, 397, 642
server-side scripting, 380, 392-397
StaticObjects collection, 392-393, 396-397
UnLock method, 392-393
applications
  code, 522
  designing (error prevention), 730-732
  error-handling code, *See* error handling
  testing, 726-727
  variables, 392
  VBScript
    alert keyword, 252
    alert method, 252
    control structures, 259
    controls, 249
    creating, 249-252
    decision structures, 259
    dim keyword, 252-254
    Do...Loop loops, 261-264
    endif, 266
    For...Next loops, 252, 259-261
    If...Then...Else structure, 264-267
    looping structures, 259
    message boxes, 249
    module variables, 257-258
    onclick method, 251
    private variables, 255-257
    public variables, 258
    Quick View, 252
    routines, 250-251
    scope, 255-259
    Select...Case...End Select structure, 267-269
    testing, 251-252
    variable declaration, 253

    variable initialization, 258
    variables, 252
    variant types, 254
    VBScript property, 249
  Web applications
    framework, 640-641
    GLOBAL.ASA file, 641-651
Arc method, 225
architecture (Web applications), 640-641
<AREA tag> (HTML)
  attributes
    HREF, 240
    NOHREF, 240
    SHAPE, 240
    TITLE, 235
  example, 239
arguments, 797
arrays, 797
arrows (blue arrows), 44
ASA (Active Server Application), 796
Asc method, 278
AscB method, 278
ASCII, 797
AscW method, 278
ASP Free For All mailing list, 794
ASP Newbies ListServ mailing list, 794
ASPChart DLL, 591-592
aspect ratio, 798
ASPs (Active Server Pages), 121
  adding to Web projects, 121, 453-455, 602-603
  CHARTING.ASP document (graphical chart report), 592

Index

ASPs (Active Server Pages)

chart data, 593
displaying, 595
FolderOnly method, 595-596
image size, 594
saving, 595
title, 593
top-level code, 592-593
COLUMNAR.ASP document (columnar report), 575
   ADO connections, 577-579
   data connection, 575-577
   data detail, displaying, 581-582
   headings, 580
   print loop, 580
copying, 583-584
creating, 386-389
current date/time, 604
data-bound grids, 452
   Button control, 459-460
   Grid control, 456-457
   HTML tables, 457-459
   Recordset control, 455
error handling, 736-737, 745-746
FileSystemObject, 664-666
   creating folders and files, 667-671
   debugging, 671
   inspecting disk storage, 666-667
   memory, 688
   reading server drives, 671-674
   security, 664
   viewing files, 678-681
   viewing folders, 674-678
GET method, GET-FORM.HTM example, 127-128

GLOBAL.ASA file, 641-642
   COM object pointers, 643-644
   Contents collections, 644-645
   data sharing, 643-644
   declaring variables, 644
   editing, 645-647
   events, 642-643
   HTML, 643
   <OBJECT>, 647-649
   type library references, 649-651
linking (Content Linker Component), 605
   text files, 606-609
   URL/title pairs, 605-606
ODBC, 381
POST method, POST-VALUES.ASP example, 121
   document file, 121
   Request object, 122
   source code listing, 122
program-based security, 711
   security code, 712-714
   session variables, 712
   tools, 711
REPORT.ASP document (tabular report)
   calling, 585-586
   copying, 583-584
   reusability, 585
server variables, 657-661
server-side include files, 652-653
   creating, 653-655
   using, 656-657
server-side scripting, 380
TABULAR.ASP document (tabular report), 583-584

TextStream object, 681-688
users
   checking for, 714-715
   login data, 715-717
   validating, 717-720

assigning permissions, 701-704

asterisks (*), displaying in place of passwords, 141-142

AtEndOfColumn property, 682

AtEndOfLine property, 682

Atn method, 273

attribute event declaration, 304-305

attributes (HTML)
   <AREA> tag
      HREF, 240
      NOHREF, 240
      SHAPE, 240
      TITLE, 235
   <BGSOUND> tag, 208
   client-side scripting, 338, 341-344
   ID attribute, 344
   <IMG> tag
      BORDER, 237
      HEIGHT, 237
      STYLE, 755-756
      USEMAP, 237
      WIDTH, 237
   <INPUT> tag
      ID, 137
      MAXLENGTH, 137
      NAME, 137
      SIZE, 137
      TYPE, 135
      VALUE, 137, 141, 148
   LANGUAGE, 338
   <OBJECT> tag, 216

Index
browsing

<OPTION> tag, 156
   order of, 145
<SCRIPT> tag, 305
<SELECT> tag, 160
<TEXTAREA> tag
   COLS, 164
   ROWS, 164
   WRAP, 165
audio files
   adding to Web projects, 210
   client-side scripts, 209
   HTML coding syntax, 207-209
   labeling, 212
   launching, 211-212
   WAV format, 209
Audio Visual Interleave (AVI) format, 215
AUTH_PASSWORD HTTP server variable, 658
AUTH_TYPE HTTP server variable, 658
AUTH_USER HTTP server variable, 658
Authority Access, 692-693
autoformatting (HTML display space), 112-113
automation objects, 798
AutoRewind parameter (ActiveMovie control), 216
autosaving records, 466
AutoStart parameter (ActiveMovie control), 216
AVI (Audio Visual Interleave) format, 215

B

B channel, 798
Back method, 359
backbone networks, 798
background styles (CSS), 187
   colors, 188
   images, 189-191
bandwidth, 798
banner ads
   creating, 69-70
   rotating, 609
      banner display pages, 611
      control files, 613-616
      hit counters, 612-613
      server-side script, 609-610
      text files, 610
<BGSOUND> tag (HTML), 207-208
binary, 798
BinaryRead method, 410
BinaryWrite method, 404
binding data, 464
bits, 798
blue arrows, 44
blue dots, 44
blurring filter, 798
BMP, 798
Boolean expressions, 798
BORDER attribute (<IMG> tag), 237
borders
   displaying, 60-61
   hiding, 61
   image map borders, removing, 237
   tables, 60-61

BorderWidth parameter (REPORT.ASP), 588
bounding boxes, 798
BreakOnColumn parameter (REPORT.ASP), 587
BRI (Basic Rate Interface), 798
brightness, 799
Broken Links Report command (View menu), 104-105
browsers
   client-side scripting, 336
   creating, 359
   display differences, 112-113
   history of sessions, 359-360
   Microsoft Internet Explorer, 336
      client-side scripting, 336
      Document object, 364-372
      DOM, 336, 346-378
      Form object, 375-378
      Frame object, 357-358
      hierarchy of objects, 347-349
      History object, 359-360
      Link object, 374-374
      Location object, 362-364
      Navigator object, 360-361
      Window object, 349-357
   Netscape, 336
   obtaining information about, 360-361, 657-661
   testing Web page layout, 60-61
   text browsers, 65
   VBScript, 381
browsing, 799

bubbling. *See* **event handling**
Buffer property, 403
Build menu, 44
built-in controls. *See* **intrinsic controls**
built-in methods. *See* **methods**
bullets, 195-196
burning, 799
Button Properties dialog box, 558
buttons
   Button control, 459, 467
      adding to tables, 469
      client-side scripting, 460
      properties, 459, 469
   data-entry form
      Cancel, 473
      Delete, 475
      List, 474
      New, 474
      Save, 473
      Update, 474
   design-time controls, 558-560
   images, 170-172
   Microsoft Internet Explorer, 351
   radio buttons, 135, 147
      event handling (VBScript), 150-152
      HTML coding syntax, 147-150
   Reset, 119
   Submit, 119
By Reference addressing, 799
By Value, 799
bytes, 799

C

CacheControl property, 403
calculations
   client-side scripting, 337
   image map coordinates, 241-243
Cancel buttons, 473
Caption property (Button control), 469
captions (DTC buttons), 558
Cascading Style Sheets. *See* **CSS**
CBool method, 290
CByte method, 290
CCS, 799
CCur method, 290
cdaoQueryDef, 524-525
CDate method, 290
CDbl method, 290
CERT_COOKIE HTTP server variable, 658
CERT_FLAGS HTTP server variable, 658
CERT_ISSUER HTTP server variable, 659
CERT_KEYSIZE HTTP server variable, 659
CERT_SECRETKEYSIZE HTTP server variable, 659
CERT_SERIALNUMBER HTTP server variable, 659
CERT_SERVER_ISSUER HTTP server variable, 659

CERT_SERVER_SUBJECT HTTP server variable, 659
CERT_SUBJECT HTTP server variable, 659
certificates, 410
CGI (Common Gateway Interface), 507, 799
change scripts (SQL)
   INSERT query scripts, 495-498
   Table Script template, 489-491
   Trigger Script template, 486-488
   View Script, 500-502
channels, 799
character codes, 799
Charset property, 403
chart reports. *See* **CHARTING.ASP document**
CHARTING.ASP document (graphical chart report), 592
   chart data, 593
   displaying, 595
   FolderOnly method, 595-596
   image size, 594
   saving, 595
   title, 593
   top-level code, 592-593
chatting, 800
Checkbox DTCs, 554
checkboxes, 135
   event handling (VBScript), 145-146
   HTML coding syntax, 143-145
CheckLogin method, 720

Index

Close method

CHECKUSER.INC file (LoginWeb project), 711, 714

Chr method, 278

ChrB method, 278

Chrome package, 224

ChrW method, 278

CInt method, 290

class modules, 800

classes (style classes), 179, 183
  applying, 199-200
  creating, 198
  example, 198

CLC (Content Linker Component), 601
  instantiating, 605
  links, creating
    text files, 606-609
    URL/title pairs, 605-606

Clear method, 226, 405, 732

clearTimeOut method, 355-357

click-throughs, counting, 612-613

client-side controls.
  See **DTCs**

client-side image maps, 235
  adding to Web pages, 237-238
  advantages, 234-235
  assocating with URLs, 242
  borders, removing, 237
  defined, 234
  image files, 236
  limitations, 235
  map coordinates, 239
    defining, 241-243
    HTML coding syntax, 239-241
  naming, 240
  sizing, 237
  target documents, 244
  testing, 244
  ToolTips, 235

client-side scripting, 336
  benefits, 337
  calculations, 337
  data-entry forms, 469
    Cancel button, 473-474
    Delete button, 475
    List button, 474
    New button, 474
    onclick events, 471-472
    Save button, 473-474
    SetInputModeTo method, 472-473
    Update button, 474
    window_onload events, 471-472
    window_unload events, 473
  DefaultClientScript property, 339, 349
  DTCs (design-time controls), 443-444, 460
  editing with server-side scripts, 384
  elements, 375-377
  forms, 375-378
  frames, 357-358
  history of browser sessions, 359-360
  HTML documents, 338
    editor, 339-341
    flexibility, 346
    FOR...EVENT method, 343-346
    HTML attributes, 341-343
    organization, 346-346
    <SCRIPT>, 339
  ID attribute, 346
  JavaScript, 336
  links, 373-374
  listening for keypresses, 337
  locating users, 362-364
  Microsoft Internet Explorer, 336, 346-347
    Document object, 364-372
    Element object, 375-377
    Form object, 375-378
    Frame object, 357-358
    hierarchy of objects, 347-349
    History object, 359-360
    Link object, 373-374
    Location object, 362-364
    Navigator object, 360-361
    Window object, 349-357
  mixing with server-side scripting, 337
  mouse movements, 337
  obtaining information, 360-367
  online help, 337
  purpose of, 337
  Visual Basic Scripting, 336
  windows
    navigating, 354-355
    opening, 353-355
    timing events, 355-357

ClientCertificate collection, 409-410

clients
  client/server architecture, 800
  thin clients, 337

CLng method, 290

Close command (File menu), 77

Close method, 682

Index

closing
  anchors of tags, 383
  database connections, 528
CMYK (Cyan, Magenta, Yellow, and Black), 800
Cobb Journal Web site, 792
code, 522
CodePage property, 399
coding. *See also* **scripting**, 336
collections, 800
  ClientCertificate collection, 409-410
  Contents collections, 644-646
    Application object, 392-397
    Session object, 398-400
  Cookies collection
    Request object, 409-412
    Response object, 403, 406-407
  Drives collection, 671, 674
  Files collection, 678-681
  Folders collection, 674-678
  Form collection, 409, 415-416
  QueryString collection, 410-415
  ServerVariables collection, 410, 657-661
  StaticContents collections, 644
  StaticObjects collections, 648
    Application object, 392-397
    Session object, 398, 401
colon (:), HTML syntax, 756

color
  8-bit color, 795
  16-bit color, 795
  24-bit color, 795
  background colors (CSS), 188
  corrections, 800
  depth, 800
  models, 800
  similarity, 800
COLS attribute (TEXTAREA tag), 164
Column property, 682
COLUMNAR.ASP document (columnar report), 575
  ADO connections, 577-578
    server objects, adding, 578
    server-side script, 578-579
  advantages, 571
  data connections, adding, 575-577
  data detail, displaying, 581-582
  defined, 570
  disadvantages, 571
  headings, 580
  print loops, 580
columns
  data binding, 464
  Grid DTC, 561
  tables, 60-62
COM
  ActiveX Data Objects (ADO), 507
  Ad Rotator component, 609
    control files, 613-616
    instantiating, 609-610
    rotating banner ads, creating, 610-613
  Content Linker Component, 601
    instantiating, 605
    links, creating, 605-609
  FileSystemObject, 664-666
    creating folders and files, 667-671
    debugging, 671
    inspecting disk storage, 666-667
    memory, 688
    reading server drives, 671-674
    security, 664
    viewing files, 678-681
    viewing folders, 674-678
  GLOBAL.ASA file, 643-644
Command object (ADO), 507, 538-539
  delete queries, 530-532
  insert queries, 530-532
  text, 509
  update queries, 528-530
commands
  Add menu
    Active Server Page, 121, 453
    Add HTML Page, 117
    Add Item, 764
    HTML Page, 462
    Style Sheet, 182
  data commands, 448
    adding to Web projects, 449
    creating, 429-430, 450-451
    Data Environment Designer, 421
    SQL statement data command, 431-433

Index — controls

table data command, 430-431
Edit menu
  Advanced, 44-45
  Select All, 102
  Set Primary Key, 485, 489
File menu
  Close, 77
  New Project, 12, 37, 136
  Open FrontPage web, 783
  Save, 63
  Save Database Diagram, 484
HTML menu
  Image, 65
  Script Block, Client, 342
Project menu
  Add Database Item, 484
  Web Project, Copy Web Application, 106
  Web Project, Working Mode, 92
SQL commands, UPDATE, 435-436
Table menu, Insert Table, 44, 60, 130, 458, 467
Tools menu, Options, 52
User menu
  New Local Group, 700
  New User, 700
View menu, 40
  Broken Links Report, 105
  Debug, 49
  Define Window Layout, 51
  Design, 49-50
  DevStudio, 49-50
  Edit HTML, 49
  Full Screen, 49
  Other Windows, Data View, 428
  Other Windows, Script Outline, 340
  Toolbars, 45-46
  Visible Borders, 60
  Visual Basic, 49
CommandText property (ADO model), 508-509
CommandType property (ADO model), 508-510
comparison operators, 801
compiled languages, 248
Component Object Model. See COM
compositing, 801
compression, 801
connecting databases
  ActiveX Data Objects (ADO), 419, 506-539
  CGI programs, 507
  closing, 528
  Data Environment Designer, 418, 421, 426-433
  escape plans, 529
  ISAPI programs, 507
  Microsoft Access databases, 420
  ODBC (Open Database Connectivity), 419-426
  OLE DB, 419-420
  Oracle databases, 420
  SQL Server databases, 420
  storage of connection data, 421
Connection object (ADO), 507, 520-523
Connection Properties dialog box, 427
ConnectionString property (ADO model), 508-509, 517-518
constants, 534, 801
CONTENT_LENGTH HTTP server variable, 659
Content Linker Component. See CLC
CONTENT_TYPE HTTP server variable, 659
Contents collections, 644-646
  Application object, 392-397
  Session object, 398-400
contents pages (VIS News Central project)
  elements, 603-604
  layout, 602-604
  server-side script, 604-606
ContentType property, 403
context menus, 34
Control Panel, 422-424
control structures (VBScript), 259
  Do...Loop loops, 261-264
  For...Next loops, 259-261
  If...Then...Else structure, 264-267
  Select...Case...End Select structure, 267-269
controls, 134-135, 154, 441-442
  ActiveX controls, 544
    ActiveMovie, 212-216, 796
    container, 796
    DirectAnimation controls, 216-232
    Path control, 220-224
    Sprite control, 218-220
    Structured Graphics control, 224-232

Index

controls

Button, 459, 467
   adding to tables, 469
   client-side scripting, 460
   properties, 459, 469
checkbox control, 135
   event handling (VBScript), 145-146
   HTML coding syntax, 143-145
converting to text, 443
creating, 441
design-time controls, 67-68, 544, 555
   ActiveX Data Objects (ADO), 506, 524
   advantages, 544-545
   buttons, 558-560
   data, 546, 552-553, 556-562
   editing, 549
   evolution of, 546
   forms, 546, 554-555
   Layout DTC, 28
   legacy, 546
   multimedia, 546, 562-567
   PageNavBar DTC, 31-32, 58, 68-75, 442
   pageTransitions DTC, 58, 68, 81-83, 563
   platforms, 545
   RecordsetNavbar, 442, 466-467
   runtime text, 544, 550-551
   scripting object model, 547-548
   scripts, 550-551
   system requirements, 74
   Web pages, 546-547
dropdown control, 155
   adding items, 157
   event handling (VBScript), 159
   example, 158
   HTML coding syntax, 156
   rearranging items, 157
   removing items, 157
file field control, 167
   displaying properties of, 169
   HTML coding syntax, 167-169
FrontPage compatibility, 786
Grid
   adding to Web projects, 456
   properties, 457
image type input control, 170-172
listbox control, 159
   event handling (VBScript), 162-163
   HTML coding syntax, 160-162
password control, 135, 141-142
radio control, 135, 147
   event handling (VBScript), 150-152
   HTML coding syntax, 147-150
Recordset
   adding to HTML documents, 463-464
   adding to Web projects, 455
scripts
   client-side scripting, 443-444
   server-side scripting, 443-444
   SOM (Scripting Object Model), 444-445
   viewing, 442
textarea control
   displaying contents of, 166-167
   HTML coding syntax, 164-166
   word wrap, 165
textbox control, 135
   adding to documents, 138, 464-466
   event handling (VBScript), 139-141
   HTML coding syntax, 136-137
   testing, 138
VBScript, 249

CONVERSION.HTM page (VBSMethods project), 291-293

converting
   data conversion methods, 290-293
   DTCs (design-time controls) to text, 443, 551

cookies, 406-407, 801
   Request object, 409-412
   Response object, 403, 406-407

coordinates (image map), 239
   defining, 241-243
   HTML coding syntax, 239-241

Copy Project dialog box, 106

Copy Web feature, 106-108

CopyFile method, 668

CopyFolder method, 668

copyrights, 207

Cos method, 273

cosines, 273

Create a New Data Source to SQL Server dialog box, 425, 482, 576

Create URL dialog box, 65
CreateFolder method, 667
CreateObject method, 390-391
CreateTextFile method, 668
cropping tools, 801
CSng method, 291
CSS (Cascading Style Sheets), 176-177
   adding to Web projects, 182
   background styles, 187
      colors, 188
      images, 189-191
   file format, 178-179
   font styles
      font families, 187
      previewing, 187
      setting, 185-186
      viewing, 187
   layout styles, 193-195
   linking to documents, 179, 184-185
   list styles, 195-197
   margin styles, 191-193
   organizing into groups, 203
   style classes, 179, 183
      applying, 199-200
      creating, 198
      example, 198
   Style Sheet Editor, 180, 183
   unique IDs, 180, 183-184
      applying, 202-203
      creating, 200-201
      example, 201
CStr method, 291
CursorLocation property (ADO model), 508-511

cursors, 510-512
CursorType property (ADO model), 508, 511-512
Customize dialog box, 47
Customize Toolbox dialog box, 215
customizing
   bulllets, 195-196
   filters, 801
   IDE views, 51-52
   layouts, 30-32
   style classes (unique ID styles), 180, 183-184
      applying, 202-203
      creating, 200-201
      example, 201
   toolbars, 34
      creating, 47-48
      naming, 48
   tools, 40
   views, 52

D

D channel, 801
DAC (Digital-to-Analog Converter), 803
dat diagrams, 802
data
   binding, 464, 801
   conversion methods, 290-293
   design-time controls, 546, 552
      Grid DTC, 560-562
      recordset DTC, 552-553
      RecordsetNavbar DTC, 556-558
   environments, 802
   ranges, 802
   sharing, 643-644

data commands, 448
   adding to Web projects, 449
   creating, 429-430, 450-451
   Data Command, 801
   Data Environment Designer, 421
   SQL statement data command, 431-433
   table data command, 430-431
Data Connection Properties dialog box, 426
data connections
   adding to Web projects, 447-448
   creating, 426-427, 575-577
   Data Connection, 802
   Data Environment Designer, 421
   Microsoft Access File DSNs, 427-429
Data Environment Designer. *See* DED
data grid (QDT), 433-434
data source names. *See* DSNs
data sources. *See* database projects
Data Tools Utilities
   Access (Microsoft), 418
   ActiveX Data Objects (ADO), 419
   Database Diagram, 483-484
      table relationships, defining, 491-493
      tables, creating, 484-486

Index

Data Tools Utilities

DED (Data Environment Designer), 418
  data commands, 421, 429-433
  data connections, 421, 426-429
  ODBC File DSNs, 424-426
limitations, 479
Microsoft Access, 418
OLE DB, 419-420
QDT (Query Designer Tool), 431-433, 483
  data grid, 433-434
  records, 494
  tables, 488-489
  views, 499-500
Table Script, 483, 489-491
uses, 418

data transfer

GET method, 123-124
  GETFORM.HTM example, 124-126
  GETVALUES.ASP example, 127-128
POST method, 115-116
  advantages, 116
  POSTFORM.HTM example, 116-121
  POSTVALUES.ASP example, 121-122

data types, 802

Data View window, 41

data-bound forms, 440

data commands, 448
  adding, 449
  creating, 450-451
data connections, 447-448
data-bound grids, 452
  ASP documents, adding, 453-455
  Button control, 459-460

Grid control, 456-457
HTML tables, 457-459
Recordset control, 455
data-entry forms, 461-462
  Button controls, 467-469
  client-side scripting, 469-475
  HTML documents, 462-463
  Recordset control, 463-464
  RecordsetNavbar control, 466-467
  testing, 476
  Textbox controls, 464-466

Database Diagram tool, 483-484

adding to Web projects, 484
creating tables, 484-486
relationships, 491-493
saving, 484

database projects, 478-479

access, 420
authentication, 426
creating, 481-482
data sources, 426
database diagrams, 484
databases (ISQL/W), 420, 480-481
debugging, 420
File DSNs, 425-426
normalization, 492
null values, 491
primary keys, 486
records
  INSERT query scripts, 495-497
  persistent INSERT queries, 497-498
  Query Designer, 494
relationships, 491-493

stored procedures
  ADO, 538-539
  creating, 502-503
  debugging, 503
  defined, 502
  results, 504
  running, 503-504
  triggers, 502
tables, 483
  Database Diagram tool, 484-486
  Query Designer tool, 488-489
  Table Script, 489-491
triggers, 486-488, 502
views, 498-499
  Query Designer tool, 499-500
  View Script, 500-502

databases, 802. *See also reports; tables*

ADO connections, 419, 506-539, 577-579
  locking, 512-513
  modes, 513
  server objects, adding, 578
  server-side script, 578-579
connections
  CGI programs, 507
  closing, 528
  creating, 575-577
  Data Environment Designer, 418, 421, 426-433
  escape plans, 529
  ISAPI programs, 507
  Microsoft Access databases, 420
  ODBC (Open Database Connectivity), 419
  ODBC File DSNs, 422-426

delete queries

    OLE DB, 419-420
    Oracle databases, 420
    SQL Server databases, 420
    storage of connection data, 421
    creating, 418
    data binding, 464
    editing (QDT), 433-434
    joins, 537
    management (Data Tool Utilities), 418
    records, 430
        autosaving, 466
        cursors, 510
        deleting with delete queries, 438
        editing with update queries, 435-436
        inserting with insert values queries, 436-438
    recordsets, 430, 556-558
    views, 537
    Web databases, 421-422

Date method, 284

date/time
    displaying, 604
    expressions, 802
    methods, 284-289

DateAdd method, 284

DateDiff method, 285

DatePart method, 285

DateSerial method, 285

DATETIME.HTM page (VBSMethods project)
    tables, 286-287
    VBScript code, 287-289

DateValue method, 285

Day method, 285

DB Connection parameter (REPORT.ASP), 587

DBForm project (data-bound form), 445-446
    creating, 446
    data commands, 448
        adding, 449
        creating, 450-451
    data connections, 447-448

Debug command (View menu), 49

Debug view (IDE), 49

debugging
    FileSystemObject, 671
    Oracle, 420
    SQL Server, 420
    stored procedures, 503

decision structures (VBScript), 259
    If...Then...Else structure, 264-267
    Select...Case...End Select structure, 267-269

declaring variables (VBScript), 253
    decision structures, 259
    GLOBAL.ASA file, 644
    looping structures, 259
    module variables, 257-258
    private variables, 255-257
    public variables, 258
    scope, 255-259
    variable initialization, 258
    variant types, 254

DED (Data Environment Designer), 418
    data commands, 421
        creating, 429-430
        SQL statement data command, 431-433
        table data command, 430-431
    data connections, 421
        creating, 426-427
        Microsoft Access File DSNs, 427-429
        ODBC File DSNs, 424-426

default settings, 802

DEFAULT.HTM page
    naming, 18-19
    specifying, 600
    VBSEvents project, 307-308
    VBSMethods project, 272

DefaultClientScript property, 339, 349

Define Window Layout command (View menu), 51

Define Window Layout dialog box, 52

defining
    document sections
        <DIV> tag, 756
        <SPAN> tag, 757
    image map coordinates, 241-243
    queries, 524-525
    styles (CSS)
        background styles, 187-191
        font styles, 185-187
        layout styles, 193-195
        list styles, 195-197
        margin styles, 191-193
        style classes, 198-200
        unique IDs, 200-203
    table relationships, 491-493

Delete buttons, 475

Delete Pages dialog box, 24

delete queries, 438, 530-532

DeleteFile method

DeleteFile method, 668
DeleteFolder method, 667
DeleteRecord method, 559
deleting
- documents from site diagrams, 22-24
- drop-down list items, 157
- permissions, 705-706
- records, 438, 530-532

Dependencies tab (Project Properties dialog box), 16
Deployment Manager, 41
Description property (Err object), 733
Design command (View menu), 49-50
design maps. *See* site diagrams
Design toolbar, 60
Design view (IDE), 49-50
design-time controls. *See* DTCs
designing
- active content, 598-599
- applications, 730-732
- data-bound forms, 440
  - *client-side scripting, 443-444*
  - *DTCs (design-time controls), 441-442*
  - *server-side scripting, 443-444*
  - *SOM (Scripting Object Model), 444-445*
- forms
  - *autoformatting, 112-113*
  - *display limitations, 112*
  - *operating modes, 114-115*
  - *stateless environment, 113-114*
  - *tables, 128-132*

Web projects, 8
- *layouts, 27-32*
- *site diagrams, 17-24*
- *themes, 24-26*

despeckle filters, 802
Developer Studio, 810
development teams, 86
- isolation, 95-96
- personal projects, 87-88
- shared projects, 86-87
- testing areas, 105-106
- working modes
  - Local mode, 90-94
  - Master mode, 89-90, 94-95
  - Offline mode, 90-91
  - setting, 91-92
  - switching, 92

DevStudio command (View menu), 49-50
DevStudio view (IDE), 49-50
DHTML (Dynamic HTML), 804
- applying, 755-757
- browser compatibility, 751
- design-time controls, 562-564
- document object model, 750
- drag-and-drop interfaces, 767-770
- element naming, 750
- event
  - *bubbling, 753-755*
  - *handling, 750-753*
- HTML content, changing at runtime, 758-762

diagrams. *See* site diagrams
dialog boxes, 802
- Add Item, 764
- Add Users and Groups, 701

Button Properties, 558
Connection Properties, 427
Copy Project, 106
Create a New Data Source to SQL Server, 425, 482, 576
Create URL, 65
Customize, 47
Customize Toolbox, 215
Data Connection Properties, 426
Define Window Layout, 52
Delete Pages, 24
Differences, 94
Directory Permissions, 703
Grid Properties, 561
input boxes, 296
Insert Image, 65
Insert Table, 60-61, 130, 467
Merge Differences, 86
message boxes
- *displaying, 297*
- *VBScript, 249*
Microsoft Internet Explorer, 351-353
modal, 115
New Folder, 640
New Local Group, 701
New Project, 12-13, 37, 136
ODBC Microsoft Access Driver 97, 423
Open FrontPage Web, 783
Options, 52-53
- *Analyzer Options, 56*
- *Data Tools, 54-55*
- *Debugger Options, 56*
- *Environment, 53*
- *HTML Options, 56*

documents

   Projects Options, 55-56
   Settings Options, 56
   Text Editor, 54
  PageNavBar Properties, 70
  PageTransitions Properties, 82
  Project Properties, 16
  Properties, 548-549
  Recordset Properties, 552-553
  RecordsetNavbar Properties, 556
  Select Background Image, 189
  Select Data Source, 426-427, 481-482, 576
  Special Directory Access, 704
  Textbox Properties, 554
  VBScript property, 249
  Web Project Wizard, 87-88

Differences dialog box, 94

diffusion dithering, 802

digital certificates, 410

digital painting, 803

digital signatures, 803

digitizing, 803-804

dim keyword (VBScript), 252-254

DirectAnimation controls, 216-217
  advantages, 217
  browser compatibility, 217
  installing, 217-218
  Path control, 220-224
    HTML coding syntax, 221-222
    scripting, 222-223
  Sprite control, 218-220

  Structured Graphics control, 224-232
    client-side script blocks, 228-229
    event handling, 231-232
    graphics, 230
    HTML coding syntax, 227
    methods, 225-226
    oval objects, 229
    rectangles, 230
    sample application, 226-227
    square objects, 229

directories, 803

Directory Permissions dialog box, 703

disk storage, 666-667

display mode, 114

display space (HTML), 112-113

dithering, 803

DIV tag (HTML), 756-757

DLLs, 591-592

DNS (Domain Name Service), 803

Do...Loop loops, 261-264

docking
  toolbars, 46
  windows, 34

Document object (Microsoft Internet Explorer), 364-367
  event handling, 313
    code listing, 315-317
    messages, 314
  methods
    execCommand method, 369-372
    Write method, 367-369
    WriteLn method, 367-369

Document Object Model. See DOM

DOCUMENT.HTM page (VBSEvents project), 314-317

documentation (online), 666

documents, 618
  ActiveX, 620-621
    adding to Web projects, 627, 630-632
    browser security, 627-628
    download speed, 635
    installation package, 628-629
    intranets, 621
    platform support, 620
    setup information files, 629-630
    startup HTML page, 632-633
    testing, 634-635
  CSS (Cascading Style Sheets), 176-177
    adding, 182
    background styles, 187-191
    file format, 178-179
    font styles, 185-187
    layout styles, 193-195
    linking, 179, 184-185
    list styles, 195-197
    margin styles, 191-193
    organizing into groups, 203
    style classes, 179, 183, 198-200
    Style Sheet Editor, 180, 183
    unique IDs, 180, 183-184, 200-203
  hosts, 618
  HTML
    adding to projects, 117, 137, 462-463

documents

client-side scripting,
  338-346
copying, 125-126
displaying information
  about, 365-367
images, 765-766,
  769-770
loading into main editor
  window, 37-38
sections, 756-757
whitespace viewing,
  44-45
merging, 86
Microsoft Office, 618
  adding to Web projects,
    621-622
  editing, 618-620
  Excel spreadsheets, 622,
    625
  viewing, 618-620
  Word 97 documents,
    625-626
site diagram documents
  adding, 19-21
  deleting, 22-24
  moving, 22
text editors, 607

dodging, 803

DOM (Document Object Model), 336, 346-347
Document object, 364-367
  execCommand method,
    369-372
  Write method, 367-369
  WriteLn method,
    367-369
Element object, 375-377
Form object, 375-378
Frame object, 357-358
hierarchy, 347-349
History object, 359-360
Link object, 373-374
Location object, 362-364
Navigator object, 360-361
Window object, 349-350
  buttons, 351
  clearTimeout method,
    355-357
  dialog boxes, 351-353
  Navigate method,
    354-355
  Open method, 353-355
  setTimeout method,
    355-357

DPI (Dots Per Inch), 803

drag-and-drop interfaces, 767-770

drawing objects (Structured Graphics control), 225-226, 230

Drive object, 671-672

drivers (ODBC), 420-422

drives (server), 671-674

Drives collection, 671, 674

drop-down lists, 155
editing items, 157
event handling (VBScript),
  159
example, 158
HTML coding syntax, 156

DSNs (data source names)
Control Panel, 422-424
creating, 424-426,
  576-577
Data Environment
  Designer, 424-426
GLOBAL.ASA file, 429
Microsoft Access, 424,
  427-429
SQL Server, 425-426

DTCs (design time controls), 544
ADO, 506, 524
advantages, 544-545
buttons, 558-560
data, 546
  Grid DTC, 560-562
  recordset DTC, 552-553
  RecordsetNavbar DTC,
    556-558
editing, 549
evolution of, 546
forms, 546, 554-555
  Checkbox DTC, 554
  inserting, 554-555
  Label DTC, 554-555
  Listbox DTC, 554-555
  OptionGroup DTC, 555
  OptionsGroup DTC, 554
  RecordsetNavbar DTC,
    556-558
  Textbox DTC, 554-555
legacy DTCs, 546
multimedia, 546, 562
  PageTransitions DTC,
    563
  Timeline DTC, 564-567
PageNavBar DTC, 68
  banners, 69-70
  links, 71-74
  navigation bars, 74-75
  site diagrams, 68-69
  tips for using, 58
PageTransitions DTC, 58,
  68, 81-83, 563
platforms, 545
runtime text, 544
  converting, 551
  viewing, 550-551
scripts
  scripting object model,
    547-548
  viewing, 550-551
system requirements, 74
Web pages, 546-547

DTCScriptingPlatform property (documents), 444

Dynamic HTML.
  See DHTML

event handling

E

Edit HTML command (View menu), 49

Edit HTML view (IDE), 49

Edit menu commands
Advanced, 44-45
Select All, 102
Set Primary Key, 485, 489

editing
custom views, 52
databases, 433-434
design-time controls, 549
GLOBAL.ASA file, 429, 645-647
main editor window, 35-39
Microsoft Office active documents, 618-620
records, 435-436
tables, 433-434
WYSIWYG, 39

Editor Defaults tab (Project Properties dialog box), 16

editors
associating, 607
client-side scripting, 339-341, 384
creating projects, 37
Design mode, 35, 38
loading HTML documents, 37-38
Quick View mode, 36, 39
Script Outline window, 340-341
Source mode, 35-39
Style Sheet Editor, 183
Table Script Editor, 483, 489-491

Element object (Microsoft Internet Explorer), 375-377
code listing, 328-331
messages, 325-326

ELEMENT.HTM page (VBSEvents project), 327-331

email mailing lists, 794

embossing, 804

empty (null) values, 491, 804

encryption, 804

End method, 405

endif, 266

environment. *See* **IDE**

EPS (Encapsulated PostScript), 804

equal sign (=), HTML syntax, 756

equalization, 804

error handling, 724
ASPs, 736-737
Err object, 732
  accessing, 734
  methods, 732
  properties, 732-733
  reporting errors, 733-734
Frontpage vinavar component, 788-789
On Error Resume Next statement, 735
runtime errors, 729-730
  defined, 724
  examples, 729-730
  preventing, 730-732
SSI error-handing files, 738
  adding to ASP documents, 745-746
  advantages, 744

creating, 739-740
designing, 738-739
ERRORTRAP.INC example, 740-744
syntax errors
  defined, 724
  example, 724-726
  preventing, 726-727
TextStream object, 685
Web-related errors, 727-728
  content-related problems, 727
  defined, 724
  hardware problems, 727

ERRORTRAP.INC file (SSI error handler), 740-744

EVENT attribute (<SCRIPT> tag), 305

event handling, 302
attribute event declaration, 304-305
DHTML (Dynamic HTML), 750
  event bubbling, 306, 753-755
  event messages, 751-752
  listening for events, 752-753
Document object events, 313
  code listing, 315-317
  messages, 314
Element object events, 325
  code listing, 328-331
  messages, 325-326
explicit event declaration, 305-306
Form object events, 318
  event-handler methods, 322-324

Index

event handling

HTML coding syntax, 320
messages, 318-319
intrinsic event declaration, 303-304
link events, 331-332
VBScript
   check boxes, 145-146
   drop-down lists, 159
   radio buttons, 150-152
   textbox controls, 139-141
VBSEvents project, 307
   DEFAULT.HTM page, 307-308
   DOCUMENT.HTM page, 314-317
   ELEMENT.HTM page, 327-331
   FORM.HTM page, 320-324
   WINDOW.HTM page, 308-312
Window object events, 308
   code blocks, 309
   code listing, 311-312
   messages, 308
   method headers, 311
   PostMsg method, 310

event object, 768-770

events, 804. *See also* **triggers**
GLOBAL.ASA file
   Application OnEnd event, 392-393, 643
   Application OnStart event, 392-393, 397, 642
   Session OnEnd event, 642
   Session OnStart event, 642
onbeforeunload, 751
onblur, 751
onclick, 251
onerror, 751
onfocus, 751
onhelp, 751
onload, 752
onmouseover, 759-762
onresize, 752
onscroll, 752
onunload, 752
Timeline DTC, 565-567

Excel spreadsheets, 622, 625

execCommand method, 369-372

Exp method, 273

Expires property, 403

ExpiresAbsolute property, 403

explicit event declaration, 305-306

Explorer. *See* **Microsoft Internet Explorer**

expressions, 804

extranets, 804

eye dropper tool, 804

F

fades, 804

FAQs (Frequently Asked Questions), 805

fields, 805

FIF (Fractal Image Format), 805

file field control, 167
displaying properties of, 169
HTML coding syntax, 167-169

File menu commands
Close, 77
New Project, 12, 37, 136
Open FrontPage web, 783
Save, 63
Save Database Diagram, 484

File object, 678-681

FileExists method, 668

files, 805
filename case sensitivity, 236
FileSystemObject
   creating files, 667-671
   debugging, 671
   documentation, 666
   FileExists method, 668
   memory, 688
   viewing files, 678-681
formats, 805
GIF (Graphical Interchange Format), 63, 218-220
GLOBAL.ASA file, 521, 641-642, 784
   Application OnEnd event, 643
   Application OnStart event, 642
   COM object pointers, 643-644
   Contents collections, 644-645
   Data Environment Designer, 421
   data sharing, 643-644
   database connection information, 521
   declaring variables, 644
   editing, 429, 645-647
   File DSNs, 429
   HTML, 643
   <OBJECT>, 647-649
   Session OnEnd event, 642

Index

forms

Session OnStart event,
  642
type library references,
  649-651
include files, 714
  ADOSTUFF.INC file,
    517-520
  ADOVBS.INC file,
    514-516
  CHECKUSER.INC file
    (LoginWeb project),
    711, 714
  ERRORTRAP.INC file
    (SSI error handler),
    740-744
INF (setup information)
  files, 629-630
JPG files, 63
managing (Active Server
  Pages), 664-681
README files, 775
RIFs (report information
  files), 586
  creating, 588
  example, 586-587
  file format, 587-588
  TEST.RIF file, 589
sound files
  adding to Web projects,
    210
  client-side scripts, 209
  HTML coding syntax,
    207-209
  labeling, 212
  launching, 211-212
  WAV format, 209
SSI (server-side include),
  714
  creating, 653-655
  nesting, 652
  using, 656-657
text files
  adding to Web projects,
    607
  TextStream object,
    683-688

video files
  ActiveMovie control,
    212-216
  AVI (Audio Visual
    Interleave) format, 215
Files collection, 678-681
FileSystemObject
  creating files, 667-671
  debugging, 671
  documentation, 666
  FileExists method, 668
  memory, 688
  viewing files, 678-681
fill tool, 805
FillSpline method, 225
Filter method, 278
filters (Link view), 98-100
finding broken links,
  104-105
firewalls, 805
FIRST.HTM document,
  180-181
Fix method, 291
flat-file databases, 588
Flush method, 405
Folder object, 674-678
FolderExists method, 667
FolderOnly method, 595
folders
  creating, 631, 640,
    667-671
  MyWeb, 9-10
  naming, 9
  ScriptLibrary, 10, 442
  viewing, 674-678
Folders collection, 674-678
fonts (CSS), 185
  font families, 187
  previewing, 187
  setting, 185-186
  viewing, 187

FOR attribute (SCRIPT
  tag), 305
FOR...EVENT method,
  338, 343-346
for...next loops, 252,
  259-261
Form collection, 409,
  415-416
Form method, 122
Form object (Microsoft
  Internet Explorer),
  375-378
  event-handler methods,
    322
  event-handling code,
    322-324
  HTML coding syntax, 320
  messages, 318-319
<FORM> tag (HTML),
  119-120
FORM.HTM page
  (VBSEvents project)
  elements, 320
  event-handling code,
    322-324
FormatCurrency method,
  294
FormatDateTime method,
  294
FormatNumber method,
  294
FormatPercent method,
  294
formatting methods,
  294-296
forms
  check boxes, 135
    event handling
      (VBScript), 145-146
    HTML coding syntax,
      143-145
  data-bound, *See* data-
    bound forms

Index

forms

design-time controls, 546, 554-555
  buttons, 558-560
  Checkbox DTC, 554
  inserting, 554-555
  Label DTC, 554-555
  Listbox DTC, 554-555
  OptionGroup DTC, 555
  OptionsGroup DTC, 554
  Textbox DTC, 554-555
displaying, 114
  autoformatted displays, 112-113
  HTML display limitations, 112
drop-down lists, 155
  adding items, 157
  event handling (VBScript), 159
  example, 158
  HTML coding syntax, 156
  rearranging items, 157
  removing items, 157
GET method of data transfer, 123-124
  GETFORM.HTM example, 124-126
  GETVALUES.ASP example, 127-128
HTML coding syntax, 119-120
list boxes, 159
  event handling (VBScript), 162-163
  HTML coding syntax, 160-162
managing, 375-378
operating modes
  display mode, 114
  multimode forms, 115, 470
  single-mode forms, 114-115

password control, 135, 141-142
POST method of data transfer, 115-116
  advantages, 116
  POSTFORM.HTM example, 116-121
  POSTVALUES.ASP example, 121-122
radio buttons, 135, 147
  event handling (VBScript), 150-152
  HTML coding syntax, 147-150
Reset buttons, 119
stateless environment, 113-114
Submit buttons, 119
tables, 128-129
  inserting, 130
  TABLEFORM.HTM example, 129-132
text areas
  displaying contents, 166-167
  HTML coding syntax, 164-166
  word wrap, 165
text boxes, 135
  adding, 138
  event handling (VBScript), 139-141
  HTML coding syntax, 136-137
  testing, 138

Forward method, 359
FPSRVADM.EXE program, 789
FPX (FrontPage Server Extensions), 776-777
fractal compression, 805

Frame object (Microsoft Internet Explorer), 357-358
frames, 357-358
FRAMESET element (HTML), 58
FrontPage, 810
installing/uninstalling, 775-776
  Personal Web Server, 777-778
  Server Extensions (FPX), 776-777
integrating with Visual InterDev
  advantages, 774-775
  cautions, 786
  Web projects, 783-784
troubleshooting problems, 787
  server connections, 787-788
  vinavar component problems, 788-789
webs
  connecting to, 779
  selecting, 780
  viewing, 781-782
  Visual InterDev 6 Script Library, 780-781

Full Screen command (View menu), 49
Full Screen view (IDE), 49
functions. *See* **methods**

G

gammas, 806
GATEWAY INTERFACE HTTP server variable, 659
Gaussian blur, 806

Index

GUID (Globally Unique ID)

General tab (Project Properties dialog box), 16
GET method, 123-124
   GETFORM.HTM example, 124-126
   GETVALUES.ASP example, 127-128
   POST method, compared, 116
getcount method, 474
GetData method, 720
getSQLText method, 456
GETUSER.ASP file (LoginWeb project), 711, 717
GIF (Graphical Interchange Format) files, 806
   sprites, creating, 218-220
   Web page templates, 63
gigabytes, 806
global variables. *See* **public variables**
GLOBAL.ASA file, 521, 641-642, 784
   Application OnEnd event, 643
   Application OnStart event, 642
   COM object pointers, 643-644
   Contents collections, 644-645
   Data Environment Designer, 421
   data sharing, 643-644
   database connection information, 521
   declaring variables, 644
   editing, 429, 645-647
   File DSNs, 429
   HTML, 643

   <OBJECT>, 647-649
   Session OnEnd event, 642
   Session OnStart event, 642
   type library references, 649-651
Go method, 359
gradient fills, 806
Graphical Interchange Format. *See* **GIF files**
graphics. *See also* **animation**
   background images (CSS), 189-191
   bullets, 195-196
   buttons, 170-172
   Chrome package, 224
   descriptive text, 65
   graphical chart reports, 573, 592
      advantages, 574
      ASPChart component, 591-592
      chart data, 593
      creating, 593-596
      defined, 570
      displaying, 595
      FolderOnly method, 595-596
      image sizes, 594
      saving, 595
      titles, 593
      top-level code, 592-593
   image maps, 235
      adding to Web pages, 237-238
      advantages, 234-235
      associating with URLs, 242
      borders, removing, 237
      defined, 234
      image files, 236
      limitations, 235
      map coordinates, 239-243
      naming, 240

      sizing, 237
      target documents, 244
      testing, 244
      ToolTips, 235
   <IMG> HTML tag, attributes, 237-238
      BORDER, 237
      HEIGHT, 237
      STYLE, 755-756
      USEMAP, 237
      WIDTH, 237
   importing into Web projects, 764
   load times, 65
   location, 63
   positioning
      HTML coding syntax, 765-766
      VBScript, 769-770
   processing, 807
   shapes, 225-226, 230
   Web page templates, 63-66
gray/color corrections, 806
grayscale, 795, 806
Grid control, 456-457
Grid DTCs, 560-562
Grid Properties dialog box, 561
grids (data-bound grids), 452
   ASP documents, adding, 453-455
   Button control, 459-460
   Grid control, 456-457
   HTML tables, 457-459
   Recordset control, 455
group breaks (tabular reports), 583
groups (Windows NT), 700-701
GUID (Globally Unique ID), 806

H

halftones, 806
HARD value (WRAP attribute), 165
headings, 580
HEIGHT attribute (<IMG> tag), 237
help
  online, 337
  systems, 235
HelpContext property (Err object), 733
HelpFile property (Err object), 733
Hex method, 291
hiding
  borders, 61
  passwords, 141-142
highlights, 806
History object (Microsoft Internet Explorer), 359-360
hit counters, creating, 612-613
HLS (Hue, Lightness, and Saturation), 806
home pages, 806
hosting active documents, 618
  ActiveX documents, 620-621, 627, 630-632
    browser security, 627-628
    installation package, 628-629
    intranets, 621
    platform support, 620
    setup information files, 629-630
  startup HTML page, 632-633
  testing, 634-635
  Microsoft Office documents, 621-622
    editing, 618-620
    Excel spreadsheets, 622, 625
    viewing, 618-620
    Word 97 documents, 625-626
hotspot graphics. *See* image maps
Hour method, 285
HREF attribute (AREA tag), 240
HSB (Hue, Saturation, and Brightness), 807
HTML (Hypertext Markup Language), 234, 807
  DHTML (Dynamic HTML), 804
    applying, 755-757
    browser compatibility, 751
    design-time controls, 562-564
    document object model, 750
    drag-and-drop interfaces, 767-770
    element naming, 750
    event, 750-755
    HTML content, changing at runtime, 758-762
  GLOBAL.ASA file, 643
HTML documents
  adding to projects, 117, 137, 462-463
  client-side scripting
    editor, 339-341
    flexibility, 346
    FOR...EVENT method, 343-346
    HTML attributes, 341-343
    ID attribute, 346
    organization, 346-346
    <SCRIPT>, 338-339
  copying, 125-126
  CSS (Cascading Style Sheets), 176-177
    adding, 182
    background styles, 187-191
    file format, 178-179
    font styles, 185-187
    layout styles, 193-195
    linking, 179, 184-185
    list styles, 195-197
    margin styles, 191-193
    organizing into groups, 203
    style classes, 179, 183, 198-200
    Style Sheet Editor, 180, 183
    unique IDs, 180, 183-184, 200-203
  displaying information about, 365-367
  images, 765-766, 769-770
  loading into main editor window, 37-38
  sections, 756-757
  server-side scripting, 383-384
  whitespace viewing, 44-45
HTML forms
  check boxes, 135
    coding syntax, 143-145
    event handling, 145-146
  displaying
    autoformatted displays, 112-113
    HTML display limitations, 112

Index

HTTP (Hypertext Transfer Protocol)

drop-down lists, 155
  adding items, 157
  coding syntax, 156
  event handling, 159
  example, 158
  rearranging items, 157
  removing items, 157
<FORM> tag, 119-120
GET method of data transfer, 123-124
  GETFORM.HTM example, 124-126
  GETVALUES.ASP example, 127-128
list boxes, 159
  coding syntax, 160-162
  event handling, 162-163
operating modes, 114
  display mode, 114
  multimode forms, 115
  single-mode forms, 114-115
password control, 135, 141-142
POST method of data transfer, 115-116
  advantages, 116
  POSTFORM.HTM example, 116-121
  POSTVALUES.ASP example, 121-122
radio buttons, 135, 147
  event handling, 150-152
  HTML coding syntax, 147-150
Reset buttons, 119
stateless environment, 113-114
Submit buttons, 119
tables, 58-62
  adding, 467-468
  inserting, 130, 457-458
  TABLEFORM.HTM example, 129-132
  titles, 458-459

text areas
  displaying contents of, 166-167
  HTML coding syntax, 164-166
  word wrap, 165
text boxes, 135
  adding, 138
  coding syntax, 136-137
  event handling (VBScript), 139-141
  testing, 138

HTML menu commands
Image, 65
Script Block, Client, 342

HTML Outline window, 41-42

HTML Page command (Add menu), 462

HTML tags
<AREA>
  example, 239
  HREF attribute, 240
  NOHREF attribute, 240
  SHAPE attribute, 240
  TITLE attribute, 235
<BGSOUND>, 207-208
closing anchors, 383
<DIV>, 756-757
<FORM>, 119-120
<FRAMESET>, 58
<IMG>
  BORDER attribute, 237
  example, 237-238
  HEIGHT attribute, 237
  STYLE attribute, 755-756
  USEMAP attribute, 237
  WIDTH attribute, 237
<INPUT>
  ID attribute, 137
  NAME attribute, 137
  SIZE attribute, 137

  TYPE attribute, 135
  VALUE attribute, 137
<LINK>, 179
<MAP>, 239
<OBJECT>, 647-649
  ActiveMovie control, 213-216
  PARAM attribute, 216
  PATH control, 221-222
  Structured Graphics control, 227
<OPTION>, 156
  VALUE attribute, 156
<SCRIPT>, 338-339, 342
  EVENT attribute, 305
  FOR attribute, 305
  LANGUAGE, 338
<SELECT>, 155
  example, 156
  MULTIPLE attribute, 160
<SPAN>, 756-757
<TABLE>, 58-62, 128, 131
<TEXTAREA>
  COLS attribute, 164
  example, 164
  ROWS attribute, 164
  WRAP attribute, 165

HTMLEncode method, 389-390

HTTP (Hypertext Transfer Protocol), 807
server-side scripting, 380
servers, 807
server variables, 657-661
  All HTTP, 658
  All RAW, 658
  APPL_MD_PATH, 658
  APPL_PHYSICAL_PATH, 658
  AUTH_PASSWORD, 658

HTTP (Hypertext Transfer Protocol)

AUTH_TYPE, 658
AUTH_USER, 658
CERT_COOKIE, 658
CERT_FLAGS, 658
CERT_ISSUER, 659
CERT_KEYSIZE, 659
CERT_SECRETKEY-SIZE, 659
CERT_SERIALNUMBER, 659
CERT_SERVER_ISSUER, 659
CERT_SERVER_SUBJECT, 659
CERT_SUBJECT, 659
CONTENT_LENGTH, 659
CONTENT_TYPE, 659
GATEWAY_INTERFACE, 659
HTTP_ACCEPT, 660
HTTP_ACCEPT_ENCODING, 660
HTTP_ACCEPT_LANGUAGE, 660
HTTP_HOST, 660
HTTP_REFERER, 660
HTTP_SECRETKEY-SIZE, 659
HTTP_USER_AGENT, 660
HTTPS, 659
HTTPS_KEYSIZE, 659
HTTPS_SERVER_ISSUER, 659
HTTPS_SERVER_SUBJECT, 659
INSTANCE_ID, 659
INSTANCE_META_PATH, 659
LOCAL_ADDR, 659
LOGON_USER, 659
PATH_INFO, 659
PATH_TRANSLATED, 659
QUERY_STRING, 659
REMOTE_ADDR, 659
REMOTE_HOST, 659
REMOTE_USER, 660
REQUEST_METHOD, 660
SCRIPT_NAME, 660
SERVER_NAME, 660
SERVER_PORT, 660
SERVER_PORT_SECURE, 660
SERVER_PROTOCOL, 660
SERVER_SOFTWARE, 660
URL, 660

HTTP_ACCEPT_ENCODING HTTP server variable, 660

HTTP_ACCEPT HTTP server variable, 660

HTTP_ACCEPT_LANGUAGE HTTP server variable, 660

HTTP_HOST HTTP server variable, 660

HTTP_REFERER HTTP server variable, 660

HTTP_USER_AGENT HTTP server variable, 660

HTTPS HTTP server variable, 659

HTTPS_KEYSIZE HTTP server variable, 659

HTTPS_SECRETKEY-SIZE HTTP server variable, 659

HTTPS_SERVER_ISSUER HTTP server variable, 659

HTTPS_SERVER_SUBJECT HTTP server variable, 659

hue, 807

Huffman compression, 807

Hungarian Naming Convention, 275

hyperlinks, 807

hypertext, 807

HyperText Markup Language. *See* HTML

HyperText Transfer Protocol. *See* HTTP

I

icons, 807

ID attribute (<INPUT tag>), 137, 346

ID property (Button control), 469

IDE (Integrated Development Environment), 34
   dockable windows, 39-43
   main editor window, 35-37
      creating projects, 37
      Design mode, 35, 38
      loading HTML documents, 37-38
      Quick View mode, 36, 39
      Source mode, 35-39
   menus, 44-45
   modifying settings, 52-56
   navigation modes, 34
   screen, 37
   toolbars, 45-48
   views, 48-49
      custom views, 51-52
      Debug view, 49
      Design view, 49-50

DevStudio view, 49-50
Edit HTML view, 49
Full Screen view, 49
   selecting, 51
Visual Basic view, 49

IDs (CSS), 180, 183-184
   applying, 202-203
   creating, 200-201
   example, 201

If...Then...Else structure, 264-267

IIS (Internet Information Server), 74, 659

Image command (HTML menu), 65

image maps (client-side), 807
   adding to Web pages, 237-238
   advantages, 234-235
   associating with URLs, 242
   borders, removing, 237
   defined, 234
   image files, 236
   limitations, 235
   map coordinates, 239-243
   naming, 240
   sizing, 237
   target documents, 244
   testing, 244
   ToolTips, 235

images. *See* **graphics**

<IMG> tag (HTML)
   attributes
      BORDER, 237
      HEIGHT, 237
      STYLE, 755-756
      USEMAP, 237
      WIDTH, 237
   example, 237-238

importing
   images, 236, 764
   Microsoft Office documents, 621-622
      Excel spreadsheets, 622, 625
      Word 97 documents, 625-626

include files, 714
   ADOSTUFF.INC file, 517-520
   ADOVBS.INC file, 514-516
   CHECKUSER.INC file (LoginWeb project), 711, 714
   ERRORTRAP.INC file (SSI error handler), 740-744
   server-side include files
      creating, 653-655
      nesting, 652
      using, 656-657

INF (setup information) files, 629-630

inline scripts, 341-342

innerHTML property, 760

innerTEXT property, 760

<INPUT> (HTML tag)
   attributes
      ID, 137
      MAXLENGTH, 137
      NAME, 137
      order of, 145
      TYPE, 135
      VALUE, 137, 141, 148

input/output methods, 296
   examples, 298-299
   Inputbox, 296
   Msgbox, 297-298

InputBox method, 296

Insert Image dialog box, 65

INSERT query scripts
   Command object (ADO), 530-532
   creating, 495-497

Insert Table command (Table menu), 44, 60, 130, 458, 467

Insert Table dialog box, 60-61, 130, 467

insert values queries, 436-438

installing
   ActiveX documents, 628-629
   ASPChart DLL, 591-592
   DirectAnimation controls, 217-218
   FrontPage, 775
      Personal Web Server, excluding, 777-778
      Server Extensions, 777
   Visual InterDev 6 Script Library, 780-781

INSTANCE_ID HTTP server variable, 659

INSTANCE_META_PATH HTTP server variable, 659

InStr method, 278

InStrB method, 278

InStrRev method, 278

Int method, 291

Integrated Development Environment. *See* **IDE**

interface, 34

Internet, 807

Internet Explorer. *See* **Microsoft Internet Explorer**

Index

Internet Information Server. *See* **IIS**
interpreted languages, 248
intranets, 695, 808
Intrinsic Constants, 808
intrinsic controls, 154
  advantages, 134
  checkbox control, 135
    event handling (VBScript), 145-146
    HTML coding syntax, 143-145
  disadvantages, 134-135
  drop-down lists, 155
    adding items, 157
    event handling (VBScript), 159
    example, 158
    HTML coding syntax, 156
    rearranging items, 157
    removing items, 157
  file field control, 167
    displaying properties of, 169
    HTML coding syntax, 167-169
  image type input control, 170-172
  list boxes, 159
    event handling (VBScript), 162-163
    HTML coding syntax, 160-162
  password control, 135, 141-142
  radio control, 135, 147
    event handling (VBScript), 150-152
    HTML coding syntax, 147-150
  text areas
    displaying contents of, 166-167
    HTML coding syntax, 164-166
    word wrap, 165
  textbox control, 135
    adding to documents, 138
    event handling (VBScript), 139-141
    HTML coding syntax, 136-137
    testing, 138
intrinsic event declaration, 303-304
invert filters, 808
IP (Internet Protocol), 808
ISAPI (Internet Server Application Programming Interface), 507, 808
IsClientConnected property, 404
ISDN (Integrated Services Digital Network), 808
ISQL/W, 480-481

J

jaggies, 808
Java, 808
JavaScript, 808
  client-side scripting, 336
  JavaScript controls, 441
Jet databases, 420
Join method, 278
joins, 537
JPEG (Joint Photographic Experts Group), 63, 809
JScript, 381, 808

K

keys
  keypress listening, 337
  primary keys, 486
keywords, 809
  alert, 252
  dim, 252-254
kilobytes, 809

L

Label DTCs, 554-555
LANGUAGE attribute, 338
languages, 248
Launch tab (Project Properties dialog box), 16
layout
  absolute positioning, 128
  applying, 27-30
  customizing, 30-32
  forms, 128-132
  styles (CSS), 193-195
  Web pages, 58-59
LayoutDTC control, 28
LCase method, 279
LCID property, 398
Left method, 279
LeftB method, 279
LeftImage parameter (REPORT.ASP), 587
legacy design-time controls, 546
legal issues, 207
Len method, 278
LenB method, 278

Index listings

libraries
   ActiveX Data Objects (ADO) library, 506
   type libraries, 649-651

lightness, 809

Line property, 682

Link object (Microsoft Internet Explorer), 373-374

<LINK> tag (HTML), 179

Link view, 96-98
   expanding Web site links, 102
   filters, 98-100
   objects, 100-102

Link View toolbar, 99

links
   ActiveX documents, 632
   broken, 104-105
   Content Linker Component, 601
      instantiating, 605
      text files, 606-609
      URL/title pairs, 605-606
   creating, 72-74
   CSS (Cascading Style Sheets), 179, 184-185
   displaying, 71-72
   elements, 331-332
   Excel spreadsheets, 624
   managing, 373-374
   projects, 87-88
   repairing, 103-105
   URLs, 103
   Web pages, 96-98

list boxes, 159
   DTCs, 554-555
   event handling, 162-163
   HTML coding syntax, 160-162

List buttons, 474

listings
   ActiveMovie control
      OBJECT tag, 213
      PARAM attribute, 216
   ActiveX Data Objects (ADO)
      Command object, 529-530, 536-539
      Connection object, 522
      Parameter object, 538-539
      parameter queries, 534-535
      QueryDefs, 535
      Recordset object, 525-527
   ActiveX startup HTML page, 633
   Ad Rotator component
      banner display page, 611
      control file, 615
      hit counter, 612
      HTML output, 616
      instantiating, 609-610
   ADOSTUFF.INC include file
      connection strings, 517
      programming objects, 518
      ShowProperties method, 518-519
      ShowRecords method, 519
   ADOVBS.INC include file, 515-516
   ASPs
      current date/time, 605
      URL/title pairs, 606
   button control attributes, 763
   check boxes
      document_onclick event, 146
      HTML coding syntax, 143-145
   client-side scripting
      <SCRIPT>, 339
      document information, 365-366
      elements, 376
      exec methods, 371-372
      FOR...EVENT method, 343-346
      forms, 376-377
      frames, 357-358
      generating HTML, 367-368
      history of browser sessions, 359-360
      HTML attributes, 342
      links, 373-374
      locating users, 362-363
      Microsoft Internet Explorer, 349-353
      navigating windows, 355
      obtaining information about browsers, 360-361
      opening windows, 353-354
      organizing client-side script blocks, 346-345
      timing window events, 356
   columnar reports
      ADO connections, 579
      ADODB Connection and Recordset objects, 578
      high-level call method, 582
      PrintDatabase method, 580
      PrintRecord method, 581
   Content Linker Component, starting, 605
   Contents collections, 646
      data storage, 644
   CSS (Cascading Style Sheets)
      background color, 188
      background image, 190
      file format, 178
      FIRST.HTM, 180-181

Index

listings

font styles, 187
layout styles, 194
linking to documents, 185
list styles, 196
margin styles, 192
style class, 199
unique IDs, 201
data-bound grid
   client-side code block, 460
   table title, 459
data-entry form
   Delete button, 475
   HTML table coding syntax, 468
   New button, 475
   onclick/onload events, 471-472
   Save/Cancel buttons, 473
   SetInputModeTo method, 472-473
   Update/List buttons, 474
   window_onload event code, 473
databases
   creating, 480
   INSERT query scripts, 495-496
   stored procedure results, 504
   stored procedures, coding, 503
   tables, creating, 491
   triggers, 487
   views, creating, 501
design-time controls
   buttons, 559-560
   runtime text, 551
   scripting object model, 548
drag-and-drop interfaces, 768-769
drop-down lists
   event handling, 159
   HTML coding syntax, 156-158

Element object events, handling, 328-331
error handling
   ASPs, example, 737
   ASPs, header code, 736, 745
   ASPs, SSI error-handling file, 746
   client-side onclick events, 735
   Err object, accessing, 734
   ERRORTRAP.INC file, 740-744
   reporting errors, 733
   runtime COM object method error, 730
   runtime file error, 731
   syntax error example, 725
event bubbling
   canceling, 754-755
   example, 753
event handling
   attribute event declaration, 304
   Document object events, 315-317
   explicit event declaration, 305
   intrinsic event declaration, 304
file field control
   displaying properties of, 169
   HTML coding syntax, 168-169
FileSystemObject
   adding first server-side script, 668-669
   adding server-side script to create folders and files, 670
   Drive object, 672
   File object, 679
   Folder object, 676

moving folders and files on the server, 670-671
releasing reference to, 688
removing folders from server, 669
Form object events, handling, 322-324
GETFORM.HTM (GET method example), 126
GETVALUES.ASP (GET method example), 127-128
GLOBAL.ASA file
   accessing COM objects using StaticObjects collections, 648
   Contents collections, 644-645
   database connection information, 521
   DSNs, 429
   session-level objects, 401
   text files, 649
   type library references, 650-651
   using <OBJECT>, 647
graphical chart reports
   chart data, 593
   extra features, 594
   FolderOnly method, 595-596
   image size, 594
   SaveChartImage method, 595
   titles, 594
   top-level code, 592
HTTP server variables, 661
image maps, HTML coding syntax
   <AREA> and <MAP> tags, 239-243
   <IMG> tag, 238
   STYLE attribute, 755-756

Index listings   849

images
   HTML coding syntax, 170, 765-766
   VBScript, 171-172, 770
link events
   coding, 331
   responding to, 332
list boxes, event handling, 162
LoginWeb project (program-based security)
   CHECKUSER.INC file, 714
   GETUSER.ASP file, 715-716
   security code, 713-714
   session variables, 712
   USERLIST.TXT file, 717
   VERIFYUSER.ASP file, 718-720
MyHobbies paragraph, 761
MyName_onmouseover event script, 760
<P> tag attributes, 759
password control
   HTML coding syntax, 141
   value, 142
Path control project
   button/image elements, 222
   OBJECT/PARAM settings, 221-222
   scripting, 223
POSTFORM.HTM (POST method example), 120-121
POSTVALUES.ASP (POST method example), 122
radio buttons
   event handling, 151-152
   HTML coding syntax, 148-150

server-side include files
   creating, 654-655
   using, 656
   viewing, 657
server-side scripting, 382-383
   Application object, 393-397
   creating scripts, 389
   mixing with HTML, 384
   Request object, 411-415
   Response object, 406-408
   Server object, 390-391
   Session object, 399-401
   VBScript, 386-387
sound files
   HTML links, 211
   launching, 211
   playing, 209
<SPAN> tag, 757
SQL Server, 538
Structured Graphics control project
   event handling, 231-232
   graphics, rotating, 230
   HTML buttons, 228
   OBJECT tag, 227
   rectangles, drawing, 230
   square/oval objects, drawing, 230
   top-level scripting, 228-229
TABLEFORM.HTM (tables), 132
tabular reports
   client-side script, 589
   sample RIF (report information file), 586-587
   submit form, 585-586
   TEST.RIF file, 589
text areas
   displaying contents of, 166
   HTML coding syntax, 164-166

textbox control
   defining, 138
   document_onclick event, 140
   HTML coding syntax, 137
TextStream object
   creating text files on server, 684
   reading data files one byte at a time, 687
   reading random lines from text file, 686
   reading text files, 687
   server-side script, 683
   writing lines to text files, 685
VBScript
   declaring variables, 253
   Do...Loop structure, 261-264
   For...Next loop, 259-261
   If...Then...Else structure, 265-267
   module variables, 258
   onclick event, 256
   private variables, 255
   Select...Case...EndSelect structure, 267-269
   variant types, 254
   Web projects, 251
VBSMethods project
   date/time methods, 288-289
   math methods, 276-277
   output formatting methods, 296
   string methods, 281-283
   user input/output methods, 299
Windows object events, handling
   code blocks, 310
   example, 311-312
   PstMsg method, 310

lists

lists
- CSS (Cascading Style Sheets), 195-197
- drop-down lists, 155
  - adding items, 157
  - event handling (VBScript), 159
  - example, 158
  - HTML coding syntax, 156
  - rearranging items, 157
  - removing items, 157
- list boxes, 159
  - event handling (VBScript), 162-163
  - HTML coding syntax, 160-162
- multiple items, selecting, 163

LOCAL_ADDR HTTP server variable, 659

Local mode, 90-94, 809

local variables. *See* **private variables**

Location object (Microsoft Internet Explorer), 362-364

Lock method, 392-393

locking databases (ADO), 512-513

LockType property (ADO model), 508, 512-513

Log method, 273

logarithms, calculating, 273

login data, 715-717

LoginWeb project (program-level security), 711
- CHECKUSER.INC file, 711, 714
- GETUSER.ASP file, 711, 717
- security code, 712-714
- session variables, 712
- USERLIST.TXT file, 712, 717
- VERIFYUSER.ASP file, 711, 717-720

LOGON_USER HTTP server variable, 659

LOOP attribute (BGSOUND tag), 208

loops (VBScript)
- Do...Loop, 261-264
- For...Next, 252, 259-261

lossey compression, 809

LPI (Lines Per Inch), 809

LTrim method, 280

Lynx, 65

LZW (Lempel Ziv Welch), 809

M

macros, 653

magazine project. *See* **VID News Central**

Magic Wand, 809

mailing lists, 794

main editor window. *See* **editors**

managers, 41

managing
- databases, 418
- files, 664-681
- forms, 375-378
- links, 373-374

map coordinates (image maps), 239
- defining, 241-243
- HTML coding syntax, 239-241
- target documents, 244

<MAP> tag (HTML), 239

MapPath method, 390

margins (CSS), 191-193

masks, 809

Master mode, 89-90, 94-95, 809

master servers. *See* **servers**

Master Web Server tab (Project Properties dialog box), 16

math methods, 273-277

MATH.HTM page (VBSMethods project)
- tables, 274
- VBScript code, 275-277

MAXLENGTH attribute (<INPUT> tag), 137, 141

megabytes, 810

Membership Access, 693-695
- defined, 692
- examples, 694
- implementing, 694

memo fields. *See* **text**

menus, 34, 810
- Build menu, 44
- context menus, 34
- Menu bar, 810

Merge Differences dialog box, 86

merging documents, 86

message boxes, 249

messages
- Document event messages, 314
- Element object events, 325-326

methods

event messages
(DHTML), 751-752
  event bubbling, 753-755
  listening for, 752-753
Form object events,
  318-319
Window event messages,
  308

metabase, 659

**METHOD attribute
(<FORM> tag), 119**

methods, 272
  addRecord method, 559
  Application object
    Lock method, 392-393
    *UnLock method,
      392-393*
  Arc, 225
  CheckLogin, 720
  Clear, 226, 732
  data conversion methods,
    290
    CBool, 290
    CByte, 290
    CCur, 290
    CDate, 290
    CDbl, 290
    CInt, 290
    CLng, 290
    CSng, 291
    CStr, 291
    examples, 291-293
    Fix, 291
    Hex, 291
    Int, 291
    Oct, 291
  date/time methods, 284
    Date, 284
    DateAdd, 284
    DateDiff, 285
    DatePart, 285
    DateSerial, 285
    DateValue, 285
    Day, 285
    examples, 286-289
    Hour, 285
    Minute, 285
    Month, 286
    MonthName, 286
    Now, 286
    Second, 286
    Time, 286
    TimeSerial, 286
    TimeValue, 286
    Weekday, 286
    WeekdayName, 286
    Year, 286
  deleteRecord method, 559
  Document object
    (Microsoft Internet
    Explorer)
      *execCommand method,
        369-372*
      Write method, 367-369
      *WriteLn method,
        367-369*
  FileSystemObject
    CopyFile method, 668
    CopyFolder method, 668
    *CreateFolder method,
      667*
    *CreateTextFile method,
      668*
    DeleteFile method, 668
    DeleteFolder method, 667
    FileExists method, 668
    FolderExists method, 667
    MoveFile method, 668
    MoveFolder method, 668
  FillSpline, 225
  FolderOnly, 595
  FOR...EVENT method,
    338, 343-344
  GET, 123-124
    *GETFORM.HTM
      example, 124-126*
    *GETVALUES.ASP
      example, 127-128*
  getcount, 474
  GetData, 720
  getSQLText, 456
  History object (Microsoft
    Internet Explorer)
      Back method, 359
      Forward method, 359
      Go method, 359
  math methods, 273
    Abs, 273
    Atn, 273
    Cos, 273
    examples, 275-277
    Exp, 273
    Log, 273
    Rnd, 274
    Sgn, 274
    Sin, 274
    Sqr, 274
    Tan, 274
  moveAbsolute, 474, 559
  movefirst, 474
  OpenDatabase, 579
  output formatting methods, 294
    examples, 295-296
    FormatCurrency, 294
    FormatDateTime, 294
    FormatNumber, 294
    FormatPercent, 294
  Oval, 225
  Pie, 225
  Polygon, 225
  PolyLine, 225
  PolySpline, 225
  POST, 115-116
    *POSTFORM.HTM
      example, 116-121*
    *POSTVALUES.ASP
      example, 121-122*
  PostMsg, 310
  PrintDatabase, 580
  PrintRecord, 581
  ProcessError, 744
  Raise, 732
  Rect, 225

Index
methods

Redirect, 612-613
ReportError, 744
requery, 456
Request object
   BinaryRead method, 410
   Form, 122
   QueryString, 127-128
   Write method, 122
Response object
   AddHeader method, 404
   AppendToLog method, 404
   BinaryWrite method, 404
   Clear method, 405
   End method, 405
   Flush method, 405
   PICS method, 404
   Redirect method, 405
   Write method, 405
revealTrans method, 81
Rotate, 226
RotateAll, 231
RoundRect, 225
SaveChartImage, 595
Scale, 226
SelfRef, 744
SendResults, 720
Server object
   CreateObject method, 390-391
   HTMLEncode method, 389-390
   MapPath method, 390
   URLEncode method, 390
Session object
   Abandon method, 399, 402
SetFillColor, 225
SetFillStyle, 225
SetFont, 225
SetGradientFill, 225
SetGradientShape, 225
SetHatchFill, 225

SetIdentity, 226
SetInputModeTo, 472-473
SetLineColor, 225
SetLineStyle, 226
setSQLText, 456
SetTextureFill, 226
string methods, 277
   Asc, 278
   AscB, 278
   AscW, 278
   Chr, 278
   ChrB, 278
   ChrW, 278
   examples, 280-283
   Filter, 278
   InStr, 278
   InStrB, 278
   InStrRev, 278
   Join, 278
   LCase, 279
   Left, 279
   LeftB, 279
   Len, 278
   LenB, 278
   LTrim, 280
   Mid, 279
   MidB, 279
   Replace, 279
   Right, 279
   RightB, 279
   RTrim, 280
   Space, 279
   Split, 279
   StrComp, 279
   String, 280
   StrReverse, 280
   Trim, 280
   UCase, 279
Text, 226
TextStream object
   Close method, 682
   Read method, 682
   ReadAll method, 682
   ReadLine method, 682
   Skip method, 682

   SkipLine method, 682
   Write method, 682
   WriteBlankLines method, 682
   WriteLine method, 682
Transform4x4, 226
Translate, 226
updateRecord method, 559
user input/output methods, 296
   examples, 298-299
   InputBox, 296
   MsgBox, 297-298
VBScript
   alert, 252
   onclick, 251
Window object (Microsoft Internet Explorer)
   clearTimeOut method, 355-357
   Navigate method, 354-355
   Open method, 353-355
   setTimeOut method, 355-357

Microsoft Developers Network Library, 666

Microsoft Internet Explorer, 336, 346-347
   client-side scripting, 336
   Document object, 364-367
      execCommand method, 369-372
      Write method, 367-369
      WriteLn method, 367-369
   Element object, 375-377
   Form object, 375-378
   Frame object, 357-358
   hierarchy of objects, 347-349
   History object, 359-360
   Link object, 373-374

Location object, 362-364
Navigator object, 360-361
Window object, 349-350
   buttons, *351*
   clearTimeOut method, 355-357
   dialog boxes, 351-353
   Navigate method, 354-355
   Open method, 353-355
   setTimeOut method, 355-357

Microsoft Transaction Server (MTS), 529

Microsoft Web sites, 792-793
   Microsoft Developer Network Web site, 422
   SQL Server page, 449

Mid method, 279

MidB method, 279

MIME (Multipurpose Internet Mail Extension), 811

Minute method, 285

modal dialog boxes, 115

Mode property (ADO model), 508, 513

models (object models)
   ADO, 419, 507-513
   Microsoft Internet Explorer, 336, 346-378
   Netscape, 336
   scripting object model, 547-548

modes, 114
   databases, 513
   display mode, 114
   multimode forms, 115
   single-mode forms, 114-115
   working modes
      Local mode, 90-94
      Master mode, 89-90, 94-95
      Offline mode, 90-91
      setting, 91-92
      switching, 92

Month method, 286

MonthName method, 286

moveabsolute method, 474, 559

MoveFile method, 668

movefirst method, 474

MoveFolder method, 668

movies
   ActiveMovie control, 212
      adding to toolbox, 215
      HTML coding syntax, 213-216
      AVI (Audio Visual Interleave) format, 215

MsgBox method, 297-298

multimedia. *See also* **graphics**
   ActiveMovie control, 212
      adding to toolbox, 215
      HTML coding syntax, 213-216
   advantages, 206
   AVI (Audio Visual Interleave) format, 215
   Chrome package, 224
   copyright restrictions, 207
   design-time controls, 546, 562
      PageTransitions DTC, 563
      Timeline DTC, 564-567
   DirectAnimation controls, 216-217
      advantages, 217
      browser compatibility, 217
      installing, 217-218
      Path control, 220-224
      Sprite control, 218-220
      Structured Graphics control, 224-232
   disadvantages, 206-207
   performance issues, 207
   sound files
      adding to Web projects, 210
      client-side scripts, 209
      HTML coding syntax, 207-209
      labeling, 212
      launching, 211-212
      WAV format, 209

MULTIPLE attribute (SELECT tag), 160

music. *See* **audio files**

MyName_onmouseover event script, 760

MyWeb folder, 9-10

N

NAME attribute (INPUT tag), 137

name servers, 811

naming
   DSNs (data source names), 576-577
   folders, 9
   image maps, 240
   naming conventions
      case sensitivity, 236
      Hungarian Naming Convention, 275
   projects, 37
   recordset DTCs, 553
   startup pages, 18-19
   toolbars, 48
   views, 52
   Web projects, 11-14

Index

Navbar control, 442
Navigate method, 354-355
navigation
   image maps, 235
      advantages, 234-235
      defined, 234
      limitations, 235
      testing, 244
      ToolTips, 235
   Integrated Development Environment (IDE), 34
   Navbar control, 442
   recordsets
      methods, 474
      RecordsetNavbar control, 442, 466-467, 556-558
   windows, 354-355
navigation bars
   creating, 74-75
   global navigation bars, 30
   site diagrams, 78-81
   troubleshooting, 788-789
Navigator object (Microsoft Internet Explorer), 360-361
nesting SSIs, 652
Netscape, 336
New buttons, 474
New Folder dialog box, 640
New Local Group command (User menu), 700
New Local Group dialog box, 701
New Project command (File menu), 12, 37, 136
New Project dialog box, 12-13, 37, 136
New User command (User menu), 700

newsgroups, 793
NI1 (National ISDN 1), 811
noise filters, 811
normalization, 492
nothing value, 811
Now method, 286
NT-1 (Network Termination 1), 811
NT/IIS4 Option Pack, 777
NTOP (NT/IIS4 Option Pack), 777
null values, 491, 811
Number property (Err object), 732

O

Object Browser, 41
object models
   ActiveX Data Object model, 507-508
      Command object, 507
      CommandText property, 508-509
      CommandType property, 508-510
      Connection object, 507
      ConnectionString property, 508-509
      CursorLocation property, 508-511
      CursorType property, 508, 511-512
      LockType property, 508, 512-513
      Mode property, 508, 513
      Recordset object, 507
   Microsoft Internet Explorer, 336, 346-347
      Document object, 364-372, 375
      Element object, 375-377
      Form object, 375-378
      Frame object, 357-358
      hierarchy, 347-349
      History object, 359-360
      Link object, 373-374
      Navigator object, 360-364
      Window object, 349-357
   Netscape, 336
<OBJECT> (HTML), 647-649
   ActiveMovie control, coding, 213-216
   PARAM attribute, 216
   Path control, coding, 221-222
   Structured Graphics control, coding, 227
objects, 811
   Ad Rotator, 609
      control files, 613-616
      instantiating, 609-610
      rotating banner ads, creating, 610-613
   ADO
      Command object, 507, 538-539
      Connection, 578
      Connection object, 507, 520-523
      Parameter object, 532-539
      Recordset, 578
      Recordset object, 524-532
   Application object
      Contents collection, 392-397
      Lock method, 392-393
      OnEnd event, 392-393
      OnStart event, 392-393, 397
      server-side scripting, 380, 392-397

Index

Onblur event

StaticObjects collection,
  392-393, 396-397
UnLock method,
  392-393
COM objects,
  FileSystemObject,
  664-681, 688
Content Linker, 601
  creating links, 605-609
  instantiating, 605
data command, 448
  adding to Web projects,
  449
  creating, 450-451
data connection, 447-448
Document, 313-317
Element, 325-331
Err, 732
  accessing, 734
  methods, 732
  properties, 732-733
  reporting errors, 733-734
event, 768-770
Form, 318-324
Link view, 100-102
Request object
  BinaryRead method, 410
  ClientCertificate collection, 409-410
  Cookies collection, 409-412
  Form method, 122, 410, 415-416
  QueryString, 127-128, 410-415
  server-side scripting, 380, 409-415
  ServerVariables collection, 410
  TotalBytes property, 410
  Write method, 122
Response object
  AddHeader method, 404
  AppendToLog method, 404
  BinaryWrite method, 405
  Buffer property, 403
  CacheControl property, 403
  Charset property, 403
  Clear method, 405
  ContentType property, 403
  Cookies collection, 403, 406-407
  End method, 405
  Expires property, 403
  ExpiresAbsolute property, 404
  Flush method, 405
  IsClientConnected property, 404
  PICS method, 404
  Redirect method, 405
  server-side scripting, 380, 387, 402-408
  Status property, 404
  Write method, 405
ScriptingContext object, 380
Server object
  CreateObject method, 390-391
  HTMLEncode method, 389-390
  MapPath method, 390
  ScriptTimeout property, 389-390
  server-side scripting, 380, 389-391
  URLEncode method, 390
Session object
  Abandon method, 399
  CodePage property, 399
  Contents collection, 398-400
  LCID property, 398
  server-side scripting, 380, 397-402
  SessionID property, 398
  Static Objects collection, 401
  StaticObjects collections, 398
  Timeout property, 398
SOM (Scripting Object Model), 444-445
TextStream object, 681-688
Window
  event handling, 308-312
  events, 751-752

Oct method, 291

ODBC (Open Database Connectivity), 419, 811
  Active Server Pages, 381
  drivers, 420-422
  File DSNs, 422-426

ODBC Data Source Administrator, 422-424

ODBC Microsoft Access Driver 97 dialog box, 423

OFF value (WRAP attribute), 165

Offline mode, 90-91

OLE Control, 811

OLE DB
  Data Tools Utilities, 419-420
  providers, 420
  queries, 509

On Error Resume Next statement, 735

Onafterupdate event, 314, 318, 325

Onbeforeunload event, 308, 751

Onbeforeupdate event, 314, 318, 325

Onblur event, 308, 325, 751

Index

Onchange event

Onchange event, 325

onclick event, 251, 314, 318, 325

onclick method, 251

Ondataavailable event, 318, 326

Ondatasetchanged event, 318, 326

Ondatasetcomplete event, 319, 326

Ondblclick event, 314, 319, 326

Ondragstart event, 314, 319, 326

OnEnd event, 392-393, 643

Onerror event, 308, 751

Onerrorupdate event, 314, 319, 326

Onfilterchange event, 319, 326

Onfocus event, 308, 326, 751

Onhelp event, 308, 314, 319, 326, 751

Onkeydown event, 314, 319, 326

Onkeypress event, 314, 319, 326

Onkeyup event, 314, 319, 326

online magazine project. *See VID News Central*

online resources
  client-side scripting, 337
  documentation, 666
  mailing lists, 794
  newsgroups, 793
  Web sites
    Using Visual InterDev 6, 791

    Visual InterDev programming resources, 792-793

Onload event, 308, 752

Onmousedown event, 314, 319, 326

Onmousemove event, 314, 326

Onmouseout event, 319, 326

Onmouseover events, 319, 326
  innerHTML property, 760
  MyName_onmouseover event script, 759-760
  VBScript, 761-762

Onmouseup event, 314, 319, 326

Onreadystatechange event, 314

Onreset event, 319

Onresize event, 308, 326, 752

Onrowenter event, 314, 319, 326

Onrowexit event, 314, 319, 326

Onscroll event, 308, 752

Onselect event, 326

Onselectstart event, 314, 319, 326

OnStart event, 392-393, 397, 642

Onsubmit event, 319

onunload event, 308, 752

Open Database Connectivity. *See ODBC*

Open FrontPage web command (File menu), 783

Open FrontPage Web dialog box, 783

Open method, 353-355

OpenDatabase method, 579

operating modes, 114-115

operating system security, 695
  advantages, 696-697
  disadvantages, 697-698
  groups, 700-701
  implementing, 698-699
  intranets, 695
  permissions
    granting, 701-704
    removing, 705-706
  users
    adding, 700
    viewing list of, 699
  Windows filenames, 236

<OPTION> tag (HTML), 156

OptionGroup DTCs, 554-555

Options command (Tools menu), 52

Options dialog box, 52-53
  Analyzer Options section, 56
  Data Tools section, 54-55
  Debugger Options section, 56
  Environment section, 53
  HTML Options section, 56
  Projects Options section, 55-56
  Security Options section, 56
  Text Editor section, 54

Oracle databases. *See database projects*

Other Windows, Data View command (View menu), 428

Other Windows, Script Outline command (View menu), 340

OTHER.HTM page (VBSMethods project)
output formatting methods, 295-296
user input/output methods, 298-299

outlines, 41-42

output formatting methods, 294-296

Output window, 41

Oval method, 225

oval objects, 229

P

Page Designer controls, 68

PageNavBar DTC, 31-32
banners, 69-70
links, 71-74
navigation bars, 74-75
site diagrams, 68-69
tips for using, 58

PageNavBar Properties dialog box, 70

pages. *See* **ASPs; Web pages**

PageTransitions DTC, 58, 68, 81-83, 563

PageTransitions Properties dialog box, 82

Paint Palette, 811

Paintbrush, 812

PARAM attribute (<OBJECT> tag), 216

Parameter object (ADO), 532-539

parameter queries
constants, 534
Parameter object (ADO), 532-537
QueryDefs, 535-537

Password parameter (REPORT.ASP), 587

passwords, 135, 141-142

Path control, 220-224
HTML coding syntax, 221-222
scripting, 222-223

PATH_INFO HTTP server variable, 659

PATH_TRANSLATED HTTP server variable, 659

PATHCONTROL.HTM project (animation), 221
button/image elements, 222
OBJECT settings, 221-222
scripting, 223

PC PaintBrush Format (PCX), 812

PCD (Photo CD format), 812

PCX files, 812

Pencil tool, 812

PerlScript, 381-383

permissions
granting, 701-704
removing, 705-706

persistent INSERT queries, 497-498

personal projects, 87-88

Personal Web Server (PWS), 777-778

Photo CD, 812

Photoshop, 812

PHYSICAL value (WRAP attribute), 165

PICS method, 404

Pie method, 225

pixels
8-bit color, 795
16-bit color, 795
24-bit color, 795

pixellization, 812

Polygon method, 225

PolyLine method, 225

PolySpline method, 225

POST method, 115
GET method, compared, 116
POSTFORM.HTM example, 116
FORM tags, 119-120
headers, 118
horizontal bars, 118
HTML code listing, 120-121
HTML document, 117
input controls, 118-119
Submit/Reset buttons, 119
POSTVALUES.ASP example, 121
document file, 121
Request object, 122
source code listing, 122

PostMsg method, 310

PowerPoint, 81

primary keys, 486

PrintDatabase method, 580

PrintRecord method, 581

private procedures, 812

private variables, 255-257

procedural textures, 812

Index

procedures, stored

procedures, stored. *See* **stored procedures**

process color, 813

ProcessError method, 744

Project Explorer, 40, 44

Project menu commands
  Add Database Item, 484
  Web Project, Copy Web Application, 106
  Web Project, Working Mode, 92

Project Properties dialog box, 16

projects. *See* **Web projects**

properties, 157, 813. *See also* **attributes**
  ADO model
    CommandText property, 508-509
    CommandType property, 508-510
    ConnectionString property, 508-509
    CursorLocation property, 508-511
    CursorType property, 508, 511-512
    LockType property, 508, 512-513
    Mode property, 508, 513
  Button controls, 459, 469
  Connection object (ADO)
    ConnectionString property, 520
    CursorLocation property, 520
  DefaultClientScript property, 339, 349
  Drive object, 671-672
  Err object, 732-734
  File object, 678-679
  Folder object, 675-676
  Grid control, 457
  innerHTML, 760
  innerTEXT, 760
  project properties, 15-16
  RecordsetNavbar control, Update on Move, 466
  Request object, TotalBytes property, 410
  Response object
    Buffer property, 403
    CacheControl property, 403
    Charset property, 403
    ContentType property, 403
    Expires property, 403
    ExpiresAbsolute property, 403
    IsClientConnected property, 404
    Status property, 404
  Server object, ScriptTimeout property, 389-390
  Session object
    CodePage property, 399
    LCID property, 398
    SessionID property, 398
    Timeout property, 398
  TextStream object
    AtEndOfColumn property, 682
    AtEndOfLine property, 682
    Column property, 682
    Line property, 682
  VBScript, 249

Properties dialog box, 548-549

Properties Window, 40

properties

providers (OLE DB), 420

proxy servers, 813

public procedures, 813

public variables, 258

PWS (Personal Web Server), 777-778

Q

QDT (Query Designer tool), 431-433, 483
  data grid, 433-434
  records, 494
  tables, 488-489
  views, 499-500

queries
  definitions, 524-525
  OLE DB, 509
  QueryDef, 524-525
  SQL queries, 433
    delete queries, 438, 530-532
    insert queries, 530-532
    insert values queries, 436-438
    parameter queries, 532-537
    Query Designer Tool, 433
    update queries, 435-436, 528-530

Query Builder. *See* **QDT**

QUERY_STRING HTTP server variable, 659

Query toolbar, 436-438

QueryDefs, 524-525, 535-537

QueryString collection, 127-128, 410-415

R

radio buttons, 135
  event handling (VBScript), 150-152

Index

reports 859

HTML coding syntax, 147-150
Raise method, 732
random numbers, 274
raster graphics, 813
Read method, 682
ReadAll method, 682
reading
  files, 685-688
  server drives, 671-674
ReadLine method, 682
README files, 775
records, 430, 813
  autosaving, 466
  cursors, 510-512
  data binding, 464
  delete queries, 438
  entering
    INSERT query scripts, 495-497
    persistent INSERT queries, 497-498
    Query Designer, 494
  insert values queries, 436-438
  update queries, 435-436
  views, 498-499
    Query Designer tool, 499-500
    View Script, 500-502
Recordset control
  adding to HTML documents, 463-464
  adding to Web projects, 455
recordset DTCs, 552-553
Recordset object (ADO), 507, 524-527
Recordset Properties dialog box, 552-553

RecordsetNavbar control, 442, 556-558
  adding to Web projects, 466-467
  properties, 466
RecordsetNavbar Properties dialog box, 556
recordsets, 430, 813
  defined, 448
  navigating
    methods, 474
    RecordsetNavbar control, 466-467
    RecordsetNavbar DTC, 556-558
Rect method, 225
rectangles, 230
Redirect method, 405, 612-613
Registry, 813
relational operators, 813
relationships
  tables, 491-493
  Web pages, 72
relative URL addressing, 607
REMOTE_ADDR HTTP server variable, 659
REMOTE_HOST HTTP server variable, 659
REMOTE_USER HTTP server variable, 660
removing. *See* **deleting**
rendering, 813
repairing links, 103-105
Replace method, 279
report information files. *See* **RIFs**

REPORT.ASP document (tabular report)
  calling, 585-586
  copying, 583-584
  reusability, 585
ReportError method, 744
reports, 570
  broken links reports, 105
  columnar reports, 570, 575
    ADO connections, 577-579
    advantages, 571
    data connections, 575-577
    data detail, 581-582
    defined, 570
    disadvantages, 571
    headings, 580
    print loops, 580
  graphical chart reports, 592
    advantages, 574
    ASPChart component, 591-592
    chart data, 593
    creating, 593-596
    defined, 570
    displaying, 595
    FolderOnly method, 595-596
    image sizes, 594
    saving, 595
    titles, 593
    top-level code, 592-593
  graphical reports, 573, 590-591
  tabular reports, 572, 583-584
    advantages, 572-573
    client-side script, 589-590
    column totals, 583
    defined, 570

Index

reports

disadvantages, 573
group breaks, 583
REPORT.ASP document, 583-586
RIFs (report information files), 586-589

ReportTitle parameter (REPORT.ASP), 587

REPOSITION.HTM document, 763

requery method, 456

REQUEST_METHOD HTTP server variable, 660

Request object
BinaryRead method, 410
ClientCertificate collection, 409-410
Cookies collection, 409-412
Form collection, 122, 410, 415-416
QueryString collection, 127-128, 412-415
server-side scripting, 380, 409-415
ServerVariables collection, 410
TotalBytes property, 410
Write method, 122

reserve cropping, 814

Reset buttons, 119

resizing, 813

resolution, 814

Response object
AddHeader method, 404
AppendToLog method, 404
BinaryWrite method, 405
Buffer property, 403
CacheControl property, 403

Charset property, 403
Clear method, 405
ContentType property, 403
Cookies collection, 403-407
End method, 405
Expires property, 403
ExpiresAbsolute property, 404
Flush method, 405
IsClientConnected property, 404
PICS method, 404
Redirect method, 405
server-side scripting, 380, 387, 402-408
Status property, 404
Write method, 405

responsiveness, 452

revealTrans method, 81

REXX, 383

RGB (Red, Green, and Blue), 814

RIFs (report information files), 586
creating, 588
example, 586-587
file format, 587-588
TEST.RIF file, 589

Right method, 279

RightB method, 279

RightImage parameter (REPORT.ASP), 588

ripple filters, 814

Rnd method, 274

Rotate method, 226

RotateAll method, 231

rotating graphics, 230

rotating banner ads, 609
banner display pages, 611
control files, 613-616
hit counters, 612-613
server-side script, 609-610
text files, 610

RoundRect method, 225

routines (VBScript), 250-251
alert method, 252
declaring variables, 253
dim keyword, 252-254
for...next loop, 252
onclick event, 251
Quick View, 252
testing, 251-252
variables, 252

ROWS attribute (TEXTAREA tag), 164

RTrim method, 280

runtime errors, 729-730, 814
defined, 724
examples, 729-730
preventing, 730-732

runtime text and design-time controls, 544
converting DTCs to runtime text, 551
viewing, 550-551

S

saturation, 814

Save buttons, 473

Save command (File menu), 63

Save Database Diagram command (File menu), 484

SaveChartImage method, 595

saving
  database diagrams, 484
  Web page templates, 63
Scale method, 226
scan rates, 814
scanlines, 814
scanners, 814
schemes, 814
scope (VBScript variables), 647, 814
  decision structures, 259
  looping structures, 259
  module variables, 257-258
  private variables, 255-257
  public variables, 258
  variable initialization, 258
SCR attribute (<BGSOUND> tag), 208
screen. *See* **IDE**
screening, 815
Script Block, Client command (HTML menu), 342
Script Library, 780-781
SCRIPT_NAME HTTP server variable, 660
Script Outline window, 41-42
  client-side scripting, 340-341
  viewing, 340
<SCRIPT> tag (HTML), 305, 338-339, 342
scripting. *See also* **VBScript**
  browser-neutral scripting, 337
  client-side scripting, 336
    benefits, 337
    Button control, 460
    calculations, 337
    DefaultClientScript property, 339, 349
    editing with server-side scripts, 384
    HTML documents, 338-346
    ID attribute, 344
    JavaScript, 336
    listening for keypresses, 337
    Microsoft Internet Explorer, 336, 346-378
    mixing with server-side scripting, 337
    monitoring mouse movements, 337
    online help, 337
    purpose of, 337
    Visual Basic Scripting, 336
  definition of, 336
  server-side scripting, 337, 380
    Active Server Pages, 380
    advantages, 381-382
    Application object, 380, 392-397
    creating scripts, 385-389
    editing client-side scripts, 384
    evolution of, 381
    HTTP, 380
    JScript, 381
    mixing with client-side scripting, 337
    mixing with HTML, 383-384
    PerlScript, 381-383
    Request object, 380, 409-415
    Response object, 380, 387, 402-408
    REXX, 383
    running scripts, 383
    ScriptingContext object, 380
    security, 389
    Server object, 380, 389-391
    Session object, 380, 397-402
    VBScript, 380-381, 386-387
    writing scripts, 382-383
  SOM (Scripting Object Model), 444-445
    design-time controls, 547-548
    enabling, 445
Scripting Object Model. *See* **SOM**
ScriptingContext object, 380
ScriptingObjectModel property (documents), 445
ScriptLibrary folder, 10, 442
scripts (VBScript). *See also* **change scripts**
  check boxes, 145-146
  client-side scripting
    data-entry forms, 469-475
    DTCs (design-time controls), 443-444, 550-551
  copying, 321-322
  DirectAnimation Path control, 223
  drag-and-drop interfaces, 768-769
  drop-down lists, 159
  DTC buttons, 559-560
  images, 769-770
  levels, 815
  list boxes, 162-163
  MyName_onmouseover, 760
  radio buttons, 150-152

Index

scripts (VBScript)

server-side scripting
  disadvantages, 452
  DTCs (design-time controls), 443-444
sound files
  launching, 211
  playing, 209
text boxes, 139-141
Timeline DTC events, 567

ScriptTimeout property, 389-390

Second method, 286

security, 692
ActiveX documents, 627-628
Authority Access, 692-693
Copy Web feature, 106-108
FileSystemObject, 664
Membership Access, 692-695
operating system security, 695
  adding users, 700
  advantages, 696-697
  defining groups, 700-701
  disadvantages, 697-698
  granting permissions, 701-704
  implementing, 698-699
  intranets, 695
  passwords, 135, 141-142
  removing permissions, 705-706
  viewing users, 699
program-based security, 708
  advantages, 708-709
  ASP example, 711-720
  disadvantages, 709-711
  implementing, 721
server-side scripting, 389

Select All command (Edit menu), 102
Select Background Image dialog box, 189
Select Data Source dialog box, 426-427, 481-482, 576
<SELECT> tag (HTML), 155
  example, 156
  MULTIPLE attribute, 160
Select...Case...End Select structure, 267-269
selections, 815
SelfRef method, 744
SendResults method, 720
SERVER_NAME HTTP server variable, 660
Server object
  CreateObject method, 390-391
  HTMLEncode method, 389-390
  MapPath method, 390
  ScriptTimeout property, 389-390
  server-side scripting, 380, 389-391
  URLEncode method, 390
SERVER_PORT HTTP server variable, 660
SERVER_PORT_SECURE HTTP server variable, 660
SERVER_PROTOCOL HTTP server variable, 660
SERVER_SOFTWARE HTTP server variable, 660

server-side controls. *See* **DTCs**
server-side image maps, 234
server-side include. *See* **SSI**
server-side scripting, 337
Active Server Pages, 380
advantages, 381-382
Application object, 380, 392-397
client-side scripts
  editing, 384
  mixing, 337
DTCs (design-time controls), 443-444
evolution, 381
HTTP, 380
Request object, 380, 409-415
Response object, 380, 387, 402-408
responsiveness, 452
REXX, 383
ScriptingContext object, 380
scripts
  creating, 385-389
  JScript, 381
  mixing with HTML, 383-384
  PerlScript, 381-383
  running, 383
  writing, 382-383
security, 389
Server object, 380, 389-391
Session object, 380, 397-402
VBScript, 380-381, 386-387
servers, 815
choosing, 11
Internet Information Server (IIS), 74, 659

Index

SQL (Structured Query Language)

Microsoft Transaction Server (MTS), 529
PWS (Personal Web Server), 777-778
scripting, 337
server drives, 671-674
specifying for Web projects, 13
troubleshooting, 787-788
variables, 657-661
Web sites, 106-108

ServerVariables collection, 410, 657-661

Session object
Abandon method, 399, 402
CodePage property, 399
Contents collections, 398-400
LCID property, 398
server-side scripting, 380, 397-402
SessionID property, 398
StaticObjects collections, 398, 401
Timeout property, 398

Session_OnEnd event, 642

Session_OnStart event, 642

SessionID property, 398

sessions, 815
code, 522
variables
LoginWeb project, 712
sharing, 400

Set Primary Key command (Edit menu), 485, 489

SetFillColor method, 225

SetFillStyle method, 225

SetFont method, 225

SetGradientFill method, 225

SetGradientShape method, 225
SetHatchFill method, 225
SetIdentity method, 226
SetInputModeTo method, 472-473
SetLineColor method, 225
SetLineStyle method, 226
setSQLText method, 456
SetTextureFill method, 226
setTimeOut method, 355-357

setup information files (ActiveX documents), 629-630

SGC. *See* **Structured Graphics control**

Sgn method, 274

shadows, 815

SHAPE attribute (<AREA> tag), 240

shapes, 225-226, 230

shareware, 815

sharpening, 815

Shockwave, 815

Sin method, 274

sines, 274

Site Designer, 77-78

Site Diagram toolbar, 79

site diagrams, 17
creating, 17, 68-69, 77-78
documents
adding, 19-21
deleting, 22-24
moving, 22
navigation bars, 78-81
property pages, 18-19

SIZE attribute (<INPUT> tag), 137
sizing image maps, 237
Skip method, 682
SkipLine method, 682
sliders, 815
smoothing, 815
SOFT value (WRAP attribute), 165
SOM (Scripting Object Model), 444-445
design-time controls, 547-548
enabling, 445

sound files. *See* **audio files**

Source property, 733
Space method, 279
<SPAN> tag (HTML), 756-757
Special Directory Access dialog box, 704
sphere filters, 816
SPID (Service Profile Identifier), 816
Split method, 279

spreadsheets. *See* **tabular reports**

Sprite control, 218-220

sprocs. *See* **stored procedures**

SQL (Structured Query Language), 816
change scripts, 486, 495-498
commands
data command, 431-433
UPDATE, 435-436
queries, 433
delete queries, 438, 530-532

Index

SQL (Structured Query Language)
   insert queries, 495-498, 530-532
   insert values queries, 436-438
   parameter queries, 532-537
   Query Designer Tool, 433
   update queries, 435-436, 528-530
   script templates
      advantages, 490
      Table Script, 483, 489-491
      Trigger Script, 486-488
      View Script, 500-502
   stored procedures
      creating, 502-503
      debugging, 503
      defined, 502
      results, 504
      running, 503-504
      triggers, compared, 502

SQL SELECT parameter (REPORT.ASP), 587

SQL Server databases. *See* **database projects**

SQL Server Web site, 449

Sqr method, 274

square objects, 229

square roots, 274

SSI (server-side include) files, 714
   creating, 653-655
   error-handling files, 738
      adding to ASP documents, 745-746
      advantages, 744
      creating, 739-740
      designing, 738-739
      ERRORTRAP.INC example, 740-744
   nesting, 652
   using, 656-657

S/T Interface, 816

startup pages
   naming, 18-19
   specifying, 600

state forms, 113-114

StaticContents collections, 644

StaticObjects collections, 648
   Application object, 392-393, 396-397
   Session object, 398, 401

Status bar, 816

Status property, 404

stored procedures
   creating, 502-503
   debugging, 503
   defined, 502
   results, 504
   running, 503-504
   SQL Server, 538-539
   triggers, 502

StrComp method, 279

streaming text, 683-688

String method, 280

string methods, 277
   Asc, 278
   AscB, 278
   AscW, 278
   Chr, 278
   ChrB, 278
   ChrW, 278
   examples, 280-283
   Filter, 278
   InStr, 278
   InStrB, 278
   InStrRev, 278
   Join, 278
   LCase, 279
   Left, 279
   LeftB, 279
   Len, 278
   LenB, 278
   LTrim, 280
   Mid, 279
   MidB, 279
   Replace, 279
   Right, 279
   RightB, 279
   RTrim, 280
   Space, 279
   Split, 279
   StrComp, 279
   String, 280
   StrReverse, 280
   Trim, 280
   UCase, 279

STRING.HTM page (VBSMethods project), 280-283

strings, 816

StrReverse method, 280

Structured Graphics control, 224-232
   client-side script blocks, 228-229
   event handling, 231-232
   graphics, rotating, 230
   HTML coding syntax, 227
   methods, 225-226
   oval objects, drawing, 229
   rectangles, drawing, 230
   sample application, 226-227
   square objects, drawing, 229

STYLE attribute (<IMG> tag), 755-756

Style Sheet command (Add Item menu), 182

Index

TCP/IP (Transmission Control Protocol/Internet Protocol) 865

Style Sheet Editor, 180, 183
   background styles, 187
      colors, 188
      images, 189-191
   CSS (Cascading Style Sheets)
      adding to Web projects, 182
      linking to documents, 184-185
   font styles, 185
      font families, 187
      setting, 185-186
      viewing, 187
   layout styles, 193-195
   list styles, 195-197
   margin styles, 191-193
   style classes, 198-200
   unique IDs, 200-203
style sheets. *See* CSS
Submit buttons, 119
submitting forms
   GET method, 123-124
      GETFORM.HTM example, 124-126
      GETVALUES.ASP example, 127-128
   POST method, 115-116
      advantages, 116
      POSTFORM.HTM example, 116-121
      POSTVALUES.ASP example, 121-122
   Reset buttons, 119
   Submit buttons, 119
SubTitle parameter (REPORT.ASP), 587
syntax errors
   defined, 724
   example, 724-726
   preventing, 726-727
system requirements, 74

T

T1-3, 816-817
table data command, 430-431
TABLE element (HTML), 58-62
Table menu commands, Insert Table, 44, 60, 130, 458, 467
Table Script, 483, 489-491
<TABLE> tag (HTML), 128, 131
TABLEFORM.HTM form (tables), 129
   source code listing, 131-132
   tables, creating, 130
tables
   adding to Web projects, 467-468
   alignment, 61
   borders, 60-61
   columns, 60-62
   creating, 483
      Database Diagram tool, 484-486
      HTML, 128-130
      Query Designer tool, 488-489
      Table Script, 489-491
   editing (Query Designer Tool), 433-434
   inserting, 457-458
   null values, 491
   primary keys, 486
   records, entering
      INSERT query scripts, 495-497
      persistent INSERT queries, 497-498
      Query Designer, 494

   relationships, 491-493
   rows, 60
   TABLEFORM.HTM example, 129-132
   titles, 458-459
   triggers, 486-488
   views (virtual tables), 498-499
      Query Designer tool, 499-500
      View Script, 500-502
   width, 60, 588
TableWidth parameter (REPORT.ASP), 588
tabular reports
   adding to Web projects, 622, 625
   advantages, 572-573
   client-side script, 589-590
   column totals, 583
   defined, 570
   disadvantages, 573
   group breaks, 583
   REPORT.ASP document, 583-584
      calling, 585-586
      copying, 583-584
      reusability, 585
   RIFs (report information files), 586
      creating, 588
      example, 586-587
      file format, 587-588
      TEST.RIF file, 589
   TABULAR.ASP document, 583-584
tags. *See* HTML
Tan method, 274
tangents, 274
Task List, 40-41
TCP/IP (Transmission Control Protocol/Internet Protocol), 817

<TD> TAG (HTML), 62

teams, 86
- isolation, 95-96
- personal projects, 87-88
- shared projects, 86-87
- testing areas, 105-106
- working modes
  - *Local mode, 90-94*
  - *Master mode, 89-90, 94-95*
  - *Offline mode, 90-91*
  - *setting, 91-92*
  - *switching, 92*

templates
- Table Script, 483, 489-491
- Trigger Script template, 486-488
- View Script template, 500-502
- Web pages, 58-59
  - *banners, 69-70*
  - *building sites with, 75-77*
  - *copying, 76*
  - *creating, 60*
  - *images, 63-66*
  - *links, 71-74*
  - *navigation bars, 74-75*
  - *saving, 63*
  - *tables, 60-62*
  - *text, 66-67*

testing
- ActiveX document installation, 634-635
- applications, 726-727
- data sources, 426
- image maps, 244
- textbox controls, 138
- Web page layouts in different browser, 60-61
- Web sites, 105-106

text
- converting DTCs (design-time controls) to, 443
- copying, 321-322
- files
  - *adding to Web projects, 607*
  - *TextStream object, 683-688*
- text areas
  - *displaying contents of, 166-167*
  - *HTML coding syntax, 164-166, 757*
  - *word wrap, 165*
- Web page templates, 66-67
- wrap, 757

text boxes, 135
- adding to documents, 138
- DTCs, 464-466, 554-555
- event handling (VBScript), 139-141
- HTML coding syntax, 136-137
- testing, 138

text browsers, 65

text editors, 607

Text method, 226

<TEXTAREA> tag (HTML), 164-165

Textbox Properties dialog box, 554

TextStream object, 681-688
- methods, 682
- properties, 682

texture mapping, 817

TGA (Targa Format), 817

themes, 24-25, 817
- applying, 25-26
- creating, 25
- previewing, 26

thin clients, 337

TIFF (Tagged Image File Format), 817

time, 604

Time method, 286

time/date methods, 284
- Date, 284
- DateAdd, 284
- DateDiff, 285
- DatePart, 285
- DateSerial, 285
- DateValue, 285
- Day, 285
- examples, 286-289
- Hour, 285
- Minute, 285
- Month, 286
- MonthName, 286
- Now, 286
- Second, 286
- Time, 286
- TimeSerial, 286
- TimeValue, 286
- Weekday, 286
- WeekdayName, 286
- Year, 286

Timeline DTC, 564-565
- inserting, 565
- scripts, 567
- timing, 565-567

Timeout property, 398

TimeSerial method, 286

TimeValue method, 286

timing
- Timeline DTC events, 565-567
- Web page transitions, 563
- windows, 355-357

TITLE attribute (<AREA> tag), 235

title bar, 817

T

toolbars
  custom toolbars, 34
    creating, 47-48
    naming, 48
  Design toolbar, 60
  displaying, 46
  docking, 46
  Link View toolbar, 99
  Query toolbar, 436-438
  Site Diagram toolbar, 79

Toolbars command (View menu), 45-46

Toolbox, 40

toolbox controls, 215

tools
  custom tools, 40
  Data Tools, 479
  Database Diagram, 483-484
    table relationships, 491-493
    tables, creating, 484-486
  ISQL/W, 480
  Query Designer, 483
    records, 494
    tables, 488-489
    views, 499-500
  Table Script, 483, 489-491
  User Manager
    adding users, 700
    viewing users, 699

Tools menu commands
  Options, 52
  View Links on WWW, 103

ToolTips, 235

TotalBytes property, 410

TotalColumns parameter (REPORT.ASP), 587

trace contours, 817

tracking user sessions, 397-402

Transaction Server (Microsoft), 529, 818

transactions, 817

Transform4x4 method, 226

Translate method, 226

triggers, 486-488

Trim method, 280

troubleshooting FrontPage/Visual InterDev integration, 787-789

true color, 818

TYPE attribute (<INPUT> tag), 135

type libraries, 649-651

U

U Interface, 818

UCase method, 279

Undo Option, 818

Uniform Resource Locators. *See* **URLs**

uninstalling FrontPage, 776

unique IDs (CSS), 180, 183-184
  applying, 202-203
  creating, 200-201
  example, 201

UnLock method, 392-393

Update buttons, 474

Update on Move property, 466

update queries, 435-436, 528-530

UPDATE SQL command, 435-436

updateRecord method, 559

URL HTTP server variable, 660

URLEncode method, 390

URLs (Uniform Resource Locators), 234, 818
  absolute addressing, 607
  image maps, 241-242
  links, 103
  redirection, 612-613
  relative addressing, 607

USEMAP attribute (<IMG> tag), 237

Usenet newsgroups, 793

user input/output methods. *See also* **forms**
  examples, 298-299
  InputBox, 296
  MsgBox, 297-298

User Manager, 699-700

User menu commands
  New Local Group, 700
  New User, 700

UserID parameter (REPORT.ASP), 587

USERLIST.TXT file (LoginWeb project), 712, 717

users
  accepting data from, 409-416
  groups, 700-701
  locating, 362-364
  redirecting, 612-613
  responding to, 402-408
  tracking sessions, 397-402
  Web sites
    checking for valid users, 714-715
    directing to, 658
    login data, 715-717
    user validation, 717-720

users

Windows NT
  adding, 700
  viewing list of, 699
Using Visual InterDev 6 Web site, 791

V

VALUE attribute
  <INPUT tag>, 137, 141, 148
  <OPTION tag>, 156
variables, 818
  application variables, 392
  declaring, 644
  HTTP server variables, 657-661
  scope, 647
  session variables
    LoginWeb project, 712
    sharing, 400
  VBScript, 252
    decision structures, 259
    declaring, 253
    looping structures, 259
    module variables, 257-258
    private variables, 255-257
    public variables, 258
    scope, 255-259
    variable initialization, 258
    variant types, 254
variants, 254
VBA/VBScript comparison, 248
vbAbortRetryIgnore button value (MsgBox method), 297
vbApplicationModel button value (MsgBox method), 297

vbCritical button value (MsgBox method), 297
vbExclamation button value (MsgBox method), 297
vbInformation button value (MsgBox method), 297
vbOKCancel button value (MsgBox method), 297
vbOKOnly button value (MsgBox method), 297
vbQuestion button value (MsgBox method), 297
vbRetryCancel button value (MsgBox method), 297
VBScript. *See also* **scripting**
  applications, 249-252
  browsers, 381
  client-side scripting, 336
  control structures, 259
    decision structures, 259
    Do...Loop loops, 261-264
    For...Next loops, 252, 259-261
    If...Then...Else structure, 264-267
    looping structures, 259
    Select...Case...End Select structure, 267-269
  controls, 249
  event handling, 302. *See also* VBSEvents project
    attribute event declaration, 304-305
    Document object events, 313-317
    Element object events, 325-331
    event bubbling, 306
    explicit event declaration, 305-306

  Form object events, 318-324
  intrinsic event declaration, 303-304
  link events, 331-332
  onclick event, 251
  Window object events, 308-312
  images, 769-770
  keywords
    alert, 252
    dim, 252-254
    endif, 266
  message boxes, 249
  methods, 272
    Abs, 273
    alert method, 252
    Asc, 278
    AscB, 278
    AscW, 278
    Atn, 273
    CBool, 290
    CByte, 290
    CCur, 290
    CDate, 290
    CDbl, 290
    Chr, 278
    ChrB, 278
    ChrW, 278
    CInt, 290
    CLng, 290
    Cos, 273
    CSng, 291
    CStr, 291
    data conversion methods, 290-293
    Date, 284
    DateAdd, 284
    DateDiff, 285
    DatePart, 285
    DateSerial, 285
    date/time methods, 284-289
    DateValue, 285
    Day, 285

Index
VI6News mailing list

examples, 275-299
Exp, 273
Filter, 278
Fix, 291
FormatCurrency, 294
FormatDateTime, 294
FormatNumber, 294
FormatPercent, 294
Hex, 291
Hour, 285
InputBox, 296
InStr, 278
InStrB, 278
InStrRev, 278
Int, 291
Join, 278
LCase, 279
Left, 279
LeftB, 279
Len, 278
LenB, 278
Log, 273
LTrim, 280
math methods, 273-277
Mid, 279
MidB, 279
Minute, 285
Month, 286
MonthName, 286
MsgBox, 297-298
Now, 286
Oct, 291
onclick method, 251
output formatting methods, 294-296
Replace, 279
Right, 279
RightB, 279
Rnd, 274
RTrim, 280
Second, 286
Sgn, 274
Sin, 274
Space, 279
Split, 279
Sqr, 274
StrComp, 279
String, 280
string methods, 277-283
StrReverse, 280
Tan, 274
Time, 286
TimeSerial, 286
TimeValue, 286
Trim, 280
UCase, 279
user input/output methods, 296-299
Weekday, 286
WeekdayName, 286
Year, 286
overview, 248-249
Quick View, 252
routines, 250-251
scope, 255-259
server-side scripting, 380-381, 386-387
testing, 251-252
variables, 252
   declaring, 253
   initialization, 258
   module variables, 257-258
   private, 255-257
   public, 258
   variant types, 254
VBA comparison, 248
VBScript property, 249
Visual Basic Setup Wizard, 627
Visual Basic view (IDE), 49

VBScript property, 249

VBSEvents project, 307
DEFAULT.HTM page, 307-308
DOCUMENT.HTM page, 314-317
ELEMENT.HTM page, 327-331
FORM.HTM page
   elements, 320
   event-handling code, 322-324
WINDOW.HTM page
   code blocks, 309
   event-handling code, 311-312
   loading, 312
   method headers, 311
   PostMsg method, 310
   TextArea control, 308

VBSMethods project
CONVERSION.HTM page, 291-293
DATETIME.HTM page
   tables, 286-287
   VBScript code, 287-289
DEFAULT.HTM page, 272
MATH.HTM page, 274-277
OTHER.HTM page
   output formatting methods, 295-296
   user input/output methods, 298-299
STRING.HTM page, 280-283

vbSystemModal button value (MsgBox method), 297

vbYesNo button value (MsgBox method), 297

vbYesNoCancel button value (MsgBox method), 297

vector graphics, 818

VERIFYUSER.ASP file (LoginWeb project), 711, 717-720

VI6News mailing list, 794

Index

VID News Central

VID News Central, 601
  contents page
    elements, 603-604
    layout, 602-604
    server-side script, 604-606
  text files, 606-609

video files
  ActiveMovie control, 212
    adding to toolbox, 215
    HTML coding syntax, 213-216
  AVI (Audio Visual Interleave) format, 215

View Links on WWW command (Tools menu), 103

View menu commands, 40
  Broken Links Report, 105
  Debug, 49
  Define Window Layout, 51
  Design, 49-50
  DevStudio, 49-50
  Edit HTML, 49
  Full Screen, 49
  Other Windows, Data View, 428
  Other Windows, Script Outline, 340
  Toolbars, 45-46
  Visible Borders, 60
  Visual Basic, 49

View Script, 500-502

viewing
  CSS (Cascading Style Sheet) styles, 187
  DTC (design-time control) scripts, 442
  files, 678-681
  folders, 674-678
  FrontPage documents, 781-782

links
  broken links, 105
  URLs, 103
  Web pages, 96-98
Microsoft Office documents, 618-620
project properties, 15-16
runtime text, 550-551
scripts, 550-551
users, 699
Web projects, 784
windows, 40, 340

views
  creating, 498-499
    Query Designer tool, 499-500
    View Script, 500-502
  databases, 537
  Integrated Development Environment, 48-49
    custom views, 51-52
    Debug view, 49
    Design view, 49-50
    DevStudio view, 49-50
    Edit HTML view, 49
    Full Screen view, 49
    selecting, 51
    Visual Basic view, 49
  Link view, 96-98
    expanding Web site links
    filters, 98-100
    objects, 100-102

vinivar component, 788-789

virtual roots, 818

VIRTUAL value (WRAP attribute), 165

Visible Borders command (View menu), 60

Visual Basic command (View menu), 49

Visual Basic Scripting language. *See* VBScript

Visual Basic Setup Wizard, 627

Visual Basic view (IDE), 49

Visual C++, 810

Visual Component Manager, 41

Visual FoxPro, 810

Visual J, 811

Visual SourceSafe, 53

W

WAV file format, 209

Web (World Wide Web), 113-114

Web applications, 818
  framework, 640-641
  GLOBAL.ASA file, 641-642
    Application OnEnd event, 643
    Application OnStart event, 642
    COM object pointers, 643-644
    Contents collections, 644-645
    data sharing, 643-644
    declaring variables, 644
    editing, 645-647
    HTML, 643
    <OBJECT>, 647-649
    Session_OnEnd event, 642
    Session_OnStart event, 642
    type library references, 649-651
  VBScript
    alert keyword, 252
    alert method, 252
    control structures, 259

Index

Web projects

controls, 249
creating, 249-252
decision structures, 259
declaring variables, 253
dim keyword, 252-254
Do...Loop loops, 261-264
endif, 266
for...next loop, 252
For...Next loops, 259-261
If...Then...Else structure, 264-267
looping structures, 259
message boxes, 249
module variables, 257-258
onclick event, 251
onclick method, 251
private variables, 255-257
properties, 249
public variables, 258
Quick View, 252
routines, 250-251
scope, 255-259
Select...Case...End Select structure, 267-269
testing, 251-252
variable initialization, 258
variables, 252
variant types, 254

Web browsers. *See* **browsers**

Web databases, 421-422

Web forms. *See* **forms**

web maps. *See* **site diagrams**

Web pages
design-time controls, 546-547
evolution of design, 59
image maps, 234
layout, 58-61

links, 96-98
relationships, 72
templates, 58-59
  banners, 69-70
  building sites with, 75-77
  copying, 76
  creating, 60
  images, 63-66
  links, 71-74
  navigation bars, 74-75
  saving, 63
  tables, 60-62
  text, 66-67
transitions, 81-83, 563
  timing, 563
  tips for using, 83

Web Project Wizard, 87-88, 91

Web Project, Copy Web Application command (Project menu), 106

Web Project, Working Mode command (Project menu), 92

Web projects. *See also* **active content; forms**
ActiveX documents, 627
  adding, 630-632
  browser security, 627-628
  installation package, 628-629
  setup information files, 629-630
  startup HTML page, 632-633
  testing, 634-635
ASPs, 121, 453-455, 602-603
data commands, 448
  adding, 449
  creating, 450-451
data connections, 447-448
databases, *See* database projects

defined, 8
designing, 8
directory locations, 8-10
drag-and-drop interfaces, 767-770
folders, 640
HTML documents, 117, 137, 462-463
image maps, 235
  adding, 237-238
  advantages, 234-235
  associating with URLs, 242
  defined, 234
  limitations, 235
  map coordinates, 239-243
  naming, 240
  sizing, 237
  target documents, 244
  testing, 244
  ToolTips, 235
images, 236, 764
inserting HTML documents, 37-38
layouts
  applying, 27-30
  customizing, 30-32
LoginWeb, 711
  CHECKUSER.INC file, 711, 714
  GETUSER.ASP file, 711, 717
  security code, 712-714
  session variables, 712
  USERLIST.TXT file, 712, 717
  VERIFYUSER.ASP file, 711, 717-720
Microsoft Office documents, adding, 621-622
  Excel spreadsheets, 622, 625
  Word 97 documents, 625-626

Index

Web projects

multimedia, *See* multimedia
naming, 11-14, 37
navigation, 30
opening, 37, 783-784
personal projects
   creating, 87-88
   linking, 87-88
shared projects, 86-87
site diagrams, 17
   adding documents, 19-21
   creating, 17
   deleting documents, 22-24
   moving documents, 22
   property pages, 18-19
start pages, 600
text files, 607
themes, 24-25
   applying, 25-26
   creating, 25
   previewing, 26
VBScript
   alert keyword, 252
   alert method, 252
   control structures, 259
   controls, 249
   creating, 12-13, 37, 136, 249-252, 446
   decision structures, 259
   declaring variables, 253
   dim keyword, 252-254
   Do...Loop loops, 261-264
   endif, 266
   for...next loop, 252
   For...Next loops, 259-261
   If...Then...Else structure, 264-267
   looping structures, 259
   message boxes, 249
   module variables, 257-258
   onclick event, 251
   onclick method, 251
   private variables, 255-257
   properties, 249
   public variables, 258
   Quick View, 252
   routines, 250-251
   scope, 255-259
   Select...Case...End Select structure, 267-269
   testing, 251-252
   variable initialization, 258
   variables, 252
   variant types, 254
viewing
   FrontPage, 784
   properties, 15-16

Web servers. *See* **servers**

Web sites
copying, 106-108
expanding links in Link view, 102
Microsoft, 792-793
   Microsoft Developer Network Web site, 422
   SQL Server page, 449
templates, 75-77
testing, 105-106
Using Visual InterDev 6, 791
Visual InterDev programming resources, 792-793

Web-related errors, 727-728
content-related problems, 727
defined, 724
hardware problems, 727

webs (FrontPage)
connecting to, 779
opening, 783-784
selecting, 780
viewing, 781-784
Visual InterDev 6 Script Library, installing, 780-781

Weekday method, 286

WeekdayName method, 286

whitespace, 44-45

WIDTH attribute (<IMG> tag), 237

widths (tables), 60

Window object (Microsoft Internet Explorer), 349-350
buttons, 351
dialog boxes, 351-353
event handling
   code blocks, 309
   code listing, 311-312
   messages, 308
   method headers, 311
   PostMsg method, 310
events, 751-752
methods
   clearTimeOut method, 355-357
   Navigate method, 354-355
   Open method, 353-355
   setTimeOut method, 355-357

WINDOW.HTM page (VBSEvents project)
code blocks, 309
event-handling code, 311-312
loading, 312
method headers, 311
PostMsg method, 310
TextArea control, 308

windows
  client-side scripts
    navigating, 354-355
    opening, 353-355
    scripting, 340-341
    timing, 355-357
  Data View window, 41
  Deployment Manager, 41
  docking, 34
  HTML Outline window, 41-42
  main editor window, 35-37
    creating projects, 37
    Design mode, 35, 38
    loading HTML documents, 37-38
    Quick View mode, 36, 39
    Source mode, 35-39
  Object Browser, 41
  Output window, 41
  Project Explorer window, 40, 44
  Properties Window, 40
  Script Outline window, 41-42, 340-341
  stacking, 42-43
  Task List window, 40-41
  Toolbox window, 40
  viewing, 40
  Visual Component Manager window, 41
Windows filenames, 236
Windows NT
  groups, 700-701
  operating system security, 695
    advantages, 696-697
    disadvantages, 697-698
    implementing, 698-699
    intranets, 695
  permissions
    granting, 701-704
    removing, 705-706
  users
    adding, 700
    viewing list of, 699
Windows NT Active Directory Services, 419
wiping, 818
wizards
  Visual Basic Setup Wizard, 627
  Web Project Wizard, 87-88, 91
word wrap (text areas), 165
Word 97 documents, 625-626
working modes
  Local mode, 90-94
  Master mode, 89-90, 94-95
  Offline mode, 90-91
  setting, 91-92
  switching, 92
worksheets (Excel), 622, 625
workstations. *See* **clients**
World Wide Web. *See* **Web**
WRAP attribute (<TEXTAREA> tag), 165
wrapping text, 757
Write method
  Document object (Microsoft Internet Explorer), 367-369
  Request object, 122
  Response object, 405
  TextStream object, 682
WriteBlankLines method, 682
WriteLine method, 682
WriteLn method, 367-369

WWW (World Wide Web). *See* **Web**
WYSIWYG Web editing, 39

X-Z

Year method, 286
Ziff-Davis/Cobb Journal Web site, 792
Zoom tool, 819

mcp.com
The Authoritative Encyclopedia of Computing

- Resource Centers
- Books & Software
- Personal Bookshelf
- WWW Yellow Pages
- Online Learning
- Special Offers
- Site Search
- Industry News

▶ *Choose the online ebooks that you can view from your personal workspace on our site.*

About MCP   Site Map   Product Support

Turn to the *Authoritative* Encyclopedia of Computing

You'll find over 150 full text books online, hundreds of shareware/freeware applications, online computing classes and 10 computing resource centers full of expert advice from the editors and publishers of:

- Adobe Press
- BradyGAMES
- Cisco Press
- Hayden Books
- Lycos Press
- New Riders
- Que
- Que Education & Training
- Sams Publishing
- Waite Group Press
- Ziff-Davis Press

mcp.com
The Authoritative Encyclopedia of Computing

Get the best information and learn about latest developments in:

- ■ Design
- ■ Graphics and Multimedia
- ■ Enterprise Computing and DBMS
- ■ General Internet Information
- ■ Operating Systems
- ■ Networking and Hardware
- ■ PC and Video Gaming
- ■ Productivity Applications
- ■ Programming
- ■ Web Programming and Administration
- ■ Web Publishing

When you're looking for computing information, consult the authority. The Authoritative Encyclopedia of Computing at mcp.com.

Other Related Titles

Sams Teach Yourself HTML 4 in 24 Hours, Second Edition
Dick Oliver
1-57521-366-4
$19.99 USA/$28.95 CAN

Sams Teach Yourself Web Publishing with HTML 4 in Week, Complete Starter Kit
Laura Lemay
0-672-31344-8
$39.99 USA/$56.95 CAN

Dynamic HTML Web Magic
Jeff Rouyer
1-56830-421-8
$39.99 USA/$56.95 CAN

Net Results: Web Marketing that Works
US Web & Rick Bruner
1-56830-414-5
$29.99 USA/$42.95 CAN

Sams Teach Yourself JBuilder2 in 21 Days
Don Doherty
0-672-31318-9
$39.99 USA/$56.95 CAN

Sams Teach Yourself JavaScript 1.3 in 21 Days, Third Edition
Arman Danesh
1-57521-304-4
$29.99 USA/$42.95 CAN

Using Visual J++ 6
Scott Mulloy
0-7897-1400-0
$29.99 USA/$42.95 CAN

Special Edition Using Visual Basic 6
Brian Siler & Jeff Spotts
0-7897-1542-2
$39.99 USA/$56.95 CAN

Sams Teach Yourself Photoshop 5 in 24 Hours
Carla Rose
0-672-31301-4
$19.99 USA/$28.95 CAN

Sams Teach Yourself TCP/IP Network Administration in 21 Days
Brian Komar
0-672-31250-6
$29.99 USA/$42.95 CAN

Special Edition Using Visual InterDev 6
Steve Bannick and Mike Morrison
ISBN: 0-7897-1549-X
$39.99 US/$57.95 CAN

Special Edition Using Active Server Pages
Scot Johnson
ISBN: 0-7897-1389-6
$49.99 US/$70.95 CAN

Active Server Pages Unleashed
Stephen Walther
ISBN: 0-57521-351-6
$49.99 US/$70.95 CAN

www.quecorp.com

All prices are subject to change.